The Media and the Rwanda Genocide

THE MEDIA AND THE RWANDA GENOCIDE

Edited by
Allan Thompson

With a Statement by
Kofi Annan

LONDON • ANN ARBOR, MI

Fountain Publishers

KAMPALA, UGANDA

International Development Research Centre

OTTAWA • CAIRO • DAKAR • MONTEVIDEO • NAIROBI • NEW DELHI • SINGAPORE

First published 2007 by Pluto Press
345 Archway Road, London N6 5AA
and 839 Greene Street, Ann Arbor, MI 48106
www.plutobooks.com

International Development Research Centre
PO Box 8500, Ottawa, ON, Canada K1G 3H9
www.idrc.ca/info@idrc.ca
ISBN 1–55250–338–0 (e-book)

Fountain Publishers Ltd
Fountain House, 55 Nkrumah Road, P.O. Box 488, Kampala, Uganda
www.fountainpublishers.co.ug
E-mail: fountain@starcom.co.ug
ISBN-10 9970–02–595–3
ISBN-13 978–9970–02–595–4

British Library Cataloguing in Publication Data
A catalogue record for this book is available from the British Library

Hardback
ISBN-13 978 0 7453 2626 9
ISBN-10 0 7453 2626 9

Paperback
ISBN-13 978 0 7453 2625 2
ISBN-10 0 7453 2625 0

Library of Congress Cataloging in Publication Data applied for

10 9 8 7 6 5 4 3 2

Designed and produced for Pluto Press by
Chase Publishing Services Ltd, Fortescue, Sidmouth, EX10 9QG, England
Typeset from disk by Stanford DTP Services, Northampton
Printed and bound in India

Contents

Message to Symposium on the Media and the Rwanda Genocide ix
Kofi Annan
Preface xi
Notes on Contributors xiii

1 Introduction 1
Allan Thompson

2 The Media Dichotomy 12
Roméo Dallaire

3 Rwanda: Walking the Road to Genocide 20
Gerald Caplan

PART ONE: HATE MEDIA IN RWANDA

4 Call to Genocide: Radio in Rwanda, 1994 41
Alison Des Forges

5 RTLM Propaganda: the Democratic Alibi 55
Jean-Pierre Chrétien

6 *Kangura*: the Triumph of Propaganda Refined 62
Marcel Kabanda

7 Rwandan Private Print Media on the Eve of the Genocide 73
Jean-Marie Vianney Higiro

8 Echoes of Violence: Considerations on Radio and Genocide in Rwanda 90
Darryl Li

9 RTLM: the Medium that Became a Tool for Mass Murder 110
Mary Kimani

10 The Effect of RTLM's Rhetoric of Ethnic Hatred in Rural Rwanda 125
Charles Mironko

11 Journalism in a Time of Hate Media 136
Thomas Kamilindi

PART TWO: INTERNATIONAL MEDIA COVERAGE OF THE GENOCIDE

12 Reporting the Genocide 145
Mark Doyle

13 Who Failed in Rwanda, Journalists or the Media? 160
Anne Chaon

14 Reporting Rwanda: the Media and the Aid Agencies 167
Lindsey Hilsum

15 Limited Vision: How Both the American Media and Government Failed Rwanda 188
Steven Livingston

16 Missing the Story: the Media and the Rwanda Genocide 198
Linda Melvern

17 What Did They Say? African Media Coverage of the First 100 Days of the Rwanda Crisis 211
Emmanuel C. Alozie

18 Exhibit 467: Genocide Through a Camera Lens 231
Nick Hughes

19 Media Failure over Rwanda's Genocide 235
Tom Giles

20 A Genocide Without Images: White Film Noirs 238
Edgar Roskis

21 Notes on Circumstances that Facilitate Genocide: the Attention Given to Rwanda by the Media and Others Outside Rwanda Before 1990 242
Mike Dottridge

22 The Media's Failure: a Reflection on the Rwanda Genocide 248
Richard Dowden

23 How the Media missed the Rwanda Genocide 256
Alan J. Kuperman

24 An Analysis of News Magazine Coverage of the Rwanda Crisis in the United States 261
Melissa Wall

PART THREE: JOURNALISM AS GENOCIDE – THE MEDIA TRIAL

25 The Verdict: Summary Judgement from the Media Trial 277

26 The Pre-Genocide Case Against Radio-Télévision Libre des Milles Collines 308
Simone Monasebian

27 The Challenges in Prosecuting Print Media for Incitement to Genocide 330
Charity Kagwi-Ndungu

28 'Hate Media' – Crimes Against Humanity and Genocide: Opportunities Missed by the International Criminal Tribunal for Rwanda 343
Jean-Marie Biju-Duval

29 A Lost Opportunity for Justice: Why Did the ICTR Not Prosecute Gender Propaganda? 362
Binaifer Nowrojee

PART FOUR: AFTER THE GENOCIDE AND THE WAY FORWARD

30 Intervening to Prevent Genocidal Violence: the Role of the Media 375
Frank Chalk

31 Information in Crisis Areas as a Tool for Peace: the Hirondelle Experience 381
Philippe Dahinden

32 The Use and Abuse of Media in Vulnerable Societies 389
Mark Frohardt and Jonathan Temin

33 Censorship and Propaganda in Post-Genocide Rwanda 404
Lars Waldorf

34 PG – Parental Guidance or Portrayal of Genocide: the Comparative Depiction of Mass Murder in Contemporary Cinema 417
Michael Dorland

35 The Responsibility to Report: a New Journalistic Paradigm 433
Allan Thompson

Bibliography 447
Index 455

UNITED NATIONS **NATIONS UNIES**

THE SECRETARY-GENERAL

MESSAGE TO SYMPOSIUM ON THE MEDIA AND THE RWANDA GENOCIDE

Carleton University School of Journalism and Communication

Ottawa, 13 March 2004

When, on 7 April, people around the world commemorate the 10th anniversary of the Rwanda genocide, that observance should be filled not only with remorse, but with resolve.

We must remember the victims – the hundreds of thousands of men, women and children abandoned to systematic slaughter while the world, which had the capacity to save most of them, failed to save more than a handful, forever sullying the collective conscience. We must also help the survivors still struggling with the physical and psychological scars. But most of all, we must pledge – to ourselves as moral beings and to each other as a human community – to act boldly, including through military action when no other course will work, to ensure that such a denial of our common humanity is never allowed to happen again.

The United Nations has now had ten years to reflect on the bitter knowledge that genocide happened while UN peacekeepers were on the ground in Rwanda, and to learn lessons that all humankind should have learned from previous genocides. We are determined to sound the alarm about emerging crises and to help countries tackle the root causes of their problems. I expect soon to appoint a United Nations special adviser on the prevention of genocide, and to make other proposals for strengthening our action in this area.

It is encouraging to know that the news media are also undertaking a process of self-examination as we collectively remember this tragedy. Media were used in Rwanda to spread hatred, to dehumanize people, and even to guide the *genocidaires* toward their victims. Three journalists have even been found guilty of genocide, incitement to genocide, conspiracy and crimes against humanity by the International Criminal Tribunal for Rwanda. We must find a way to respond to such abuses of power without violating the principles of freedom, which are an indispensable cornerstone of democracy.

I am glad that you are confronting these and other questions, including the role of the international media, especially at a school where future journalists are being trained. Such training must include reflection on the responsibilities of their chosen profession.

There can be no more important issue, and no more binding obligation, than the prevention of genocide. The world has made some progress in understanding the responsibility to protect. Yet it is still not clear, were the signs of impending genocide to be seen somewhere today, that the world would mount an effective response. I hope that all of us, as diplomats, journalists, government officials or just concerned citizens, will act promptly and effectively, each within our sphere of influence, to halt genocide wherever it occurs – or better still, to make sure there is no 'next time'.

Preface

It was the French philosopher, Voltaire, who wrote: 'We owe respect to the living; to the dead we owe only truth.'

In the case of the 1994 genocide in Rwanda, the news media accomplished neither of Voltaire's admonitions. Confronted by Rwanda's horrors, Western news media for the most part turned away, then muddled the story when they did pay attention. And hate media organs in Rwanda – through their journalists, broadcasters and media executives – played an instrumental role in laying the groundwork for genocide, then actively participated in the extermination campaign.

On the eve of the tenth anniversary of the Rwanda genocide, the School of Journalism and Communication at Carleton University in Ottawa hosted a one-day symposium on 13 March 2004, entitled 'The Media and the Rwanda Genocide.' The symposium examined in tandem the role of both the international media and Rwanda's domestic news organizations in the cataclysmic events of 1994. The Carleton symposium brought together for the first time an international collection of experts as well as some of the actors from the Rwandan drama; it also inspired this collection of papers. Many of the contributions found here are based on papers delivered at the Carleton event, but others were commissioned or have been reprinted here because of their valuable contribution to the debate.

The symposium was made possible by generous contributions from the International Development Research Centre (IDRC) and the Government of Canada, through the Global Issues Bureau of the Foreign Affairs department and the Canadian International Development Agency. The IDRC has also played a key role in the publication of this collection; it continues to support Carleton's efforts to build a Media and Genocide Archive and to establish a partnership with the School of Journalism and Communication at the National University of Rwanda in Butare through a project called The Rwanda Initiative.

I would like to thank all those who contributed to the symposium and to this collection, most notably the authors of the papers you are about to read. Special thanks are due to Chris Dornan, who was director of the School of Journalism and Communication when this project began, Pamela Scholey and Bill Carman from the IDRC, Roméo Dallaire, who lent considerable moral support to this project, and Sandra Garland, who did wonderful work as a copy-editor. Finally, I would like to thank my wife Roula El-Rifai and our son, Laith Rifai-Thompson. My passion for Rwanda has often consumed time and energy that should have been devoted to my family.

For my part, I came to Rwanda late. Before joining the faculty at Carleton in 2003, I was a career journalist with the *Toronto Star*. I was not in Rwanda in 1994. I first visited in 1996 to report on the repatriation of Hutu refugees from the Goma region of what was then eastern Zaire. But Rwanda does get inside you and, since then, I think I have been trying to some degree to make amends for not having been there in 1994. Reviewing the *Toronto Star* archives, I found an article of mine published on 9 April 1994. I had forgotten ever having written it; perhaps it left my memory because it was such a dreadful piece of journalism. Written three days into the genocide, the article focused entirely on the evacuation of Canadian expatriates from Kigali and invoked every cliché of tribal conflict, chaos and anarchy.

Two months later, in early June, while Roméo Dallaire and his beleaguered contingent watched helplessly as the slaughter continued in Rwanda, I reported for the *Star* from Normandy, France, where then Canadian Prime Minister Jean Chrétien was participating in ceremonies to mark the fiftieth anniversary of D-Day. In my experience, major events taking place elsewhere in the world often become a preoccupation for the journalists reporting on such international gatherings. But as I recall, during that weekend of speeches and press conferences in Normandy commemorating a war that ended half a century earlier, there was nary a mention of what was going on at that moment in Rwanda. None of the leaders mentioned the Rwanda genocide. Nor did any in the media throng covering the D-Day commemorations ask about Rwanda.

The collection you are about to read explores the role of hate media in the Rwanda genocide and examines international media coverage of the genocide. Then it turns to an assessment of the guilty verdict in the international criminal tribunal for Rwanda's 'Media Trial' and finally concludes with a section on the aftermath, examining the current media climate in Rwanda, media intervention strategies and the place of the Rwanda genocide in popular culture.

The purpose of looking back at the media's role in the Rwanda events is not just to remember. We still have some learning to do on this subject and examining the way journalists and news organizations conducted themselves in 1994 is not just a historical exercise. Sadly, we don't yet seem to have fully discerned or absorbed the lessons from Rwanda.

Ultimately, this collection is dedicated to those who perished in 1994. To underline the point, I would like to borrow a comparison used by British journalist, Scott Peterson. To understand the number of dead, imagine that every word in this book is the name of a victim. This entire volume would list only 200,000 of the dead, a fraction of the estimated toll of nearly one million people. As you read this collection, look at every word. Then think of someone you know.

Allan Thompson
Ottawa, 2006

Notes on Contributors

Emmanuel C. Alozie is university professor of media communications at Governors State University, University Park, Illinois. His research interests are in development communication, international/cultural journalism, advertising and public relations. Alozie is former assistant editor with Democratic Communiqué, author of *Cultural Reflections and the Role of Advertising in the Socio-economic and National Development of Nigeria* (2005, Edwin Mellen Press), and co-edited, *Toward the Common Good: Perspectives in International Public Relations* (2004, Ally & Bacon).

Jean-Marie Biju-Duval is a Paris-based lawyer who was engaged as the defence counsel for Ferdinand Nahimana, the former Rwandan media executive who was convicted in the Media Trial.

Gerald Caplan is a leading Canadian authority on genocide prevention. He is the author of *Rwanda: The Preventable Genocide*, the 2000 report of the International Panel of Eminent Personalities appointed by the Organization of African Unity to investigate the 1994 Rwanda genocide. He is also founder of Remembering Rwanda, the Rwanda genocide tenth anniversary memorial project and has developed and teaches a course on the role of the media in the Rwanda genocide.

Frank Chalk is a professor in the Department of History, Concordia University, Montreal, Canada, and the co-director of the Montreal Institute for Genocide and Human Rights Studies. He is co-author (with Kurt Jonassohn) of *The History and Sociology of Genocide*.

Anne Chaon is a journalist with Agence France-Presse (AFP). In the first weeks of the 1994 Rwanda genocide, she was based in Paris, working on AFP's Africa desk. She reported from Rwanda for AFP in June, before heading to eastern Zaire in July of that year. She testified against RTLM media executive Ferdinand Nahimana in Paris and before the International Criminal Tribunal for Rwanda in the Media Trial.

Jean-Pierre Chrétien is a historian and co-author of *Rwanda: les médias du Génocide*. He has held teaching positions at l'École normale supérieure du Burundi, l'Université de Lille III, and since 1973 has been a researcher in African history at the Centre National de la Recherche Scientifique (CNRS) in Paris.

Philippe Dahinden is a Swiss journalist who is cofounder of and former editor-in-chief at the Hirondelle Foundation, an international organization of journalists that establishes media operations in crisis areas. He founded and managed the independent radio station, Radio Agatashya, which covered Rwanda, Burundi and the Kivu after July 1994 in an attempt to counter the destructive messages of hate radio. He also set up and managed Radio Okapi in the Democratic Republic of Congo.

Roméo Dallaire is a retired Lieutenant-General. He led the United Nations Assistance Mission for Rwanda (UNAMIR) to help implement the Arusha accords. He is the author of *Shake Hands with the Devil: The Failure of Humanity in Rwanda* and now sits in the Senate of Canada as a member of the Liberal party.

Michael Dorland is professor of communication in the School of Journalism and Communication at Carleton University. A former film critic before his return to the academy in 1992, his current research concerns the medical aspects of Holocaust survival.

Mike Dottridge was a desk officer with Amnesty International during the 1980s, covering Rwanda and other countries in the Great Lakes region. At the time of the genocide (and until 1995) he was supervising Amnesty's work throughout sub-Saharan Africa. He is currently a consultant on human rights issues.

Richard Dowden was Africa editor for a British newspaper, the *Independent*, in 1994. He is now director of the Royal African Society.

Mark Doyle has worked for the BBC since 1986 and was its east Africa correspondent in 1993–94. He spent much of the period of the genocide in Rwanda and, on several occasions, he was the only foreign reporter in Kigali.

Alison Des Forges is senior advisor to the Africa division of Human Rights Watch. She is also the author of *Leave None to Tell the Story: Genocide in Rwanda* and has served as expert witness in genocide proceedings at the International Criminal Tribunal for Rwanda, U.S. Federal Court, and in Belgian and Swiss courts.

Mark Frohardt is Internews Network's regional director for Africa and former deputy chief of mission for the United Nations Human Rights Field Operation in Rwanda (May 1995 to June 1997).

Tom Giles covered the Rwanda genocide as a producer for BBC News. He won a Royal Television Society award in 'international current affairs' for his Panorama production on the war in Iraq – *In the Line of Fire*.

Jean-Marie Vianney Higiro is an associate professor in the Department of Communication at Western New England College in Springfield, Massachusetts. From 31 July 1993 to 6 April 1994, he was director of the Rwandan Information Office (ORINFOR) in Kigali.

Lindsey Hilsum was one of only two Western journalists on the ground in Rwanda at the time of the genocide and is in a unique position to describe media coverage of the genocide and the disproportionate attention paid to the plight of Hutu refugees who had fled to Goma. She is China correspondent for Channel 4 News in Britain.

Nick Hughes is a British director/cameraman who captured some of the only known media images of killings during the 1994 genocide in Rwanda. He later testified as a prosecution witness before the International Criminal Tribunal for Rwanda, where his footage was entered as a piece of evidence, exhibit 467, in the trial of George Rutaganda. Hughes later produced the film *100 Days*, the first cinematic treatment of the Rwanda genocide.

Marcel Kabanda is a Rwandan historian and a consultant with the United Nations Educational, Scientific and Cultural Organization (UNESCO) in Paris. He is also a co-author of *Rwanda: les médias du Genocide*.

Charity Kagwi-Ndungu is a trial attorney with the United Nations International Criminal Tribunal for Rwanda and was a prosecutor in the Media Trial.

Thomas Kamilindi is a former Radio Rwanda journalist, based in Kigali. He resigned a few months before the genocide started. He was among the many liberal Hutus accused of sympathizing with the Tutsi-led rebel forces of the Rwandan Patriotic Front and narrowly escaped death during the genocide. In 2005, he left Rwanda, where he had been working as a BBC correspondent, to accept a Knight-Wallace Fellowship at the University of Michigan.

Mary Kimani is a journalist who covered the Media Trial and conducted a series of interviews with an RTLM journalist. The work reported in this volume formed part of a thesis completed for a master's degree in communication psychology at the University of Warnborough, Canterbury, United Kingdom.

Alan Kuperman is assistant professor at the LBJ School of Public Affairs, University of Texas at Austin.

Darryl Li is completing a PhD in Anthropology and Middle Eastern Studies at Harvard University and a JD at Yale Law School. In three months of fieldwork, he explored the impact of RTLM on its listeners by interviewing dozens of Rwandans who were part of the station's audience and who admitted to taking part in the genocide.

Steven Livingston is associate professor of political communication and international affairs and director, School of Media and Public Affairs, The George Washington University.

Linda Melvern is an investigative journalist and author of *A People Betrayed: The Role of the West in Rwanda's Genocide* and *Conspiracy to Murder: The Rwandan Genocide*.

Charles Mironko is a cultural anthropologist whose work focuses on genocide perpetrators. He was formerly Associate Director of the Genocide Studies Program at Yale University, and chief of the Culture Section at the Organization of African Unity. He is currently a Humanitarian Officer in Darfur, under the African Union Mission in Sudan.

Simone Monasebian was a trial attorney with the United Nations International Criminal Tribunal for Rwanda and one of the prosecutors in the Media Trial. Later, she was principal defender at the Sierra Leone tribunal before her appointment as chief of the New York office of the United Nations Office on Drugs and Crime as well as a CourtTV legal analyst.

Binaifer Nowrojee is Lecturer on Law at Harvard Law School. She was counsel with Human Rights Watch/Africa and the author of the Human Rights Watch report, *Shattered Lives: Sexual Violence during the Rwandan Genocide and its Aftermath*. She has testified as an expert witness before the International Criminal Tribunal for Rwanda on sexual violence and in 2005 became director of the Open Society Initiative for East Africa.

Edgar Roskis (1952–2003) was a journalist with *Le Monde diplomatique* and a senior lecturer in the Department of Information and Communication, Université Paris-X, Nanterre, France.

Jonathan Temin is a senior programme officer with the CHF International and former programme associate with Internews Network.

Lars Waldorf is currently affiliated with the World Policy Institute at The New School. From 2002 to 2004, he ran Human Rights Watch's field office in Rwanda. He is now writing a book on the genocide trials before Rwanda's community courts (gacaca).

Melissa Wall is a journalism professor at California State University, Northridge. A former journalist, she has trained journalists in Ethiopia and researched township newspapers in Zimbabwe.

Allan Thompson is a professor at Carleton University's School of Journalism and Communication. He joined the faculty at Carleton in 2003 after spending 17 years as a reporter with the *Toronto Star*, Canada's largest circulation daily newspaper. He worked for a decade as a correspondent for the *Star* on Parliament Hill in Ottawa and also undertook frequent reporting assignments in Africa, reporting from Rwanda a number of times. At Carleton, he leads the Rwanda Initiative, a media capacity-building partnership with the journalism school at the National University of Rwanda.

1
Introduction

Allan Thompson

The images are so disturbing they are difficult to watch. Two women kneel amid the bodies of those who have already been slain. They are at the side of a dirt road in Kigali, the capital of Rwanda. Their final moments are captured on video by a British journalist, one of only a few foreign reporters left in the country, who is recording clandestinely from the top of a building nearby.[1] Remarkably, during a genocide that claimed as many as a million lives, this is one of the only times a killing is recorded by the media. In the footage, one of the women is pleading, first clasping her hands in front of her, as if in prayer, then throwing open her arms, appealing to the throng of men who are milling about nearby, holding machetes and sticks. Further along the road are the bodies of others who have been dragged out of their homes and killed. The woman continues to beg, but the men seem to be oblivious to her. A young boy dressed in a T-shirt strolls past, giving the women only a backward glance. At one point, you can see a man in the crowd clutching something in his left hand. It appears to be a radio.

Minutes go by and the woman continues to plead for her life. The other figure crouched beside her barely flinches. Men wielding sticks in one hand and machetes in the other move forward and begin to pound the bodies that are strewn around the two women, striking the corpses again and again. One man gives the bodies a final crack, as if driving a stake into the ground, then slings his stick over his shoulder and ambles off. All the while, the woman continues to wave her arms and plead. A white pickup truck approaches and drives through the scene. The windshield wipers are flopping back and forth. One of the men huddled in the back of the vehicle waves a hand at the woman who is kneeling on the ground. He taunts her with a greeting.

Finally, two other men approach. One, dressed in dark trousers and a white shirt, winds up to strike the pleading woman. He has the posture of someone who is about to whip an animal. She recoils. Then he strikes her on the head with the stick he is clutching in his right hand. She crumples to the ground, then suffers more blows from her murderer. Almost at the same moment, the other woman is struck down as well by another assailant, her head very nearly lopped off by the initial blow. Finally, the two men walk away casually, leaving the bodies to squirm. In the distance, there is the sound of birdsong.

The date is 18 April 1994, nearly two weeks after the 6 April plane crash that claimed the life of Rwandan President Juvénal Habyarimana and plunged

Rwanda into the abyss. The tiny central African country, a mere dot on the world map, garnered virtually no international media attention before the killing spree that followed the president's death. No one had paid much attention to a fledgling peace accord signed in Arusha, Tanzania in 1993, setting out the details for a power-sharing arrangement between the majority Hutu population and the minority Tutsi, represented in the talks by the rebels from the Tutsi-dominated Rwandan Patriotic Front (RPF). An international peacekeeping force, commanded by a Canadian general, Roméo Dallaire, was dispatched to oversee implementation of the accord. Dallaire and his peacekeepers were only vaguely aware of the mounting tensions in the autumn of 1993, but heard rumblings about a 'third force' – Hutu extremists who opposed the power-sharing arrangement.

The voice of Hutu Power was the private radio station RTLM, established by extremists who surrounded the president. And RTLM was an echo of other extremist media, notably the newspaper *Kangura*. Once the president's plane was shot down by unknown assailants, the message from RTLM was unmistakable: the Tutsi were to blame; they were the enemy and Rwanda would be better off without them. The killings began almost immediately in Kigali through the night of 6–7 April. Hutu moderates, who were willing to share power, were among the first targeted, along with Tutsi marked for extermination in a campaign that eventually fanned out across the country. Many of the hundreds of thousands of Rwandans who were slaughtered had huddled in churches for sanctuary. Death squads lobbed in grenades. In their frenzy, killers severed the Achilles tendons on the heels of their victims, so they could return and finish the job later. Teachers killed students, neighbours slaughtered neighbours as local officials helped organize the killing.

In its 2003 verdict in the 'Media Trial' of executives from RTLM and *Kangura*, the International Criminal Tribunal for Rwanda (ICTR) confirmed the undoubted role of Rwandan hate media in the killing:

> The newspaper and the radio explicitly and repeatedly, in fact relentlessly, targeted the Tutsi population for destruction. Demonizing the Tutsi as having inherently evil qualities, equating the ethnic group with 'the enemy' and portraying its women as seductive enemy agents, the media called for the extermination of the Tutsi ethnic group as a response to the political threat that they associated with Tutsi ethnicity. (ICTR 2003: para. 72)

(The full text of the judgement summary can be found in Part Three of this collection.)

Most international news organizations initially misunderstood the nature of the killing in Rwanda, portraying it as the result of tribal warfare, rather than genocide. Much of the international coverage focused on the scramble to evacuate expatriates from the country. In mid-April, when the killing intensified, the volume of news reports actually declined. Most journalists had left along with the other foreigners.

The grainy video captured on 18 April by Nick Hughes, who was positioned on the top floor of the French School, is truly the exception that proves the rule. Hughes looked first through the scope of a rocket launcher, borrowed from a Belgian soldier stationed in the school. Then he trained his camera on what he saw taking place in the road below. Hughes would recount later that he had to stop shooting at several points for fear that his lone remaining battery pack would expire and, as a result, there are 'jump cuts' in the video at points when he briefly turned off his camera. Because he was shooting from such a distance, the sound on the audio track is the background noise in the school and, occasionally, the voice of Hughes and an associate. 'She's praying over the person that has just been killed,' he comments at one point. 'They're going to kill her, you can see that,' he says later.

Eventually, the international media reports on Rwanda were replete with images of bloated corpses, strewn at the roadside or choking Rwanda's rivers. But because there were so few foreign journalists on the ground at the height of the killing and because the domestic media had either been cowed or co-opted into the massacres, there are no other known images of the crime itself, the crime of genocide. Would the world have reacted differently if confronted daily by images of people being slaughtered rather than the static, disembodied pictures of disfigured corpses? More informed and comprehensive coverage of the Rwanda genocide, particularly in those early days, might well have mitigated or even halted the killing by sparking an international outcry. The news media could have made a difference. But within Rwanda, the only news media making a difference were hate media, such as RTLM, which proved instrumental in fanning the flames and implicating tens of thousands of ordinary people in the genocide.

Journalists could have had an impact in Rwanda – a sort of Heisenberg effect – had there been a significant enough media presence to influence events. The Heisenberg effect, named for German physicist Werner Heisenberg, describes how the act of observing a particle actually changes the behaviour of that particle, its velocity or direction. Arguably, more comprehensive and accurate reporting about the Rwanda genocide could have changed the behaviour of the perpetrators, mitigating the slaughter. Instead, the lack of international media attention contributed to what I would call a sort of inverse Heisenberg effect. Through their absence and a failure to adequately observe and record events, journalists contributed to the behaviour of the perpetrators of the genocide – who were encouraged by the world's apathy and acted with impunity.

At every turn, it seems, we return to this troubling equation, implicating news media – both within Rwanda and internationally – in the genocide. In looking back on this period, it is important to examine the role of domestic hate media and the international media in tandem in one collection of papers. As uncomfortable as this connection may seem, we cannot separate the two. We are looking at the role of the media, the power of its message and the impact of an information vacuum.

There is a considerable and growing body of literature on the Rwanda genocide in general and the role of the media in particular. Indeed, a number of authors have focused intently on the role of hate media in fostering and fomenting the genocide and that important work is reflected and elaborated upon in the collection of papers you are about to read. This collection takes the crucial step of juxtaposing analysis of the Rwandan media with analysis of coverage by the international media, thus encouraging a broader reflection on the role of the media as a whole. No other publication brings together both sides of the topic in this way. The role of hate media in the Rwanda genocide is in some ways self-evident. But it is not so clear, or at least not as universally accepted, that international media played a role in the genocide as well.

In the autumn of 1994, French journalist Edgar Roskis, wrote in *Le Monde Diplomatique* of 'un genocide sans images', a genocide without images. His article, translated and reprinted in this collection, underlines the point that because most foreign journalists fled the country, the indisputable crime of genocide very nearly went unrecorded. Roskis cites French photographer, Patrick Robert, who was working in Rwanda at the time for the Paris-based Sygma photo agency. 'There were six American correspondents,' Robert recounted. 'They had scarcely arrived when their editors gave them all orders to come home. At the Hôtel des Mille Collines, I picked up snatches of their conversations: "Too dangerous, not enough interest ... deep Africa, you know ... middle of nowhere."'

From 6 April until the middle of May, when the bulk of the genocide took place, Rwanda was still relegated to the inside pages of most newspapers, Roskis notes. The photos that were published were small and often old, the accounts second-hand, with little if any news appearing for days at a time.

The international media really only began to pay attention once Hutu refugees began to pour out of Rwanda into neighbouring countries. As Roskis contends, it was the 'humanitarian melodrama' of Goma that finally garnered the full attention of the international media. The Rwanda genocide was a media event, without question. And yet, it never quite graduated to the rank of 'mega-event', the kind of sensation that frequently attracts hundreds of international reporters, camera crews and satellite uplinks.

There is irony here. Dallaire continues to insist that with an intervention force of 5,000 troops, he could have put a halt to the killing. But the world's power brokers – chief among them the United States, Great Britain and France – used their positions on the United Nations Security Council to argue against intervention. The lack of focused, persistent media coverage of events in Rwanda only served to help the cause of those foot-draggers who did not want to get involved. Many blame American unwillingness to be drawn into Rwanda on 'Somalia fatigue', a reference to its humiliating withdrawal from Mogadishu in 1993 after 18 US rangers died in an abortive mission. The bodies of some of the helicopter pilots were later mutilated and dragged through the streets of the Somali capital by a jeering crowd. Canadian journalist, Paul Watson, then working for the *Toronto Star*, captured a Pulitzer-prize-winning photograph of the body of one of the American pilots as it was being hauled through the streets. That searing media image was published by many US newspapers and is widely credited with prompting the Clinton administration to withdraw from Somalia.

A media image contributed to US withdrawal from one African mission. A year later, at the height of the Rwanda genocide, the lack of media images probably helped the cause of those in Washington, London, Paris and other major capitals who wanted to avoid mounting an international intervention in another African country. As Dallaire puts it in his overview chapter in this collection, the world turned its back on Rwanda, not least because international news organizations initially downplayed the story. The Rwanda genocide, as a news event, simply did not break through.

By most accounts, there were only two foreign journalists in Rwanda on 6 April 1994, when Habyarimana's plane was shot down: Katrin van der Schoot, a freelance Flemish reporter for Belgian radio, and Lindsey Hilsum (the author of 'Reporting Rwanda: the Media and the Aid Agencies', in Part Two of this collection). Hilsum was in Rwanda on a temporary contract for UNICEF, although she also worked as a freelance reporter for the BBC, the *Guardian* and the *Observer*. As Hilsum recounts in her paper, some Nairobi-based journalists managed to move southward from Uganda with the RPF. Others – among them the BBC's Mark Doyle, who recounts his experiences in this volume – persuaded a World Food Programme official in Entebbe to fly them into Kigali on a plane being used to evacuate foreigners. A few others drove up from Burundi, but for most of April, there were no more than 10 to 15 reporters in the country at any time.

As Hilsum describes, most of the journalists were Africa specialists, but even they did not understand what was happening at first. 'With a shooting war in the east and the north and massacres in much of the country, for most of April it was genuinely confusing,' Hilsum writes. The journalists who did remain were mainly British, French and Belgian. Most US reporters had been ordered to leave by their employers because it was too dangerous. Although a significant number of reporters arrived on the scene shortly after the killing began, most were there with instructions to cover the attempts to rescue foreign nationals. And all but a handful left along with the evacuees in mid-April. There was virtually no 'real time' TV news out of Rwanda for the first weeks of the genocide because it was too risky to send an expensive satellite uplink into the country. The first satellite uplink was erected in Kigali only in late May, after the RPF had secured the airport.

As French journalist, Anne Chaon, notes in her contribution to this collection, the media muddled the story from June onward, when the French military began 'Operation Turquoise' in southwest Rwanda. 'Dozens of reporters returned to Rwanda. And while they were able at that time to discover the enormity of the killing campaign in this area ... they reported also on the humanitarian and military intervention from abroad. The result was that the reality of genocide was, once again, submerged in too much information.'

* * *

This collection of papers grew out of the 13 March 2004 symposium at Carleton University, organized by Canada's best-known and oldest journalism school.

The purpose of the event was to make a direct and explicit connection between the conduct of Rwandan media in the genocide and the role played by the international media. Like the symposium, the collection of papers follows the same structure, with an added focus in the final section on events since 1994 and the current state of the media in post-genocide Rwanda.

A substantial introductory section includes a historical overview by Gerry Caplan, author of the Organization of African Unity report, *Rwanda: the Preventable Genocide* (IPEP 2000). Retired Canadian General Roméo Dallaire speaks from the unique vantage point of a key player during the period, with first-hand knowledge of the role of the media, his failed attempts to shut down or jam RTLM hate radio and his efforts to attract international media attention to the genocide in Rwanda. Dallaire argues that hate media were essentially the soundtrack of the genocide and were deployed as a weapon. He also recounts how, in his view, the international media influenced events by their absence, at a time when so much attention was focused on the war in the Balkans, where white Europeans were the victims.

This central contention – that local hate media fomented the genocide and international media essentially facilitated the process by turning their backs – is the crux of this collection of papers. This collection is, in essence, a journey through the media role in the events in Rwanda, a journey that has not yet reached its destination.

HATE MEDIA IN RWANDA

It is logical to begin with an examination of the evolution of hate media in Rwanda and the particular role played by radio station RTLM and the newspaper *Kangura*. Alison Des Forges, senior advisor to Human Rights Watch's Africa Division and the author of the definitive work *Leave None to Tell the Story: Genocide in Rwanda* (Des Forges 1999), sets the scene with a broad historical overview of the development of hate media in Rwanda and the world's failure to deal effectively with the phenomena. French historian Jean-Pierre Chrétien, co-author of *Rwanda: les Médias du Génocide* (Chrétien et al. 1995), traces the evolution of RTLM in Rwandan society. He describes how the organizers of the genocide plotted to use the airwaves to instill the notion of 'the democratic alibi', justifying the extermination of the Tutsi on the grounds that they posed a threat to the majority Hutu. Marcel Kabanda, a Rwandan historian and also co-author of *Rwanda: les Médias du Génocide* (Chrétien et al. 1995), focuses on the role of print media in the lead-up to the genocide, specifically the bimonthly newspaper *Kangura*. Jean-Marie Higiro, now an associate professor in the Department of Communication at Western New England College in Springfield, Massachusetts, was director of the Rwandan Information Office in Kigali from 31 July 1993 to 6 April 1994. He examines the impact of the private print press on Rwandan politics before the genocide. Darryl Li, explores more fully the impact of RTLM on its listeners by interviewing dozens of Rwandans who were part of the RTLM audience and admitted to taking part in the genocide. Charles Mironko uses data from interviews with nearly 100 confessed genocide perpetrators to analyze critically the relationship between the rhetoric of ethnic hatred so prevalent among Rwandan political elites and the forces that propelled ordinary Rwandan Hutu to participate in killing Tutsi. Kenyan journalist Mary Kimani, who worked for a number of years with Internews Rwanda, uses a detailed content analysis of recordings of RTLM broadcasts to make the case that individual broadcasters – not their guests or government officials – were most likely to use the airwaves to disseminate hate.

And finally we hear from Thomas Kamilindi, a former Radio Rwanda journalist based in Kigali, who later worked as a freelance correspondent in Rwanda for the BBC and other media outlets. In a personal reporter's memoir, he recounts how he resigned from state-run radio in Rwanda a few months before the 1994 genocide started because he had sometimes been asked to broadcast news repugnant to him.

INTERNATIONAL MEDIA COVERAGE OF THE GENOCIDE

Part Two turns to the other side of the equation to examine the role of international media coverage of the genocide. The contention is that while hate media in Rwanda contributed to the genocide by playing a proactive role, the international media also played a role by, in essence, acquiescing to the killing campaign by downplaying it. But that is the critique writ large. Through a combination of journalistic memoirs from reporters who were in the field and academic studies by observers of the international media coverage, this section canvasses such issues as the responsibility of individual journalists and the constraints faced by journalists reporting from war zones.

The first contributor is Mark Doyle, the BBC journalist who spent more time on the ground in Rwanda during the genocide than any other foreign reporter. His paper navigates the first days of the genocide through the eyes of a reporter and, notably, includes numerous extracts from the transcripts of his crucial broadcasts from Rwanda in the midst of the killing. He discusses his own deliberations over when and how to use the word genocide to describe what was going on around him. Anne Chaon is a journalist with Agence France-Presse, who worked on AFP's Africa desk in Paris during the first weeks of the genocide, then reported from Rwanda in June before heading to eastern Zaire in July. Chaon takes issue with the conventional wisdom that individual journalists missed the story in Rwanda and, instead, argues that journalists did the best they could under the circumstances and that the problem was that readers and decision-makers didn't care about a tiny country in Africa. As one of only two foreign reporters on the ground when the genocide began, Lindsey Hilsum is in a unique position to describe media coverage of the genocide and the disproportionate attention paid in July and August to the plight of Hutu refugees who had fled to Goma, in eastern Zaire. She contends that the complex political causes of the exodus to Goma were not understood by the public nor by many of the journalists who covered Goma as a humanitarian story. Steven Livingston, associate professor of political communication and international affairs at The George Washington University in Washington, DC, analyzes American television coverage of the genocide and concludes that the US stood at arm's length from events in Rwanda in the spring of 1994 because policymakers believed their predecessors in the George H.W. Bush administration were lured into Somalia by television pictures. Linda Melvern, investigative journalist and author of *A People Betrayed: The Role of the West in Rwanda's Genocide* (Melvern 2000) and *Conspiracy to Murder: The Rwandan Genocide* (Melvern 2004), argues that international media contributed directly to the genocide by misconstruing the killing in the first weeks as spontaneous, tribal warfare rather than a systematic campaign to exterminate a minority. Nigerian-born researcher Emmanuel Alozie is one of the few to seriously examine African media coverage of the genocide. Alozie, professor of media communications at Governors State University in Illinois, analyzes coverage of the Rwanda genocide in *The Nation* newspaper in Kenya and Nigeria's *Guardian* and makes some comparisons with African media coverage of Darfur a decade later. Nick Hughes, the British cameraman and later film producer, describes the important footage he captured in Rwanda, one of the only known instances of a killing during the genocide recorded by the media. Mike Dottridge, who was a desk officer with Amnesty International at the time of the genocide, takes a step back from the issue of media coverage to explore the fact that so little attention was paid to events in Rwanda before the genocide, particularly in the late 1980s and between 1990 and 1994, despite abundant evidence of unrest. His paper situates the three and a half years of inaction, as RTLM broadcast its messages of hate, in a broader context in which journalists and others based outside Rwanda share responsibility for this inaction.

Part Two also reprints accounts by several journalists who reported from Rwanda during the genocide, including Tom Giles, who was a BBC producer in Rwanda in 1994, and Richard Dowden, who was Africa editor for the British newspaper the *Independent* at the time. It also includes the piece by French journalist Edgar Roskis, who wrote in *Le Monde Diplomatique* in the autumn of 1994 about the impact of the lack of images from the Rwanda genocide. We also reprint a paper by Alan J. Kuperman, now assistant professor at the University of Texas. Kuperman argues that international media were guilty of several key lapses: they mistook the killing for a resumption of the civil war, grossly underestimated the death counts, left en masse at a critical moment and those who remained focused almost exclusively on Kigali. The exploration of international media coverage of the genocide is rounded out with an analysis by Melissa Wall, a journalism professor of news magazine coverage at California State University, Northridge. Wall, whose paper was first published in *Gazette: The International Journal for Communication Studies*, discovered several disturbing themes in coverage: Rwandan violence was the result of irrational tribalism, Rwandan people were little better than animals, the violence was incomprehensible, neighbouring countries were just as violent and only the West was capable of solving Rwanda's problems.

JOURNALISM AS GENOCIDE – THE MEDIA TRIAL

Part Three explores the 3 December 2003 guilty verdict in the so-called 'Media Trial' before the ICTR. The tribunal convicted Ferdinand Nahimana, Jean-Bosco Barayagwiza and Hassan Ngeze of genocide, direct and public incitement to commit genocide, conspiracy to commit genocide and crimes against humanity (persecution and extermination). Nahimana and Barayagwiza were the directors of RTLM, which was found to have fanned the flames of hate and genocide in Rwanda. Ngeze was the editor of the extremist newspaper *Kangura*. The full text of the summary of the verdict, issued by judges Navanethem Pillay, Erik Møse and Asoka de Zoysa Gunawardana, is included in this section as a key reference document.

The rest of the section explores the Media Trial from four key vantage points. Simone Monasebian, who was one of the trial attorneys with the ICTR and a prosecutor in the Media Trial, focuses specifically on RTLM broadcasts before 6 April 1994. She argues that the world community had grounds to intervene well before RTLM used its broadcasts to goad the killers and that RTLM broadcasts after 6 April could not have had the impact they did without the several months of conditioning of the population. In a direct retort to Monasebian, Jean-Marie Biju-Duval, a Paris-based lawyer who served as defence counsel for Ferdinand Nahimana, takes issue with the legal arguments that were central to the guilty verdict in the Media Trial. Biju-Duval attacks the tribunal's ruling on the question of the criminality of the propaganda that was broadcast and published before 6 April 1994, when the attack on the president's plane precipitated the massacres and genocide of April to July 1994, during which he concedes the media did make direct calls for extermination. Charity Kagwi–Ndungu, who was also a prosecutor in the trial, examines the difficulty of prosecuting the crime of incitement to genocide in print media. She argues, 'The challenge is how to counter war propaganda and speeches in the future that jeopardize the lives of minority groups.' Finally, Binaifer Nowrojee, author of *Shattered Lives: Sexual Violence During the Rwandan Genocide and its Aftermath* (Nowrojee 1996) focuses on the direct link between the sexually graphic and offensive depiction of Tutsi women in the pages of *Kangura* before the genocide and the brutal sexual violence and rape that became a stock in trade of the killers during the genocide. Nowrojee takes issue with the Rwanda tribunal's failure to prosecute journalists specifically for inciting sexual violence.

AFTER THE GENOCIDE AND THE WAY FORWARD

Part Four of this collection explores issues that emerged after the Rwanda genocide – such questions as appropriate strategies for media intervention in such a situation, the role of the media in peace-building and in cases where the media in vulnerable societies are being abused. This concluding section also looks at the media climate in Rwanda and, finally, the portrayal of the Rwanda genocide in popular culture.

Frank Chalk, co-director of the Montreal Institute for Genocide and Human Rights Studies and co-author of *History and Sociology of Genocide: Analyses and Case Studies* (Chalk and Jonassohn 1990), makes blunt recommendations for aggressive intervention in situations where media are being manipulated. Chalk recommends three possible forms of intervention: early-stage interventions in conflict situations where mass killing has not begun; medium-stage interventions in societies just beginning to suffer genocidal massacres; and late-stage interventions launched when genocide is underway, which could require actually destroying the transmitters and printing presses of the hate media outlets.

Philippe Dahinden, a Swiss journalist, focuses on his experience founding and managing the independent station Radio Agatashya, which covered Rwanda, Burundi and the Kivu after July 1994 in an attempt to counter the destructive messages of hate radio. This led to the creation of the Hirondelle Foundation, an international organization of journalists that establishes media operations in crisis areas.

Mark Frohardt, Africa regional director for Internews and former deputy chief of mission for the United Nations Human Rights Field Operation in Rwanda (May 1995 to June 1997), describes a groundbreaking analysis on the role of media in vulnerable societies. According to Frohardt and co-author Jonathan Temin, vulnerable societies are highly susceptible to movement toward civil conflict or repressive rule or both. They advocate *structural interventions,* such as strengthening domestic and international journalist networks; *content-specific interventions,* such as issue-oriented training; and *aggressive interventions,* such as radio and television jamming.

The current media climate in Rwanda is the subject of a paper by Lars Waldorf, a former Human Rights Watch staffer in Rwanda. He describes how an authoritarian regime in Rwanda continues to justify censorship and propaganda as a necessary safeguard against the recrudescence of genocide. Waldorf contends that after the RPF stopped the genocide and took control in July 1994, it retooled the previous regime's information agency and the official media to disseminate its own propaganda.

Carleton University professor Michael Dorland writes about the place of the Rwanda genocide in popular culture, with particular reference to the film 'Hotel Rwanda'. Dorland, an expert on the Holocaust film genre, reflects on what happens to this genre when the subjects are not Jewish.

Finally, in an epilogue written in 2006 – some twelve years after the genocide – I reflect on what, if anything, has changed in the meantime. If we can't figure out the structural flaws in the news media that resulted in the failure to provide adequate coverage of the Rwanda genocide or the more recent crisis in Darfur, surely that difficulty should not prevent us from trying to change the structure one small piece at a time, through the work of individual journalists. The collection ends with a rallying cry to journalists, to assume their responsibilities.

It is our hope that this collection of papers will foster a more critical and comprehensive examination of the role of the news media in the Rwanda genocide. The stark reality is that all these years later, we have barely begun to learn the lessons of Rwanda.

NOTES

1. A copy of the raw footage shot by journalist Nick Hughes has been deposited in the Media and Genocide Archive at Carleton University. The footage was also entered as Exhibit 467 at the trial of Georges Rutaganda before the International Criminal Tribunal for Rwanda in Arusha, Tanzania.

REFERENCES

Chalk, F. and K. Jonassohn. 1990. *History and Sociology of Genocide: Analyses and Case Studies.* Yale University Press, New Haven, CT, 624 pp.

Chrétien, J.P., J.F. Dupaquier and M. Kabanda. 1995. *Rwanda: les Médias du Génocide.* Karthala, Paris, France. 397 pp.

Des Forges, A. 1999. *Leave None to Tell the Story: Genocide in Rwanda.* Human Rights Watch and the International Federation of Human Rights Leagues, New York, NY, USA. Available at <www.hrw.org/reports/1999/rwanda/> (accessed 30 August 2005).

ICTR (International Criminal Tribunal for Rwanda). 2003. Summary judgement. In *The Prosecutor* v. *Ferdinand Nahimana, Jean-Bosco Barayagwiza, Hassan Ngeze.* ICTR-99–52-T. ICTR, Arusha, Tanzania, 3 December. Available at <http://65.18.216.88/> (accessed 30 August 2005).

IPEP (International Panel of Eminent Personalities). 2000. *Rwanda: the Preventable Genocide.* Organization of African Unity, Addis Ababa, Ethiopia.

Melvern, L. 2000. *A People Betrayed: the Role of the West in Rwanda's Genocide.* Zed Books, London, UK.

—— 2004. *Conspiracy to Murder: the Rwandan Genocide.* Verso, New York, NY, USA. 358 pp.

Nowrojee, B. 1996. *Shattered Lives: Sexual Violence During the Rwandan Genocide and its Aftermath.* Human Rights Watch, New York, NY, USA.

2
The Media Dichotomy

Roméo Dallaire

The news media – both domestic and international – played a crucial role in the 1994 Rwanda genocide. From my vantage point as commander of the United Nations Assistance Mission for Rwanda (UNAMIR), I was able to watch the strange dichotomy of local media, on one side, fuelling the killing while international media, on the other side, virtually ignored or misunderstood what was happening.

The local media, particularly the extremist radio station Radio-Télévision Libre des Milles Collines (RTLM), were literally part of the genocide. The *genocidaires* used the media like a weapon. The haunting image of killers with a machete in one hand and a radio in the other never leaves you.

The international media initially affected events by their absence. A tree was falling in the forest and no one was there to hear it. Only those of us in Rwanda, it seemed, could hear the sound, because the international media were not there in any appreciable numbers at the outset.

And my mission, especially in those early days, was ill equipped to monitor what was being broadcast in the local media or to counteract it with strong messages of our own about the UN and its role in Rwanda.

To step back for a moment, it is important to set the scene in Rwanda in 1993–94, then to look at the ways in which the media were involved, both locally and internationally. This was a time when Rwanda had, in theory, finished a civil war. Enemies had signed a peace agreement, some of them under duress. In the course of a year, the country moved from a peace agreement through political stagnation to assassinations, massacres, civil war and, ultimately, genocide. In the end, the Tutsi minority actually won the war, gained control of the whole country and is now on a different path.

In my view, 1993–94 was an era in the 'new world disorder', not the 'new world order', as George Bush, Sr, called it. No new military thinking, no new diplomatic thinking was coming to the fore.

We were entering an era of conflict into which many diplomats, politicians, soldiers and humanitarian relief workers stumbled. They did a lot of on-the-job training, a lot of crisis management. In some cases they applied too many resources, at a terrible cost of life. In Rwanda, they didn't want to get involved at all, creating an orphan nation, where the people simply didn't count.

The American experience in Mogadishu in October 1993 significantly changed the will of the Western world to commit itself to the betterment of the developing world. Eighteen American soldiers were killed. They were professional soldiers who knew that every day when they woke up, they risked their lives. It was part of their way of life, their professional commitment. But after 18 military deaths in Somalia, the imperial power turned tail and ran.

The Americans had entered Somalia, along with Canadians and soldiers from many other countries, because hundreds of thousands of Somalis were dying of thirst and lack of food and medical supplies. When the Americans eventually pulled out – and pulled the heart out of the mission leaving it in the hands of Pakistanis, Italians, Canadians and the UN – there were still hundreds of thousands of Somalis dying. But for the United States, the price had become too high. The price of 18 soldiers was too high for the American government to continue with its stated aim of helping Somalia.

In Rwanda, in the first 24 hours of the genocide, the death of ten Belgian soldiers was too much for Belgium, the ex-colonial power, to sustain. It was a massive shock, I agree, and the Belgians pulled out and tried to convince everybody else that we should leave. They said we would all be massacred and nobody wanted to get involved in another African escapade where the risk of soldiers' lives was too high.

A representative of one major power came to me within the first weeks of the genocide and said quite clearly that, after doing an assessment, they had decided that they were not going to come and stop the carnage. There were bodies all over. We were already burning bodies with diesel fuel, because of the fear of disease, the smell and the wild dogs. This representative said, 'You know, this country is of no strategic value. Geographically, it provides us nothing. It's not even worth putting a radar station here. Economically it's nothing, because there's no strategic resources, only tea and coffee, and the bottom is falling out of those markets.'

This person said, 'In fact what there's too much of here is people. Well, we're not going to come because of people.' In quantifying that, he went on to say that his government could only reconsider its decision not to intervene if for every one if its soldiers either killed or injured, there would be an equivalent of 85,000 dead Rwandans.

Are all humans human or are some more human than others? Do some count more than others? Millions of dollars were pouring into Yugoslavia in 1994 along with tens of thousands of troops. Everybody was looking at Yugoslavia. Nobody came to Rwanda. They pulled everything out and abandoned us in the field. There were more people killed, injured, internally displaced and turned into refugees in 100 days in Rwanda than during the six years of the Yugoslav campaign. And yet, the powers that be ripped the heart out of the possibility of stopping, or at least curtailing, the killing or saving of black Africans. It was as if those people didn't count.

In Yugoslavia, the problems were portrayed as long-standing divisions that educated people had debated. It was religious and ethnic conflict, something studied and analyzed. As such, we brought in new terms, like 'ethnic cleansing' to describe Yugoslavia. In Rwanda, it was just a bunch of tribes going at each other, like they always do. Rwanda was black. Yugoslavia was white European.

And where were the media? Where were the media in that debate? How many were taken in or set up? In terms of humanity, the real crisis at that time was in a small country in black Africa that nobody was interested in. The media for the most part travelled down the road of the mainstream thinking of the world powers – it was Yugoslavia that mattered, not Rwanda.

While the killing raged on in Rwanda, the O.J. Simpson case dominated the airwaves. Tonya Harding's kneecapping of her figure skating competitor was there as well. You had Nelson Mandela's election in South Africa. You had Yugoslavia. And, oh yes, somewhere in there, a bunch of black tribesmen in Africa were killing each other. During the 100 days of the Rwanda genocide, there was more coverage of Tonya Harding by ABC, CBS and NBC than of the genocide itself. Was that because of a love of pathos? Was it because of the excitement? Was it because the Harding story was on CNN's radar screen? Or was it the hand of someone above, guiding the media and getting across the subtle message, 'Listen, we have absolutely no interest in going into another hellhole in Africa. We do not want to get involved in Rwanda. So don't get us involved.'

The media, like so many others in Rwanda, failed. The world powers failed. Individually we failed.

Major news agencies devote fewer resources to Africa to begin with and virtually ignore small countries like Rwanda, which are deemed to be of little strategic value. There is no context, no general understanding of situations like the one that evolved in Rwanda. As I say in my book, when I was asked to go and serve as commander of the mission in Rwanda, I had to ask, 'Rwanda, that's in Africa isn't it?'

Before the genocide, the media scene in Rwanda was essentially internal with some local stringers, who were responding more often than not to the international journalists based in Nairobi. Until the start of the war, international media involvement amounted to: 'Is there an event? Do we go or do we just get the stringer?'

Months before the genocide, when we opened our mission headquarters with President Habyarimana in attendance, a number of journalists from international agencies were there. When the president was sworn in as part of the new government, there was international media coverage. When there was a massacre in the northwest of the country, there was international coverage.

But in essence, the international press were neophytes when it came to Rwanda. In fact, one international media organization was using a Rwandan stringer in Kigali who was part of the extremist movement. I had a call from a London journalist, who asked questions that were clearly based on false information. Thank God a person like Mark Doyle of the BBC spent considerable time on the ground and worked to set the record straight.

In my view, most of the journalists who came into Rwanda after the war started knew little or nothing of the country. Those who *did* know a lot were not necessarily listened to. Many stories were simply gruesome accounts of killings. There was little analysis of why we let a potential peace process fall into disarray.

After years of ignoring the place, after 6 April, all of a sudden every journalist wanted to jump on whatever aircraft or truck was available to get to Kigali. They didn't know what they were looking for, but there was excitement and it had reached the CNN radar screen. So, in the first days, a number of journalists did appear; within the first week, more than 200 were sitting in Nairobi.

They came to report that people were being slaughtered. Platoons of journalists would come in for three or four days, then leave so I could bring more in. We guaranteed their safety and provided them with transport, food and lodging. To me it was absolutely essential that they get their story. I put the lives of my troops on the line to guarantee that people got their daily story. Not only to get to the places where the catastrophe was evolving, but also to get their stories out. I had officers and soldiers run the gauntlet to get television tapes to my headquarters in Uganda, then to Kampala and then Nairobi where the technology existed to transmit images.

It took some time before the big media outfits arrived and set up their international capabilities. Within the third week of the genocide, when the UN had buckled under and decided that it was not only *not* going to reinforce the mission, but that it was also going to abandon Rwanda, the only voice, the only weapon that I had, was the media. If, through the media, I could shame the international community into acting, then I would have achieved my aim. But despite the courageous work done by reporters in the field, the stories often didn't get past the editor's desk. The story never really got told and that's why O.J. Simpson and Tonya Harding got a lot more press than 800,000 human beings being slaughtered.

The media can be a two-way street. I tried to give journalists what they required and some of them were instrumental in providing me with information. Many journalists were courageous enough to go between the lines. I opened my headquarters to them. The only time I didn't want them there was when we were planning operations. At other times, I would see journalists standing at the big map boards with my operations duty officers. They would be marking the map and saying, 'Yes, I've been through there and, yeah, there is a massacre site there and, yes, there are about 50,000 people on the side of that hill over there.' The exchange was transparent.

But after the initial flurry of attention in the first few days of April, most international media representatives were evacuated with the other expatriates and it seemed like there was no one left, like no one cared.

When news reaches the general population, it shapes public opinion. When there is a lack of statesmanship, public opinion can force a government to make decisions. Getting information out to the general population and holding decision-makers accountable – by continuously berating them about what is going on and what they are doing or not doing – is more crucial than a few talk shows and a couple of newscasts. In the case of Rwanda, that's where the process broke down. The events in Rwanda simply did not break through to such an extent as to create momentum.

From mid-April into the beginning of May, only a handful of international reporters were on the ground to witness the genocide. I went to great lengths during that period to attract international media attention. I wanted journalists to get their stories and, as I said, I used UNAMIR resources to get tapes up to the Ugandan border, so that they could eventually reach Europe. The BBC's Mark Doyle used my satellite phone from time to time. I felt that one good journalist on the ground was worth a battalion of troops, because I realized they could bring pressure to bear.

I had a policy of taking all media calls in the evening and gave instructions to my staff to facilitate those interviews. I had frequent conversations with Michael Enright on the Canadian Broadcasting Corporation's radio programme 'As it Happens'. But the media coverage wasn't enough to create an outcry in the international community. The ambivalence of the great powers toward Rwanda was too imbedded; they had reason to be disinterested, to turn away, because of 'Somalia fatigue'.

Ironically, the news media finally descended in hordes once the genocide was over and the 'refugee crisis' occurred in Goma. A clouded picture of the suffering appeared, as *genocidaires* were among those who fled and were now getting ten times the media attention given to the genocide itself.

I have been asked why I didn't leak the famous 11 January cable, with its warning about *Interahamwe* militia training to kill thousands, making lists and hiding weapons. There has been much debate about my message to the UN in New York, about an informant who provided information about arms caches and the preparation of lists of people to be exterminated. I informed New York of my intention to raid some of the arms caches, but was ordered not to intervene. Once it was clear the UN system was not going to act on those warnings, should I have leaked the information to *The New York Times* or the *Washington Post*?

If the media had come and asked me what was going on, if they had come and queried me about the stagnation and the political and security process and asked me what we were doing, they would have got the answer. And they could have reported what was happening. But I was not going to leak that document. You cannot be ethical and fiddle with the media.

Within the country, Rwandan media played an exceptionally important role in the genocide. The country is known as a radio country. In some villages, radio was like the voice of God. At the height of the killing, in the camps for the displaced and refugees, you could still find people with portable radios. I wondered where they got the batteries. We couldn't even get batteries for our flashlights.

RTLM was created specifically as a tool of the *genocidaires* to demonize the Tutsi, lay the groundwork, then literally drive on the killing once the genocide started.

A great handicap for UNAMIR (in effect the representative on the ground of the world community) was our initial ignorance of what was really happening and of the mixed media messages. We had so little capacity to monitor broadcasts, particularly those in the local language, Kinyarwanda. For a long time, we didn't notice the difference in tone between RTLM broadcasts in French and those in Kinyarwanda. We missed this vital early-warning sign of what was to come because, in effect, we weren't listening properly to local media and what it was telling people in January, February and March 1994.

I still believe it would have made a significant difference if we had had the capacity to monitor local media comprehensively from the outset. This was one of the lessons learned from Rwanda – that part of the role of an international force is to get the whole picture, to realize the importance of media messaging.

In the first few days after 6 April, it was Rwanda's prime minister designate, Faustin Twagiramungu, who was in hiding in my headquarters, who acted as my media monitor, listening to RTLM and translating from Kinyarwanda. Later, we hired a young man who could speak English and French and trained him to perform the same task.

Missions such as ours need people with media and linguistic skills. You ignore the local media at your peril. And there was another lesson in this volatile situation: UNAMIR desperately needed its own media outlet, its own radio station. We were unarmed in the media war that was going on and had virtually no capacity to explain ourselves to the local community to whom radio was so important. People were turning to the extremist RTLM, the state-run Radio Rwanda and the rebel-controlled Radio Muhaburu. In Cambodia, for example, the UN's use of radio was essential. But in our case, the equipment was unavailable, so it was dropped from the budget for our mission. In January and February, when it became apparent that we needed a media outlet to explain ourselves, we begged the UN for that facility. We knew that equipment from the UN station in Cambodia was in storage in Italy, but although we pleaded for it, we didn't receive the gear until well after the genocide.

We did not have a radio station to take part in the debate or to sell our 'product'. It became clear to me that none of the radio stations in Rwanda actually told people why we were there. No information from us was being passed on. People saw a white vehicle with a blue flag going by at 70 kilometres an hour, but many Rwandans had no idea why we were there. Those who *did* know were led to believe that we could do much more than our mandate actually permitted.

In fairness, before 6 April, at the behest of Jean-Marie Higiro, then the director of Radio Rwanda, we were allowed 30 minutes a week on the air. But we discovered that no one in our small mission had the skill to do 30 minutes of programming. In fact, some weeks we didn't even go on the air. Without interpreters or media analysts, we didn't even have the ability to present a lucid programme.

Once the killing started, I would meet displaced people and Rwandans would always have this sort of look of astonishment with regard to the Blue Berets. They believed that the UNAMIR mandate was to protect and defend the Rwandans, whereas, in fact, the Security Council limited it to assisting in establishing an atmosphere of security. The limitations of our mandate were never really explained to the whole of the nation, and that is one of the great tragedies of the mission.

Another tragedy was our failure to intervene early to shut down RTLM, which had become the voice of the devil in Rwanda. Through January, February and March 1994, before the genocide began, the radio station stepped up its campaign, delivering the message that there were people who should not live in Rwanda. It even described ways to eliminate them. Failing all else, we should have shut down RTLM. I repeatedly asked for the capability to jam RTLM, but the request was denied. The argument was that this would amount to a violation of state sovereignty and that there was also a very high cost attached to maintaining jamming equipment.

In my view, it was time to question the absolute of state sovereignty and to ask whether it was becoming an impediment to humanity. When RTLM started to attack not only the mission, but also myself, when RTLM was launching its descriptions of how to kill, it was obvious to everyone that RTLM was operating without any rules. It was beyond rules. It was beyond limits. And it was an overt instrument of genocide. I went to the UN and the big powers, and said, 'I need two things. One is a radio station and, second, I need somebody to find that RTLM emitter and close her down, either by jamming it or ultimately destroying it.' At the height of the genocide, the response was that Rwanda is a sovereign state, the airwaves belong to that sovereign state and we cannot intervene. Sovereignty became an instrument for not doing something.

In fact, on 25 May 1994 in a convocation speech at the US Naval Academy in Annapolis, Maryland, President Clinton said the US could not be the policeman of the world and would only participate in and fully support UN peacekeeping operations that were deemed to be in the vital interests of the US. 'We cannot solve every such outburst of civil strife or militant nationalism simply by sending in our forces,' Clinton said. 'We cannot turn away from them. But our interests are not sufficiently at stake in so many of them to justify a commitment of our folks.'

This doctrine was spelled out in Presidential Decision Directive 25, unveiled that same month, even as the killing went on unabated across Rwanda. That directive codified and complicated US participation in peacekeeping operations. Indeed, it is my understanding that weeks earlier, on 7 April, in the working room of the Security Council, Madeleine Albright and her colleagues said bluntly about Rwanda, 'The Americans are not going to intervene, and they're not going to help anybody who wants to.'

The world failed utterly to deal with one of the century's most clear-cut examples of abuse of the media. Sadly, we dealt with it only in hindsight through the 'Media Trial', the important prosecution at the International Criminal Tribunal for Rwanda.

As for the international media, I think we need to ask ourselves, did the lack of attention and understanding by the international media actually contribute to the genocide? Did the decision to ignore Rwanda border on complicity by letting this atrocity go unreported?

The media can be both a weapon and a conscience to humanity. Journalists can be powerful, individually and collectively. But they can also be manipulated very easily if the depth of the subject is not there. For future journalists, my advice is get yourselves a lot more cultured, learn some geography, some anthropology, some sociology and maybe even some philosophy. Bring more depth to your questions and to your analysis. And stay dynamic in the search for the truth, for you are an instrument of the absolute called 'justice'. If you abdicate or if you are perfunctory, then we will all be weakened.

3
Rwanda: Walking the Road to Genocide

Gerald Caplan

BEFORE INDEPENDENCE

It is not difficult to isolate the key steps that led from the late pre-colonial period in Rwanda to the genocide a full century later. There was nothing inexorable about this process. At its heart was the deliberate choice of successive elites to deepen the cleavages between the country's two main ethnic groups, to dehumanize the group that was out of power and to legitimate the use of violence against that group. In hindsight, two almost competing historical evolutions can be seen: the series of building blocks that paved the way to the point where genocide became conceivable; and the numerous occasions when it was not yet too late to reverse this destructive pattern.

It was under *Mwami* (King) Rwabugiri, a Tutsi who ruled during the late 1800s, that the chief characteristics of modern Rwanda were fixed for the next 100 years. A powerful head of a centralized state, he provided firm direction to an elaborate series of subordinate structures. In the colonial era, under German and then Belgian rule, Roman Catholic missionaries, inspired by the overtly racist theories of nineteenth-century Europe, concocted a bizarre ideology of ethnic cleavage and racial rankings that attributed superior qualities to the country's Tutsi minority. This 15 per cent of the population, it was announced, were approaching, however gradually, the exalted level of white people, in contrast with the declared brutishness and innate inferiority of the 'Bantu' (Hutu) majority. Because the missionaries ran the colonial-era schools, these pernicious values were systematically transmitted to several generations of Rwandans along with more conventional Catholic teachings.

The alleged differences between ethnic groups were arbitrary and baseless, yet they soon took on a life of their own. The Belgians made the *Mwami*'s complex structures more rigid and ethnically inflexible. They institutionalized the split between the two groups, culminating in the issuance to every Rwandan of an ethnic identity card. This card system was maintained for over 60 years until, with tragic irony, during the genocide it became the instrument that enabled Hutu killers in urban areas to identify the Tutsi who were its original beneficiaries.

While it served them, the Tutsi elite were only too pleased to believe in their own natural superiority and to run the country for their Belgian patrons. The majority Hutu were treated with harshness appropriate to a lower caste. Soon many Hutu came to agree that the two ethnic groups, distinguished mostly by vocation in prior centuries, were indeed fundamentally dissimilar in nature and irreconcilable in practice. The Tutsi came to be demonized as a foreign invading power with no entitlements in Rwanda.

As the colonial era drew to a close, democracy in the colonies became synonymous with majority rule. The tragedy of Rwanda is that the majority came to be defined by ethnicity alone. A national independence movement, an umbrella under which all citizens united to oppose colonial rule, failed to thrive in Rwanda. Voices of moderation and inclusiveness were drowned out by extremists advocating ethnic exclusivity.

Yet, there had been little open violence before independence. Hutu were unquestionably considered the 'serfs', but only some Tutsi benefited from colonialism; many led lives no better than the Hutu peasantry. Then, as always, the notion of ethnic homogeneity was contradicted by the actual divisions within both Hutu and Tutsi communities.

Although Hutu surely resented their status and treatment, considerable intermarriage took place between the two groups, which after all shared a common language, religion, geography and, often as not, appearance. Tutsi cattle herders and Hutu farmers complemented each other. Hatred between the two groups needed careful nurturing. Until political parties formed on the basis of ethnic origins, there were no massacres of either ethnic group by the other.

Instead of an independence struggle directed against their colonial masters, the Hutu party targeted their masters' Tutsi surrogates. Surprisingly enough, Hutu politicians now found themselves actively supported by the Belgians and the Catholic Church, both reversing their original stance once they realized that Hutu rule was inevitable. This support continued even when anti-Tutsi violence broke out. Between 1959 and 1967, 20,000 Tutsi were killed and 300,000 fled in terror to neighbouring countries. In the eyes of some Tutsi today, these attacks constitute either a prelude to genocide or genocide itself.

THE FIRST AFRICAN GOVERNMENTS

The newly independent government of Grégoire Kayibanda made its colours apparent from the start. As early as 1961, the United Nations reported that 'the developments of these last 18 months have brought about the racial dictatorship of one party ... An oppressive system has been replaced by another one.' The Hutu government pleased no one, not even the large majority of its fellow Hutu. Life for the peasantry remained precarious, while a small Hutu elite from the north and northwest grew increasingly dissatisfied with their marginal role in Kayibanda's southern-dominated government.

As pressure on Kayibanda grew, he unleashed ethnic terror once again, hoping to save his regime by uniting the Hutu against the common Tutsi enemy. At the same time, ethnic cleavages were reinforced, neither for the first nor last time, by events south of the border in Burundi. In 1972, after an appalling massacre of the Hutu majority by the Tutsi government there, terrorized Burundian Hutu flooded into Rwanda to inflame ethnic tensions and to join in anti-Tutsi attacks.

Although relatively few Tutsi were killed, many thousands were driven out to join their ethnic kin in exile.

But Kayibanda's exploitation of ethnic fears failed to save his regime and, in 1973, he was replaced by Juvénal Habyarimana, head of the Rwandan army. For the next 15 years, Rwanda enjoyed relatively good times and little ethnic violence. Habyarimana opened the country to the world and efficient, stable little Rwanda soon became the darling of the West's burgeoning development industry. As for the Tutsi, they were now safe for the first time in almost 15 years. It is true they suffered significant institutional discrimination. They were allowed to play only a marginal role in politics, were shut out of the military and were limited by quota to 10 per cent of education placements. But they thrived in the private sector and were successful in the liberal professions as well as some public service institutions.

More than 60 per cent of Rwandans were Catholic, and the church remained a trusted ally and reliable bulwark of the regime, giving it legitimacy and comfort literally until the end. In common with the foreign governments and aid agencies that were involved with Rwanda, church leaders rarely challenged the ethnic basis of public life or Habyarimana's one-party military dictatorship; indeed, they embraced without reservation the notion of demographic democracy based on the Hutu's overwhelming majority.

By the late 1980s, however, economic progress stalled. Government revenues declined as coffee and tea prices dropped. International financial institutions, indifferent to the social and political consequences of their demands, imposed programmes that exacerbated inflation, land scarcity and unemployment. Young men were hit particularly hard. The mood of the country was raw.

It was at this vulnerable moment, on 1 October 1990, that the children of the Tutsi refugees who had earlier fled into English-speaking Uganda re-emerged as a rebel army, the Rwandan Patriotic Front (RPF). Often made scapegoats and persecuted in exile, Rwandan Tutsi also remained unwelcome back in Rwanda. According to Habyarimana, the country was too poor, too crowded and had too little land to accommodate the exiled community – all plausible propositions.

The RPF invasion and the government's response constituted a giant step on the road to genocide. The RPF was not constrained by the knowledge that incursions by Tutsi exiles in the 1960s had led to great brutality against other Tutsi. As for Habyarimana, he had a choice in October 1990. Contrary to RPF expectations, few Rwandans of any background welcomed these unknown 'Ugandan' soldiers. A united front among *all* Rwandans against outside invaders was perfectly plausible. But an opportunistic and threatened government chose the opposite course; with great deliberation, to further their own self-interest, they reawakened the sleeping dogs of ethnic division. All Tutsi, both citizens and RPF soldiers, were portrayed as alien invaders, while divisions among Hutu had to be submerged in a common front against the intruders. All Tutsi were denounced as fifth columnists, secret supporters of the RPF. Anti-Tutsi propaganda, largely muted for the previous 17 years, was unleashed anew.

At the same time, Habyarimana called on his foreign friends for military help. The French responded most positively. Their forces prevented a swift RPF victory over the hapless Rwandan army, and French soldiers and advisors remained in the country counselling Habyarimana's people politically and militarily on keeping these 'anglo-saxon' interlopers at bay. The government learned that, whatever it did, it could always count on the unconditional public and private support of the French government.

Immediately after the RPF raid, the Organization of African Unity (OAU) threw itself into peacemaking and attempts to resolve the conflict. For the OAU in Rwanda and then the Great Lakes region, the 1990s were a time of well-meant initiatives, incessant meetings, commitments made and commitments broken. In the end, the OAU had only enough resources and power to bring adversaries together, hope they agreed and pray they did not violate their agreements.

The impact of the RPF raid was devastating in every way. Its advances, together with the government's anti-Tutsi propaganda, drove terrified Hutu into internal settlement camps. In a short time, close to 300,000 Rwandans had been driven from or fled their land to become 'internally displaced persons' (IDPs). In early 1993, another large-scale RPF attack led to a further million, mostly Hutu, IDPs. The country was in turmoil. The ailing economy had little chance to recover. Anti-Tutsi violence, organized by the government or its allies, spread like wildfire, while the RPF insurgents similarly showed little restraint in dealing brutally with Hutu civilians in the areas they 'liberated'.

Within the Habyarimana government, real power increasingly resided with a small faction of insiders from the northwest called the *Akazu*, 'the little house'; it was also widely known as '*le Clan de Madame*', as its core was the president's wife, family and close associates, who were the chief beneficiaries of the corruption that characterized the regime. As the economic collapse significantly reduced the available spoils of power and called into question the very legitimacy of the regime, the *Akazu* began playing the ethnic card to divert attention away from serious divisions among the Hutu.

This should not be taken to mean that planning of the genocide was initiated at a precise moment. Both physical and rhetorical violence against the Tutsi continued to escalate from the RPF incursion until the genocide actually started in April 1994. There is no question that this campaign was organized and promoted and that at some point it turned into a strategy for genocide. But that exact point remains unknown. For Rwanda, the 'smoking gun' that nails the perpetrators and their fanatical plot is not a single meeting or a particular letter, but rather a cumulative series of events.

Rwanda endured three and a half years of violent anti-Tutsi incidents. In retrospect, most of these can be interpreted as deliberate steps in a vast conspiracy culminating in the shooting down of the president's plane on the evening of 6 April 1994 and the unleashing of the genocide. But this interpretation remains somewhat speculative. No one yet knows who shot down the plane, nor can it be demonstrated that every one of the countless manifestations of anti-Tutsi sentiment in these years was part of a diabolical master plan. The evidence most plausibly suggests that the idea of genocide emerged only gradually through 1991 and 1992, accelerating in determination through 1993 and into 1994.

Later, when it was finally over, a great international argument broke out over who knew what about the events unfolding in Rwanda. There can be no debate here; the facts speak for themselves. The world that mattered to Rwanda – its Great Lakes neighbours, the United Nations, all the major Western powers – knew exactly what was happening and that it was being masterminded at the highest levels of the state. They knew that this was no senseless case of 'Hutu killing Tutsi and Tutsi killing Hutu', as it was sometimes dismissively described. They knew that a terrible fate had befallen Rwanda. They even knew that some Hutu Power extremists were talking openly of eliminating all Tutsi, although few could then conceive that an actual genocide was being plotted.

Anti-Tutsi violence, it was widely known, was revived immediately after the RPF invasion when organized anti-Tutsi massacres began – and ended only when the genocide itself ended. Massacres of Tutsi were carried out in October 1990, January 1991, February 1991, March 1992, August 1992, January 1993, March 1993 and February 1994. On each occasion, scores of Tutsi were killed by mobs and militiamen associated with various political parties, sometimes with the involvement of the police and army, incited by the media, directed by local government officials and encouraged by some national politicians.

As the terror heightened, the organizers learned that they could not only massacre large numbers of people quickly and efficiently, they could get away with it. Wholehearted backing of the regime by the French government and general indifference to the escalating racism by the churches reinforced this feeling. A culture of impunity developed as the conspirators grew bolder. Extremist army officers colluded with the circles surrounding Habyarimana and the *Akazu* to form secret societies and Latin American-style death squads known as '*Amasasu*' (bullets) and the 'Zero Network'. They did not long remain secret; in 1992, their existence and connections were publicly exposed.

But contrary forces were at work at the same time. Pressure for democratization from both within and outside the country forced Habyarimana to accept multiparty politics. The apparent advance toward democracy, however, had several unanticipated consequences, all of them unwelcome. A host of new parties emerged, most of them Hutu, wanting to participate in the process. One of these new parties, the Coalition for the Defence of the Republic, represented Hutu radicals and had links to the death squads. What was worse, parties organized their own youth militias, the most notorious being the *Interahamwe* formed by Habyarimana's own *Mouvement Républicain National pour la Democratie et le Développement* (MRND). At the same time, new hate-propagating media sprang up, most infamously a private radio station calling itself Radio-Télévision Libre des Milles Collines (RTLM), which was financed and controlled by the *Akazu* faction. While his militia terrorized opponents and beat up Tutsi and his radio station incited ethnic hatred and violence, Habyarimana, with great reluctance, agreed to accept a coalition government.

Immediately, the new ministers joined with the OAU and Western powers to pressure Habyarimana to agree to negotiations with the RPF in Arusha,

Tanzania. In August 1993, after long, drawn-out sessions, agreement was reached on a series of key issues. But these were never implemented. Ultimately, Arusha backfired. The more it appeared that power and the limited spoils of office would have to be shared not only with other Hutu parties but also with the RPF, the more determined the *Akazu* insiders grew to share nothing with anyone.

At the same moment, a deadly new weapon was unexpectedly delivered into the hands of the Rwandan Hutu. The assassination in October 1993 by Tutsi officers of Burundi's democratically elected Hutu president and the appalling massacres that followed were taken by many Hutu as final proof that power-sharing between Tutsi and Hutu was forever doomed; the Tutsi could never be trusted. The emergence of Hutu Power, an explicit and public organizing concept, was the immediate consequence of the Burundi upheaval. Large Hutu Power rallies attracted members of all parties, attesting to the new reality that ethnic solidarity trumped party allegiances. Political life, in these last turbulent months before the genocide, was reorganized strictly around the two ethnic poles.

As the conspiracy widened and deepened, so did knowledge of the conspirators' intentions. Virtually everyone in Rwanda associated with the United Nations, the diplomatic community or human rights groups knew about death lists, accelerating massacres, arms proliferation and threats to opposition politicians. The UN military mission uncovered a high-level *Interahamwe* informant, whose revelations led its commander, Major General Roméo Dallaire, to send his famous 11 January 1994 message – the so-called 'genocide fax' – to New York headquarters: 'Jean-Pierre,' Dallaire reported, 'has been ordered to register all Tutsi in Kigali. He suspects it is for their extermination. Example he gave was that in 20 minutes his personnel could kill up to 1,000 Tutsi.' Dallaire's superiors at the Department of Peacekeeping Operations replied with the perverse instruction to inform the president and take no further action. Another opportunity to expose the conspiracy was lost.

When it was finally unleashed only three months later, hours after Habyarimana went down with his plane, the violence was organized and coordinated. Its goal was explicit: genocide. A clique of Rwandan Hutu planned to mobilize the Hutu people with the explicit intention of exterminating all Tutsi in the country, including women and children. The rest of the world knew that a great disaster loomed for Rwanda, but few envisaged the possibility that the radicals would resort to outright genocide. It was a prospect simply too appalling to contemplate. But for the extremist Hutu leadership, no other response to their situation any longer seemed adequate.

THE EXTERNAL ACTORS BEFORE THE GENOCIDE

Several outside actors carried a heavy responsibility for the events that were now unfolding. Some were guilty of crimes of commission, others crimes of omission. But one way or another, as they had for the entire century, outsiders had great influence on Rwanda's fate, much of it malevolent.

Within Rwanda itself, the chief culprits were the Catholic and Anglican hierarchies and the French government, all active supporters of the Habyarimana government. Church leaders failed to use their unique moral position among the overwhelmingly Christian population to denounce ethnic hatred and human rights abuse. The French government was guilty of the same failure at the elite level. Its public backing constituted a major disincentive for the radicals to make concessions or to think in terms of compromise. Although some French officials knew that many of their clients at the highest echelons of the Rwandan regime were guilty of human rights violations, they failed to use their influence to demand that such violations stop. At the same time, they continued to act as senior political and military advisors to the government. The radicals drew the obvious lesson: they could get away with anything.

At the United Nations, the Security Council, led unremittingly by the United States, simply did not care enough about Rwanda to intervene appropriately. There were no economic or strategic interests at play. What makes this betrayal of their responsibility even more intolerable is that the genocide was in no way inevitable. It could have been prevented entirely. Even once it was allowed to begin, the destruction could have been significantly mitigated. All that was required was a relatively modest international military force, perhaps 5000 properly trained troops, with a strong mandate to enforce the Arusha agreements. Nothing of the kind was authorized by the Security Council before the genocide, and the force that was approved during the genocide was not permitted to intervene until the slaughter was over.

The United States has formally apologized for its failure to prevent the genocide. President Clinton insisted that it was a function of ignorance. The evidence shows that the American government knew precisely what was happening, not least during the months of the genocide. Domestic politics took priority over the lives of helpless Africans. After losing 18 soldiers in Somalia in October 1993, the US was unwilling to participate in further peacekeeping missions and was largely opposed to the Security Council authorizing any new serious missions at all, with or without American participation.

In October 1993, the first UN mission to Rwanda (UNAMIR) was set up; it was notable mostly for its weak mandate and minimal capacity. No amount of credible early warnings could persuade the members of the Security Council to treat the mission seriously or the UN Secretariat to interpret its mandate flexibly. In fact, the single occasion on which UNAMIR was authorized to go beyond its passive observer mandate was at the very outbreak of the genocide. Several European nations flew planes in to evacuate their nationals, and UNAMIR was authorized not only to assist the evacuation, but also to go beyond its mandate, if required, to assure the safety of foreign nationals. Never was such permission granted for the protection of Rwandans. And none of the 2,500 European and American troops used in the evacuation or on standby in the region offered to work with UNAMIR to stop the genocide.

The significance of the Security Council's action should not be underestimated: its refusal to sanction a serious mission made the genocide more likely. The feeble UN effort helped persuade the Hutu radicals that they had nothing to fear from the outside world, regardless of their deeds. This assessment proved only too accurate. Once the genocide began, the US, backed most forcefully by Britain, repeatedly and deliberately undermined all attempts to strengthen the UN military presence in Rwanda.

Belgium became an unexpected ally in this goal. On day two of the crisis, ten Belgian soldiers were murdered by Rwandan soldiers. As the radicals had anticipated, Belgium swiftly decided to pull out all its troops, leaving the 2,500 Tutsi they were protecting at a school site to be slaughtered within hours. The Belgian government decided that its shameful retreat would be at least tempered if it were shared by others, and strenuously lobbied to disband UNAMIR entirely. Although the US supported the idea, it was too outrageous to pursue. Instead, with the genocide costing tens of thousands of lives daily, and ignoring the vigorous opposition of the OAU and African governments, the Security Council chose to cut the UN force by 90 per cent at the exact moment it needed massive reinforcement. For most of the 100 days of the genocide, General Dallaire commanded a force of only 400, many of them inadequately trained or equipped. As horror stories accelerated, the council authorized a stronger mission, UNAMIR II, but once again the US did all in its power to undermine its effectiveness. In the end, not a single new soldier or piece of military hardware reached the country before the genocide ended.

THE GENOCIDE

The two rockets that brought down President Habyarimana's plane became the catalysts for one of the great calamities of our age: a genocide and a civil war, separate but simultaneous. To this day, controversy reigns over the responsibility for this attack. Most students of the genocide believe the finger most plausibly points to Habyarimana's extremist allies, fed up with his attempts to placate outsiders. Deniers of the genocide – still active to this day – insist it was the RPF leadership. There has been no investigation and no one can say with certainty.

A certain chaos reigned for the few days following the crash, although the conspirators had control enough to begin systematic search-and-murder missions against their leading opponents, both Hutu and Tutsi. But soon enough, all sense of uncertainty ended. The government's military structure that had been built since 1990 was now swiftly mobilized to execute the genocide as well as to fight a civil war. It could now be seen clearly that its creators had an overall strategy that it implemented with scrupulous planning and organization, control of the levers of government, highly motivated soldiers and militia, the means to kill vast numbers of people, the capacity to identify and kill the victims and tight control of the media (specifically RTLM) to disseminate the right messages both inside and outside the country.

When the genocide ended little more than 100 days later, perhaps as many as a million women, children and men, the vast majority of them Tutsi, lay dead. Thousands more were raped, tortured and maimed for life. Victims were treated with sadistic cruelty and suffered unimaginable agony.

The attacks had many targets. A clear priority list for elimination included anti-Habyarimana government and opposition members; Hutu who opposed the extremists, thousands of whom were slaughtered without mercy in the first days; critics such as journalists and human rights activists; any Tutsi seen as community leaders, including professionals, political activists, lawyers and teachers; as well as priests, nuns and other clergy who were Tutsi or who sheltered intended victims.

Together, military leaders and the new interim government of Hutu Power supporters that was sworn in after the plane crash made the overall decisions, while Rwanda's elaborate governing structure implemented the genocide with remarkable efficiency. The Hutu leadership of the Catholic and Anglican churches, with a few notably courageous exceptions, played a conspicuously scandalous role in these months, often directly complicit in aiding the *genocidaires*, at best remaining silent or explicitly neutral. This stance was easily interpreted by ordinary Christians as an implicit endorsement of the killings, as was the close association of church leaders with the leaders of the genocide. Perhaps this helps explain the greatest mystery about the genocide: the terrible success of Hutu Power in turning so many ordinary people into accomplices in genocide. In no other way could so many have been killed so swiftly.

It has always been difficult to establish the numbers killed in the genocide. The highest persuasive figure for Tutsi killed seems to be near one million, the very lowest, 500,000. Government spokespeople have often used a figure of 'more than a million', while a new official figure is 937,000 dead. More research is needed to be certain. Even if the most conservative figure is used, it still means that over three-quarters of the entire population registered as Tutsi were systematically killed in just over 100 days. As well, millions of Rwandan Hutu became internally displaced within the country or fled to become refugees in neighbouring countries.

THE WORLD DURING THE GENOCIDE

Until the day it ended with the RPF's military victory, the UN, the governments of the US, France and Belgium, most African governments and the OAU all failed to define the events in Rwanda as full-blown genocide and all continued to recognize members of the *genocidaire* government as legitimate official representatives of their country. All except the French government remained publicly neutral between a government that was executing the genocide and their RPF adversaries, the only force fighting that government.

Throughout the genocide, France remained openly hostile to the RPF. After two months of conflict, the French government, in a so-called humanitarian mission known as Operation Turquoise, sent a force to create a safe zone in the southwest of the country. It probably saved the lives of 10–15,000 Tutsi, although it jeopardized other Tutsi by giving them a false sense of security. Far more consequentially, as the RPF advanced, many government and military leaders responsible for the genocide and many government soldiers and militia escaped to the safety and protection of this zone. They were then permitted by the French force to cross the border into eastern Zaire, joining fellow *genocidaires* who had escaped through other routes, all of them ready to resume their war against the new Kigali government. When the French troops pulled out in August 1994, not a single *genocidaire* had been arrested in their safe zone. The consequences for later conflict in the Great Lakes Region can hardly be exaggerated.

The facts are not in question: a small number of major actors could have prevented, halted or reduced the slaughter. They include France in Rwanda itself; the United States at the Security Council, loyally supported by Britain; Belgium, whose soldiers knew they could save countless lives if they were allowed to remain in the country; and Rwanda's church leaders. In the bitter words of the commander of the UN's military mission, the 'international community has blood on its hands'.

In the years since, the leaders of the UN, the United States, Belgium and the Anglican Church have all apologized for their failure to stop the genocide. Yet none has suggested that Rwanda is owed restitution for these failures, and in no single case has any responsible individual resigned in protest or been held to account for his or her actions. Neither the French government nor the Roman Catholic hierarchy (including the late Pope John Paul II) has apologized or accepted responsibility for its role.

RWANDA SINCE THE GENOCIDE

When the war and the genocide ended on 18 July 1994, the situation in Rwanda was almost indescribably grim. Rarely had a people anywhere had to face so many seemingly insuperable obstacles with so few resources. Their physical and psychological scars were likely to linger for decades.

The country was wrecked – a wasteland. Of seven million inhabitants before the genocide, as many as 15 per cent were dead, two million were internally displaced and another two million had become refugees. Many of those who remained had suffered horribly. Large numbers had been tortured and wounded. Many women had been raped, tortured and humiliated, some becoming infected with AIDS. Of the children who survived, 90 per cent had witnessed bloodshed or worse. An entire nation was brutalized and traumatized. They were, in their own phrase, 'the walking dead'. Yet killers and survivors had no alternative but to resume living side-by-side on Rwanda's hills.

This was the situation a new inexperienced government had to face. Its challenges were monumental and its strategies not always convincing. Although it has always called itself a government of national unity and included prominent Hutu in high-profile offices, most observers believe that real power in the land – political and military – has been exercised by a small group of the original 'RPF Tutsi', the English-speakers from Uganda. Paul Kagame, leader of the RFP forces during the civil war and genocide, and vice-president and minister of defence until he became president in 2000, has universally been seen as the government's indispensable man.

Some saw it as a government that was not trusted by its people and a people not trusted by its government. Under the circumstances, neither was surprising. A major insurgency by *genocidaires* based in the Democratic Republic of the Congo (DRC) into northwestern Rwanda caused havoc through the late 1990s. The government, suspicious of all Hutu, responded with brute force, frequently failing to distinguish between *genocidaires* and ordinary peasants. The latter, in turn, were reinforced in their belief that the RPF government was not theirs.

Nor, for very compelling reasons, did the new government trust the international community, although it immediately found itself overwhelmingly dependent on Western nations and international agencies and financial institutions to begin reconstruction. Given its past record, the world's response to Rwanda's needs ranged from modest to disappointing to downright scandalous. Although the government eventually began to find favour among various Western countries, notably the US and United Kingdom, which led to somewhat more generous aid packages, nothing like restitution or the cancellation of the odious debts incurred by the Habyarimana regime has ever been contemplated.

To make matters worse, only months after the genocide ended, many of the foreigners who had come to 'help' the country began to argue that Rwandans ought to get on with the task of rebuilding their society. 'Quit dwelling on the past and concentrate on rebuilding for the future,' they were advised. Within six months of the end of the genocide, relief workers were already telling a traumatized people, 'Yes, the genocide happened, but it's time to get over it and move on.' Rwandans believed, not without reason, that such insensitivity and lack of empathy could only be directed at Africans. In fact, as research from the Holocaust and Armenian genocides has shown, the traumas from a disaster of this order are multi-generational in their impact. Certainly today, for survivors and perpetrators alike, Rwanda remains very much a traumatized nation.

'Getting over it' is an enormously difficult task. As with all societies in transition from tyranny and terror, among an endless host of problems that continue to bedevil Rwanda are highly complex questions and dilemmas of justice, guilt and reconciliation. In the insightful words of scholar Mahmood Mamdani (2002),

> The Tutsi want justice above all else and the Hutu want democracy above all else. The minority fears democracy. The majority fears justice. The minority fears that the demand for democracy is a mask for finishing an unfinished genocide. The majority fears the demand for justice is a minority ploy to usurp power forever.

As hundreds of thousands of ordinary Rwandans had picked up their machetes and actively participated in the genocide, Rwanda faced an unprecedented situation. The UN set up an International Criminal Tribunal for Rwanda (ICTR) in Arusha, Tanzania, aimed at trying 'the big fish', while Rwanda is now experimenting with two parallel judicial systems. In all of these, the process of trying accused *genocidaires* is long, laborious and frustrating. But if there are more effective ways to deal with this issue, they are not readily apparent.

The ICTR has been a source of controversy from its inception. Foes, not least the Rwandan government, must acknowledge its groundbreaking jurisprudence, while supporters have difficulty justifying its huge budget and enormous staff – in 2004–05, US$ 231 million and 1,042 authorized posts. Although 60 people have been detained, as of mid-2005, after almost a decade of work, the court has convicted only 22 people and acquitted 3 others. Nevertheless, even within this almost derisory number, the ICTR's achievements must be recorded:

- The court interpreted the definition of genocide as presented in the 1948 *Convention for the Prevention and Punishment of Genocide*.
- It defined the crime of rape as a crime against humanity.
- It convicted, for the first time, a leader of a government for the crime of genocide.
- It ruled that the media can be a tool of genocide for which those in charge are responsible.

In Rwanda, a decimated judicial system had the responsibility for dealing with some 120,000 Hutu rotting in prisons in appalling circumstances, often without proper charges. The task defied capacity. As of 2004, some 6,500 had been tried. At this rate, it was estimated, it would take two to four centuries to clear the backlog. The government resorted to two dramatic steps. To the chagrin of the voluble survivors' umbrella organization, *Ibuka*, it released some 20,000 of those charged with lesser crimes or for whom no credible documentation existed. Beyond that, it embarked on one of the most remarkable social experiments of our time: local courts called *gacaca,* an attempt to blend traditional and contemporary mechanisms to expedite the justice process in a manner that is meant to promote reconciliation. To clear the enormous backlog of cases, 12,000 *gacaca* courts have been appointed, each made up of 19 locally elected judges. A staggering 250,000 Rwandans have been trained for their roles.

Some human rights advocates are concerned that these grass-roots courts will operate as a kind of mob justice, with no properly trained professionals and no capacity to adhere to international standards. However, most observers feel there was little practical alternative and are watching the *gacaca* panels with much interest. Already unexpected consequences are emerging. Ordinary Rwandans are accusing their neighbours of participating in the genocide, adding thousands of new names to the lists of those to be tried. Equally dramatic, Rwandans prominent in public life today have been accused of genocidal activities, most notably the minister of defence, and they too will be obligated to make their case before a *gacaca* panel. It will be some time before a balanced judgement about the effectiveness and fairness of this bold innovation can be made.

In the meantime, questions of justice and reconciliation, perplexing in any post-conflict situation let alone a genocide, will remain to bedevil official actions and popular expectations. The government has created a series of structures and institutions designed to foster reconciliation and unity, but on its own terms. Ethnicity can no longer be recognized except as a destructive aberration of the past – a radical proposition given the past century. There can be only one identity – Rwandan – and any attempt to resurrect old ethnic issues is pounced on as unacceptable 'divisionism'. Government argues this is the only way to forge a united people. To the government's opponents, it is merely a convenient excuse to suppress legitimate democratic opposition. What the vast majority of Rwandans in the hills think, what young Rwandans think, whether traditional stereotypes have evaporated because they are no longer legal is not easy to say.

THE REGIONAL CONSEQUENCES

While these questions absorbed Rwandans internally, beyond its borders the genocide had created another monumental crisis. By the end of the 100 days, two million citizens had fled the conflict in every direction – more than half a million east to Tanzania, more than a quarter million south to Burundi and, most dramatically, at least 1.2 million west to the eastern Kivu region of Zaire. As the fighting and genocide drew to a close, thanks to France's Operation Turquoise much of the leadership and many of the troops and militia of the genocide had escaped from Rwanda into eastern Zaire, where they had unlimited access to weapons. This was a sure-fire formula for disaster.

The international media had first ignored, then largely misinterpreted the genocide as nothing more than another example of African savagery; now they made the Kivu refugee camps a universal cause célèbre. Foreign aid and foreign aid workers flooded in, vastly more than went to Rwanda itself. Unfortunately, the *genocidaire* army (former Forces Armées Rwandaises (FAR)) and the *Interahamwe* militia had almost completely taken over the camps and were benefiting enormously from the work of the humanitarian community; genuine refugee needs could be met only when the NGOs finished meeting the demands of the military controlling the camps.

The goals of Hutu Power were transparent and well known to everyone involved in dealing with the Kivu crisis: to overthrow the new government in Kigali and return to power. Almost immediately they began raids back into the country, providing yet another major emergency for the new Rwandan rulers to deal with. Widespread demands for the 'international community' to disarm the killers went nowhere. Once again, the leaders of the Security Council badly failed Rwanda. In some ways, they actually added to Rwanda's woes. The French government, with tacit American approval, supported Zaire's President Mobutu as the only person who could help with the refugee crisis in his country. In fact, Zairian groups associated with Mobutu's notoriously corrupt government became the primary suppliers of arms to the ex-FAR and militia in the Kivu camps, although many other countries and groups were involved in weapons trading as well.

The consequences of these international decisions for Africa were largely foreseeable and wholly disastrous. The post-genocide Rwandan government had long made it abundantly clear that it would not continue to tolerate the use of the camps in Zaire as launching pads for the *genocidaires*' return. By late 1996, they had had enough. Hostility toward the many former Rwandan Tutsi who lived in the Kivu region had increased ominously, and the Rwanda government had secretly begun training them. Under the flag of an alliance of anti-Mobutu Zairians headed by the dissolute Laurent Kabila, and with the active support of Uganda, the Rwandan army launched a vicious attack on the entire complex of Kivu camps in October and November. The cost in human life was enormous and a flood of refugees swarmed back into Rwanda. But substantial numbers of camp dwellers fled deeper into Zaire. Some of these were genuine refugees, some ex-FAR and *Interahamwe*. Led by the Rwandan army, the anti-Mobutu alliance pursued them ruthlessly, killing large numbers including women and children. In the process, they perpetrated atrocious human rights abuses whose actual magnitude is still not known.

But the military action soon spread far beyond eastern Zaire. The emboldened anti-Mobutu alliance, still led by the Rwandan army and bolstered by the forces of Uganda, Angola and Burundi, now set its sights on Mobutu himself. Within nine months, Mobutu fled and Kinshasa fell to the rebels. But there was to be no happy ending to the saga. The new head of the rechristened Democratic Republic of the Congo (DRC), Laurent Kabila, soon clashed with his Rwandan advisors, and in July 1998, little more than a year after they had helped him become president, Kabila threw the Rwandan and Ugandan military out of the DRC.

Within days they returned as an enemy force. The second Congo war in two years now began, but almost immediately escalated to continental dimensions. It became Africa's first great war. Directly or indirectly, more than a fifth of all African governments or armies from across the continent have been involved, as well as perhaps a dozen or more armed groups; the alliances between and among these groups, with their varied and conflicting interests, have been bewildering. Kabila's major military allies were Zimbabwe, Angola and Namibia; facing them were the Rwandans, Ugandans and Burundians. The situation is further endlessly complicated by the DRC's enormous mineral resources, an irresistible lure for governments, rogue gangs, warlords and powerful foreign corporations alike, and by the continuing problem of arms proliferation sponsored by governments throughout the world as well as a multitude of unscrupulous private hustlers.

One year after the new war began, the Lusaka agreement on a ceasefire and peace process was signed. Although the ceasefire was repeatedly violated, attempts to implement a genuine peace continued and in 2000 the Security Council sent a small peacekeeping mission (MONUC) to the Congo.

Violence continued, however. Although most of the DRC remained beyond the control of government, in eastern Congo full-scale anarchy and terror was unleashed. Rwanda and Uganda found the pursuit of mineral wealth at least as compelling as the destruction of the remaining *Interahamwe* fighters, and fought the DRC army and various armed gangs over these riches. Coltan, a metal ore used in cell phones and computers, previously unknown except to experts, became everyone's favourite plunder. Soon open warfare broke out between erstwhile allies – Ugandan and Rwandan troops – over control of territory and resources. While a truce was eventually reached, the bitterness between the rulers of the two countries has not entirely dissipated and remains a source of potentially serious instability.

Through these years ordinary Congolese died in huge numbers. Including those killed in conflict and those who died of the famine and disease spread by the conflict, they may now number close to four million (although all statistics are very rough approximations). Gang rape of girls and women on a mass level, often followed by further torture and violent death, has become commonplace. By all accounts, this constitutes the greatest human-inflicted disaster since World War II. Those directly responsible include the governments of the DRC, Rwanda and Uganda and an assortment of proxy gangs and warlords all competing for mineral resources. Those indirectly responsible are the Western countries backing the various belligerent governments and the Western mining companies who have moved into the middle of the action. Many have been named in UN investigative reports. What all have in common is a refusal to acknowledge the slightest responsibility.

Laurent Kabila was assassinated in 2001 and replaced by his son, Joseph. The following year, peace negotiations led Uganda and Rwanda to promise to withdraw their armies and the DRC promised the demobilization and disarmament of Rwandan Hutu rebels in eastern Congo. By the end of 2002, Rwanda and Uganda claimed they had fully withdrawn from the DRC, although their proxies remained. At times it was difficult to tell which proxies were which. At all times, innocent Congolese paid the cost in suffering and death.

In Kinshasa, a power-sharing unity government was set up under Joseph Kabila in 2003, but it is now stalled and is at risk of failure. Meanwhile, a long-simmering conflict over land and mineral wealth in the northeastern Ituri region broke into widespread interethnic violence and massacres in 2002–03. Once again Rwandan and Ugandan proxies were said to be involved, although the two countries vehemently denied the charges. But recent history shows that today's denial has often enough become tomorrow's acknowledgement. Although a strengthened UN mission (MONUC II) has now been deployed in the Congo, various armed groups continue to threaten its stability.

The Congo's neighbours continue to perceive the situation as a threat to their interests and have taken interventionist actions that further destabilize the fragile process of transition. Some 8,000 to 10,000 anti-RPF Rwandan rebels, including the remaining *Interahamwe*, still operate in eastern DRC under the umbrella of the Forces Démocratique pour la Liberation du Rwanda. The Kigali government will never let its guard down as long as their threat continues. The events in Kivu in 2004, when Rwandan troops crossed into the DRC (an action formally denied and universally believed in Kigali), the current violence in Ituri, ongoing tensions in Kinshasa and other parts of the DRC are stark warnings that the conflict in the Congo could quickly spiral into another large-scale war.

Burundi too remains unpredictable. The civil war that effectively began in 1993 with the murder by Tutsi officers of the first democratically elected president, a Hutu, has now largely ended, although some rebels refuse to give up their arms. A great international effort has been invested in ending this murderous conflict and getting all factions to agree to multiparty elections with both Hutu and Tutsi guaranteed representation and influence. The late President Nyerere of Tanzania and Nelson Mandela were both immersed in the process for some time, and the government of South Africa continues to play a central role. Efforts at reconciliation and nation-building have been extensive and there is real reason for optimism. But given its bloody and violent history, the future of Burundi, ranked 173rd of 177 countries on the United Nations Development Programme's (UNDP's) human development index, remains very much an open question.

Although each of these Great Lakes nations has its own multiple challenges to meet, their interconnectedness can hardly be overestimated. Tensions between Rwanda and Uganda, which has its own intractable conflict in the north of the country, merely aggravate the situation. It hardly needs saying, but without peace the futures of Rwanda, Uganda, Burundi and the DRC are all jeopardized, with incalculable consequences not only for their own citizens, but also for the entire continent.

RWANDA TODAY AND TOMORROW

Predicting the future of Rwanda and the Great Lakes Region is not easy. Looking at Rwanda itself, it is possible to be either mildly optimistic or quite pessimistic.

In many ways, the progress the country has made since 1994 is remarkable. The ubiquitous devastation has completely vanished, manifested now only in the damaged walls of the National Assembly and the genocide memorial sites with their eerie skeletons throughout the country. Yet both the assembly and the sites have been left deliberately as memories of the genocide. Kigali now boasts a new expensive luxury hotel, high-rise office buildings, a large new estate of mansions and an elite that crowds the clubs and hotels on Saturday night. Economic growth has been relatively strong. To the superficial observer, Rwanda has returned to normality, even to a certain prosperity.

At best, however, that means it has returned to the status of being a desperately poor underdeveloped country, now ranked 159th of 177 countries on the UNDP's human development index. The gap between the small privileged elite and the vast majority is great and growing. Life expectancy at birth is 39 years and 60 per cent of the population lives on less than US$ 1 a day. Of the eight million population, close to 90 per cent live in rural areas, most of them very poor.

Yet Rwanda's challenges go well beyond the usual litany of deep-rooted social and economic problems faced by any poor country with scarce land and a swelling population. There is the onerous and 'odious' debt, meaning that it was incurred largely by the previous government for weapons that were used in the genocide. (Some debt relief has just been announced.) Then there are the enormous funding needs that spring directly from the genocide: for assistance to survivors, for orphans, traumatized children, street children, children-headed households, for widows, for violated women, for women with HIV/AIDS, for the great burdens of the two parallel justice systems, for programmes to inculcate national reconciliation and human rights, for resettling the millions of refugees and IDPs, for demobilizing and re-educating ex-FAR troops, for ex-child soldiers, for the army, for the battered education and health systems, for continuing research on the genocide – the list is limitless. This burden is the consequence of a tragedy that could have been prevented or mitigated. Yet Rwanda today is dependent on foreign sources for much of its meagre budget, while most initiatives crucial to rehabilitation, reconciliation and a culture of rights depend for their viability on outside funding sources.

Views on Rwanda today remain remarkably diverse. Hutu Power advocates, still thriving outside the country, continue perversely to deny the genocide with a series of self-contradictory propositions. It never happened. Or, Hutu were enraged that the RPF murdered Habyarimana and spontaneously lashed out. Or, people were killed in a civil war. Or, if there was a genocide at all, it was perpetrated by the RPF both in Rwanda and in the DRC. Or, there was a 'double genocide'. The ugly phenomenon of denial is particularly widespread in the French-speaking countries of Europe and Africa and in Quebec. It would be useful to expose the network of European politicians, priests and academics who continue to fund and support this malignant force and who actively foment hatred against the present government of Rwanda.

Hostility to Rwanda for its human rights abuses is also widespread. Some prominent former foreign friends of Rwanda have emerged as bitter critics, sometimes describing the country as virtually a totalitarian dictatorship. Instances of intimidated human rights activists, jailed reporters, threatened media and opponents of the government forced to flee the country are not hard to come by. The presidential election of 2003, the first since 1994, was won by Paul Kagame with an almost unbelievable 95 per cent of the vote. But there was criticism of the way the 'divisionist' card was played against Kagame's main opponent, and his opponents accused the RPF of beating up their campaign workers.

Yet, typical of Rwanda, others insist that such attacks are excessive. Some see an unfair double standard imposed on the RPF government. Corruption is a great deal less widespread than among its neighbours. Security obtains in most of the country. The election process appeared to be mostly fair. In the subsequent elections for the National Assembly, opposition parties won a credible 25 per cent of the vote. Beyond that, almost half the legislators are women, the largest proportion of any parliament in the world. This should have positive repercussions for all Rwandan women. Within certain boundaries, mostly understood, the media are cut a good deal of slack; in any event, the BBC and Voice of America are now easily available in the three national languages. Although some accuse Kagame and his government of exploiting the genocide for their own self-interest, others argue the opposite: considering that it has been only twelve years since the genocide, the number of *Interahamwe* still active in eastern Congo and the uncertain loyalty of the country's 85 per cent Hutu majority, it can just as convincingly be argued that the government allows a substantial amount of freedom and openness. But no one, on any side, doubts Kagame's steely determination and his readiness to take whatever steps are necessary, barring none, to keep his country secure and his government in power.

Eleven years after the genocide, Rwanda remains impenetrable, opaque, mysterious, a source of puzzlement and controversy to all who know it – a country that found itself making history that it never sought and is now attempting to forge a new path in the face of spectacular odds. Terribly poor, badly traumatized, deeply divided, a precarious entity in a fragile and explosive region, Rwanda is a country that is now bound to make history once again. It has only two paths to choose. It can once again succumb to its history and regress to yet another unspeakable conflict. Or it can transcend its past and attempt to defeat poverty and underdevelopment as a united, secure and stable country. As has been true for more than a century, both Rwandans and outsiders will play central roles in determining the future.

Part One

Hate Media in Rwanda

4
Call to Genocide: Radio in Rwanda, 1994

Alison Des Forges

Eleven years after the end of the Rwandan genocide, two films were released for popular audiences, greatly increasing widespread realization of the horror that had taken the lives of more than half a million Tutsi. In both cases, the film-makers highlighted the importance of radio in mobilizing people to kill. Audiences leave the theatre wondering how it was possible for genocide to occur in full public view at the end of the twentieth century and why no action had been taken to halt the broadcasts that were promoting the worst of all crimes.

LEAD-UP TO GENOCIDE

At the end of the 1980s, Juvénal Habyarimana saw his power slipping after nearly 20 years. Even though he was a member of the Hutu ethnic group, who formed some 90 per cent of the population, he had lost much of his popular base. For years he had favoured his own region and, even more, his own family circle, as the rest of the country experienced an economic crisis due to the falling prices of coffee and tea, the country's major exports. The voices of dissent grew, taking the form of a demand to end the monopoly of power held by the president's political party, the *Mouvement Républicain National pour la Démocratie et le Développement* (MRND).

In 1990, Rwanda was attacked by the Rwandan Patriotic Front (RPF), a movement consisting mostly of refugees and children of refugees of the Tutsi ethnic group. Once the ruling elite of Rwanda, the Tutsi had been overthrown in a revolution beginning in 1959 and many had fled the country. In the early 1960s these Tutsi refugees had led a series of incursions into Rwanda, each of which provoked reprisals against the Tutsi who still lived in the country. After Habyarimana came to power in 1973, there was a period of calm with neither attacks from the outside, nor killings of the Tutsi minority in Rwanda.

With the 1990 attack by the RPF, Habyarimana and some around him saw the chance to stop the erosion of their popularity and to try to craft a new Hutu solidarity by turning against the Tutsi minority inside the country, labelling them traitors and accusing them of supporting the RPF attackers. Within days of the first attack, the government had rounded up thousands of Tutsi and Hutu opposed to the regime; it would hold some for months without trial in inhumane conditions. Many were tortured and scores died. Two weeks after the RPF attack, government officials carried out the first of a series of massacres of Tutsi civilians, killing hundreds at the commune of Kibilira. Over the next three years, there would be another 15 such massacres before the genocide of 1994 began (Des Forges 1994: 87; International Commission 1993: 11–29).

From the opening days of the war, the government understood the importance of using media to rally Rwandans around the regime. Believing that the government-controlled media were not up to the task of carrying forward a vigorous propaganda campaign, Habyarimana named a promising young intellectual and university professor, Ferdinand Nahimana, to take over the official information office, a post that included authority over the national radio station (Chrétien et al. 1995: 51–2).

THE ROLE OF RADIO

A large number of Rwandans could not read or write and, as a result, radio was an important way for the government to deliver messages to the population. In addition to the usual news, the radio broadcast official notification of appointments to and dismissals from government posts, announcements of government meetings and lists of candidates admitted to secondary schools. It also broadcast daily reminders from the president, exhorting Rwandans to work hard and live clean, moral lives. So long as Rwanda was a single-party state – that is until June 1991 – the radio also disseminated propaganda for the president's party, the MRND. Not just an official voice of the state and a propaganda channel for the single party, the national radio also helped link families whose relatives were distant, broadcasting news of deaths so that relatives could return home for funerals.

In March 1992, Radio Rwanda was first used in directly promoting the killing of Tutsi in a place called Bugesera, south of the national capital. On 3 March, the radio repeatedly broadcast a communiqué supposedly sent by a human rights group based in Nairobi warning that Hutu in Bugesera would be attacked by Tutsi. Local officials built on the radio announcement to convince Hutu that they needed to protect themselves by attacking first. Led by soldiers from a nearby military base, Hutu civilians, members of the *Interahamwe*, a militia attached to the MRND party, and local Hutu civilians attacked and killed hundreds of Tutsi (International Commission 1993: 13–14).

The role of the radio in inciting killing demonstrated the importance of controlling the media. Opposition parties, having proved their strength in massive street demonstrations, were able to push Habyarimana into conceding to them the right to participate in government and one of the ministries they wanted to control was a newly created ministry of information. In the new coalition government formed just after the Bugesera massacre, a member of one of the opposition parties was named to head this ministry. He gradually instituted policies meant to end the MRND monopoly on the media and to guarantee equal access to members of other political parties. Nahimana was removed as head of the information office and so lost control of the radio as well (Chrétien 1995: 61).

Other voices were also beginning to be heard. The RPF broadcast through a station called Radio Muhabura, although its signal did not reach all of Rwanda. Some civil society groups also drew up proposals for independent radio stations, such as one to serve the rural poor.

RADIO AS PART OF THE 'SELF-DEFENCE'

The war dragged on through 1991 and 1992, punctuated by occasional ceasefires and sporadic negotiations, but without any real settlement. In January 1993, the RPF was able to force some major concessions on the government during a negotiating session, a diplomatic success they followed by a stunning military advance in early February – in violation of an existing ceasefire agreement. Until this time, Habyarimana had been able to count on France as a reliable supplier of arms and political support. French troops, supposedly in Rwanda to protect French citizens, were decisive in stopping the RPF advance on several occasions, including in early 1993. But some French authorities were becoming convinced that the Rwandan government would need substantial additional support if it were to continue to resist the RPF and the French were increasingly unwilling to supply this.

In that atmosphere of growing RPF strength and weakening French support, some Habyarimana supporters – and perhaps Habyarimana himself – turned to the idea of mobilizing large numbers of civilians as a 'self-defence' force to back up the national army. Military correspondence, as well as propaganda, had made clear in the preceding months that the 'enemy' included Tutsi civilians as well as RPF combatants. Thus the self-defence force was apparently meant as much to attack these civilians as to confront the soldiers of the RPF force.

The general outlines of the self-defence force were sketched out by Colonel Théoneste Bagosora in the first pages of his 1993 engagement book. Bagosora, who would take the lead in national affairs after President Habyarimana was killed on 6 April 1994, was known for his hostile attitude toward Tutsi. Many of the details jotted down in his 1993 engagement book were later replicated in a secret national self-defence plan drawn up in the early months of 1994, then implemented in April 1994 when the civilian population was mobilized to kill Tutsi civilians. Even in his preliminary notes, Bagosora suggested that the radio should be used in the self-defence effort. He even noted the name of Simon Bikindi, one of the most popular musicians in Rwanda, who would become famous for his songs extolling Hutu solidarity and denouncing supposed Tutsi crimes (Bagosora 1993).

AN END TO WAR: THE ARUSHA ACCORDS

Nearly four years of war between the Rwandan government and the RPF ended with the signing of the Arusha accords in August 1993. At that time the signatories already recognized the importance of propaganda in contributing to tensions between parties and agreed to end such propaganda.

But despite the carefully detailed accords, some elements in both the Rwandan government and the RPF were not ready to make peace and continued preparations for further war.

As part of the accords, a United Nations (UN) peacekeeping force was created to help implement the agreement. Known as the United Nations Assistance Mission for Rwanda (UNAMIR), it arrived later than expected – most of the peacekeepers came only in December – and was smaller than thought necessary by its commanding officer, Canadian General Roméo Dallaire. UNAMIR was poorly equipped and poorly supplied throughout its time in Rwanda. Taking into consideration its weaknesses, the UN Security Council gave the force a mandate that was far less robust than originally envisioned in the accords.

RTLM MAKES ITSELF HEARD

Radio-Télévision Libre des Milles Collines (RTLM) began its broadcasts just after the accords were signed. In the context of multiplying voices, adamant supporters of the MRND and of a new, related party called the Coalition for the Defence of the Republic (CDR) decided to launch a radio station to broadcast the message that used to be the only one heard on Radio Rwanda. Nahimana, well acquainted with the power of radio, did much of the work organizing the new station. Habyarimana himself was the most important of its backers, which comprised many of the ruling elite, including ministers and other government officials, bankers and high-ranking military officers. But the station was meant to be the voice of the people and the price for a single share was kept low to attract ordinary citizens to support the effort (ICTR 2003: para. 4.2).

RTLM was also meant to reach out to the ordinary citizen in its programming. It aired the latest music, especially popular Congolese songs, while Radio Rwanda was still broadcasting old standard tunes. Unlike the official Radio Rwanda, which spoke in the ponderous tones of state officials, RTLM was informal and lively. Several of its announcers were known for their quick wit, which was appreciated even by those who were the butt of their humour. According to one Rwandan well-acquainted with the media in his country, RTLM offered comments that sounded like 'a conversation among Rwandans who knew each other well and were relaxing over some banana beer or a bottle of Primus in a bar' (Higiro 1996).

RTLM brought the voice of ordinary people to the airwaves. Listeners could call in to request their favourite tunes or to exchange gossip with announcers and a wider audience. RTLM journalists went out into the streets and invited passers-by to comment on topics of the day. This populist approach allowed RTLM to claim a legitimacy different from that of Radio Rwanda; it still broadcast official voices often enough to continue to enjoy the authoritativeness of national radio, but to that it added the appeal of being the station to speak for the people.

But in late October 1993, the president of neighbouring Burundi and the first Hutu to hold that post, was assassinated by military officers who had seemed to accept his popular election by majority vote several months before. As soon as the news of the assassination became known, Burundian Hutu – in some cases led by local government officials or political leaders – began attacking Tutsi. The Tutsi-led army then carried out extensive reprisal killings of Hutu civilians, sometimes in areas where Tutsi had not actually been killed. The final death toll was tens of thousands of dead in both groups.

These events in Burundi further polarized Rwandans, many of whom were quick to draw lessons from the neighbouring state, whose Hutu–Tutsi population mirrored their own. For many Tutsi, the attacks on other Tutsi in Burundi demonstrated the vulnerability of a minority in situations of ethnic conflict and made them even more afraid to put their trust in a Hutu-led government. Meanwhile, some Hutu speculated that the RPF had assisted Burundian Tutsi soldiers in the assassination and claimed that the crime proved that Rwandan Tutsi could not be trusted to implement the Arusha accords as they had agreed to do.

Two important opposition parties split over the question of the desirability of continuing with efforts to implement the accords, while their anti-Arusha accord members formed a new coalition with Habyarimana's MRND and the CDR. The coalition became known by its rallying cry 'Hutu Power' and its voice became the RTLM.

RTLM reported the assassination of the Burundi president in a highly sensationalized way to underline supposed Tutsi brutality and heighten Hutu fears of Tutsi (RTLM transcripts: 25 October; 20, 29, 30 November; 12 December 1993). The president was actually killed by a bayonet blow to the chest, but RTLM reported details of supposed torture, including castration of the victim. In pre-colonial times, some Tutsi kings castrated defeated enemy rulers and decorated their royal drums with the genitalia. The false report of the castration of the Burundi president was intended to remind Hutu listeners of this practice and to elicit their fear and repulsion; it did so with great success.

From late October on, RTLM repeatedly and forcefully underlined many of the themes developed for years by the extremist written press, including the inherent differences between Hutu and Tutsi, the foreign origin of Tutsi and, hence, their lack of rights to claim to be Rwandan, the disproportionate share of wealth and power held by Tutsi and the horrors of past Tutsi rule. It continually stressed the need to be alert to Tutsi plots and possible attacks and demanded that Hutu prepare to 'defend' themselves against the Tutsi threat (RTLM transcripts: 25 October; 12, 20, 24 November 1993; 29 March; 1, 3 June 1994).

In addition to the increasingly virulent propaganda against Tutsi, the radio spewed forth attacks on Hutu who were willing to continue cooperating with them. In some cases, the radio moved from general denunciations to naming specific people, including the Hutu prime minister, as enemies of the nation who should be eliminated one way or another from the public scene. It used increasingly violent language, saying, for example, that the *Interahamwe* militia might rip into little pieces those thought to support the RPF (Article 19 1996: 92–3, 96–7, Sénat de Belgique 1997: 70).

In February 1994, RTLM showed that it could be used just as Radio Rwanda was used at the time of the 1992 Bugesera massacre, to pinpoint targets for attack. An opposition politician was assassinated and, in reprisal, the head of the CDR party was lynched by militia members of the opposition party (Sénat de Belgique 1997: 38–9, 71–2). RTLM warned that the RPF were going to attack the capital, a report that was false. It demanded that listeners protect themselves against RPF supporters in certain parts of the city. Hutu in those neighbourhoods, led by militia, killed about 70 people, thus foreshadowing the bloody events to come two months later (Article 19 1996: 97).

FEAR AND FOREBODING

In December 1993, some 600 RPF soldiers moved into Kigali, implementing a provision of the accords that allowed the RPF to station troops in the capital to protect their political leaders during the period of transition to a new government. At the same time, preparations for renewed war increased. Political leaders of Hutu Power parties recruited thousands of militia members and arranged for their training. Officials and military officers distributed thousands of weapons to civilians, an effort so widespread and public that it drew condemnation from a Catholic bishop who asked authorities to explain why the firearms were being handed out (Kalibushi et al. 1993). In December and throughout the early months of 1994, RTLM stepped up the pace and bitterness of its attack on Tutsi, Hutu opposition figures, leaders of civil society and even the UN peacekeepers, all of whom it accused of favouring the RPF. In several cases, the peacekeepers did behave badly toward Habyarimana supporters, thus providing a kernel of truth on which RTLM expanded very successfully (Belgium 1994).

Rwandan and international human rights organizations and other members of Rwandan civil society denounced these preparations publicly while diplomats cabled their capitals more discretely, warning of the growing risk of renewed war and violence (Sénat de Belgique 1997: 41, 85–6). Dallaire notified UN headquarters in New York about caches of arms hidden in the capital and he reported that militia were highly organized and prepared to kill 1,000 Tutsi in the first 20 minutes after the signal for attack was given. His warnings, like his efforts to win permission to confiscate arms and his pleas for more supplies and equipment, went unheeded.

Those who tried to raise the alarm about the preparations for violence frequently drew attention specifically to the radio. Dallaire, who had once hoped for radio equipment to permit the UN force to inform the public in a responsible fashion, notified New York about the broadcasts against his force, but to no avail. One RTLM announcer warned that the UN peacekeepers from Belgium – particularly disliked because Belgium, the former colonial power, had refused to provide arms to the Rwandan government – would face ‘a fight without pity’ and ‘hatred without mercy’ unless they gave up and returned home (Sénat de Belgique 1997: 49). The Belgian ambassador told authorities at the Belgian Foreign Ministry that RTLM was disseminating 'inflammatory statements calling for the hatred – indeed for the extermination' of Tutsi. Days before the start of the genocide, the German ambassador, then serving as head of the European community in Rwanda, called attention to the 'unacceptable role of some media' (Adelman and Suhrke 1996: 32, Prunier 1995: 209). When diplomats protested to Habyarimana and other officials about the broadcasts, they claimed that the radio station was a private enterprise, merely exercising its right to free speech.

The minister of information, under whose authority the radio station operated, tried to call the directors of RTLM to account for the content of its broadcasts. In correspondence and in meetings, he insisted that the incitement to fear and hatred must stop. On at least one occasion, RTLM leadership promised to moderate the tone of the broadcasts, but did not do so. The attorney general registered civil complaints against RTLM but, under pressure from the president, had not yet taken action on them by early April (ICTR 2003: para. 4.3).

Critics of RTLM all asked for changes in the content of the broadcasts; none went so far as to ask for the station to be closed down completely.

RADIO IN THE GENOCIDE

President Habyarimana, the president of Burundi and leading military and civilian officials of the Rwandan government were killed on the evening of 6 April 1994 when their plane was shot down on its approach to Kigali airport. Within hours, military, administrative and political authorities ordered the killing of leading members of parties opposed to Hutu Power and of Tutsi. Under the guidance of Colonel Bagosora and other Hutu Power officers and officials, a new interim government was installed. It included political leaders ready to implement a 'self-defence' plan that included widespread killing of Tutsi civilians.

The killings began first in the capital and some outlying areas where Hutu Power leaders were strongest; authorities in other regions, particularly the south and centre of the country, resisted the killing for the first two weeks. On 7 April, the RPF attacked the Rwandan government army, thus beginning full-scale war once again. From this time forward, the war and the genocide were intertwined, making it easier to direct the killing of Tutsi civilians as if it were part of the war effort.

Assailants searched out Tutsi, moving from house to house in a neighbourhood; they massacred them by the thousands in churches and other public buildings where Tutsi sought refuge; and they picked them out at barriers set up to impede their flight on roads and paths throughout the country.

Authorities used RTLM and Radio Rwanda to spur and direct killings both in those areas most eager to attack Tutsi and members of the Hutu opposition and in areas where the killings initially were resisted. They relied on both radio stations to incite and mobilize, then to give specific directions for carrying out the killings (RTLM transcripts: 13, 29 April; 15, 20 May; 1, 5, 9, 19 June 1994).

Incitement

As RTLM had forewarned, it turned its full force against the Belgian peacekeepers, accusing them of having shot down – or helping to shoot down – the president's plane. Under the stimulus of these broadcasts, some soldiers of the Rwandan army brutally murdered ten UN troops of the Belgian contingent. Some Hutu Power leaders had foreseen that the Belgian government would withdraw its troops from the peacekeeping force should some of its soldiers be killed, and it did just that soon after the murders. This withdrawal so badly weakened the force that the Security Council initially favoured the withdrawal of the whole force, although it finally permitted a token force to remain in the country with orders to keep a low profile, concentrating on protecting itself and taking no risks to save Rwandans (UN 1996: 37–44).

After 6 April, RTLM called on all Hutu to 'rise up as a single man' to defend their country in what was said to be the 'final' war. One announcer predicted that the war 'would exterminate the Tutsi from the globe … make them disappear once and for all' (Chrétien et al. 1995: 205). RTLM staff carried forward all the themes so vigorously developed in previous months, emphasizing the cruelty and ruthlessness of the Tutsi (RTLM transcripts: 15 May; 9, 14, 19, 20 June 1994). As one announcer said, using the term *inyenzi* or cockroach to refer to the RPF and its supporters, 'the cruelty of the *inyenzi* can be cured only by their total extermination' (Chrétien et al. 1995: 204; RTLM transcript: 3 June 1994).

RTLM used terms like *inyenzi* and Tutsi interchangeably with others referring to RPF combatants, leading listeners to believe that all Tutsi were necessarily supporters of the RPF force fighting against the government. RTLM announcers warned specifically that combatants dressed in civilian clothes were mingling among displaced people fleeing combat zones, and they encouraged people along their route to be vigilant in searching out any refugees who looked like they might be RPF in disguise, that is, who looked like they might be Tutsi (RTLM transcripts: 1, 2 February; 29 April; 4–6, 20 June 1994).

After 6 April, the director of Radio Rwanda, himself a member of the political opposition, fled and the national radio station took up the anti-Tutsi messages of RTLM. One RTLM announcer commented that Radio Rwanda had changed from 'rival' to 'sister' (Chrétien et al. 1995: 79). On 21 April, Radio Rwanda broadcast a debate by political leaders, during which one politician insisted that Tutsi returning from exile abroad intended to 'exterminate, exterminate, exterminate, exterminate'. Tutsi, he said, were going to 'exterminate you until they are the only ones left in the country so that they can keep for a thousand years the power that their fathers had kept for four hundred years ... You must not let up in your efforts,' he told his listeners (Chrétien et al. 1995: 300).

On some occasions, national authorities were heard on Radio Rwanda, delivering a similar message but one that carried additional weight because of the respect attached to their offices. In an effort to force the people of the southern prefecture of Butare to begin killing, the government removed the prefect (governor) in a humiliating way that left no doubt about why he had lost his post. At the ceremony installing his successor, broadcast by Radio Rwanda, the interim president of Rwanda, who had been set up by the Hutu Power faction, exhorted all citizens to see killing Tutsi as their responsibility. He said that any not ready to do so should step aside for those ready to 'work', a common euphemism for killing. He warned further that those not willing to 'work' should be eliminated by others, by the good 'workers who want to work' for their country (Sindikubwabo 1994).

Directives

Authorities used both radio stations to give instructions and orders to listeners. RTLM announcers identified specific targets to attack, sending assailants on 8 April to the home of Tutsi businessman Antoine Sebera and later to the home of Joseph Kahabaye. One identified a hill in the capital where Tutsi were said to be hiding in the woods and another provided a list of 13 people and their locations. On one occasion, an announcer urged people guarding a barrier in Kigali city to eliminate Tutsi in a vehicle just nearing that checkpoint. Notified soon after that the Tutsi had been caught and killed, the announcer congratulated the killers on the air. In yet another case, the station directed assailants to attack a mosque in Kigali where Tutsi were seeking shelter and on another day, urged an attack on a convoy that was attempting to evacuate Tutsi and Hutu opponents of Hutu Power from the Hotel Mille Collines, a gathering point for people at risk (RTLM transcripts: 13, 29 April; 15, 20 May; 1, 5, 9, 19 June 1994). Later in May, RTLM said that General Dallaire should be killed, identifying him as a white man with a moustache (Dallaire 2004: 379–80). Leaders of the militia used RTLM to call their men to meetings in the capital or to send them off to other parts of the country (Kamanzi n.d.: 146).

Radio Rwanda conveyed orders from the authorities, including a message from the prefect of Kigali telling residents to 'close ranks, remember how to use the usual tools [weapons] to defend themselves' (Kayishema 1994). He went on to specify that citizens should clear the brush in which Tutsi might hide. He directed them to 'search houses, beginning with those that are abandoned, to search the marshes of the area to be sure no *inyenzi* have slipped in to hide there ... and to search the drains and ditches.' He said that 'reliable' people should be chosen for these tasks, meaning those who supported the Hutu Power line, and that they should be given what they need for the work, meaning weapons. Radio Rwanda served to summon drivers of bulldozers needed to dig mass graves for the thousands of bodies (Chrétien et al. 1995: 298).

Authorities relied on the radio stations to congratulate those who were 'vigilant' and performed well and to castigate those who hesitated to join in the killing. On occasion, when they wanted to limit the violence, authorities used radio to deliver this message as well. In early May, when the UN commissioner for human rights was about to arrive, RTLM told listeners to abstain from attacks on Tutsi. In another incident a short time later, the interim government was seeking to win renewed French support and found the French unwilling to commit much assistance to a government then beginning to come under criticism for its genocidal policy. To help persuade the French that the genocide would not pose a problem to the delivery of aid, RTLM told listeners to please behave in a more dignified fashion. Listeners were told to make sure that bodies were not left on the roads to be seen by foreigners and to please not stand around barriers laughing when someone's throat was cut (Chrétien et al. 1995: 316–17; Human Rights Watch 1994).

The impact of the radio

Authorities supporting the genocide urged citizens to listen to the radio. One official even told the residents of his area that they should regard what the radio told them as having the same importance as direct orders from him. In some cases, authorities picked up radio messages and used them to mobilize local people more effectively. Thus when the radio claimed that supporters of the RPF had hidden weapons in or near churches, local authorities staged incidents in which they 'discovered' planted weapons to give credence to the reports of secret preparations for attacks against Hutu.

Conversely, authorities who tried to resist or limit the killings asked national officials to halt the broadcasts or moderate their content; in one case, two prefects advised the people in their prefectures to listen to the radio with a very critical ear.

In addition to this indication of the importance that authorities attached to the radio, there is considerable evidence from the perpetrators themselves about the impact of radio and RTLM, in particular. One foreign religious sister crossed dozens of barriers as she moved across Rwanda during the genocide; at each one, she found the guards listening to the radio. Others have testified that bands of killers set off to 'work', singing the anti-Tutsi songs they had learned from RTLM. One witness said that it was RTLM who said that the Tutsi were to be killed and another said the radio had taught people that they must 'kill them before they kill you' (Human Rights Watch/International Federation of Human Rights Leagues interviews: Kigali, 16 July 1995; Musebeya, 7 June and 28 August 1995; Butare, 19 October 1995).

Throughout the genocide, RTLM continued the interactive broadcasting that it had begun in the months before. Its journalists went out around the city of Kigali, interviewing ordinary people at the barriers, giving them an opportunity to explain on air what they were doing and why they were doing it. This confirmation by ordinary people of the 'rightness' of what they were doing contributed to the legitimacy of the genocide for radio listeners.

When foreign observers began to criticize the genocide, RTLM sought to bolster the legitimacy of the authorities by discounting all negative comments and by reminding its listeners that all they had to do was to win the war and then foreign critics would forget any crimes they had committed (Chrétien et al. 1995).

Demands for action

As the death toll mounted, human rights and humanitarian organizations sought without success to persuade leading UN members to increase the number of peacekeeping troops in Rwanda. On 30 April, the Security Council did direct the Secretary General to examine ways to expand the force, but it was another two and a half weeks before the resolution calling for an enlarged force was approved. Because of the difficulties securing, equipping and transporting the new peacekeepers, the reinforcements did not arrive in Rwanda until the interim government had been defeated by the RPF and had fled the country.

Unable at first to obtain assurance of reinforcements, activists sought help from the United States (US), France and the UN with the more limited objective of closing down the radio stations that were inciting and directing the violence.

The argument developed by Human Rights Watch and followed by some other international nongovernmental organizations was that international silence on the genocide and failure to interrupt the broadcasts made it possible for the interim authorities to continue to claim that they constituted a legitimate government, recognized by other governments. The fact that Rwanda continued to sit as a non-permanent member of the Security Council throughout the genocide reinforced its claim to international legitimacy. Human Rights Watch argued that jamming radio broadcasts would disrupt incitements to genocidal violence and would limit the delivery of genocidal directives. And, argued the human rights group, jamming the broadcasts would deliver a broader message as well: it would make clear international condemnation of the genocide, thus weakening the claim of the authorities to legitimacy and perhaps encouraging resistance against the killings.

In early May, US State Department staff who shared concern over the role of the radio stations in the genocide had their legal staff consider the implications of jamming the radio. In accordance with the usual strong US support for freedom of speech as guaranteed by international conventions and telecommunications law, the State Department lawyers concluded that the US should not interrupt RTLM broadcasts. At a congressional hearing on 4 May, George Moose, assistant secretary of state for African affairs, said that the issue was moot because a military attack by the RPF had silenced RTLM, an assertion contradicted immediately by a Human Rights Watch representative who said that the station had resumed broadcasting from a mobile transmitter (Des Forges 1994). On the same day, national security advisor Anthony Lake, who had been pressed by human rights activists to interrupt the radio broadcasts, raised the issue with the secretary of defence. Within 24 hours, the Department of Defence replied that the radio could be jammed from a specially equipped aircraft, but that it would be 'ineffective and expensive', costing about US$ 8,500 for each hour (Wisner 1994).

On 1 June, Ted Kennedy, an influential senator, made a new effort to get action and asked the US Secretary of State to cooperate with the UN in ending 'the unconscionable incitement to genocide' being carried out by radio stations in Rwanda. Once again the official response described jamming as 'legally contentious', an assertion to which officials again added arguments concerning the cost and supposed ineffectiveness of jamming the radios (Acting Undersecretary of Defence for Policy 1994).

In fact, the legal arguments against jamming could have been countered by another set of arguments in its favour – arguments used previously by the US when it silenced radio broadcasting in Haiti and during the 1991 Persian Gulf War. Had the US lawyers been willing to recognize the killings in Rwanda as genocide – an action delayed until June – lawyers could also have justified halting the broadcasts by referring to that part of the *Convention on the Prevention and Punishment of the Crime of Genocide* (UN 1951) that prohibited 'direct and public incitement to commit genocide' (Metzl 1997).

Arguments concerning cost and effectiveness could also have been debunked had officials with sufficient clout wished to do so. In the end, the ultimate consideration was simply to avoid getting involved in what US officials saw as becoming a complicated conflict and especially to avoid becoming enmeshed in a conflict that might require the deployment of US forces. From that perspective, jamming the radio carried a significant risk: if the US judged that the situation was serious enough to merit this first step, it would find it difficult not to move to a further stage of involvement if the jamming itself proved insufficient to stop the killings. It was probably this consideration that moved a defence department official to advise that jamming could be a very 'dangerous and open-ended prospect' (Acting Undersecretary of Defence for Policy 1994). Having suffered the loss of 18 soldiers in a peacekeeping operation in Somalia the previous year, US officials were determined to avoid any 'dangerous and open-ended' commitments, especially on the African continent.

The UN Security Council was finally moved to action by RTLM threats against General Dallaire and the peacekeeping troops under his command. In late June, the president of the council asked the interim government to close down RTLM. At first the Rwandan representative, still sitting as a nonpermanent member of the council, put forward arguments about the private nature of the enterprise and guarantees of freedom of speech. After further pressure, he agreed to end the broadcasts, but they continued, his commitment notwithstanding (Haq 1994).

In late June, the French government sent a military force to Rwanda, purportedly to protect civilians. At first, interim government officials expected that the deployment, known as Operation Turquoise, would support its troops in opposing further RPF advance. RTLM and Radio Rwanda hailed the arrival of the French soldiers and gave instruction on how to welcome the troops warmly. By the first week of July it was clear that the French did not intend to support the interim government and its army – at least not openly – and French soldiers began protecting Tutsi and dismantling some of the barriers. The tone of RTLM commentary changed abruptly and the radio began criticizing the French presence. The French, with experienced, highly qualified troops on the ground, lost little time in destroying at least one and possibly more radio transmitters used by RTLM and the national radio. When RTLM continued to broadcast, although apparently to a more limited area, French officials were able to oblige the stations to halt verbal attacks on French troops. They also brought in equipment to jam the radio, although they did not use it.

NEW ATTITUDES TOWARD JAMMING RADIO

In mid-July the RPF defeated the Rwandan army and both army and interim government officials led a massive exodus of nearly two million Rwandan Hutus into neighbouring countries. This caused an enormous humanitarian crisis and the loss of even more human lives, this time mostly Hutu. Recognizing that the outflow threatened to destabilize the entire region and cause far larger problems, the UN and the US hoped to limit the crisis by persuading the refugees to return home rapidly; but RTLM, still broadcasting from a mobile transmitter, encouraged the refugees to remain outside Rwanda. In late August, the US asked the French to jam the radio and offered to help them do it; however, the French had sent their equipment home (Quiles et al. 1998: 329–30). In October, the US and the UN discussed cooperating in jamming the broadcasts, but before they could act, the radio vanished from the airwaves.

Having seen the power of hate radio in Rwanda, US officials were ready to act in 1995 when a Burundian station called Radio Rutomorangingo began broadcasting anti-Tutsi messages. A policymaking group decided that the US could 'technically and legally contribute to silencing the radio' (Young 1994). In the end, the station moderated its broadcasts and the US took no action against it, although the Burundian government jammed its broadcasts a year later, using equipment from Israel. As a result of the Rwandan experience, President Bill Clinton issued a policy directive in 1999 permitting US interventions in any future cases in which radio stations called for violence (Clinton 1999).

The importance of the radio, which was recognized by policymakers in the United States in the years after the Rwanda genocide, was spread to wider audiences with the showing of the popular films in 2005. Perhaps this recognition of the role of the radio by a broader audience will help ensure that policymakers actually act to stop the voices of hate in similar tragedies in the future.

ACKNOWLEDGEMENTS

Memoranda originating in the Department of Defense were provided by the National Security Archive, an organization that assists researchers in obtaining access to previously classified US government documents. I thank William Ferroggiaro of the archive for his kind assistance.

REFERENCES

Acting Undersecretary of Defence for Policy. 1994. Senator Kennedy: Letter on jamming of Rwandan radio broadcasts: memorandum for secretary of defence and deputy secretary of defence, June 9. Department of Defence, Washington, DC, USA.

Adelman, H. and Suhrke, A. For Steering Committee of the Joint Evaluation of Emergency Assistance to Rwanda. 1996. The international response to conflict and genocide: lessons from the Rwandan experience. Study 2: Early warning and conflict management. *Journal of Humanitarian Assistance*, March. Available at <www.jha.ac/Ref/aar003c.pdf> (accessed 23 August 2005).

Article 19. 1996. *Broadcasting Genocide, Censorship, Propaganda and State-Sponsored Violence in Rwanda, 1990–1994.* Article 19, London, UK. Available at <www.article19.org/pdfs/publications/rwanda-broadcasting-genocide.pdf> (accessed 23 August 2005).

Bagosora, T. 1993. Agenda 93 (personal appointment book). Kigali, Rwanda. Examined and copied by Human Rights Watch.

Belgium. 1994. Military intelligence reports: 7 (9 January); 14 (27 January); 16 (1 February). Government of Belgium, Brussels, Belgium.

Chrétien, J.P., J.F. Dupaquier and M. Kabanda. 1995. *Rwanda: les médias du génocide.* Karthala, Paris, France. 397 pp.

Clinton, W.J. 1999. Presidential decision directive NSC-68. Government of the United States, Washington, DC, 30 April.

Dallaire, R.A. 2004. *Shake Hands with the Devil: the Failure of Humanity in Rwanda.* Random House, Toronto, Canada.

Des Forges, A. 1994. Testimony on the crisis in Rwanda. Subcommittee on Africa, House Committee on Foreign Affairs, Washington, DC, USA, 4 May, 103rd Congress.

—— 1999. *Leave None to Tell the Story: Genocide in Rwanda.* Human Rights Watch and the International Federation of Human Rights Leagues, New York, NY, USA. Available at <www.hrw.org/reports/1999/rwanda/> (accessed 30 August 2005).

Haq, F. 1994. Rwanda: close down anti-Tutsi radio, says the U.N. Security Council. InterPress Service, Rome, Italy, June.

Higiro, J.M.V. 1996. 'Distorsions et omissions'. In Rwanda: les médias du génocide. *Dialogue*, 190 (April-May): 171.

Human Rights Watch. 1994. Press release, 11 May. Human Rights Watch, New York, NY, USA.

ICTR (International Criminal Tribunal for Rwanda). 2003. *The Prosecutor v. Ferdinand Nahimana, Jean-Bosco Barayagwiza and Hassan Ngeze.* Case no. ICTR-99–52-T: Judgement and sentence. Arusha, Tanzania, 3 December.

International Commission of Investigation on Human Right Violations in Rwanda since October 1, 1990. 1993. *Final report.* Africa Watch, International Federation of Human Rights Leagues, Interafrican Union for Human and Peoples' Rights, and the International Center for Human Rights and Democratic Development, New York and Paris, March.

Kamanzi, N. n.d. *Rwanda: du genocide à la défaite.* Édition Reberoi, Kigali, Rwanda.

Kalibushi, W. and priests of Kibuye and Gisenyi. 1993. Press release. 28 December.

Kayishema, C. 1994. Kibuye prefecture, Kigali, Rwanda, 2 June.

Metzl, J.F. 1997. Rwandan Genocide and the International Law of Radio Jamming. *American Journal of International Law,* 91(4): 628–651.

Prunier, G. 1995. The Rwanda Crisis: History of a Genocide. Columbia University Press, New York, NY, USA.

Quiles, P., P. Brana and B. Cazeneuve. 1998. *Enquete sur la tragédie rwandaise (1990–1994).* Assemblée Nationale, Paris, France.

RTLM. Transcripts of RTLM broadcasts are held by the Office of the Prosecutor, International Criminal Tribunal for Rwanda

Sénat de Belgique. 1997. *Rapport du groupe ad-hoc Rwanda à la Commission des Affaires Etrangères.* Government of Belgium, Brussels, Belgium, 7 January.

Sindikubwabo, T. 1994. Discours du Président Théodore Sindikubwabo prononcé le 19 avril à la Préfecture de Butare. Government of Rwanda, Kigali, Rwanda.

UN (United Nations). 1951. *Convention on the prevention and punishment of the crime of genocide.* Adopted by Resolution 260 (III) of the UN General Assembly, 9 December. 1948. *UN Treaty Series* no. 1021, vol. 78: 277. Available at <www.preventgenocide.org/law/convention/text.htm> (accessed 6 September 2005).

—— 1996. *The United Nations and Rwanda, 1993–1996.* UN Department of Public Information, New York, NY, USA. Blue Book vol. X.

Wisner, F.G. 1994. Memorandum for deputy assistant to the president for national security affairs, National Security Council, 5 May. Department of Defence, Washington, DC, USA. Available at <www.gwu.edu/~nsarchiv/NSAEBB/NSAEBB53/rw050594.pdf> (accessed 23 August 2005).

Young, C.D.R. 1994. Memo to deputy director, Pms and Chief MEAF Div. Subject: peace-keeping core group SVTS, 21 July, 1994. National Security Archive, George Washington University, Washington, DC, USA.

5
RTLM Propaganda: the Democratic Alibi

Jean-Pierre Chrétien

Among the testimonials of participants in the Rwanda genocide gathered by journalist Jean Hatzfeld is this passage:

> Killing is very discouraging if you must decide to do so yourself ... but if you are obeying orders from the authorities, if you are adequately conditioned, if you feel pushed and pulled, if you see that the carnage will have absolutely no adverse effects in future, you feel comforted and revitalized. You do it without shame ... We envisaged this relief with no reluctance whatsoever ... we were efficiently conditioned by radio broadcasts and advice we heard. (Hatzfeld 2003: 85)

This psychology of killers perpetrating mass slaughter makes the most sense not when it is seen as some kind of exotic, ethnocultural way of thinking, but rather when situated among the methods of an eminently modern propaganda. The psychology is explained in a handbook written by French psychosociologist Roger Mucchielli (1972), *Psychologie de la Publicité et de la Propagande: Connaissance du Problème, Applications Pratiques*. A training handbook in the field of humanities designed for psychologists, facilitators and leaders, it can be found along with the rest of Mucchielli's works in the library of the National University of Rwanda, Butare. The handbook inspired a note 'regarding expansion and recruitment propaganda', written by a Butare intellectual and later found by the team headed by human rights researcher Alison Des Forges (1999: 65–6). The Mucchielli manual explains – without moral or ideological expectation – the mechanisms of mass conditioning and mobilization required to create a mass movement. It describes methods for moulding a good conscience based on indignation toward an enemy perceived as a scapegoat. It describes such tactics as 'mirror propaganda' or 'accusations in a mirror', the notion of ascribing to others what we ourselves are preparing to do. The good conscience would legitimize collective action based on widespread certainty of being on the side of the strongest and the just. In other words, the collective action would be the embodiment of the 'people'.

The fascination that some genocide organizers displayed for Mucchielli's work is quite understandable. All the ingredients for such conditioning existed in Rwanda: a low literacy rate, a proclivity for a unanimous partisan approach surrounding moralistic assertions, a well-established potential scapegoat in the Tutsi minority and enduring references to the 'majority people' (*rubanda nyamwinshi*).

From an ideologic point of view, this socioethnic populism entailed the pre-eminence of the 'Hutu people', whose absolute right was based on the fact that this community constituted the majority (perceived as homogeneous). The right was also based on the assertion of the community's indigenous character, in contrast with the so-called foreign nature of the Tutsi community (also seen as naturally homogeneous).

From the early 1960s, this ideology had infiltrated all spheres of public life in Rwanda, evolving from a distinctive pre-colonial and colonial history and the subsequent process of decolonization. It is impossible here to review the details of twentieth century Rwandan history; however, it seems important to recognize that the roots of the extremist propaganda that prepared and accompanied the genocide are twofold. First, the propaganda is set within a traditional socioracial policy that had been refined for a generation. Second, changes within Rwanda's political and social conditions in the generation since independence meant that, after 1990, the sense of belonging among the Hutu was no longer the sole factor leading to political mobilization. As a result, this propaganda was grounded in the sheer efficiency of its arguments (combined with sufficient provocation and violence) and became a tool for disqualifying all opponents and for uniting the Hutu masses around the so-called Hutu Power movement, thus facilitating 'recruitment and expansion'. From then on, the use of democratic language became a 'technology' designed for totalitarian mobilization, under the guise of freedom of speech – the democratic alibi.

A review of the propaganda themes exploited by Radio-Télévision Libre des Milles Collines (RTLM) highlights its obvious inclination to play on two fronts. The first is associated with racist ardour against the Tutsi 'cockroaches' and the second pertains to the legitimacy of the elimination of these 'cockroaches' by the 'majority people'. The first front, which is ethnoracial, surfaces when journalists use epithets such as 'dogs' or 'snakes' when referring to Tutsi, accusing them of cannibalism and mercilessly welcoming their disappearance. It is also apparent when journalists start theorizing about the primacy of ethnic considerations, about the final battle of the Bantu and Hima–Tutsi and about the need to eliminate people who do not have an identity card at checkpoints. In fact, the 'interethnic' aspect of the conflict was emphasized near the end of the massacres and in the aftermath of the genocide as growing awareness of international disapproval set in. When he was questioned in Goma in July 1994, Gaspard Gahigi, editor-in-chief of RTLM, invoked his right to speak about the 'ethnic problem' as this problem led to the 'humanitarian catastrophe' that was then unfolding in the refugee camps in eastern Zaire. On 3 July 1994, Kantano Habimana, the most popular journalist host on RTLM, was still advising his audience to 'keep this small thing in your heart', meaning the intent to eradicate the arrogant and ferocious 'hyenas' (Chrétien et al. 1995: 317).[1]

When the French Operation Turquoise reached Rwanda in June, RTLM dispensed advice from 'our intellectuals' on the need to legitimize, for the benefit of these foreign friends, the role of barriers during 'a war'. The station also advised of the necessity to approach foreign journalists with great caution. 'Today, everyone knows that it was an ethnic war,' Gahigi explained on 15 May 1994 (Chrétien 1995: 137). In other words, racism is either coded or benignly portrayed as natural, in accordance with ethnographic beliefs prevailing among Europeans. According to this way of thinking, hatred was quite natural between these ethnic groups, public anger was spontaneous and authorities did everything in their power to prevent the worst from happening. This would become the central theme of information campaigns led by those who had close ties to the genocidal regime and oversaw the refugee camps of Kivu between 1994 and 1996.

In the months preceding the genocide – from October 1993 to April 1994 – and during the slaughter in April and May 1994, the essential reference is that of the majority people and the legitimacy of self-defence against a 'feudal clique'. The reference normalized the massacre perpetrated by the majority, which becomes an expression of democratic anger. 'If the Hutu who represent 90 per cent in our country ... if we can be defeated by a clique of 10 per cent, the Tutsi population, it means that we have not demonstrated our full strength,' said the leader of MRND, Joseph Nzirorera, on 28 May 1994 (Chrétien 1995: 118–19). Just two weeks earlier, on 14 May, Kantano Habimana talked about the fact that 'the small-size family in Rwanda' is that of the *Inkotanyi* [the RPF guerrillas symbolizing all the Tutsi] ... 'It is a minuscule group descending from those we call Tutsi. The Tutsi are few, estimated at 10 per cent,' he added. Already, on 23 March 1994, Kantano Habimana was defending the logic of Hutu Power to fight the logic underlying the Arusha accords. 'This Rwanda is mine. I am of the majority. It is I, first and foremost who will decide, it is not you.'

The aim of this thesis regarding Hutu majority is very clear: to achieve, through propaganda methods identified earlier, a massive and violent mobilization of the Rwandan Hutu in support of extremist factions, such as the Coalition pour la Défense de la République (CDR), which was the soul of RTLM. On 3 April 1994, Noël Hitimana spelled it out very clearly:

> The people are the actual shield. They are the truly powerful army ... On the day when people rise up and don't want you [Tutsi] anymore, when they hate you as one and from the bottom of their hearts, when you'll make them feel sick, I wonder how you will escape.

Hence, it was freely recognized that the systematic slaughter of Tutsi was legitimate: 'The proof that we will exterminate them is that they represent only one ethnic group. Look at one person, at his height and physical features, look closely at his cute little nose and then break it,' Kantano Habimana proclaimed on 4 June 1994 (Chrétien 1995: 193). As early as 13 May, he observed:

> The Tutsi are very few. They were estimated at 10 per cent. The war must have brought them down to 8 per cent. Will these people really continue to kill themselves? Do they not risk extermination if they persist in this suicidal behaviour of throwing themselves against far more numerous people? (Chrétien 1995: 205)

Three days later, Habimana proclaimed the expected victory of the 'Sons of the Cultivators' (*Benesabahinzi*, meaning the Hutu) who 'slowly exterminate' their enemies. These types of declarations of war, labelling the disappearance of the Tutsi a 'mass suicide', were widespread. They weave together the notions of demographic strength, the certainty of victory and the good conscience of a citizen's struggle. As it had claimed since October 1993, RTLM aimed to 'tell the truth' – the truth of numbers and the truth of right. Georges Ruggiu, Belgian announcer for French-language broadcasts on RTLM, calmly explained at the end of June that, as reported by Radio France International, 50 people killed in a commune merely represent 9 per cent of the population of the commune, which is 'approximately the proportion of individuals who might have helped the RPF'. In other words, their eradication was normal. Hence, we should be talking about the 'media of genocide' rather than the 'hate media' because they were conveying and justifying cold and deliberate propaganda.

The democratic alibi that this propaganda so busily sustains is also discernible in historical references. For example, on 23 May 1994, RTLM, via Ananie Nkurunziza (closely associated with the police and acting as an intellectual analyst), linked the prevailing circumstances with all that happened in Rwanda between 1959 and 1967, that is, the way in which a so-called 'social' revolution had been accompanied by populist movements against the Tutsi (including the acts of genocide of December 1963 to January 1964, perpetrated in Gikongoro). In his view, these acts arose from 'a realization' or 'an awakening'. That is precisely what RTLM, pursuing the work of the periodical *Kangura*, was trying to do: to restore the logic of socioracial mobilization, which had been so efficient 30 years earlier.

As Parmehutu did in the 1960s, the extremists in 1993–94 likened their actions to those that took place during the great European revolutionary and liberation movements, such as the French Revolution. For example, on 17 June 2004, just as the French government had announced its plan to intervene, Kantano Habimana compared 'the final war in progress' to the French Revolution (Chrétien 1995: 331). On 30 June, Georges Ruggiu, referring to the 'furious population', stated: 'Has Robespierre not done exactly the same in France?' (Chrétien 1995: 204). On 3 June, RTLM editor-in-chief Gaspard Gahigi awaited international assistance, which he equated to the Normandy landings of 1944 (Chrétien 1995: 331). It would also be appropriate to consider the divine justifications that were invoked, whereby God, the Holy Family and the Virgin Mary were all mobilized for the sacred cause of the Hutu people (Chrétien and Rafiki 2004: 283).

This calculated populism was designed to 'awaken' the Hutu masses. It also served to comfort the usual biases that prevailed in France and in Belgium, notably within democratic-Christian circles and also among leftists, about the nature of the Rwandan regime. In Western media there is an apparent intertwining of ethnographic analysis (atavistic antagonisms, etc.) and a 'democratic' interpretation of 'majority power', to the extent that during the 1980s, President Habyarimana was often portrayed as a democratic state leader, a representative of the Hutu majority. Other factors defining democratic culture (human rights, respect for minorities, refusal to recognize the exclusion of communities, rule of law, social justice) were considered to be ancillary under the tropical sky.

Georges Ruggiu's biography is mainly the account of a young Third World activist who, when he first landed in Kigali, compared the suburbs of the capital to the Brazilian *favelas* he had visited.[2] In Belgium, he had had the opportunity through the social-Christian movement to mingle with Rwandan militant students who were members of the sole party (MRND). As if spontaneously, without possessing an extensive knowledge of Rwandan history, he adhered to the dogmas of the majority people and of a democracy that in his view would be set back by the Arusha compromise. His populist beliefs almost naturally connected with the racial ideology of the extremists with whom he associated.

From a broader standpoint, we know that this belief was also brought forth by President Mitterrand to vindicate France's steadfast support for Habyarimana and later for the Kambanda government, including the Operation Turquoise endeavour. When surveying the French written press in May and June 1994, one notices that various articles printed in *Le Monde*, *Libération* or *Le Nouvel Observateur* combine ethnographic factors (under the 'old demon' of Hutu–Tutsi antagonism) with suggestions of 'popular defence'. One Belgian media report plainly condemned the 'sanctioned racism' prevalent in Rwanda and within a number of the country's Western partners (Cros 1994). On 26 June, reporter Jean Hélène from *Le Monde*, who was on site in Cyangugu with the French army, alludes to 'popular exultation', 'the relief of villagers' and the concern of 'Rwandan authorities' to 'track down the enemies of the nation who threaten the population' (Hélène 1994). On 4 July, French missionary Father Maindron, even though he had witnessed events in the Kibuye region, declared to a French journalist that the killing was 'a spontaneous popular rage' (Luizet 1994). He was echoed by the prefect of Cyangugu, when he talked to French soldiers about 'legitimate self-defence ... against an enemy from within' (Smith 1994).

What is manifest today is the obvious continuum from the propaganda devised by RTLM through to current theses denying the genocide. In fact, these viewpoints do not attempt to deny the massacres, but rather to justify them in terms of 'ethnic hatred', 'spontaneous rage', 'legitimate popular uprising' or 'international disinformation'. An editorial by Jacques Amalric (1994) was prescient:

> Are we next going to lend credence to Capitaine Baril's utterances, who would have Tutsi being responsible for their own extermination ... We can fear the worst, after hearing the content of some private conversations, supposedly

held confidentially: 'Things are not as simple as you believe. It is not a question of all innocents on one side and culprits on the other.'

In fact, racist propaganda wearing the mask of democracy – the common thread of extremist media – was also voiced by official channels and managed to find assent, whether through distraction or genuine conversion, among Western partners. This would largely explain why it took two months to clearly identify, in Western media, the nature of the events taking place in Rwanda. The president of Médecins Sans Frontières very adequately summarized the situation: 'Neither France, nor the international community gave themselves the means to characterize the genocide and to promptly assume its implications' (Biberson 1994).

Alfred Grosser (1989) wrote: 'No, it is not true that the slaughter of Africans is felt in the same way as is the slaughter of Europeans.' This rings terribly true in the case of Rwanda. Although this could be blamed on a level of indifference toward far away tragedies, more likely it is due to significant exotic ethnographic factors that still hinder a more sensible perception of African societies. But first and foremost in this case, it is because of the effectiveness of modern propaganda – propaganda that was well thought out, constructed, refined and of unyielding efficiency, both within and outside the country. This propaganda succeeded in camouflaging genocide and making it appear to be a vast democratic mobilization, consequently trapping an entire population.

NOTES

1. The RTLM broadcasts cited in this article were transcribed from tape recordings used during preparation of expert testimony for the Media Trial in 2002 by J.F. Dupaquier, M. Kabanda, J. Ngarambe and J.P. Chrétien. The tapes that remain are part of the documentation of the International Criminal Tribunal for Rwanda. We have noted variations in the numbering of the tapes between 2000 and 2002. Thus citations are based on the date of broadcast and the name of the journalist. When the transcripts were also mentioned in our book *les médias du génocide* (Chrétien et al. 1995), we indicated the appropriate page number.
2. Ruggiu, G. *Dans la tourmente rwandaise*. Unpublished journal. 127 pp. This journal was presented as evidence to the International Criminal Tribunal for Rwanda on 16 June 2003 as exhibit no. K0269165–K0269292.

REFERENCES

Amalric, J. 1994. Génocide et neutralité. *Libération*, 5 July.

Biberson, P. 1994. Rwanda: le piège humanitaire. *Le Figaro*, 15 July.

Chrétien, J.P., J.F. Dupaquier, M. Kabanda and J. Ngarambe. 1995. *Rwanda: les médias du génocide.* Karthala (with Reporters Sans Frontières), Paris, France.

Chrétien, J.P. and U. Rafiki. 2004, L'église de Kibeho au Rwanda, lieu de culte ou lieu de mémoire du génocide de 1994? *Revue d'histoire de la Shoah*, 181, July-December (Génocides lieux et non-lieux de mémoire): 277–90.

Cros, M.F. 1994. Un racisme de bon aloi. *La Libre Belgique*, 1 June.

Des Forges, A. 1999. *Leave None to Tell the Story: Genocide in Rwanda.* Human Rights Watch and the International Federation of Human Rights Leagues, New York, NY, USA.

Grosser, A. 1989. *Le crime et la mémoire.* Flammarion, Paris, France.

Hatzfeld, J. 2003. *Une saison de machettes.* Le Seuil, Paris, France.
Hélène, J. 1994. Liesse chez les Hutus, soulagement chez les Tutsis. *Le Monde*, 26–7 June.
Luizet, F. 1994. Le 'journal de guerre' du père Maindron. *Le Figaro*, 4 July.
Mucchielli, R. 1972. *Psychologie de la publicité et de la propagande.* Les éditions ESF, Paris, France.
Smith, S. 1994. Im Land der Massengräber. *Der Spiegel*, 4 July.

6
Kangura: the Triumph of Propaganda Refined

Marcel Kabanda

In Rwanda's print media of the 1990s, the publication that had the most impact on the country was the bimonthly newspaper *Kangura*. It was well known for its hysterical hatred of Tutsi and any Hutu who expressed a desire for change, freedom and democratic openness. Established in May 1990, and headed from beginning to end by Mr Hassan Ngeze, *Kangura* soon became famous for its publication of what was commonly referred to as the 'Ten Commandments' of the Bahutu (Anon. 1990: 6). Through these commandments, the paper strongly exhorted the Bahutu to understand that the Tutsi were first and foremost an enemy and that they should break all ties with them, whether those links derived from marriage, business or professional relations.

Kangura also called for the dissolution of the historical, political and cultural community of Rwanda and for the building of a new community, one that would supposedly be authentic and pure. Alongside this new community could subsist a nonindigenous category that would be tolerated, but closely monitored, because its ambition was to dominate. To convince its readers, *Kangura* proceeded to display flagrant exhibitions of a mummified, pre-revolutionary Rwanda – albeit wearing its best modern attire – so that it would have some appeal to readers. Deliberately overlooking all changes that had taken place in the previous 30 years with regard to distribution of power and national wealth, Hassan Ngeze delved into history's attic and revealed a picture that was initially put to use by the Parmehutu Party. Essentially, this representation was one of a country dominated, indeed 'colonized', by Tutsi. *Kangura* brought the Rwanda of the 1990s back to its 1957 version, when Hutu leaders wrote the *Bahutu Manifesto* denouncing their exclusion.

In 1990, Rwanda was at a crossroads. Refugees who had lived outside the country for 20 or 30 years were asking to come back. They insisted on the abolition of ethnic quotas – between groups and between regions. Within the country, more and more people were demanding a multiparty system. Opposition to refugee repatriation, and the stronghold on state governance and markets exercised by a few people close to the president's family, were in clear contradiction to the principles that legitimized the revolution of 1959, namely democracy. Thus, a sense of asphyxia within the country and a feeling of abandonment by those who were exiled converged to condemn the hypocrisy of a system that, while claiming to be republican and democratic, overtly practiced discrimination and tyranny.

Faced with war and requests for political openness, the regime reacted by alluding to the 1959 revolution, which had brought a dual benefit. It allowed the branding of armed opponents as nostalgic feudal groups and called on the majority to mobilize and fight to keep the advantages it had gained. On the other hand, it served to remind people of the populist resistance movement and the first aggression by refugees in December 1963, an event used to justify the most extreme violence. From 1990 to 1994 – but particularly during 1991 – *Kangura* contained a number of articles that repeatedly agitated against the Tutsi scapegoat. The Tutsi became those 'who took everything', 'who are everywhere', who control the business sector, who govern despite appearances, who constitute the majority in the school system, both in terms of teachers and students, in the church and within all spheres that symbolize progress.

Kangura aimed to awaken the Hutu, not from a sleep, but from what *Kangura* saw as a state of unconsciousness that made them unaware of the fact that the Tutsi had secretly led a contra-revolution. Hassan Ngeze attempted to demonstrate that through relentless erosion, the Tutsi had managed to reverse the former position of the Hutu on the social, cultural and political fronts. But the Ten Commandments were not enough to draw in followers. *Kangura* worked to provide its readers with reasons to believe in its credo, to convince them of imminent danger and to persuade them that they needed messiahs.

Kangura was active in a context wrought with undeniable difficulties, where increasing poverty hindered access to education, health care and employment and within a society that lived by agriculture, while land became less and less available and fertile. Within this setting, accusing Tutsi of grabbing all privileges and identifying them as scapegoats was a sure-fire mobilization tactic. It successfully mustered the support of a majority of young people who were non-schooled, unemployed and without hope for a better future. It also appealed to a great number of graduates who could no longer be hired by a government that was complying with structural adjustment programmes set up by the International Monetary Fund. *Kangura* revived the *Bahutu Manifesto* of 1957. This document, considered to be the soul of the Hutu emancipation movement, described the *Muhutu–Mututsi* social problem:

> First and foremost, the problem is one of political monopoly enjoyed by one particular race, the Mututsi: political monopoly that under existing structures, develops into social and economic monopoly, which in turn, because of de facto selection in education, becomes a monopoly that pigeonholes the Bahutu as perpetual unskilled subordinates.

Attempting to superimpose 1957 values on 1990 Rwandan society, *Kangura* denounced the so-called Tutsi hegemony and the perceived injustice toward the Hutu, the majority people. First, it insisted that the Hutu remember the revolution of 1959 and the conditions under which democracy could continue.

> The fact that the Batutsi are fighting to restore monarchy should incite a number of Bahutu to fight for democracy, to remember the roots of the 1959 revolution. If they do not fully appreciate this fact, then the revolution loses its purpose. And, as the majority people well know, the revolution was justified. They will have to live with the consequences. (Anon. 1990: 6)

The paper pointed out that the contra-revolutionary war conducted by the Tutsi had never stopped.

> Remember also, at the beginning of November 1959, the Batutsi provoked inter-ethnic massacres in trying to eliminate the Hutu elite who were calling for democracy and social justice for the benefit of the Bahutu masses, until then crushed under the feudal and minority power of the Batutsi ... Since the revolution of 1959, the Batutsi have not for one moment relinquished the notion of reconquering power in Rwanda, of exterminating intellectuals and of dominating Bahutu farmers ... The war declared against Rwanda in October 1990 is undoubtedly aimed at achieving what the Batutsi had attempted to accomplish through guerrilla warfare and terrorism, from 1962 to 1967, harassing the Hutu population through nocturnal Inyenzi attacks. (Anon. 1990: 6–7)

The paper suggested that, on this path to conquest and power, the Tutsi had made considerable progress, and that they were monopolizing areas such as the workplace, trade and finance.

> The Batutsi comprise 50 per cent of government officials, 70 per cent of private business employees, 90 per cent of staff in embassies and international organizations, and they hold prominent positions everywhere. However, this ethnic group constitutes 10 per cent of the population. National wealth, trade and industry are in the hands of the Batutsi, who often use civil and military authorities as a cover-up. It is to the Batutsi that banks award substantial loans, it is them who benefit from considerable tax exemptions, import and export licences, etc. (Anon. 1991a: 3)

Immediately before the 1959 revolution, one of the central factors that polarized the debate around social relations between Tutsi and Hutu was schools. At the time, research was being conducted to ascertain the proportion of Hutu and Tutsi youth who were educated. According to the Rwandan *Comité d'étude du Conseil supérieur du pays* (1958):

> Twenty-nine elementary establishments of 114 responded, which is 24 per cent of the total: total numbers in these schools: 29,953 Bahutu, which represents 67.81 per cent; 14,211 Batutsi, or 31.70 per cent; 32 Batwa, or 0.01 per cent. Secondary institutions: 29 of 47 establishments responded: 1,116 Bahutu, 39.20 per cent; 1,740 Batutsi, that is 60.80 per cent; 0 Batwa.

In the 1990s, extremist propaganda spoke as if these circumstances still prevailed and education had remained a Tutsi monopoly:

> Regarding completed education, the minority remains in the lead ... They have fought incessantly and with courage for their people to massively pursue their education, in such high proportion, when compared to the percentage of the population they represent, which is 10 per cent. Through their cold and calculated expansion, the Tutsi managed to so condition the Second Republic that policies now privatized foreign student scholarships. It is obvious that it was not privatization of scholarships per se, but rather the unprecedented and official award of scholarships to the minority ... Since the 1960s, the Hutu have clumsily directed the conquest of administration, while the Tutsi concentrated on teaching so as to retain a positive image of their people. They have advised their little Tutsi brothers to seek higher education, which is so important in the workplace, particularly in English and computer sciences, among other fields. As soon as they left their classrooms and auditoriums, the Tutsi laureates overwhelmed the Hutu within international projects and organizations, not to mention the administrative sphere. As for trade! Nothing more to say. It is their preserve. Whose preserve is it? The Tutsi's, of course. Their secret lies in that their refugee brothers facilitate imports and they don't have to leave the country. They also benefit more than the Hutu from loans awarded by Rwandan banks ... With this overall intellectual and economic might, the Tutsi progresses without obstacles on the road to his moral revolution. Vague and nebulous are the means chosen by the 1959 revolution to force him to back off, because at the time when the majority was liberating itself, the minority was aiming at the mortal target that is the human psyche. And it is precisely there that we must look for the causes of the October war. (Anon. 1992a: 11)

In another article published in the international issue:

> Supposing that statistics relative to teaching at all levels of secondary and superior education were carefully recorded, one would unfortunately be surprised to recognize that the Tutsi is omnipresent. Those who are in establishments of higher education well know the actual situation. Ethnic proportions are unequal and crystal-clear. In public and private affairs, power is undoubtedly secured. The minority managed to seduce Rwandan society and it is now clustered around its core. Some areas have become Tutsi strongholds, namely the Rwandan clergy, etc ... Everywhere, members of the Tutsi ethnic group are united and are forever faithful travellers forming networks, aiming to conquer power. (Anon. 1992b: 3)

Kangura blamed the 'negligent manner with which ethnic classification was carried out' for the increasingly prominent positions held by Tutsi within the realm of Rwandan social and economic spheres. It criticized the country's authorities for a lack of vigilance and for providing Tutsi with identity cards attesting that they were Hutu, which made control and discrimination impossible.

> Due to the practice of identity falsification, the policy aiming for ethnic balance has failed. This explains why the Tutsi – those who kept their identity and those who modified it – now make up 80 per cent of staff in our schools. But who would be surprised by this? Those who should implement this policy are themselves Tutsi, pretending they are Hutu. (Anon. 1991b: 13)

The impact of this lack of control on Tutsi movements is considered to be equivalent to the 'programmed disappearance' of the Hutu from all sectors that symbolize modernity – including cities – and setting the Hutu back to rural life, which in turn leads to unequal distribution of the fruits of progress. If the programmed disappearance succeeded, the Hutus would lose everything they had gained during the revolution:

> Did you know that Tutsi represent 85 per cent of the population living in the city of Kigali? When all those who had no job were sent away, only the Hutu left. As for the Tutsi, they managed to obtain work certificates through their brothers who attested that they used them as maids and servants. Furthermore, after their liberation, their accomplices piled into Kigali in order to be better protected by the international community. What is missing that would unite the Bahutu in such a way? If the Hutu are not careful, they will soon be sent back to the countryside, leaving only the Tutsi to reside in cities. Just look at Kigali, Bujumbura, Kinshasa and Kampala. (Anon. 1991c: 10)

The reference to 1959 is also used against opposition parties but, in this case, the receding timeline is supplemented by role inversion. Some facts might improve understanding of the scope of a campaign that is more akin to a political swindle than to a normal public debate. Historically, the leader of the social revolution is considered to have been President Grégoire Kayibanda. Co-signer of the *Bahutu Manifesto*, in 1959 he established the Mouvement Démocratique Républicain (MDR) Parmehutu party that would spearhead the revolution. In 1960, elected representatives from the Parmehutu proclaimed the advent of the republic.

In July 1973, President Kayibanda was deposed by a military coup led by Major Juvénal Habyarimana, who later became a major general. Kayibanda and a number of his collaborators were arrested and tried for treason. Some were executed. The death sentence proclaimed against Kayibanda was later commuted to life imprisonment. Held in residence in Kavumu, in his native prefecture of Gitarama, Kayibanda died in 1975 under suspicious circumstances. In the 1980s, Kayibanda's name was revived and the international airport in Kigali was named after him. But his political party remained prohibited. In 1991, during overtures to a multiparty system, a number of political leaders from the centre and south of the country attempted to reinstate the party. *Kangura* accused them of treason.

> These cowardly traitors have succumbed to the temptation of using the people against themselves, in collusion with the unfortunate aggressor who has already lost the battle in the ground. In doing this, they usurped the glory of the MDR-Parmehutu party and lured the people who spearheaded the 1959 Revolution to free the Rwandan people from the yoke of feudalism, into the trap set by the *Inyenzi*. That is how they hurriedly adopted the name MDR, making sure they removed 'Parmehutu,' in order to appease the Tutsi extremist who had in the past preferred exile to being led by a Hutu elected by the majority, in accordance with the principles of democracy. Through this trickery, they managed to lure to their side some of the citizens who fondly remember ... At a time when the Bantu people of our sub-region are fighting a legitimate battle to free themselves from the tutsi hegemony; at a time when the blood is filling the Akanyaru and its tributaries in the South; it is not the time to fool anyone. The war is between the Tutsis and the Hutus and the only solution is public awakening. (Anon. 1991d: 4)

In so clearly usurping heritage and patrimony, Hassan Ngeze strove to depict President Habyarimana as the legitimate representative of Kayibanda. In a politically skewed message, published in January 1991, the international issue of *Kangura* stated that the leader of the 1973 coup and gravedigger of the Parmehutu was the best person to incarnate the ideals of the man he had left to die 15 years earlier in devastating isolation and destitution.

> *Kangura* informs you that the RDP (Republican Democratic Party) is born
>
> After witnessing the need for the majority people to have its own party, able to lead it towards authentic democracy, a party through which it can express itself and speak in the name of those who cannot, we ask that all Rwandans, whatever their religious beliefs, adhere to the RDP. This party already has a large number of members in Rwanda, notably those who support the beliefs of Dr. Grégoire Kayibanda – to protect the interests of the majority – and those of Habyarimana, who promotes a policy based on peace and development. It is not customary for Rwandans to denigrate. You are well aware of the fact that some say successive governments, whether led by Habyarimana or by Kayibanda, have brought us nothing. In our opinion, the most important issue is to appreciate the good that was accomplished by those who have presided over Rwanda since the end of monarchy and to examine together the means for us to do better. (Anon. 1991e: 7)

At a time when the country faced war and others discussed the possibility of moving toward a multiparty system, *Kangura* ignored current affairs and problems. It was mainly preoccupied with convincing Rwandans that they were still living under the circumstances prevailing in 1957. Consequently, it forced those who wanted change to position themselves with respect to the only worthwhile battle, that is, the battle fought by their ancestors. So as to highlight how clearly this debate was rooted in the past, *Kangura* not only repainted the present with archaic colours, but it also strove to revive the feelings and emotions that inspired revolutionary action, by giving a voice to those who, from 1957 to 1960, acted as charismatic and uncontested leaders of the Hutu cause.

These men were called on because of their knowledge of Rwanda and their expertise on the issues at hand. In the December 1990 issue of *Kangura*, Hassan Ngeze, as though wanting to support the decalogue of Tutsi hatred by drawing on the perspective of a wise man, well-versed in Hutu–Tutsi relations, published a text supposedly written in 1976 that he attributed to Joseph Gitera. In response to President Habyarimana who, at the time, had allegedly interrogated him on ways to facilitate reconciliation among Rwandans, this early leader of Hutu emancipation apparently depicted the Tutsi as a *Mugome*:

> It is the pretentious Tutsi, with his Muhutu slave and his Mutwa clown and hunting dog, who chose exile from Rwanda because of his misdeeds and is now scheming against Rwanda and Rwandans. Again, it is this grudge-holding Mututsi who, with his courtesan Muhutu and his subservient Mutwa, is nesting like a snake ready to devour Rwanda and oblivious Rwandans. This one and the other are constantly communicating and co-operating, to eventually take revenge on the Rwandan Republic, its authors and its perpetrators of insult and lese majesty: '*Banze Umwami*.' This is the two-headed dragon, one head outside Rwanda and the other inside. Here then is the '*Umugome*.' Is he merely a fantasy? Absolutely not. (Gitera 1990: 12)

Kangura's diagnosis of the Hutu situation in Rwanda was catastrophic. The solution it put forward was radical and unyielding. In November 1991, Hassan Ngeze asks one question: 'What tools will we use to defeat the Inyenzi once and for all?' The answer is in the adjacent illustration where Kayibanda and a 'beautiful' machete appear alongside each other (Anon. 1991f). This allegory intends to demonstrate the rationale for the elimination of Tutsi by means of murder, implying that this is inscribed in the republic's history and that it is based on the need to protect the Hutu from the permanent threat of feudal bondage. *Kangura* refers to past violence as examples to follow. The bloodbath of December 1963 is prominently highlighted. In Hassan Ngeze's opinion, this event holds information that would offer a final resolution to the Tutsi problem within the republic.

In fact, there are similarities between the 1963 episode and the 1990 crisis. On the night of 20 December 1963, a few hundred Tutsi refugees armed with bows and makeshift guns arrived from Burundi, entering southeast Rwanda (in Bugesera). They proceeded to attack the military camp of Gako where they killed four soldiers, then took the road to Kigali after stealing weapons, ammunition and two jeeps. Along the way, they recruited displaced Tutsi at camp Nyamata and their ranks grew to approximately 1,000 men. They were arrested on the Nyabarongo bridge, south of the capital city, by the army aided by Belgian advisors (Segal 1964). This raid, led by 'cockroaches' (*inyenzi*) – to borrow a term they were given to characterize their nocturnal activities – was followed by similar fruitless ventures. But this time, retaliation tactics were such that the crisis renewed the atmosphere of 1959.

It seems that Ngeze was fascinated by the way in which the Kayibanda government handled that crisis. Reprisal tactics were of unprecedented magnitude. All influential Tutsi were arrested. Some were released after being mistreated, while others were executed without trial in Ruhengeri (in the north of the country). This was the case for senior officials and leaders of both the UNAR party (Union Nationale Rwandaise) and the moderate Rassemblement Démocratique Rwandais, well known for their opposition to *Mwami* Mutara Rudahigwa and for their struggle for a political system that would be more respectful of human dignity and personal freedom.

Tutsi who remained in the country were considered, as a whole, to be suspect and accomplices of enemies from the outside – justification for taking them hostage and legitimizing retaliation against them. Members of Parliament and government were sent back to their prefectures to plan the people's 'self-defence', with prefects and burgomasters. These events were truly foreboding of the 1994 genocide. Particularly in Gikongoro, in the south of the country, more than 10,000 people were atrociously massacred between 24 and 29 December that year, their bodies thrown in rivers. According to witnesses, the man orchestrating these massacres, who was frequently seen on site and whose statements were more favourable to the killers than to the victims and escapees of the murders, was then minister of agriculture Nkezabera Damien, an early militant within the Parmehutu.

At the time, Bertrand Russell spoke of the 'most horrible and systematic massacre since the extermination of Jews by the Nazis' (*Le Monde*, 6 Feb. 1964). On 6 February 1964, the French periodical *Témoignage Chrétien* published an account of the mass murders that occurred in Gikongoro. Following are two excerpts attesting to the fact that in Rwanda, even after a generation had passed, we could not ignore what would eventually emerge from the propaganda devised by the media:

> In the afternoon of December 25th [1963] would begin a 'plan of repression' that, simply put, consisted of exterminating all Tutsi residents from the prefecture of Ginkogoro.

> The entire population – Christians and Pagans alike, catechisers and catechumens – in groups of roughly one hundred, led by propagandists of the Party and with the authorities' blessings, attacked the Tutsi. This time, the goal was not to loot but to kill, to exterminate all that bore the Tutsi name. In order to prevent potential humanitarian reactions, organizers of the massacre had avoided targeting the killers' immediate neighbours; hillside residents killed people from a faraway hill, and vice versa.

Giles-Denis Vuillemin, a Swiss professor who was in Rwanda through UNESCO, witnessed the events and recorded entries in his journal:

> January 3rd, I travel to Kigeme where I meet Dr. Hendersen. At the hospital, there are only a few refugees and authorities are attempting to chase them

> off. Dr. Hendersen tells me that the hill of Kigeme was spared because of the influence of the director of schools, a respected member of Parmehutu. On the other hand, trucks are preventing access to the hospital. Dr. Hendersen estimates a total of 5,000 dead in the region. From Kigeme, I go to Cyanaka. The mission is full of refugees (1,500 to 2,000). The Fathers there are clearly talking about genocide; in their opinion, only international pressure could prompt authorities to change their policy. In the long term, they say, Rwandan Batutsi are doomed. They would have to be provided with another country, under international control and assistance. (Vuillemin 1964)

In December 1990 (*Kangura* issue 7: 5) and December 1991 (*Kangura* issue 28: 3), Hassan Ngeze republished a declaration made in April 1964. In it, Grégoire Kayibanda, president of the First Republic warned Rwandan Tutsi:

> You have witnessed the unrest from which we are only now emerging, that was caused by the provocative and irresponsible meanness of the refugees – inyenzi. Residents of Nyamata know, those from Burundi witnessed it: blame it on the secular (and incurable) meanness of what is the true essence of the Buhake. Gashaka-Buhake and the footmen who followed him in his flight are still digging the trenches they had started in 1959 …
>
> We have told you what we expect from you in our 1963 speech: awaken to democracy, follow the new custom in Rwanda. What we want is brotherhood amongst citizens … Goodness and wisdom will be our weapons. But if you resist the wisdom of democracy, you can blame no one. (Kayibanda 1964)

In February 1991, *Kangura* republished a speech given in Paris, on 3 April 1964, by Anasthase Makuza, at the time president of the National Assembly of Rwanda, in which this great militant of Parmehutu attempted to justify the aforementioned massacres:

> The population did not succumb to panic. It did not extend its neck so that the Inyenzi could cut its throat, according to plan. As soon as the Hutu became aware of the atrocities perpetrated in Bugesera, they understood the great danger of returning to prior circumstances. They remembered the abuse they endured under feudal rule. They glanced at the scars the Tutsi regime had left on their bodies. They remembered hard labour, the contempt they withstood and the practice by which a Tutsi could ask another to lend him a Hutu to murder. They then felt a great anger and vowed not to fall victim to the fate of losers. This anger was intensified by the fact that the former servant had, for four years, experienced the flavourful treats of democracy and that it is those he had called upon – invited to do so by his leaders – to share in the delights, that threatened to deprive him of his satisfaction. (Makuza 1991: 4)

Reference to the anger of parents is meant to inspire that of their children. Thus, *Kangura* is highlighting what it is normal to expect from sons who are worthy of their fathers.

> It is incredible and intolerable, but here all limits have been transgressed. We have to show these accomplices that it is not they who govern us. It is troubling and it is a genuine problem to consider that the national army has just spent more than a year in the maquis, fighting against the *Inkotanyi* opponent. In the meantime, the brothers of this enemy come and go freely inside the country, spreading false information, thus demoralizing the national army and the majority people. Obviously, if this is allowed to go on, the people will engage in a battle using alternative means. All is fair in war. How is it that newspapers published by the *Inkotanyi* draw false lists of their alleged dead and that the Hutu keep silent even though they were killed in greater numbers since the beginning of this war? (Ngeze 1991: 2)

In revisiting these articles, one is particularly struck by the publisher's interest in history. Why did *Kangura* need to refer to the speeches made in 1964 by Kayibanda and Makuza, or by Joseph Gitera in 1976? In a society where age and experience bestow authority, the voices of elders constitute an excellent argument. The past provided evidence that violence against the Tutsi was normal and legitimate. However, it is clear that those historical references favoured a particular trend, that of the Parmehutu.

In reading these documents, one is amazed by the precision with which the logic of genocide is exposed: identification of the Tutsi from within, as being obvious accomplices in any action undertaken by refugees; a whole component of the population whose members are taken hostage and accused of being, through heredity, enemies of the republic; the justification of massacres if these people would not 'obey'.

They are, in fact, a call to kill, sanctioned by arguments drawn from past experience. In the end, reference to the revolutionary period, both in the print media and in RTLM propaganda (see Chrétien, Chapter 5), demonstrates that the genocide bloomed on the soil planted by the 'Barwanashyaka' of the Parmehutu and abundantly irrigated by MRND militants.

REFERENCES

Anonymous. 1990. Appel à la conscience des Bahutu. *Kangura*, 6 (December).

—— 1991a. Si on demandait au général pourquoi il a favorisé les Batutsi. [What if we asked the general why he favoured the Batutsi]. *Kangura*, 25 (November).

—— 1991b. N'est-ce pas une infraction que de changer d'ethnie? [Is it not a crime to change one's ethnicity?]. *Kangura*, 12 (March).

—— 1991c. [No title]. *Kangura*, 18 (July).

—— 1991d. Le comité de concertation MDR-PL-PSD coince sous la ditature de l'alliance FPR-UPR des Inkotanyi. *Kangura* (international edition), 3 (January).

—— 1991e. Publicité. *Kangura* (international edition), 3 (January): 7.

—— 1991f. Cover. Kangura, 26 (November).

—— 1992a. À vos armes, Hutu [Take up arms, Hutu]. *Kangura*, (international edition), 10 (May).

—— 1992b. Rwanda: pourquoi la solicarité de la majorité doit-elle provoquer des insomnies? *Kangura* (international edition), 10 (May).

Chrétien, J.P., J.F. Dupaquier, M. Kabande and J. Nagarambe. 1995. *Rwanda: les médias du génocide*. Karthala, Paris, France.

Comité d'étude du Conseil supérieur du pays. 1958. Compte rendu, session spéciale, 4–7 juin. Government of Rwanda, Kigali, Rwanda.

Gitera, J.H. 1990. Par qui et comment reconcilier les twa, les Hutu, les Tutsi du Rwanda entre eux? *Kangura*, 6 (December).

Kayibanda, G. 1964. Ubutegetsi ni demokarasi. *Imvaho*, II-96 (special ed.), April.

Makuza, A. 1991. Repubulika ya mbere nayo yagombye guhatana itazuyaza n'ibinyoma by'inyenzi-nkotanyi. Gatutse-nyenzi yateye yiyahura! *Kangura*, 10 (February): 4–9.

Ngeze, H. 1991. Editorial. *Kangura*, 25 (November).

Segal, A. 1964. *Massacre in Rwanda*. Fabian Society, London, UK.

Vuillemin, G.D. 1964. Personal journal, 3 January.

7
Rwandan Private Print Media on the Eve of the Genocide

Jean-Marie Vianney Higiro

In April 1994, I was director of the Office Rwandais d'Information (ORINFOR), a government agency that managed public media: Radio Rwanda, Rwandan Television, Agence Rwandaise de Presse and the government-published newspapers, *Imvaho* and *La Relève*. I had been appointed by the coalition government led by Prime Minister Agathe Uwilingiyimana on 31 July 1993 and, in this role, I collected a significant volume of information about the media.

Early in the morning of 7 April, when I realized that the Forces Armées Rwandaises (FAR) had taken over Radio Rwanda and that my assassination and that of my family was likely and potentially imminent, my family and I left our residence to hide at a friend's house; we took only the clothes on our backs. A group of presidential guards sent to kill us arrived about 30 minutes later.

On 9 April, I called the United States embassy, in Kigali, to evacuate my daughter, who was born in Austin, Texas, when I was in graduate school there. We rushed into the car the embassy sent and drove to Bujumbura, Burundi, where we boarded a plane to Nairobi, Kenya, accompanied by US marines.

My exhaustive documentation on the Rwandan media was totally lost. For this paper, I have to rely on my memory and the messages I exchanged with some Rwandan newspaper editors after the genocide. (For their security, I cannot disclose their names.) [Editor's note: The author also referred to the material listed in the bibliography at the end of this paper to refresh his memory.]

TYPES OF PUBLICATIONS

The privately owned print media in pre-1994 Rwanda can be divided into four categories based on their political bias:

- Newspapers aligned with the Mouvement Républicain National pour la Démocratie et le Développement (MRND) and the Coalition pour la Défense de la République (CDR);
- Political opposition newspapers;
- Rwandan Patriotic Front (RPF) newspapers;
- The print media of the Rwandan Tutsi diaspora.

Pro-MRND and CDR newspapers

Newspapers in this group were: *Akanyange*, *Umurwanashyaka*, *Écho des Mille Collines/Impanda*, *Intera*, *Interahamwe*, *Kamarampaka*, *Kangura*, *La Médaille Nyiramacibili*, *Umurava*, *Le Courrier du Peuple* and *Shishoza*. Most of their editors were Hutus from northern Rwanda.

They praised the MRND and President Juvénal Habyarimana's leadership and offered space to MRND leaders to respond to criticism levelled at them by the editors of other newspapers and leaders of opposition parties. They depicted Habyarimana as the guarantor of peace and the MRND as the political party of true patriots.

Opposition leaders were portrayed as RPF puppets, traitors and embezzlers of public funds, demagogues, opportunists and idiots motivated by the desire to settle scores with President Habyarimana. The papers saw the RPF as Tutsi supremacists whose goal was to restore the Tutsi monarchy and enslave Hutus. To them, the invasion by the RPF from Uganda was an attempt to roll back the social and economic progress made by Hutus since the social revolution of 1959. In these pro-MRND media, Tutsi leaders were portrayed as cunning, bloodthirsty, untrustworthy and natural power mongers.

These negative representations tap into Rwandan history and old stereotypes exemplified in such sayings as '*Umututsi umucumbikira mu kirambi akagukura ku buliri*' (You give shelter to a Tutsi in your living room, he chases you out of your bedroom) and '*Umututsi umuvura imisuha akakwendera umugore*' (You cure a Tutsi of inflammation of the genitals, he makes love to your wife).

Kangura stands out among these newspapers. From its inception, its mission was the defence of Hutu interests and it published many articles dehumanizing Tutsis and depicting them as the enemy. *Kangura* articulated pan-Hutuism and strived to raise the awareness of the Hutus of Rwanda, Burundi and the eastern part of Zaire (now the Democratic Republic of the Congo) about the perceived threat presented by the Tutsis of Rwanda and Burundi and the Himas of Uganda.

These newspapers were funded by northern Hutus who viewed the birth of a private press as an assault on the social and economic accomplishments of the Habyarimana regime. For example, Seraphin Rwabukumba, President Habyarimana's brother-in-law, and Pasteur Musabe, the director general of the Banque Continentale Africaine, launched *Intera* after *Kinyamateka* (the newspaper owned by the Catholic Church) and *Umuranga* (a newspaper founded by Félicien Semusambi) published articles criticizing the Habyarimana regime. The Service Central de Renseignements launched *Kangura* with Hassan Ngeze as the cover to counter the articles published by *Kanguka*, a newspaper funded by Valens Kajeguhakwa, a Tutsi businessman and a member of the RPF. High-ranking northern Hutus believed that some southern Hutus, along with some Tutsis, were attempting to destroy the Habyarimana regime and that it was important to counter their attacks. As the name suggests, *Intera*'s objective was to convince the public of the economic progress made by the Habyarimana regime since it came to power in 1973.

Opposition newspapers

Opposition political parties, particularly the Mouvement Démocratique Républicain (MDR) and the Parti Social Démocrate (PSD), were associated with *Agatashya*, *Ibyikigihe*, *Ikindi*, *Ijambo*, *Intwali-Ijwi rya J.D.R.*, *Intumwa/Le Méssager*, *Isibo*, *Izuba/Le Soleil*, *La Griffe*, *L'Ère de Liberté*, *Umuranga*, *Nouvelle Génération*, *Nyabarongo*, *Republika*, *Rukokoma*, *Soma*, *Verités d'Afrique*, *Umuturage w'U Rwanda*, *Urumuli rwa Demokarasi* and *Umurangi*. Their editors came from southern Rwanda. After the split of the MDR into two factions in 1993, *Umurangi* and *Umuranga* went along with the MDR power faction, a group who felt that the Arusha agreement between the RPF and the Rwandan government gave too much power to the RPF.

Pro-opposition newspapers presented MRND leaders as evil and corrupt: liars, idiots, animals, bloodthirsty murderers and warmongers. Some published drawings of President Habyarimana covered with blood. *Intumwa/Le Méssager* (no. 10, 30 December 1991) published a cartoon featuring Prime Minister Sylvestre Nsanzimana carrying a hyena on his shoulders; the hyena stood for the MRND. In its 25 July 1992 issue, the newspaper depicted the secretary general of the MRND as a bird with a snake around its wing and neck, biting his head; the MRND is the snake in this cartoon. *Ijambo* (no. 54, 31 May 1993) published a cartoon featuring a gorilla wearing the hat of the CDR. In other words, these newspapers dehumanized the MRND and the CDR, and the newspapers associated with the MRND and CDR responded in kind.

Umurangi frequently published cartoons portraying Prime Minister Agathe Uwilingiyimana as a prostitute or sexual object and other opposition political leaders as dogs. In Rwandan culture a person considered dishonest, untrustworthy, cowardly and corrupt is usually labelled '*imbwa*' or dog.

These newspapers portrayed opposition leaders as peace-loving people capable of ending the war. They disseminated the view that expansion of the war was something that President Habyarimana and the MRND wanted to keep them in power. According to these newspapers, opposition leaders had a solution to the war: peace with the RPF. Some represented opposition leaders as medical doctors administering medicine to a confused patient, President Habyarimana. *Intumwa/Le Méssager* (no. 20, 15 August 1992) ran a cartoon of Habyarimana lying on a hospital bed and being forced to drink a medication administered by the leaders of the MDR, PSD and Parti Libéral.

Pro-RPF newspapers

Buracyeye, *Kanyarwanda*, *Kanguka*, *Kiberinka*, *Le Flambeau*, *Rwanda Rushya* and *Le Tribun du Peuple* (also known as *Umuvugizi wa Rubanda et Le Partisan*) strived to be the voice of the Tutsi. Their founders and editors were all Tutsi and members of the RPF living in Rwanda.

These newspapers denounced the MRND regime and its human rights records. They too contended that President Habyarimana and his party, the MRND, did not want peace. Examples of dehumanization of ideological opponents were also found in these papers. For instance, *Kanyarwanda* (no. 1, 23 September 1992) and *Rwanda Rushya* (no. 18, 22 February 1992) published cartoons depicting the MRND and the CDR as monsters that thrive on human flesh. *Kanguka* (no. 58, May 1992) published a cartoon showing the members of the CDR as monkeys. A cartoon published by *Kiberinka* (no. 8, April 1992) warns Prime Minister Nsengiyaremye not to carry the hyena (meaning the MRND) on his shoulders. In these newspapers MRND and CDR leaders and supporters were depicted as killers.

These papers hailed the RPF armed struggle. They published interviews with RPF leaders, and provided information about its political agenda and the territory the RPF had conquered. They never published stories about the assassinations, the abductions or the destruction for which the RPF was responsible as it advanced from southern Uganda in its quest for power. If they printed stories about violence in the demilitarized zone or buffer zone separating Rwandan government forces and RPF forces, they attributed it to 'the army of Habyarimana', a derogatory label for the FAR.

The front page of *Le Flambeau*, *Rwanda Rushya*, *Kanguka* and *Le Tribun du Peuple* quite often carried a photograph of RPF soldiers. Furthermore, the editors of this group of newspapers were the only ones allowed to visit the Rwandan Patriotic Army. Jean Pierre Mugabe, the chief editor of *Le Tribune du Peuple*, frequently visited the zone occupied by the RPF in Rwanda. He even produced a video documentary depicting the RPF military living in the areas under its occupation at a time when the Rwandan government was telling the world that there were no RPF soldiers on Rwandan territory, that they were in Uganda. The government strategy was to refuse to negotiate with the RPF, but rather to deal with the government of Uganda. This video omits any discussion of the destruction of villages and displacement of populations resulting from the war, and instead glamourizes the RPF and its leaders.

In 1993, Jean Pierre Mugabe fled Rwanda and joined Radio Muhabura, the radio station of the RPF. Charles Kanamugire, the chief editor of *Le Flambeau*, always wore around his neck a photograph of General Fred Rwigema, a founder and commander of the RPF. Vincent Rwabukwisi, the chief editor and owner of *Kanguka*, wrote in every issue of his paper that he could not get along with a person who did not call him an RPF militant or *inkotanyi*. His paper even organized a contest to promote the political platform of the RPF. André Kameya, the editor-in-chief of *Rwanda Rushya*, published many articles supporting the RPF and, as one of the leaders of the Parti Libéral, he repeated RPF messages at press conferences.

The media of the Rwandan Tutsi diaspora

Rwandan Tutsi refugees had their own publications: for example, *Alliance* edited by Alliance National Unity (RANU), an organization that later changed its name to the Rwandan Patriotic Front (RPF); *Congo Nil*, edited by Francois Rutanga in Belgium; *Impuruza*, edited by Alexander Kimenyi in the United States; *Inkotanyi*, edited by the RPF; *Intego*, edited by Jose Kagabo in France; *Munyarwanda*, edited by the Association of Concerned Banyarwanda in Canada; *Avant Garde*; *Le Patriote*; *Huguka*; and *Umulinzi*. These publications were circulated clandestinely in Rwanda.

The best known paper in this group is *Impuruza*, published in the United States from 1984 to 1994. Tutsi refugees and Roger Winter, the director of the United States Committee for Refugees, provided financial assistance to the publication. *Impuruza* is the name of a drum, which in pre-colonial Rwanda was beaten to call able men to war. In the first issue of *Impuruza*, its editor, Alexander Kimenyi, a Rwandan national and a professor at California State University, explained, 'The reason why we chose this name is to remind us that we too are at war and that we have to continue to show heroism.'

Impuruza published articles on the condition of the Rwandan Tutsi diaspora and on the authoritarian nature of Habyarimana's regime. It accused Belgium and the Catholic Church of being responsible for ethnic conflict in Rwanda because of their colonial policies and called for a round table between the Rwandan government and the representatives of the Tutsi refugees.

Although this paper was not sold in Rwanda, it circulated among Hutu and Tutsi elite in the country. Some Hutu elite saw it as the true reflection of an agenda for Tutsi hegemony in the Great Lakes of Africa even though the publication purported to defend the rights of Rwandan refugees to a homeland. Examples of statements suggesting Tutsi hegemony may be found in the name *Impuruza* and in the article written by Festo Habimana, the president of the Association of Banyarwanda in Diaspora USA in the first issue:

> A nation in exile, a people without leadership, 'the Jews of Africa,' a stateless nation, all these could very well make wonderful titles to depict the 'saga' of our people. A nation in exile because we are a group of people who are of the same origin, speak the same language distinct from the rest of the surroundings; a people who have been victimized for a long period of time yet survived and excelled under oppression ... It is no secret, as it is not our fault that we happen to be scattered in five or six different countries in which we are outnumbered, and the consequent problems are not of our making that the partition of Africa left us in such dilemma we find ourselves in.

He calls for the unity of Tutsi refugees saying:

> But our success will depend entirely upon our own effort and unity, not through world community as some perceive – in 25 years, what have they achieved for us in terms of concrete settlements for those who were displaced in [the] late 50s and early 60s? It will be only when they see us in charge of ourselves, and in control, that they will respond and listen. As long as we are scattered, with no leadership, business as usual on their part shall always be their policy. We are a very able and capable people with abundant blessings. What are we waiting for? Genocide?

It should be noted that the Association of Banyarwanda in Diaspora USA – assisted by Roger Winter – organized the International Conference on the Status of Banyarwanda Refugees held in Washington, DC, in 1988. It was at this conference that Tutsi refugees presumably chose armed struggle as the solution to the refugee problem. Winter, two US State Department officials and a Ugandan diplomat participated in the conference. At the invitation of the president of the association, I attended the opening session. I was then a graduate student in the United States.

After the RPF launched the war in October 1990, pro-MRND and CDR newspapers frequently reminded their readers that the ultimate goal of the RPF was the creation of a Tutsi–Hima empire in the Great Lakes of Africa.

To Hutu elite, *Impuruza* articulated a racist ideology that predated colonial rule. They particularly singled out a poem Alexandre Kimenyi wrote to honour General Fred Rwigema, the commander-in-chief of the RPF who died in the early days of the invasion of Rwanda in 1990. The poem, called 'Nsingize Gisa umusore utagira uko asa' (A tribute to Gisa, a young man with an indescribable beauty), appeared in *Impuruza* (no. 17) in December 1990. Here is an excerpt translated into English by Dr Froduald Harelimana:

> You are a bullfighter who launched a war to free the Nobles [Tutsi]
> Since you decided to use the entire arsenal
> The termites [Hutu] will run out of the country
> Just a few days before the first shell has landed
> Those wild rats, corrupted crooks [Hutu] are already panic-stricken
> They are looters, hooligans, and killers [Hutu]
> I see those traitors with bloated cheeks [Hutu] running in panic and disarray
> Those thieves [Hutu] are troublemakers.
> The ugly creatures [the Tutsi mythology preaches that people of Hamitic origin are generally handsome, whereas people of Bantu origin are ugly] are insane and furious
> They are the enemies of Rwanda; they are nothing but a bunch of dishonorable dirt.

The Hutu elite regarded *Impuruza* as the voice of the Tutsi refugees and its editor as the ideologue of the RPF. Kimenyi, the editor, served as the director of research of the RPF: Rwandan officials took this publication very seriously.

JOURNALISM AND POLITICAL ACTIVISM

Except for the government journalists, most journalists in Rwanda did not have college degrees or professional training. Many editors and journalists were militants in the political parties they worked for and were well respected in those political parties. The journalists who were on the side of the ruling party, the MRND, behaved as intelligence agents of the state: ordinary citizens were afraid of them.

Some journalists held positions in political parties. Gaspard Gahigi, editor-in-chief of *Umurwanashyaka* and Radio-Télévision Libre des Milles Collines (RTLM), was a member of the central committee of MRND; Ngeze, owner and director of *Kangura,* was an advisor to the CDR; Sylvestre Nkubili, a journalist at *Kinyamateka*, was vice-president of the Union Démocratique Populaire de Rwanda (UDPR); Andre Kameya, owner and director of *Rwanda Rushya*, was the director of the commission of information of the Parti Libéral; Vincent Rwabukwisi, owner and director of *Kanguka*, was president of the UDPR.

Rwandan newspapers looked very similar in format and presentation. Most of them were tabloids; they published articles in Kinyarwanda (the language spoken in Rwanda) and used cartoons to portray political leaders. They watched each other closely and tried to emulate or outsmart each other.

Some cartoons looked alike. For example, *Izuba/Le Soleil* (no. 12) of 1 April 1992 published a cartoon that had already appeared in *Le Tribun du Peuple* (*Umuvugizi wa Rubanda*). It showed the minister of public works, Joseph Nzirorera, hanged by dogs for corruption and embezzlement. *Kanguka* (no. 51) of 13 January 1992 published a cartoon showing Félicien Ngango and Félicien Gatabazi, respectively first vice-president and executive secretary of the PSD, hanged by dogs for corruption and embezzlement. Finally, *La Griffe* (no. 6) of 11 April 1992 printed a cartoon showing Ferdinand Nahimana, then director of ORINFOR, caught by dogs for his use of public media to spread hatred against Tutsi.

Examples of dehumanization could be found in many of these papers, including those associated with political opposition and the RPF.

To improve the quality of the Rwandan press, the Friedrich Naumann Foundation, a German organization, included independent journalists in its international training programmes. In the mid-1980s, this foundation initiated a training programme for journalists of the Economic Community of the Great Lakes, of which Burundi, Rwanda and the Democratic Republic of the Congo are members. After the legalization of political parties, the American and Belgian embassies also organized seminars for Rwandan journalists. These seminars attracted many editors very eager to learn. After the signing of the Arusha peace agreement, organizers of these seminars even invited journalists from Radio Muhabura, the clandestine radio station of the RPF. I was an instructor at these seminars. Instructors always insisted that the media not be used to promote war, hatred or racist ideology. Such messages went unheeded.

PROFIT AND THE NEWSPAPER BUSINESS

According to some editors, the financial viability of a newspaper depended on its readers. The number of readers a newspaper had depended on its political leanings. The buyers of the newspaper and the financial supporters were members of the political party the newspaper had chosen to support. The newspapers that sided with political parties that had money were the ones that were viable and published regularly. Those supporting the MRND and the RPF fall into this category.

Newspapers supporting the MRND included *Kangura*, *Umurwanashyaka*, *Interahamwe*, *Kamarampaka*, *Écho des Mille Collines* and *La Médaille Nyiramacibili*.

Among those supporting the RPF were *Kanguka*, *Rwanda Rushya* and *Le Flambeau*. These newspapers and their editors had financial resources that came from wealthy Tutsis, such as Valence Kajeguhakwa, the director of planning of the RPF. The three newspapers had an office, a telephone and other office equipment.

Other editors frequently published articles supporting RPF views, usually from RPF supporters living inside Rwanda. To have these articles published, RPF supporters had to pay substantial sums of money. Some editors who received such funding were Elie Mpayimana of *L'Ère de Liberté*, Theoneste Muberantwali of *Nyabarongo*, Édouard Mutsinzi of *Le Méssager*, Édouard Mpongebuke of *Umuturage* and Augustin Hangimana of *Ijambo*.

A former Rwandan editor who now lives in exile wrote to me:

> When we launched independent news organizations in 1990 (I launched mine in June 1990) we had many contacts with RPF milieus. However, at that time, these milieus were called Rwanda National Unity. There were individuals who gave us articles to publish using Tutsi channels (business people) and there were individuals who gave us money for subscriptions of support (for instance a person would say I have read your articles and I liked them, here is a contribution to publish in the next issue of your newspaper). I later found out that there was also some confusion since there were powerful Tutsi who knew there was something in preparation but did not have necessary contacts and thought we had them, and they asked us for them. Some would ask to meet with me and whenever they saw me and realized I did not look like them, they were disappointed. After the war broke out, some people accused me of supporting the enemy; there were powerful Tutsis who were convinced I was a member of the RPF, and they asked me for contacts ... However later they found the proper channels of establishing links with the RPF.

Some newspapers received financial assistance from people who were only motivated to bring about democratic change in the country. Among them are *Isibo* and *Ikindi,* which received financial assistance from the United States embassy and wealthy supporters of the opposition MDR. Some received a budget from their founders. Among these were state-run newspapers; *Kinyamateka*, a Catholic-owned newspaper; *Imbaga*, a newspaper owned by Centre Iwacu, a private nongovernmental organization (NGO); and the newspapers owned by political parties. Other newspapers and their editorial staff did not make a profit and journalists who worked for them were poor.

Selling newspapers was a major problem. Every editor had to find a market and organize a distribution system. In Kigali, newspapers were sold at the central bus station and children sold newspapers on the street. Usually the editors did not receive the money collected by these street children. Quite often I visited kiosks where newspapers were sold to observe reading behaviours and talk to newspaper boys. I could see many unsold issues.

When the private press was first established, a newspaper sold for 50 Rwandan francs (about US$ 0.30). After devaluation of the Rwandan franc by 67 per cent in November 1990, under an International Monetary Fund (IMF) structural adjustment programme, the cost of a copy doubled. Reading a newspaper became very expensive even for me, the director of a state agency. It was too costly to buy all the newspapers that were published in Kigali. I observed that a reader could give 50 Rwandan francs to a newspaper boy, read a copy standing at the kiosk and return it.

Based on discussions with many of the editors of these newspapers, whom I met at seminars and other events in Kigali, the circulation of a newspaper was 2,000–3,000 copies. When an issue sold well, the editor would order another printing. Hassan Ngeze of *Kangura* told me on several occasions that the circulation of his newspaper was 10,000 copies and sometimes 30,000. I always doubted these figures; visiting the kiosks in Kigali, I found many unsold issues of *Kangura*.

DISTRIBUTION IN THE COUNTRYSIDE

There were many obstacles to the distribution of these newspapers outside Kigali. The first was the high illiteracy rate. To emphasize the impact of Rwandan media on the genocide, Professor Alison Des Forges, a Human Rights Watch researcher and an expert on Rwandan history, wrote:

> Some 66 per cent of Rwandans are literate and those who knew how to read were accustomed to reading for others. In many cases, the written word was underscored by cartoons, most of which were so graphic that they could not be misinterpreted. (Des Forges 1999)

However, the general census of the population conducted on 15 August 1991 indicates that: 'The population that cannot read nor write represents 44 per cent of people who are more than six years.'

In other words, only 56 per cent of the population could read and write in 1991. The same general census adds: 'In comparison to 1978, this represents a decrease of 13.4 per cent, since the illiteracy rate was 57.4 per cent for the entire country.' Des Forges' literacy figure suggests that there had been a dramatic change of 10 per cent between August 1991 and 6 April 1994. However, during that time there was no documented campaign to increase the literacy level of the population.

Buying a paper was expensive: the cost of a newspaper was 100 Rwandan francs before 6 April 1994 (US$ 0.75) or the average day's salary of a migrant worker in rural areas of Rwanda. The drop in coffee prices on the world market and the IMF's structural adjustment programme worsened the situation. Potential consumers, such as elementary school teachers, did not have money to spend on print media. In fact, the Rwandan government was not even paying the salaries of teachers on time because it was almost bankrupt.

The newspapers of the government, the Catholic Church and the political parties reached rural areas. The political parties sent their papers to their supporters in the prefectures and communes. Others reached rural areas through people who travelled to Kigali. People living outside the capital did not realize that many newspapers existed.

Editors could put advertisements on Radio Rwanda to announce that a new issue of their newspaper was available, but they could not hint at the content. For publicity, they had to count on the weekly review of the print press, a Radio Rwanda programme produced by Tharcisse Rubwiliza. Those who did not like this weekly review regarded this journalist as an accomplice of the RPF; in April 1994 *Interahamwe* killed Rubwiliza at his house in Gikondo.

There were no places in the provinces or communes where newspapers could be sold. The administrative structure of Rwanda was still dominated by the MRND and did not allow easy dissemination of any information opposed to it. However, political parties that had organizational structures in the countryside used them to distribute newspapers to local leaders and supporters free of charge.

FREEDOM OF THE PRESS

With the sudden emergence of an aggressive press early in 1990, the government reacted by issuing statements broadcast by Radio Rwanda asking journalists not to abuse the freedom of the press. When those statements went unheeded, the chief of the Service Central de Renseignements (SCR), an agency based in the president's office, called a meeting with journalists in early 1990 and dictated issues that were off limits for discussion. Such issues included the head of state and his family, regionalism or relations between southerners (*abanyenduga*) and northerners (*abakiga*), religion and government officials. The SCR chief even designated an intelligence officer to serve as an advisor to the press. His restrictions would have left little freedom and no one accepted these injunctions.

The regime engaged in persecution of the private press, particularly newspapers that were critical of the MRND and its leaders. Editors were frequently jailed, interrogated by the SCR or beaten by its agents. Among those who were jailed were Thaddée Nsengiyaremye of *Ikindi*, Théoneste Muberantwali of *Nyabarongo*, Janvier Afrika of *Umurava*, Julien Uwimana of *Ibyikigihe* and *Urumuli rwa Demokarasi* and Sixbert Musangamfura of *Isibo*.

Many issues of some newspapers were not allowed to leave the print shop because they contained articles critical of the Habyarimana regime. Politicians took editors to court. Joseph Nzirorera, a minister of public works sued Sixbert Musangamfura because he had published an article on mismanagement in the ministry. Other editors were targeted by car 'accidents', that is, attempted assassinations. Félicien Semusambi survived a car accident, while Father Silvio Sindambiwe did not.

To silence dissent in the private print press, Nahimana Ferdinand, then director of ORINFOR, convened a meeting of all Rwandan journalists. His idea was to create an association of journalists supposedly to defend their interests, but in fact he wanted to use it to influence the content of newspapers. The journalists affiliated with opposition papers and the representatives of

Kinyamateka, a Catholic newspaper, and *Imbaga*, a newspaper funded by Centre Iwacu, walked out of the meeting and created the Association des Journalistes du Rwanda (AJR). Those who remained formed a pro-regime government association, the Union des Journalistes du Rwanda (UJR).

In June 1991, a new constitution legalized multiparty democracy, and political parties began to publish their own newspapers. Some politicians and parties provided funds to newspapers and used them to defend themselves against political attacks or to disseminate their views. Thus, these newspapers were published regularly. For example, the pro-MRND and pro-CDR newspapers *Kangura*, *Umurwanashyaka*, *Interahamwe*, *Kamarampaka*, *Écho des Mille Collines/Impanda* and *La Médaille/Nyiramacibili* came out at least twice a month; pro-RPF newspapers *Kanguka*, *Rwanda Rushya* and *Le Flambeau*, and pro-MDR newspapers, *Isibo* and *Umurangi*, were also published at least twice a month. Their resources came from political parties or their supporters, who were very often wealthy businessmen. Some newspapers had two or three people working for them, an office and a telephone; others were a one-person operation without a known address.

Finally, a law of the press was promulgated in 1992. While claiming to recognize the freedom of the press, its emphasis was on how to restrict that freedom. The Rwandan law on the press recognized the right of any Rwandan to publish a newspaper. It stated that a person who wanted to launch a newspaper had to write a letter to the minister of information and the local prosecutor informing them of his intentions and providing the name of the newspaper, its goals and the identity of the editorial team. Once the person received authorization from both officials, he could begin publishing. If after 30 days the minister of information and the local prosecutor had not responded to the letter, the person could start a newspaper anyway. The law also provided that the owner of the newspaper had to send three copies of each issue to the minister of information and the local prosecutor.

IMPACT OF THE PRIVATE PRINT PRESS ON RWANDAN POLITICS

Erosion of power

The private print media represented the first political opposition to the Habyarimana regime. Until 1989, only *Kinyamateka* – under the leadership of Father Silvio Sindambiwe and André Sibomana – could publish articles critical of the regime. Under government pressure, Silvio Sindambiwe was replaced by André Sibomana, who used the newspaper as a platform to defend human rights. The regime used all sorts of intimidation tactics, including taking him to court. The birth of independent newspapers followed his example.

The resistance of these editors to the authoritarian regime of Juvénal Habyarimana convinced the Rwandan elite that if they needed political change they had to fight for it. The negative representation of Habyarimana and his associates as warmongers, murderers, monsters, liars and embezzlers lifted all the taboos that had surrounded the regime. The regime lost its essential attribute of instilling terror in the population. When multiparty democracy became legal, opposition supporters in Kigali chanted '*navaho impundu zizavuga*' (when he [Habyarimana] is removed from office cries of joy will resonate throughout Rwanda). In Rwandan political culture, this type of discourse was previously unthinkable.

Influence on the political process

I believe the private print media influenced the Rwandan political elite. For instance, in 1991 pro-opposition media called for the abolition of the annual compulsory contribution each public- and private-sector employee was obligated to pay as a member of the MRND. (According to the country's constitution of 1978, all Rwandans were members of the MRND.) The contribution was deducted from the pay cheque at the beginning of a new year. Although the constitution was not changed until June 1992, the secretary general of the MRND abolished the annual compulsory contribution.

During the coalition government led by Prime Minister Dismas Nsengiyaremye, pro-MRND and pro-CDR newspapers monitored and denounced many abuses committed by some members of his cabinet who belonged to opposition parties. At the time, the media accused the members of the PSD of diverting public resources toward their political party. The accusation of mismanagement put these ministers on the defensive.

The dehumanization practices mentioned earlier made the political discourse vitriolic. For example, when a newspaper published a cartoon depicting a political leader as a dog, a murderer or a monster, a newspaper favourable to this political leader would retaliate by publishing a cartoon depicting an opponent as a dog or a monster, or he would dehumanize the other or the other's political party during a speech at a political rally. These dehumanization practices found in the media led to the escalation of conflicts between the MRND and the CDR and opposition parties, and it caused the escalation of conflicts among opposition parties themselves. It was common to see politicians depicted in newspapers as a cow, goat, dog, hyena, lion, monkey, gorilla, pig, snake, shark, eagle or mouse. In other words, the media were used as proxies in the struggle for power and reflected the anger and even hatred the political parties harboured toward each other.

To illustrate the impact of dehumanization on the escalation of violence, I have selected three examples mentioned earlier to relate them to Rwandan political culture.

Inyenzi: *Inyenzi* means cockroach, which is of course demeaning. Originally the word *inyenzi* had a positive connotation, to do with the Tutsi rebel movement that devastated Rwanda throughout the 1960s and 1970s. In a BBC interview broadcast on 8 November 2003, Aloys Ngurumbe explained that *Inyenzi* is the acronym of '*Ingangurarugo yemeye kuba ingenzi.*' *Ingangurarugo* was an army division under Kigeli Rwabugili, a Tutsi king who ruled Rwanda at the end of the nineteenth century. Hence, *Inyenzi* means 'a member of *Ingangurarugo* who has committed himself to bravery.' Rwabugili, the son of King Rwogera belonged to this division. The word *ingangurarugo* comes from '*kugangura urugo* *rw'ibwami*' or to provoke trouble at the king's court. When Rwabugili was a child, he and his friends attacked Rwogera's court and took away his cattle. More broadly, *ingangurarugo* then means troublemakers. During his reign, Rwabugili waged war throughout the Great Lakes of Africa until his death in 1895. Ngurumbe stated that his supporters chose the label, not extremist Hutus, to whom it is attributed in many writings on the 1994 Rwanda genocide.

In the 1960s and 1970s, *Inyenzi* would attack at night and kill innocent civilians. Then they would rapidly vanish in the countryside or retreat into Burundi, Tanzania, Uganda or Zaire. Due to this ability to terrorize the country and to disappear, the population associated the attackers with cockroaches instead of bravery. Cockroaches are annoying insects that disappear when somebody turns on the light. The only way to get rid of them is to kill all of them. *Inyenzi* became a generic term for Tutsis. By extension, the supporters of the Habyarimana regime and other Hutus opposed to the RPF applied the label *inyenzi* to their political opponents.

By virtue of this exclusionary practice, during a political rally held in October 1993 to remember the assassination of Melchior Ndadaye, the first democratically elected Hutu president of Burundi, Froduald Karamira, the second vice-president of MDR declared that Radio Rwanda had fallen into the hands of *inyenzi* and that *inyenzi* Higiro should be fired. Karamira was referring to me. Given the volatile political climate of the time, labelling a person or a group of people cockroaches was similar to sentencing somebody to death. The Radio Rwanda reporter informed me of this hate language and I ordered him to omit that part of the speech from his report. In compliance with the Arusha accord between the Rwandan government and the RPF, I had ordered state-run media not to use the word *inyenzi* when referring to the RPF and to avoid all language that incited violence. This policy applied to the news coverage of political rallies, the broadcast time allocated to political parties and all press releases sent to ORINFOR, including those of MDR, the party to which I belonged. Whenever a news release of a political party came across my desk and contained language inciting violence or dehumanizing a group of people, I would cross out that language and initial the crossed out paragraphs or sentences before sending it to the news desk of Radio Rwanda. My family and I almost lost our lives because of this policy.

***Hyena**:* In Rwandan culture a hyena is the worst animal. Rwandans use the name to label a dirty person or a person who has a bad look. Saying that a person is a hyena is to wish him death. It is a very bad insult. In Rwanda it is common to carry a baby or a person one likes or who needs care on one's back or shoulders. Showing someone carrying a hyena like that is the worst possible insult.

The editor who published the cartoon portraying Prime Minister Nsanzimana carrying a hyena on his shoulders wanted to express empathy with him. I think he meant that Nsanzimana was sentenced to death because he was given the tough responsibility of leading Rwanda during a political and economic crisis. I doubt that in the volatile situation Rwanda was undergoing, MRND members decoded this intended meaning. I rather think that they saw the cartoon as very offensive.

Monkey or gorilla: Likening the rally of the CDR to a bunch of monkeys or gorillas is to draw on deep stereotypes or even the hatred that Tutsi supremacists felt for Hutus. There is a Rwandan tradition known as '*kwishongora*' – an oratory skill consisting of either putting down a speaker or a group of speakers, or deflecting an attack from a speaker or group of speakers. Tutsi aristocrats had to master this skill to be able to socialize with their peers. Tutsi supremacists compared Hutus to monkeys or gorillas as part of this oratory practice because they were confident that they were superior to Hutus and the indigenous Twas. Since the CDR was made up of Hutus, a rally of gorillas was a rally of Hutus. Again the editor's intended message was to ridicule the emphasis on Hutu identity, but it rekindled deeply seated racism. In a politically charged atmosphere, such as the one prevailing in Rwanda at the time of publication, the cartoon was very provocative.

Role in the genocide

Many newspapers welcomed the signing of the Arusha peace agreement between the Rwandan government and the RPF. *Interahamwe*, a pro-MRND newspaper devoted a special issue to the Arusha talks, with many photos of the representatives of the RPF. The political atmosphere was one of relief and hope. However, the positive news coverage did not last long, for opposition parties split into pro-MRND and pro-RPF factions, and newspaper editors aligned themselves accordingly.

During the genocide these newspapers stopped publication. Most of the journalists were killed.

Did the content of these newspapers serve as the catalyst of the genocide? The media have the potential to shape the views of their readers. As said earlier, Rwandan newspapers reached a small proportion of the population because of their high cost and the high illiteracy rate. They certainly shaped the world view of the political elite, as evidenced by the example regarding the abolition of the compulsory annual contribution to the MRND, and they probably contributed to the escalation of violence.

Having said that, the Rwanda genocide cannot be solely attributed to Rwandan media. The media tapped into a context of social discontent, war, high population growth rate, economic crisis, regionalism, historical ethnic conflict opposing Hutus to Tutsis, bad leadership and such external forces as the structural adjustment programme and the rivalries between foreign powers. It is the combination of these factors that led to the genocide.

CONCLUSION

Basic human rights – such as freedom of speech and freedom of the press – should be guaranteed to Rwandan citizens, otherwise underground networks will channel social discontent and an explosion of violence will likely occur again. These basic human rights should be sustained by economic development.

Economic development that favours one group over others will inevitably create social inequalities and discontent and, in the long run, likely lead to violence. The MRND regime favoured northern Hutu elite; today the RPF regime favours Tutsi refugees who returned from Uganda.

Journalism is an established academic discipline. It is important that Rwandan journalists learn the professional values of this field and understand the requirements and responsibilities of the profession.

Foreign donors should support the development of a free press by funding the training of professional communicators in Rwanda and by encouraging the Rwandan government to open up the political arena and the state-run media to pluralistic ideas.

Alternative media, such as Internet newspapers or magazines, may reach only those Rwandan elite with access to this technology. It is these elite who are involved in the struggle for power. Cultural centres and libraries may play a major role by making the Internet accessible at a low cost.

For the majority of the population, radio remains the medium through which news and ideas are disseminated most widely. As long as Rwanda is ruled by authoritarian regimes, broadcasting will remain under government control. That is why international radio stations that broadcast in Kinyarwanda and Kirundi – such as the BBC and the Voice of America – are essential to provide information on topics that are off limits in Rwanda. I realize that these radio stations have their own political agenda; however, it is my conviction that so far they have offered space to political diversity in their programming. Providing space in which differences are articulated is one way to prevent conflicts.

To prevent abuses perpetrated in the name of freedom of speech and freedom of the press, there is a need for local independent NGOs to defend these basic freedoms. These organizations may monitor violations of these freedoms by both the government and journalists and remind them of their obligation to maintain a free society.

Some 'experts' on Rwanda relay the RPF propaganda according to which a racist ideology originated from the teaching of Catholic missionaries, the policies of Belgian colonizers and the social revolution of 1959 that overthrew the Tutsi monarchy. These 'experts' then emphasize the role of *Kangura* and the RTLM in the mobilization of Hutus around a racist ideology that instilled hatred in Rwanda before 1994. These experts create only two social categories among Hutus: Hutu 'extremists' and Hutu 'moderates'.

In 1992, my parents fled our village near the Rwanda–Uganda border as a result of the RPF 'scorched earth' policy. They moved from one internally displaced camp to another until they reached Zaire, then Kenya. They returned to Rwanda in 1998 only to find the ruins of their home. In which category do they fit? During this entire period they were always on the run. Many other people like them just ran to save their lives. The narrow social categories of 'extremist' and 'moderate' are, therefore, meaningless.

When it comes to the media as well, some experts adopt a binary analysis: the media of hate and the media of democracy. Such a representation of events is, of course, valuable in Western movies or other artistic creations. Rarely do these experts realize that practices of racism and exclusion in Rwanda have indigenous seeds in Rwandan proverbs that stereotype ethnic groups, myths that legitimize the superiority of Tutsis over Hutus and Twas and other social practices.

When I was growing up, no Hutu or Tutsi drank at the same jar of *ikigage* (beer of sorghum) or *urwagwa* (banana wine) with a Twa or partook of the same meal in a basket with a Twa. This exclusionary practice was still alive in 1994. Likewise, before the social revolution of 1959, Tutsi aristocrats never socialized with Hutus. Only impoverished Tutsis mixed with Hutus – impoverished Tutsis and Hutus made up of what the Hutu leaders of the social revolution of 1959 called '*rubanda rugufi*' or the low or oppressed people. Racism and exclusionary practices are not confined to one ethnic group or one group of media as the Hollywood approach suggests.

Before the social revolution of 1959, Tutsi supremacists called Hutus '*ibimonyo*' or ants. *Ibimonyo* are a type of ant that lives in colonies of thousands. They are big and work very hard tilling the soil, but they are considered worthless. If a person steps on them and kills them, it does not matter. The Rwandan name '*Sekimonyo*' means the son of an ant or the son of a Hutu. To my knowledge only Hutu parents gave this name to a child. This suggests that Hutus had internalized their oppressor.

As discussed earlier, after Tutsi rebels launched the *Inyenzi* movement in the 1960s and 1970s to retake power, Hutu elite turned the acronym on its head and labelled all Tutsis *inyenzi* or cockroaches. Under the RPF regime, Tutsi elite labelled Hutus '*genocidaires*' or genocide perpetrators. Unlike Hutu elite, Tutsi elite are careful not to use such a label in writings and speeches at public events. Since the victory of the RPF, Tutsi elite have added a new label to the Rwandan dictionary of exclusionary practices, the word '*ibipinga*' from a Swahili word '*kupinga*', which means to reject what another person says. Thus *ibipinga* means those who reject RPF policies, and the word has become a generic term used by the RPF to mean Hutus. By extension, the label also applies to Tutsis who oppose the RPF. As a consequence of this exclusionary discourse, *ibipinga* have to be eliminated in the elite pro-Tutsi regime by assassinating them or forcing them into exile.

Rwandans who are committed to building a democratic society in Rwanda and to understanding the racism and exclusionary practices that have both historically and contemporarily pervaded Rwandan society, should beware of the limited narratives of experts and the discourse of the RPF. An open discussion on this issue may result in the adoption of policies and behaviours that will lead to peaceful coexistence among the three Rwandan ethnic groups: the Hutus, the Tutsis and the Twas. Shifting the blame on to foreigners and ignoring deep-seated racism will only lead to cyclical violence as each ethnic group strives to achieve a zero-sum solution to oppression.

ACKNOWLEDGEMENTS

I thank Keith Harmon Snow, a researcher at Survivor's Rights International, for his editorial suggestions and insight into the politics of the Great Lakes of central Africa. I also thank Ms Maya Graf for providing many of the cartoons I referred to in writing this article. Ms Graf, a Swiss national, helped launch *Makuru ki i Butare?* the first independent newspaper that existed in Butare, Rwanda, before the war broke out in October 1990.

REFERENCES AND FURTHER READING

Centre Culturel Americain. 1992. Media situation in Rwanda. Embassy of the United States of America, Kigali, Rwanda.

Chrétien, J.P., J.F. Dupaquier and M. Kabanda. 1995. *Rwanda: les médias du génocide.* Karthala, Paris, France. 397 pp.

Des Forges, A. 1999. *Leave None to Tell the Story: Genocide in Rwanda.* Human Rights Watch and the International Federation of Human Rights Leagues, New York, NY, USA. Available at <www.hrw.org/reports/1999/rwanda/> (accessed 30 August 2005).

Government of Rwanda. 1993. Recensement général de la population et de l'habitat au 15 août 1991. Analyse des principaux résultats. Government of Rwanda, Kigali, Rwanda, July.

Guichaoua, A. (ed.). 1995. *Les crises politiques au Burundi et au Rwanda (1993–1994).* Karthala, Paris, France. 790 pp.

Habimana, F. 1984. A Nation in Exile. *Impuruza*, 1. Sacramento, California.

Hall, S. 1980. 'Encoding and decoding' (revised extract). In S. Hall, D. Hobson, A. Lowe, P. Willis (eds). *Culture, Media, Language.* Hutchinson, London, UK.

Kelman, H.C. 1998. Social-psychological Dimensions of International Conflict. In W. Zartman and J. Rasmussen (eds). *Peacemaking in International Conflicts: Methods and Techniques.* United States Institute of Peace, Washington, DC, USA.

Kimenyi, A. 1984. Editorial. *Impuruza*, 1. Sacramento, California.

—— 1990. Nsingize Gisa umusore utagira uko asa. *Impuruza*, 17. Sacramento, California.

Ministère des Finances et de la Planification Économique. 2004. *Recensement 2002 en bref.* Government of Rwanda, Kigali, Rwanda.

Ministeri y'Amashuli Makuru n'Ubushakashatsi mu by'Ubuhanga. 1988. *Ingoma ya Kigeli Rwabugili na Nyirayuhi Kanjogera.* Government of Rwanda, Kigali, Rwanda.

RSF (Reporters Sans Frontières). 1994. *Rwanda: médias de la haine ou presse démocratique.* RSF, Paris, France.

—— 1995. *Rwanda: l'impasse? La liberté d'expression après le génocide.* RSF, Paris, France.

—— 2004. *Rwanda 2004, Annual Report.* RSF, Paris, France.

Staub, E. 1989. *The Roots of Evil.* Cambridge University Press, Cambridge, UK.

8
Echoes of Violence: Considerations on Radio and Genocide in Rwanda

Darryl Li

For 100 days in the spring and summer of 1994, millions of Rwandans witnessed, participated in or otherwise lived through a nationwide campaign of extermination – a collective effort whose rhythm was in many ways regulated by the broadcasts of Radio-Télévision Libre des Milles Collines (RTLM). 'The graves are only half empty; who will help us fill them?' an RTLM announcer is reputed to have wondered out loud in one of the station's less subtle moments. The semi-private radio station, reportedly linked to a circle of high-ranking Hutu extremists, has achieved an infamous, if not legendary, reputation for allegedly inciting Rwandan Hutu to participate in massacring the country's Tutsi minority on a scale and scope without precedent in the country's history.[1] Aside from acting as a surrogate information network for the *Interahamwe* militia and other organized groups dedicated to the killing, RTLM was also the most popular station in the country during the genocide;[2] it was perceived as a reliable political barometer, a source of entertainment and a provider of breaking news. Yet in many ways, despite a burgeoning literature on the Rwanda genocide (notably African Rights 1995; Des Forges 1999; Gourevitch 1998; Mamdani 2001; Prunier 1995) and even specific studies on radio's role (Chalk 1999; Chrétien et al. 1995; Kellow and Steeves 1998; Kirschke 1996; Nkusi et al. 1998), its impact on listeners remains relatively unexplored and its overall place in encouraging mass participation in the killings largely under theorized.

This enquiry, based in part on three months of fieldwork conducted in Rwanda in the summer of 2000,[3] seeks to integrate the perspectives and experiences of radio listeners with broader considerations about the study of the Rwanda genocide and mass atrocity more generally. Specifically, I will argue that the question of RTLM's role in the genocide can be elucidated through three aspects: *ideologically*, it played on existing dominant discourses in Rwandan public life for the purposes of encouraging listeners to participate in the killings; *performatively*, the station's animateurs[4] skilfully exploited the possibilities of the medium to create a dynamic relationship with and among listeners; and, finally, RTLM helped the Rwandan state appropriate one of the most innocuous

This paper originally appeared in the *Journal of Genocide Research*, 6(1), March 2004.

aspects of everyday life in the service of the genocide. Taken together, these three aspects make radio a useful prism through which one can approach the question of mass participation in a genocide that was diffuse, routinized and intimate in nature.

OPENING QUESTIONS

An enquiry into the Rwanda genocide and RTLM's role in it reveals parallel questions and gaps in the existing literature on collective violence and media studies, both essentially revolving around the question of subjectivity and action. Commentators have frequently remarked on the highly centralized and labour-intensive nature of the killing campaign, involving the direct or indirect efforts of hundreds of thousands of ordinary citizens working under the direction of a strong state using a dense network of local administration and parastatal entities. Although it was spearheaded and guided at the local level by bureaucrats, party cadres and armed elements (military, police, militia), what sets the Rwanda genocide apart from many other contemporary mass atrocities was the participation of such a sizeable and heterogeneous portion of the population (farmers, businessmen, journalists, nongovernmental organization (NGO) workers, clergy, teachers) as killers, lookouts, informants, looters, logisticians and cheerleaders.

The fact of mass participation in the genocide, however, needs to be further understood through three particular aspects that frequently elude systematic enquiry. First, the killing was highly diffuse. Although it did not unfold evenly or simultaneously across the country, it left no region untouched, and the killing itself was carried out in spaces both public and private, including churches, roadblocks, homes, schools, fields and government office buildings, obviating the need to relocate and concentrate large numbers of victims to distant, secluded institutions such as camps or prisons. Second, in the vacuum left by the absence of much cultivation, business and study, the genocide established its own rhythm; participation (construed broadly, not necessarily killing) was routinized. Although orgiastic massacres did occur, many of the day-to-day activities of the genocide (primarily roadblock duty, patrols and searches) were carried out by work crews rotating according to set schedules, sometimes electing their own leaders. Third, the genocide was a project in which mass violence relied on social intimacy. Systematic identification and pursuit of Tutsi depended on the compilation of comprehensive lists at the local level; such surveillance, coupled with movement restrictions, made escape and anonymity extremely difficult. Moreover, the killing involved widespread denunciation and betrayal of friends, neighbours and loved ones.[5]

Scholars have drawn from many of the existing theories of collective violence to explain the Rwanda genocide. So-called 'primordialist' approaches, based on the idea of reified 'ancient ethnic [or tribal] hatreds' (teleologically drawing on earlier episodes of anti-Tutsi violence in the late 1950s and 1960s), initially dominated much of the media coverage of and some of the scholarship on the genocide. However, these have been widely criticized to the extent that they now serve as little more than an academic pinata, although their political potency cannot be underestimated (and their potential analytical value, if properly revised, is perhaps under-appreciated at this time). Primordialist approaches have been largely displaced by explanations that emphasize the historicity/contingency of ethnic identities, the role of manipulative and self-serving political elites, crushing economic and demographic pressures, the importance of racist anti-Tutsi ideologies or often some combination thereof. Although these diverse theories (at times grouped together as 'instrumentalist') have provided a useful critique of primordialism and have made a number of positive contributions to the study of the genocide, the question of how mass participation was secured and sustained is often effaced (notable exceptions include Mamdani 2001 and Uvin 1998).[6] Indeed, in the face of such widespread participation in diffused, routinized and intimate killing, it seems difficult to rely on existing explanations – ideas such as cultural norms of obedience, elite-driven manipulation and socio-economic pressures – without somehow speaking of Rwandans as easily open to manipulation and control. Yet at the same time, one cannot lose sight of the fact that the genocide came immediately after the period of multipartyism, which was marked by unprecedented political openness and opposition to the state, including intra-Hutu violence.

Interestingly, the holes in the extant literature on RTLM and the genocide are similarly shaped. Pictures of *Interahamwe* militia with their ears glued to radios and stories of RTLM's more gory announcements were easily incorporated into atavistic explanations of the genocide. The first in-depth studies (Chrétien et al. 1995; Kirschke 1996) reviewed the kinds of racist stereotyping used in the station's broadcasts or unearthed the overlapping networks of power, money, patronage and ideology that brought RTLM and other extremist media to life. Others have analyzed the question from the perspective of sociolinguistics (Nkusi et al. 1998) and media studies (Kellow and Steeves 1998). In extensively cataloguing and analyzing the broadcasts of RTLM, these works highlight the station's role in disseminating racist stereotypes and inciting specific killings. However, they say little about how media messages were received by their intended audiences and how such broadcasts interacted with other factors at the local level (especially state coercion and mobilization). This empirical gap often allows analyses to fall back on older 'magic-bullet' theories of media studies in which, as Jean-Marie Higiro, a Hutu opposition journalist, put it, 'human beings are considered as automatons' (Higiro 1996: 170). Chrétien's thorough catalogue of ideological themes and tropes in newspapers and radio, considered the authoritative work on media in the genocide, essentially relies on this theory: 'Two tools, one very modern, the other less so, were particularly used during the genocide of the Tutsi in Rwanda: the radio and the machete, the first to give and receive orders, the second to carry them out!' (Chrétien et al. 1995: 191). He says little of the perspective of listeners or their immediate contexts. In a similar vein, Kellow and Steeves write: 'some African countries have strong traditions of hierarchy and authoritarianism, which increase the likelihood of blind obedience to the orders of officials on the radio. Norms of rote obedience were and continue to be, exceptionally strong in Rwanda' (Kellow and Steeves 1998: 116). Yet such an argument is undermined by the fact that RTLM, started just months before the genocide, was younger than both the familiar state-controlled Radio Rwanda and the rebel Rwandan Patriotic Front's (RPF) Radio Muhabura. Moreover, many of the Rwandans I interviewed recalled actively debating, comparing and doubting broadcasts from different radio stations, including RTLM, and still do. At the same time, however, it is clear that media audiences do not exist in a cultural vacuum that allows them to 'objectively' evaluate different radio stations; although RTLM was popular and many Rwandans *did* indeed obey orders to kill, the connection between these two facts must be analyzed rather than taken for granted.

Accounts of the genocide and of radio's role in it share a problematic approach to the role of the human as subject; both tend to assume uncritically the existence of an ordinary farmer/citizen/radio listener, open to manipulation, mobilization and stimulation. These perspectives can find their parallels in the rich and long-running tradition of scholarship that seeks to explain collective action, especially in relation to violence. It is of little surprise, then, that the old dyads of structure versus agency and materialism versus idealism that have long dogged social science research should re-emerge here.

RADIO AND THE IDEOLOGY OF GENOCIDE

There is little disagreement that RTLM propagated a racist anti-Tutsi ideology, drawing on historical myths, stereotypes of the Tutsi and appeals to Hutu unity and that it often did so in a thinly veiled code referring to 'work' instead of killing and 'cockroaches' (*inyenzi*) instead of Tutsi. Furthermore, the station described gruesome acts of violence attributed to Tutsi as a means of implying what should be done to them (the so-called 'accusation in a mirror' technique: see Des Forges 1999: 65–6). Yet accounts of RTLM's ideological role that focus solely on racist aspects do not explain why the station's particular ideological world views caught on more than those of other stations; moreover, they fail to show how RTLM transcended ordinary propaganda, from simply propagating certain beliefs or feelings about Tutsi as an ethnic category, to encouraging and facilitating participation in the murder of friends, neighbours and relatives.

To address these two points, the analysis of the ideology of the genocide as propagated through RTLM needs to be widened beyond its amply documented anti-Tutsi imagery. In light of the near-absence of anti-Tutsi propaganda or policy in Rwanda from the early 1970s to the 1990s, I would like to draw attention to how RTLM appropriated and transformed elements of three dominant public discourses of post-colonial Rwandan modernity: *history* (as a particular way of thinking of the past); *democracy* (as a particular way of thinking about governance); and *development* (as a particular way of thinking about economy and work). RTLM built on these discourses while responding to the particular contingencies of the post-1990 political situation in a way that neither Radio Rwanda nor Radio Muhabura appeared to match. Moreover, RTLM helped Rwandans make sense of their active participation in the genocide in terms that were broader than simple hatred or fear of Tutsi by creating a context in which euphemisms such as 'work' and 'cockroaches' could be easily understood through an indirectness that left nothing unsaid.

The discourse of history in Rwanda was a product of late colonial modernity, a particular way of looking at the past based on a unified national narrative incorporating the lives of all its people past and present and cast in the mould of linear progress, whose dominant theme was Hutu victimization (in the colonial era) and emancipation (1959 onward). In this formulation, the 'Hutu revolution' of 1959 that precipitated the end of elite Tutsi hegemony (many Tutsi were as poor as their Hutu neighbours) and Belgian rule represented a radical and emancipatory leap forward, the *raison d'être* of the post-colonial Rwandan state that had always implicitly legitimized itself in opposition to the past.

During the genocide, however, RTLM portrayed the progress achieved since the revolution as under threat from the RPF, collapsing past into present and calling on Rwandans to re-enact the do-or-die moment of 1959. Georges Ruggiu, RTLM's Belgian animateur, recalled that the station's management issued explicit instructions to make such historical comparisons and that he said on the air that 'the 1959 revolution ought to be completed in order to preserve its achievements' (ICTR-97–32-DP2000., paras 110, 186). Kantano Habimana, arguably RTLM's most popular animateur, once told listeners: 'Masses, be vigilant … Your property is being taken away. What you fought for in '59 is being taken away' (RTLM, 21 January 1994). Venant, a 69-year-old Tutsi, told me that RTLM 'made [people's] heads hot *[ashyushe imitkwe]*' when speaking of how the RPF intended to restore the monarchy and reinstate dreaded colonial-era clientship institutions, while another farmer said he feared a repetition of the events of 1959 (interviews, 8 and 11 August 2000).

I do not wish to imply, however, that the simple invocation of specific historical memories had a predetermined effect. What is important about the examples above is not simply that they alluded to the past (after all, one could easily mention a past characterized by Hutu–Tutsi cooperation or even indistinction, as official RPF rhetoric does), but that they built on the discourse of history while undermining its *structure* as a discourse, specifically by removing the element of progress.[7] The linear shape of history, implying inevitable teleological progress, had long been used to legitimize the regime through implicit comparison with the colonial era. By disrupting linearity and folding 1959 into 1994, not only did RTLM evoke negative historical memories of colonial rule but it also contributed to a deep sense of crisis, in which the nation was suddenly and violently derailed from the path it had been on. While the state had earlier evoked a fear of the past based on comparison to produce assent, RTLM brought the past into the present, producing a more profound horror intended to prompt action.

The discourse of democracy was built around a congruence between ethnicity and nation (specifically the Hutu as the Rwandan nation, with the Tutsi transformed from exotic aristocrats to parasitic outsiders) and a notion of ethnic majoritarianism, in which the president rules by virtue of his membership in and representation of an ethnic majority that will always be entitled to rule by virtue of its numerical preponderance. Not only did this allow the state to demonize the Tutsi as a hostile minority bent on restoring its old dominance (especially early years of the post-colonial state, when monarchist Tutsi guerrillas continued to launch raids from neighbouring countries, prompting bloody reprisals against the Tutsi who stayed behind), but more importantly, it squelched economic, regional and ideological differences between Hutu in the name of ethnic solidarity.

During the genocide, RTLM, the self-styled voice of the *rubanda nyamwinshi* ('numerous people', that is, majority or masses), drew on this discourse of democracy in its frequent appeals to ethnic majoritarianism, while at the same time attempting to channel the participatory potential of opposition politics rather than simply suppress it. Because the genocide was preceded by a period of multipartyism that witnessed intense and at times violent opposition by various Hutu parties, a priority of the regime was to co-opt or split the opposition as a means of promoting ethnic solidarity (or vice versa). The many such 'conversions' I was told about included a Hutu opposition activist called Ngerageze who, according to an acquaintance, 'heard on RTLM that you had to forget about parties and think only of ethnicity' and became a local militia leader during the genocide (interview, 9 August 2000). Although it may be impossible to say how much Ngerageze's decision was influenced by RTLM, it is clear that re-establishing ethnicity as the supreme principle of democracy was a priority of the genocidal regime. It is in this context that one can make sense of the following remark by RTLM animateur Valérie Bemeriki, a sample typical of the station's broadcasts:

> Now, we seem to have forgotten political parties and it is understandable since the enemy who harasses us is unique ... In the meantime, we have put aside matters of political parties even if the international community is shouting: '*lnterahamwe*! *Interahamwe*!'... But for us, we apply that word to all of us, to all Rwandans who stood up together, at the same time, who got united in order to beat the *Inyenzi Inkotanyi*. (RTLM, 22 June 1994)

The station also played on the idea of democracy by reminding people of the numerical weakness of the country's Tutsi minority, which would not only guarantee their defeat but absolve Hutu of any blame, since an enemy resisting in the face of such odds could be nothing but suicidal. 'These are *Inkotanyi* [nickname for RPF fighters or Tutsi generally], they come from a very tiny minority called the Tutsi,' Kantano once explained. 'Will those people truly continue to commit suicide against the majority? Will they not be exterminated?' (RTLM, 12 May 1994).

The discourse of development in post-colonial Rwanda defined the relationship between state and economy after the abolition of colonial-era forms of often coercive 'customary' clientship. It was especially important in legitimizing President Juvénal Habyarimana's regime from the early 1970s onward (Uvin 1998: 23–4).[8] The consequences were both symbolic (Habyarimana's party called itself *Mouvement Républicain National pour la Democratie et le Développement* (MRND); the rubber-stamp parliament of the regime was the *Conseil National pour le Développement*) and material (foreign aid inflows comprised 22 per cent of the country's GNP by 1991 (Prunier 1995: 79). The centrepiece of development was *umuganda*, obligatory communal labour mandated on nearly the entire population on a weekly basis, enforced through dense administrative networks of both state functionaries and party cadres (*umuganda* was officially an MRND activity) at the local level.

RTLM's notorious use of 'work' as a euphemism (with machetes as 'tools') needs to be understood in the context of development, with participation (manning roadblocks, taking part in night patrols, conducting house searches, clearing fields) being likened to *umuganda* on a number of occasions. RTLM's invocation of work drew upon the existing discourses of development while simultaneously recasting communal labour as an exercise in national survival (sometimes described as 'civil defence') at a moment of crisis. 'Mobilize yourselves,' animateur Georges Ruggiu told listeners during the killings. 'Work you the youth, everywhere in the country, come to work with your army. Come to work with your government to defend your country' (RTLM, 5 June 1994). A Western missionary who spoke fluent Kinyarwanda recalled: 'Every morning, RTLM was in the habit of asking listeners, "Hello, good day, have you started to work yet?"' (interview, 29 April 1997, supplied by an anonymous source). It is important to emphasize that work had a value beyond *umuganda*, which was so burdensome that it more or less fell into disuse during the era of post-1990 multipartyism. The value of work was also tied to the virtues espoused by the Catholic Church (Prunier 1995: 77; Verwimp 2000: 338) and to the dignity of being associated with the activities of the state (Taylor 1999: 141).

It is also important to note that state-controlled Radio Rwanda, which had been broadcasting since the eve of independence in 1962, played a pivotal role in propagating each of these discourses (history, democracy, development) in post-colonial Rwanda; the majority of those I spoke to learned much of their country's past through the radio. Radio was a key site for the articulation of democracy, and Radio Rwanda regularly exhorted listeners to work harder and advised them on agricultural techniques.[9]

Yet in the context of instability caused by the RPF invasion in 1990, Radio Rwanda's reticence about the progress of the war began to raise listeners' suspicions that it was withholding the full extent of the truth; this stiltedness was amplified in the opening weeks of the genocide, when the station was largely paralyzed by internal power struggles between MRND supporters and opposition sympathizers. Radio Rwanda's inability to adjust to the fluid political situation in the early 1990s is best captured by the memory of many Rwandans of Habyarimana's death; Domitille, 57, an accused *génocidaire*, recalled listening to the radio the morning after the crash in which Habyarimana was killed: 'While Radio Rwanda played classical music, RTLM gave news about the situation' (interview, 11 July 2000).

On the other hand, the RPF's Radio Muhabura remained limited (although it sought to tap into anti-regime sentiment and many of the people I spoke to listened clandestinely out of curiosity, despite potential repercussions). Aside from its dull and propagandistic style (even RPF soldiers were said to prefer

RTLM), its ideological vision was perhaps too radical for much of the Rwandan population; not only did it espouse a view of politics that entirely ignored ethnicity (or reduced it to an imperialist plot), but it also raised fears of a radical change in the country's demographic, economic and political makeup by billing itself as the 'voice that repatriates' (Kirschke 1996: 50) – a reference to the diaspora of predominantly Tutsi refugees in neighbouring states who fled Rwanda in 1959.

While Radio Rwanda appeared mired in the past and Radio Muhabura seemed to foreshadow a frightening future, RTLM somehow struck a balance between continuity and change, positioning itself in relation to dominant discourses while departing from them in specifically compelling ways. At the same time, it appropriated ideologies that had previously produced acquiescence and depoliticization and gave them a participatory, mobilizational edge, which resonated with the dynamism of political plurality that marked the period of the early 1990s.

RADIO AND PERFORMANCE IN THE GENOCIDE

RTLM did more than merely articulate the ideological world view of genocide; after all, there were dozens of Hutu newspapers that did so as well. Also important was its use of radio's specific properties as a medium of broadcast performance, where oral texts are perfectly reproduced but uniquely received in thousands of different locales as specific events in time.[10] With a virtuosic flare, RTLM's animateurs played off and around the ideological agenda they sought to promote, developed distinctive on-air personalities and sought to implicate listeners in the project of the genocide.

Although the extant literature on the genocide has cited RTLM's informal atmosphere, lively style, good music, off-colour jokes and the introduction of 'western-style interactive broadcasting' to explain its appeal (Chrétien et al. 1995: 73–4; Des Forges 1999: 70; Higiro 1996: 1; Kirschke 1996: 84–5; Prunier 1995: 189), it has often been understood simply as a means by which the station could easily 'manipulate' audiences, a kind of Rwandan breads and circuses.[11] Instead, it is also necessary to grasp how listeners interacted with RTLM's broadcasts, and how animateurs consciously or unconsciously exploited the possibilities and limits of the medium.

One key performative aspect was the skill with which RTLM's animateurs played off the ideologies of the genocide, giving an impression of frankness and trustworthiness that also gave the ideology resilience in dealing with contingency. In doing so, RTLM did what any good propaganda must do: provide specific responses to opposing arguments ('balance'), even if they are based on non-falsifiable assumptions. On 6 January 1994, RTLM broadcast an interview with Tito Rutaremara, a high official in the RPF, in which he was allowed to voice harsh criticism of the MRND. Yet Kantano prefaced the interview with a long monologue peppered with numerous jokes and attempts to discredit Rutaremara, referring to him as 'that tall Tutsi' and reporting that he was surrounded by other Tutsi drinking milk (milk, metonymous with cattle, is often considered a symbol of Tutsi refinement or snobbery); after playing back the recording, Kantano noted that Rutaremara 'was of course answering [the questions] in the *Inkotanyi* way'. RTLM also corrected itself, especially in cases where it retracted denunciations (which were effectively death warrants), paradoxically bolstering its claims to tell 'only the truth'. The performative contingency of the moment allowed RTLM's animateurs to depart from the ideological script of the genocide to strengthen it.[12]

RTLM animateurs themselves became personalities, known and invested with certain meanings by many of their listeners, often fitting into typecast roles: for example, Ananie Nkurunziza, a former intelligence officer, as the serious political analyst; and editor-in-chief Gaspard Gahigi as political pundit. However, Kantano Habimana was by far the most popular animateur ('Kantano talked as if people were right in front of him, which was good for getting their attention,' recalled James, a 41-year-old farmer (interview, 6 August 2000)), a sentiment echoed by many others I spoke to, both Hutu and Tutsi.

Perhaps the most interesting example of the personal authority of animateurs is the strange case of Georges Ruggiu, a Belgian citizen newly arrived in Rwanda, hired at Habyarimana's behest despite having barely any journalism experience and no knowledge of Kinyarwanda (ICTR-97–32-DP2000:, para. 87–90). Although there has been speculation as to why Ruggiu was hired, most Rwandans I spoke to believe it was because he was white.[13] Both Hutu detainees and Tutsi survivors I spoke to said that the presence of a *muzuungu* (white man) at RTLM gave it the appearance of strength, perhaps even international sanction. Indeed, some of Ruggiu's monologues seem to serve little purpose other than to leverage his Europeanness for credibility. Several weeks before the genocide, Ruggiu engaged in one of RTLM's routine denunciations of the Arusha accords before adding a unique twist:

> Then, this evening in order to feed your thoughts, we thought of searching in our library. We then chose for you two extracts from *The Prince* by Nicholas [sic] Machiavelli. That book about government and political principles was written in 1514, that is more than 490 years ago now. But good ideas don't die … These two extracts are going to feed your thoughts and we remain open to others; dialogue and mutual listening seem to us profitable to everyone and if you have written comments, we remain always available to be acquainted with them and perhaps even to broadcast them if they are worth it. Here then is Nicholas Machiavelli who speaks through my voice. (RTLM, 15 March 1994)

After relaying Machiavelli's advice about how a prince must learn not to be good (Chapter 15) and that he must be loved and feared (Chapter 18), Ruggiu signed off in a din of classical European music. In this performance, one can see how the invocation of a founding treatise of modern Western political thought, the emphasis on its age, the use of European classical music (probably not contemporaneous with *The Prince*), and the alignment of Machiavelli the author with Ruggiu the performer ('speak[ing] through my voice') were brought together to create an inter-textual narrative linking the political situation in Rwanda to a construction of European thought and authority, dangling the weight of centuries of 'civilization' in the air before RTLM's listeners.

The power of the myth of whiteness in sub-Saharan Africa is a thing that cannot be discarded, yet, at the same time, must be invoked with the greatest caution. A priori, Ruggiu's authority or credibility as a white man with Rwandan farmers who could not understand his words would seem at best dubious, one must recall that radio often feeds into the dynamics of other enduring social hierarchies and relations. As Immaculée, 36, a detainee accused of participation in the genocide, explained: 'Those who understood French liked to listen to the *muzuungu* and said he was on the side of the Hutu, and that he spoke well and was against the Tutsi. Educated people and *bourgmestres* would explain the French broadcasts to others' (interview, 11 July 2000). Here, one can see radio broadcasts as events in which different actors create multiple meanings. In a mutually reinforcing process, local elites could play upon and enhance their credibility as educated Francophones vis-à-vis those who could not speak French, while Ruggiu's reach was extended and his own authority strengthened by the endorsement of such notables.[14]

Besides apparently alerting listeners to specific targets and hiding places,[15] RTLM's animateurs also implicated ordinary listeners in the activities of the genocide; farmers at roadblocks or on the street were frequently interviewed, and RTLM employed techniques that acted on relations among listeners. During an interview at a roadblock, a man once told Kantano that he and his colleagues had killed five *inyenzi*. After encouraging them to 'keep it up,' Kantano asked: 'When testing if people like a radio station, you ask the following question: who are the speakers of that radio whom you know? Who are the RTLM speakers you know? ... If you do not know them that means that you do not like this radio' (RTLM, 29 May 1994).

In another instance, Kantano called on Tutsi who were not RPF accomplices to man the roadblocks with the Hutu. The following day, while addressing the people manning the roadblocks, he suggested, 'look around you, the enemy is among you' (interview, 18 September 1995, supplied anonymously). Whether intended or not, such tactics probably indirectly pressured people to listen to RTLM or at least to conceal any opposition to it. 'Some people were against RTLM but didn't have the strength to say so in public,' recalled Jamad, 48, a mason (interview, 17 August 2000); one Tutsi I met was so afraid that he went so far as to purchase a recording of the music of Simon Bikindi, whose anti-Tutsi songs were played repeatedly on RTLM before the genocide, to demonstrate his loyalty to the regime (interview, 11 August 2000).

RTLM explicitly informed conversations that took place away from the physical contexts of listening as well. Broadcasts were often reincarnated elsewhere as rumour, where the possibilities for exaggeration or reinterpretation could only expand. According to one of his neighbours, a militia member named Hakiri used to spend mornings on the roof of his shop with a radio clutched to his ear, listening to RTLM. When he listened, 'his mood changed' and he would climb down and gather people to tell them what he had heard (interview, 22 July 2000). Even if one assumes that Hakiri relayed the content and tone of these broadcasts as faithfully and uncritically as possible, he was still engaging in a process of performance, acting as a medium through which the project of the genocide manifested itself and could possibly be shaped. Across the country, thousands of listeners were relaying, embellishing and even misrepresenting RTLM's broadcasts. One prominent Hutu extremist, taking pity on some Tutsi children at a roadblock, reportedly admonished the militiaman harassing them: 'Don't you listen to the radio? The French said if we don't stop killing children they'll stop arming and helping us' (Gourevitch 1998: 130).

The process of re-performance is even more interesting in the case of oral texts, such as songs, which are repeatedly played and thus more likely to be remembered and passed on in everyday speech. The music of Simon Bikindi, with its rousing tunes and anti-Tutsi lyrics, was part of RTLM's regular fare and provided many of the anthems of Hutu Power. Many Hutu sang along with Bikindi's songs on RTLM in bars and in streets, and even after 'work' shifts. Bikindi's songs, however, could somehow take on a life of their own in different contexts of performance. Immaculée told of an old Tutsi woman who was hiding in a cassava field when some passing militia, ignorant of her presence, started singing one of Bikindi's songs. 'When the old woman heard the song, she thought she had been found and so she ran from the bush,' Immaculée explained; the old woman barely managed to relay her story to Immaculée before being found and killed by the militia (interview, 11 July 2000).

As the old woman's 'accidental' interpretation suggests, each context of re-performance beyond the physical site of listening presents opportunities for different meanings to be derived, thus adding a crucial dimension of versatility to the circulation of oral texts. Although the Hutu were not reshaping the message of the song (in the way that a rumour may mutate), the old woman's behaviour was not a reaction to a song per se, but to an oral text relayed by particular actors (a gang of armed Hutu) and heard in a particular context (while hiding in a cassava field). In short, she was shaping meaning in the context of performance, however inadvertently. In this way, ordinary people became a medium through which the inescapability of the genocidal project manifested itself, and the old woman's 'mistaken' interpretation serves as a reminder of how contextualized creativity can work in unpredictable and unintended ways.

RTLM sustained the larger edifice of the ideology of the genocide on a continuously shifting foundation of smaller truths, performative moments that rendered animateurs endearing or familiar or otherwise authoritative to listeners. Moreover, the animateurs did not simply perform the genocide before captive audiences, but indirectly implicated them in the performance of the project itself.

RADIO IN THE TIME OF GENOCIDE

In contemplating the question of obedience in the genocide, it is important to note that the capture and mobilization of state resources by its orchestrators mirrored a gradual appropriation of the cornerstones of collective life for the purposes of the killing. The genocide extended beyond bureaucracies to other everyday routines and contexts. From the point of view of most Rwandans, it was not simply that the priest, the schoolteacher and the radio animateur spoke of the same necessity to work, but that they sometimes did so as part of the weekly sermon, the daily lesson, the hourly bulletin. Indeed, one of the most pervasive and overlooked aspects of RTLM's influence on listeners was its quotidian role.

Radio, which bookends and punctuates the daily routine of many ordinary Rwandans, continued to do so during the genocide. RTLM did not simply whip Hutu into a frenzy to channel fear and anger into sudden attacks. Rather, through the daily diet of informational updates, operational details (not to leave bodies on the road in view of Western journalists, for example) and encouraging monologues, it contributed to the framing of schedules and the routinization of 'work'. According to one survivor, local Hutu would gather at the nearby government office, then spend the day performing the mundane tasks of the genocide, occasionally coming upon and killing Tutsi. During that time, many people would listen to RTLM at roadblocks, in homes and in bars during breaks. Sometimes they would listen outdoors in groups as large as 100, closely following the information relayed to plan the next day's activities. When asked if this took place every day, one man replied, 'Of course. It was work. It was to know what to do' (interview, 18 August 2000). Regardless of whether all of the news it passed on was true (and many Rwandans recognized that at times it was not), those who killed still built their schedules in part around RTLM and used its broadcasts to help guide the details and schedules of work. 'Kantano said there are no RPF here, so we can continue our work,' one Hutu cultivator recalled hearing some locals say (interview, 6 August 2000).

Even Rwandans who did not kill still arranged their activities around and took advantage of the rhythms of 'work'. Knowing when certain teams would be called up could help some Hutu evade roadblock duty by hiding or feigning illness. And, as in ordinary times, listening schedules were also shaped by gender. While the men were at work, women often listened and followed RTLM's advice in other ways. Bonfride, a 21-year-old Tutsi, spent several weeks sheltered in the homes of sympathetic Hutu neighbours, often with families that had no sons. Although they risked their lives to hide a Tutsi, women in these families also liked RTLM's broadcasts and heeded the station's entreaties to go out and pillage the belongings of those who had been killed (interview, 2 September 2000).[16]

One of the most apparent ways in which RTLM placed itself in the daily routines of listeners was through one of its star animateurs, Noël (Noheli) Hitimana, who had become a household name after working at Radio Rwanda from the late 1970s until the early 1990s. During the early shift when farmers rose to tend the fields, one of Hitimana's trademarks was to call out to the furthest mountains in the country, issue personal greetings to specific regions of Rwanda and salute named individuals with whom he had met or shared a drink the night before. He was also known for his quick wit, his adroit word play (alluding to his name while giving Christmas greetings, for example) and his fondness of alcohol (he was supposedly fired from Radio Rwanda after insulting President Habyarimana during an inebriated on-air gaffe). Despite (or perhaps because of) these antics, Hitimana was well liked by radio listeners throughout the country.

During my time in Rwanda, I knew professionals of both ethnicities who spoke highly of him as a kind man with no particular hatred or animosities for anyone before the period of multipartyism. Moreover, people appreciated his recognition of and speaking to audiences while on the air. 'He showed that Radio Rwanda was interested in its listeners,' said Elie, 30, imprisoned after the genocide, adding that being mentioned by name over the radio was a small honour for anyone, a moment's celebrity and recognition for hard work (interview, 5 July 2000). Philip, 56, also awaiting trial, claimed that two of his own friends were once saluted by Hitimana on Radio Rwanda. 'He would say hello to this secteur and hello to that secteur. He had his own style, and people liked him and knew his voice' (interview, 10 July 2000). Listening to Noël Hitimana at dawn while heading out to the fields was itself a cultural practice, part of the daily process through which meanings – pertaining to the nation as an imagined community, or to the value of hard work as frequently extolled on Radio Rwanda – were brought to life.

Whether as a deliberate strategy or out of habit, Hitimana's work at RTLM continued in the vein of many of his old practices at Radio Rwanda. For example, in response to criticisms of RTLM broadcast over Radio Muhabura, he responded with a litany of areas that had experienced RPF attacks:

> It's ridiculous to hear them declaring on their radio: 'That murderer, Noel!' Ha! Ha! If you go to Ruhengeri or Byumba and walk around to the communes of Butaro, Kidaho, Cyeru, Cyumba, Kivuye, Mukarange, until Muvumba, if you come back to Kigombe or even to Mukingo, or up to Kora, you'll understand who has suffered and who's the murderer. You'll understand how deep their sorrow is. Their sorrow! When you go on until Base, Nyamugali, or Nyakinama and Nyamutera, you find sad people everywhere. Sad. Really sad. Ask them who's responsible for their sorrow. (RTLM, 1 April 1994)

Here, one does not simply see an animateur invoking the names of specific locales; it is Noheli Hitimana, who for years has been known to salute and greet individuals in all of the country's communes and secteurs. Hitimana's invocation of locales capitalizes on the earlier variants of the practice to convince listeners of a particular world view (in this case, that the Hutu are the victim of the Tutsi) while simultaneously implicating listeners in the areas cited as fellow sufferers. Once the genocide began, the naming of places by Hitimana and other animateurs became associated with exhortations to rush to specific areas where there were still Tutsi to be found.

Similarly, Hitimana's habit of saluting individuals also shaped his work on RTLM. Several days before the genocide, during a commentary on an unrelated subject, he suddenly launched into an attack on opposition journalist Joseph Mudatsikira:

> Let me say hello, child of my mother. Let me salute you, as you are the same as Noheli [i.e., also a journalist] ... If you die just as everyone has been speaking about you, it is not like dying like a sheep, without having been spoken of. When we have spoken about you, you have effectively been spoken of. (Kirschke 1996: 93)

The playful familiarity adopted vis-à-vis Mudatsikira is typical of Hitimana's style, even in the context of a death threat (Mudatsikira was killed several days after the broadcast). Kirschke adds that Hitimana 'joked about the fact that he was singling out a journalist, as if it were an honour to be mentioned on RTLM'. Yet if one considers Hitimana's longstanding relationship with Rwandan radio listeners and his habit of naming personal acquaintances, then such an attitude may seem almost normal, which became the case as Hitimana began threatening individuals with increasing regularity. In the above examples, Hitimana converts his everyday habit of naming, recognizing and saluting individuals into a means of denouncing, targeting and threatening them, all within the boundaries of the same style and the same medium. In his invocation of names and places, Hitimana's broadcasts at RTLM exploited a quotidian familiarity established over a decade's worth of performative participation in the lives of listeners, casting the genocide in the mould of a daily routine.

More important, however, the reliance on familiarity made Hitimana's actions more than mere threats. It made them betrayals, signals to listeners that underneath all that defines their social world, even routines followed in the privacy of the home, lies the possibility of treachery, of being attacked by a Tutsi neighbour or falsely accused of treason by a Hutu friend. Providing an example of what to emulate and a warning of what to avoid, Hitimana showed that it was better to denounce than to be denounced, and that even personal ties of mutual benefit or affection could be subordinated to the imperatives of the genocide. By setting this example in the intimacy of the home and implicitly telling Hutu that they too should denounce friends if need be, Hitimana was, ironically, educating listeners in the rules of the genocide, helping them build trust in a world that was built on the mistrust of others.

Based on available information, I would like tentatively to suggest that the appropriation of the rhythms of everyday life by the proponents of the genocide was part of a dialogic process through which Rwandans actively sought to understand and confront a social world disrupted by four years of civil war, political instability and economic crisis, now coming to a head with the assassination of Habyarimana and the eruption of widespread violence. The process of balancing predictability and possibility is central to any notion of human subjectivity, for the complete absence of either renders human action impossible. Thus, just as RTLM's ideological tropes and performative aspects successfully mimed the familiar while resonating with the contingent, its appropriation of everyday routines contributed to a context that shaped the incentives and categories of thought behind choices but did not determine them.

Although they do not directly involve radio, two sharply contrasting anecdotes may shed light on this idea. In early 1995, researchers for the NGO African Rights interviewed Zakia Uwamugira, then 42, from Gisenyi, in northwestern Rwanda. Having just returned from a refugee camp in Zaire, she admitted to having encouraged *Interahamwe* through song during the genocide:

> I am accused of being there when people were being killed and singing. I admit I did this. I was there when people were being killed. Many people. I joined the [*animasiyo*] just as I would join any other choir ... I decided to come back because I realised I had not done anything that was wrong. (African Rights 1995: 72)

In full awareness of the murders being committed around her, Uwamugira repeatedly insisted that she had done nothing wrong, justifying her actions through the lens of the weekly state-sponsored ritual of *animasiyo* (in which farmers were obliged to sing songs in praise of the state, the MRND or the president, often after participating in *umuganda*). Similarly, many who opposed the genocide also carried out their struggles in the vein of normality rather than nobility. Philip Gourevitch grapples with this apparent blandness in his profile of Paul Rusesabagina, the Hutu manager of the Hotel Mille Collines in Kigali who saved hundreds of lives through his resourceful use of contacts in the regime, money and alcohol. 'Paul is a mild-mannered man, sturdily built and rather ordinary-looking – a bourgeois hotel manager, after all – and that is how he seemed to regard himself as well, as an ordinary person who did nothing extraordinary in refusing to cave in to the insanity that swirled around him' (Gourevitch 1998: 127).[17] Rusesabagina's resistance of the genocide on its own terms and from within its own structures required a degree of trust in the system itself and in his ability to manipulate it.

Even as everydayness came to be defined according to the imperatives of the project of extermination, different paths of action carved out by circumstance and will remained open: 'under conditions of terror most people will comply *but some people will not* ... Humanly speaking, no more is required, and no more can reasonably be asked, for this planet to remain a place fit for human habitation' (Arendt 1964: 233). Despite the impossibility of morally comparing the actions of Zakia Uwamugira and Paul Rusesabagina, it is their common appeal to normality in a shared social world defined by such 'conditions of terror' that is so striking. Indeed, while it is often noted that the road to genocide is paved with smaller massacres, it may be more appropriate in this case to say that rather than violence becoming normal, it was normality itself that was co-opted in the service of violence.

REVERBERATIONS

This paper hardly represents a comprehensive study of RTLM radio's role in the genocide; at the very least, that would require extensive analysis of Kinyarwanda rhetoric in the broadcasts, more in-depth fieldwork with listeners and more research on Radio Rwanda and Radio Muhabura. Nevertheless, I hope that this enquiry has helped shed some light on issues of relevance to the study of mass atrocity and mass media. In the above arguments, a broad theme emerges of radio implicating rather than manipulating its listeners, informing but not determining their choices. In its various aspects, RTLM's activities intertwined with Rwandans' efforts to make sense of and navigate the world in which they lived during such difficult times. Radio served as a medium through which Rwandans experienced and enacted the genocide, its broadcasts reverberating in the thoughts and actions of millions of people, both participants and witnesses, alongside and at times in opposition to other social forces based on coercion, interest or fear. Its intangible power did not rest solely in words, memory, the psyche, the state or some combination of causal factors, but was produced in the process of articulation and rearticulation by animateurs and listeners.

Such a perspective on radio's role is possible only if one regards listeners (or farmers or killers) as constituted subjects rather than through a concept of agency that depends on unitary, autonomous actors, for whom radio is simply a source of information or misinformation, a stimulus eliciting a certain response. If the subject is permeable to mediated discourses, firmly embedded in an ever-shifting set of forces, structures and meanings, it may be that choices are shaped by and made in the spaces and tensions between these currents. Although this is hardly a novel insight given the contemporary trajectories of much of Western philosophy and social theory (and, subsequently, in some areas of anthropology and history), such developments – including the diverse and rigorous critiques of positivism in social science – have yet to be adequately confronted by much of the comparative and theoretical literature on mass atrocity. The fact that this literature takes such important human events as its object of study only makes this gap more saddening and only makes bridging it more urgent.

ACKNOWLEDGEMENTS

With the greatest appreciation to all of those who agreed to speak to me in the course of research in Rwanda. Thanks also to Alison Des Forges, Samba Diop, Shakirah Hudani, Mahmood Mamdani, Pauline Peters and Sayres Rudy for their comments and the Weatherhead Centre for International Affairs at Harvard University, the Harvard Committee on African Studies, and the Harvard College Research Program for generous research funding.

NOTES

1. Though not without precedent in the region, unfortunately, given large-scale massacres of Hutu in Burundi in the early 1970s and 1990s. It is important to interpret Rwanda's history of violence in non-teleological terms. The 1959 'Hutu revolution' was marked by violence aimed at driving out Tutsi chiefs; after independence, monarchist Tutsi guerrillas attacked the new state from neighbouring countries, providing a pretext for pogroms against Tutsi in the country. Before such violence subsided in 1967, up to 20,000 Tutsi were massacred and 300,000 were forced to flee (Prunier 1995: 62), creating one of the first major refugee crises in Africa. In 1973, President Grégoire Kayibanda's largely unsuccessful attempt to incite violence against

Tutsi was the last card he played before being overthrown in a coup by Juvénal Habyarimana, who remained president until his death in 1994. Although Tutsi were excluded from public life and faced harsh discrimination, little ethnic violence was directed against them until the 1990 civil war; between 1990 and 1994, tens of thousands of Tutsi were killed in a series of tightly focused and planned massacres.

2. Kirschke (1996) argues that 'outside Kigali and other urban centres, the station is reported to have attracted people from urban backgrounds ... rather than peasants from rural areas,' a claim which is not supported by the fieldwork undertaken for this essay. As one imprisoned Hutu told me, 'it's a lie if a farmer says he didn't listen to RTLM' (interview, 8 July 2000). The station began broadcasting in late 1993, with range limited to the Kigali area; from early 1994 onwards, its reach was more or less nationwide.
3. This research is based on a number of sources, including interviews and documentation. Interviews were conducted in the summer of 2000 with approximately 30 inmates in Rwandan prisons who had already pleaded guilty to some form of participation in the genocide and approximately 60 farmers living in rural Rwanda; conversations also took place with various Rwandan academics, activists and officials. Interviews in the first two groups were conducted through interpreters speaking French and Kinyarwanda. Other interview transcripts were provided by anonymous sources. The documentation reviewed included several dozen transcripts of RTLM broadcasts translated into English and French, documents of the United Nations' International Criminal Tribunal for Rwanda (ICTR) and relevant writings by Rwandan public figures and academics.

   In this essay, surnames of interviewees are omitted. Ages listed are those at the time of the interview. It is important to point out several empirical and methodological limitations to this enquiry. I have been unable to locate extensive documentary evidence (including transcripts) on RTLM's competitors, namely, Radio Rwanda and Radio Muhabura (although the rival stations were often discussed in interviews). My lack of fluency in Kinyarwanda, the short timeframe of field research and security considerations (regarding the prison) made it impossible for me to achieve the level of trust and familiarity with interviewees ideal for ethnographic work. Indeed, I would be the first to acknowledge the limitations of studying radio in a language one does not understand.
4. In describing on-air radio workers, especially those of RTLM, I decided to employ the French *animateur/animatrice* to emphasize the crucial performative and directive aspect of their work. The English equivalents of 'journalist', 'broadcaster', 'disc jockey' and 'personality' do not capture this dimension, nor does the Kinyarwanda word '*umunyamakuru*' (literally, 'one of the news' or 'newsman'). RTLM's best-known animateurs included Kantano Habimana (who allegedly died of AIDS in the Congo), Valérie Bemeriki (currently in detention in Rwanda), Noël Hitimana (who died in a Rwandan prison), Georges Ruggiu (who pleaded guilty to the ICTR and was sentenced to twelve years' imprisonment in 2000) and Ananie Nkurunziza (missing?). Other participants included editor-in-chief Gaspard Gahigi (missing?), manager Phocas Habimana (dead?), alleged founder and leading Rwandan historian Ferdinand Nahimana (sentenced to life in prison in 2003). The singer Simon Bikindi, whose music was featured regularly on RTLM, was arrested in the Netherlands in the summer of 2001 and is awaiting trial at the ICTR.
5. At the same time, it is crucial to recall the extent to which Rwandans either resisted the genocide or merely sought to avoid it. Numerous Hutu risked their lives to save Tutsi, whether out of altruism or greed, while many avoided work for reasons of disgust, laziness or conscience. Indeed, it was not uncommon for individuals to have both taken lives and saved them, severely testing the familiar categories of perpetrator, victim and bystander.
6. Mahmood Mamdani sums up these difficulties well in noting the application of these arguments to hostel violence in apartheid South Africa: 'All of these explanations contain a grain of truth, and none can be ignored. The argument of [manipulative elite] forces is compelling, but it cannot by itself explain the violence: conspiracies exist, but that fact on its own cannot explain why some succeed and others fail. Sociological conditions ... do explain why [people] are more disposed towards mobilization, as economic conditions in deprived communities explain the acute desperation that marks the quest to sustain life, but neither explains the

ways in which people actually mobilize or act. Although material conditions do explain the constraints under which we make real choices in real life, they cannot by themselves explain the choices we do make within those constraints. The old argument between structure and agency, between sociological and historical constraint and human will, cannot be resolved simply by holding up one end of the pole' (Mamdani 1996: 225–26).

7. Rwandan elites, casting themselves in the mould of Jacobins, emphasized progress in nearly all discussions of the past. School textbooks cleanly segment the Rwandan past into the pre-colonial, colonial and post-colonial stages, each new phase foreclosing any possibility of returning to the previous ones. A book by the son of a prominent Hutu revolutionary charting the anti-monarchist struggle and the subsequent achievements of the post-colonial state (complete with a timeline from 1884 to 1994) is dedicated to those who fought for the 'grands principes de Liberté, de Justice, et de Progrès pour nous' (Mbonyumutwa 1990: 5).
8. The Rwandan state dedicated entire years to specific development goals, such as the augmentation of production (1975), education (1979) and soil conservation (1980). In addition, state-controlled mass media were actively used to sensitize the population to such campaigns (Mfizi 1983: 57).
9. Indeed, one cannot underestimate radio's importance as the dominant medium of orality and communication in the post-colonial era. In a country without a daily newspaper and few television sets, radio was the dominant mass medium, one whose emergence marginalized earlier forms of orality to reflect a new sense of nationness, making radio a dynamic site for the creation of 'imagined communities' in ways beyond the nexus of 'print capital' envisioned by Benedict Anderson in his discussion of how newspapers contributed to the rise of nationalism: 'The significance of this mass ceremony – Hegel observed that newspapers serve modern man as a substitute for morning prayers – is paradoxical. It is performed in silent privacy, in the lair of the skull. Yet each communicant is well aware that the ceremony he performs is being replicated simultaneously by thousands (or millions) of others of whose existence he is confident, yet of whose identity he has not the slightest notion. Furthermore, this ceremony is incessantly repeated at daily or half-daily intervals throughout the calendar. What more vivid figure for the secular, historically clocked, imagined community can be envisioned?' (Anderson 1991: 35). In Rwanda, the answer to Anderson's rhetorical question is radio.
10. As I do not speak Kinyarwanda and my work is based mostly on RTLM transcripts rather than tapes, the analyses of performance here are obviously biased toward forms amenable to textual interpretation and are, therefore, far from comprehensive.
11. Interviews indicate that the station's popularity and importance during the genocide stem from other reasons as well. Some of those I spoke to recalled being drawn to RTLM's liveliness, but only when specifically asked about it; more general questions about the sources of the station's popularity almost never received replies such as 'because it was funny' or 'because the animateurs spoke well'. This suggests that RTLM's entertaining style was not necessarily its most important aspect. Interestingly, educated Rwandans, primarily Tutsi, always pointed out RTLM's 'street style' as the primary reason for its appeal. It is possible that the reliance of some published accounts on educated, urban informants magnified or reproduced certain presumptions shared by elites.
12. At times, they were even forced to contradict the code of their rhetoric to avoid the pervasive influence of euphemism. As news spread that France was preparing to intervene in Rwanda, Valérie Bemeriki instructed Hutu to welcome them with flowers and greetings of '*bon jour*' and '*soyez le bienvenu*'. Still, after months of whipping up hatred against whites in general and Belgians in particular, and mixing anti-Tutsi invective with superficial reassurances that not all Tutsi were bad, it was only sensible to make the instructions absolutely clear. 'If you are told to do something, you are not told to do the opposite,' Bemeriki announced to listeners. 'If we are saying that we should welcome the French, that does not mean that we should throw stones at them' (RTLM, 22 June 1994).
13. Ruggiu made some 60 hours' worth of confessions to ICTR prosecutors, during which he presumably discussed in detail how he was hired and the nature of his work at RTLM, as both topics are featured in his plea agreement. The content of these sessions, however, remains

confidential. My numerous requests to ICTR for access to the tapes and to Ruggiu himself received no official replies.

14. Ruggiu's case also provides an example of the oversights that can come with an overly textual perspective in understanding radio. In June 2000, Ruggiu was sentenced to twelve years' imprisonment by ICTR after pleading guilty to inciting genocide. In the judgement, the tribunal's judges cited Ruggiu's European background and consequent ignorance of the complexities of the situation in Rwanda as mitigating factors in the sentencing. The significance of his European background to his involvement with RTLM was not mentioned.
15. In one incident, the station issued the licence plate number of a red van reported to be 'full of accomplices'; the passengers of the vehicle, Hutu dissidents, were stopped at a nearby checkpoint the same day and executed (Kirschke 1996: 121). Interestingly, Ruggiu also told ICTR prosecutors that at the behest of the Rwandan military, he once relayed a message to have a red Volkswagen stopped, giving registration number and general location, but did not know the result of the broadcast (ICTR–97–32–DP2000: para 171).
16. The ones who needed most to adapt to the rhythms of work crews were the Tutsi who managed to go into hiding. Observing patrol patterns while hiding in the fields during the day, they came out at night to find food, new sanctuaries or to get news from friends. In exploiting the regularity of schedules, even these Tutsi seem to have developed some sense of mastery over how the system of the genocide worked, even if it was working against them.
17. Resistance, of course, took on multiple and diverse forms, of which only some occurred in the framework of the genocide. In some instances, large groups of Tutsi were able to organize and defend themselves for some time, fending off multiple attacks before succumbing to superior military force (Des Forges 1999: 216–20).

REFERENCES

African Rights. 1995. *Rwanda: Death, Despair, and Defiance.* African Rights, London, UK.

Anderson, B. 1991. *Imagined Communities: Reflections on the Origin and Spread of Nationalism.* Verso, London, UK.

Arendt, H. 1964. *Eichmann in Jerusalem: a Report on the Banality of Evil.* Penguin Books, New York, NY, USA.

Chalk, F. 1999. Hate Radio in Rwanda. In H. Adelman and A. Suhkre (eds). *The Path of a Genocide: the Rwanda Crisis from Uganda to Zaire.* Transaction Publishers, New Brunswick, NJ, USA.

Chrétien, J.P., J.F. Dupaquier and M. Kabanda. 1995. *Rwanda: les médias du génocide.* Karthala, Paris, France. 397 pp.

Des Forges, A. 1999. *Leave None to Tell the Story: Genocide in Rwanda.* Human Rights Watch and the International Federation of Human Rights Leagues, New York, NY, USA. Available at <www.hrw.org/reports/1999/rwanda/> (accessed 30 August 2005).

Gourevitch, P. 1998. *We Wish to Inform you that Tomorrow we Will be Killed with our Families: Stories from Rwanda.* Farrar, Straus and Giroux, New York, NY, USA.

Higiro, J.M.V. 1996. 'Distorsions et omissions'. In Rwanda, les médias du génocide. *Dialogue* 190 (April-May):160–78.

ICTR-97–32-DP (International Criminal Tribunal for Rwanda). 2000. *Le Procureur contre Georges Ruggiu: convention de plaidoyer aux fins de donner acte d'un accord d'aveu entre Georges Ruggiu et le Bureau du procureur*. ICTR, Arusha, Tanzania, April.

Kellow, C. and H. Steeves. 1998. The Role of Radio in the Rwandan Genocide. *Journal of Communication,* 48(3): 107–28.

Kirschke, L.1996. *Broadcasting Genocide: Censorship, Propaganda and State-Sponsored Violence in Rwanda, 1990–1994.* Article 19, London, UK. Available at <http://www.article19.org/pdfs/publications/rwanda-broadcasting-genocide.pdf> (accessed 23 August 2005).

Mamdani, M. 1996. *Citizen and Subject: Contemporary Africa and the Legacy of Late Colonialism.* Princeton University Press, Princeton, NJ, USA.

—— 2001. *When Victims Become Killers: Colonialism, Nativism, and the Genocide in Rwanda.* Princeton University Press, Princeton, NJ, USA.

Mbonyumutwa, S. 1990. *Rwanda: gouverner autrement.* Imprimerie Nationale, Kigali, Rwanda.

Mfizi, C. 1983. *Les lignes de faite du Rwanda indépendant.* Office Rwandais d'Information, Kigali, Rwanda.

Nkusi, L., M. Ruzindana and B. Rwigamba. 1998. *The Kinyarwanda language: its use and impact in the various media during the period 1990–1994: a sociolinguistic study*. Report commissioned by the United Nations International Criminal Tribunal for Rwanda, Arusha, Tanzania.

Prunier, G. 1995. *The Rwanda Crisis: History of a Genocide.* Columbia University Press, New York, NY, USA.

Taylor, C. 1999. *Sacrifice as Terror: the Rwandan Genocide of 1994*. Berg, Oxford, UK.

Uvin, P. 1998. *Aiding Violence: the Development Enterprise in Rwanda.* Kumarian Press, West Hartford, CT, USA.

Verwimp, P. 2000. Development Ideology, the Peasantry, and Genocide: Rwanda Represented in Habyarimana's Speeches. *Journal of Genocide Research,* 2(3): 325–61. Available at <http://www.yale.edu/gsp/publications/Rwanda.pdf> (accessed 5 September 2005).

9
RTLM: the Medium that Became a Tool for Mass Murder

Mary Kimani

The birth of Radio-Télévision Libre des Milles Collines (RTLM) in 1993 could not have come at a better time for Rwanda's Hutu elite. Finally, here was a radio station they could use as a mouthpiece for their ideals and a means to propagate their ethno-political war against the Tutsi-dominated Rwandan Patriotic Front (RPF).

A detailed analysis of the content of RTLM broadcasts makes clear that individual broadcasters – not their guests or government officials – were most likely to use the airwaves to disseminate hate. Based on a sample of taped broadcasts, individual journalists dominated the station's programming and accounted for most of the inflammatory statements. In a departure from usual radio programming, monologues by the station's personalities were the most common format of RTLM broadcasts, followed by interviews. News items took up less than 2 per cent of airtime, whereas instructions and directives issued by the station took up less than 3 per cent.

Three-quarters of the time used to make inflammatory statements occurred when there were no guests in the studio; that is, RTLM's on-air personalities were responsible for most of the station's inflammatory statements.

It is important to remember that RTLM broadcasts were *not* responsible for introducing the language and ideology of hatred into the Rwandan community. Such language and the ideology of ethnic conflict and polarization already existed in Rwanda in the form of a powerful social construct involving ethnic identity. The language had been further developed in 1990–93 by *Kangura* and other media allied with Hutu Power.

RTLM, coming at the very end of the conflict, drew its commentary, arguments and interpretation of issues from this existing framework. For example, certain words initially used by *Kangura* over its four years of publication, 1990–94, would become popular and the vocabulary of the ensuing genocide. According to the testimony of language expert Matthias Ruzindana at the ICTR on 21 March 2002, *Kangura* popularized words like *kurimbura* and *gutsemba* (to massacre), *gutsembatsemba* (to exterminate), *kumara* (to eat up), *gutikiza* and *gusakumba* (to clean), *kumarira kw'icumu* (to spear), *gutema* (to cut); others related to 'working', such as *gukora* (to work), *ibikorwa* (the work), *ibikoresho* (the working), *abakozi* (the workers), *umuganda* (communal work); and words for nocturnal patrols, *irondo*, and the people's war, *intambara y'abaturage*. In those four years *Kangura* set a trend. By 1994, the media had a language and tools with which to convince the population to undertake violence as a form of 'self-defence'.

The media served the narrow political ends of their owners by playing on the ordinary Hutu's fear of dispossession, violence and displacement. To do this the media relied heavily on half-truths and sometimes-outright lies and threats. The media defined who the enemy was, and why. Later on, they would also explain what was to be done to this enemy.

By 1994, history and reality had been skewed by both politicians and their media to the maximum effect, as the late Archbishop of Rwanda and former journalist André Sibomana outlines, resurrecting patterns of ethnic conflict and making them a norm.

> Through a game of repetition, drop by drop, the media build up moral and cultural constructs which eventually become permanent features ... This failure on the part of party officials and media to stem the progress into the abyss contributed significantly to fuelling a climate of intolerance and turned them into agents of destruction of Rwandan society. (Sibomana 1999: 49)

It was into this politically charged environment that RTLM was born in July 1993, a few months before immense international pressure was brought to bear on the parties in the conflict. The result was that the combined weight of the Rwandan Patriotic Army (RPA) and opposition party representation in the new government seemed to effectively marginalize the former ruling party, *Mouvement Républicain Nationale pour la Democratie et le Développement* (MRND), and its allies.

> The composition of the parliament meant that agreement from at least four parties was required to reach a majority. From a government's perspective, it was clear that the RPF would have an easier time mastering the opposition votes than would MRND. (Jones 1999: 139)

In the following months, tensions increased. In particular, the assassination of Burundi's first Hutu president would be a turning point. Melchior Ndandaye was assassinated by soldiers in the almost exclusively Tutsi Burundi army barely four months after winning a landslide election victory. The assassination gave Hutu politicians in Rwanda reason to wonder if the RPA (another largely Tutsi army) would be satisfied with a negotiated solution to power sharing in Rwanda or if it would seek to extend its control. The assassination was also a convenient example that media such as *Kangura* used to illustrate the 'power hungry nature' of the Tutsi.

What RTLM clearly did was to reach a greater number of people than *Kangura* or other media had access to. It popularized the *Kangura* version of reality. Indeed as the judges at the International Criminal Tribunal for Rwanda stated in their judgement against the founders of RTLM and *Kangura*:

> 29. … RTLM broadcasts exploited the history of Tutsi privilege and Hutu disadvantage, and the fear of armed insurrection, to mobilize the population, whipping them into a frenzy of hatred and violence that was directed largely against the Tutsi ethnic group.
>
> 99. … Unlike print media, radio is immediately present and active. The power of the human voice, heard by the Chamber when the broadcast tapes were played in Kinyarwanda, adds a quality and dimension beyond language to the message conveyed. Radio heightened the sense of fear, the sense of danger and the sense of urgency giving rise to the need for action by listeners. The denigration of Tutsi ethnicity was augmented by the visceral scorn coming out of the airwaves – the ridiculing laugh and the nasty sneer. These elements greatly amplified the impact of RTLM broadcasts. (ICTR summary judgement, see Chapter 25)

Through RTLM, the Hutu elite of the time created an environment in which the 'Tutsis of the past' and the 'Tutsis of the present' became the same. The 'Tutsis of the past', who had – according to mistaken beliefs of the past and contemporary histories – ruled Rwanda with an iron fist and exploited the Hutu mercilessly, and the 'Tutsis of the present', who were – allegedly – invading and trying to take over power, were one and the same. They had to be fought and they had to be taught that the Hutu would never submit to them again.

The general picture painted of the Tutsi community by RTLM was that of a treacherous people, people who had hoodwinked the Hutu, living with them in apparent peace while all the while planning an attack.

In the last months before the genocide, RTLM emphasized the similarity between what was happening in 1994 and what had happened in 1959. It was a choice of going back to the slavery that preceded 1959 or rising up and protecting one's freedom, even one's life. For that, one could not trust any Tutsi civilian because it was not possible to know how deeply the RPF had infiltrated such people.

On 23 May 1994, Ananie Nkurunziza, responsible for political analysis in RTLM, made one of these comparisons between the past and the present. He drew on comments made by a politician in one of the parties formed during independence.

> Recently, I am always dealing with similarities; those Tutsis killed the president of the Republic. Therefore the masses got up. The population stood up at once. With the attacks of 1966, which are similar to those of 1994, the population has always been vigilant. In addition, Thaddeus Bagaragaza (of APROSOMA) was asked the reason why, during the 1959 revolution, so many Tutsis were killed, whether they all were on the king's side. He well answered that even Tutsis who were not chiefs were all on the king's side. Here we have to see the similarity of things.
>
> Kantano, we've already said it, Tutsis, Rwandan Tutsis, will understand later perhaps that they shouldn't cling on one fixed idea. Clinging to their Tutsi hood is not a sort of loneliness but a constant will to dominate, a feeling

of being special, supreme beings. That's why according to Bagaragaza, a so big number died, because even those who weren't chiefs considered themselves as superior to Hutus.[1]

Five days later, Kantano Habimana, another RTLM journalist adds:

Wait until we get enough bullets to chase them away, they will regret what brought them here. They said they will kill all Hutus but what can they use to decimate Hutus? One Tutsi may kill one Hutu, but in the end 6 million Hutus can survive, then what ethnic group would be injured the most? (Kantano Habimana, RTLM broadcast)

After 6 April, RTLM criticized and gave instructions and orders to people in the government. RTLM journalists and government officials sent out mutually reinforcing statements targeting sections of the population that were alleged members of RPA or its political wing RPF and anyone believed or suspected to be supporting it. The political elite made sure that people understood that the government supported the message of RTLM. Prime Minister Jean Kambanda called on the station and in a broadcast told the population that RTLM was 'one of the key weapons in the war'.

The station and government officials reinforced each other's call for all able-bodied people in Rwanda to actively participate in the campaign to find the RPF, the RPA and all persons associated with them. Participation was made an imperative. Those who did not participate and wanted to flee the war were mocked by RTLM and sometimes targeted for death. RTLM, as well as political leaders, made it clear that killing 'the enemy' was the duty of every Rwandan.

RTLM's role in the genocide was to reinforce distorted notions of Rwandan history. It used these notions to describe to the ordinary population the 'threat' posed by RPA and an amorphous group of supporters that ranged from innocent Tutsis to the commander of the UNAMIR forces. It used these mythical images of Tutsi cruelty and treachery to spur people into action by presenting a fait accompli; participate or be subjected to slavery and extermination by the blood thirsty RPA. Kill or be killed.

ANALYSIS OF RTLM BROADCASTS

As part of a master's degree in communication psychology, I conducted a content analysis of RTLM broadcasts. Written transcripts of a selection of broadcasts were used; in some instances, the transcripts were compared with audio recordings. I relied on a database created by the International Monitor group, which contained transcripts of 99 tapes, 56 of which were RTLM broadcasts. The recordings varied in length from 60 minutes to several hours. I also had access to a CD-ROM database used by the International Criminal Tribunal for Rwanda (ICTR) prosecution team, which contained more than 100 transcripts of other broadcasts. Of the transcripts obtained from the ICTR, 16 were examined as part of the content analysis. Thus, in total, 72 transcripts of

RTLM broadcasts, ranging in length from one to three hours were examined. The tapes had been transcribed into English and French. I am fluent in English and read French with relative ease.

CLASSIFICATION OF DATA AND DEFINITION OF TERMS

The broadcasts were classified according to the following characteristics:

- Format of broadcast;
- Name of broadcaster;
- Name of guest or interviewee;
- Theme or subject of the broadcast;
- Group targeted for violence or hatred by the particular broadcast;
- Type of statement that targets a group or person for violence or hatred.

Format of broadcast

The format of RTLM broadcasts included monologues, dialogues, group discussions, interviews, speeches or statements, songs, news, interrogations, instructions.

'Dialogue' is defined as a conversation between two people while 'group discussion' involves three or more people.

An 'interview' is a formal question-and-answer session, making it different from a dialogue, which is an informal exchange of views. RTLM broadcasts used the interview format with guests, but broadcasters also discussed issues with each other. 'Discussion' has, therefore, been used to describe programmes in which two members of the team are talking about an issue while 'interview' applies when questions are put to outsiders.

'Instructions' are directives on what to do and how to act.

Certain broadcasts were difficult to categorize. For example, like other African radio stations, RTLM often broadcast programmes in which the broadcaster read out greetings and messages from the audience, often interspersed with music and the broadcaster's own commentary and witticisms. I have categorized all such broadcasts as 'other' (see Table 9.1).

Name of broadcaster

Only seven RTLM journalists were well known. However, other freelance journalists could be heard from time to time. The staff who transcribed the tapes were sometimes unable to identify the journalist; these are grouped under 'unknown' as opposed to 'other' who were not regular journalists but were recognized. Jean Baptiste Bamwanga is a Radio Rwanda journalist, for example; however, RTLM borrowed Radio Rwanda material and he is included because of the frequency with which he appeared (see Table 9.2).

Name of guest or interviewee

Those interviewed by RTLM are of particular importance to this research as this is where we begin our study of the interaction of the message and the authority figures. The list (Table 9.3) includes a number of known political and military figures and certain persons linked to the launch of RTLM and *Kangura* newspaper, in addition to representatives of important parties and groups. This is accurate only insofar as these people speak on behalf of the party or militia they claim to represent.

Theme or subject of the broadcast

From study of an initial sample, it was apparent that the classification in this area should indicate the general tone in which the subject matter was discussed. In addition, certain subjects are classified as general, as the subject matter, which was not political, was neither positive nor negative, but purely information, e.g., sports news, news of other countries, etc. (see Table 9.5).

Group targeted for violence or hatred

This category deals with whether the broadcast called for action against a particular group of people and what kind of action was called for. I classified the data into two broad areas: a broadcast that warned people to beware, watch closely for, be vigilant and wary of infiltration by targeted persons; and directives. In the latter, the broadcaster asks for violent action to be taken against the targeted group (beaten, killed, exterminated) or gives instructions for people to go to a certain area and take similar action against a targeted group (see Table 9.6).

I distinguished between use of the words *Inyenzi* and *Inkotanyi*. *Inyenzi* has connotations that go beyond meaning the RPA and could mean a Tutsi or an associate of the RPF. Broadcasts targeting the *Inkotanyi* are classified as targeting the RPF.

Type of statement that targets a group or person for violence or hatred

Broadcasts including statements used to target people for harm or violence were more difficult to categorize. In deciding what to call a broadcast likely to create hatred or harm, I relied heavily on Article 20 of the *International Covenant on Civil and Political Rights* (UN 1966). I also considered what would be considered provocative in the Rwandan context.

The definition I have come up with in describing what I was looking for is: a statement that was likely, not only to portray a group, issue or person in a threatening light, but also likely to impute ill or anti-social motives to a group or person, thereby justifying a response for self-defence, or any direct call for negative action, such as killing, and justification for such action.

In some cases, the broadcast may be justified; for instance the negative portrayal of the RPA after a spate of crippling bombing raids by that group cannot be called calls to hatred. However, these have also been identified and classified as they form part of the debate on what role the RTLM played.

I classified insults and allegations of social deviancy separately. Allegations of social deviance imply that a group or person is no longer acceptable in society and is a threat; for instance allegations of cannibalism have very different implications compared with calling a person a dog.

By the end of the research, I found that some of the categories had no entries or that the type of content I had found in a category did not have any relevance to the research, such categories were subsequently removed from the results (see Table 9.7).

RESULTS

Format of broadcast

The most common format of RTLM broadcasts was monologues by the station's own journalists (Table 9.1). This type of broadcast took up 66.29 per cent of instances. Second to monologues, RTLM relied on interviews. It is interesting to note that news items accounted for only 1.52 per cent of all formats, and instructions and directives issued by the station accounted for 2.56 per cent.

Speeches and statements were also more common than news items, taking up 5.84 per cent of segments. The station also aired interrogations of alleged soldiers of the RPA conducted by officers of the Rwandan Armed Forces. These make up 1.28 per cent of the broadcasts, and one of the interrogations featured an alleged RPA member.

RTLM's format is a bit unusual for a news organization. One ordinarily expects to find news, interviews and other forms of programming taking more airtime than monologues by journalists. Standard practice on many broadcast stations is not to have a person talk on air for longer than a few seconds. Even news bites are short and are structured in that manner on the assumption that lengthy monologues lose audience attention.

Table 9.1 Format of broadcast

Category	*No. of segments*	*% of total*
Monologue	828	66.29
Interview	236	18.90
Speech or statement	73	5.84
Instructions	32	2.56
Dialogue	25	2.00
News	19	1.52
Interrogation	16	1.28
Group discussion	15	1.20
Other	4	0.32
Song	1	0.08
Total	1,249	99.99*

*Total may not equal 100% due to rounding

Name of broadcaster

In the research sample, Kantano Habimana was the broadcaster on air most frequently (33.51 per cent of instances), almost twice as often as his editor-in-chief, Gaspard Gahigi (Table 9.2). The second most frequent broadcaster was Valérie Bemeriki, followed by Gahigi. RTLM political analyst Ananie

Nkurunziza was the broadcaster in 10.65 per cent of instances. These four RTLM journalists account for 75.76 per cent of appearances by broadcasters.

Ruggiu, broadcasting only in French, accounted for 7.97 per cent of appearances, while Noël Hitimana, who left the service in April after being wounded in a mortar explosion, accounted for 5.02 per cent. Unidentified journalists make up 4.16 per cent, and other journalists visiting RTLM take up 4.24 per cent of the total.

Nkomati does not feature much, which can be explained by the allegation that he was sacked in May for failure to appear at work. It is unclear why Rucogoza is not on air more frequently. Mbilizi, a Congolese national, left RTLM in April and attempted to go back to his home country. Ruggiu probably fails to feature prominently because he could not broadcast in Kinyarwanda.

Table 9.2 Name of broadcaster

Category	*Instances*	*% of total*
Kantano Habimana	387	33.51
Valérie Bemeriki	195	16.88
Editor-in-chief Gaspard Gahigi	170	14.72
Ananie Nkurunziza	123	10.65
Georges Ruggiu	92	7.97
Noël Hitimana	58	5.02
Other	49	4.24
Unknown	48	4.16
Emmanuel Rucogoza	14	1.21
Phillipe Mbilizi	11	0.95
Nkomati	6	0.52
Jean Baptiste Bamwanga	2	0.17
Total	1,155	100.00

Name of guest or interviewee

Analysis of the data on interviews indicates that 74.91 per cent of the time, there was no guest at the station. Kambanda accounted for 2.53 per cent of interviews; government officials, 3.34 per cent; unidentified militiamen and women, 2.17 per cent; CDR militia official Stanislas Simbizi and MDR party official Frodould Karamira accounted for 1.53 and 0.99 per cent, respectively; while 1.45 per cent of interviews were with members of the RPA and RPF. Ordinary civilians took up 7.76 per cent (Table 9.3).

To give a clearer picture of how much airtime each interviewee was given, I recalculated the data based on the proportion of interviews of each as a percentage of total interviews (Table 9.4), that is, I excluded the 830 instances reported in Table 9.3 in which there was no interviewee.

Theme or subject of the broadcast

Analysis of the content of the study sample indicates that 16.32 per cent of RTLM broadcasts studied contained statements alleging atrocities carried out

Table 9.3 Name of guest or interviewee

Category	*Instances*	*% of total*
No guest	830	74.91
Other	86	7.76
Government official	37	3.34
Prime Minister Jean Kambanda	28	2.53
Ferdinand Nahimana	27	2.44
Unidentified militia member	24	2.17
CDR militia official	17	1.53
Rwanda Patriotic Army officer	15	1.35
MDR party official	11	0.99
Rwanda Armed Forces officer	11	0.99
Hassan Ngeze	8	0.72
Jean Bosco Barayagwiza	6	0.54
President Théodore Sikubwabo	4	0.36
PL party official	1	0.09
Gendarmerie officer	1	0.09
UNAMIR representative	1	0.09
Juvénal Habyarimana	1	0.09
Total	1,108	99.99*

* Total may not equal 100% due to rounding

Table 9.4 Time spent interviewing various people as a proportion of total interview time

Category	*Instances*	*% of total interview segments*
Other	86	30.93
Government official	37	13.31
Prime Minister Jean Kambanda	28	10.07
Ferdinand Nahimana	27	9.71
Unidentified militia member	24	8.63
CDR militia official	17	6.11
Rwanda Patriotic Army officer	15	5.39
MDR party official	11	3.96
Rwanda Armed Forces officer	11	3.96
Hassan Ngeze	8	2.87
Jean-Bosco Barayagwiza	6	2.16
President Théodore Sikubwabo	4	1.44
PL party official	1	0.36
Gendarmerie officer	1	0.36
UNAMIR representative	1	0.36
Juvénal Habyarimana	1	0.36
Total	278	99.98*

* Total may not equal 100% due to rounding

by the RPA (Table 9.5), including indiscriminate bombing of civilians, hospitals and orphanages, indiscriminate killings of civilians and extermination of Hutu populations in areas and zones occupied by the RPA. No inflammatory content was found in 13.21 per cent of the broadcasts studied.

Table 9.5 Inflammatory content of broadcasts

Category	*Instances*	*% of total*
Allegations of RPA atrocities	294	16.32
Encouragement to Hutus to fight, kill	252	13.99
No inflammatory content	238	13.21
Direct calls for extermination	165	9.16
Allegations that RPA wants power and control over Hutu	106	5.89
Allegations that Tutsis in the region are helping those within	127	7.05
Insults to Tutsis and RPA	88	4.89
Description of how the past influences present events	70	3.89
Congratulations to FAR	60	3.33
Allegations that Tutsis plan to subjugate the Hutu	57	3.16
Allegations that RPA killed Habyarimana	50	2.78
Allegations that political parties are supporting RPA	45	2.50
Broadcast insults/slurs against Hutus sympathizing with the RPA	41	2.28
Tutsis, RPA are social deviants, abnormal	41	2.28
Allegations that Tutsis are exterminating Hutus	39	2.17
Attack or harm Belgians or UNAMIR personnel	36	2.00
Threats to Hutus sympathizing with RPA, fleeing war	24	1.33
Allegations that invalids, women, old men armed, support RPA	24	1.33
Broadcast justifies massacres	20	1.11
Not all Tutsis are enemies; should live together with Hutus	16	0.89
Allegations that Tutsis killed Habyarimana	8	0.44
Total	1,801	100.00

A clear reminder that Tutsi civilians are not necessarily linked to the RPA and its activities and that the two groups should live together peacefully took up only 0.89 per cent of all broadcasts studied. The call on Hutu civilians to fight for their country, look out for infiltrators, avoid re-enslavement and kill all RPA members and their accomplices took up 13.99 per cent. Direct calls for the extermination of members of the RPA and all its supporters, as well as congratulatory messages on the extermination of RPA members and supporters – *Inyenzi*, *Inkotanyi*, accomplices – took up 9.16 per cent of the broadcasts.

Allegations that RPA members were not Rwandans and formed part of a regional conspiracy to dominate Tutsis and set up a Tutsi–Hima empire in central Africa took up 7.05 per cent of the broadcasts; allegations that the RPA wanted to take over the country and reinstate the monarchy, subjugating all Hutus accounted for 5.89 per cent.

Other allegations included statements that Tutsi civilians were part of the regional plan by Tutsis to take over power, or that they were actively helping RPA in this cause and stood to benefit from it (3.16 per cent); that Tutsi civilians were actively exterminating Hutus, making such plans, or supporting them (2.17 per cent); that RPA members killed president Habyarimana, precipitating the unrest in the country (2.78 per cent); and that some political parties were helping the RPA (2.50 per cent).

Insults and ethnic slurs directed at the RPA and Tutsis took up 4.89 per cent, and comments depicting the RPA and Tutsis as social deviants – cannibals, sorcerers, vampires – accounted for 2.28 per cent. Reminders about the history of Rwanda, the fall of the monarchy in 1959 during the Hutu revolution and similarities of those events with the present occurred in 3.89 per cent of the broadcasts. Threats of death or harm to the Belgian contingent of UNAMIR and the UNAMIR commander Roméo Dallaire made up 2.00 per cent. Death threats to Hutu supporters of the RPA or those accepting the fact that RPA was winning the war took up 1.33 per cent of the time, while slurs and insults directed at the two groups made up 2.28 per cent.

In the tapes studied, a total of 69.24 per cent of inflammatory messages were linked to either the RPA or Tutsis.

Group targeted for violence or hatred

Calls for the audience to be on the look out for Tutsis accounted for 10.59 per cent of all warnings and directives (Table 9.6). Words that characterized this type of statement were: look out for, tricks, malice, activities of the Tutsi, Tutsi accomplices, *Inyenzi*-Tutsi and *Inyenzi* wherever it was not qualified by the addition of *Inkotanyi*.

Table 9.6 Group targeted for violence or hatred

Category	*Instances*	*% of total*
Warnings		
Seek, watch out for RPF, RPA, *Inkotanyi*	598	38.61
Seek, watch out for *Inyenzi*, Tutsi	164	10.59
Seek, watch out for individual	76	4.91
Seek, watch out for members of particular party	9	0.58
Directives		
No targeting of any group for harm	287	18.53
Harm or kill members of RPA/*Inkotanyi*	149	9.62
Identification of person/groups as accomplices of *Inyenzi*	89	5.75
Kill or harm *Inyenzi*, Tutsi	55	3.55
Identified accomplice should be sought	35	2.26
Kill or harm individual	25	1.61
Specific targeting of Tutsi females as tools of RPA to be resisted or harmed	21	1.36
Specific and direct call for restraint	14	0.90
Targeting Belgians for hatred or violence	14	0.90
Identified accomplice should be harmed or killed	9	0.58
Encouragement of Hutu females to participate at roadblocks/fighting	4	0.26
Total	1,549	100.00

Directives included targeting of Tutsis for murder or extermination (3.55 per cent); calls to kill or harm RPA soldiers (9.62 per cent); identification of individuals as supporters or accomplices of the RPA (5.75 per cent); instructions to seek out accomplices named on RTLM (2.26 per cent); and instructions to kill such accomplices (0.58 per cent). Warnings to watch the activities of named individuals took up 4.91 per cent of the total, while instructions to kill such individuals accounted for 1.61 per cent.

Broadcasts citing Tutsi women as spies and asking people to watch out for them occurred in 1.36 per cent of all cases, while those calling on Hutu women to actively participate at roadblocks and in fighting the enemy took up 0.26 per cent.

Statements targeting the Belgian UNAMIR contingent took up 0.90 per cent.

The content analysis indicates that 75.14 per cent of all inflammatory statements occurred when there were no interviewees. Consequently, it is accurate to say that RTLM journalists, rather than their interviewees, made most of the inflammatory statements.

Inflammatory comments by civilian interviewees accounted for 6.44 per cent of the total. Out of the total airtime taken up by inflammatory comments, Prime Minister Jean Kambanda accounts for 3.66 per cent; Ferdinand Nahimana, 2.33 per cent; CDR member and militia man Stanley Simbizi, 2.50 per cent; MDR official Frodouald Karamira, 2.00 per cent; unidentified militia, 1.89 per cent; and government officials (mostly burgomasters), 2.33 per cent.

Out of the 7.16 per cent of airtime taken up by comments that RPA members were not Rwandans and formed part of the regional conspiracy to take over central Africa, 5.99 per cent were made in the absence of any interviewees. Similarly, during the 9.32 per cent airtime when direct calls for extermination were made, there were virtually no interviewees present. It is important to note that only 0.06 per cent of the airtime was taken up by Rwanda government officials participating in RTLM interviews to explain that Tutsis were distinct from RPA and not necessarily linked with its activities, and to encourage coexistence.

Out of the total airtime devoted to allegations of RPA atrocities, those made by government officials during interviews account for 0.50 per cent. Out of the calls alleging that Tutsis as a group were planning or committing extermination campaigns against Hutus, Kambanda was responsible for 0.11 per cent.

Of the 9.35 per cent of airtime taken up in direct calls for extermination, RTLM journalists were responsible for 8.10 per cent while Kambanda accounts for 0.11. Allegations that Tutsis and RPA were social deviants, namely cannibals, vampires, or unfit for society took 2.28 per cent of the airtime; RTLM journalists accounted for 2.00 per cent of this airtime while Kambanda accounted for 0.06 per cent.

The call for all Hutus to participate actively in the events accounts for 14.10 per cent of the airtime. Of this, RTLM journalists were responsible for 9.05 per cent, government officials for 0.78 per cent and Kambanda for 0.62 per cent.

Of 3.27 per cent of the time taken up by allegations that the Tutsi community was planning to take over power and subjugate Hutus, 2.16 per cent can be allocated to RTLM journalists, while Kambanda was responsible for 0.06 per cent.

A study of the types of statements used to rouse the Hutu population to fight, defend themselves and actively participate in the events (Table 9.7) showed that 33.33 per cent were accompanied by allegations of RPA atrocities – claims of indiscriminate bombing, massacres and extermination of Hutus. These allegations also included claims that RPA was eviscerating people. In 24.24 per cent of cases, they were accompanied by the allegation that RPA were not

Rwandans and were part of a conspiracy to establish a Hima–Tutsi monarchy in the region; 16.16 per cent included allegations that the RPA wanted power and control over the Hutu and might reinstate the monarchy. Reminders of past evils of the monarchy and links with the armed insurgencies of the 1960s accompanied 14.14 per cent of the calls to violence. These also included reminders of how the Hutus had freed themselves from slavery and subjugation.

Table 9.7 Context in which inflammatory statements were made

Category	*Instances*	*% of total*
Reports of RPA atrocities	33	33.33
Allegations that Tutsis in the region were involved in the war or a conspiracy	24	24.24
Allegations that RPA wants power and control over Hutus	16	16.16
Reminders of Rwanda's past and its relation to the present	14	14.14
Claims that Tutsis, RPA are social deviants	7	7.07
Allegations of Tutsis are exterminating Hutus	3	3.03
Allegations that Tutsis plan to subjugate Hutus	2	2.02
Total	99	100

In 7.07 per cent of the airtime, calls on the Hutu were accompanied by descriptions of Tutsi civilians and RPA as social deviants. This included claims of cannibalism, drinking victims' blood, sorcery, and unredeemable evil natures that did not belong to normal society. In 2.02 per cent, allegations were made that Tutsi civilians were out to subjugate Hutus, were actively helping the RPA in that cause or hoped to benefit from it. In 3.03 per cent, it was announced that Tutsi civilians were killing Hutus, or planning to do so.

CONCLUSIONS

Those who argue that RTLM was set up with the express aim of instigating mass murder right from the start miss the point. They fail to see the frightening process by which a station that was set up merely to air the political views of one group became the megaphone through which people were incited to mass murder.

The content analysis revealed that each time the RPA made advances, the tenor of the broadcasts would change, becoming more extreme, and more blatantly so, as time went on. The level of inflammatory content began climbing in January 1994 – as it became obvious that implementation of the Arusha accords had floundered – and rose steadily until March. With the April assassination of President Habyarimana, the level reached new heights and continued to rise steadily through June as it became evident that the RPA was winning the war.

Until about the beginning of April, RTLM broadcasts tended to focus on anti-RPA, anti-Arusha peace accords propaganda. Broadcasters focused on renditions of the history of Tutsi–Hutu antagonism and allegations that the opposition parties were helping the RPA block installation of the negotiated government. There was a clear change in tone after the assassination on 6 April and even more so after 11 April as the RPA took over parts of Kigali, forcing the provisional government to flee to Gitarama.

During this second phase, which lasted until mid-May, there were clear calls for extermination of the RPA and elimination of Tutsis and all other accomplices. Names of people were broadcast, sometimes along with instructions on what to do to them. The word extermination was used repeatedly during this period. RTLM also broadcast allegations that Tutsi children, women and old men were being armed, making them legitimate targets.

The messages were very clear: the RPA was advancing to take over the country, Tutsis were helping them and they were working together with the Hima and other Tutsis in the region to install a monarchy in the central African region with the intention of subjugating the Hutu. To achieve their end, the RPA and their Tutsi supporters were willing to do anything including exterminating all Hutu.

RTLM told its listeners that the only way to avoid what was coming was for everyone to look out for the 'enemy in their midst' and work with the authorities to ensure the extermination of the RPA and all its accomplices. It was a fait accompli – kill or be killed. Faced with this constant message and the follow-up actions of their leaders, who organized and led militia in attacks against Tutsi, many ordinary civilians believed the propaganda and actively took part in the killing campaign. Those who were not convinced were often coerced and threatened, sometimes even treated as accomplices to 'the enemy'.

Extermination became a project in which lack of involvement or even fleeing into RPA-controlled sectors signified support for the target group.[2] Radio had become a tool for directing mass murder.

NOTES

1. It is likely that RTLM was actually mistaken in the identity of the person they quoted. I have been told that Thaddeus actually belonged to MDR–Parmehutu and not APROSOMA. It is also likely that the spelling is Thadée and not Thaddeus.
2. 'I have always told you. All the people who joined the part controlled by the *Inyenzi Inkotanyi* are *Inyenzi* themselves. They approve the killings perpetrated by *Inyenzi*. They are criminals like the *Inyenzi Inkotanyi*. They are all *Inyenzi*. When our armed forces will get there, they will get what they deserve. They will not spare anyone since everybody turned *Inyenzi*. All those who stayed there are all Inyenzi since those who were against *Inyenzi* have been killed by *Inyenzi*. Those who suceeded to escape run away to Ngara, Burundi and to the western part of our country. Those who stayed are accomplices and acolytes of the *Inyenzi*.' (Valérie Bemeriki, RTML broadcast, 28 June 1994)

REFERENCES

Jones, B. 1999. 'The Arusha Peace Process'. In H. Adelman and A. Suhkre (eds). *The Path of a Genocide: the Rwanda Crisis from Uganda to Zaire.* Transaction Publishers, New Brunswick, NJ, USA.

Sibomana, A. 1999. *Hope for Rwanda: Conversations with Laure Guilbert and Harve Deguine*. Pluto Press, London, UK, 205 pp.

UN (United Nations). 1966. *International Covenant on civil and political rights*. General Assembly Resolution 2200A (XXI), 16 December. Available at <www.unhchr.ch/html/menu3/b/a_ccpr.htm> (accessed 6 September 2005).

10
The Effect of RTLM's Rhetoric of Ethnic Hatred in Rural Rwanda

Charles Mironko

Because of its inflammatory rhetoric and extremist views, much has been made of the role of RTLM in the genocide of 1994. According to Des Forges (1999: 71), it was the 'sole source of news as well as the sole authority for interpreting its meaning' during the genocide. Although no one really disputes the genocidal overtones of RTLM's broadcasting, there *is* disagreement about the causal link between the words on the air and the violence on the ground.

Some feel that without the assistance of RTLM, the *genocidaires* could not have succeeded to the extent that they did. Mahmood Mandani's thesis about Tutsi as a racialized political identity cites RTLM as one of 'two propaganda organs [that] were central to this effort [recasting Tutsi as a race]' (Mandani 2001:190). The US State Department asserted that RTLM broadcasts 'ultimately had a lethal effect, calling on the Hutu majority to destroy the Tutsi minority. Experts cite RTML as an important factor in the spread of genocide in the hours and days following Habyarimana's death' (Chalk 1999: 97). Chrétien and his colleagues, authors of the most comprehensive analysis of the role of media in the genocide to date, give central importance to radio (including RTLM), saying, 'Two tools, one very modern, the other less [modern] were particularly used during the genocide against the Tutsis in Rwanda: the radio and the machete. The former to give and receive orders, the second to carry them out' (Chrétien et al. 1995: 191).

But some scholars have contested the role of radio, specifically RTLM, in the genocide. For example, Richard Carver writes that:

> Most commentary on Rwandan hate radio has worked on the simple assumption that since RTLM broadcast propaganda for genocide and genocide did indeed occur, there must be a causal relationship between the two ... the notion that people could be incited to acts of extreme violence by the radio is *only tenable if* it is accepted that RTLM propaganda unlocked profound or even primordial hatred. [Milles Collines] may have produced propaganda for the genocide but it did not incite it. (Carver 2000:190, emphasis added)

Carver identifies the leap of logic in relating hate speech to murder, without more compelling evidence that the murderers were, in fact, somehow motivated or crucially affected by the radio's message. Carver makes an interesting observation:

> RTLM broadcast hate propaganda, there was genocide, and therefore one caused another. If we were talking about almost any other issue – violence on television, pornography or whatever – those arguing in favour of a ban would attempt to demonstrate at least a cursory link between the broadcast and the action. There is now an abundant research to suggest that it is impossible to draw a linear causal link between what people see or hear in the media and how they behave. But because it is genocide we abandon our critical faculties. (Carver 1996)

The purpose of this paper is to explore the relation between the rhetoric of ethnic hatred so prevalent among Rwandan political elites and the forces that propelled ordinary Rwandan Hutus to participate in killing Tutsis. Information was collected in conversations conducted in 2000 with nearly 100 confessed perpetrators held in six Rwandan prisons: Kigali, Butare, Rilima, Gitarama, Gisenyi and Ruhengeri.

OVERVIEW OF RTLM, FORM AND FUNCTION

The RTLM signal originally reached only greater Kigali and part of the surrounding countryside, but from 8 July 1993 it could also be heard throughout the country and in the north of Burundi. RTLM broadcast every night on FM 106 for a few hours – more if there were major events to report – but it also used FM 94, one of Radio Rwanda's transmitter frequencies.

RTLM was especially popular among the youth, because it played up-to-date music from Zaire. RTLM recruited the best Kinyarwanda and French speakers and journalists including foreigners. These journalists promoted the station, which they called 'Radio Sympa' (lovely radio), claiming that it was the radio 'of the people, for the people.' For example, one broadcaster, Gaspard Gahigi, welcomes ordinary citizens:

> We have a radio here, even a peasant who wants to say something can come, and we will give him the floor. Then, other peasants will be able to hear what peasants think. Personally, I think what complicates things is that ordinary citizens have no forum where they can speak. Normally, for ordinary citizens to speak, they speak through elections and elections are impossible. So, in fact, ordinary citizens have been deprived of a say but RTLM is there, we will give them the floor. (Gaspard Gahigi, RTLM, 19 March 1994)

> What makes us happy here at RTLM is that we broadcast your announcements quickly, very quickly, I mean, it is just like making wood fire glow [*kwenyegeza*]. You bring a message any time and you say: 'Ha! Put it now, and then we put it in very quickly so that your messages reach … whoever you want.' (Gaspard Gahigi, RTLM, 15 December 1993)

Kantano Habimana, a popular RTLM broadcaster, bragged that people could not follow foreign news because it was in French or English. In contrast, RTLM's Ananie Nkurunziza monitored foreign news for 'our RTLM' (31 May 1993). Nkurunziza's spin on international reports was an analysis that justified RTLM hate speech, discredited the Arusha peace talks and condemned the international community because it was supposedly on the side of the Rwandan Patriotic Front (RPF). Likewise, Kantano spoke against the rival RPF radio station, Muhabura.

> I don't understand how a Rwandan can follow what Muhabura radio says ... Muhabura radio broadcasts from far away in the bush. Instead of trusting RTLM radio, which broadcasts near him, they are together and they are also together with journalists whom he can see and even ask them the situation. So, those people who listen to Muhabura radio, let them get lost [mentally lost], let them get lost but they will regret it for a long time. (Kantano Habimana, RTLM, 25 May 1993)

RTLM broadcasts also trumpeted a version of Rwandan history that pitted Hutu against Tutsi in a story of foreign invasion and ethnic domination.

> Tutsi are nomads and invaders who came to Rwanda in search of pasture, but because they are so cunning and malicious, the Tutsi managed to stay and rule. If you allow the Tutsi–Hamites to come back, they will not only rule you in Rwanda, but will also extend their power throughout the Great Lakes Region. (RTLM, 2 December 1993, author's translation from Kinyarwanda)

ETHNIC CONSCIOUSNESS OF CONFESSED PERPETRATORS

My line of questioning in interviews with confessed genocide perpetrators focused on the practices of media consumption in Rwanda. Ideally, I would have observed people listening to the radio, discussing its content and circulating these ideas in their everyday lives, but this was not possible during the genocide. Instead, I collected the comments and reflections of low-level perpetrators six years after the fact, during interviews conducted in 2000.

During the interviews, I discerned differences between the possible impact of RTLM on people in urban areas and on ordinary peasants (*abaturage*) who lived in remote villages (*ibyaro*). RTLM appears to have been especially effective in Kigali, where it issued vehement instructions to foment violence at roadblocks, broadcast names of escaped Tutsi and their hiding places, threatened Tutsi youth, broadcast lists of 'accomplices' (*ibyitso*) to kill and encouraged listeners to 'get rid of the dirt' (*gukuraho umwanda*).

Interviews with genocide perpetrators also led me to make a distinction between the responses to RTLM hate speech and propaganda of two distinct audiences. One audience was the urban jobless youth, trained and operating under the umbrella of the *Interahamwe.* These young people held portable radios to their ears on roadblocks and around commercial centres. The other was pro-government middle-class urban dwellers, including civil servants, professionals and businessmen.

According to Debra Spitulnik's approach to understanding the role of media in social life, it is important to

> factor in what is happening at the levels of reception and *lateral communication*, such as the social circulation of media discourse outside of contexts of direct media consumption. I suggest ... that the repeating, recycling, and recontextualizing of media discourse is an important component in the formation of community in a kind of subterranean way, because it establishes an indirect connectivity or intertextuality across media consumers and across instances of media consumption. (Spitulnik 2001: 98, emphasis added)

In the cities in the former Belgian colonies, lateral communication took place via a broad urban gossip network called *radio trottoir* (sidewalk radio), which transmitted 'counter-hegemonic' popular discourses that often contested information dispensed by official media. Writing with respect to Kinshasa, Schoepf (1993) talks about *radio trottoir*, an urban version of the 'bush-telephone' that used talking drums to carry news to settlements separated by long distances.[1] Bourgault (1995: 201–3) describes the *radio trottoir* alternative to the official press in the francophone West African countries of Togo and Cameroon. He suggests that even if masses at the bottom of society are passive, they have evolved their own discursive means to resist oppressive discourse from above. In densely populated rural Rwanda, a 'bush-telephone' operated with great efficiency using word-of-mouth, without recourse to drums.

By exploring the theme of radio and radio consumption with groups of prisoners, I have been able to glimpse some of this 'lateral communication' and 'circulation' in a newly fashioned community – the community of confessed perpetrators. For my analysis, I drew on three key concepts from Spitulnik's (1996) article 'The Social Circulation of Media Discourse and the Mediation of communities': consumption, circulation and community.

Examining radio and language in contemporary Zambia, Spitulnik argues that radio today achieves what newspapers did in the colonial world. Drawing on Benedict Anderson's (1983) concept of 'imagined communities', she writes that it creates a shared cognitive space, a *community* of listeners who incorporate its linguistic elements into their everyday lives in both conscious and unconscious ways. Spitulnik focuses on the circulation of language – lexical items, catchphrases, semantic fields, and discourse styles – as evidence of this community of people who cannot see each other. I will consider the additional possibility that radio might affect more than symbolic behaviour, that is, speech, and actually contribute to the commission of violent actions, that is, murder.

Spitulnik locates radio within a broader discursive context and seeks to understand the inter-textualities or cross-linkages between mass media and other forms of discourse. It has been established that the ethnically divisive rhetoric that characterized RTLM broadcasts overlapped with, and borrowed from, the social scientific discourse from the colonial period and with political speech from the first and second republics. The importance of radio in a place like Zambia, as in Rwanda, is related to the fact that it is the most widely consumed medium in the country and 'the same broadcasts are accessible to the entire national population at the same time and, thus, allow for the possibility of producing a degree of shared *linguistic* knowledge across a population of roughly 9.1 million' (Spitulnik 2001: 99, emphasis added).

If we substitute the word 'ideological' for 'linguistic', we begin to see the potential for RTLM to serve both as 'reservoir and reference point' for ideas of ethnic hatred and violence for five or six million Rwandans. If we add that radio audiences were well aware that they were audiences (not individuals), that millions of others were simultaneously listening as well, the intensity of their potential is increased.

However, Spitulnik advances the idea that language broadcast on the radio is not passively consumed by listeners, but is actively re-centred, reinterpreted and re-circulated. The listeners are 'active decoders ... of media messages, who accept, reject, or resist what is conveyed based on their own class position within society' (Spitulnik 1993: 297). This latter point is crucial to understanding the listenership of RTLM and prevents us from assuming that what elites, professionals and townspeople 'heard' on RTLM is the same as what rural dwellers 'heard'.

This could not have been made more clear to me in my interviews with confessors. The first response to my questions was often a claim of ignorance of RTLM. Some professed to know nothing of its message or its role in inciting violence. Many informants told me that they did not listen to RTLM at all, either because they did not own radios (or had no batteries) or because they did not perceive themselves to be part of the target audience for this radio station. Radio technology in general was presented by the perpetrators as something alien to the rural peasantry, a medium of information that requires special education or political credentials to make sense of its messages.

> I was a cultivator, so what can I tell you about it? I don't know anything about the radio. (Interview, Kigali prison, 20 September 2000)

> In the countryside, things of radio do not exist. (Interview, Kigali prison, September 2000)

> I don't know anything about it. This is the first time [I am hearing about this]. (Interview, Rilima prison, 21 September 2000)

> We had a radio but I did not hear anything. (Interview, Rilima prison, September 2000)

> Except that I am a peasant and it does not concern me. Do you think I even know what RTLM stands for? Not at all! (Interview, Gitarama prison, 9 September 2000)

> How can you listen to the radio when you did not go to school? When you can't read and write? (Interview, Butare prison, 29 September 2000)

Given these informants' apparent lack of identification with the political message of RTLM, it was interesting to explore their awareness and understanding of the messages broadcast on Radio Muhabura, the station run by the RPF, from the National Park (*Parc National des Volcans*) at the Rwanda–Uganda border. Radio Muhabura broadcast in full AM frequency and could be heard in most parts of Rwanda except the south (Chrétien et al. 1995). In separate interviews, all the confessors expressed the same thing: it was strictly forbidden to listen to Radio Muhabura in Rwanda, and anyone found doing so was beaten or otherwise punished.

One informant told me that I should have an equal or greater understanding of RTLM's broadcasts than he did, as if it broadcast to educated elites around the world, but was somehow opaque and foreign to Rwandan peasants:

> Q: Now, do you think that in the situation you went through there is something, which could be attributed to what the radio broadcast?
> A: Peasants [*Abaturage*] like us did not even have any radios.
> Q: Why do they say it anyway? So, you never heard anyone saying it?
> A: Radio? A person who did not have a radio heard it from someone else. For example, RTLM said that ...
> Q: But what do you think? Telling you: 'kill or do this' or hearing it from the radio, is it the same thing?
> A: No. Hearing it only could not have any impact. People were forced to kill by those soldiers. But simply hearing from the radio could not do anything.
> Q: You heard it from the radio and you saw people killing?
> A: I mean, soldiers brought it [the killing] and then RTLM reported it. For example, I had a small radio. The radio used to broadcast it. You found out that what it broadcast was what the soldiers were doing. So, it was necessary that we do it too. Because the leadership supported it, we accepted it. (Interview, Ruhengeri prison, 27 September 2000)

By claiming ignorance of the radio and its message, by suggesting that they were essentially incapable of participating in the political project that the radio represents, these perpetrators position themselves as bystanders or even victims of the larger struggle between Hutu political elites in Kigali and the invading force of Tutsi exiles in the RPF. This idea of being caught between two powerful and dangerous forces pervades the perpetrators' narratives and finds expression in a well-known proverb: 'In a war between elephants, it's the grass that gets trampled. We are the grass' (Interview, Gisenyi prison, 25 September 2000).

Far from being unable to understand what RTLM was exhorting them to do, though, these perpetrators offer ample evidence that they understood the radio's message and that they themselves *were*, in fact, a specifically targeted audience, precisely because they were seen as being on the margins of ethnic politics and not naturally inclined to take up arms against their Tutsi neighbours. In other words, the radio messages were needed to involve them in killings that many were not initially inclined to perform. The interviews offer further emphasis against the primordial hypothesis.

> Q: Sure, I understand you. So, there is the issue … of RTLM? I would like to understand also how a radio announces something and people do it. Can you give me an example?
> A: In fact, I don't own a radio because I am a cultivator [*umuhinzi*]. From the fact that I was a cultivator, I had no radio. But in fact, [some people] used to say that radio RTLM was urging us [*idushishikarije*] to kill people … killings. It said: 'the enemy is Tutsi.' And when a peasant hears that, that person has no choice … When he meets a person he doesn't know, he says to himself: 'this is the one who came to eradicate us, he came to fight us.'... You understand that, this also brought a bad atmosphere [*umwuka mubi*; literally, bad air] among people. (Interview, Ruhengeri prison, 27 September 2000)

Another genocide confessor confirmed:

> A: RTLM? You mean that radio? People who owned radios are the ones who listened to it.
> Q: No, you can tell me what you heard from other people.
> A: The so-called radios [*ibyo biradiyo*] of RTLM … [implies a bad thing. With a dismissive tone, he looks away.] Except that they announced: 'find out who the enemy is.' Then they announced that: 'the Tutsi is the enemy.'
> (Interview, Gisenyi prison, 25 September 2000)

The same informant recalled a particular announcer on RTLM encouraging peasants to cultivate and to be armed and vigilant while waiting for the enemy from outside.

> Then they said: 'Look, while a Hutu is cultivating, he has a gun because they were distributed to them. You should have them with you when you are cultivating. When the enemy comes up, you shoot at each other. When he retreats, then you take up your hoe and cultivate!'... Such things were also announced. That is, they were doing sensitization about those things [*kubisansibiliza*] among peasants. They told them: 'Follow what the radio is saying.' (Interview, Gisenyi prison, 25 September 2000)

Did RTLM get its message of hatred across to different audiences to the same degree? Mindful of Spitulnik's idea of a mass-mediated community of active consumers or, put differently, with common reference points but the potential for different reactions to them, let us turn to the perpetrators' reflections about radio.

Beyond the initial claims of ignorance of RTLM's presence, its mission and its intended audience, a closer analysis of the perpetrators' reflections suggests that they had a clear understanding of what they were being told to do.

On 6 April 1994, when the president's plane was shot down, RTLM announced that Habyarimana had been killed by the RPF and that everyone in the country should stay where they were. In interview after interview, nearly every informant recalled this directive disseminated via the radio. Subsequently, RTLM, aka 'Radio *Rutwitsi*' (the radio that sets fire) encouraged the *Interahamwe* in their mission of defeating the *Inkotanyi* (Rwandan Patriotic Army). It emphasized the message that *all* Hutu were at risk of being attacked, overwhelmed, recolonized and exploited by *all* Tutsi and that appropriate measures should be taken to prevent this.

According to the interviewees, RTLM preached fear of and hatred toward Tutsi and told its listeners to avenge the 'head of the nation'. Some recalled that RTLM insisted that Hutu should separate themselves from Tutsi because of war. They remembered that the Tutsi were identified as their enemies, outsiders, invaders and cunning manipulators. They recalled that RTLM said that the only way to defend the nation in general, and one's own safety and security in particular, was to pre-emptively destroy not only the Rwandan Patriotic Front, but also every Tutsi, even the unborn.

> Don't you know that after Habyarimana's death, radios announced that: '*Inkotanyi* are barking ... *hohoohohooo*!!!' Also that: '*Inkotanyi* attacked before us. They [Tutsi] had said that they would kill Hutu and now they have pre-empted us. Women should go nowhere.' (Interview, Rilima prison, 21 September 2000)

Many of the perpetrators I spoke with expressed ambivalence about RTLM's message that 'cultivators' (understood to be synonymous with 'peasants') stood for all Hutu and the only legitimate Rwandans. One man stated: 'RTLM talked about Hutu as cultivators, the children of cultivators' (*Benesebahinzi*) and said that 'everyone should join in the violence against the enemy.' The enemy was not limited to the RPF alone. 'RTLM said that the enemy was your accomplice neighbour (*icyitso*), so you must be vigilant.'

To the extent that these perpetrators bring into the discussion the ideological conflation of the Hutu extremist elites with all Hutu and the rebel army of Tutsi exiles with all Tutsi, they are implicitly resisting the interpretation that the genocide was fundamentally rooted in primordial ethnic sentiments and hatred. In fact some explicitly stated the opposite:

> In fact, the way everything came up, we were not ... we appeared like people who did not know beforehand. We were all united together. We even started to fight what is known as *Interahamwe*. We were defeated later because *Interahamwe* had guns. At that point, they started convincing us [*kutwinjizamo*; literally, to push into us] that Tutsi are our enemies.
>
> We shared, we were the same, we intermarried [and] there was no problem between us. Then, it happened just like that, eh ... even when that radio RTLM was talking about 'ethnicity' [*ubwoko*], *Interahamwe* had already been killed in Kamonyi. They were killed by villagers and commune police. They were

fighting together … even bourgmester was fighting … fighting *Interahamwe* at Taba in Kamonyi.[2]

When RTLM broadcast that Tutsi have finished off Hutu, then we started being afraid. So, how did it happen? We noticed that it came from Runda. They came saying that … in fact, we spent the day on the hill waiting for *Interahamwe* in order to fight them. At around 3 p.m. people from Igihinga came and ordered us to eat cows belonging to other people. We took cows belonging to a Tutsi who was there. His cattle keeper had fled with them for security, but he lived in Runda. So, they forced us to eat them. Eeh! They then took four, we took three. Good. At dawn they came back and took another cow. Then they killed the first person. They killed him because of people from Igihinga. That is how things started and then it grew tougher [*ibintu birakomera*; literally, it became hardened, i.e., more serious] from there onwards. (Interview, Gitarama prison, 29 September 2000)

Informants suggest that the rhetoric of the radio implicitly acknowledged the lack of ethnic division among rural peasants. The messages recalled by the perpetrators seem designed to induce rural dwellers to break the bonds of neighbourhood solidarity (see also Longman 1995). Perhaps in an effort to appeal directly to those who were less willing to kill their neighbours, this rhetoric often took the form of agrarian metaphors:

The radio told us to clear the bushes. There was no person who did not hear that! (Interview, Gisenyi prison)

RTLM said to 'separate the grass from the millet' [i.e., weed out the Tutsi]. (Interview, Gisenyi prison, 25 September 2000)

Bikindi told people 'to pull out the poison ivy together with its roots.' (Interview, Gisenyi prison, 25 September 2000)

In another interview that began with denial, the informant shared euphemisms learned through lateral communication.

Q: Uuh, so, did you listen to RTLM radio in you area?
A: Radio, where?
Q: Uuh …
A: I didn't even own a radio then.
Q: No, you did not listen to radio RTLM. So, you didn't hear anything from other people. Is it the first time you hear about it?
A: RTLM?
Q: Uuh, of Kantano, etc. No … is this the first time you hear about it?
A: RTLM was that radio which broadcast hot news [*yashyushyaga amakuru*], telling people: 'Work!'[*Mukore*] I heard about it from what people told me, because I did not own a radio. Or from people in a place where I would be staying because I did not own a radio at that time.

Q: Uuuh, uuh, telling people to work [*gukora*]?
A: It told people to kill Tutsi. After all, wasn't [it] explained openly? … Through conversations with other people, I heard that [RTLM] had very hot news during that period of killings. (Interview, Butare prison, September 2000)

Although these comments buttress arguments about the power of radio to demonize, incite and perhaps even direct violence, they also yield evidence that as active (re)interpreters of RTLM's message, many ordinary peasants in the ranks of the low-level perpetrators did not swallow everything they heard whole. Even as they reflected on the role of the radio six years after the fact, these people make it clear that for most ordinary Rwandan peasants (*abaturage*), radio was viewed as a medium for the urban, the educated and the elite.[3] This resonates strongly with Spitulnik's argument that 'the communities mediated by radio broadcasting are several. Since media discourse is not uniformly accessible or even uniformly seized upon and interpreted in the same ways, all kinds of outcomes are possible' (Spitulnik 2001: 113).

Similarly, while some Rwandan villagers may have listened to broadcasts, many stated that they did not. They heard the messages from others, however, and understood the ideological significance of certain songs, speeches and the reporting of current events from others. Nevertheless, this information *alone* did not cause them to kill. It is, therefore, necessary to explore other reasons why these Rwandans took part in the genocide.

NOTES

1. The Connaissida Project in Kinshasa, in which I participated in 1985–98 highlighted the importance of *radio trottoir* in changing perceptions of AIDS.
2. Survivors' testimony collected by African Rights from Gikongoro and Butare prefectures also mentions initial flight and fighting by Hutu and Tutsi neighbours against *Interahamwe* from outside. The Hutu who were with them, they said, did not understand that only Tutsi were being targeted for killing (African Rights 1995: 329, 330, 332).
3. To some extent, however, it seems likely that some confessed perpetrators were seeking to distance themselves from the local rural elites who were leaders of genocide.

REFERENCES

African Rights. 1995. *Rwanda: Death, Despair and Defiance* (2nd edn.). African Rights, London, UK.

Anderson, B. 1983. *Imagined Communities*. Verso, London, UK.

Bourgault, L.M. 1995. *Mass Media in sub-Saharan Africa*. Indiana University Press, Bloomington, IN, USA: 201–3.

Carver, R. 1996. Speech delivered at the Annual General Meeting of the Freedom of Expression Institute, Johannesburg, South Africa, 23 May 1996.

—— 2000. 'Broadcasting and Political Transition: Rwanda and Beyond'. In R. Fardon and G. Furniss (eds). *African Broadcast Cultures: Radio in Transition*. David Philip, Capetown, South Africa. 239 pp.

Chalk, F. 1999. 'Hate Radio in Rwanda'. In H. Adelman and A. Suhrke (eds). 1999. *The Path of a Genocide: the Rwanda Crisis from Uganda to Zaire.* Transaction, New Brunswick, NJ, USA. 414 pp.

Chrétien, J.P., J.F. Dupaquier, M. Kabanda and J. Ngarambe. 1995. *Rwanda: les médias du génocide.* Karthala, Paris, France.

Des Forges, A. 1999. *Leave None to Tell the Story: Genocide in Rwanda.* Human Rights Watch and the International Federation of Human Rights Leagues, New York, NY, USA. Available at <www.hrw.org/reports/1999/rwanda/> (accessed 30 August 2005).

Longman, T. 1995. Genocide and Socio-Political Change: Massacres in Two Rwandan Villages. *Issues*, 23(2): 18–21.

Mandani, M. 2001. *When Victims become Killers.* Princeton University Press, Princeton, NJ, USA.

Schoepf, B.G. 1993. AIDS Action Research with Women in Kinshasa. *Social Science & Medicine*, 37(11): 1401–13.

Spitulnik, D. 1993. Anthropology and Mass Media. *Annual Review of Anthropology*, 22: 293–315.

—— 1996. The Social Circulation of Media Discourse and the Mediation of communities. *Journal of Linguistic Anthropology*, 6(2): 161–87.

—— 2001. 'The Social Circulation of Media Discourse and the Mediation of Communities'. In A. Duranti (ed.). *Linguistic Anthropology: a Reader*. Blackwell Publishers, Oxford, UK.

11
Journalism in a Time of Hate Media

Thomas Kamilindi

I have been a journalist in Rwanda for 20 years; the only time I stopped working was during the 1994 genocide. I think the first question we should ask is should journalists be put on trial? Should they be judged? My answer is yes. And that's why I chose to testify before the International Criminal Tribunal for Rwanda as a prosecution witness. I testified because I consider journalists to be citizens like any other members of society. They should be held accountable for their actions and if need be prosecuted. I also testified because of my belief that journalists have a major role to play for the good of society and should be held to account when, instead, they cause harm. Grave problems were created in my society. Evil took place and journalists played an important role.

Before dealing with my own experience, I think it is important to provide some background on the media in Rwanda, to place it in context. When we talk about the media, people in the West think in terms of what the news media are like in the Western world. That is simply not the case with Rwanda.

The written press has existed in Rwanda only since 1933, when the first newspaper was established – a newspaper still published by the Catholic Church, which is a very important institution in my country. Decades later, in the 1960s, a government newspaper was set up. Both of these were published in Kinyarwanda, my mother tongue and the native language of Rwanda. Other attempts to create newspapers were short-lived until 1991, when there was a kind of democratic explosion, and a large number of newspapers were established.

Until the creation of RTLM in 1993, there was only one radio station: the government-run Radio Rwanda, which began operations in 1961. Radio Rwanda was the voice of authority, and authority is respected in Rwanda. People are raised and taught to take what they hear on the radio as gospel truth.

In 1992, the first television station emerged and remains the only one. It too belongs to the government.

RTLM (Radio-Télévision Libre des Milles Collines) was created in 1993 by people who were, for the most part, close to or from the stronghold of President Habyarimana. They presented it as a commercial venture. Indeed, to be a member, it was necessary to purchase a share valued at 5,000 Rwandan francs (RWF), about US$ 30 at the time. But RTLM's programming was not commercial; it was all about politics and centred on ethnic cleavages. RTLM followed directly from *Kangura*, the extremist newspaper created by a former bus driver, Hassan Ngeze. *Kangura* was backed by financiers who were well placed in the army and the civil administration. It is known particularly for its publication of the famous Hutu 'Ten Commandments'.

No one succeeded in combating these hate media in Rwanda. They were very powerful and entrenched with those who held power – in the military, in government and in business. Even the information minister, Faustin Rucogoza, failed in his efforts to sanction or close down these hate media outlets. He was among the first assassinated by the *Interahamwe* militia, on the morning of 7 April 1994.

As a simple journalist, the only weapon I had was to report the facts and only verifiable facts. But even that was difficult because it brought me many problems.

In 1991, I was suspended from my job at Radio Rwanda. I learned later that this suspension was intended to be permanent. But I managed to get my job back, thanks to some good legal work by a friend who was a lawyer and also because of intense diplomatic and political pressure on President Habyarimana, who was the ultimate authority for Radio Rwanda.

In 1992, the head of the Conseil d'Administration of l'ORINFOR (Office Rwandais d'Information), which was responsible for all of the state-owned media in Rwanda (Radio Rwanda, Télévision Nationale Rwandaise and the written press), called me into his office. He told me I was going to be arrested and that he couldn't protect me. This was after broadcasts I had made about an attempted coup against the prime minister of the day. Once again, I was saved by political and diplomatic pressure, because the coup attempt was very real.

Another way to fight against hate media as a journalist is to have no part of it. In my case, I could have bought shares in RTLM because it was the first private radio station that was going to break the monopoly of the state; to support it could have been seen as supporting the emergence of pluralism in the media. But I did not get involved because I saw who the real instigators of this new station were. The editor-in-chief, Gaspard Gahigi, who had been my boss at Radio Rwanda, asked me many times to come and work with him at RTLM. He said I was a good journalist who could add a lot of credibility to the new station. But time and again I refused because I would not use my professional talent or influence to stigmatize the Tutsi.

Then, in April 1994, came the genocide. What could the media have done? The media are not there to fight, but to set things right, to provide accurate information. Instead, there was much propaganda and people received messages of hate. You simply cannot imagine it.

For example, on 3 May 1994, the United Nations Assistance Mission for Rwanda (UNAMIR) came looking for a group of us at the Hotel Mille Collines. We were about 40 and UNAMIR wanted to evacuate us from the country. We hadn't even left the lobby of the hotel when RTLM began to broadcast a list of our names, including that of my daughter and even a newborn child. RTLM called on the *Interahamwe* not to allow these *inyenzi* to be evacuated by UNAMIR, because 'they would come back with weapons in their hands'. In fact, the militia blocked us on the road to the airport. We were attacked and some of us were injured. In the end, after many hours of negotiations, UNAMIR brought us back safely to the hotel.

I have a daughter. She's twelve now but she was very small at the time. One day, somebody said, 'That one is a snake. They have to kill her.' She wasn't even two years old. My daughter asked me, 'Am I a snake? Am I a snake?' Is that the role of the press? Is it the role of the media to harm people?

Imagine journalists who would enthusiastically applaud militia for the good work they had done at such and such a location. The journalists from RTLM did this each time a Tutsi family was killed. And they regarded as cowards the militiamen and soldiers who did not have as much zeal for the massacres.

It was a hard time to work as a journalist. In fact it seemed as if the only journalists who could function properly were the ones who were in the camp of the killers. I wasn't in their camp, so I had to give up my job. But there were still ways to be a journalist – someone who bears witness to events and informs others.

I resigned from Radio Rwanda a few months before the genocide started and, as it happened, my last day was 6 April. In a sense, I think I knew what was coming. As a journalist, I had been asked to broadcast news that was repugnant to me.

Radio Rwanda was in effect the voice of President Habyarimana. It was difficult to do truly professional work as we were constantly faced with demands from the authorities on the manner in which we should work, right down to the formulation of a phrase.

I recall one time when the director of ORINFOR came to the studio with a text that he had written about a meeting of the central committee of the president's party – the only party allowed at the time – the MRND (*Mouvement Républicain National pour la Democratie et le Développement*). Instead of reading this statement word for word, as he wished, I reworked the text. I hadn't even left the studio after the broadcast when the phones began to ring. The members of the central committee, including their leader, the upper ranks of the army and the director of ORINFOR were furious with me and some insulted me personally.

In 1992, we rebelled against this situation. The journalists of Radio Rwanda organized a series of strikes and I was appointed to head this protest movement. It was following these strikes, which resulted in many threats against me, that I decided to leave Radio Rwanda because it seemed impossible for me to bring about any change. The pro-Habyarimana forces had an enormous influence.

During the massacres that followed President Habyarimana's death in the plane crash on 6 April, I was among many liberal Hutus accused of sympathizing with the Tutsi-led rebel forces of the Rwandan Patriotic Front (RPF).

I had grown up Hutu. That is what was marked on my identity card. But I was born to a Hutu mother and a Tutsi father, who had taken steps to change his ethnicity in 1959 (he was 21 years old at the time) to survive the first pogroms against Tutsis. I was born in the south of the country, considered at the time to be a largely Tutsi region and later supportive of the RPF. I was married to a woman whose parents were also in a mixed marriage. These conditions, among many other factors, meant that after 6 April, I was one of the targets of the Hutu militia, directed notably by RTLM. Journalists like Kantano and Bemeriki who knew me very well didn't hesitate to say over the air, 'Does Kamilindi think the Mille Collines hotel is a bunker?' They revealed to the militia where I was in hiding and how to find me.

As it happened, on the evening of 6 April, I was in high spirits. My wife, Jacqueline, had baked a cake for a festive dinner at our home in Kigali. It was my 33rd birthday and that afternoon I had completed my last day of work at Radio Rwanda. After ten years at the government radio station, I had resigned in protest against the lack of political balance in news programming.

I remember very clearly, I was taking a shower that evening when Jacqueline began pounding on the bathroom door. 'Hurry up!' she shouted. 'The president has been attacked!' I locked the doors of the house and sat by the radio listening to RTLM. Of course I detested RTLM's violent propaganda, but the way things were going in Rwanda, that propaganda often served as a highly accurate political forecast.

RTLM reported that President Habyarimana's plane, returning from Dar es Salaam, Tanzania, had been shot down over Kigali and had crashed into the grounds of his own palace. The new Hutu president of Burundi and several of Habyarimana's top advisors had also been on board. There were no survivors.

In the days before, I had heard through sources about preparations for large-scale massacres of Tutsis nationwide by the president's extremist entourage and about lists of moderate Hutu that had been drawn up for the first wave of killings. But I never imagined that Habyarimana himself might be targeted. I thought to myself, if Hutu Power had sacrificed him, who was safe?

Along with 700 others, I took refuge in the Mille Collines hotel, where manager Paul Rusesabagina negotiated to save our lives, using the liquor from the hotel basement to buy off bands of killers who showed up with lists of victims. Leaving the hotel meant you risked dying.

But, as I said, as a journalist, there are many ways in which you can work. As a refugee at the Mille Collines, I asked people, 'What are you doing so that people will know that you're here?' They said, 'We're not doing anything.' So I worked with other refugees who had contacts, like François-Xavier Nsanzuwera. He was a human rights activist and had a lot of fax numbers, telephone numbers, all sorts of contacts. We sent fax after fax, one on top of the other when the telephone worked. We informed the world of what was happening. That was how we spoke out. We did something.

There has been a lot of discussion about the role of the international media. For the most part, the international media weren't there. On 12 April 1994, all foreigners were evacuated. All international public servants, aid workers, journalists – they were all evacuated. The genocide began in earnest in those first two weeks and nobody knew anything about it. It was done in secrecy at a time when what we needed were a few courageous people to come and report on this country – this country, which, for many news organizations, didn't seem to exist.

But there was no structure left. You can't imagine what it was like. By the time the world began to learn about what was happening in Rwanda, it was too late. Thousands and thousands of people were killed. I can't help thinking that if the media had been there, maybe the harm would have been less.

In their absence, I took it upon myself to try and get the word out. On 26 April, when the telephones were briefly restored, I called some friends at Radio France International (RFI) in Paris and I said, 'We're still alive.' They said, 'We have no news, what's going on? Can we interview you? Can you explain to us what's going on?' I said, 'Yes.'

So they asked me how we were living, how many of us were there. I told them there were about 700 refugees, and we were drinking water from the swimming pool, the same pool the soldiers were using to wash their clothes and which eventually turned into a toilet. We had to drink that water without being able to boil it.

They asked me, 'What's going on in military terms?' I said that government forces were, in fact, losing ground. There were defeats everywhere. I spoke about the massacres, although as I explained to them, they were indescribable. There were no words to use.

As a journalist, I wanted the world to know about the atrocities taking place inside Rwanda. I probably signed my own death warrant by calling attention to the massacres during the RFI interview.

After that, local radio started calling the Hotel Mille Collines a home for 'cockroaches'. I was told they were coming for me. But the others there stopped me from giving myself up. I wanted to go out because I was the source of the problem and I thought that if I left, maybe they wouldn't kill the others. If I were to be killed, maybe the others wouldn't be bombed.

The day after that interview was broadcast, a soldier arrived at the hotel to kill me. But as was often the case in the genocide where most people knew their killers, the man who had been sent to kill me had been a friend since childhood. He explained that the military command wanted me dead. Then he said, in effect, 'I don't know who's going to kill you. I can't do it. But I'm leaving the hotel and they'll send someone for sure to kill you.' Nobody else came for me, at least not to my knowledge. Some years later I heard Paul Rusesabagina say in a radio interview that an army colonel had come to see him at one point to establish whether I was alive. Paul refused to tell him anything, then negotiated with the soldiers, gave them drinks and, in the process, saved my life.

It became clear to me that the message I managed to get out through RFI was something that the government didn't want the world to know. If the media had played its role, things probably wouldn't have happened the way they did.

At another point, when I was facing death, they gave me a piece of paper and a pen and told me to write. I wrote to my wife saying I loved her, that she should be strong and look after the children and that I was leaving everything behind for her spiritually and materially. That was one of three times that I was nearly killed; that time, the soldiers who had come to kill me allowed me to write a message before putting the gun to my head.

My wife was pregnant with our third child, and I wrote, if God wishes, you will have the baby. By that time I didn't know about my firstborn because she was not with us. I mentioned my three children and told my wife to start her life again if she survived. I said don't be alone, carry on, keep going.

The soldier told everyone to get back because he was going to finish me off. Curiously, I was not scared. I was prepared for death. It was like a dream. This guy cocked the pistol and just then miraculously a tank arrived while the gun was at my temple. It was like a movie. The commander in the tank shouted 'Thomas what's going on?' I turned to look at him and said 'They want to kill me.'

The commander stopped the killing. But while I survived, my firstborn daughter did not. I later discovered that she had been murdered while on a visit to her grandparents.

It is very difficult to put my life experiences behind me and to forget. My wife and I live with it all the time. It is part of me. Sometimes I shut myself in a room and cry when I think about my little girl. It's difficult when you know you could have been killed and you survived, but your child was killed. Every time I go to the memorial sites and see the skulls, I can't help myself. When I look at them, I cry because I remember my daughter. Maybe her skull is somewhere, but I don't know where.

But I cannot give up my career as a journalist because life has to go on. I have to keep living. After all, I survived. I returned to full-time journalism in December 1994, once the phone lines in Rwanda started to work again and I was able to do freelance work for foreign news outlets. Since then I've worked for Voice of America and the BBC. I think one of the reasons I have to continue my work as a journalist is so that I can contribute toward preventing genocide from ever happening again.

I do believe that despite the genocide and the media's role in inciting the mass violence, there is still a new generation who want to become journalists. I have spoken to students and they have sought my advice. But there are still many troubling questions. How does a journalist become a criminal? It's extremely difficult to answer that question, because journalists are human like everyone else. Sometimes reporters think they are supermen or women, but we are human beings. We have feelings like everyone else, and we are members of society. We can be caught up in the circle of violence like anyone else. We can identify with the group responsible for violence. That is why, as reporters, we should be more objective.

In April 2003, I was in Côte d'Ivoire as a guest at a seminar on 'Conflict, Peace and Media', and I spoke to journalists about what we lived through in Rwanda. I said that certain reporters participated in the violence, while others spoke out against it. I reminded them that 48 journalists had been killed in Rwanda because they spoke out. The reporters in Côte d'Ivoire asked me, 'How can we know if what we're doing is wrong?' They didn't know the answer to that question. Some of them had already gone too far. They had become part of the hate media without knowing it. So I told them, 'look at what you write. Listen to what you say, and analyze yourself. If you are demonizing people, if you are stigmatizing other tribes, other clans, you're involved in violence.'

'How did you go this far,' I asked. They didn't know. So I said, 'You're no longer reporters. You're no longer journalists, and I would like to congratulate the politicians who managed to co-opt you, and co-opt you without your knowing it. I congratulate these politicians. They're good politicians, very effective. Now stand up and be reporters, do your job, report the facts objectively.' And one of them replied, 'Well there was a politician who has said we want Côte d'Ivoire for the people from Côte d'Ivoire. Can we repeat that?' Well yes, you can say that, you can say that this politician said that. You can report that, and public opinion will know how to react to this politician. You can report the facts, but don't get involved.

I have to admit, it's hard to know as a reporter when you've taken the wrong turn. All I can say is, be brave and stand up for your work.

Part Two

International Media Coverage of the Genocide

12
Reporting the Genocide

Mark Doyle

It was late April 1994. I was in Kigali, doing a question-and-answer session with a BBC presenter in London and the presenter asked me to clarify what all this shooting and killing was about. I found myself saying,

> Look you have to understand that there are two wars going on here. There's a shooting war and a genocide war. The two are connected, but also distinct. In the shooting war, there are two conventional armies at each other, and in the genocide war, one of those armies – the government side with help from civilians – is involved in mass killings.

That may seem simplistic, but I think it is a useful way of understanding what happened.

I am writing about my own experiences reporting the war and the genocide for the BBC, filing both radio and television reports. Normally based in Nairobi, Kenya, I spent much of the 100 days after 6 April 1994 reporting from Rwanda, at times, as one of the only Western reporters still in the capital. In this paper, I won't draw comparisons with other media reporting, because, quite frankly, I was so busy during those 100 days that I didn't catch much of it. But I think it is important to go into some detail about what I did before I started reporting on the genocide *as genocide.*

I have to admit that during the first few days, I, like others, got the story terribly wrong. Down on the ground, up-close – if you could get close enough, safely enough – it did look at first like chaos. I said so. I used the word chaos. What I could see clearly in the first few days was the shooting war between the Rwandan Patriotic Front (RPF) and the government, and the dead bodies. It was not clear who had killed whom, not at first, and the shooting war appeared chaotic with shifting front lines, a lot of noise and a lot of red hot lead flying around.

In a way, the shooting war was easy to describe. The genocide war took a little longer to confirm. But I got there in the end. In fact, looking back now at the scripts of my reports broadcast on the BBC, within little more than a week of the beginning of the killing on 6–7 April, there were clear references to government-backed massacres of ethnic Tutsis and Hutu opponents of the regime. In other words, within the first few weeks of the killing, there was reportage from the field sketching out the true nature of the massacres.

My focus here will be on what I know best: the reporting I did on the ground.

My first two trips to Rwanda were in late 1993 and early 1994, before the genocide. The installation of the broad-based transitional government was continually postponed. I didn't really understand why this was happening until I visited an African embassy in Kigali and asked the ambassador if he would give me an off-the-record briefing on the political situation. I can't identify which ambassador it was, of course, because he spoke off the record.

This ambassador astonished me by not only explaining in some detail and very frankly how the various extremist Hutu parties were blocking the installation of the power-sharing government, but also by keeping me there, in his private office, for more than four hours.

I was a bit embarrassed at first. I didn't even have an appointment. But every time I looked at my watch or started to leave, the ambassador said, 'No no, sit down. I want to make sure the BBC understands this – do you understand it? Do you realize now what is going on and how dangerous it is?' Thanks to that ambassador, I was just beginning to realize.

The ambassador kept me so long because he was frustrated that the world didn't seem to be paying attention to Rwanda or realizing the dangers. When I left his office he said something like 'Don't forget Rwanda, Mark, something big could happen here.'

There are some events that make us all remember exactly what we were doing at the time. For my parents' generation, it was John F. Kennedy's assassination. For me, it was the day the plane carrying Rwandan President Juvénal Habyarimana and President Cyprien Ntaryamira of Burundi was brought down – late on the evening of 6 April 1994.

I was working late in the BBC office in Nairobi. At about 11 p.m., the phone rang. It was one of the editors in London, a man by the name of David Eades, who is now a BBC-TV presenter. David said they were getting news agency reports that a plane carrying the presidents of Burundi and Rwanda had crashed. I remember with crystal clarity what I said. 'Oh my God,' I said, remembering the ambassador's warning. 'Oh my God, this is going to be a huge story!' David was taken aback by my response.

I told David I had to go to Rwanda immediately, because this event was going to have major ramifications.

That night, I filed a report based on information that I could gather by phone from Nairobi, citing information from United Nations (UN) and diplomatic sources and residents on the ground in Rwanda.

My first report focused, not surprisingly, on the reports of the plane crash and 'urgent discussions' between the UN commander, Roméo Dallaire, and members of the Rwandan government.

The next day, the machinery was set in motion. Colleagues from Reuters news agency chartered a plane from Nairobi to Mbarara in southern Uganda and I bought a seat. Kigali airport was closed, of course, so that destination was out of the question. Heading for northern Rwanda, for the RPF-held zone, seemed the best way to get some sort of angle on the story immediately. It took us most of the day and night to get to Mbarara, then most of the next day to reach Kabale on the Uganda–Rwanda border. After many hours waiting at the border, we negotiated entry into the RPF-held zone and Paul Kagame's headquarters in the manager's offices of an old tea estate in Mulindi in northern Rwanda.

My memory of arriving there has a digital clarity. I remember looking down from the hill where Kagame had his headquarters, down to the old, long-abandoned tea plantations. The field of bright green tea bushes was in such stark contrast to the dark green trees around the edges of the valley that the expanse of tea looked like a placid lake of green water.

I stayed for a couple of days near Mulindi and saw the start of the shooting war between the RPF lines just north of the town of Byumba and the government lines on the outskirts of the town. On 8 April, I reported on an interview with the RPF Secretary General Theogene Rudasingwa, who said the RPF intended to take military and political action to restore order in Kigali and throughout Rwanda. A report on 9 April, from Byumba, focused on the RPF attack against government troops and the RPF plan to send a detachment into Kigali to shore up the rebel garrison there. I signed off this way:

> The strategic outcome of the current hostilities is impossible to predict, but it's a certainty that the ordinary Rwandan people, who have suffered years of ethnic and political violence, will be adversely affected in the short term.

When it became clear from what I saw around Byumba that the shooting war had started again in earnest, I decided I had to try to get to Kigali. There was no way I could get through those front lines and travel south toward the capital by land, so I took a risk and went back north into Uganda, driving through the night to Entebbe airport.

By an extraordinary fluke and some negotiations, a few other journalists and I met an aid worker at the airport who had a plane, which he was going to fly from Entebbe to Kigali. It was half empty, except for some food supplies, and he agreed to give us a lift. Again, I don't think I'll tell you the aid worker's name, because he got into a furious argument with General Dallaire when he turned up in Kigali, unannounced, with a planeful of journalists.

I don't think General Dallaire was in a particularly good mood at the time. After months of asking for more and better troops for his UN mission and being told none were available, he suddenly saw hundreds of them arrive, but not to help in his mission of pacifying Rwanda, but to take part in an entirely different mission – saving expatriates.

The scene at Kigali airport was extraordinary. The shooting war was clearly in full flow. We could hear constant small arms and mortar fire from inside the town. At night, we could see tracers and explosions. On the apron of the airfield, there were numerous French, Italian and Belgian military planes disgorging European paratroopers who had come to save European lives.

I spent a few nights sleeping on the airport floor and eating French military rations – which are, by the way, infinitely superior to those of most other countries. By day, I went on short trips with the French military as they drove into town to rescue French and other European citizens. I went on these trips not because I thought rescuing Europeans was the main story, but because it was the only story I could cover safely, or at least relatively safely. It was the only way I could get into town to see what was going on. No one in their right mind would have voluntarily gone into the city of Kigali in those early days without a serious armed escort.

On 11 April, I filed this report from Kigali:

> The capital of Rwanda is in chaos. Three main military groups are contesting positions in the centre of the city: the rebel Rwandan Patriotic Front and two components of the government forces, regular army troops and elements of the Presidential Guard, loyal to the late head of state. Reinforcements [plural] for the rebels are moving towards Kigali from their stronghold in the north. In addition to those military forces, various militias are settling ethnic and political scores, which broadly reflect animosity between the Hutu and Tutsi tribes. But this is not just a tribal war. The Hutu are split politically and former neighbours are now at each other's throats. I have definite evidence that at least a dozen people were killed this morning. The total for those few hours alone is certainly many more. An experienced aid worker said tens of thousands of people had died in the last five days. Foreign residents are being evacuated from Rwanda in an air bridge to Nairobi and other regional capitals. The United Nations forces, which came here to monitor a ceasefire between government and rebels, have found themselves in the middle of a vicious war. Loud explosions, believed to be mortar fire, could be heard sporadically throughout the day near the airport compound, which is controlled by UN forces and French troops brought here to evacuate their nationals. It is not thought that the airport is being targeted, but it is close to positions held by the three main military groups.

It was on one of those evacuation trips with the French military that I realized something other than just the shooting war was going on. Standing on the back of a truck I looked down to see a Rwandan man attacking another Rwandan, in the head, with a screwdriver, clearly intent on killing him. I saw several dead bodies of people who had been killed with machetes. Colleagues at the other end of the convoy of trucks saw someone being attacked with machetes. The French soldiers controlling the convoy just drove past all these incidents, heading for the house of a European who was to be rescued.

In a contribution to another news package broadcast 11 April, I filed this report:

> As the convoy left the airport to collect its mainly Belgian passengers, snaking its way through outlying suburbs and farms, I counted three recently killed people, probably Rwandans, lying in a pool of blood. Large groups of men armed with clubs and machetes stood around. An hour later as the convoy returned, there were at least eight bodies. Reporters at the front of the convoy saw at least two people being hacked to death. The killing is continuing.

It wasn't until about a fortnight after the plane went down that we started piecing together a clear picture of what happened starting on the night of 6 April. We all know now, of course, thanks to the various inquiries, that the *Interahamwe* and the army set up roadblocks within hours or even minutes of the signal, if it was a signal, of the plane going down. And we all know now the purpose of those roadblocks.

In a live interview on 12 April, I relayed news that the interim government of Rwanda had reportedly fled to Gitarama and that thousands of refugees were apparently leaving Kigali by road, heading south in the direction of Burundi. Another report that day quoted Dallaire as confirming that the RPF force sent down from the north had now linked up with the RPF battalion based in Kigali.

A report from 13 April focused on the fight for Kigali:

> The battle for Kigali continues. Small arms, automatic weapons and grenades are being used as rebel and government forces struggle for advantage. On Tuesday (April 12), the UN commander in Rwanda said the rebel forces were not encountering strong resistance. However, there was heavy fighting at dawn on Wednesday. The conflict began when the president's plane was shot down seven days ago. The president's supporters blamed rival tribal and ethnic groups and the massacres of civilians began. Tens of thousands of people were killed and hundreds of thousands displaced by the unrest. Now the fighting has a more military aspect with two highly trained armies attacking each other. The rebels say they are fighting to restore order in Kigali and then in the longer term to introduce democracy to Rwanda. The government army may be fighting for its own survival. The government it was supposed to be protecting fled on Tuesday for a regional town. Different groups are in charge of various parts of Kigali, while much of the population has fled. Whichever group comes out on top will have to manage a huge humanitarian crisis. Over a million people were critically short of food before the Rwandan civil war resumed because of drought and earlier conflict. Hundreds of thousands of others will now be dependent on food aid.

Later the same day, in a report about ceasefire negotiations, I referred to the RPF contention that it had no interest in a ceasefire 'while innocent people were being killed in Kigali'. I reported on:

> … rebel allegations that thousands of political opponents of the late president, who died when his plane was shot down last week, have been systematically murdered by the government army and militias loyal to the former head of state. These allegations are supported by numerous eyewitnesses. However, the RPF advance has also undoubtedly led to many deaths. The main army base in western Kigali and the area that surrounds it is still firmly in government hands. The streets around the base are patrolled by government soldiers in armoured cars and tanks. Several evacuated foreign embassies in the zone are untouched by looters. In other parts of the west of the city, however, thugs

mounting roadblocks are continuing to kill people they consider to be their ethnic or political opponents.

Many reports, including my own, made reference to the 'tribal' nature of the conflict and militias settling scores. But the outlines of genocide began to appear in news reports, even before we first used the word to describe the killing. Here is a report from 14 April that began with the sound of gunfire:

> One of the many front lines in Kigali. The city is now divided into rebel and government-held zones. Where there aren't soldiers from one side or the other, militias with machetes and clubs rule the streets. Neighbourhood boundaries are defined by roadblocks, often with piles of bodies next to them. Militias loyal to the government have killed many ethnic Tutsis. Militias loyal to the rebels have killed Hutus. Before the rebels came to Kigali a few days ago, what appears to have been a deliberate plan by Hutu militias to massacre Tutsis or rebel supporters was instigated – thousands were executed by bullet or by knife. There have been some reports that rebel soldiers are taking revenge. This afternoon, a reliable eyewitness saw an RPF soldier force five people into a house and shoot them dead. The rebels hold positions near the United Nations headquarters and several other areas. The government holds the western zone, where empty foreign embassies stand, positions around the airport and other areas. The deafening sound of gunfire and mortar echo around the misty valleys of this once beautiful city. The sickening stench of bodies on the streets is common, despite the mass graves – some containing thousands of bodies – which have been filling up. The United Nations operation in Rwanda was helpless as the carnage gathered pace. Now its commander, General Dallaire, is shuttling between the two sides trying to arrange a meeting, which might lead to a ceasefire. The rebels have vowed to capture the whole city, but they have failed to take several key points because of government resistance. The battle for the Rwandan capital continues.

On 15 April, I reported on the decision by the International Committee of the Red Cross to suspend its operations in Rwanda following an attack on a Red Cross ambulance, during which six wounded being carried in the ambulance were killed at a roadblock. The report also noted the continued intensity of the military battle:

> The fighting is fierce. Mortar and heavy-calibre automatic weapons were heard at various times throughout the night. Tens of thousands of people have been killed in the last week in clashes, which have involved tribal militias at least as much as regular government and rebel troops. The capital of Rwanda is anarchic. UN peacekeepers have failed to stop the fighting but are trying at least to organize a meeting between the two sides.

Another report on 15 April painted a more detailed picture of the suffering on the ground:

> The displaced people I have been able to see in the capital are undoubtedly but a drop in the ocean of human suffering caused by the political and military unrest. Five thousand Rwandans have taken refuge in a football stadium in which Bangladeshi UN soldiers are billetted and a similar number fled to a UN hospital. Thousands more are in churches or in other places of refuge. The 5,000 displaced in the main Kigali football stadium are being protected by the Bangladeshis, but have very little food, no running water and no medical supplies. Many of them were wounded in the fighting or are suffering from malaria and other easily preventable diseases. There are several Rwandan doctors in the football stadium, but they have no drugs or bandages. The Bangladeshis have shared some of their combat rations with the refugees. At a makeshift clinic under one of the main spectator stands, a Rwandan volunteer was handing out small sachets of apricot jam to sick people. 'It's all we've got,' he said. 'I know it's not medicine but I've got to give them something.' With almost all United Nations civilians and other aid personnel evacuated from Rwanda, there are virtually no foreign aid organizations here to address the catastrophe caused by the war. The main exception is the International Committee of the Red Cross, but even this organization has had considerable difficulties operating. Several aid groups are said to be standing by in Nairobi to bring in much-needed food and medical supplies, but until the fighting dies down and airport security is guaranteed by the UN, aid flights can't come in. The UN force commander said improving airport security was one of his top priorities.

My reports over the next few days focused on the withdrawal of Belgian troops, the appointment of Augustin Bizimungu as the new Rwandan army chief of staff, the government's claim that two million people had been displaced by the fighting and the intense battle for strategic hilltops south of Kigali.

But a dispatch on 16 April, about attempts at ceasefire talks, cited senior UN officers who said the killing of the president's political opponents began soon after the 6 April plane crash:

> The immediate aim of the talks is clearly a ceasefire so a semblance of order can be restored to the capital. Currently, apart from the two warring military sides, there are militias, bandits and looters on the streets. Near-anarchy prevails and hundreds of thousands of people have been displaced by the war. There is no effective government and the RPF rebels don't recognize the interim administration, which has now fled the capital and is based in the town of Butare in the south. Meanwhile, for the first time since the president's plane was brought down over a week ago, a clearer picture is emerging of what United Nations peacekeepers think happened after the crash. Senior UN officers say massacres of the president's political opponents from both Tutsi and Hutu tribes began just a few minutes after the plane was brought down. UN officers said they appealed to the presidential guard to stop the killing, but failed. According to the UN officers, it was this mass killing which prompted the rebels to break out of their United Nations designated

> cantonment to mount what the rebels described as a rescue mission. The city is now divided into government and rebel-held zones which ethnic and political militias are protecting as a first line of defence. UN military officers said the rebels were also fighting for the northern towns of Ruhengeri and Byumba, which are held by government soldiers but which have come under rebel shelling. The UN asked for a pause in the shelling, so it could pull back some of its units to the capital.

A report the next day, 17 April, repeated the summary, by stating:

> It's estimated that tens of thousands of people have been killed in Kigali since the president's plane was brought down by still unknown gunmen. First the president's supporters massacred his political opponents, then the rebels marched on the city and military clashes began …

An 18 April report gave some credence to the Rwandan army claim that the RPF had rounded up 250 civilians and killed them. But the report also stated that:

> Most independent eyewitness accounts of killings in the Rwandan capital in the last few weeks have accused government soldiers and militias loyal to the government of killing political opponents in very large numbers. The presidential guard in particular is accused of massacring ethnic Tutsis and Hutu members of political parties opposed to the late president who died when his plane was shot down almost two weeks ago by unknown gunmen.

Another file that day contained this reference: 'Camps full of ethnic Tutsis, fleeing violence from government-sponsored ethnic Hutu militias, are said by Rwandan army officers to have been created in several parts of the country.'

In a 19 April report about the withdrawal of UN military observers, I stated that:

> On the streets leading to the main government army base, militias armed with machetes are directed by soldiers and form a first line of defence against rebels and rebel sympathizers, who are often taken by the militia to include any ethnic Tutsis.

Monitoring events from Nairobi on 20 April, I reported that 'thousands of people have been killed with machetes and clubs by the government militia, who have targeted opposition sympathizers and members of the minority Tutsi tribe who dominate the rebels forces.'

And again on 22 April, I made a reference to 'militias loyal to the memory of the Rwandan president who was killed in a plane crash two weeks ago. The militias are killing political and ethnic opponents of the late president in large numbers.' The same tone permeates my 23 April report, once again from Kigali, which is bolstered by information from the Red Cross:

> Massacres of ethnic or political opponents of the late president, who died in a plane crash which rekindled the war, are continuing. Most of the massacres are committed by militias loyal to the late president's memory – sometimes with government army soldiers present. The Red Cross estimates that up to 100,000 people have been killed in the past two weeks.

My report from Kigali on 24 April painted a clear picture of what was happening on the ground:

> It's difficult to imagine the scale of the human disaster in Rwanda unless you've seen some of the many piles of bodies heaped on the streets of Kigali and on roadsides in the rural areas. There is little dignity for the main victims of this war which General Dallaire reluctantly believes still has some time to run. The Canadian commander is keeping lines of communication open, is protecting those civilians that he can and is working hard for a ceasefire. But he said it was not clear to him that the tactical aims of the two armies had yet been achieved. Most of the killing is being done not by soldiers or rebels, but by machete-wielding militias who seek out ethnic and political opponents. The worst killing so far has been in the capital and the worst culprits have been militias opposed to the ethnic group from which the rebels are drawn, the Tutsi. Other political opponents from the Hutu tribe have also been killed. While this slaughter continues, there is a more conventional war between the government and rebel armies taking place …

Short of using the word genocide, my report from Kigali on 26 April, echoing charges levelled by Amnesty International, challenged the notion that the killing was a simple tribal conflict.

> Amnesty's main charge is that the killings have been part of a deliberate political plan, rather than pure tribal violence. The main culprits, according to the human rights organisation, have been supporters of the late president who have systematically executed known or suspected opponents of his former rule. This thesis fits broadly with the facts. It was only a matter of minutes after the late night plane crash three weeks ago before elements of the former leader's presidential guard began killing opponents of their late head of state. By morning the next day, militias loyal to President Habyarimana's party were on the streets seeking out opposition sympathizers. They included members of the Tutsi tribe, from which the rebels draw most of their support and ethnic Hutus from opposition parties. According to the International Committee of the Red Cross, up to 100,000 people have been killed. Despite the undoubted political motivation behind many of the killings, it is nevertheless probable that the majority of those to have died are Tutsi. Politics and ethnicity are inextricably linked in Rwanda. While many Rwandan intellectuals, particularly

opponents of the former president's military rule oppose tribal politics, it is still a factor in most political calculations and is likely to be for some time to come.

Looking back through my reports, it appears I didn't use the word 'genocide' until 29 April, in a report filed from Nairobi that noted that the British aid agency Oxfam had described the killing in Rwanda as 'genocide'. But my reports had for some time been replete with references to the massacres of Tutsi civilians and moderate Hutus by government-backed militias.

After that, as it became clear to me what was happening, I used the word genocide more often. But one of the problems we faced in reporting the genocide as genocide – apart from, of course, confirming the facts on the ground – was that it took the rest of the world, including some of my editors in London, some time to take it in. I'm not saying I was censored, or anything like that. Far from it. I think every word I sent to London was rebroadcast. But the BBC often uses sources of information and interviewees other than its own correspondents on the ground. That's quite right and healthy, of course, but it sometimes meant parts of the BBC were at odds with what I was saying.

The first problem was a general one. There is a general tendency to portray Africa as chaotic, the Dark Continent, and so on. Sometimes indeed, it is very dark. It was in Rwanda in 1994. But Rwanda was not, after a while, chaotic or impenetrable. It was, as we now know, a very well planned political and ethnic genocide. That didn't really fit the media image of chaotic Africa and various things flowed from that.

For example, I used to take regular calls from BBC editors in London asking me to make sure I 'put the other side'. The implication, of course, was that the RPF must be killing as many as the *Interahamwe* and the government army, and that I should be reporting this. During calls like this, I had to control my inner fury at the implication that I was somehow biased. But, from a London perspective, I could see why they were asking the question. I told them what I knew, that this was not a balanced picture in terms of killings, and that was that – whether it fitted what we might have expected or not. My editors trusted me and used my material, but I still had a feeling they were a bit uneasy.

Sometimes, if I took my eye off the ball and didn't carefully monitor the output from London, I found that BBC newsrooms in London would revert to using phrases like 'chaos' and 'indiscriminate mass killings'. It wasn't chaotic, on the whole, and it wasn't, on the whole, indiscriminate. I sometimes found myself sending my editors what for me were highly unusual memos, not for broadcast, asking them please to stick to my words. In response they usually did.

I sent one such memo on 20 June, headed 'Rwanda/Guidance.' It read as follows:

> It is a very serious misrepresentation of the situation in Rwanda to describe the killings simply as 'the slaughter of civilians' or 'the mass killings,' without explaining who is killing whom. The vast majority of the hundreds of thousands of killings in Rwanda have been committed by the government

> militia and government army who have been implementing a well-organized plan of genocide of Tutsis, the tribe from which the rebels draw most support, and ethnic Hutu government opponents. These killings preceded, or coincided with, the military offensive by the main[ly] Tutsi Rwandan Patriotic Front rebels. The BBC should not fall into the trap of bland and misleading descriptions of Africans massacring Africans without explaining why, as the news agencies are doing most of the time. The killings in Rwanda are political as well as ethnic. A BBC correspondent who has spent much of the last three months in Rwanda says the government militia and the government armed forces are responsible for most of the bodies being found in mass graves in Rwanda and floating in rivers leading from Rwanda to Lake Victoria in Uganda.

Nevertheless, the 'spin doctors' sometimes won bizarre victories. In July 1994, a few dozen British and American soldiers arrived at Kigali airport to help distribute some aid. The United States and British army media relations staff promptly announced to the world, in keeping with the usual image of Western troops arriving in Africa, that they had 'taken control' of the airport. This was, of course, ridiculous. The RPF was by this time in control of almost the whole country, and had been in complete control of the airport for many weeks. A few lines of this 'taken control of the airport' rubbish crept into BBC news bulletins written in London. The phrase gave the desired impression, of course, that the United States and the United Kingdom had finally arrived to sort out the squabbling natives, when this was complete nonsense.

There were more serious attempts to 'balance' what was essentially an unbalanced story. A few weeks into the genocide, some RPF soldiers killed five churchmen. I'm not sure of the exact circumstances, but it was public knowledge soon afterward because the RPF leadership publicly denounced it. Newsrooms around the Western world seized on the killings with undisguised glee – it was as if here, at last, was proof that the 'other side' was just as evil. The problem was, this was *not* the proof of moral equivalence that could make the world feel okay about dismissing the whole Rwanda business as African chaos. This was *not* the balancing item that would make it okay to forget about the genocide and say, with the warring parties at each other's throats, nothing could be done. Five murders, condemnable and awful though they may be, cannot, in my book, equate with 5,000 or 50,000 or however many had been committed by the other side by that time. I believe that highlighting this case, giving it the prominence it got, was misleading.

On another occasion, a senior spokeswoman for a UN agency told a press conference in Geneva that the Hutus in southwest Rwanda, who were mainly fleeing the shooting war, had good reason to fear being massacred by the advancing RPF. At this point there was, to my knowledge, no evidence of mass killings by the RPF, and this UN spokeswoman was simply wrong. Perhaps she, too, was seeking a moral equivalence. But she had clearly not understood the difference between the shooting war and the genocide war, and who was doing what to whom. And yet, as a senior UN official, she surely should have done. Her remarks were given wide credence, but again, were misleading.

I filed this copy on 1 May:

> The statement by the UNHCR spokeswoman, Sylvana Foa, to the effect that the mainly Hutu people in southeastern Rwanda are in danger of being massacred appears to be based on mis-information. Ms Foa said that the Hutus are desperately afraid of the RPF and that tens of thousands of them are in danger of being massacred. The clear implication was that the rebels would do the massacring. A BBC correspondent who has spent much of the last three weeks in Rwanda, said there had been no convincing evidence of the RPF massacring civilians. The RPF have openly admitted to killing government militias whom they consider armed combatants. Our correspondent says it is likely that the Hutus in southeastern Rwanda are scared of the RPF military advance, because they don't want to be caught in the crossfire with government troops, but that the allegation that they fear being massacred by rebels does not appear to have any evidence to back it up. The vast majority of the killing in Rwanda has been done by government militias, murdering ethnic Tutsis and Hutu members of the opposition parties.

In addition to filing the news copy, I added this guidance to the desk: 'I suggest that we do not broadcast Sylvana Foa's statement about the alleged fear of massacres by the RPF until some convincing evidence emerges to back it up.'

After the front lines began to stabilize a bit in Kigali, I ventured out of the airport and away from the protection of the French military. I went into town on my own. My first stop was the Mille Collines hotel.

I managed to get a share of a room in the hotel and decided – rather foolishly, in retrospect – to go to the Red Cross hospital. It was a rather dangerous thing to do. But I suppose I'm pleased I ventured out because I learned a lot that day about the genocide war. There were about six roadblocks between the Mille Collines and the Red Cross, with militiamen and soldiers on them. As we made our way toward the hospital, there was a comparatively small number of bodies next to each roadblock. (This is of course an extraordinary way to describe dead fellow humans. But Rwanda seemed to change the way we all saw things, including the scale. Never before then would I have used a phrase like 'a comparatively small number of bodies.')

With some bluffing we managed to get past the militiamen and reached the hospital. I was with fellow journalist Catherine Bond. We did the necessary interviews with Red Cross officials and patients and, after about two hours, started to make our way back to the hotel. The piles of bodies at the roadblocks had grown. For the first time, I had personal eyewitness evidence that pro-government militias were killing people. There was no doubt about it. I remember Catherine turning to me in the car and saying we should describe that road between the Mille Collines and the Red Cross as 'Machete Avenue'.

'If they can have "Sniper Ally" in Sarajevo,' she said, 'we can have "Machete Avenue" in Kigali.'

I think I stayed at the Mille Collines for a few more days, then I became too scared by the militias at the doors, and I sought a kind of refuge at the Red Cross offices. The incredibly brave Red Cross representative, Philippe Gaillard, who used to cross the front lines every day doing his humanitarian work, tolerated me on his floor for a few days. But Philippe made it clear that I would be kicked out if any of my reports ever compromised his neutrality. I didn't like putting him in this position, so I moved out when I realized that the Meridien Hotel, on the other side of town, had some UN officials staying in it and, consequently, had a few Tunisian UN soldiers on guard.

Staying at the Meridien was surreal. The hotel was actually *on* the front line when I moved in and, again in retrospect, it was absurdly dangerous being there. The RPF had dug trenches in the road just outside the entrance lobby and we used to actually watch them exchanging fire with the government forces. It was also surreal staying there because although two of the floors were full of refugees, one of the managers of the hotel had stayed on and still had the keys to the kitchens and the wine cellar. Every night she served us a meal, which we paid for in dollars and ate while the shooting war raged, literally, outside our front windows.

A colleague from Reuters news agency had a bullet come through his window and into his bathroom. The most sought-after rooms were at the back.

Gradually, the RPF won the initiative in the shooting war in the capital and took the area encompassing the UN headquarters at the Amahoro stadium, the Meridien Hotel and the airport. This meant that there was some freedom of movement in this area, and fairly quickly the UN headquarters became a focus of my activity – it was a relatively safe place to be and the UN was a good source of information. Not all of the UN officials were happy for me to be there, but most came round after a bit of persuasion. Some of them let me go on trips with them and briefed me about their version of events. Ceasefire meetings were held at the Amahoro and that meant I had regular access to both RPF and Rwandan government officials. This would have been impossible without the UN.

General Dallaire himself was quite canny with the press. He would talk to us when he could and was quite friendly. I remember once going to his room to interview him. I hadn't shaved for several days, and the first thing he did was to open his personal suitcase and give me a disposable razor. But at the same time, I realized that Dallaire was *using* the press. If he turned up at a meeting with, say, Kagame or Bagasora, with a posse of journalists in tow, it allowed him to get the belligerents to say, on camera – when they wanted to of course – that they agreed with this or that ceasefire proposal.

I was quite happy to be used in this way if it meant I got better access to the key actors in the two wars.

But on one occasion I deeply regretted travelling with Dallaire to a ceasefire negotiation. He went across Kigali, across the front line, to meet with the government side in the Mille Collines hotel. The top government army and gendarmerie brass were there. After the talks, the press were invited in to record some prepared statements. At this ceremony, a senior gendarmerie officer suddenly started publicly berating the press, especially the BBC, for spending too much time with the RPF and not telling the government side of the story. Now, let's be clear. There were very good reasons why we didn't spend much time on the government side. It was hostile and extremely dangerous. For one thing, the RPF were winning the shooting war and the government positions were being overrun. For another, the genocide war was taking place on the government side and it was a distinctly unhealthy place to be, of course for Rwandans, but also for foreign journalists. I'd been there many times and it was, quite frankly, terrifying.

Nevertheless, some misplaced pride in my objectivity persuaded me to answer the gendarmerie officer's complaints by saying, in public, that I would welcome the opportunity to accompany him on a visit to the government front lines. I regretted it almost as soon as I had opened my mouth, but I realized that once I had said it, I had to go through with it.

And so I set off, very reluctantly, again with my colleague Catherine Bond, on a tour of government positions near the centre of Kigali and in the district of Nyamirambo. I deeply regretted our itinerary, in a government military vehicle, because I knew, from independent sources, that the RPF had firing positions in the hills above Nyamirambo.

At one point a mortar round landed quite near to us, quite possibly targeting the officers I was travelling with. But, on the other hand, I did learn some important things that day. One, the killing was continuing. I saw a deep well full of bodies. And, two, the government military were working in direct collaboration with the civilian militia. I knew this because I saw it for myself. I saw the barriers with bodies next to them, and I drove in a car with army officers who ordered the civilian militiamen to let them through. I also saw a senior civilian militiaman give orders to men in uniform. It was direct collaboration.

Once the RPF had more or less firm control of most of Kigali, more and more journalists started arriving in the capital by road from the north, and the RPF began showing us things for themselves, especially genocide sites. I went with them a few times including, once, to the church at Nyamata where several hundred people were killed. But on the whole I preferred to stay near the UN because that way I could get parts of both sides of the story, hitching rides with UN officers as they shuttled between the two sides. I travelled, for example, to Gitarama to interview Theodore Sindikubwabo, the man who was briefly appointed interim president after the remnants of the government had fled the capital. I got there thanks to some friendly Ghanaian military observers. I also made many trips outside the capital independently.

My last trip before leaving Rwanda in late July 1994 was an independent journey to the town of Gisenyi on the border with what was then known, and I still think of, as Zaire. The RPF had claimed to have taken Gisenyi, and since it would be the last major town to fall to them, meaning they would have won the shooting war, I decided to go and check.

Again, there is a crystal clear picture in my mind. Gisenyi was littered with red beer crates, which had been looted from the brewery, and the hills around the town were dotted every few metres with the little piles of stones Rwandans use to balance their cooking pots. Hundreds of thousands of Hutus had camped there, in the open, before flooding into Zaire as the *genocidaires* made what I am convinced they thought of, at the time, as a tactical retreat.

There was a petrol tanker on fire at a crossroads in Gisenyi where I met a tall RPF officer called Bruce Munyango. Someone had told him I was coming and he greeted me. As we shook hands, I noted that one finger was missing on his right hand. 'I'm going to take you right up to the border,' he said, 'to show you we're in full control.'

He did just that. The RPF had won one of the wars, the shooting war. But it didn't feel like a triumph, because the other side had almost won the genocide war.

13
Who Failed in Rwanda, Journalists or the Media?

Anne Chaon

Did the media fail in Rwanda? Or did individual journalists fail in Rwanda? In his analysis of the world's reaction to the genocide in Rwanda, Alan Kuperman (2000) wrote in an International Press Institute report:

> Western media blame the international community for not intervening quickly, but the media must share blame for not immediately recognizing the extent of the carnage and mobilizing world attention to it.

Kuperman says the media must share the blame for the world's failure to stop the genocide. I would like to be the devil's advocate, to explain a bit about how we worked as reporters in Rwanda in 1994.

Before I take issue with Kuperman's point, let me cite a few words written by my friend and colleague Annie Thomas, the first and principal Agence France-Presse (AFP) special correspondent in Rwanda. She was based in Nairobi at the time, but left Kenya immediately after the 6 April 1994 attack on President Juvénal Habyarimana's plane and took the first flight to Bujumbura. Then she drove north into Rwanda and made her way to Kigali through Butare. (Annie is still with the AFP, now based in Dakar.) Here is what she wrote:

> You ask me if I think about Rwanda sometimes: much more than sometimes. It has become a kind of obsession.
>
> An obsession because of the event itself: massacres, mutilated children; people I met on both sides: victims and killers. I still have some faces before my eyes. I had nightmares every night for at least two years and, since then, occasionally.
>
> An obsession because of our inability to describe properly those events during the first few days. Being caught in Kigali for a long time, first on the Hutu side, and then on the RPF side, it was simply impossible to say that hundreds of thousands of people were killed. 'Acts of genocide,' or 'genocide' are words, which only came later.
>
> An obsession because of the accusations that arose later against journalists who were there, especially those who were with the 'genocidaires.' As journalists, as an agency, we couldn't avoid listening to them and quoting

them. Jean Helene (Radio France International correspondent, killed in Abidjan in the autumn of 2003) suffered a lot because of those accusations and even AFP, afterward, has been described as '*Interahamwe*.' (Annie Thomas, AFP, personal communication, February 2004)

Annie spent weeks in Rwanda in 1994, at least three weeks a month for the first three months. She spent most of her time in Kigali or in Gitarama and Butare. She was an eyewitness to a massacre at Kigali hospital on 11 April, when soldiers entered the premises, dragged injured young men from their beds, pushed them toward a pile of corpses in the yard and killed them with bayonets. She reported that scene the very same day on the wire.

Later, she crossed the front line and joined other journalists who had come from Uganda to reach the RPF zone. 'Honestly,' she writes, 'for my intellectual comfort, I would have been much more comfortable on that side than being with militiamen, their machetes still dripping with blood, professing how much they loved France' (Annie Thomas, AFP, personal communication, February 2004).

In the first weeks of the genocide, from April to late June 1994, I was still in Paris, working on the desk at AFP, editing Annie's copy. In late June, I went to Rwanda to report, mainly in the northwest of the country, the heartland of the former President Habyarimana, where militias were acting as the real authority.

It is important to understand what it was like to work as a journalist in Rwanda. There was shelling. There were hundreds of thousands of people on the roads. There were bombs. There was a civil war. There were roadblocks with militias, drunk or stoned, with grenades, machetes, AK-47s.

The militia would come to get Tutsis. They would ask people for their ID cards and check journalists' papers. They were looking for two RFI French journalists, Monique Mass and Jean Hélène, to kill them – just because they were able to understand their broadcasts, which were in French (they may not have heard the BBC broadcasts or read the newspapers). They also described their position very simply: Hutu majority; Tutsi minority. That's what we worked on reporting every day, every hour for radio.

Did the media fail in Rwanda? Yes, definitely. Did journalists fail in Rwanda? No.

Journalists who went to Rwanda were very strongly committed to being there – to report and to testify. Even journalists from France, where the authorities were so involved with the Habyarimana regime, did as much as they could.

During three months of genocide, from 7 April to the beginning of July when the rebels came into Kigali, AFP was one of the rare media outlets to speak out. Sometimes, we were virtually the only international agency on the ground. Mark Doyle from the BBC also stayed most of the time, as did Radio France International (RFI). But very few media were there all the time. Why? Aspiring young journalists should not forget that the media are businesses. Media companies want to be profitable and such reporting costs a lot of money, particularly if it involves the use of satellite phones.

Another factor was the international situation at the time, the global context. In Bosnia, Gorazde was under siege and was bombed for weeks. South Africa was holding its first multiracial elections, celebrating the end of apartheid. In the United States, people were more interested in O.J. Simpson than Rwanda. The French were concerned by the death of Ayrton Seyna, the Brazilian formula 1 driver.

At the international level at that time, people were more interested in Bosnia than Rwanda. The conflict in Bosnia had started in 1992 and in Yugoslavia in 1991. The genocide in Rwanda would have to have lasted for two or three years to garner as much media attention as Bosnia. What we saw in the media in France was similar to that in North America. There was very little coverage of the genocide.

Nonetheless, AFP kept at least two people in Rwanda, usually more. After the expatriates had been evacuated, in mid-April, most of the media pulled their journalists out for safety reasons. They would come back later, especially in June, with the French intervention. But AFP's Annie Thomas stayed, along with representatives from RFI, the BBC and a handful of others. At times, AFP was the only wire service on the ground in Rwanda.

In a 1996 study, Garth Myers and colleagues (1996) compared news coverage of Rwanda and Bosnia in six major American newspapers: *The New York Times*, *Los Angeles Times*, *Washington Post*, *Chicago Tribune*, *Christian Science Monitor* and *Boston Globe*. In April 1994, there were twice as many articles about the conflict in Bosnia as Rwanda.

In all of 1994, the French daily *Le Monde* published 1,665 articles on Bosnia and only 576 on Rwanda. And the Rwanda tally includes coverage of the evacuation of foreigners and the outbreak in June and July of cholera in the Zaire refugee camps (Rabechault 2000). Among the articles in *Le Monde*, more than 60 per cent were short pieces, mainly news agency dispatches. In other words, some 220 articles on Rwanda that appeared in *Le Monde* that year were not bylined pieces by the newspaper's own journalists, nor their own analysis or commentary.

Most journalists are not experts in genocide. Many of them – myself included – arrived in Rwanda with very little knowledge of the country. So, it was tempting, especially at the beginning, to speak of the civil war, of these massacres as a perverse return of a civil war, and to link these massacres to previous massacres since 1959. We failed to understand that the killing was something totally new, that this was not a continuity of what had happened before.

During those first few days in April, special correspondents were much more likely to use words like 'chaos', 'anarchy' and 'furore'. They were reporting on a resumption of the civil war. In the field, it was easy to be confused and view the massacres as a 'side effect' of the fighting.

Then, on 12 April, the main story became the evacuation of foreigners and the closing of embassies. A special correspondent for the French public TV channel recalls that he had very strict orders: cover the evacuation of the French people, then get out. Actually, most of the TV teams came and left with the military planes.

Newspapers generally gave the same amount of space to the evacuation as to the massacres, then reduced their coverage of Rwanda to focus on Bosnia and the elections in South Africa. Photographers arrived quickly, but what they got were pictures of corpses, never photos of massacres at the moment they took place. To my knowledge, there is only one video image of a massacre taking place (the film shot by British camerman, Nick Hughes, in April 1994).

Patrick Robert, from Sygma Corbis Agency, explained that a month after he returned to Paris from Rwanda, he had still sold almost none of his pictures from Rwanda. He was there, but no one wanted to see. Journalists were there: but who would listen to them, or read their stories?

The first time AFP used the term 'genocide' was on 20 April. In the weeks before, AFP referred to 'massacres', 'killings', 'ethnic cleansing'. It was all too easy to link the situation with the past, to recall the waves of killings in Rwanda since 1959 and also in Burundi with massacres that followed the October 1993 assassination of President Melchior Ndadaye.

AFP's use of the term 'genocide' was in the context of a report quoting Human Rights Watch, which had warned the United Nations (UN) against reducing the extent of its mission in Rwanda. The executive director of Human Rights Watch, Kenneth Roth, said in New York that 'Rwandans, mostly Tutsis, could face certain death in what would amount to genocide.'

AFP used the term again on 28 April, this time quoting Médecins Sans Frontières, and again on 3 May, quoting the Council of Europe. On 16 May, the French foreign minister, Alain Juppe, referred to 'genocide' in Rwanda. Finally, 'genocide' came into common media usage when the UN Committee for Human Rights adopted a resolution – on 25 May – acknowledging that genocide was being perpetrated in Rwanda.

We all know now why the international community was so reluctant to qualify the situation so strongly. Using the word genocide would have necessitated action, under the genocide convention (UN 1951). For weeks, AFP and other media used the word only if it was able to quote a source using that term. Thanks to Human Rights Watch, Oxfam, Médecins Sans Frontières and others, the reality of the genocide finally made its way into the media. As journalists, we probably avoided many errors because of these nongovernmental organizations (NGOs). In my view, the NGOs and independent organizations did an excellent job, conducting inquiries and producing reports. But for weeks, the media underestimated what was actually going on in Rwanda.

Is it the reporter's fault? I would say no. Even if they did not have the complete picture of what was going on in the whole country, they described what was happening. Reporting on a daily basis – on an hourly basis for a wire service, if you consider that you're almost always on a deadline for some part of the world – they had to provide an overall picture of the situation: fighting between government troops and the RPF, rebel progress, attempts to reach a ceasefire agreement, political developments, refugees and displaced people and also, of course, killings.

In my view, the media failure came much more from those who were out of the country, in Paris, London, Washington and Ottawa. Given all the material coming in from the field, editors should have the responsibility to qualify the events. But news agencies are very careful about the use of words. At AFP we have a strong policy about the use of words and we have often been too cautious. In 1989, in Timisoara, northern Romania, some reporters described mass graves, with dozens of corpses, including babies. The truth was far from this: the graves actually contained dead from a nearby hospital, the baby was stillborn. After this outrageous mistake, editors at AFP, like others, too often decided that emotional factors were overwhelming a reporter in the field.

Another glaring failure of the media occurred at the very end of the genocide, when the French began 'Operation Turquoise' in southwest Rwanda. Dozens of reporters returned to the country. Although they were able at that time to discover the enormity of the killing campaign in this area – in such places as Kibuye, Cyangugu and Bisesero – they also reported on the humanitarian and military intervention from abroad. The result was that the reality of genocide was, once again, submerged in too much information.

It became worse in mid-July, when a million Hutus crossed the border into Zaire and cholera flared up in the camps. The humanitarian catastrophe overwhelmed the real story of the genocide. Everybody ran to Goma, because the story there was so easy to cover. After months of genocide, the issue of good guys and bad guys disappeared completely. The enemy was cholera, but no political issue surrounded cholera in the camps. It seemed as if journalists were more comfortable covering cholera than genocide.

But there are some other basic facts to remember. There is what one would call in French 'le concept du rapport mort/kilometre' – in essence, the notion that deaths at home or close to home seem to matter more than those at a distance. So five French dead are more important to French readers than ten German dead and more important than one hundred African dead. In this sense, the news media reflect the public's state of mind.

As well, during the spring of 1994, while events were unfolding in Rwanda, those who wanted to know what was going on, knew. The details arrived late, but those who wanted to know, knew. Reporters were there, not all the time, but often. And their testimony was emerging from Rwanda. AFP was almost always there. The BBC was there. Individual reporters in the field showed their determination. They wanted to report, to bear witness to the killing.

To answer Alan Kuperman, I would say, 'Yes we missed the Rwanda genocide.' But Kuperman wrote in 2000, six years after the event. Journalists are neither historians nor sociologists. They do not work in the quiet of their study. Their reports become part of history, but history is knitted day by day, before their eyes. They don't benefit from the distance required to quickly understand the whole scene.

To their credit, individual journalists kept on working in Rwanda in the months and years that followed the genocide. American newspapers were eventually able to tell the truth about the UN and Rwanda, about Lieutenant General Roméo Dallaire's famous 11 January fax. French newspapers were able to push for the establishment of an information mission on Rwanda in the national assembly. It was far from a full commission of inquiry, but it was the first time that parliament questioned the presidency and the government about foreign policy. And a clear picture emerged of the ties between Paris and Kigali in the early 1990s and well into the spring of 1994.

A final word: what can the media do when the world doesn't want to listen or to hear?

And what about Africa itself, so silent except for the Organization of African Unity's attempts to convene a summit to achieve a ceasefire? In mid-May 1994, we asked all the AFP offices in Africa to send to Paris press reviews and remarks in the African media on the Rwanda issue. What reactions had they picked up in the press and among intellectuals? What actions, if any, were undertaken? Were there any demonstrations? Any concerts like the Band Aid effort years earlier for Ethiopia?

But our survey of African media coverage found the same troubling apathy that was prevalent in the Western media – with only a few exceptions. In the end, we wrote a synthesis of the African reports under the headline: 'The deepening silence in Africa on the drama in Rwanda' (Anon. 1994).

After the genocide, we all tried to understand how the world missed the Rwanda story. But in the end, I can only conclude that for those of us who thought their work could change something in the world, Rwanda was a cruel disillusionment, a major failure. Reporters were there. Pictures were available. Stories were filed. But if readers, if the people you speak to do not want to listen, you can't force them. They can just turn the dial. And editors can refuse to publish your reports.

A final example: some time ago, in early 2004, Roméo Dallaire gave a terrific interview to TF1, the most popular French TV channel. It was broadcast in prime time. For such a channel, it was a very courageous move to broadcast the interview, but the audience declined. The number of people listening decreased during the programme.

Those who don't want to listen shut their ears. That's what happened for Rwanda. We can say, 'Oh it's the fault of the United States that didn't want to intervene. It's the fault of the government of France.' But the public could have done something.

When I returned from Rwanda in 1994, I went to my little village in eastern France. A fisherman said, 'Oh were you there? Well, don't talk about it any more. We've had enough. We see these terrible pictures at 8 p.m., right when we're eating. But what can we do? We can't do anything.'

For a long time I never spoke to anyone about Rwanda and when I did it was when the International Criminal Tribunal for Rwanda called on me three years later to ask me for details about some of my reporting. In the meantime, I understood that no one else wanted to hear from me about Rwanda. I could not force them to listen, nor did I want to.

REFERENCES

Anonymous. 1994. The Deepening Silence in Africa on the Drama in Rwanda. AFP International, Paris, France, 29 May.

Kuperman, A. 2000. How Media Missed Rwandan Genocide. *IPI Report*, 6(1).

Myers, G., T. Klak and T. Koehl. 1996. The Inscription of Difference: News Coverage of the Conflicts in Rwanda and Bosnia. *Political Geography,* 15(1): 21–46.

Rabechault, M. 2000. *La presse au Rwanda: des massacres à la mission d'information parlementaire: une analyse dans la presse française de la couverture médiatique du conflit rwandais et du rôle que la France y a joué*. Institut d'Etudes Politiques, Université de Strasbourg III, Strasbourg, France.

UN (United Nations). 1951. *Convention on the prevention and punishment of the crime of genocide*. Adopted by Resolution 260 (III) of the UN General Assembly, 9 December 1948. UN Treaty Series no. 1021, vol. 78: 277. Available at <www.preventgenocide.org/law/convention/text.htm> (accessed 6 September 2005).

14
Reporting Rwanda: the Media and the Aid Agencies

Lindsey Hilsum

In late July 1994, some 500 journalists and media technicians gathered in the town of Goma in eastern Zaire (now the Democratic Republic of the Congo) to cover the influx of an estimated one million Rwandan refugees. They brought with them the technology of instant, 'real time' news: satellite uplinks for transmitting pictures and sound, satellite phones for sending newspaper copy and computer equipment connected to satellite phones to transmit still photographs.

From the point of view of aid workers trying to cope with the needs of refugees, the journalists were in many ways a nuisance. They added to the chaos of clogged roads. They inflated the cost of hiring a car or an interpreter. Nurses resuscitating children with cholera found themselves tripping over tripods and cameramen looking for a better angle.

But aid agency press officers – ever mindful of the hot competition for funds back home – pursued journalists, proffering not only updates and interviews, but free transport and accommodation in return for covering their agency's programme. The aid agencies needed the journalists, and the journalists needed the aid agencies.

In Britain, Newsnight called it 'the largest ever concentration of refugees in recorded history.' The exodus and the subsequent cholera epidemic became a huge story around the world. It led television news bulletins in Europe and North America for two to three weeks and was front-page news in the British tabloids, which rarely cover Africa. Rwanda was on the front page of the *New York Times* for six weeks in July and August.

But the public did not understand the complex political causes of the exodus to Goma. And they were probably not understood by many of the journalists who covered Goma as a humanitarian story, nor by the dozens of young, inexperienced aid workers for whom Goma was their first mission.

This paper was prepared for the Joint Evaluation of Emergency Assistance to Rwanda, Study III (1996, vol. 3), and is published here in its entirety for the first time. It was written before the events of November 1996, when the Hutu refugee camps located in eastern Zaire (now the Congo) were cleared and an estimated 700,000 people returned to Rwanda. Much of the information is based on interviews conducted between May and August 1995; the names of interviewees are listed at the end of the paper.

The events that led up to the exodus – the massacre of Rwanda's Tutsi population and moderate Hutu opposition and the war between Rwandan government forces and the Rwandan Patriotic Front (RPF) – were given far less space and airtime. In most Western countries, with the exception of the former colonial power, Belgium, coverage was largely restricted to 'serious' newspapers and some radio and television reports. The story was dangerous to cover and difficult to understand. It was a big story, but not a massive one.

This is not a new issue: in the late 1960s, coverage of the war in Biafra had little impact on the public as long as the story was Africans killing Africans. The moment the story became pitiful – skeletal African babies dying of starvation – the imagination and the conscience of the public was engaged and it became a massive story.

Decades after Biafra, a number of new factors are relevant to this study. First, satellite technology means TV reports can be transmitted and broadcast as they happen rather than days or weeks after filming. Second, a proliferation of aid agencies are competing for funds. Third, the international climate has changed since the end of the Cold War, and Western governments have little strategic or political interest in Africa. These factors have implications for the way coverage of humanitarian disasters affects aid policy and practice.

In this paper, I attempt to clarify the role the media played in the humanitarian effort in Rwanda and on its borders in 1994. The first part provides the context of the disaster and pointers about how media influence works. The second part is a chronology of the coverage until the exodus to Goma, with reference to the relation between aid agencies and the media. The third part is an analysis of the impact of media presence and coverage on the aid effort in Goma. It concludes with a number of points for further discussion.

CONTEXT: A FOREIGN POLICY VACUUM

In most Western countries there is a vacuum where there used to be a policy on Africa. The vacuum is filled by aid, much of it directed through nongovernmental organizations (NGOs).

Western countries had no policy to prevent or stop the killing in Rwanda or to contain the flow of refugees. They did not actively back the RPF or the government. The only exception was France, which pursued a complex policy in which a military intervention with several aims was characterized as humanitarian.

Media influence in the foreign policy vacuum

According to Nik Gowing (1995), former diplomatic editor of ITN's Channel Four News and now a BBC World presenter, 'Neither TV journalists nor humanitarian organisations should delude themselves about the impact of their images on the making of foreign policy' (for further detail, see Gowing 1994). Certainly, editorials and pressure from aid agencies failed to persuade the West to intervene when the killing was at its height in April, May and early June 1994.

The high-profile response of governments to the humanitarian crisis in Goma came as thousands of members of the public – voters – gave money to NGOs and demanded that 'something should be done.'

> I would argue that dispatching water trucks from California or logisticians from Frankfurt in response to TV pictures of bodies being tipped into the cholera pits of Goma was not a fundamental foreign policy switch designed to end a crisis. It was a knee-jerk, high-profile response, which carried little political risk or cost. It made good television. It also gave the impression of engagement and deep concern at a time when – in President Clinton's case – domestic policies like healthcare reform and gun control had hit the rocks. (Gowing 1995)

Governments failed to come to the aid of the victims of genocide, but provided succour to many of the perpetrators. It was, of course, much easier to provide humanitarian aid than to try to prevent or stop the genocide, and how much outside powers could have done is still arguable. But the relatively light coverage of the genocide and the heavy coverage of the refugee crisis helped governments appear to be responding to the most important aspect of the drama.

It was not the intention of aid agencies or journalists to help Western governments use humanitarian aid as a fig leaf for the lack of policy on genocide. One can cite several examples of in-depth coverage and criticism of the failures of the United Nations (UN) and national governments. But the issue is quantity of coverage. One of the major outcomes of the imbalance in reporting of different aspects of the story was that governments were able to hide behind a humanitarian screen.

Relation between aid workers and journalists

'The media presence changed the perception of the Rwandan crisis in a very damaging way,' said Anne-Marie Huby, who was executive director of Médecins Sans Frontières (MSF)–UK in the mid-1990s. 'In the general public's memory, the Rwanda crisis was people who die of cholera. I think people forgot the long-lens coverage of genocide. [In Goma,] I remember CNN saying "This is genocide again." We told the reporter that dying of diseases is not genocide.'

The distinction was not as important to CNN as to Huby. 'We see a compelling news story, not whether it's genocide or refugees or whatever,' said Larry Register, senior international editor at the time at CNN's headquarters in Atlanta. 'Rwanda was such a straightforward story – a humanitarian tragedy unfolding daily.'

There is something ironic about an aid worker telling a journalist that a medical tragedy is not the key event. Aid workers, after all, were a major part of the humanitarian story and Samantha Bolton, then the MSF's regional information officer for East Africa and spokesperson in Goma, was interviewed on British television more than any other aid agency official in Goma during the first week of the crisis (Glasgow Media Group 1994). But MSF–France did have a clear idea of its own limitations – in May it launched a campaign with the slogan 'You can't stop genocide with doctors.'

But the interest of journalists in covering humanitarian aid sometimes overwhelms their responsibility to expose underlying issues. Timothy Weaver of FirstLine News, wrote:

> During the emergency period [of a humanitarian disaster] the difference between a humanitarian agency and the media should be at its most marked. The aid agency should be concerned with delivering aid, and the news agency should be reporting what is happening. Yet nowadays the two tend to be blurred. The aid agencies are the news, and the news becomes a charity appeal. Reporters become crusaders, demanding action to be taken, money to be spent, and something to be done (but not by me, because I am off to my next assignment, thank you very much). (Weaver 1995)

In a situation like Goma, where the human tragedy was so desperate and so visual, it is inevitable that some blurring will occur. But reporting on Goma should not be seen in isolation. From Afghanistan to Somalia, wars in what used to be called the Third World are increasingly being reported with an emphasis on the humanitarian over the political or military. This is partly because editors think their viewers and readers have a limited interest in complex political events far away. It is also a reflection of the lack of political or strategic interests of outside powers – the political story is remote because it does not involve us.

Moreover, the aid worker and the journalist are often the only foreigners in a dangerous and threatening situation. They speak the same language and they stick together. Their perspectives merge and it becomes hard to maintain strictly distinct roles.

CHRONOLOGY OF MEDIA COVERAGE OF RWANDA UP TO 1994

October 1990 – RPF invades Rwanda

The story of the first three years of the war and the 1993 Arusha accords was scarcely covered at all in the anglophone press. It received regular attention from BBC World Service radio and TV. The French and Belgian media covered it more because of former colonial and linguistic ties.

September 1993 – attempted coup and refugee crisis in Burundi

The killing of between 50,000 and 100,000 Burundians and the subsequent exodus of 700,000 people to Rwanda, Tanzania and Zaire was not big news in Britain or the United States. It was slightly bigger in France and much bigger in Belgium. Aid agencies lobbied for coverage and failed. In the end, Oxfam offered to fly George Alaigiah, then BBC TV developing world correspondent, to Bujumbura. The images Alaigiah came back with were strong and the story compelling, but they did not spark more coverage. After seeing the BBC reports, Sue Inglish, associate editor of Channel Four News, said 'they kicked themselves for not sending a reporter,' but once the BBC had carried the story felt they had missed the boat.

Anglophone aid agencies that were already in the region strengthened their emergency programmes, but most of the aid agencies that went out in response to the emergency were French and Belgian.

It is hard to say definitively why this huge massacre and humanitarian disaster did not capture the attention of the press. At the time, the media were dominated by the Middle East peace agreement – the handshake between Yasser Arafat and Yitzak Rabin on the White House lawn took place on 13 September. Previous massacres in Burundi – in 1988, for example – had been covered in a similarly limited way in anglophone countries. There was a sense of déjà vu and a lack of interest in the complex political causes of the tragedy.

December 1993 – food for Burundi refugees dries up

The World Food Programme (WFP) failed to get enough food to the Burundi refugees in Rwanda. The WFP said the problem was insufficient resources from donors and inefficiency and corruption within the agencies distributing food. NGOs and donors blamed a weak WFP office in Kigali for incompetence in managing the food pipeline and reducing rations without informing anyone. Thousands of children began to die of diseases related to malnutrition, and MSF used the media to bring pressure on the WFP.

'If we really want to put pressure on the UN or the donors, we'll work out where the weakness is and expose it,' said Samantha Bolton of MSF. 'They generally react to media pressure – they're petrified of bad publicity.' Bolton, who was based in Nairobi, briefed the Nairobi press corps and organized trips to the affected camps. 'It became a huge scandal and there was a lot of interest. Because WFP was so frightened, they started pumping out press releases. It made them much more efficient.'

This use of the media to pressure the UN and donors is typical of MSF. Other NGOs, anxious to maintain good working relations with UN agencies on the ground, are more reluctant to go public and prefer to talk to journalists off the record. One result of Bolton's work was that the WFP scandal brought the forgotten story of the Burundi refugees back into the news.

Whether the WFP in Kigali became more efficient because of direct media pressure is open to question. By March, the food pipeline was being managed more efficiently. Donors, including Echo, had been leaning on the WFP, which had sent senior staff to Kigali to try to sort out the problem. It seems likely that the media pressure did not work directly on WFP in Kigali but on donors and on the WFP in Rome and Nairobi.

January–April 1994 – build up to the crisis

The mounting tension as President Habyarimana delayed implementing the Arusha accords received little coverage in the anglophone press and only slightly more in the francophone. The media were dominated by the violent build-up to the South African elections – at this point, Chief Buthelezi was still boycotting the poll. Rwanda was a very difficult story to report, requiring good contacts and an understanding of Rwandan politics.

6 April 1994 – the plane comes down, the massacres start

When the plane carrying presidents Habyarimana and Ntaryamira was shot down over Kigali, there were two foreign correspondents in Kigali: Katrin van der Schoot, a freelance Flemish reporter for Belgian radio; and Lindsey Hilsum (the author of this paper), in Rwanda on a temporary contract for UNICEF and normally a freelance reporter for the BBC, *Guardian* and *Observer*.

Some Nairobi-based journalists managed to move south from Uganda with the RPF. Others persuaded a WFP official in Entebbe to fly them into Kigali on a plane being used to evacuate foreigners. Others drove up from Burundi. For most of April, there were no more than 10–15 reporters in the country at any time.

After foreign embassies and most aid workers left Rwanda at the end of the second week of April, the only real sources of information in Kigali were these journalists and the UN contingent. Journalists travelling with the RPF were strictly supervised.

Although most of the journalists were Africa specialists, even they did not understand what was happening at first. With a shooting war in the east and the north and massacres in much of the country, for most of April it was genuinely confusing. The journalists in Kigali depended on the UN for protection. After a while, the UN limited their numbers, saying it could not accommodate more than half a dozen or so. The journalists were mainly British, French and Belgian. Most United States reporters had been ordered to leave by their employers because the situation was too dangerous. A French cameraman was shot and injured in Kigali.

It was extremely difficult to cover the story thoroughly. 'It was a story we wanted to tell but it was appallingly dangerous,' explained Mike Jermey of ITN, which sent a staff correspondent to Rwanda in May. Mark Doyle was in Kigali for most of April and May reporting for the BBC. His reports indicating the progress of the RPF advance and the scale of the civilian slaughter by government forces were frequently broadcast on the BBC World Service. When another BBC reporter, Fergal Keane, was stopped at a checkpoint near Butare in late May, the machete-wielding thugs manning it said that if they ever saw Doyle they would kill him.

There was no 'real time' TV news because it was too risky to send an expensive satellite uplink into Rwanda. Channel Four News had reports from Catherine Bond, who had covered the war since 1990, but these were not 'real time' so their impact was limited. 'There were a number of attempts to get in, but it looked so disastrous and we could not get the pictures out,' said Sue Inglish of Channel Four News. The first satellite uplink was erected in Kigali in late May, after the RPF had secured the airport and most of the massacres were over.

In April and early May, the media had little influence on the aid agencies, but were an important source of information because most agencies had lost touch with their local staff (many of whom were dead, while others were participating in the killing). Agencies distributed goods to a trickle of refugees in neighbouring countries and managed to get some supplies to people in locations guarded by the UN. They stockpiled goods and held anxious meetings in Bujumbura trying to prepare for a likely exodus of refugees. The media coverage of these efforts did not spur aid agency supporters to send money. 'It looked like a bloodbath, a civil war, so sending money wasn't going to help,' said one press officer working with a US-based organization.

Agencies such as Oxfam concentrated on advocating UN intervention to stop the killing. Others tried to publicize small efforts at humanitarian aid.

Benaco and Ngara – the story takes off

The first large wave of refugees crossed into Tanzania on 28 April, the last day of voting in the South African elections.

'For me the world became aware of Rwanda on the 29th April,' said Geoff Lone, head of the International Committee of the Red Cross (ICRC) regional delegation for East Africa. 'Suddenly it was a humanitarian problem. The refugee situation translated the crisis into terms which could be understood by the world at large.'

By this time, news editors were aware that something major was going on and they were missing it because it was too dangerous and too complicated. But Benaco was much, much easier. It was safe – neither the journalists nor the expensive satellite equipment were at risk. It was accessible – the Red Cross would fly you direct from Nairobi. The story made sense – refugees fleeing war, being looked after by aid workers. And, for TV, the visual images were very strong but not so offensive that you could not show them.

News organizations started to pull reporters out of South Africa, where the smooth electoral process had made the story less eventful than predicted, and send them to Tanzania.

Of course, the story was not simple – were these people fleeing war or retribution? Were they victims or perpetrators? But the images were simple and recognizable: Africans on the move, living in camps, at the mercy of the generosity of the outside world. The aid agencies, thrilled that at last there was something concrete they could do, flocked to Benaco and eventually had their numbers restricted by the UN High Commissioner for Refugees (UNHCR). As money began to flow in to fundraisers in Europe and the United States, competition for media coverage became acute. One press officer relates how the Red Cross hospital was at the entrance to Benaco, next to the camp where journalists slept. 'It was impossible to get the journalists out of the hands of the Red Cross.'

May – genocide continues while the UN dithers

By May, more journalists were trying to cover the genocide, but it was still very difficult and dangerous to get access except via Uganda under the watchful eyes of the RPF.

Newspaper editorials and opinion pieces ('op-eds') by human rights workers or aid agency officials advocated UN intervention to stop the killing. This had some influence within the UN. Karel Kovanda, Czech ambassador to the UN and a member of the Security Council at the time, pushed hard for the UN Security Council's 17 May Resolution to send 5,500 troops to Rwanda to try to stop the genocide. Kovanda said the turning point was an op-ed by Human Rights Watch, published in *The New York Times* in mid-April. 'It explained the role of France arming Habyarimana and so on. That article was an eye-opener, a key to understanding Rwanda,' Kovanda said. He contacted the writer, Alison Des Forges, and she provided him and other concerned members of the Security Council with information to supplement (and at times contradict) what they heard through official channels.

Aid agencies and editorials pressured Western countries to back up the 17 May Security Council Resolution. But the United States, bruised by its failure in Somalia, scuppered the plan by quibbling over details and delaying sending equipment that the African peacekeepers were to use.

In the end, it was the RPF that stopped the genocide by winning the war. It is interesting to note that no NGOs and few journalists were advocating that Western countries take a political stance and back the rebels.

Operation Turquoise – the French intervene

There was limited coverage of Rwanda in the French press after the withdrawal of French military trainers and embassy staff from Kigali in mid-April. During May, when the full horror of genocide was emerging, liberal newspapers such as *Libération* challenged the role France had played in arming the Habyarimana regime.

The French administration was divided about what to do and some parts of the media started to push for action – what kind of action was unclear. 'The military officers who disagreed with the decision on 8 April to withdraw everything used press coverage to say the decision had been racist, because [the government] didn't care about people in Africa,' said Stephen Smith, then Africa editor of *Libération*. 'They used the media as a tool within the state apparatus, saying the French colonial past was being betrayed. So the media was used in the context of rivalry within the state apparatus, rather than as overall pressure on a coherent, monolithic state.'

MSF–France, with its campaign of 'You can't stop genocide with doctors,' fed into the calls for action, and its campaign – which was purely advocacy – nonetheless brought in significant donations from the public. But when President Mitterand announced in mid-June that he was sending troops unilaterally rather than as part of a UN contingent, MSF–France was against the move because French troops were seen as politically aligned with the government that was committing genocide.

> When [French troops] intervened in the southwest and didn't show independence from the former government, we in other MSF sections were very angry. When one MSF makes a mistake it becomes a problem for all the others. The French prime minister's ratings went through the roof. Antenne 2 was practically writing lines for visiting generals – there was collusion between

> the press and the army. It was impossible for MSF to raise any dissenting voice. (Anne-Marie Huby, MSF–UK, interview)

The French government had motives too complex to explore in this report, but humanitarianism was the factor they wanted to advertise. They had backed the Hutu government and they wanted to be seen saving Tutsis.

Stephen Smith agrees that the coverage in France of the French army's 'humanitarian mission' was largely positive. 'The broad public opinion is that France was the only nation to care about human suffering. They did something and then got out, but by that time everyone wanted them to stay. Most people would say it was a success.'

When the French press started to criticize MSF for refusing to cooperate with the French army in southwest Rwanda, Samantha Bolton was dispatched to make MSF's case. 'It was a disaster for MSF,' she said. 'There were constant quotes like Colonel Gil saying "medical organizations whose job it is to do medical work refuse to do it. They are letting children die."'

The problem was image rather than money. MSF looked inconsistent because it had called for intervention then didn't like the result.

Bolton had more luck with the anglophone press, but although all major British TV and print media were there, as well as CNN (although not the American networks), June was a low point for coverage in the English-speaking world. This made it hard for NGOs to raise funds, even though they were now active in Tanzania, Burundi and some in the French protection zone. CARE–USA ran an advertisement in the major American newspapers (*The New York Times*, *Washington Post*, *Boston Globe*, etc.) and the response did not even cover its costs. In July after Goma, an almost identical advertisement did phenomenally well.

From April to June, the UN had come under considerable criticism in the media for failing to do anything. The Security Council, Secretariat, Department of Peacekeeping Operations, UNAMIR and the specialized agencies were all portrayed as impotent and useless. The French intervention pointed up the UN's failure.

THE IMPACT OF MEDIA PRESENCE AND COVERAGE ON THE AID EFFORT IN GOMA

The impact of the media on the aid effort in Goma is difficult to define or quantify because aid agencies are reluctant to ascribe anything they do to media influence. According to most agency press officers and workers, pandering to the media is something that *other* agencies do.

For NGOs, the main impact was, of course, on fundraising. The predominant TV image was the dying African child being saved by a foreign (white) nurse. For Mike Jermey of ITN, the most memorable image was Kevin Noone, a young Irish aid worker from GOAL Ireland, who rolled up his sleeves and threw the bodies of dead cholera victims into trucks to clear room for the living.

Media coverage of general humanitarian issues is essential to persuade regular supporters to give money to their chosen NGO. Specific attention raises the profile of an organization and will attract new supporters. In Britain, a threshold is passed when the tabloids cover the story. John Grain, operations room manager for Oxfam, logs credit card donations. He noted that the number of calls and donations mirrored almost exactly the ebbs and flows of TV and tabloid coverage of Rwanda: May, 1,000 calls; June, 134; July, 6,000 (the largest *ever* response to an appeal in a month); August, 2,500; September, 100.

Did the media influence the decision of agencies and governments to go to Goma and how long to stay? Did it influence what they did while there?

The proliferation of NGOs

'The most important aspect of "the CNN factor" was that it sent dozens of NGOs we didn't want,' said Joel Boutroue, head of the UNHCR sub-delegation in Goma. 'This took an inordinate amount of our time and complicated our job. You cannot coordinate 100 NGOs; it made for a very expensive programme and we're still suffering from it.'

The most extreme example of an agency driven by the media was Operation Blessing, based in Virginia, USA. Operation Blessing was a department within the Christian Broadcasting Network, right-wing evangelist Pat Robertson's own TV network. It existed simply as a function of television. Robertson and his TV crew, plus satellite uplink, flew to Goma very early in the crisis. 'He implied the Hutus were heroes. Maybe he got confused,' said Richard Walden, president of Operation USA, a secular outfit that collects and transports donations in kind to disaster zones.

On his daily TV show 'The 700 Club,' Robertson appealed for doctors to come and save dying Rwandans. 'We sent six medical teams each with 15 people, so a total of 90 people,' said Hanan Kassir, head of international centres for Operation Blessing. Staff rotated every two weeks. For nearly all, it was their first experience in Africa. The 700 Club filmed their work, thus generating more volunteers, more sponsorship and – according to Walden who watches Operation Blessing closely – more general funds for Robertson's political-religious campaign in the US. The teams evangelized as well as treating the refugees. 'Faith is something you cling to,' explained Kassir.

Operation Blessing volunteers believe they were useful. 'We sent 80,000 pounds of medicines and supplies and must have treated 80,000 patients,' said Kassir. Boutroue disagrees. 'Operation Blessing … tried to cure cholera with the laying on of hands. They are nutcases,' he said. Experienced health workers point out that two-week rotations are expensive and inefficient and that people with no previous experience of Africa could not possibly be useful in such a short time frame.

Operation Blessing pulled out of Goma in February. 'We had no more funds,' said Kassir. 'We can't take from the existing program. We'd had a good appeal and had used it up. We can't just keep on helping everybody all the time.' In other words, Operation Blessing only works in places while it is generating media coverage and thus attracting volunteers and funds.

Boutroue is equally critical of CARE–Germany. 'They came late, 200 Germans at a time rotating every two weeks, a lot of students giving the wrong drugs, creating resistance to diseases and giving inadequate treatment. They were working in total isolation and they created a lot of havoc.' CARE–Germany's refusal to coordinate with other agencies was revealed in the German press. 'There was a decision made by the board not to cooperate with other NGOs … This showed the competition inside Germany,' said Manuela Rosper, programme manager with CARE–Germany. 'We got an extremely bad press. Once you have a bad press and you are not in a position to defend yourself properly, it does not get any better.' Rosper defends the work their doctors did in the field. 'We were well prepared for the whole thing and continued until the end of the year … It did not affect our work in the field but affected fundraising at home.' The board of CARE–Germany has since changed.

CARE–Germany's experience reveals the power of the media over some organizations – the agency was in such competition with others, it refused to coordinate with them and, when it got bad press, it could not raise money and left.

There was an opportunity cost in the arrival of inefficient organizations, especially at the beginning of the disaster when thousands of refugees were dying daily. 'For every loony that rolled into the place, 20 kilos of water equipment didn't get onto a plane,' said Nic Stockton, head of Oxfam's emergencies unit.

'Media supply side' NGOs do not impress experienced journalists who have seen this kind of thing before. However, some of the reporters covering Goma were 'firefighters' – gullible novices with little prior experience of Africa or of emergency situations.

Aid agencies that stayed away or left

The fact that so many agencies went to Goma meant that some experienced agencies stayed away, notably Save the Children Fund, United Kingdom (SCF–UK). 'We looked at what was happening with cholera and dysentery and – given the lack of preparation – felt a lot of people were going to die whatever anyone did, and the key to that was the large concentration [of refugees],' said Don Redding, press officer for SCF–UK. 'The problem was so many agencies piling in without coordination.' Rather than add one more agency, SCF–UK decided to concentrate on working inside Rwanda. 'We felt right from the start that refugee cities of that size were not sustainable and very politicised.'

Redding says that not being seen in the media to be active in Goma probably cost SCF money in resources not raised. However, being a member of the Disasters Emergency Committee, which raises money collectively for five major British NGOs, SCF received a share of money anyway, and felt it could afford to ride on the general coverage rather than needing specific reporting of its own activities.

Geoff Lone, head of the ICRC regional delegation in Nairobi, said the media presence took the pressure off his organization, which had some food stockpiled in Goma before the exodus. 'Because the media was there, other humanitarian actors came … If the media had not been there, we would have had to get stuck in with [UN]HCR just to keep the situation going ... We would have been left doing more.' ICRC puts a lot of energy into liaising with the media these days, but, because of the ubiquitous nature of the Red Cross logo, the organization's long-established reputation and the fact that it gets money more from governments than private donations, it does not have to be seen to be there quite as much as other agencies. The arrival of other agencies gave it freedom to move on and apply more resources in Bukavu, where there were fewer agencies.

Small agencies and individuals

Aid agency managers do not usually read the newspapers or watch television before deciding they must do something about whatever disaster is featured. But they are susceptible to pressure from their supporters for whom the media is the only source of information. Whereas large agencies have stockpiles and the financial security to borrow against expected income, young and small agencies can only respond to a crisis once they have raised funds. This makes them extremely vulnerable to media interest and means they cannot start doing anything before the media get there.

Feed the Children was founded in 1990 to take gifts in kind from Britain to Romania and Bulgaria; its slogan is 'Taking the Aid Direct.' Its awareness of the importance of news coverage for fundraising is shown by newspaper advertisements that are headed 'Report from Bosnia' or 'Report from Rwanda' and imitate the layout and writing style of a news report. Feed the Children had not worked in Africa before. Goma provided the opportunity.

'By July our supporters were calling to say what were we doing?' said Stuart Crocker, deputy director. 'We are responsive to the wishes and intentions of our supporters. We don't want to let them down ... Being so young, we have no underpinning levels so we are constantly working at keeping fundraising up and we have to focus on activities which raise money.' They launched a Rwanda appeal and raised US$ 600,000 in seven weeks.

In mid-July, Feed the Children sent out two people to see what they could do. Interestingly, they decided Goma was too crowded with NGOs and opted to work in the French Protection Zone where they felt they could make more of a contribution. It was, therefore, the general media coverage of human suffering rather than specific coverage of their own activities that was most important. Their supporters are loyal.

Crocker is keen to stress that they do not want to pack up and leave with the journalists. 'If we did that our integrity would be questionable ... We see our operation as a bridgehead, possibly expanding to Burundi and maybe Angola.' But the short attention span of the media is a problem. 'Seven weeks after we started, the media got more interested in political conferences and money dried up immediately. It was like turning off a tap.' Feed the Children is, however, still working in Rwanda.

Between April and July, better established agencies such as MSF and Oxfam were pushing for more coverage of the background to the crisis – the genocide, the failures of the UN, the need for international action on a political front. Crocker has a different perspective. 'We wish the media would focus more on people, the human side … In Bosnia, for example, as soon as the political and military viewpoint of the story dies, they discontinue interest in the continuing needs of the people.'

Governments

On 28 July, approximately ten days after the Goma media barrage started on US television, President Clinton held a meeting in the White House with representatives of 15 American NGOs. 'The vice-president was there, the secretary of defence, the deputy secretary of state [for foreign affairs], the head of USAID and the joint chief of staff of the US Army,' said Richard Walden of Operation USA, one of the chosen NGOs.

> The media was waiting outside. The meeting was a direct result of media pressure and of lobbying by all of us [NGOs] … They gave us a presentation – the joint chief of staff said they would do what they had done for the Kurds. They said we should look to them for our transport needs and they'd be pulling water tankers out of the Gulf. They said 3,000 Americans would be involved, including those in Frankfurt, Entebbe and so on.

In fact, the US military effort in Goma was already underway, so the meeting underscored and gave further publicity to US efforts.

The Clinton administration had been criticized in the media for holding up the deployment of UN peacekeepers to try to stop the genocide. This was an opportunity to show the US army saving lives, without the risks of Somalia. Some journalists who saw it as a domestic rather than an international story and who had not followed Rwanda before were easily misled. 'In July there was a story "American troops have secured Kigali airport," quoting sources in Washington. But the airport had been secure for two months,' said Mark Doyle of the BBC.

The British government also sent troops for the aid effort and spent approximately US$ 45 million on the Rwandan emergency in 1994–95. 'There was day in, day out pressure from the media. What can you do? You throw money at the problem. I'm sure we gave more money because of that,' said one official. The British did not concentrate on Goma, but worked inside Rwanda as well from July onward. Baroness Chalker, then minister for overseas development, visited Goma as a side-trip from a planned trip to Uganda at the end of July. Her visit was a big story especially in the tabloid press and provided an opportunity to publicize the aid programme and British NGOs, many of which were funded by the ministry.

It is important to note that NGOs in Goma were looking to governments for funding as much as to the general public. Press officers say that the messages they put across through the media are directed at donors – who are thinking of political capital at home – as much as the general public.

Did the media influence what agencies did?

Within two weeks of their arrival, journalists were wondering whether the refugees should go back. This was mainly because they were looking for new angles after endless reports of overcrowding and cholera, and those who had not covered Rwanda before were beginning to understand the political complexities and implications of the refugees' continued presence in Zaire. Ray Wilkinson of UNHCR was asked quite aggressive questions about UNHCR's policy on repatriation. His response was confused – an accurate reflection of UNHCR's uncertain policy.

Stockton and several other senior aid workers believe UNHCR was diverted into thinking about repatriation when it should have been concentrating on keeping people alive where they were. The WFP got into the repatriation issue by holding up trucks delivering food to Kibumba camp, so that any refugee who wanted to go home to Rwanda could hop on board for the return journey. Only a handful of refugees took up the offer – but it gave flagging journalists a new angle.

The WFP itself provided a different example to illustrate how they resisted media pressure. 'We were pressured by journalists to distribute food, and from a PR point of view we should have pushed a couple of trucks into a camp, but we didn't,' said Brenda Barton, WFP information officer. She said they also resisted the temptation to airlift food —always a more dramatic media concept than trucking – and gave up air slots to allow more urgently needed water equipment to get in.

Publicity stunts

The US army took a different approach, in what has become a classic example of how a publicity stunt during a disaster can backfire. On 24 July, before the world media, three US army C130s airdropped food parcels in a banana plantation somewhere near Katale camp north of Goma. According to Jenny Matthews, a British photographer who witnessed the drop, the parcels contained dirty clothes, Gruyère cheese (labelled 'perishable, needs refrigeration'), ski-mittens, biscuits (labelled 'do not drop'), chocolate and flour from Sainsbury's.

There was no need for an airdrop – food was coming in by road, and there had been a distribution in Katale that morning. The food was obviously inappropriate. Airdrops are expensive. Worst of all, the Americans persuaded CARE to let them have several Action Aid/Assist trucks that were desperately needed to transport water equipment.

The trucks couldn't reach the place where the food had landed, so a French army fork-lift, which had been used for digging graves, arrived with a crane. Machine guns slung across their shoulders, the French troops 'liberated' the chocolate and cheese. CARE loaded some items onto the trucks to take to a warehouse. They dispelled local Zaireans who – encouraged by journalists – had arrived to help themselves. The airdrop was sharply criticized in the American media.

Americares, an NGO based in Connecticut, flew in 10,000 cases of Gatorade, a soda drink containing electrolites preferred by athletes. It was clearly inappropriate, but according to Richard Walden of Operation USA, Americares nonetheless got a favourable mention for acting quickly from Dr Bob Arnott, the CBS medical correspondent, who flew into Goma on the same flight. It was an example of an agency sacrificing appropriateness to act quickly and get into the media spotlight. *The New York Times* was critical.

Many agencies decided to help orphans and abandoned children, either in Goma or within Rwanda. This decision was often media-driven – children are the most popular subject for stories about human suffering. By contrast, few NGOs or governments wanted to deal with the urgent need for latrines, the least popular aspect of the story. UNHCR had tremendous trouble persuading anyone, including governments, to work on latrines, even though they said it was the most crucial intervention needed after water.

These examples illustrate that the media did influence how agencies operated in Goma. NGOs with set agendas did what they always do: MSF addressed health problems while CARE did camp management and logistics. But some agencies rushed in without thinking properly about what they had to offer. UN agencies and governments revealed themselves to be as susceptible to media pressure as NGOs, despite the fact that they do not rely on the public for donations. They are afraid of bad publicity, which would challenge their legitimacy.

Visibilty and profile

'To the newly arrived, Goma looks as if it is hosting some kind of competition election,' wrote Richard Dowden in the *Independent on Sunday*. 'Oxfam, Goal, Care, World Vision: WFP, UNHCR blare out their names and logos like soft drink manufacturers ... Echo stickers have appeared on lamp-posts all over Goma.'

Oxfam's water tanks in Kibumba were the largest structure in the camp, and you knew who donated them by reading the six-foot high black letters an the side. 'I got a sign writer in Goma to write OXFAM on the side of the tanks,' said Oxfam press officer Ian Bray. 'It was a backdrop for TV interviews.' The decision provoked a mixed reaction within the organization. According to Bray, locally recruited workers liked the sign and the Oxfam T-shirt they were given to wear, possibly because it gave them a sense of identity and belonging. 'I was appalled,' said Nic Stockton. 'It doesn't make us friends in the media – it's a turnoff. The old image is of the Oxfam water engineer in a scruffy T-shirt doing a good job. I think that's better.'

Stockton is right that branding is a turn-off for serious journalists such as Dowden. But if the aim was to get the logo on TV to raise visibility, Oxfam needed to do more. In the first week of the Goma crisis (15–21 July), the Oxfam logo was featured only once on British TV news compared with twelve appearances of the MSF logo.

Tension between fundraisers pushing for visibility and workers in the field guarding their integrity is nothing new, but with the proliferation of NGOs, the stakes were higher. Many agencies say branding is part of security – MSF workers always wear MSF T-shirts so they can be clearly identified in a crisis. But branding has gone to an extreme. 'MSF is over the top on PR – adhesive bandages, needles sticking into arms had the MSF logo,' said Richard Walden of Operation USA after seeing close-ups of the offending bandages on US television.

Press officers

As agencies feel vulnerable to the power of the media, the job of press officers has become more important. Goma marked a watershed, with large numbers of press officers present, leading to great competition for exposure. The fact that press officers are seen as so important in gaining media coverage and, therefore, raising money means their power within their organizations is increasing.

Over the last few years, under the guidance of former UPI bureau chief Sylvana Foa, UNHCR has appointed journalists as press officers. They are inclined toward openness, in contrast with the UN bureaucrat's traditional instinct for silence and obfuscation. Ray Wilkinson, one of the chief UNHCR spokespeople in Goma, used to be the Newsweek correspondent in East Africa, and knew very well what constitutes a story and what journalists need.

'The media is your greatest asset in a crisis and you should be as open and frank as possible,' said Wilkinson. 'If the media is talked to as an adult and they believe you, they are very sympathetic.' UNHCR admitted to mistakes in Goma, and this may have increased their credibility because they were seen to be open rather than trying to hide.

Other UN organizations rushed to keep up with UNHCR. The WFP always had two press officers in Goma, even though food was not the focus of the story. UNICEF had an easy time attracting coverage because orphans and abandoned children make natural, heart-rending TV pictures. NGO press officers took the pressure off water engineers and nurses who needed to get on with the job; their main task, on the other hand, was to promote their organization and boost donations.

The 'war of the press officers' has become legendary, and everyone has a story of a press officer (from another agency) who refused to let journalists talk to 'the opposition'.

The same problems apply with press officers as with branding. Press officers who shamelessly plug their organization, exaggerate the issues and know nothing about the context will alienate serious journalists and attract bad publicity in the quality press. Some agencies take the attitude that publicity is publicity, it doesn't matter if it's good or bad because the mere mention of the name raises profile. However, journalists writing tabloid stories may welcome a simple PR approach of the 'white angel saves dying black baby' kind.

The following analysis of TV coverage in the United Kingdom reveals the success of press officers in getting their view into the media. Several reported that their status and influence within their organization has increased since Goma. 'CARE had never had media coverage like that in the UK before,' said Alison Campbell, CARE–UK media liaison officer. 'We raised 1 million pounds in three or four weeks. The perception was that massive media coverage brought in the money.'

Some of the income was credited to Campbell's budget, an acknowledgement of the central role she played. CARE has been criticized by other agencies for courting publicity before their programmes were established, but Campbell's technique was simple. She was always available, she would talk about almost any aspect of the crisis including the politics, she helped journalists with practical problems such as communication and transport and she was not afraid to be controversial.

This caused tension within CARE. Campbell highlighted the issue of killers in the camps and – during an interview on CNN – criticized the US airdrop.

> The next day CARE–USA sent out its PR person on a damage limitation exercise,' Campbell said. 'They'd had complaints from Denver, Colorado saying that CARE was unpatriotic. Within an hour of arriving, the PR officer told us not to mention the killers in the camps ... [Afterwards] CARE did an assessment and said the remarks had caused trouble at the time, but were later shown to be true. It helped us push the idea of advocacy within the organization, which is traditionally conservative.

The most prominent press officers were the most proactive. Samantha Bolton of MSF was in Goma before the influx. She described later how she was at the border at dawn on 15 July when the first large wave came across. By this point, Oxfam and MSF had been predicting the influx publicly for more than a week and were frustrated with a lack of response from UNHCR. 'I ran back to the house and rang the Today programme [BBC Radio 4], the World Service and CNN,' Bolton said. Bolton was not promoting MSF in what she said, but the fact that she, as an MSF employee, was savvy enough to know whom to call and how to tell the story meant she became a sought-after interviewee. (For a week afterward, she had a daily slot on the most popular TV morning news programme in the US, Good Morning America.)

What Bolton did next reveals how NGOs can use the media to pressure the UN. 'I took a journalist from Associated Press with me to the UNHCR house to say the refugees were arriving. I said [to the UNHCR representative], "You'd better get down there." He said, "Why don't you tell them to go up beyond the airport?"' According to Bolton, the HCR representative repeated this even after she had pointed out she had a journalist with her. The journalist went off to write the story of how the UN was unprepared for the influx, despite warnings from NGOs.

Fact inflation

In Goma, there was what Richard Dowden of the *Independent* has called 'fact inflation'. Ray Wilkinson described how it worked at the daily press conference:

> I'd say something and I'd be contradicted down the line. In a lot of circumstances it was a deliberate grab for headlines. MSF announced a study of deaths in Katale. Journalists were briefed to ask a follow-up question. I

was asked if I could extrapolate to the whole population – MSF had said you could. Whenever I gave death figures I said that this was ballpark – approximately 20,000 dead. If you extrapolated the MSF figures you got 30,000 deaths. Inevitably they got headlines.

'Speculation inflation' was also an occupational hazard of journalists and aid workers in Goma. Both frequently speculated that the exodus to Bukavu was going to be even bigger and more catastrophic. It was a kind of insurance against being caught off guard as they had been over Goma. The noise of collective excitement drowned out more measured interpretation. One correspondent described seeing several thousand people on the roads leading to Bukavu in mid-August. Her newspaper found on the news wire a quote from an aid worker who thought a million were on the way. The aid worker and the reporter had been in exactly the same place at the same time, but the aid worker's estimate prevailed because it fit the mood of the moment. In the end, the reporter was proved right – but that was after the story had been printed.

Another connected issue was the down-playing of long-term health problems in favour of short-term issues. Cholera, with its resonance of medieval plague and its instant horrific impact, was clearly a major story. Dysentery, which health experts say killed more people over a longer time, was scarcely a story at all. It is inevitable that journalists will report what is happening at the time more than what experts predict. The emphasis on the immediate and things that happen quickly is another hazard of 'real time' coverage. The only way to improve understanding of these health issues is for journalists to become better educated, for aid workers to explain the issues clearly and in a more compelling way.

One problem with Goma was that the catastrophe was so enormous and so sudden that it raised the stakes for other emergencies. It became more difficult for journalists to raise editors' interest in long-term humanitarian disasters such as Sudan or Angola. The only exception was Burundi, which – like a watched pot – refused to boil over in the way journalists and aid workers breathlessly anticipated.

The Goma effect was felt by agencies too: 'It's changed our perspective in that region. Before, 10,000 refugees was a lot,' said Samantha Bolton of MSF. 'Now, if there are 10,000 refugees, we say, let another smaller agency do it.'

High- and low-profile agencies

Cholera inevitably turned attention to medical organizations, especially MSF, even though water and sanitation were in some ways more important in stemming the disease. This is partly because Western culture values medical science over environmental issues. 'Medical aid is sexy – it's like [the TV programme] ER,' said Anne-Marie Huby of MSF. 'And everyone in MSF can talk, even the truck drivers. You don't have to ask Geneva [for permission]. Our people are volunteers. They're very flexible and very young. And we have so many nationalities, we can talk to every journalist in his or her mother tongue.'

Journalists have been criticized for speaking only to foreigners and not to Africans when covering stores like Goma. The criticism is valid, but the pressures of 'real time' reporting mean the problem is likely to get worse, not better. A nurse or doctor working for MSF is familiar with the language of television and knows more or less what the journalist wants. It's a quick and relatively easy exchange. Interviewing African players in the drama is much more time-consuming and complicated. You have to find out who exactly the person is as well as engaging an interpreter. Otherwise, you don't know what question to ask or how to interpret the answer.

Aftermath

In 1995, journalists continued to visit Goma, but obviously in much smaller numbers. Boutroue believes the wide publicity given to the internal UNHCR report by Robert Gersony – which alleged widespread atrocities by the RPF against Hutus – slowed the return of refugees to Rwanda. One can argue that the return was slowed because the report was right (that is, refugees had experienced atrocities so wouldn't return) or because UNHCR commissioned the report (that is, information about the report would have circulated in the camps whether the foreign media got hold of it or not). The impact of media coverage in slowing the return cannot be clearly established.

Despite the debate within aid agencies about the morality of continuing to work in Goma given the presence of killers in the camps, most aid workers there appeared unconcerned about the question. The moral issue of giving succour to killers has not affected the image of aid agencies very much. Although press officers, such as Alison Campbell and Samantha Bolton, spoke openly about the issue from the start, only a few reporters challenged the agencies and negative publicity was minimal. MSF got some publicity when their French and Belgian chapters withdrew, citing moral issues as the reason (actually they withdrew at about the time MSF normally withdraws from emergencies), but the Dutch chapter remained, taking much of the sting out of the tail of their decision.

CONCLUSIONS FOR DISCUSSION

1. The proliferation of NGOs was a direct result of media coverage. Only when media coverage started in earnest could NGOs raise funds. Goma, with its massive media coverage, thus became an opportunity for smaller, less experienced agencies. This lowered standards and complicated coordination.
2. Better-established agencies, seeing the influx of new actors, felt they had to guard their market share by promoting their agencies more aggressively. They did not, on the whole, change their programmes, but they used their logo and name as extensively as possible and employed more press officers.
3. UN agencies are very afraid of bad publicity. UN press officers tried to use the media to improve the efficiency and increase openness in the UN bureaucracy. There are divergent views on whether this succeeded.

4. NGOs, especially MSF, used the media to pressure UNHCR and other UN agencies to be more responsive and efficient. This had varied results.
5. Governments responded to the crisis in Goma by sending soldiers. They were 'flying the flag' and tried high-profile interventions that were at times expensive and inappropriate.
6. In Goma, journalists added to the general sense of chaos but did not significantly disrupt the relief effort.
7. Because the media were so important in Goma, the power of press officers within organizations increased. Many press officers pushed for agencies to speak out on political issues.
8. The suddenness and gravity of the Goma crisis, combined with the massive media attention, has dwarfed other emergencies and relief efforts in Africa, with implications for fundraising and continued aid agency interest.
9. The massive media and aid agency attention paid to Goma helped governments promote their humanitarian aid programme and hide their lack of policy on genocide.
10. The media coverage of Rwanda hugely increased the public's awareness of aid agencies, but did virtually nothing to increase knowledge of what caused the exodus to Goma or of what happened to Rwanda's Tutsi people and members of the Hutu opposition.

INTERVIEWEES

Interviews were conducted between May and August 1995.

Sue Adams, head of external affairs, Action Aid.
Andy Babcock, head of emergencies, ODA.
Brenda Barton, regional public information officer, World Food Programme, Nairobi.
Chris Beer, chief executive, Helpage International.
Samantha Bolton, regional information officer, Médecins sans Frontières, Nairobi.
Joel Boutroue, head of United Nations High Commissioner for Refugees sub-delegation, Goma.
Ian Bray, press officer, Oxfam.
Alison Campbell, media liaison officer, CARE, London.
Stuart Crocker, deputy director, Feed the Children.
Mark Doyle, East Africa correspondent, BBC.
John Grain, head of operations room, Oxfam.
Anne-Marie Huby, executive director, Médecins sans Frontières–United Kingdom.
Sue Inglish, associate editor, Channel Four News, London.
Mike Jermey, head of ITN programming on ITV.
Hanan Kassir, head of international centres, Operation Blessing.
Mike Kiernen, media director, Interaction, Washington.

Geoff Lone, head of the International Committee of the Red Cross, Regional Delegation for East Africa, Nairobi.
Jenny Matthews, photographer, Network, London.
Colin McCullum, chief press officer, British Red Cross,
Don Redding, press officer, Save the Children Fund, United Kindom.
Larry Register, senior international editor, CNN, Atlanta.
Manuela Rosper, programme officer, CARE–Germany.
Stephen Smith, Africa editor, *Libération*, Paris.
Nic Stockton, head of emergencies unit, Oxfam.
Nigel Twose, director of international division, Action Aid.
Richard Walden, president, Operation USA, Los Angeles.
Ray Wilkinson, public information officer, United Nations High Commissioner for Refugees, London.

REFERENCES

Glasgow Media Group. 1994. British television news and the Rwanda crisis, 15–21 July (part 4). Glasgow Media Group, University of Glasgow, Glasgow, UK.

Gowing, N. 1994. *Real-Time Television coverage of armed conflicts and diplomatic crises: does it pressure or distort foreign policy decisions?* Joan Shorenstein Barone Centre on the Press, Politics and Public Policy, John F. Kennedy School, Harvard University, Cambridge, MA, USA. Working paper 94–1.

—— 1995. 'Television and Foreign Policy'. In *Crosslines Global Report* 14–15, April/May. Crosslines, Geneva, Switzerland.

Weaver, T. 1995. 'Prostituting the Facts: Aid and the Media'. In *Crosslines Global Report* 14–15, April/May. Crosslines, Geneva, Switzerland.

15
Limited Vision: How Both the American Media and Government Failed Rwanda

Steven Livingston

To understand American news coverage and government policy concerning the 1994 Rwanda genocide, one must begin with the 1992–93 United States intervention in Somalia. Why did the Bush administration decide to intervene in the Somali crisis in the first place? Conventional wisdom at the time suggested that the only viable explanation was the television coverage of the horrific famine, fighting and disease that plagued the country. American statesman and scholar, George Kennan, made this argument when he explained the acceptance of the mission by Congress and the public.

> There can be no question that the reason for this acceptance lies primarily with the exposure of the Somalia situation by the American media, above all, television. The reaction would have been unthinkable without this exposure. The reaction was an emotional one, occasioned by the sight of the suffering of the starving people in question. (Kennan 1993a)

The idea that media attention to distant crises can trigger policy responses is typically referred to as the CNN effect (for a full description of this phenomenon, see Livingston 1997; Livingston and Eachus 1995–96; Robinson 2002). Foreign policy priorities are established and public attention is directed to issues that happen to be in the news, rather than toward strategic objectives defined by national interest. As Kennan (1993b) put it, foreign policy should not be determined by news stories that are 'fleeting, disjointed, visual glimpses of reality, flickering on and off the screen, here today and gone tomorrow'.

Foreign policy conducted in such a manner is not only irresponsible; it may actually undermine the constitutive authority of elected government.

> If American policy, particularly policy involving the uses of our armed forces abroad, is to be controlled by popular emotional impulses, and particularly ones invoked by the contemporary commercial television industry, then there is no place – not only for myself, but for what have traditionally been regarded as the responsible deliberative organs of our government, in both executive and legislative branches. (Kennan 1993b)

In this chapter we consider the realist critique of media and humanitarian interventions. At the heart of that critique is the claim that news of international affairs in the US media – when it is found at all – tends to be fleeting, ephemeral and all too typically frivolous. We present evidence that suggests critics on this score are largely correct.

Implicit in this criticism is the idea that media content, frivolous and fleeting as it sometimes may be, has the capacity to reorder US foreign policy priorities. Kennan's assumptions concerning Somalia offer one example of this faith in the power of media. This assumption is also held by the activist community that lobbied for US intervention in Rwanda (and elsewhere). Both the realists and interventionists (for lack of a better term) share the common belief that media content spurs intervention, although, of course, they hold opposing views regarding the wisdom of such a thing.

We argue that this assumption regarding the power of the news media is mistaken. Realists' worries and interventionists' hopes are misplaced. In most instances, media do not have the ability to reprioritize policy objectives and policymakers' attention.

Why is this important in developing our case concerning Rwanda? The United States stood at arm's length from events in Rwanda in the spring of 1994 because policymakers believed their predecessors in the George H.W. Bush administration were lured into Somalia by television pictures. Although this assumption was fundamentally inaccurate, it prevailed and coloured the US response to the genocide in Rwanda. As a result, Rwanda became a test case for a new-found commitment to realist principles. Television and talk of genocide, no matter how compelling and emotional, would not be allowed to sway the steely-eyed pursuit of national interests. In short, the non-intervention in Rwanda was predicated on a misunderstanding of the causes of intervention in Somalia.

THE REALIST CRITIQUE OF MEDIA

It cannot be said that realist foreign policy theorists have given sustained attention to the issue of media and foreign affairs. The critique is more oblique. What is said, however, has roots in a core philosophical component of realist belief: foreign policy conducted properly keeps a cold eye on the rational pursuit of interests clearly understood. Anything else, including sentimentality, is regarded, at best, as distraction. Media content is heavily laden with emotional freight concerning distant injustices and brewing evil. In populating the news with victims of one sort or another, calculations of national interest are supplanted by mere sentimentality. This is the core principle at the heart of the realist critique of the media and foreign policymaking.

Even if emotion weren't such a poor substitute for the rational calculation of national interest, news would still serve as a poor guide to a foreign policy process based on the more emotional landscape of international affairs. The news media, particularly television news, is fickle, shifting from one crisis to the next. As a result, even a foreign policy based on the pursuit of morally derived duties to right wrongs would be ill-served. This criticism comes most often not just from realists, such as Kennan, but also from those I have referred to above as interventionists – those who believe media have a responsibility to alert the world to circumstances such as Rwanda early, loud and unwaveringly (see Livingston and Eachus 1999). What evidence supports these claims? What do we know about media content patterns?

Systematic empirical investigation of news content supports these criticisms of the American news media. From 1990 to1998, American television networks more than doubled the time devoted to celebrity and entertainment, disasters, accidents and crime, while decreasing the time spent on policy and international affairs (Patterson 2000). Indeed, until the September 2001 attacks on the United States and the war in Afghanistan, international news almost disappeared from American television news. Foreign affairs coverage on network television declined from 45 per cent of stories in the 1970s to 13.5 per cent in 1995 (Hoge 1997). Similar trends were evident in American newspapers. International news coverage in newspapers shrank from over 10 per cent of non-advertising space in the early 1970s to 6 per cent in the early 1980s and less than 3 per cent in the 1990s (Hoge 1997). Similarly, between 1985 and 1995, international news in the national weekly news magazines declined from 24 to 14 per cent in *Time,* from 22 to 12 per cent in *Newsweek*, and from 20 to 14 per cent in *U.S. News and World Report* (Hickey 1998).

A Pew Project for Excellence in Journalism found similar results. By 2001, the three nightly network newscasts were devoting fully a third of their broadcasts to stories in the categories of lifestyle, features and crime (Kurtz 2002). In a study of 5,000 news stories taken from television, magazines and newspapers, Patterson (2000) found similar patterns in content. Other studies confirm these findings. Livingston and Stephen (1998) found a steady decline in international news content offered by the broadcast television networks between 1972 and 1995 (Figure 15.1).

Figure 15.1 illustrates the trends in international news content as a percentage of total news content per year. Several high-water marks in coverage occurred during or near the end of the Cold War. Interestingly, the low-water mark also occurred during the Cold War; Watergate dominated news in 1973–74. The Soviet invasion of Afghanistan, the Iranian hostage crisis and the Cold War politics of the Reagan administration led the post-Watergate resurgence in international news content. The collapse of the Soviet Union and the Eastern Bloc in 1989–90 received the greatest share of attention by the networks.

What in general is revealed in Figure 15.1? In the 20-year period between 1972 and 1991, 40 per cent of the network's news content focused on international events. The end of the Cold War marked a dramatic shift in focus.[1] In the four years after 1991 that are represented in Figure 15.1, the networks' international news content averaged about 27 per cent. The Rwanda massacre occurred during this second period of relative journalistic inattentiveness to international affairs. Looking more closely at the crucial years when Rwanda was – or could have been – the focus of media attention in the US (1993–95), we see that only one in four network news stories concerned international events (Figure 15.2). In general, following the end of the Cold War, American networks paid less attention to international events.

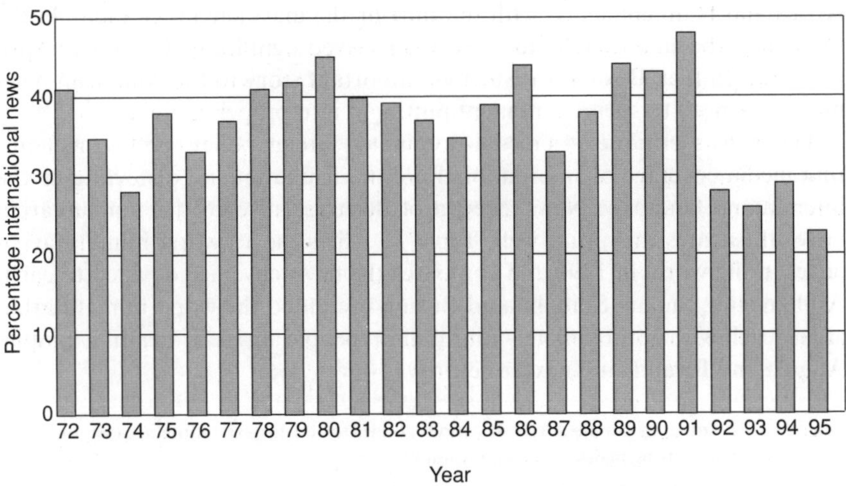

Figure 15.1 International news as a percentage of total television network newscasts, 1972–75

Source: Livingston and Stephen 1998.

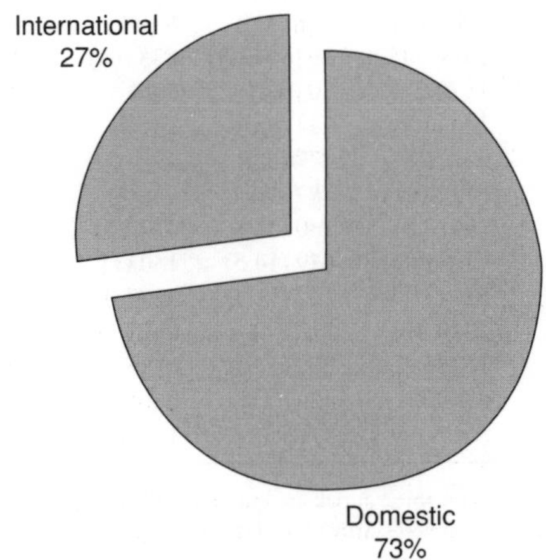

Figure 15.2 Proportion of domestic versus international news stories, 1993–95

Source: Livingston and Stephen 1998.

What was covered in the 1990s? Figure 15.3 (p. 193) tracks several events that occurred during the Rwanda crisis. A coup and civil unrest in Haiti leading to a mass exodus of refugees to Florida was the object of considerable media attention. The refugees made Haiti both a domestic and international news story. The election and inauguration of Nelson Mandela in South Africa also peaked in May. The networks devoted significant resources, including mobile 'flyaway' units used to cover events in locations without sufficient satellite uplink capacity, to the coverage of the South African elections in 1994. Both South

Africa and Haiti coincided with the start of the massacre in Rwanda. At the same time, the bloody civil war in Bosnia received significant attention in April and May. In fact, Bosnia was such an important story to the American news media, we need to spend a moment putting it into proper context.

The realists' critique of a media-dominated foreign policy centres on claims that media coverage of international politics is uneven and distorting of the international landscape. News coverage of Bosnia relative to other humanitarian crises illustrates this point well. Table 15.1 lists the 13 worst humanitarian crises in the world in 1996 and compares the news coverage devoted to each. Afghanistan, Sudan, Somalia and Bosnia presented the worst humanitarian crises, each with approximately four million people at risk of death. Ethiopia, Angola and Rwanda are next in severity.

Table 15.1 Number of people at risk in various countries and corresponding number and percentage of reports by major news organizations

Country	*Millions of people at risk (% of column total)*	*No. (%) mentions in various media* The New York Times	Washington Post	*ABC*	*CNN*	*NPR*
Afghanistan	4 (14)	274 (4.7)	225 (4.8)	19 (1.5)	57 (1.2)	57 (2.9)
Sudan	4 (14)	190 (3.3)	166 (3.5)	8 (0.6)	54 (1.1)	31 (1.5)
Bosnia	3.7 (13)	2,633 (45.8)	2046 (43.7)	833 (66)	3062 (66.7)	1204 (61.3)
Ethiopia	3–4 (11)	15 (0.2)	10 (0.2)	0 (0)	3 (0)	6 (0.3)
Angola	2.5 (9)	120 (2.0)	144 (3.0)	9 (0.7)	22 (0.4)	34 (1.7)
Rwanda	2.5 (9)	401 (6.9)	277 (5.9)	49 (3.9)	150 (9.8)	118 (6.0)
Sierra Leone	1.8 (6)	63 (1.0)	78 (1.6)	4 (0.3)	26 (0.5)	20 (1.0)
Liberia	1.5 (5)	164 (2.8)	150 (3.2)	32 (2.5)	49 (1.0)	46 (2.3)
Iraq	1.3–<4 (5)	839 (14.6)	679 (14.5)	150 (11.9)	540 (11.7)	201 (10.2)
Haiti	0.9–1.3 (3)	654 (11.3)	522 (11.1)	89 (7.0)	316 (6.8)	132 (6.7)
Eritrea	1 (4)	28 (0.4)	21 (0.4)	0 (0)	3 (0)	4 (0.2)
Somalia	4 (14)	312 (5.4)	309 (6.6)	69 (5.5)	294 (6.4)	102 (5.1)
Tajikistan	1 (5)	45 (0.7)	52 (1.1)	0 (0)	13 (0.2)	9 (0.4)
Total*	28.2† (100)	5,738 (99.1)	4,679 (99.6)	1,262 (99.9)	4,589 (99.2)	1,964 (99.6)

Source: Livingston 1996. The totals for those at risk are found in USMUN 1996.
* Due to rounding, percentages do not necessarily total 100 per cent in any column.
† Based on the low-end figure where a range has been given.

Moving to measures of news coverage, each cell in a column shows the number of reports on the crises along with the percentage of total coverage of all 13 crises that it represents. For example, of all articles published in *The New York Times* on these 13 crises in 1996, 6.9 per cent (401 articles) were devoted to Rwanda. Of all *Washington Post* articles on these 13 crises, 5.9 per cent (277 articles) mentioned Rwanda.

The figures for Bosnia reveal the sort of distortion that concerns critics of US news coverage of humanitarian crises. With 3.7 million people at risk, Bosnia received nearly 46 per cent of the total coverage of these crises in the *The New York Times*, nearly 44 per cent of the *Washington Post* total and 66 and 67 per cent of the coverage on ABC and CNN, respectively. National Public Radio devoted about 61 per cent of its total coverage to Bosnia alone. On the other hand, Afghanistan and the Sudan – the two places in the world that we would later discover harboured Osama bin Laden and al Qaeda – had more people at risk than Bosnia, but *together* received only 12 per cent of the total media coverage of all 13 crises concerning the worst humanitarian crises in the world – affecting nearly 30 million people. Nearly half were devoted to the crisis in Bosnia where 3.7 million people were at risk.

This is not to say that Bosnia wasn't important. Nor is it to say that populations at risk are necessarily the only or best dimension for calibrating the importance of a crisis. But it does illustrate that US news coverage tends not to be calibrated to more complex determinants. Bosnia coverage reflected its proximity to major European cities – all major operational bases for the news media – and its geostrategic importance. Second, Bosnia and the rest of the Balkans sit on the southern edge of Europe and indirectly involve at least two key NATO member states: Greece and Turkey. Instability along NATO's southern tier was as much a catalyst for US intervention as was news coverage. Indeed, as we will argue below, news coverage followed US involvement.

Table 15.1 illustrates the distortions that occur within the universe of humanitarian crisis reporting. But the distortions don't end there. Most often, humanitarian crises are shunted aside by news of another sort.

Turning to Figure 15.3, we can see that, beginning toward the end of May and peaking in the summer of 1994, the O.J. Simpson drama received more attention than any other news story. The Rwanda massacre received relatively

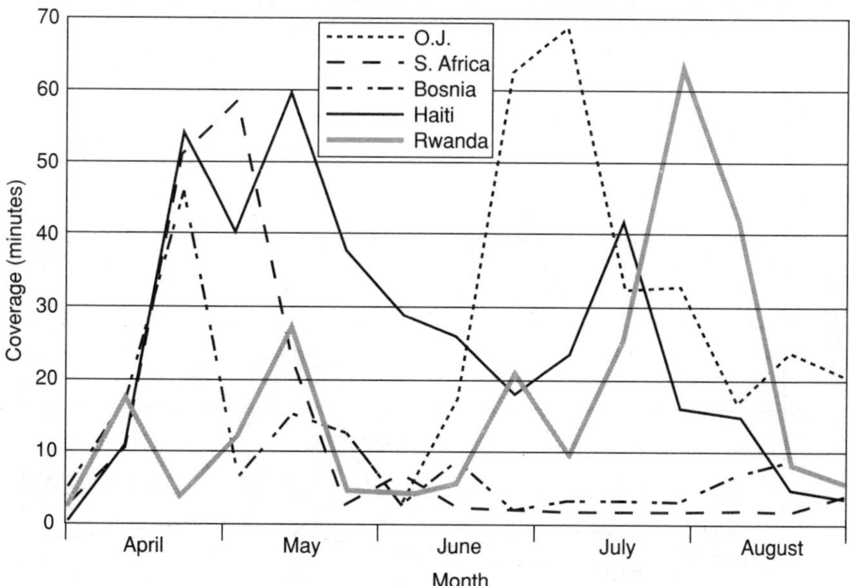

Figure 15.3 Coverage (in minutes) of various topics in ABC, CBS and NBC nightly newscasts, 1994

Source: Livingston and Stephen 1998.

little attention; it wasn't until later, when events in the Great Lakes region of Africa shifted, did the news media pay significant attention. By July and August the crisis in Rwanda centred on the hundreds of thousands of Hutu refugees in camps such as in Goma, Zaire.

In short, during the crucial spring months of 1994, the American broadcast television networks devoted relatively little attention to the systematic extermination of nearly a million people. Figure 15.3 highlights aggregate news coverage of Rwanda by the (then) three major American broadcast network newscasts. O.J. Simpson's trial received more American network news coverage than the systematic murder of over 800,000 people.

MEDIA EFFECTS ON POLICY

What effect does news content have on policy decision-making? Clearly, the foreign policy realists have a point when they argue that news content offers an uncertain guide to international events. But this fails to address the question of whether media content of any kind has the capacity to affect foreign affairs decision-making.

Critics and policymakers alike assume that it does. Critics who favour robust international responses to humanitarian crises tend to fault the news media for not paying more attention to Rwanda in the early weeks and months of the crisis, implicitly suggesting that, had more attention been given by the news media, Western policymakers might have responded differently. It is indeed true that most of the attention was paid to the Hutu refugees in the camps around

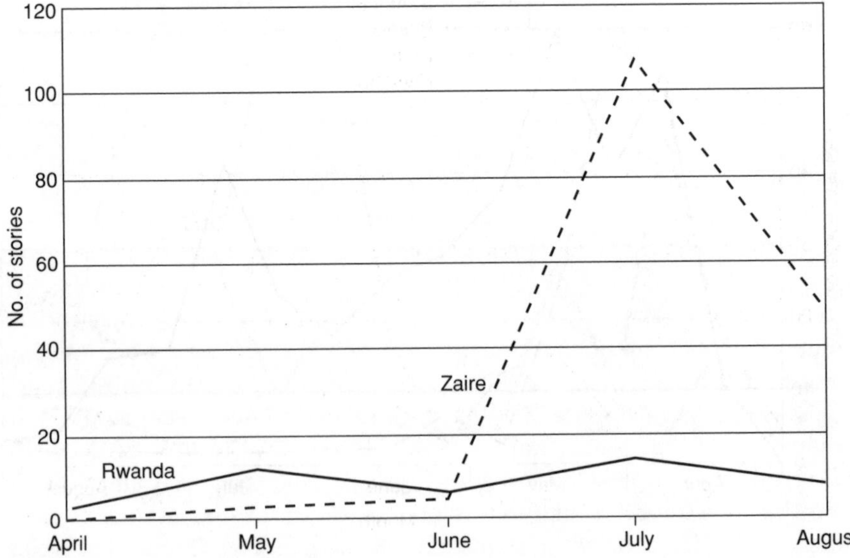

Figure 15.4 CNN coverage of the Rwanda genocide and refugee crisis 1994

Source: Livingston and Stephen 1998.

Rwanda, rather than to the Hutu massacre of Tutsi in Rwanda earlier. Figure 15.4 shows the frequency of CNN datelines (the locations from which a report is filed or transmitted) over the course of the massacre and humanitarian crisis in the refugee camps in Zaire.

The vast majority of CNN news stories about Rwanda were not about the Hutu massacre of Tutsi and moderate Hutu; instead, they were about the Hutu refugees who fled Rwanda on the heels of the RPF military campaign to stop the genocide and unseat the Hutu government. My own observations of the Western press operating in Nairobi, Kenya, at the time indicated an initial mix of fatigue (Somalia had demoralized journalists working out of Nairobi, the hub of the Western press corps for much of Africa) and a sense of danger that prevented closer coverage at the time. This certainly was not universally true. Mark Doyle and Fergal Keane of the BBC, Terry Leonard of the Associated Press and Donatella Lorch, then with *The New York Times*, took enormous personal risks in their attempts to cover the massacre, as did many others. Yet, despite these efforts, most media attention failed to focus on the start of the crisis when, presumably, something could have been done to stop the massacre. But does media coverage actually have the presumed effect implied by the criticism? If more media attention had been given to events in Rwanda early in 1994, could the massacre have been prevented?

By the spring of 1994, American policymakers and pundits *assumed* that coverage of the Somalia crisis drove the US decision to intervene. CNN and other television networks covered the suffering of the Somali people and US policymakers responded with the intervention. Wanting to 'learn the lessons of Somalia', the Clinton administration was adamant: it would not allow pictures of yet another humanitarian crisis in Africa to drive foreign policy decision-making. That is what happened in Somalia and it would not happen in Rwanda.

The only problem with that lesson of history is that it is wrong. The American inaction in Rwanda was the consequence of a fundamental misunderstanding of the policy decisions made by the Bush administration going into Somalia in 1992. In their analysis of US media coverage of events in Somalia in 1991–92, Livingston and Eachus (1995–6) found no evidence to suggest that media determined or otherwise served as the primary cause of the administration's decision to intervene in Somalia. Instead, the decision was the consequence of political pressure put on the administration by key members of Congress, and even from officials within the administration itself. Livingston and Eachus's findings have been substantiated numerous times by subsequent analyses. In a summary of a decade of fairly intense scholarly investigation of the CNN effect, media researcher Piers Robinson (2000) concluded that only under certain and generally unlikely conditions might one expect media coverage to force intervention decisions on policymakers. 'No evidence was found that media coverage could cause policymakers to pursue the more risky option of deploying ground troops during humanitarian crises. The idea of media driving this kind of intervention is a myth' (Robinson 2000: 128). After noting the lack of effect television coverage of Bosnia had on US policymaking, Susan Moeller (1999: 225) reached similar conclusions concerning Rwanda:

> And the Holocaust language and images of genocide in Rwanda did not force American military intervention there either. Stabilizing the internal situation appeared to officials at the Pentagon and elsewhere to be a black hole of commitment. But once the slaughter ended and the refugees settled in camps at the borders, the potential debacle turned into a doable humanitarian effort that the U.S. forces were well-equipped to solve. So the Americans went in.

Yet the conventional wisdom was that media were responsible for setting US policy priorities in Somalia and, therefore, posed that same risk (in the view of those who wished to avoid intervention) or promise (for those who viewed the lack of massacre coverage as the missing ingredient in what would otherwise surely have been an intervention). Media simply do not have that capability, however understood.

That said, it is important to note that media content can indeed have an effect on policy. Television diplomacy in a global information environment, for example, accelerates deliberations. Rather than communicating through traditional diplomatic channels, leaders communicate through media programming of various types. There are other obvious effects. Military operations are vulnerable to disruption by media images in at least two ways. First, such coverage may sap morale. During war, US and civilian casualty coverage is avoided at all costs for fear that support for the war will be adversely affected. Second, in this era of global real-time television coverage using highly mobile satellite technology, reporters may compromise operational security, the secrecy concerning military plans and manoeuvres essential to modern warfare (Livingston 1997). But these effects are not the same as those implied by Kennan and others who have argued that media can establish foreign policy priorities. Policy agenda-setting is left to policymakers.

NOTES

1. It would be inaccurate to ascribe the shift in focus away from international news solely to the end of the Cold War. Important changes to the internal dynamics of news and news culture in the United States were occurring simultaneously. Growing concentration of media ownership is pointed to by many scholars as a principle cause of the erosion of international news, and serious news generally. With an eye toward the bottom line, corporate media began filling airtime with exactly the sort of stories identified in the content analysis results mentioned: crime, scandal and features. International news is expensive to produce and often, it is sometimes argued, unimportant to American audiences – except when the story from abroad involves Americans. See Bagdikian (1997) for a full discussion of the concentration of media ownership.

REFERENCES

Bagdikian, B. 1997. *The Media Monopoly* (5th edn.). Beacon Press, Boston, MA, USA.

Hickey, N. 1998. Money Lust: How Pressure for Profit is Perverting Journalism. *Columbia Journalism Review*, July/August: 32–3.

Hoge, J.F., Jr 1997. Foreign News: Who Gives a Damn? *Columbia Journalism Review*, November/December: 49.

Kennan, G. 1993a. Through a Glass Darkly. *The New York Times*, 30 September 25.

—— 1993b. If TV Drives Foreign Policy, we're in Trouble. *The New York Times*, 24 October 14.

Kurtz, H. 2002. Start Shredding the News: are the Revenue-Hungry Networks Ready to Dump Dinner Hour Broadcasts? *Washington Post National Weekly Edition*, 18–24 March: 6–7.

Livingston, S. 1996. *Beyond the CNN Effect: an Examination of Media Effects According to Type of Intervention.* Shorenstein Center on Press, Politics and Public Policy, Kennedy School of Government, Harvard University, Cambridge, MA, USA.

—— 1997. 'Beyond the CNN Effect: the Media-Foreign Policy Dynamic'. In P. Norris (ed.). *Politics and the Press: the News Media and their Influences*. Lynne Rienner Publishers, Boulder, CO, USA.

Livingston, S. and T. Eachus. 1995–96. Humanitarian Crises and U.S. Foreign Policy: Somalia and the CNN Effect Reconsidered. *Political Communication*, Winter.

—— 1999. 'Too Little Too Late: American Television Coverage of the Rwandan Crisis of 1994'. In H. Adelman and A. Suhrke (eds). *Path to a Genocide: the Rwandan Crisis from Uganda to Zaire*. Transaction Publishers, Brunswick, NJ, USA.

Livingston, S. and D. Stephen. 1998. 'American Network Coverage of Genocide in Rwanda in the Context of General Trends in International News'. In S. Schmeidl and H. Adelman (eds). *Early Warning and Early Response*. Columbia International Affairs Online, New York, NY, USA: 1–18.

Moeller, S. 1999. *Compassion Fatigue: How the Media Sell Disease, Famine, War and Death.* Routledge, New York, NY, USA.

Robinson, P. 2002. *The CNN Effect: the Myth of News, Foreign Policy and Intervention.* Routledge, New York, NY, USA.

Patterson, T.E. 2000. *Doing Well and Doing Good: How Soft News and Critical Journalism are Shrinking the News Audience and Weakening Democracy – and What News Outlets Can Do About it.* Joan Shorenstein Center on Press, Politics, and Public Policy, Kennedy School of Government, Harvard University, Cambridge, MA, USA.

USMUN (United States Mission to the United Nations). 1996. *Global Humanitarian Emergencies, 1996*. USMUN, New York, NY, USA. Available at <www.reliefweb.int/library/usglobal/ghe96_1.html> (accessed 16 September 2005).

16
Missing the Story: the Media and the Rwanda Genocide

Linda Melvern

In the course of a few terrible months in 1994, one million people were killed in Rwanda. It was slaughter on a scale not seen since the Nazi extermination programme. The killing rate in Rwanda was five times that achieved by the Nazis. Such a crime requires motives, means and opportunity. The motive of those responsible for the genocide was to continue to monopolize power and seek a 'final solution' to the political opposition. The means was the mobilization of militia and use of the civil administration to encourage people to take part. Both methods of mass killing had already been tried successfully in Rwanda and were well documented in human rights reports (Ndiaye 1993).

The opportunity for genocide was provided by a conjunction of circumstances, allowing the hard-liners to confuse the international community long enough to be able to perpetrate the crime with extraordinarily little international response. These circumstances, contrived or fortuitous, included the almost immediate withdrawal of international groups when the killing began, the resumption of a civil war and an inaccurate portrayal of the killing by the international press as 'tribal violence'.

It is the initial inaccurate reporting of the genocide by the Western press that is the subject of this paper. There is no doubt that the events in Rwanda in April 1994 took the British and the American media by surprise, but the message that the violence in Rwanda was the result of ancient tribal hatreds was quite simply wrong. The use of this cliché dominated the early reports on the genocide. The basic inference was that the killing represented uncontrollable tribal savagery about which nothing could be done. One British newspaper reported without question the view of a Western diplomat in the capital, Kigali, who told a journalist how 'various clans were murdering others.' Rwanda was described as a failed state. There was chaos and anarchy (Hilsum 1994a).

In reality, a planned annihilation was taking place. This was not a sudden eruption of long-simmering hatred. Genocide does not take place in a context of anarchy. What was happening was the deliberate slaughter of Hutu moderates and all Tutsis, in carefully planned and clinically carried out massacres. There were daily deliveries of weapons to the roadblocks. There were dustcarts touring the capital into which prisoners who had been seconded to 'clean' the streets

This paper first appeared in *Contemporary Security Policy*, 2001: 22(3).

threw bodies. There were no sealed trains or secluded camps in Rwanda. The genocide took place in broad daylight and was broadcast on the radio. The vast majority of victims in Rwanda, it has since been ascertained, died in the first six weeks of the genocide, in large-scale and organized massacres (Des Forges 1999).

The first large-scale massacre to be discovered by United Nations (UN) peacekeepers was at a parish called Gikondo, a stronghold of the Hutu Power faction in the heart of the capital city, Kigali. It was Saturday 9 April. A few weeks before, in March, a Major Podevijn had reported to the headquarters of the UN mission in Rwanda that weapons had been distributed to the members of the *Interahamwe* in Gikondo. On this particular Saturday, the UN peacekeepers were answering a desperate call from two Polish military observers living in Gikondo.

Setting out for the parish that day were two Polish majors, Stefan Stec and Maric Pazik. They were experienced peacekeepers and they had served in the UN mission to Cambodia. With them went Major Brent Beardsley. Beardsley was the staff officer of the force commander, Major General Roméo Dallaire.

The peacekeepers travelled to Gikondo in the one working Czech-made armoured personnel carrier (APC) with a three-man Bangladeshi crew. They were warned that the APC could break down at any moment. As they made their way through the streets, a group of people screamed at them to stop. They drove on. None of them spoke as they passed bodies that were littering the streets. The climb up the hill at Gikondo was laborious for the road was steep and there were deep ruts made by torrential downpours. At the top of the hill was a Catholic mission, operated by Polish priests and nuns and set in terraced gardens surrounded by eucalyptus trees. It was a large mission, self-contained and dominated by a brick church.

When they reached the church the peacekeepers left the Bangladeshi crew with the APC, and walked into the garden. It was there they found the bodies. Whole families had been killed together, each person hacked to death with machetes. There were terrible wounds to the genitalia. Some people were not dead. There was a three-month-old baby, the mother raped and the baby killed with a terrible wound. There were children, some with their legs or feet cut off, and their throats cut. Most of the victims had bled to death.

Stec returned to the APC. He wanted to get his camcorder to film it. There must be proof. They found the UN observers huddled together in the church. Military observers (MILOBS) consisted of commissioned officers from the rank of captain to lieutenant colonel, who were deployed around the country to monitor and ensure that all parties followed the peace agreement.

The peacekeepers in the UN Assistance Mission for Rwanda (UNAMIR) had come to Rwanda to monitor a peace agreement, the Arusha accords, signed in 1993, ending a civil war between the mainly Tutsi rebels, the Rwandan Patriotic Front (RPF) and the Hutu dictatorship that had ruled Rwanda for 20 years. The Arusha accords provided for radical change – political, military and constitutional reform. Rwanda was to have a broad-based transitional government until a democratically elected government was installed. The RPF and the Rwandan army would integrate; there would be disarmament and demobilization. Some 900,000 Tutsi refugees, expelled in the anti-Tutsi pogroms that had taken place since 1959, were to be allowed to return home.

At first, the job of the UN peacekeepers had seemed unambiguous: this was classic UN peacekeeping with the soldiers acting as a buffer between two former enemies. The peacekeepers observe and they mediate. But it was not so simple. By April 1994 the peace agreement had stalled. There were delays in its implementation and the peacekeeping force was too weak to make any difference.

The UN military observers in Gikondo were part of a team of officers from 16 different countries under the command of Colonel Tikoca from Fiji, and supported by operations officer Lieutenant Colonel Somalia Iliya from Nigeria. It was the Polish observers who reported that the *Interahamwe* militia had carried out the killing in Gikondo under the direction of the Presidential Guard. On Saturday morning, 9 April, at about 9 a.m. the priests had organized a mass and about 500 people, sheltering in the compound, turned up at the church. During the mass, there were the sounds of shooting and grenades. There was a commotion. Then two Presidential Guards and two gendarmes burst into the church, followed by *Interahamwe*. The *Interahamwe* wore their distinctive clothing, the *Kitenge*, their multicoloured pants and tunics.

After the massacre was over the priests had tried to gather the wounded in the porch. The priests said that the Rwandan army had cordoned off the parish. They said some of their parishioners did the killing. When the president's plane went down (Wednesday, 6 April) there had been shooting all night long. The next day Tutsi had fled to the church for safety and some people were so afraid that they hid beneath floors, in cupboards or in the rafters.

Another witness to the massacre recalled: 'The militia began slashing away ... They were hacking at the arms, legs, genitals, breasts, faces and necks.' There was total panic. Some people were dragged outside and beaten to death. The killing lasted about two hours and then the killers had walked slowly among the bodies and looted them or finished off the wounded.

One of the Polish military observers had watched the local police entering the buildings in the compound, followed by militia armed with machetes and clubs. One of the militia had what looked like a Kalashnikov. The Polish observer had seen militia climb over the fence and said he had tried to contact UNAMIR headquarters, but the radio channels were jammed. He helped the wounded and had noticed how ears and mouths were slashed, clothes had been pulled off and the genitals of men and women mutilated. He took photographs. There was a pile of identification cards with the ethnic designation of Tutsi, burned in an attempt to eradicate all evidence that these people had existed. The next day the *Interahamwe* came back. They discovered that the survivors were hiding in a small chapel. When they failed to break down the door, the militia poured petrol in through the windows of the chapel followed by hand grenades (Melvern 2000).

In the next three months massacres like this became commonplace. But at Gikondo, there was film and proof. The Polish peacekeepers thought that

Gikondo should alert the world, for they recognized what was happening as genocide.

Two days after the attack on the church in Gikondo, the story of what had happened there appeared in a French newspaper, *Libération*, written by journalist Jean-Philippe Ceppi (1994). Ceppi described seeing mutilated bodies, the men with their penises cut, and the women their breasts. Only a dozen people had survived the massacre and they were not expected to live. In the roads around Gikondo and all over Kigali, murders were taking place. Everywhere there were sounds of screams and gunfire. Presidential Guards toured the city in APCs, carrying lists of victims. The *Interahamwe* battered down doors, chasing Tutsi from house to house, and room to room. Nowhere was safe for Tutsi, not even the hospitals, where Rwandan soldiers were rampaging through the wards looking for them. So many bodies were delivered to the city morgue that they had to be stacked outside.

The French daily *Le Monde* also carried a story about Gikondo, published on Tuesday 12 April by journalist Jean Hélène (1994). Hélène described how the victims of the killing in Kigali were mostly Tutsi. According to the chief delegate of the International Committee of the Red Cross, Philippe Gaillard, who had organized vehicles and delegates to go and help the wounded of Gikondo, an estimated 10,000 people had already been murdered in Kigali. Jean Hélène speculated that by the time the RPF reached Kigali, all the Tutsi would be dead.

But in the Ceppi article in *Libération* the word 'genocide' was used. Ceppi wrote that the RPF was advancing on Kigali and, according to some reports, was only 15 kilometres from the capital. 'But by the time they arrive,' Ceppi reported, 'a genocide of the Tutsi would already have taken place.' Ceppi told me recently that when he got to Kigali on 8 April, over land from Burundi, everyone was using the word genocide. He had met Gaillard, who told him that a genocide of the Tutsi had just begun. Ceppi's story in *Libération* on 11 April, as far as can be ascertained, was the first mention of the word genocide in the media in relation to what was happening. On that day in Britain a broadsheet published a report from Rwanda about the evacuation of a French woman's poodle as a 'veteran of African conflict', and the first paragraph described the evacuation of foreigners from Rwanda. The headline ran: 'Foreigners flee bloody horrors of Rwanda,' and the story explained that there was bloodletting between the majority Hutu and minority Tutsi groups (Hilsum 1994b).

The word genocide disappeared from news reports after that mention in *Libération* and, for the next few weeks, a fog of misinformation shrouded what was happening. Roger Winter, the director of the United States Committee for Refugees, who had known about the problems of Rwanda since 1983, had just returned from Rwanda when the genocide started and he became quite desperate to change the perception in the press that this was tribal warfare. He wrote an article to explain how the violence was political in nature and that what was happening was a plot by an extremist clique to cling to power. This clique was using ethnicity to achieve its aims. Winter's article was rejected by most American papers, including the *Washington Post* and *The New York*

Times. It was eventually published in Toronto's *Globe and Mail* on 14 April (Winter 1994).

The next day an article in *The New York Times* described Rwanda as small, poor and globally insignificant (Sciolino 1994). Rwanda, the newspaper explained, was in an 'uncontrollable spasm of lawlessness and terror'. No member of the UN with an army strong enough to make a difference was willing to risk the lives of its troops for this 'failed central African nation-state with a centuries-old history of tribal warfare and deep distrust of outside intervention'. The newspaper explained that the American strategy was to keep expectations as low as possible. The headline on the story ran: 'For West, Rwanda is not worth the political candle.'

In the first days of the genocide the commander of UNAMIR, Major General Roméo Dallaire from Canada, thought that what was going on was a power grab by extremists, a military coup with the intention of eliminating all opposing politicians and ruining forever the possibility of reconciliation. But the situation soon became clear to him. On 8 April, Dallaire cabled UN headquarters in New York with his first detailed assessment. In this cable, he described a campaign of terror that was well planned and organized. There must be no doubt, he told New York, without the presence of UNAMIR the situation would be much worse.

Dallaire wanted reinforcements. He wanted to take action to try to stop the bloodshed and he believed that with a minimum reinforcement of some 5,000 armed and trained troops, a signal could be sent to those who were organizing the bloodshed. A show of force by the UN would intimidate the gangs of militia. Protected sites could be set up for civilians. Only a lack of means prevented him taking action. Dallaire argued that reinforcements could stop the terror from spreading. He later explained that there was a window of opportunity when the political leaders of the genocide were susceptible to international influence. But there seemed little chance of any reinforcements. At the UN Secretariat in New York the focus was either on the evacuation of expatriates or the possibility of obtaining a ceasefire in the renewed civil war. In the Security Council, there were similar concerns. On 12 April in a secret and informal meeting of the council, the British and American governments made it clear that the best course of action was to pull out all but a token force of the UN peacekeepers from Rwanda.

The issue of reinforcements was not discussed in any depth in the press, although there was a reference to it in a *New York Times* editorial on 23 April on the need to consider whether a mobile quick-response force under UN aegis was necessary to deal with such calamities. The editorial began with the words: 'What looks very much like genocide has been taking place in Rwanda ... The world has few ways of responding effectively when violence within a nation leads to massacres and the breakdown of civil order' (NYT Editors 1994). The Security Council had thrown in the bloodied towel when it decided unanimously to cut back the blue helmets. The editorial ended that without a rapid reaction force 'the world has little choice but to stand aside and hope for the best.'

There remains to this day a lack of interest in the circumstances of the genocide. In the US there have been no congressional hearings into the decision-making process within the US government. In Britain, both the press and Parliament have failed to question the policies of the British government of John Major toward Rwanda. Britain is, after all, a permanent member of the Security Council with a special responsibility for UN policy. Although the former president Bill Clinton later apologized for the international community's failure over Rwanda, the British government, a bystander to genocide, has yet to recognize its own role. Britain had voted for a peacekeeping mission for Rwanda in October 1993. Was there no subsequent monitoring of what was taking place there? What did Britain know of the unfolding of the genocide? What was Britain's role in decision-making in the Security Council?

The meetings held by the Security Council to discuss what to do about the peacekeeping mission and the crisis in Rwanda took place behind closed doors. Twenty years ago, when most council meetings were held in public, it would have been possible to hear the options discussed, but nowadays most debates take place in a side room where the deals are concluded that make up 'UN policy'. This means that the policies of each member government are hidden from public scrutiny. Throughout the genocide, the Security Council was in almost constant secret session, meeting sometimes twice daily and long into the night.

These meetings would usually have remained secret forever were it not for the leak to me from within the council of a remarkable 155-page document containing an account of them. This invaluable primary source gives a unique view of the council's secret world and, without it, an account of the international failure over Rwanda would be incomplete (Melvern 2000). This document exposes some unpleasant truths – not the least of which is the fact that Dallaire's military estimate to try to prevent the spread of organized killings of civilians was not even put to the council for discussion in the first crucial weeks. Just five days after the genocide began, the British raised the issue of reinforcements, but then only to dismiss the idea.

Sir David Hannay, the UK's ambassador to the UN, had put forward four options. The first was to reinforce the troops. But this, Hannay warned, could be a repetition of Somalia. Peacekeeping was not appropriate for civil war, for situations where there was no peace to keep and where fighting factions were unwilling to cooperate. Inadequate effort was worse than no effort at all. Second, UNAMIR could pull out completely but the negative signal that this would send would be damaging. Third, the troops could stay on, although Hannay did query what they could effectively do, for there was no evidence that UNAMIR was in any position to protect civilians. The fourth and last idea was to pull most of the peacekeepers out, leaving behind 'some elements'. Although this might initially attract public criticism, it seemed to be the safest course. There were no press reports about these choices. Whatever official briefing information that comes out of any closed-door session of the council is censored – a culture of secrecy nowadays taken for granted.

In April 1994, the council did not address the question of genocide in Rwanda until three weeks after it had begun. By this time, the evidence was leaking from

Rwanda as hundreds of bodies clogged the Kagera River flowing out of the country. The aid charity, Oxfam, had already determined that genocide was under way and on 28 April had issued a press release with the headline, 'Oxfam fears genocide is happening in Rwanda' (Oxfam 1994).

There was a flicker of interest in the press, but not a lot, for another story was now grabbing the headlines. Thousands of people were pouring out of Rwanda into Tanzania, the fastest exodus the world had ever seen. In Oxford, the press officer for Oxfam, John Magrath, noted the huge numbers of journalists in South Africa covering elections for a new multiracial parliament. Magrath dryly recorded in his diary: 'The South African elections were over and all the crews were diverted to Tanzania – the refugees became the story, not the genocide.' While the genocide took place in Rwanda, the number of reporters never rose above a maximum of 15. In South Africa, in early May, there had been 2,500 accredited press.

On 29 April, the day after Oxfam's press release, there was a long discussion about Rwanda in the Security Council. The president of the council, the New Zealand ambassador Colin Keating, who had been given a briefing on the slaughter by Médecins Sans Frontières, had proposed a presidential statement to recognize that genocide was under way in Rwanda. Keating believed that if the Security Council was to admit that this was genocide, then the states that had signed the 1948 *Convention on the Prevention and Punishment of the Crime of Genocide* (UN 1951) were legally bound to act.[1]

The ambassador for the Czech Republic, Karel Kovanda, had already confronted the council with the fact of genocide at an informal meeting a day earlier, telling ambassadors that it was scandalous that so far 80 per cent of council efforts had been spent discussing withdrawing the peacekeepers, and 20 per cent trying to get a ceasefire in the civil war. He told them: 'It was rather like wanting Hitler to reach a ceasefire with the Jews.' What was happening in Rwanda was genocide, conducted by the interim Hutu regime, he said. Yet the council had totally avoided the question of mass killing. There were objections to Kovanda's outburst and afterward Kovanda said that British and American diplomats quietly told him on no account was he to use such inflammatory language outside the council. It was not helpful.

What Keating proposed in his presidential statement was to give the killing in Rwanda its rightful name – genocide. The statement included the paragraph:

> The horror of Rwanda's killing fields has few precedents in the recent history of the world. The Security Council reaffirms that the systematic killing of any ethnic group, with intent to destroy it in whole or in part constitutes an act of genocide as defined by relevant provisions of international law ... the council further points out that an important body of international law exists that deals with perpetrators of genocide.

The draft warned the 'interim government of its responsibility for immediately reining in and disciplining those responsible for the brutality.'

There were objections. Hannay did not want the word 'genocide' to appear in the statement, and he argued that were the statement to be used in an official UN document, then the council would become a 'laughing stock'. To name this genocide and not to act on it would be ridiculous. Nor did the US want the word used, and China argued against it. The Rwandan ambassador said that the civilian deaths were the result of civil war and he was ably supported in this by the French-influenced ally, Djibouti. The debate went round in circles.

Keating, whose term as president of the council would end the following day, tried the somewhat desperate measure of threatening a draft resolution, tabled in his national capacity. This would require a vote, and a vote was always taken in public. This would expose the positions of each country to public scrutiny. Only after this threat was a compromise reached. Thanks to the drafting ability of the British, known for resolutions with mind-numbing ambiguity, a watered-down statement was issued, and while the statement quoted directly from the genocide convention, it did not use the word genocide.

> The Security Council condemns all these breaches of international humanitarian law in Rwanda, particularly those perpetrated against the civilian population, and recalls that persons who instigate or participate in such acts are individually responsible ... the Security Council recalls that the killing of members of an ethnic group with the intention of destroying such a group in whole or in part constitutes a crime punishable by international law. (Security Council 1994)

The statement recognized that the massacres were systematic, although it did not identify the targets. It read: 'Attacks on defenceless civilians have occurred throughout the country, especially in areas under the control of members or supporters of the armed forces of the interim Government of Rwanda.' To satisfy French insistence that massacres had also been conducted by the RPF, the statement went on: 'The Security Council demands that the interim Government of Rwanda and the Rwandese Patriotic Front take effective measures to prevent any attacks on civilians in areas under their control.' The statement appealed to all states to refrain from providing arms or any military assistance to the two sides in Rwanda and reiterated the call for a ceasefire. It requests that the Secretary General investigate 'serious violations of international humanitarian law'. The statement was finally voted on at 1.15 a.m. on Saturday 30 April. 'We ended April exhausted but hopeful that the first few weeks of May would bring action to reinforce UNAMIR with a real force capable of doing what Dallaire had been urging,' Keating said.

Some years later, in December 1998, in a BBC Radio Four interview, Hannay talked specifically about the genocide convention in relation to Rwanda: 'Nobody ever started to say who will actually do the intervening and how will it be done' (Glenny 1998). In an interview with me in December 1999, Hannay pointed out that the council could not conjure up troops and, although he believes that Dallaire did a fantastic job, Hannay remains deeply sceptical of Dallaire's belief that 5,000 troops could have prevented much of the slaughter.

In any case, to have mounted an enforcement mission with so few troops was totally against US military doctrine. Hannay explained that the British were 'extremely unsighted' over Rwanda. There was no British embassy there. There were no British interests. Rwanda was a long way down the list of priorities and the telegrams about Rwanda, received from British embassies in Brussels, Paris and Washington were not treated as high grade. In April 1994, a lot of time and resources were being channelled into the problems of Bosnia and in trying to disarm Iraq. The staff at the British mission in New York was overstretched.

Hannay says the information coming from the Secretariat was insufficient; he complained about the inadequate briefings available to the Security Council. Secretary General Dr Boutros Boutros-Ghali controlled the flow of information to the council, Hannay said, allowing only those officials with his permission to brief ambassadors.

In all the discussions held about Rwanda before the genocide began, the focus had been on how to implement the Arusha accords. 'Events proved,' said Hannay, 'we were looking in the wrong direction, and that the Secretariat was telling us to look in that direction.' He had seen none of the force commander's cables from Rwanda because the council was not meant to be involved in the day-to-day running of peacekeeping missions. Even so, Hannay is convinced that there was nothing the UN could have done to prevent the genocide in Rwanda, not with a Hutu-led government intent on it. Even had the Security Council recognized the killing as genocide, it would not have saved any lives. Hannay said that he was not a lawyer and was, therefore, not in a position to decide whether what was happening was genocide. 'We knew a lot of Tutsi were being killed by a lot of Hutu,' he said.

Another glimpse into British government thinking is afforded in a letter sent in July 1995 by the Foreign and Commonwealth Office (FCO), to an international enquiry. In this letter, written a year after the genocide ended, the FCO said it did not accept the term genocide. The FCO was inclined to regard a discussion of whether the massacres constituted genocide as 'sterile'. The FCO approach was characterized from the outset by a determination to play the matter down and, for a body that once regarded Africa as its area of special interest, an almost deliberate ignorance. For instance, on 9 May in the House of Commons, and in response to a question about Rwanda, Parliament was told: 'More than 200,000 may have perished in the recent fighting in Rwanda' (Lennox-Boyd 1994).

This was an extraordinary statement. The estimated death toll had reached 500,000 – whole families killed in organized massacres taking place nowhere near the renewed civil war. The lack of Parliamentary scrutiny of British policy is evidenced in the fact that a debate on Rwanda was not held until 24 May 1994 – some six weeks after the genocide began – when Labour Party MP Tony Worthington expressed shock that so little attention had been paid to Rwanda. Worthington told an almost empty House at 11 p.m.: 'It is inconceivable that an atrocity in which half a million white people had died would not have been extensively debated in the House' (Worthington 1994). Worthington said that the press had a terrible tendency to dismiss the events as tribalism. 'Genocide is certainly involved,' Worthington told the House. Britain was a signatory to the genocide convention. 'Has there ever been a clearer example of genocide?' he asked.

The Labour Party had waited until May before putting pressure on the government to act, and only then because Oxfam telephoned the office of David Clark, shadow Secretary of State for defence. Clark called for the UN and the Organization of African Unity (OAU) to organize an immediate deployment of forces to try to end the mass killing of civilians and appealed to Malcolm Rifkind, the Secretary of State for defence, so that the 'advice and expertise that our armed forces possess could be made available to the UN'. On 23 May, Rifkind wrote back to say that troops for Rwanda would 'probably come from regional forces in Africa'.

The UK, wrote Rifkind, 'has not been asked to provide any personnel for the operation'. It was an extraordinary sentence for Rifkind to write. Only a few days earlier Britain had voted in the Security Council to authorize more troops for Rwanda and, at the time, officials in the Secretariat were making desperate efforts to find soldiers. This was repeated in the House of Commons on 14 June when, in a written answer, Douglas Hogg claimed that the UK government had not been asked to contribute troops to the UN peacekeeping operation in Rwanda (Hogg 1994). In fact, the head of the UN's peacekeeping department, Kofi Annan, said that every UN member government with spare military capacity had received a fax with a list of urgently needed troops and equipment.

In July 1994, Britain's minister for overseas development, Baroness Lynda Chalker, visited Kigali. She met Dallaire and she asked him what he needed. Dallaire had showed Chalker his list of basic requirements, which by then had been faxed around the world. 'I gave her my shopping list,' he remembered. 'I was up to my knees in bodies by then.' Britain had previously promised Dallaire 50 four-ton four-wheel-drive trucks, but they had not materialized.

On a BBC 2 Newsnight programme about Rwanda, Baroness Chalker later blamed Dallaire's lack of resources on 'the UN', which, she explained, ought to 'get its procurement right'. No one challenged this remark. Only after the genocide was over, and in response to another massive flight of people from Rwanda, this time into Zaire, did Britain become more generous. Chalker called the refugee tragedy the most ghastly in living memory, a replay of the Middle Ages and, on 28 July, Britain offered military assistance in the form of 600 personnel from the Royal Electrical and Mechanical Engineers (REME) to repair the large number of unroadworthy vehicles that belonged to Dallaire's mission, a field ambulance and a field squadron of Royal Engineers to repair roads and drill wells. Dallaire's only offers during the genocide, as a matter of record, were 50 trucks from Britain; a promise from Italy of one C130 aircraft plus crew; 6 water trucks, a signals squadron plus aircraft from Canada; from the US 50 armoured personnel carriers, leasehold; and from Japan, US$ 3 million toward the cost of equipment. Nothing materialized.

In the years since the genocide, the shortage of accurate media coverage has been placed high on the list of reasons for Western inaction. One international report concluded that the Western media's failure to adequately report that genocide was taking place, and thereby generate public pressure for something to be done to stop it, had contributed to international indifference and inaction, and possibly to the crime itself. Although the coverage had been handicapped by danger on the ground, the press, in generally characterizing the genocide as tribal anarchy, was fundamentally irresponsible (Millwood 1996). It was left to nongovernmental organizations – most notably Oxfam and Amnesty International – to lead a call for something to be done in Rwanda, to draw attention in those first crucial weeks to what was really happening.

In a letter to the *Guardian* on 16 April 1994, Stewart Willis, the overseas director of Oxfam, had pleaded for the UN to immediately reinforce its peacekeepers in Rwanda: 'It is outrageous and despicable that at the same time as the UN Security Council is acting with vigour to protect civilians in Gorazde, French and Belgian troops have to look away while people are hacked to death' (Wallis 1994). At the time, the Serb bombing of the safe area of Gorazde was grabbing the headlines.

On 20 April, Jeri Laber, executive director, Human Rights Watch–Helsinki, wrote to the *New York Times* that the UN should find a means to protect the innocent. To describe ancient hatreds in Rwanda was deplorable, faulty and dangerous (Laber 1994). Another letter said: 'One has to wonder why the atrocities in Bosnia receive the widespread attention they do while the massacres of tens of thousands in an African country is met with a collective denial of responsibility and a hasty retreat.' It was from William F. Schulz (1994), executive director of Amnesty International to the *Washington Post* on 1 May.

With no outcry about genocide in the press, no choices were given and no risks were taken. At the very least the genocide should have been condemned in the strongest possible terms by the press. Those responsible for the genocide, and their names were known, should have been publicly denounced. Even the story of Dallaire and the gallant contingent of the International Committee of the Red Cross (ICRC) under chief delegate, Philippe Gaillard, remained unreported. Indeed, there was later criticism of UNAMIR. One US journalist, Philip Gourevitch, wrote how in the summer of 1994 UN troops had killed dogs feeding off the corpses. Gourevitch (1998: 148) noted: 'After months during which Rwandans had been left to wonder whether the UN troops knew how to shoot, because they never used their excellent weapons to stop the extermination of civilians, it turned out that the peacekeepers were very good shots.'

While some 470 volunteer peacekeepers stayed on in Rwanda, the UN failed even to resupply them; at the same time, the ICRC had managed to get tonnes of medical equipment into Rwanda. When Dr James Orbinksi of Médecins Sans Frontières arrived in Kigali in June 1994, he was shocked at the state of the peacekeepers, astonished that they were obliged to limit their rescue attempts for lack of petrol. Orbinski said of their commander: 'His tenacity and sheer drive to maximise the impact of UNAMIR was extraordinary.'

While diplomats and politicians were arguing that nothing could be done, these people were doing all they could to try to ease the suffering of the Rwandan people. Gaillard estimated that during the three months of genocide, the ICRC looked after 9,000 injured people and a further 100,000 people were saved because of the work of ICRC delegates elsewhere in the country. In Kigali, there had been 1,200 surgical operations and hundreds more people were treated from the back of ambulances. At the end of the genocide there were 2,500 people in the ICRC hospital compound in Kigali. Gaillard told me that this was 'no more than a drop of humanity in an ocean of blood'. It was the most extraordinary humanitarian operation since World War II, and my book told for the first time the amazing story of these people (Melvern 2000).

The international community could have publicly condemned the interim government in Rwanda for flagrantly failing to fulfil its obligations under international law, notably the *Convention on Genocide*, which it signed in 1975. Countries should have severed diplomatic ties with Rwanda and expelled Rwandan ambassadors.

Anyone who tried to represent a government that was presiding over genocide – in fact was perpetrating it – should have been refused a place anywhere in the civilized world. Instead there was silence. For three months the British and US administrations played down the crisis and tried to impede effective intervention by UN forces. There was even reluctance to take the slightest action, such as jamming the hate radio, which could have saved lives. The lack of action over Rwanda should be the defining scandal of the presidency of Bill Clinton. Yet in the slew of articles on the Clinton years that followed Clinton's departure from power, there was barely a mention of the genocide. Only Christopher Hitchens (2001), one of several journalists interviewed about the Clinton legacy, mentioned how Clinton had 'vetoed the rescue of Rwanda'.

If the media forget this story, then the media have failed. Why this pitiful lack of coverage in this great age of information? The lack of adequate reporting of the genocide in Rwanda raises some serious questions and most of them have yet to be adequately addressed. It is an unpalatable fact, but this story has a tragic contemporary resonance, for the scars and the consequences of the genocide, largely unreported, are with us today.

NOTE

1. In April 1994, the nonpermanent members of the Security Council were: Argentina, Brazil, Czech Republic, Djibouti, New Zealand, Nigeria, Oman, Pakistan, Rwanda and Spain. All but three of these states – Djibouti, Nigeria and Oman – had signed the genocide convention.

REFERENCES

Ceppi, J.P. 1994. Kigali livre a la fureur des tueurs Hutus. *Libération*, 11 April.

Des Forges, A. 1999. *Leave None to Tell the Story: Genocide in Rwanda*. Human Rights Watch and the International Federation of Human Rights Leagues, New York, NY, USA. Available at <www.hrw.org/reports/1999/rwanda/> (accessed 30 August 2005).

Glenny, M. 1998. War radio. BBC Radio 4, 10 December.

Gourevitch, P. 1998. *We Wish to Inform You that Tomorrow We Will be Killed with our Families*. Picador, London, UK.

Hélène, J. 1994. Le Rwanda feet a sang. *Le Monde*, 12 April.

Hilsum, L. 1994a. Rwandan PM Killed as Troops Wreak Carnage. *Guardian*, 8 April.

—— 1994b. Foreigners Flee Bloody Horrors of Rwanda. *Guardian*, 11 April.

Hitchens, C. 2001. The Clinton Years. *Observer*, 7 January.

Hogg, D. 1994. *Hansard: written answers to questions*. House of Commons, London, UK, 14 June.

Laber, J. 1994. Don't write off Rwandan violence as ethnic (letter to the editor). *The New York Times*, 20 April.

Lennox-Boyd, M. 1994. *Hansard: written answers to questions*. House of Commons, London, UK, 9 May.

Melvern, L. 2000. *A People Betrayed: the Role of the West in Rwanda's Genocide*. Zed Books, London, UK.

Melvern, L. 2004. *Conspiracy to Murder: the Rwandan Genocide*. Verso, New York, NY, USA.

Millwood, D. (ed.). 1996. The international response to conflict and genocide: lessons from the Rwandan experience. Steering Committee of the Joint Evaluation of Emergency Assistance to Rwanda, Copenhagen, Denmark. Available at <www.jha.ac/Ref/aar003e.pdf> (accessed 20 September 2005).

Ndiaye, B.W. 1993. *Report of the International Commission of Investigation of Human Rights Violations in Rwanda since 1 Oct 1990*. Fédération internationale des ligues des droits de l'homme, Paris, France. E/CN.4/1994/7/add 1.

NYT Editors. 1994. Cold Choice in Rwanda. *The New York Times*, 23 April.

Oxfam. 1994. Oxfam fears genocide is happening in Rwanda (press release). Oxfam, Oxford, UK.

Schulz, W.F. 1994. US leadership in Rwanda's crisis (letter to the editor). *Washington Post*, 1 May.

Sciolino, E. 1994. For West, Rwanda is Not Worth the Political Candle. *The New York Times*, 15 April.

Security Council. 1994. Statement by the president of the Security Council. United Nations, New York, NY, USA, 30 April. S/PRST/1994/21. Available at <daccessdds.un.org/doc/UNDOC/GEN/N94/199/86/PDF/N9419986.pdf?OpenElement> (accessed 20 September 2005).

UN (United Nations). 1951. *Convention on the prevention and punishment of the crime of genocide*. Adopted by Resolution 260 (III) of the UN General Assembly, 9 December 1948. *UN Treaty Series* no. 1021, vol. 78: 277. Available at <www.preventgenocide.org/law/convention/text.htm> (accessed 6 September 2005).

Wallis, S. 1994. Looking the other way in Rwanda (letter to the editor). *Guardian*, 16 April.

Winter, R. 1994. [Title unknown]. *Globe and Mail*, 14 April.

Worthington, T. 1994. *Hansard: debates*. House of Commons, London, UK, 24 May. Available at <www.publications.parliament.uk/pa/cm199394/cmhansrd/1994–05–24/Debate-17.html> (accessed 20 September 2005).

17
What Did They Say? African Media Coverage of the First 100 Days of the Rwanda Crisis

Emmanuel C. Alozie

Issues and events in Africa attract little attention in the world press (Livingston and Eachus 2000). The deficiencies in international media coverage of the 1994 Rwanda genocide have been well established, and there is a considerable body of literature on Western media coverage of Africa in general (Alozie 2005a). But most researchers have focused on the performance of European or Western news media. Few have examined the coverage that African media outlets in one country afford to events taking place in another African country. Do African media, by virtue of geographic proximity or their situation in the African context, do a better job in their analyses and news reports of events on the continent?

This study attempts to discern the frames that dominated the coverage of the 1994 Rwandan crisis and genocide in two leading African newspapers: Kenya's *Daily Nation* and Nigeria's *Guardian*. It looks at the period from the start of the genocide, on 7 April 1994 through to the end of June. These two newspapers were chosen because of their prominence in their regions and indeed in Africa and also because one is published in Kenya – one of Rwanda's neighbours – while the other is in Nigeria on the other side of the continent.

There was a great deal of overlap between the two newspapers with regard to the major frames established. Both papers also went to considerable lengths to explore the background to the crisis and its greater implications. This is important considering that Western media are often accused of failing to do just that. However, there were also differences in coverage. The national/regional interest emerged as a theme in the *Daily Nation* but did not develop in coverage by the *Guardian*. This focus was evidently a result of Kenya's proximity to Rwanda – not the fact that the *Nation* is an African newspaper. And although both papers devoted considerable space and resources to covering the Rwanda events, over time, the *Daily Nation* offered more comprehensive accounts while the *Guardian*'s attention waned.

THE ROLE OF THE MASS MEDIA IN AFRICA

The establishment of national media outlets and telecommunication components, coupled with cooperative efforts among African countries to develop communication links, attest to the fact that governments realize the importance of effective communication for promoting national development and international diplomacy (Pratt 1996). However, Africa still lags woefully behind in the development of media and information and communications technologies (De Beer 2004). Hachten (2004) blames the underdeveloped status of African media and communications on the inadequate financial, technical and telecommunications resources and the lack of professional manpower. De Beer (2004) includes the legacy of slavery, apartheid, colonialism and imperialism as contributing factors. Zaffiro (1993) identified characteristics of both democratic and autocratic African states:

- Skewed, urban-based centralization of infrastructure, resources and audiences;
- Emphasis on comings and goings and images of top national political leaders, particularly the president;
- Heavy and often conflicting demands on media institutions to serve national development, to inform, educate and entertain;
- General lack of diversity of information and focus between different national media organs;
- Structure that ensures top-down communications flow and is susceptible to monopolization and political manipulation.

In this era of globalization, when information and communications technologies have become a mainstay of international economic and political activities, many African governments are shifting their policies to enhance the growth of the communication sector and engaging in cooperative efforts to improve communications. The revival can be attributed to press freedom and economic liberalization that have promoted private ownership, technical acquisition and enhanced professional assistance and development (Alozie 2005b; Onwudiwe and Ibelema 2003). But development of information and communications technologies is still slow (Eribo 2004) and the rate of progress differs from one nation to another. Few Africans are regular Internet users, for example, owing to cost and access problems.

The degree of control over and restrictions on freedom of the press vary greatly among African countries. For example, Kenya and Nigeria have a tradition of a relatively liberal and independent press, whereas Rwanda is restrictive (BBC 2005a). Kenya is one of the few African countries where the existence of a large middle class provides substantial advertising revenue. Like most Africans, Kenyans rely on the broadcast media, particularly radio, for news. Although electronic and print media are in both private and government hands following recent liberalization, in the past the government dominated and owned the broadcast station. The reach of radio and television is expanding nationally, unlike in the past when only Nairobi and other major cities enjoyed adequate coverage. The BBC World Service, the Voice of America and Radio France Internationale are relayed on full-time FM stations in various parts of the country.

In Nigeria, ownership of print media is in both private and government hands. Currently, Nigeria has about 150 consumer publications including dailies, magazines, periodicals and industrial and professional journals (BBC 2005b). All 36 states run their own radio stations and most of them operate television services. Broadcast services reach rural and urban areas in most regions, but television viewing tends to be concentrated more in urban areas and among the affluent. Nigeria has a handful of privately owned broadcasting outlets, but the television industry is limited by high costs and scarce advertising revenues. International services are reaching Nigeria through the Internet, cable and satellite services. Radio is very common and serves as the main source of information for Nigerians of all socio-economic and educational levels.

The government of Rwanda owns the only television network in the country and a large number of the radio stations (BBC 2005c). It regulates electronic broadcasting and imposes censorship on the press. The first privately owned radio station since 1994 was established in 2004 and has since been joined by a cluster of competitors. Radio played a significant propaganda role during the 1994 crisis. Rwanda's growing numbers of newspapers face government restrictions and generally exercise self-censorship. Some are outright pro-government. The BBC World Service, Voice of America and Deutsche Welle broadcast on FM in Kigali.

REVIEW OF THE LITERATURE

Interest in international communications and the number of studies of international news coverage and analysis have been on the rise for more than 30 years. The increase can be attributed to the greater interaction among people and nations, the need to examine and understand the flow and exchange of mass media artefacts and news across boundaries, coupled with the need to promote international diplomacy and understanding (Anokwa et al. 2003; Herman and Chomsky 1988; Kamalipour 2002; Strobel 1997). Research has examined who controls international communications, news content, news selection and news flow – attributes that affect news content and how national and international relations affect news coverage and analyses (Chang 1993; Galtung and Ruge 1970; Pool 1952; Shoemaker et al. 1991).

Most studies have concluded that national interest, trade volume, cultural affinity, political relations, conflicts and disaster and the presence of international news agencies influence international news coverage and coverage exerts an influence on public policy and the public. They have also found that the West and a small number of supra-news organizations in developed nations dominate international news and communications (Cho 2003; Golan 2003; Wanta et al. 2004; Wu 2000).

However, despite the rising interest and growing number of studies, little or nothing exists with regard to African mass media coverage and analysis of international issues and events. This is especially true of studies that deal with how the press in one African country monitors, covers and analyzes events, conflicts and related issues in another African country (Edeani 1994; Emenyonu

1995). This shortcoming exists despite the fact that, of all regions in the world, Africa has experienced and continues to experience the greatest number of internal and external conflicts as well as economic, social and political woes. A paucity of qualified researchers, lack of avenues for publication, inadequate financial and technical resources and government pressures have all been blamed for the gulf (Alozie 2005b; Ochola 1980). It could be argued that this failure hinders the promotion of knowledge about events and the role of the press in Africa. It also prevents African leaders and government from monitoring how their policies and actions are viewed, leading them to feel less accountable.

The few studies that do exist on African press coverage of international issues have often dealt with their coverage of events, issues and nations outside the continent or personalities visiting the continent who may have limited impact in Africa (Alozie 2004; Idowu 1987; Ibelema 2001; St. Clair 2004). Critics have alleged that these studies do not necessarily promote knowledge of Africa, influence events or have a direct impact on Africa because they are not focused on Africa. (It must be noted that some studies have examined domestic media and have dealt with development, internal strife and other related issues (Edeani 1994; Emenyonu 1995; Nwokeafor and Nwankwo 1993; Umaru Pate cited in Onwumechili and M'Bayo 1995).)

Critics argue that studies of African mass media and international news coverage have often focused on only a few countries and have been limited in scope (Ochola 1980). This is true in terms of the work of Nwokeafor and Nwankwo (1993), Edeani (1994) and Emenyonu (1995) on Nigerian mass media coverage of Africa. Umaru Pate's work on African press coverage of international concerns is important. The content analysis found that African mass media paid more attention to events outside the continent – especially those in Europe and the United States – than they did to events in Africa (Onwumechili and M'Bayo 1995). Critics who find these results startling contend that the African media have failed to monitor the governments in the region to hold them accountable for their policies and actions. On the other hand, those who are not surprised at Pate's findings contend that the greater attention paid to Europe and America is influenced by European colonization and African dependence on Europe and the United States for aid, trade and economic welfare.

Numerous studies have examined the portrayal of Africa in Western and other regional media (Biko et al. 2000; Fair 1996; Hawk 1992). Their common finding reveals that according to the Western press, Africa is plagued with political and socio-economic upheavals, is prone to violent conflicts and often suffers from natural disasters as well as disasters caused by human beings. Critics point out that Western news media tend to pay attention to Africa only when crises occur and fail to contextualize the stories they are covering. This practice has resulted in a negative image of Africa as a place where nothing works in spite of the progress the continent has made, considering its longstanding sufferings from slavery, colonialism and a battleground during the Cold War (Onwudiwe and Ibelema 2003).

METHODS

In this study, I use framing to examine the coverage and analyses of the 1994 Rwandan crisis and genocide from the outset of the genocide on 7 April 1994 through to 29 June 1994. Two leading African newspapers were chosen for study because of their prominence in their regions, and indeed in Africa, and also because one (the *Daily Nation*) is situated in Kenya, one of Rwanda's neighbours, and the other (the *Guardian*) is in Nigeria, an African giant to be sure, but located on the other side of the continent from Rwanda. The reliance on framing allows us to discern whether the focus of these newspapers overlaps or whether there were marked differences in content.

The approach

The process was straightforward. Using microfilm copies, a research assistant examined every page of the issues published during the period under study. He extracted every account that mentioned the Rwanda genocide in any way. The machine he was using allowed him to create portable document format (PDF) images of the pages containing the identified articles.

Qualitative analysis calls for sequential and multiple reading of the texts. The first step entailed a general reading to gain an understanding of the stories, while making descriptive notes about the content of the articles (Gavrilos 2002). The articles were read a second time, during which detailed notes were taken identifying certain recurring themes, frames, values and topic categories. These were used to develop a framework for a third reading – an in-depth interpretation of the articles. This third reading involved applying critical analysis techniques to gain a deeper understanding of the messages conveyed in the texts and thus discern their implications, connections, omissions, stance and values in relation to the theoretical underpinning and research questions being explored. The words 'international' and 'world' are used interchangeably to refer to countries and organizations outside the continent of Africa, while Africa or African refer to countries and organizations in Africa.

It is important to note that there is no 'correct' interpretation of these texts because a researcher's reading, like a journalist's, is filtered through the lens of that person's own experiences and opinions (Kellner 2003). Kellner points out that an analyst's interpretation of a text is only one probable understanding from a critic's subjective position, no matter how multiperspective, and may not necessarily be the assessment the audience prefers or the one offered by others.

The newspapers

The *Daily Nation* is a member of the Nation Media Group (NMG), founded by His Highness the Aga Khan and the largest independent media group in East Africa. The newspaper started publishing in 1960 with a promise to do its utmost to help Kenya and the other East African territories make the perilous transition to African majority rule and full independence as peacefully and constructively as possible. The newspaper has been characterized as a Kenyan national daily with a regional outlook. In its own promotional material, the newspaper says its history is closely entwined with that of modern Kenya, and the newspaper has remained true to its mission to be independent. Viewed as the leading multimedia house in the East African region with its major publications, *The East African*, *The Advertiser*, *Monitor* (Uganda) and Kiswahili papers *Mwananchi* and *Mwana Spoti* (Tanzania), the NMG has a strong presence in both print and electronic media as well as on the Internet, attracting a regular audience unparalleled in East Africa (Daily Nation 2005).

Since its inception more than 25 years ago, the *Guardian* has been consistently ranked as one of the leading dailies in Nigeria and enjoys a reputation as an independent voice because of its stand against military regimes, its critical examination of Nigeria's internal problems and its informed discussions of foreign affairs. Founded by Alex Ibru, one of Nigeria's foremost industrialists, the *Guardian* has a liberal philosophy, with the motto: 'Conscience, Nurtured by Truth'. Known for its balanced coverage of events and issues, on the domestic front, the paper is

> committed to the best traditions and ideals of republican democracy. It believes that it is the responsibility of the state not only to protect and defend the citizen, but also to create the conditions, political, social, economic and cultural, in which all citizens may achieve their highest potential as human beings. It is committed to the principle of individual freedom, but believes that all citizens have duties as well as rights.

Its international mission states that it

> believes that Nigeria is a legitimate member of the international community, but holds that she can best fulfill her international obligations only if her own security and integrity are assured. (Guardian 2005)

Framing: theoretical and methodological implications

The mass media use the relaying of information and news to influence society. Although they attempt to be objective, objectivity is difficult to achieve because the training, upbringing, religious, political and cultural orientations of journalists tend to influence how they report and analyze events and issues (Severin and Tankard 2001). Framing is used to understand the process that the mass media use in selecting content for public communication (Wikipedia 2005). The frame is an abstract notion that organizes or structures the meaning of artefacts. Mass media frames influence the audience's perception of the news; 'this form of agenda-setting not only tells *what* to think about an issue (agenda setting theory), but also *how* think to about that issue' (Value Based Management.net 2005). Auerbach and Bloch-Elkon (2005: 85) describe framing as a pattern for presenting and commenting on the news that organizes the political debate into what is comprehensible to the public.

Framing has grown as a methodological approach to discerning and interpreting the values and meaning conveyed in news. Employing framing requires 'constructing and processing discourse or characteristics of the discourse itself' (Pan and Kosicki 2003: 57). The process helps analysts determine what influenced and controlled the coverage of an issue or event. Entman (1993) and others have stated that framing can be used to unmask the ideology, values, implications, orientations, views and aims conveyed in media artefacts like news, commentaries and features (Alozie 2005a, b; Bishop 2005; Goffman 1974; Scheufele 1999; Tuchman 1978).

However, some say that framing lacks rigorous conceptualization. Carragee and Roefs (2004: 214) cite the conceptual 'problems in the definition of frames, the inattention to frame sponsorship, the failure to examine framing contexts within wider political and social contexts, and the reduction of framing to a form of media effects'. They advise that framing studies should take a cue from their sociological origins that relied on the holistic approach through an exploration of the wider historical, political, economic and cultural environment that affects the coverage of a subject.

In spite of the debate over the appropriateness of framing, it remains one of the most useful and powerful mechanisms for examining texts and artefacts, which usually convey multiple meanings because of the social and cultural differences that may exist within and across borders. News aims at providing objective facts to the public to enable them to make informed decisions on a variety of issues. News tells the public what has occurred, what is occurring and what is most likely to occur. It tells the story of those who do not want to or cannot tell their own stories. It tells the story of the victor and vanquished. It exposes the evils of the powerful or even good deeds that might not otherwise come to the forefront. It takes the weak and beleaguered into account. It holds individuals and societies responsible for their conditions and gives them hope by seeking help when the facts are presented. It surveys the environment to shine the searchlight on every human conduct no matter where, when, how, why and what occurs. It guides the human experience.

Because framing requires in-depth analysis of texts, it helps us achieve the secondary purpose of this study: to determine if, in their coverage of the Rwanda genocide, the focus of the two newspapers overlapped (synchronization) or if there were marked differences in their content (heterogeneity). This distinction will help determine whether mass media closer to Rwanda covered the events in a different fashion than media at a distance. Does national interest relate to geography and the neighbourhood in which a society exists? As a neighbour, Kenya might have greater socio-economic ties with Rwanda than Nigeria on the other side of the continent. On the other hand, South Africa and Nigeria are regarded as the most influential nations in sub-Saharan Africa and, since independence, Nigeria has played an important role in the affairs of Africa economically and politically.

FINDINGS

Examination of coverage of the 1994 Rwandan crisis and genocide in the *Guardian* and *Daily Nation* revealed four discourses: bane of a nation; Rwandan national introspection; African cataclysm and introspection; and world inaction and indifference.

Bane of a nation

The phenomenon of ethnic violence, killings and refugee flights in Rwanda can be traced to Hutu efforts to dislodge the colonial administration and end centuries of Tutsi domination. The Hutus took a major step in this regard when they overthrew the reigning Tutsi king in 1959, which helped them ascend to power at independence in 1962. Since then, Rwandan political and social institutions have been beset by one upheaval after another. Over the years, these sprees of violence, pogroms and refugee flights planted the seeds of the 1994 crisis and genocide that cost about 800,000 lives and displaced three million people (Talentino 1999). The immediate catalysts of the 1994 disorder and massacre were the Rwandan Patriotic Front's (RPF's) October 1990 invasion, the protracted and stalled peace negotiations, the failure to implement the Arusha accords and the deaths of the presidents of Rwanda and Burundi (Habyarimana and Ntaryamira, respectively) in a plane crash while they were returning from a peace mission.

When the *Daily Nation* (1994a) reported the deaths of Habyarimana and Ntaryamira it highlighted historical violent events in Rwanda and Burundi:

- 1959 – Hutus overthrow Tutsi kings;
- 1965 – Attempted Hutu coup;
- 1972 – Over 100,000 Hutus massacred;
- 1993 – Peace accord signed in Arusha;
- 1993 – Melchior Ndadaye (the first elected president of Burundi) killed in coup bid;
- 1994 – President Habyarimana of Rwanda and President Cyprien Ntaryamira killed.

The report, which traced and focused on Rwanda's political crisis since the RPF's invasion in 1990, tended to describe the RPF's military exploits as 'stunning and successful' and as forcing the Rwandan government to enter into negotiations and make concessions to the rebels. The article stated:

> Since 1959 and in subsequent Tutsi massacres at the hands of Hutus in Rwanda, large numbers sought refuge in the neighbouring countries of Tanzania, Zaire and Uganda. Others sought refuge far away in Kenya and Europe, but all nursed a dream of returning back. Numbering between two and three million worldwide, they offered an elaborate system of financing and support for the rebels. (Daily Nation 1994a)

If the Tutsi viewed the invasion as an attempt to return to their homeland, 'to the Hutus, both in Rwanda and Burundi, the rebels were no freedom fighters, but Tutsi seeking to hoist and reclaim their past dominance.' Another article on 8 April contended:

> What is interesting about the tribal tensions is that they are a relatively new phenomenon. In pre-colonial era, Hutus and Tutsis were on equal footing and inter-marriage was common. It was Belgium modernization and democratization that undermined local elites; tension then rose. (*Daily Nation* 1994b)

On 9 April, *Daily Nation* (1994c) reported that within hours after the deaths of the presidents, 'out-of-control soldiers were on the streets of Kigali, killing, terrorizing, kidnapping and looting'. The same article reported that Rwanda's acting Prime Minister Agathe Uwilingiyamana and scores of civilians including Christian missionaries were also killed. *Daily Nation* reports implied that the continued and ensuing political instability, insecurity, violence and killings that turned hundreds of thousands of Tutsis and Hutu moderates into refugees had become a national bane for the Rwandese. It attributed the bane to various groups, including government and opposition groups, who were using the upheaval as an excuse to settle scores and had turned the country into an unstable and destabilizing entity.

The *Guardian* expressed similar views. Reporting on the deaths of the presidents, the *Guardian on Sunday* of 10 April stated that they had 'given feathers to the wings of despondency and cynicism with which people like Kayibanda approach the seeming endless crisis in both Burundi and Rwanda' (*Guardian* 1994a). Recounting Rwanda's history, the article added:

> Hostilities between the two tribes are nothing new. The majority Hutu ended Tutsi dominance of the country in a bloody rebellion in 1959, three years before independence. That year and over the next 15 years, tens of thousands of Tutsi fled to neighboring [countries] mostly Uganda. At least 100,000 were killed in the fighting. Nearly a million Rwandese had been driven from their homes by the civil war since 1990 pitting the government against Tutsi-dominated rebels who invaded from Uganda. (*Guardian* 1994a)

Since independence in 1962, thousands of Tutsis and moderate Hutus have been killed in various pogroms and by the 1980s over 600 were displaced as a result of political crises, ethnic rivalries and economic malaise (Des Forges 1999). During the 1994 crisis and genocide, both the *Daily Nation* (1994d) and the *Guardian* (1994b) tended to blame the various Hutu-dominated governments for the atrocities and for failure to compromise and implement peace agreements. They attributed these failures to the need to remain in power. However, the RPF was not absolved from atrocities. For example, the *Daily Nation* (1994e) blamed the RPF for the killing of the archbishop of Kigali, while the the *Guardian* (1994b) recalled that the current crisis arose from the RPF invasion of Rwanda in 1990.

In a *Daily Nation* article (1994f), the political and socio-economic crisis in Burundi was often mentioned, probably because of the close history of the two nations and the fact that the presidents of both countries died in the 6 April plane crash. Most Hutus blamed the crash on the RPF, although the RPF denied responsibility.

Rwandan national introspection

The second theme that emerged from the analysis was the need to stop Rwanda's cycle of violence and conflagration. It explored the history of Rwanda with regard to the socio-economic and political structure that existed before colonization, how colonial administrations affected the traditional structures and the post-independence negative consequences of colonial policies and the need for Rwandans to eschew violence and resolve their problems peacefully.

As stated earlier, since the 1994 crisis and genocide, scholarly works on the history of Rwanda have called attention to the fact that for centuries Rwanda's three major ethnic groups (Hutus, Tutsis and Twas) coexisted peacefully under the dominion of Tutsi kings. Rwanda remained at peace until the arrival of Europeans who introduced ethnic prejudice by favouring the minority Tutsis over the Hutus and Twas in social, economic and political endeavours (Jones 2001; Talentino 1999). Assuming that the majority Hutus and Twas were docile for centuries while acquiescing to Tutsi dominion, it could be argued that Hutus became radicalized as they gained access to education and employment. They began to organize to oppose colonial and Tutsi dominion, culminating in their ascension to power at independence (*Daily Nation* 1994g; *Guardian* 1994b).

The Hutus' struggle for power threatened entrenched Tutsi elites whom the colonial masters favoured over the years and provoked them to undermine the Hutus. Between 1959 and 1962, Tutsis organized a campaign to eliminate the Hutu leaders and retain power. Historians point out that if the Belgium colonial authorities had acquiesced, the Tutsi were likely to have succeeded. Their campaign to dislodge their Hutu counterparts and be at the helm of government after independence marked the beginning of modern ethnic division and hatred between the two groups (Jones 2001; Talentino 1999).

Taking into account Rwanda's political violence, massacres, refugee flights, famines and the economic malaise that political instability generated, the *Daily Nation* and the *Guardian* urged the Rwandese to engage in a national dialogue and introspection to stop the cycle of violence and coexist peacefully.

Addressing the concerns of Hutus, the *Daily Nation* reflected on the military successes of the RPF, offered a poser and issued a caution to Rwandans when it stated:

> Rwanda is made of Hutus and Tutsi. As well as being numerically dominant, the Hutus in Rwanda have been exposed to the instruments of government and opportunities for enlightenment, without which experience they would have been open to minority domination like their cousins in neighboring [Burundi], who for years have had to live with a Tutsi control of the Civil Service, military and other levers of power. (*Daily Nation* 1994h)

The article implies that Hutus must compromise and find ways to accommodate the interests and safety of the Tutsi who would always clamour for their rights in Rwanda. The same article warned the Tutsi and the Tutsi-dominated RPF of the need to come to mutual agreement:

> In the unlikely event of Government forces being driven out of the capital, the new guerrilla-controlled authority will require public acceptance to rule without wielding the big stick. Can [they] suppress a Hutu majority and conduct the business of government as if nothing is amiss? Could they possibly hold against Hutu military incursions if the population they ruled gave saccour [sic] to the enemy hiding rebels, feeding them and providing vital intelligence?

Condemning the lack of compromise between the Hutu-dominated government and the Tutsi-dominated RPF, the *Daily Nation* contended that the only way to stop the continued human, political and economic carnage in Rwanda was for warring groups to engage in soul-searching if the people of Rwanda ever again expected to 'settle in the same neighbourhood, walk the same streets and work from dawn to dusk in the same factories without a secret murderous thought' (*Daily Nation* 1994e).

The *Guardian* (1994b) offered an answer and advice. It stated that to build confidence and resuscitate their country, Rwandans must examine and deal with the root causes of the fratricides through reallocation of resources on the 'basis of equity and justice'. If the Hutus and Tutsis can 'ever again share the challenges of nation building and pursue political rivalries in democratic good nature' or allow a 'multi-tribal nation once called Banyarwanda to roll up into one again', the *Daily Nation* advised, they must rid themselves of current divisions and motives, which the paper described as primitive, reckless and a throwback to a distant age (*Daily Nation* 1994e).

The *Guardian* agreed. The paper noted that, when President Theodore Kubwabo set up an interim government, which the *Guardian* described as nationalist, he made overtures to the RPF for reconciliation, as the rebel group's military success threatened the interim government (*Guardian* 1994c). The paper contended that the only way forward was for Rwandan leaders (especially the RPF's) 'to agree to a path of reason and de-emphasize their expansionist ambition ... [because] indeed there has to be a limit to the agony' for Rwandans. Underscoring the need for national introspection among Rwandese, the *Guardian* concluded that the 'need for a re-arrangement of the political structure of Rwanda is not in doubt. A broad-based power-sharing equation should be adopted in Rwanda to accommodate the feuding tribes. The present arrangement where domination is perceived is hardly healthy.'

African cataclysm and introspection

Covering the 1994 crisis provided these leading dailies with an opportunity to take stock of events throughout Africa since the end of colonialism, to point out Africa's problems and failures and to indict governments all over the continent for making the region the world's abyss despite its human and mineral wealth. Like Rwandan national introspection, this theme uses the Rwandan turmoil and carnage and the consequent regional instability, insecurity and humanitarian crisis it produced to examine the political, economic and social events that had resulted in wars, famine, deaths, economic malaise and human degradation throughout Africa. The discourse urged Africans to engage in self-examination, eschew violence and seek solutions to their internal and external disagreements (whether political, economic, ethnic or religious) to avoid the destructive consequences that have been visited on African societies historically and help the continent attain its place and promise in the wider world.

If the seeds of the 1994 genocide in Rwanda were sowed by ethnic hatred and distrust, competition for power, political instability, discrimination, famine and presidential deaths, the *Daily Nation* (1994i) and the *Guardian* (1994d) emphasized that these problems were not limited to Rwanda. Both pointed out that half a century after African nations gained independence, most had not fulfilled the political, economic and social promises that self-government offered them. Using Rwanda as an example of what had happened and continues to happen in African nations, the *Daily Nation* and the *Guardian* implied that the continent is a place where one violent incident or crisis begats another, one killing and pogrom leads to another and ethnic hatred and distrust results in more of the same. The *Guardian* pointed out that:

> The story follows the same refrain. Ethnic nationalities lumped together join hands together to win political independence from colonial masters, so that they can handle their own affairs and hold their destinies in their own hands. As has been shown in different parts of [the] world, [especially Africa] from the northern to southern hemisphere, as soon as the colonialists depart, the union wielded together usually by force begins groaning over strains of diversity. (*Guardian* 1994d: 17)

In the same vein, the *Daily Nation* (1994i) stated:

> The Rwanda cauldron has followed classic African lines: an eruptive event (often a coup but in this case the apparent assassination of two presidents) followed by retributive violence against perceived enemies plus anyone who gets in the way, a deterioration into aimless drunken anarchy, evacuations, and panic-stricken refugee columns, and the disposition of so-called government against the so-called rebels for overall control of the state which is about where we are now in Rwanda.

Both dailies tended to blame the colonial powers and the inheritors of power for a lack of understanding, a failure to recognize ethnic differences and a tendency to gloss over differences. They contended that Africa's historical orientation would consume the people if the leaders failed to deal with the cataclysmic nature of African crises through continental introspection. They proposed introspection as a viable vehicle for resolving domestic and international disagreements and to promote peace, understanding and prosperity (*Daily Nation* 1994i, j; *Guardian* 1994d).

The *Guardian* (1994d: 17) warned that

> it is hardly noticed that once there is a threat of survival, politically, economically, and culturally to its ethnic group, something sweeps through their psyche and the people of that stock quickly bind together to defend themselves – regardless of their stations in life.

Reflecting on the Rwandan crisis, killings and other problems plaguing Africa, the *Daily Nation* (1994k) argued that African lives and freedom are devalued in a continent that maintains a culture where one crisis begats another. It asked: 'How long can Africans continue to look on as their brothers [Rwandans and others] are being slaughtered?' (Daily Nation 1994i). The *Daily Nation* pointed to the lack of attention from and the inaction of the international community during the Rwandan crisis (and other crises that have plagued Africa) and urged African leaders to develop institutions, infrastructure, resources, political will and treaties to deal with the problems that plagued their nations (*Daily Nation* 1994i, l).

Both papers implied that Africa would remain the world's bottomless pit if its leaders did not develop policies to help their nations and each other to help themselves (*Daily Nation* 1994j; *Guardian* 1994e). While underscoring the need to stop African crises, the *Daily Nation* (1994j) stated that the Rwandan situation would 'be a lesson enough to those African heads of states, their cronies and henchmen who take the peace and prosperity of their countries for granted'.

Although these papers tended to blame outside forces and centuries-long exploitation for sowing the seeds of violence, ethnic hatred and distrust, it must be pointed out that corruption, lust for power, poor management of resources and ethical indifference since independence half a century ago account for the lack of development in Africa. And although outsiders have not come to Africa's aid many times when they were needed, they did respond during the Ethiopian famine in the 1980s and the civil war in Somalia.

World inaction and indifference

The *Daily Nation* and the *Guardian* also explored the failure of the international community (the United Nations, foreign governments, colonial masters, other African countries and the Organization of African Unity (OAU)) to take military action to stop the massacre of non-combatants in Rwanda. In addition to blaming the international community for its failures, this discourse includes reports of the concerted efforts of Western countries and organizations to evacuate their foreign nationals while abandoning Rwandan.

As mentioned above, one of the factors contributing to the 1994 Rwanda crisis and genocide was the invasion of the RPF three years earlier. Since independence, Rwanda had been afflicted by a cycle of pogroms between ethnic groups as they jostled for political and economic power (Des Forges 1999; Kuperman 2000). However, Rwanda's strife remained off the radar screens of the world press. As in other cases, the press paid little or no attention to the historical crises in Rwanda (Livingston and Eachus 2000) and this inattention continued until the deaths of presidents Habyarimana and Ntaryamira, which resulted in a few reports in the international press.

However, attention waned within weeks (Kuperman 2000) even though the deaths precipitated violence as Hutu militias and government forces took to the streets to massacre Tutsi, whom they blamed for sabotaging the plane and killing the presidents. When the situation regained world attention, the reaction was mixed. The *Guardian* and the *Daily Nation* contended that, instead of taking action to stop the killing, the UN engaged in protracted debate, offered weak resolutions and vowed to disengage (*Daily Nation* 1994m, n; *Guardian* 1994f, g). Promises of financial, capital, moral and logistic support were made, but failed to materialize (*Daily Nation* 1994m). Countries outside Africa refused to send troops, while the international presence was withdrawn (*Daily Nation* 1994o; *Guardian* 1994f). The OAU seemed moribund, unable to make decisions and take initiatives or action without UN approval and assistance (*Guardian* 1994h).

As fighting intensified and killings increased, rather than increasing its presence in Rwanda, the UN threatened to withdraw its peacekeepers (*Guardian* 1994i, j). Foreign governments (especially Western nations) evacuated their citizens (*Guardian* 1994g). With the death toll mounting and the world press focusing on Rwanda temporarily as the world community and UN waffled on what to do, the *Guardian* accused the UN of adopting 'half-measures' by failing to fulfil its mission by expanding the mandate of the United Nations Assistance Mission for Rwanda (UNAMIR) – 'originally sent to Rwanda to monitor the implementation of the Arusha Peace Accord between the Rwandese Government and the RPF, to protect civilians in the country as well as provide security for humanitarian relief operations' (*Guardian* 1994k). In 1993, after the OAU brokered a ceasefire treaty between the Rwandan government and the rebels, the UN sent a contingent of about 2,500 peacekeepers to monitor the implementation of the Arusha accords. The OAU had a transition team in the demilitarized zone (*Guardian* 1994l). Despite the presence of these peacekeepers, calls from General Roméo Dallaire, head of UNAMIR, and from nongovernmental organizations for prompt action to end the ensuing violence (Kuperman 2000), the world community seemed to turn a deaf ear (*Daily Nation* 1994n; *Guardian* 1994l).

Blaming the international community for inaction and indifference in the face of the deaths of the thousands of black Africans, the *Guardian* (1994l) argued that there was a need for imagination from the international community to resolve the crisis in Rwanda. While calling for quick, swift and thorough investigation of the crash that killed the presidents of Rwanda and Burundi and condemning Rwandan presidential guardsmen for cordoning off the crash scene, the *Guardian* warned:

> The present slaughter, like those before it, will of course, come to an end: The people will be exhausted and riotous soldiers will need to replenish their arsenals. But violence will erupt again unless there is a wise intervention. And this will be effective only if it goes beyond the political stereotypes now being known at Africa's delinquent leadership. (*Guardian* 1994l)

Considering Rwanda's cycle of violence, the *Guardian* contended that it would take bold imagination on the part of the international community to find lasting solutions to the current violence. It suggested that offering each of Rwanda's ethnic groups political autonomy and guaranteeing their security and the power to manage their resources represented ways to establish lasting peace in Rwanda. The *Guardian* explained, 'It should be clear that Euro-American concept of democracy (one man, one vote) taken in isolation and applied mechanically, cannot resolve the conflict in Rwanda' (Guardian 1994l). The *Guardian* concluded, 'If the practical implication is the physical separation of the two ethnic groups, then the peacemakers should boldly look at the option.'

The world's inaction and indifference, the *Daily Nation* (1994n) pointed out, could be attributed to the fact 'the industrialized world, after a burst of optimism about Africa's prospect, is coming to the conclusion that many African countries are hopeless cases'. While expressing disgust at the failure of forces outside Africa, both the *Guardian* (1994d) and the *Daily Nation* (1994n) condemned African leaders and the OAU for bickering and for their inability to muster financial, physical and human resources to tackle this and other African tragedies. However, the *Daily Nation* noted that ending the conflict and restoring peace

> is a responsibility not only for African countries, but also for the international community [because] ignoring the problems African countries face and marginalising sub-Saharan Africa in the world economy will only increase the chances of more Rwandas. (*Daily Nation* 1994n)

CONCLUSION AND DISCUSSION

The study used framing to discern the patterns that dominated the coverage and analyses of the 1994 Rwandan crisis and genocide in two leading African newspapers: the *Daily Nation* of Kenya and the *Guardian* of Nigeria within the first 100 days of the genocide. Framing allowed us to determine whether the focus of these newspapers overlapped (synchronization) or whether there were marked differences in content (heterogeneity).

Although the four themes described above dominated both papers, arguments, rationale and opinions tended to differ. For example, with regard to the origin of the crisis, the *Daily Nation* (1994b) believed it to be relatively recent, whereas the *Guardian* described the causes as long standing (*Guardian* 1994a). While the *Daily Nation* tended to be sympathetic and praised the RPF's military successes (*Daily Nation* 1994a), some articles in the *Guardian* revealed scepticism with regard to the intention of the RPF, whom it viewed as somewhat arrogant (*Guardian* 1994c). However, neither paper absolved the Hutu-dominated government of responsibility (*Daily Nation* 1994j; *Guardian* 1994e).

Reports in both papers attempted to explore the background of the crisis and its greater implications. This is important considering that the world press is often accused of failing to do so. The ability of the African press to provide background could be attributed to their greater understanding of underlying matters that affect the continent.

Although national/regional interest emerged as a theme in the *Daily Nation* (1994p, q), it did not develop in the *Guardian*'s coverage. The national/regional interest frame focused on the need to find lasting solutions to the Rwandan crisis if the Great Lakes Region and Eastern Africa is to achieve political, economic and social stability. This theme included the need to evacuate Kenyans and other foreigners from the country at the height of the crisis. It demonstrated the economic links between the two countries and other countries in the region and showed that there were many Kenyans living in Rwanda and many Rwandans living in Kenya. Reporting on the evacuation of foreigners, the *Daily Nation* tended to give accounts of Kenyans who experienced the crisis. The discourse tended to urge the Kenyan government to take concrete steps to find peace. This focus may be a result of the proximity of Kenya to Rwanda.

At the onset of the Rwandan crisis (within the first three weeks), the *Guardian* and the *Daily Nation* published a considerable number of daily accounts of events; later, the *Daily Nation* offered more daily accounts over a longer time than the *Guardian*.

In terms of in-depth articles, the *Guardian* tended to quote Nigerian experts more often than the *Daily Nation* quoted Kenyan experts. However, both papers quoted national and international officials liberally.

Although the role of the media in conflict situations remains crucial (Obinor 2005), it is important to note, that the ability of the mass media to influence the cause of the war remains neither simple nor clear, as this and other studies demonstrate (Ross 2003; Wolfsfeld 1997a). The themes established in this study (bane of a nation, Rwandan national introspection, African cataclysm and introspection, and world inaction and indifference as well as national/regional interest) seem to be in keeping with those established in other studies dealing with mass media coverage and analysis of conflict. Depending on where the media place themselves on a continuum of four key roles – aggressive watchdog of government (power corrupts frame); advocate of the downtrodden (brutal repression frame); semi-honest broker (responsible citizen frame); and faithful servant parroting government (law and order frame) – they tend to adopt either a 'law and order' frame or an 'injustice and defiance' one (Wolfsfeld 1997b, 2001).

> The media have long been characterised as a social force used to the benefit or detriment of the society within which they operate. When used to promote justice, morality, unity and harmony in society, they can act as facilitators of peace in times of crisis. However, they can also be used as instigators of conflict and for other destructive purposes. (Obinor 2005)

Obinor advocates continuing to examine the role of African mass media during domestic and international crises, because

> studies point to the possibility that besides its other roles, the press, particularly the elite press, may contribute to transforming a crisis from a macro-systematic crisis, hardly noted by the decision-makers, into a micro-perceptional crisis, receiving higher priority from them. (Auerbach and Bloch-Elkon 2005: 16)

That is, by framing the story in terms that show its pertinence and relevance to the local context. This is especially important in Africa where domestic and international crises continue unabated in the twenty-first century.

REFERENCES

Alozie, E.C. 2004. 'How sub-Saharan African Mass Media Covered Events Leading to the Anglo-Iraqi War of 2003'. In R. Berenger (ed.). *Global Media Go to War: the Role of News and Entertainment Media During the 2003 Iraq War.* Marquette Books, Spokane, WA, USA: 39–58.

—— 2005a. Sudan and South Africa – a Framing Analysis of *Mail* and *Guardian Online*'s Coverage of Darfur. *Ecquid Novi* 26(1): 63–84.

—— 2005b. *Cultural Reflections and the Role of Advertising in the Socioeconomic and National Development of Nigeria.* Edwin Mellen Press, Lewiston, NY, USA.

Anokwa, K., C.A. Lin and M.B. Salwen (eds). 2003. *International Communication: Concepts and Cases.* Thomson/Wadsworth, Belmont, CA, USA. 297 pp.

Auerbach, Y. and Y. Bloch-Elkon. 2005. Media Framing and Foreign Policy: the Elite Press vis-à-vis US policy in Bosnia, 1992–95. *Journal of Peace Research*, 42(1): 83–99. Available at <jpr.sagepub.com/cgi/content/abstract/42/1/83> (accessed 28 December 2005).

BBC (British Broadcasting Company). 2005a. Country profile: Kenya. BBC, London, UK. Available at: <www.news.bbc.co.uk/1/hi/world/africa/country_profiles/1024563.stm> (accessed 12 Nov. 2005).

—— 2005b. Country profile: Nigeria. BBC, London, UK. Available at <www.news.bbc.co.uk/1/hi/world/africa/country_profiles/1064557.stm> (accessed 12 November 2005).

—— 2005c. Country profile: Rwanda. BBC, London, UK. Available at <www.news.bbc.co.uk/1/hi/world/africa/country_profiles/1070265.stm> (accessed 12 November 2005).

Biko, H., K. Gore and H. Watson. 2000. *Press Coverage of Africa.* TransAfrica Forum, Washington, DC, USA. Issue brief. Available at <www.transafricaforum.org/documents/PresscoverageAfrica2000.pdf> (accessed 17 December 2005).

Bishop, R. 2005. A Philosophy of Exhibitionism: Exploring Media Coverage of Al Roker's and Carnie Wilson's Gastric Bypass Surgeries. *Journal of Communication Inquiry*, 29(2): 119–40.

Carragee, K.M. and W. Roefs. 2004. The Neglect of Power in Recent Framing Research. *Journal of Communication*, 54: 214–33. Available at <www.joc.oxfordjournals.org/cgi/content/abstract/54/2/214> (accessed 17 December 2005).

Chang, T.K. 1993. *The Press and China Policy: the Illusion of Sino-American Relations, 1950–1984.* Ablex, Norwood, NJ, USA.

Cho, J. 2003. Media, Terrorism, and Emotionality, Emotional Differences in Media Content and Public Reactions to the September 11th Terrorist Attacks. *Journal of Broadcasting and Electronic Media*, 47: 309–28.

Daily Nation. 1994a. Rebels Stunned World with Lightning Attacks. *Daily Nation*, 8 April: 8.

—— 1994b. A Catastrophe for Rwanda, Burundi. *Daily Nation*, 8 April.

—— 1994c. Rwanda Must Look to Truth to Survive. *Daily Nation*, 9 April.

—— 1994d. Leader Leaves Nations in Disarray. *Daily Nation*, 8 April: 8.

—— 1994e. Murder Most Foul in Tragic Rwanda. *Daily Nation*, 11 June.

—— 1994f. Rebels Suspected in Presidents' Death. *Daily Nation*, 8 April: 2.

—— 1994g. Colonialism to Blame in Rwanda. *Daily Nation*, 3 May.

—— 1994h. The Real Folly of Rwanda's Killings. *Daily Nation*, 9 June.

—— 1994i. Africa Must Stop Rwanda Carnage. *Daily Nation*, 16 April.

—— 1994j. Rwandan Killings a Lesson to All. *Daily Nation*, 5 May.
—— 1994k. Killings Devalue Africa's Freedom. *Daily Nation*, 27 April: 9.
—— 1994l. Rwanda Shouldn't Bleed to Death. *Daily Nation*, 2 May.
—— 1994m. Rwanda: New Evidence of the UN as a Paper Tiger. *Daily Nation*, 18 April: 18.
—— 1994n. What Can be Done to End the Carnage in Rwanda. *Daily Nation*, 9 May.
—— 1994o. UN Evacuates Soldiers from Rwandan Capital. *Daily Nation*, 20 April: 8.
—— 1994p. Kenya Flee Kigali Bloodbath. *Daily Nation*, 12 April: 1.
—— 1994q. Strife in Rwanda Worries Traders. *Daily Nation*, n.d.
—— 2005. Company profile. *Daily Nation*. Nairobi, Kenya. Available at <www.nationmedia.com/dailynation/about_us.asp> (accessed 12 November 2005).
De Beer, A. 2004. 'The Internet in Africa: Leapfrogging to a Global Future'. In C. Okigbo and F. Eribo (eds). 2004. *Development and communication in Africa*. Rowman & Littlefield, Lanham, MD, USA:157–64.
Des Forges, A. 1999. *Leave None to Tell the Story: Genocide in Rwanda*. Human Rights Watch and the International Federation of Human Rights Leagues, New York, NY, USA. Available at <www.hrw.org/reports/1999/Rwanda/> (accessed 30 August 2005).
Edeani, D. 1994. Nigerian Mass Media Handling of Conflict Situations in the West African Sub-region. *Africa Media Review*, 8(1): 1–24.
Emenyonu, N. 1995. Africa's Image in the Local Press: An Analysis of African News in Some Nigerian Media. *Africa Media Review*, 9(2): 82–104.
Entman, R.M. 1993. Framing: Toward Clarification of a Fractured Paradigm. *Journal of Communication*, 43(4): 51–8.
Eribo, F. 2004. 'African Development and Innovation of Communication Technologies'. In C. Okigbo and F. Eribo (eds). 2004. *Development and Communication in Africa*. Rowman & Littlefield, Lanham, MD, USA.
Fair, J.E. 1996. The Body Politic, the Bodies of Women, and the Politics of Famine in U.S. Television Coverage of Famine in the Horn of Africa. *Journalism and Mass Communication Monographs*, 158.
Galtung, J. and Ruge, M.H. 1970. 'The Structure of Foreign News'. In J. Tunstall (ed.). *Media Sociology: a Reader.* University of Illinois Press, Urbana, IL, USA: 259–98.
Guardian. 1994a. Burundi, Rwanda: a Hurl Back into the Dark Ages. *Guardian on Sunday*, 10 April: A19.
—— 1994b. Battling Mayhem in Rwanda. *Guardian*, 13 May: 9.
—— 1994c. Rwanda's Gambit Goes Beserk. *Guardian on Sunday*, 19 June: A17.
—— 1994d. The Horror in Rwanda. *Guardian*, 12 May: 17.
—— 1994e. On Rwanda's Agony. *Guardian*, 16 May: 10.
—— 1994f. Nigeria May Initiate UN Peace Action in Rwanda. *Guardian*, 4 May.
—— 1994g. Western Nations Evacuate Citizens from Rwanda. *Guardian*, 11 April: 1, 7.
—— 1994h. UN-OAU Bureaucracy Stalls Troop Deployment to Rwanda. *Guardian*, 8 June: 1.
—— 1994i. Rwanda Fighting Intensifies as Rebels Deny Peace Talks. *Guardian*, 15 April: 6.
—— 1994j. OAU, Red Cross, Reject UN Withdrawal Plan in Rwanda. *Guardian*, 7 May.
—— 1994k. Security Council Adopts Half-Measures on Rwanda. *Guardian,* 18 May: 1, 5.
—— 1994l. Rwanda–Burundi: the Need for Imagination. *Guardian*, 16 April: 16.
—— 2005. About Us: What We Stand For. *Guardian*, Lagos, Nigeria. Available at <www.guardiannewsngr.com/about_us/> (accessed 12 November 2005).
Gavrilos, D. 2002. Arab Americans in a Nation's Imagined Community: How News Constructed Arab American Reactions to the Gulf War. *Journal of Communication Inquiry*, 26(4): 426–45.
Goffman, E. 1974. *Frame Analysis*. Free Press, New York, NY, USA.
Golan, G. 2003. America's Narrow Window to the World: an Analysis of Network Global Coverage. *International Communication Bulletin,* 38(3–4): 2–11.
Hachten, W.A. 2004. 'Reporting Africa's Problems'. In C. Okigbo and F. Eribo (eds). *Development and Communication in Africa*. Rowman & Littlefield, Lanham, MD, USA: 79–87.
Hawk, B. (ed.). 1992. *Africa's Media Image*. Praeger, New York, NY, USA.
Herman, E.S., and N. Chomsky. 1988. *Manufacturing Consent: the Political Economy of the Mass Media*. Pantheon Books, New York, NY, USA.

Ibelema, M. 2001. Welcoming a visiting in-law: racial solidarity and President Clinton's image in the Nigerian press. Presented at the Association for Education in Journalism and Mass Communication annual conference, 5–8 August 2001, Washington, DC, USA. AEJMC, Columbia, SC, USA.

Idowu, S. 1987. Images of the Third World Through the Eyes of Five Nigerian Newspapers. *Africa Media Review*, 2(1): 52–65.

Jones, B.D. 2001. *Peacemaking in Rwanda: the Dynamics of Failure*. Lynne Reinner, London, UK.

Kamalipour, Y.R. 2002. *Global Communication*. Wadsworth/Thomson, Belmont, CA, USA.

Kellner, D. 2003. 'Cultural Studies, Multiculturalism, and Media Culture'. In G. Dines and J. Humex (eds). *Gender, Race, and Class in Media: a Text-reader.* Sage Publications, Thousand Oaks, CA, USA: 9–20.

Kupermann, A. 2000. Rwanda in Retrospect. *Foreign Affairs*, 79(1): 94–118.

Livingston, S. and T. Eachus. 2000. 'Rwanda: U.S. Policy and Television Coverage'. In H. Adelman and A. Suhrke (eds). *The Path of a Genocide: the Rwanda Crisis From Uganda to Zaire.* Transaction Publishers, New Brunwick, NJ, USA: 209–28.

Nwokeafor, C. and R. Nwankwo. 1993. Development Information Content in the African Mass Media: a Study of two Nigerian Dailies. *Africa Media Review*, 7: 75–95.

Obinor, F. 2005. Reporting Conflicts in African Way. *Guardian Online*, 14 November. Available at <www.ngrguardiannews.com> (accessed 14 November 2005).

Ochola, F. 1980. Aspects of Mass Communication Research in Africa on Black Africa, With Special Reference to U.S. Doctoral and Masters Studies, a 20-Year Perspective, 1960–1979. University of Georgia, Athens, GA, USA. Master of Arts thesis.

Onwudiwe, E. and M. Ibelema (eds). 2003. Afro-Optimism: Perspectives on Africa's Advances. Praeger, Westport, CT, USA.

Onwumechili, C. and R. M'Bayo. 1995. 'Structure and Functions of the Mass Media in National Development in Africa: Systematic Considerations'. In P. Nwosu, C. Onwumechili and R. M'Bayo (eds). *Communication and the Transformation of Society: a Developing Region's Perspective*. University Press of America, Lantham, MD, USA: 53–75.

Pan, Z. and G. Kosicki. 2003. Framing Analysis: an Approach to News Discourse. *Political Communication*, 10: 55–75.

Pool, D. 1952. *Symbols of Democracy*. Stanford University Press, Stanford, CA, USA.

Pratt, C. 1996. 'Africa South of the Sahara'. In P. Jeter, K. Rampal, V. Cambridge and C. Pratt (eds). *International Afro Mass Media: a Reference Guide*. Greenwood Press, Westport, CT, USA: 3–61.

Ross, S. 2003. Framing of the Palestinian–Israeli Conflict in Thirteen Months of New York Editorials Surrounding the Attack of September 11, 2004. *Conflict and Communication Online*, 2(2). Available at <www.cco.regener-online.de/2003> (accessed 5 January 2005).

Scheufele, D.A. 1999. Framing as a Theory of Media Effects. *Journal of Communication*, 49(4): 103–22.

Severin, W.J. and J.W. Tankard, Jr 2001. *Communication Theories: Origins, Methods, and Uses in Mass Media* (5th edn.). Addison Wesley Longman, New York, NY, USA.

Shoemaker, P.J., L. H. Danielian and N. Brendlinger. 1991. Deviant Acts, Risky Business, and U.S. Interests: the Newsworthiness of World Events. *Journalism Quarterly*, 68(4): 781–95.

St. Clair, D. 2004. President Bush visits Africa: an analysis of Botswana's *Daily News* and South Africa's *Mail & Guardian*. Presented at the Association for Education in Journalism and Mass Communication annual conference, 4–7 August 2004, Toronto, Canada. AEJMC, Columbia, SC, USA.

Strobel, W. 1997. *Late-breaking Foreign Policy: the News Media's Influence on Peace Operations*. United States Institute of Peace, Washington, DC, USA.

Talentino, A. 1999. 'Rwanda'. In M. Brown and R. Rosecrance (eds). *The Costs of Conflicts: Prevention and Cure in the Global Arena*. Rowan & Littlefield, Lanham, MD, USA: 53–73.

Tuchman, G. 1978. *Making News*. Free Press, New York, NY, USA.

Value Based Management.net. 2005. Framing explained. Value Based Management.net, Bilthoven, The Netherlands. Available at <www.valuebasedmanagement.net/methods_tversky_framing.html> (accessed 16 November 2005).

Wanta, W., G. Golan and C. Lee. 2004. Agenda Setting and International News: Media Influence on Public Perceptions of Foreign Nations. *Journalism & Mass Communication Quarterly*, 81(2): 364–77.

Wikipedia. 2005. Framing (communication theory). Wikimedia Foundation Inc., Saint Petersburg, FL, USA. Available at <www.en.wikipedia.org/wiki/Political_framing> (accessed 15 November 2005).

Wolfsfeld, G. 1997a. Fair Weather Friends: the Varying Role of the News Media in the Arab–Israeli Peace Process. *Political Communication*, 14(1), 29–48.

—— 1997b. *Media and Political Conflict*. Cambridge University Press, New York, NY, USA.

—— 2001. The News Media and Peace Processes, the Middle East and Northern Ireland. *Peaceworks*, 37(2).

Wu, H. 2000. Systemic Determinants of International News Coverage: a Comparison of 38 Countries. *Journal of Communication*, 50: 110–30.

Zaffiro, J.J. 1993. Mass Media, Politics and Society in Botswana: the 1990s and Beyond. *Africa Today*, 40(1): 7–25.

18
Exhibit 467: Genocide Through a Camera Lens

Nick Hughes

To be a journalist in Rwanda in April of 1994 was to have a window on Auschwitz. Yet, there are precious few records of the genocide as it took place. There are pictures of rotting bodies around churches, but few images of the killing itself. What I know is that on three different occasions, killing was filmed by a Reuters camera operator, an unknown Rwandan camera operator and me. Killing surrounded each of us, and we were only able to record briefly. From the top of a building called the French School, I filmed across a valley to record a street that was being cleared of Tutsi. These images are among the only known pictures of the genocide and they are shocking. In a sense, they are the only reminders that this event really happened. If only there had been more such images.

As a journalist and cameraman, I was in Rwanda in the first few days after the genocide began on 6 April. Years later, I agreed to testify before the International Criminal Tribunal for Rwanda in the trial of George Rutaganda. The tribunal wanted to use my footage as evidence and asked me to testify. What follows is my description of that footage. As I told the tribunal, in the first few days after 6 April, we knew that there was killing going on. We could see bodies in the streets. I also knew that there was a resumption of hostilities, as I had passed through Rwandan Patriotic Front (RPF) territory when they declared that they were marching on Kigali.

* * *

The war had started again with ferocity. But what we didn't know was the sheer scale and how organized the systematic killing of Tutsi civilians was. When we began to see the number of bodies increase and the way in which people were being killed, the nature of the killing began to sink in, but usually in recollection, not at the moment when we were witnessing events. I recall looking back on an event, four or five days later, and thinking to myself, 'Now hold on, what I have just filmed is not a normal event. I haven't seen that anywhere else.' I knew that whenever there was hostility in Rwanda, civilians got killed. There had been ethnic killing many times before. You expect that in Rwanda. But the events we were witnessing in April 1994 made us begin to realize there was something more this time – there was the magnitude of the killing. It was not so sporadic. We noticed gangs roaming the streets looking for somebody to kill, in a systematic way.

On the day I shot the footage of people being killed, I was in a building of the French School, in central Kigali. Belgian paratroopers were there, which made it a relatively secure place from which to observe. The soldiers had a rocket launcher in the top room of the school, a building that extends up the side of the valley and overlooks another road going up the other side. Through the sights on the rocket launcher, the soldiers could see people being killed on the other side of the valley. I was told about this and went up to look and, indeed, there were bodies on the other side of the road. I set up my camera in the room next door to where the soldiers were located. At this point I was a bit short of charged batteries and tapes for my camera, so I wanted to be careful about what I was filming. Looking across the valley, I could see groups of people walking up and down the dirt road and I could see piles of bodies.

At one point, I turned my camera away to look at other activity on the road. By the time I panned back to the first spot, two or three men had been brought out and killed. You can see that on the footage. You can see them still being beaten. What is notable is that they weren't killed instantly; they were slowly beaten to death, tortured. When I focused my camera that second time, I could see two women among one pile of bodies. There must have been about eight bodies by then and a group of men on the other side of the road, investigating something.

Both women were kneeling. One was begging, arms outstretched. Nonchalantly, the killers would come over and beat the men who were dying in front of these two women, then stroll away.

Most of the men were carrying something in their right hand – a machete or club of some sort. Then I could see a child walking down the road with a club, coming up to the other side of the group. At the top of the road at a T-junction, people were going about their business, not paying attention.

I saw quite clearly another woman who apparently lived next door; she was very much at home. She put her head around the door to see what was happening to her neighbour – to watch her neighbours being murdered in the street.

The woman on the ground pleaded for about 20 minutes. I could not film the whole thing because I was concerned about my batteries and tape. She pleaded the entire time, pleaded for her life. At one point a little boy walked past and a man strolled into a house nearby. He had one hand in his pocket and was just wandering in. He had probably known this woman all her life.

Then a pickup truck drove down the road, with about three men in the back. No one questioned them or impeded their progress. The driver paused the vehicle by the begging woman. They weren't fleeing the city. One was in uniform. They were checking that the killing was going ahead.

Finally, a man came across the street and hit one woman on the head with such a force that he broke the stick he was using. She fell back. She put her arm up to ward off the blow, and he must have broken it. The second blow hit her on the side of her head and neck. I could see her head jerk away.

No one questioned why these people were there, why they were doing this. The neighbour standing in her doorway wasn't questioning what was going on, even though the woman who was struck might have been her neighbour for years. It was as if the two women who were being attacked in the street knew they were going to be killed. It was as if these people had the authority to kill them. The women knew they couldn't run away. People living on the street could have stopped them. There was no attempt to escape and no possibility of escape.

This was going on up and down the street. People were brought out of their houses and killed on the street, systematically. It was not a rampage into someone's house, to smash in the door and kill those in the front room. They were being dragged out and killed, their bodies piled outside so that they could be more easily picked up and taken away. There seems to be no question that the killers believed they had the right to be there, doing what they were doing.

It was nonchalant and it was tiring. It was work. In the space of about 100 metres, there were eleven, maybe twelve, bodies on the street.

When the truck went past, the woman was still begging for her life, crouching there in a pile of bodies. The people on the truck knew what was going on. They knew who the people on that street were. They knew what they were going to do. As they drove by, one of them gave a quick wave. There was no attempt by anybody to help the women. It was not as if they were being punished, attacked, for being a member of the opposition and given a beating. This woman was going to die. Everybody on the street knew that. They knew what was going on. There is no other explanation, but that this was systematic killing.

The organization and, above all, the nonchalance of the killers was a perfect vignette for the genocide, during which thousands were killed each day.

Eventually, someone killed the two women with severe blows. I caught that on tape, one of the only instances, I believe, of an actual killing being recorded by the media. Looking back, it is surprising that given the number of bodies we saw around the city when we travelled with military convoys, we hadn't witnessed the killing of more people. But nobody was going to kill in front of a camera if they knew it was recording. I suppose, in this instance, they didn't know they were being watched because we were across the valley.

What I saw through my camera lens was not just killing, but the systematic searching of that street. People were going from house to house. You could see them walking back and forth across the street. You could see more bodies appearing on the side of the road. I think they were probably looting the houses as well as dragging people out and killing them.

Most of the killers appeared to be 20 to 30 years old. They were obviously quite at home. This was their area and they knew where they were. A lot of people were just walking around the streets as well, mostly men. They had no uniform. They were dressed in shabby clothing, trousers and T-shirts. Almost universally, they were armed with a machete or a club or both. In some cases, you could see a stick grenade in their hand.

As I have said, we expected ethnic killing. The full gravity of what we witnessed really only sank in after we left. I remember being on a flight to Ethiopia with some journalists I was working with. We got to talking about how this killing was not normal by Rwandan standards. I remember endlessly repeating to the other journalists and to myself, 'How can someone just go and cut the legs off a woman. How can they do that?' I remember mood swings as a result of the killing and the bodies that I had seen. The day I left, I began to realize that this was something different – the ferocity, the nonchalant killings, the systematic killings that I had seen in Kigali, the endless bodies and the way the people were killed. I remember a British journalist, my friend Catherine Bond, saying, 'There won't be any Tutsi left by the time this war is over.' That is how it was dawning on us after a week or so on the ground.

In early April, I was travelling from Kigali airport to the centre of town in the back of a small car, in the middle of a convoy of French troops. We passed a few bodies, then gangs of men waving machetes. On one side of the road, a young boy about ten years old was running through the tall grass in a field. He stopped to beg, but he wasn't pleading for his life. He turned and with both hands pointed at his younger brother who was too young to get through the long grass. He pleaded for his brother's life, but we drove on. I cannot have that moment back, to insist that the driver of our car stop, that the whole convoy should stop. Two young boys, like my two sons.

A week later, a convoy of Belgian paratroopers was going to a Catholic mission to rescue a white expatriate. The Belgian captain refused to allow me, with my camera, to ride on one of his trucks. My producer and I followed the convoy in a small saloon car, left abandoned by an expatriate evacuee. The convoy made its way through the centre of Kigali. There were a few bodies by the side of the road. The convoy turned into a heavily populated residential area and along this stretch were roadblocks every 100 metres, manned by the *Interahamwe*. The men were armed with stick grenades and they shouted, '*Vive la France*', and attempted karate kicks.

Every 20 metres, there was a line of bodies neatly laid out. In some cases, blood poured from fatal head wounds; in places, bloodstains showed where more bodies had been laid out some time before. The blood ran down the side of the road and collected in the gutter. The gutters actually flowed with blood. Between the frenzied roadblocks, the bodies and the small shops, some residents went about seemingly normal business, some walking slowly in conversation. I couldn't use my camera during that ride. I did not have the courage.

I know now that what I saw was human evil in majesty. Many of those who were there later felt a bond – a need to explain what had happened to anyone who would listen.

19
Media Failure Over Rwanda's Genocide

Tom Giles

By late afternoon, they looked like water lilies cloaking the river's surface.

Only when the light reflected off the water did you catch a truer glimpse of them: bodies by the dozen, bloated and obscene, floating together downstream. Bit by bit, you built up a picture of something human in the expanse – a back, an arm, the slope of a neck.

After minutes of concentration, perhaps, you could get a hint of someone's father, someone's brother or daughter – lost in the eddying circles that swept them on to Lake Victoria.

We stood on the bridge above the Rusumo Falls along the Kagera River – the crossing that marked the border between Rwanda and Tanzania. Behind us were the newly erected tents and plastic sheeting of the makeshift Ngara Camp.

Hundreds of thousands of Hutu refugees had fled Rwanda just days before, seeking shelter in this grim settlement. Hidden among them were some of the killers.

These were members of the Hutu gangs that were already responsible for the slaughter of hundreds of thousands of their Tutsi neighbours. They had encouraged this exodus, fearful of revenge from the Tutsi army – the RPF – which had managed to liberate a small part of Rwanda over the border.

A few weeks later, as the extermination continued in the vast areas the Tutsi army could not reach, some 800,000 would be dead. For all our frantic efforts, we didn't realize we were already too late. Nothing would be done to stop the killing.

'Watch the smell!' my colleague gestured, choking. The wind must have turned suddenly. I looked away – in time to see a figure flushed out over the crest of the falls, tumbling down into a pool far below.

It surfaced, a black body whitened by death but distinct – a small boy, a baby – perhaps no older than my nine-month-old son. He bobbed stiffly – 30 or so feet beneath – the saddest thing you could imagine, testing and taunting your humanity, burnt in the mind forever.

Two days before, at home in London, I had received a message from my TV news editor saying 250,000 Rwandan refugees had just crossed into Tanzania that day – 30 April.

This article appeared originally on the BBC website on 7 April 2004 as *Media Failure Over Rwanda's Genocide*. It is also available on the BBC website at <www.news.bbc.co.uk/2/hi/programmes/panorama/3599423.stm>.

Camps of that size were always news, and they were there to be filmed. I would fly out that day. Although I was aware of the killings that had begun in the Rwandan capital, Kigali, on 6 April, I and the rest of the world had seen little since to suggest the scale of what was happening.

Apart from the images bravely snatched by the fleeing press corps in the genocide's first days, there were few pictures. Once the UN had all but left the country, the hazards for journalists trying to get back in by land were too great.

For nearly three weeks in April, after its first days had passed, the story of one of the twentieth century's worst crimes had failed – in an age of global satellite broadcasting – to make the top of the TV news bulletins.

This was mainly due to the difficulty of access into Rwanda. But there were other issues. Most senior correspondents were down in South Africa covering the election of its first black president. In comparison, this story seemed at first too obscure for them – an African blood feud. The problem was to be compounded by the appalling nature of the pictures.

Months earlier, the BBC newsroom had been bombarded with complaints when a small massacre in neighbouring Burundi had been shown in dreadful detail, once, on the lunchtime news. Someone had issued a directive about pictures. This was allowed to set the tone, in the BBC at least, for a story of unimaginably greater consequence.

On my way to the airport, I had hoped to make copies of the rushes that had been sent from Rwanda. But there were almost none. The worst – the ones that actually showed the scale of the slaughter – had never been aired.

They were sent to London in mid-April when the need to alert the world to what was happening was at its greatest. An entire news piece, gathered at great risk to the BBC team filming it, was dropped. It had been deemed too graphic for British viewers.

The next day, I met the same BBC team in Nairobi. With polite exasperation, the cameraman explained how he had been told to make future pictures wider – less distinct, more impressionistic.

He had been unable to achieve this with the offending shots, as he had tried to do what he thought would be right in the circumstances – to get some record, from a moving car and without being seen by the killers themselves, of the piles of bodies nine feet high that lined both sides of the road.

With our BBC colleague, Mark Doyle, still negotiating to fly with the UN peacekeepers back into the Rwandan capital, Kigali – I took another team in a small chartered plane to the camps. After hours of flying, we reached an isolated airstrip then drove for hours more through appalling mud-clogged tracks to reach the Hutu refugees at Ngara.

We had little time to take in the scene – filming mass human misery in cold, scattergun fashion. Some of these Hutus were perpetrators or accomplices to the killings – not the victims. None of them would suffer too much. Ngara was at least full of crops, food and aid agencies.

We had to press on, crossing the border at the Rusumo bridge. Soon after, the scale of the Hutus' work became clear.

This corner of Rwanda had been liberated days before by the advancing Tutsi-led army, but all around there was silence. Apart from the flies and vultures, it felt as if all nature had fled the earth.

Ahead lay towns and villages abandoned by the living, among them those soon to become infamous like Nyarubuye – with its church full of bodies. It would be more than six weeks before the full graphic horror of these scenes would be broadcast on the BBC.

For now, I had to record a voice-track with the reporter and turn back with my rushes to reach Nairobi and the satellite feed. Alone, and abandoned by the pilot who had promised to return, I had to hire a passing plane on the spot and fly back through a lightning storm.

With a minute to spare, the piece was edited and rushed through the Nairobi traffic to be fed by satellite to London. Finally, the story led the news again – though I regret much of the horror was carefully self-censored.

For this much at least, I was commended. London now wanted human stories from the camps, of getting aid to the refugees, of babies born in misery.

It was clear even then that this was not a story of refugees or of some distant civil war but of a systematic genocide still being carried out. But it was hard to get this message across – this was a complicated story in a country few people had heard of. Refugees were, at least, a simpler issue.

Weeks of frustration followed. Pieces were often re-edited in London – shots of bodies removed. On one occasion, a shot of a sack on the ground edited in by us to avoid showing bodies was removed because, I was told, the viewers might still have thought it was a body.

What the viewers in London weren't seeing in scale was what I saw in pictures arriving back in Nairobi – corpses piled high, decaying skulls and skeletons, terribly injured children.

What they did see often were images of refugees in camps and of gunfire in the heat of the battle that raged for control of Kigali. Only one BBC team, from Newsnight, ventured further into the active killing zones at this time.

The producer, a friend, has never forgotten the hollow faces of those Tutsis he met, trapped and abandoned, waiting to die in a camp south of Kigali.

Three and a half weeks after I had flown out, I returned to London, exhausted and overwhelmed by a sense of failure. Weeks later – long after the vast bulk of the killing had stopped – another decision was made.

Fergal Keane's extraordinary Panorama – 'Journey into Darkness' – on the killings at Nyarubuye would be broadcast with, at last, pictures showing the true scale of the horror, uncensored.

It went out on 27 June. It was the first of many harrowing and moving documentaries about what happened to Rwanda's Tutsis in the weeks from April to June 1994. All of them, unfortunately, were broadcast too late to prevent it.

As journalists, we were rightly quick to condemn the inaction of the UN and the wider international community over Rwanda. But many of those who tried to cover this appalling story as it happened around them still harbour, as I do, a lingering sense of helplessness – a sense of guilt, perhaps shame, that we didn't do more to apply pressure for action when it might have made a difference.

20
A Genocide Without Images: White Film Noirs

Edgar Roskis

'For photographers, Rwanda was like an open-air workshop,' says François Huguier, one of the photographers who know Africa best (see Huguier and Cressole 1990). And indeed, we all recall the flood of images from July 1994, none of them any less terrible for being so artistically wrought. During the Rwandan tragedy, there were so many journalists in the field – but only at certain times – and so many images sent out around the world – but only from certain places – that it is easy to get the impression that this event was 'over-covered' by the media.

But in reality, what Rony Brauman (1994: 7), former president of Médecins Sans Frontières, describes as 'a planned extermination … a campaign of butchery organized by the legally constituted authorities, in which no opponent, real or imagined, was ever supposed to survive' – in short, an indisputable crime of genocide – was never captured in still or moving images.

The signal for the massacres was given on 6 April 1994. 'Less than one hour after the president's Falcon 50 aircraft (a gift from France, a friendly country) was shot down, militiamen had erected the first barriers on the road to the airport and in the capital … In the Gikongo district of Kigali, in a single day (April 10), the street was covered with corpses for an entire kilometre' (Brauman 1994: 11–12).

At that time, the media did not yet regard Rwanda as a 'subject'. French photo agencies dispatched only two photographers: Patrick Robert from Sygma and Luc Delahaye from SIPA, who reached Kigali on 9 April with a Red Cross convoy from Bujumbura, Burundi.

'There were six American correspondents,' recalls Patrick Robert. 'They had scarcely arrived when their editors gave them all orders to come home. At the Hôtel des Mille Collines, I picked up snatches of their conversations: "Too dangerous, not enough interest … deep Africa, you know… middle of nowhere"'.

THE MEDIA HAVE LANDED

Robert and Delahaye stayed there almost alone, aside from a handful of correspondents from regional media outlets. In the coming days, they would

This article is reprinted in translation from *Le Monde Diplomatique* of November 1994.

photograph dozens of corpses abandoned on farms, Tutsis massacred with hand grenades and automatic weapons, struck down with machetes, sometimes left for dead. 'But always after the fact, without ever seeing the actual executions themselves. The Hutu militias were too cunning for that.'

The two photographers moved on into territory controlled by the Rwandan Patriotic Front (RPF), where they met some 15 survivors and gathered their stories. But the photographers' raw, unadorned images and the survivors' simple accounts left editors cold. Patrick Robert returned to Paris in early May scarcely having sold a single photo.

From 6 April to mid-May, while the bulk of the massacres were being perpetrated silently yet systematically (100,000 dead in Butare, out of a population of 800,000, as of 23 April), Rwanda was still relegated to the inside pages of the newspapers. The photos that were published were small and often old, the accounts second-hand, with little if any news appearing for days at a time.[1]

Not until 18 May did a photograph of the Rwandan atrocities make it onto the front page of a French newspaper, the *Quotidien de Paris*. And even this image, of a dozen decapitated bodies in Rukara, mangled and partly eaten by animals, was just a snapshot taken by a doctor, Eric Girard, not by a photojournalist. That same day, another Paris daily, *Libération*, was headlined 'Rwanda: France's guilty friendships', but except for another photo by Eric Girard, the accompanying photos showed only some Rwandan refugees in Tanzania.[2]

From that time until the end of Operation Turquoise, the journalists on the Rwanda story depended on humanitarian groups for transport, and their coverage reflected this fact: it was limited to the refugee camps, at first in Tanzania, and then mainly in Zaire. Patrick Robert recalls ruefully, 'In the early days of May, before that famous exodus into Tanzania, which was really quite spectacular, not many people were all that interested in Rwanda.' In other words, what inspired the picture-takers, the newspapers, the magazines and television the most was not the civil war or the planned massacres of hundreds of thousands of Tutsis and moderate Hutus,[3] but the humanitarian melodrama, 'the endless lines of refugees, the sacks of rice, the orphans and field hospitals, the images of downtrodden humanity and resolute volunteers, of suffering and salvation' (Brauman 1994: 78).

The peak of this coverage – when the numbers of special correspondents and news reports were at their highest – occurred between 14 and 20 July. 'In the space of a few hours, a flood of 200,000 Hutu refugees arrived, followed soon in the Goma region [Zaire] by a veritable tidal wave of 600,000 to 700,000 people' (Brauman 1994: 74–5). The Goma refugees were stricken almost immediately by a cholera epidemic. It was the cholera, followed by dysentery for good measure, plus all the spectacular visuals that came with such a massive displacement of population and such an unprecedented, unmanageable flood of refugees, that really triggered the media influx to the region.

Relying on the resources of the military forces and humanitarian groups in the region to take them where they could observe this phenomenon close up, picture-chasers from all over the globe, from the most timid to the boldest, the most sensitive to the most cynical, poured into the area. As Jean-Michel Turpin, of the Gamma agency, describes it,

> The hotels, campgrounds, and airports were packed with photographers and television crews. Not really much more media than for any big event, but this time, we were all concentrated in a very small area, about 50 kilometres of highway starting at Goma. The number of journalists was unbelievable, and there really were dead and dying everywhere.

It was along this highway in Zaire that Turpin took that terrible photo, perhaps more terrifying than any other because it juxtaposed a white adult with a black child in a position that was intolerable and that, even though it was only a picture, bespoke a certain truth.

> 'At first,' Turpin relates, 'I didn't want to take that picture. Showing a colleague under those conditions – it was just too easy. Writers can do their jobs more discreetly, but when you work with a camera, you have to get up very close to your subjects and look them in the face. You have to get into some positions that are going to be grotesque. But that day, I had just seen this poor little kid grab onto a television reporter's pant leg, and the reporter's reaction was to whip out his point-and-shoot and take a close-up of the kid just hanging on there. This guy wasn't even a cameraman, he was just somebody who does stand-ups and talks into a microphone. He didn't need that photo for anything – he was just taking it for a souvenir. Who could want a souvenir like that? Then half a second later, I saw a photographer who was almost sitting on top of a dead child to get a shot. He obviously hadn't realized it, but at that point, I had had enough. (Joannès 1994; Roskis 1994)

It was there, in Zaire, that most of the other images of 'Rwanda' that are imprinted on our memory were photographed. The Goma region and the triangular 'safe humanitarian zone' created by the French military gave the photo stylists and other photo award hunters one compact, convenient location where they could instantly access an inexhaustible supply of the raw materials they needed to produce images of Africa for Western consumption: large, anonymous groups of people floating through ethereal clouds of dust; the beautiful bodies of the ill and the injured; the wide, imploring eyes of children; infants latched on to their mother's empty – or, with a bit of luck, her dead – breast; the mandatory pushing and shoving at food-distribution points, the struggle for the tiniest scrap; and, most of all, courtesy of Operation Turquoise, images of the good White Man, hale and hearty, feared as much as admired by the dark masses held in awe by his confident gaze – the White Man, ready to go anywhere, any time, to help the widows, the orphans and the sick, heedless of adversity, disdainful of danger. In the end, these were comforting, iconic images for Western eyes and easy pickings for the media.

THE NEED TO SHOCK

'In Rwanda more than anywhere else, I was forced to confront the shame in what I do for a living,' confesses Luc Delahaye, now with Magnum. 'The shame of stopping in front of someone at the side of the road, watching their agony, and then taking their photo.' But Albert Facelly, of SIPA, sees it differently. 'If we want our pictures to serve any useful purpose, then they have to shock people' (Facelly 1994: 12–13).

This idea – that pictures must shock to serve a purpose, including one's own – has been fully embraced by the NGOs, who apply it skilfully and somewhat cold-bloodedly in their communication campaigns, responding to the laws of a new marketplace. But this kind of shock is highly questionable, and so is the cause that it pretends to serve. At best these images of the dead and dying attract our charity. They don't keep us from living, or even from sleeping at night, and they don't keep the people who take these pictures from winning awards.

What would we think of a Pulitzer Prize won at Auschwitz? The comparison may seem sacrilegious. But the fate promised the Tutsis was indeed a 'final solution', a political and military crime compounded by a sinister movement, a 'tropical Nazism' (Bensussan 1995; Chrétien 1994) that was the direct source of this 'humanitarian disaster'.

Unfortunately, in our mental image of the world, the African dead remain eternally remote and exotic, and we want to be kept blind to the circumstances in which they were murdered. And that is what pictures do: they hide as much as they show. Behind the screen of those ever-so-photogenic refugee camps, the Hutu slaughterers were rebuilding their civil and military might, preparing, perhaps, for the next bloodbath.

NOTES

1. And yet on 27 April, *Le Monde* published the account of a volunteer from International Action Against Hunger under the headline 'A monstrous manhunt in Rwanda', followed the next day by a long report from a Red Cross representative, with a front page 'teaser' that read 'The massacres in Rwanda'.
2. See in particular Sebastiao Salgado's photos of Benako, 'the largest refugee camp in the world', in the 26 May edition of *Paris-Match*, and those of Gilles Peress (Magnum) in the 27 May and 4 June editions of *Libération*.
3. In *Le Monde*, 20 May 1994, but no earlier, Bernard Kouchner offered an initial estimate of its extent: 'between 200,000 and 500,000 dead'.

REFERENCES

Bensussan, G. 1994. Les génocides de l'après-Shoah. *Libération*, 12 October: 9.
Brauman, R. 1994. *Devant le mal. Rwanda: un génocide en direct.* Arléa, Paris, France.
Chrétien, J.P. 1994. Un nazisme tropical. *Libération*, 26 April: 7.
Facelly, A. 1994. *InfoMatin*, 13 September.
Huguier, F. and Cressole, M. 1990. *Sur les traces de l'Afrique fantôme*. Maeght Editeur, Paris, France.
Joannès, A. 1994. Rwanda, l'imagerie de l'horreur. *Télescope*, 76, September.
Roskis, E. 1994. Retour sur une image choc. *Télescope*, 81, October.

21
Notes on Circumstances that Facilitate Genocide: the Attention Given to Rwanda by the Media and Others Outside Rwanda Before 1990

Mike Dottridge

Most reports focusing on the role of Radio-Télévision Libre des Milles Collines (RTLM) and other media in Rwanda's genocide pay little or no attention to events before 1990 and say little about the extraordinary profile that Rwanda managed to maintain for most of the previous two decades. A few months after the 1994 genocide, I made a comment along the same lines as many others, that the tragedy which started on 6 April this year occurred because governments and others turned a determined deaf ear to the reports being issued by human rights nongovernmental organizations and eventually even to a report by one of the United Nations Commission on Human Rights' own experts. This note is intended to put that 'deafness' into a longer-term context: before 1990, it was evident that very few people listened for information coming out of Rwanda.

A lot has been written and said about why governments and intergovernmental organizations turned a deaf ear to the rising tide of genocidal violence between October 1990 and April 1994. This three and a half years of inaction is part of a broader context in which journalists and others based outside Rwanda share responsibility for inaction.

I suppose anyone who documents political repression that involves murder or disappearances is haunted by ghosts afterward. Those of us who observed the pogroms that preceded Rwanda's 1994 genocide and tried helplessly to react once the full horror began in April 1994 are probably more haunted by both guilt and memories of individuals whom we knew and who were slaughtered than those who arrived in Rwanda to witness the bloodshed or skeletons afterward. We know, or we think we know, that the scale of the extermination could have been prevented if the world had paid some attention before 6 April and if the world's great powers had felt the inclination to react once the killings got underway.

As a desk officer monitoring political imprisonment in Rwanda (along with the some ten other countries in central Africa) for Amnesty International from 1979 until 1987 and supervising Amnesty's work in sub-Saharan Africa (including the Great Lakes region) until 1995, I became involved with Rwanda at a time when the killing and persecution of Rwandese Tutsi from 1959 until

1966 was regarded by the outside world as a thing of the past. Further anti-Tutsi violence in 1973 had received little media attention and was generally dismissed as a relatively minor hiccup provoked by the preceding year's political violence in Burundi. However, little was published about Rwanda outside its frontiers and, as I started digging for information about political prisoners in 1979, I had no idea that the fate of more than 50 people detained five years earlier remained unclear and was a cause for great concern.

I do not look back with great pride on what we (Amnesty International and others) managed to achieve during the 1980s through external pressure on the government of Rwanda. We focused on abuses of human rights concerning prisoners, principally political prisoners, and attempted to ascertain whether those we learned about were 'prisoners of conscience'. If the information we obtained – for example on the basis of sedition charges leading to prisoners' convictions – indicated that someone was in jail for expressing his or her non-violent opinions, Amnesty 'adopted' that person and sought his or her release.

With the benefit of hindsight, it is obvious that the terms of reference with which we approached Rwanda, and consequently the human rights questions we raised, were far too narrow. Even in the specific field of political imprisonment and abuse against political prisoners, we tended to base the assessment of whether an individual was a prisoner of conscience on the formal record (the charges on which someone was convicted), when in practice the authorities were arresting people for all sorts of reasons and using whatever charges they thought would sound acceptable to Rwanda's public and result in the imposition of a prison sentence of a suitable length. In terms of the broader field of human rights associated with political repression, we did not address the country's structural problems until far too late.

However, it is not this mea culpa that I want to focus on here, but rather the implications of what we and others did or did not do when information about political repression and abuses of human rights in Rwanda was made available. For despite the inadequacy of what was achieved, it was possible to sneak under the fence of silence that Rwanda had constructed (by keeping its media almost exclusively in Kinyarwanda and under the control of ORINFOR, one of the region's more formidable propaganda agencies) and to ferret out information from all sorts of places, including the dungeons of Rwanda's most secretive prison. The government's newspaper and the Catholic Church's weekly both published details about political trials in Kinyarwanda, which were fairly accessible to anyone who sought the services of a translator.

It took a while for me to get the personal testimony of someone who had experienced torture and imprisonment in Rwanda, for the prisoners associated with the Kayibanda government had been wiped out, leaving no one to interview. However, in 1985, a detailed interview with a former political prisoner provided a great deal of detail that could be used to corroborate other second-hand accounts of the violence used against prisoners, and also served as an indictment of practices in Rwanda.

The ghosts I remember from the 1980s include a host of people (a much smaller host than in 1994) who had been killed well before the Rwandan

Patriotic Front (RPF) launched its offensive against the Habyarimana regime in October 1990 – in particular, a group of more than 50 people who were arrested soon after General Juvénal Habyarimana seized power in June 1973. They included individuals who had been well known outside Rwanda, such as Gaspard Harelimana, a member of the government from 1964 until 1973, and Aloys Munyaneza, the foreign minister in 1972 and 1973. However, the 1970s was a period when political repression and secret executions became the norm in much of Africa, to such an extent that they passed either unremarked or without provoking protests from either other Africans or non-Africans who were aware of what was occurring.

Remarkably, however, I received almost no complaints about human rights abuse from members of Rwanda's Tutsi minority. Those with experience in interviewing members of repressed minorities will not be surprised by this: from Egypt's Copts to Pakistan's Hindus and Christians, both religious and ethnic minorities often conclude that making a fuss is counterproductive and that those in power are probably less nasty than others who might take their place.

During the 1980s, the amount of interest I or others were able to generate among journalists and political circles in Europe and North America in political repression in individual African countries varied according to some obvious criteria:

- Whose colony the country had been (if Belgian, Spanish or Portuguese, it usually attracted less attention than others, unless it involved a monstrous dictator doing something ludicrous);
- What European language was in use in the country;
- How strong the vested interests in Africa, Europe or North America were to maintain silence;
- Whether a journalist who knew the country and was inclined to report on events there was already tied up with other stories;
- What else was going on in Africa and the rest of the developing world at the same time.

There was little in terms of 'joined up reporting' (that is, reporting that identifies the connections between developments in neighbouring countries or within entire subregions), which has become more common since 1994 as the regional nature of conflict in the Great Lakes region of Africa and in the vicinity of Liberia and Sierra Leone in West Africa has become obvious. Consequently, from 1982 through 1986, when massacres were a daily occurrence in southern and southwestern Uganda and the persecution of Rwandese in Uganda[1] resulted in Rwandese refugees seeking shelter back in Rwanda, there was little or no independent reporting to assess the level of oppression that Tutsi in Rwanda were being subjected to. The world was told (by President Habyarimana) that Rwanda was overpopulated and had 'no more room'. Similarly, there was next to no journalistic investigation of the supply lines of Yoweri Museveni's guerrilla force in Uganda (which depended heavily on the logistic support it received via Bujumbura, resulting in occasional arrests of Ugandans travelling through Rwanda), possibly because the journalists who reported on the conflict in Uganda were so appalled by what was going on that they inevitably took a pro-Museveni line.

Stamped on my memory is a visit to Rwanda's high-security prison – Ruhengeri in the northwest, where many of the prisoners associated with Rwanda's first government led by Grégoire Kayibanda had been murdered in the 1970s. I was accompanied by Alpha-Abdoulaye Diallo, a former foreign minister from Guinea who had been imprisoned for a long period in his own country and who had managed to avoid being starved to death – the fate of many hundreds of prisoners in Sékou Touré's Guinea. The prisoners we saw in May 1986 in Ruhengeri prison's 'special section' included the former head of security, Théoneste Lizinde, who had orchestrated most of the killings in the 1970s.

I recall three aspects of the visit particularly vividly: the large Catholic confessional that hid the entrance to the special section off the prison's main courtyard; the three completely black, unlit punishment cells ('*cachots noirs*') that you passed as you walked into the special section, where members of the Kayibanda government had been starved to death and more recently political prisoners whose cases I had handled had been confined for long periods; and Lizinde himself, the only one of the 30-odd prisoners in the special section who defied the order not to speak to the Amnesty visitors (he had, after all, been sentenced to death twice by that time, so possibly felt he had little to lose). Always one to speak out, after serving as a provincial governor after the RPF took power in Rwanda in 1994, he parted company again with the RPF, left the country again and was murdered in Kenya.[2]

I mention the prison visit because it illustrates for me a number of Rwanda's characteristics in the 1980s, which helped facilitate the disasters of the early 1990s. First, the fate of the Kayibanda government received virtually no attention from either journalists outside Rwanda or others with a possible professional interest. Indeed, when I looked at Amnesty's almost non-existent records on Rwanda in 1979, I found that the organization had congratulated President Habyarimana for an amnesty he had announced following Kayibanda's death, without realizing that this was part of the cover-up for both the former president's disappearance and that of others. At the time, the only humanitarian organization that was aware of these deaths was probably the International Committee of the Red Cross. At the end of the 1970s, there was just one Belgian academic who came to visit me at my office in London to voice concern about political repression in Rwanda and to suggest that, alongside Amnesty's protests at torture and other human rights violations in neighbouring Burundi, Congo, Uganda and Zaire, we should also be doing something about Rwanda.

Even when the international community descended on Rwanda in 1979 with a human rights focus,[3] no attention was given to the fate of members of the previous government. Within a few months, there were further political arrests, of Lizinde and others, signifying a major fall out among those in power. Nothing of this was mentioned in the Western media.

It was not until 1982 that Amnesty International began publishing a significant amount of information about political imprisonment in Rwanda, but even then it was hidden away in the annual report, among a mountain of other stories of sordid murders and torture around the world. It was not surprising that no one noticed. Well, that is not quite true. It was noticed in Rwanda itself and by some of the regime's supporters in Belgium. When I met the Archbishop of Kigali on the visit to Kigali in 1986 (at that time he was still a member of the central committee of Rwanda's ruling party, the only party allowed), he told us that he had not known anything about Amnesty before 1982 and that once he started reading our reports, he had 'noted a lot of inaccuracies', such as our failure to mention when a particular prisoner had been released. More significantly, in 1983 he was reported to have been one of the first people outside Rwanda's security service to be allowed to visit the inmates of Ruhengeri's special section, along with Minister of Justice Jean-Marie Vianny Mugemana; this visit led to some improvements in prison conditions there.

Soon afterward, a number of journalists (three, I think) were dispatched to Rwanda from Belgium to prepare reports on how rosy everything was there. I wish I had kept verbatim notes of my encounter with these journalists, for they represented a range of points of view within Belgium's pro-Rwandese political spectrum, from the genuinely right wing to a newspaper traditionally associated with 'Catholic trade unionism'. However, I recall that all were only too ready to whitewash the Rwandese government's record. Why?

I am not satisfied that the international community has adequately analyzed and understood the inclination of Western media to misreport or simply *not* report on abuses by governments for which they have a liking. I was astounded by it in the late 1970s when the government of Angola was able to get away with hundreds of secret executions (following an unsuccessful coup attempt in May 1977) without a word about them abroad.

It was equally shocking in the early 1980s, when some London-based journalists attempted to deny that massacres and torture had become daily events in Uganda. Rwanda represented something similar, but over a much longer period. The results were obvious within days of the RPF's first assault from Uganda into Rwanda in October 1990. When government forces themselves organized an incident in Kigali, claiming it was an RPF attack, to justify mass round-ups of both Tutsi and suspected government opponents, the Western press swallowed the government version and no one was alerted to the sordid cases of torture and murder that followed.

Of course, there is an important distinction between the media taking no interest (and possibly peddling inaccurate information as a result) and the media actively siding with a repressive regime. However, the consequences of both attitudes need analyzing if we are to understand what has to be done to avoid facilitating genocide.

And what is it that inspires journalists to support governments that are quite obviously tyrannical? In the case of Rwanda from 1960 to 1990, we know it was a follow-on to the support that both Belgian and some Catholic interests gave to the ousting of Rwanda's *mwami* shortly before independence and the installation of a government that was viewed by most Belgian Rwanda-watchers as more 'democratic', simply because it was composed of Hutu.

Some of the support that Western newspapers have given to the governments of countries in the Great Lakes region since 1994 has been just as bizarre and misplaced. It is probably born out of good motives, a view of the world that divides political protagonists into 'good' and 'bad', seeking to support the good and retaining this view whatever level of evidence is available to indicate that it is foolhardy! However, my own assessment of the work I was involved in during the 1980s is that everyone should be held accountable for the consequences of their own actions, both journalists and human rights organizations and, of course, political leaders responsible for murder and torture – even those whom someone assesses to be 'not as bad as their opponents' and who, consequently, are allowed to get away with murder.

NOTES

1. Both Rwandese refugees who had fled from Rwanda between 1958 and 1966 and ethnic Rwandese (Banyarwanda) whose families had lived in Uganda for many generations.
2. I saw Théoneste Lizinde only once again, equally briefly, in London, after he had been freed during a daring raid by the RPF on Ruhengeri in 1992 or 1993. He was accompanied by RPF minders on his visit to London.
3. The Franco-African summit held in Kigali decided to set up a commission of inquiry into the reported murder of imprisoned schoolchildren in Bokassa's Central African Empire, and a human rights seminar was organized in Kigali at much the same time. The commission of inquiry included a senior Rwandese judge who became involved in trying to penetrate the secret part of Ngaragba prison in Bangui and whom we later approached in order to bring about an inquiry into the secret executions in Rwanda. At the time of the summit, Burundi exiles in Rwanda sought to exploit the current international interest in human rights violations by claiming that massacres were occurring in Burundi, allegations which proved unfounded.

22
The Media's Failure: a Reflection on the Rwanda Genocide

Richard Dowden

In their article 'Britannia waived the rules' in the January 2004 issue of *African Affairs*, Linda Melvern and Paul Williams argue that during the Rwanda genocide: 'Britain and other great powers signalled their intention to let the killers conduct their grisly business unimpeded' (Melvern and Williams 2004). They point out that while members of the United Nations (UN) Security Council may not have recognized that genocide was taking place, they were aware that hundreds of thousands of people were being killed when they decided to withdraw the UN peacekeepers. They accuse the British government of a 'deliberately misconceived version' of what was happening in Rwanda and a 'wilful neglect of its obligations under the genocide convention.'

With hindsight, it is obvious that the world's political leaders and opinion formers failed Rwanda in 1994. Bill Clinton, then United States president, and Madeleine Albright, his representative at the UN and later Secretary of State, have recognized this and expressed regret for their part in withdrawing the UN force from Rwanda as the genocide started. Their British equivalents, John Major, then prime minister, Douglas Hurd, foreign secretary, and Baroness Lynda Chalker, the minister for Africa, have been less forthright. At the time, no one resigned and nobody's career has been damaged by the failure in Rwanda. Indeed, the pivotal player at the UN at the time, Kofi Annan, undersecretary general for peacekeeping, who dealt with the dispatches from the UN force commander in Kigali, later became secretary general. Annan's deputy and successor at peacekeeping, Syed Iqbal Riza, was later to serve as Annan's *chef de cabinet*.

The aim of this commentary is not to pass judgement on these players, but to try to recall the thinking of the time and revisit the context in which decisions about Rwanda and Africa were made. Because the genocide in Rwanda itself has challenged assumptions and changed perspectives, it requires a mental repositioning that goes further than asking who knew what when. I begin with my own experience as a journalist covering Africa at the time, then go on to examine some of the early coverage of the genocide that appeared in Britain's press.

This paper first appeared in *African Affairs*, volume 103, number 411, April 2004.

In 1994, I was Africa editor for the *Independent*. I had been in Kigali briefly in January that year on my way to Zaire, as Congo was then called. All the diplomats, politicians and aid workers I spoke to in Kigali talked about the fragile but functioning Arusha peace accords, the complex power-sharing agreement between the Tutsi-led Rwandan Patriotic Front (RPF), the Habyarimana government and several small political parties. After two years of bitter fighting and heavy negotiations, an agreement had at last been reached and signed. The delicate and dangerous task of implementation was then reaching its final stages. Only one person in Kigali had warned me that there could be genocide: Philippe Gaillard of the International Committee of the Red Cross. He told me that militias were being armed by the government and that plans were being laid to promote mass killings of Tutsis throughout the country.

I thought long and hard about writing a story called 'Genocide looms in Rwanda.' It might have made the front page – the aspiration of every journalist – but I had only one source. Everyone else I spoke to talked up the Arusha peace process. I did not sense anything sinister on the streets of Kigali that might have made me skeptical. And, as the world-weary diplomats said, the worst that would happen if the accord did not work would be another round of fighting. I had not been in Kigali long enough to make a judgement or doubt my interlocutors, so to write a sensational story about impending genocide would have been dishonest and irresponsible. It might even prompt genocide. I put down my pen and went off to eastern Congo.

On 6 April, I was packing my bag for South Africa to cover the impending election when the *Independent*'s foreign editor, Harvey Morris, called to tell me about the plane crash that had killed President Juvénal Habyarimana. After some discussion, we agreed that I should continue to South Africa but watch developments in Rwanda. I wrote a background article and caught the plane to Johannesburg. For the next three weeks the newspaper carried agency reports on Rwanda. As the South African polls closed, I flew to Kampala to try to find out what was happening in Rwanda.

Getting to the action was not easy. There were no flights to Kigali or anywhere else in the country. The route from Zaire in the west was impossible as President Mobutu Sese Seko did not allow journalists into the country except by special invitation. To try to get in from the south through Burundi might be impossible and dangerous, as that country too had been destabilized by the death of its president. The other viable routes were through Tanzania to southeastern Rwanda – a journey of at least three days, or across the Uganda border, which was officially closed. However, the World Food Programme (WFP) was running a cross-border feeding operation to eastern Rwanda, encouraged by the RPF, which controlled the border on the Rwandan side.

The WFP lent me a vehicle and a driver and we drove into Rwanda. Once inside, the RPF took over and kept us waiting near the border for a couple of days. Eventually, the RPF gave me a guide and bodyguard and, on 2 May, we drove down through Rwanda to the Kagera River on the Tanzanian border. I learned later that the best road from Uganda into the northeast was being used for military supplies, something that neither the RPF nor the Ugandan government wanted outsiders to see. We, therefore, had to take ill-maintained dirt roads.

The country was almost completely deserted. Africa's roads, especially in a crowded country like Rwanda, are usually dotted with pickup trucks, walkers and cyclists. In two days of driving, we saw no more than a dozen people. The Kagera River carried scores of bloated dead bodies downstream. At the rate I saw them – one every four or five minutes – I estimated that hundreds of people were being killed every day further upstream. It was hard to get close enough to see the cause of death, but some seemed to have their hands tied.

From there we drove across to the refugee camps on the Tanzania side, leaving our RPF guide and guard in Rwanda. Here thousands of Hutus who had fled eastern Rwanda told us that RPF Tutsis were murdering Hutus and they had come across the border to escape. Some journalists bought this story at face value. Although we had seen few people on the way, I had seen no evidence of killing and little sign of destruction and I did not believe it. My instincts were confirmed when two people separately drew me aside and whispered that what I was being told was untrue. I found them convincing. They were clearly frightened but desperate to tell their story. They said that it was these refugees who had done the killing and they had fled to escape RPF revenge.

On the way back, I saw some of the massacre sites that have been extensively reported and recorded. Then we turned west to Kigali and joined the RPF front line in the hills overlooking the city from the northeast. From a distance it looked peaceful. It was impossible to know what was happening there.

It was also impossible to get the story out without leaving Rwanda. Telephones did not work and mobile phones did not reach that far in those days. To send reports back to the newspaper meant going all the way back to Uganda, another day's journey on roads where you had to drive permanently in second gear. Once out, it might be impossible to get back in again as the WFP vehicle had to go back to Kampala and no other vehicles were available.

I should also add that it was difficult for me to find words to describe what was happening. I had covered nearly 20 wars, but the usual clichés of death and destruction mocked Rwanda's horrors. I could find no new words to describe what I was seeing. Furthermore, all the usual human and journalistic instincts to tell an important story to the world shrivelled in the face of what I was seeing and hearing. I began my main report with the words: 'I do not want to tell you what I saw today….' Why should my aged parents be presented with this vision of hell at their breakfast table? How could I tell my wife what I had seen and smelled? And what of my children as they got ready for school? What if they caught a glimpse of it? Why should anyone at all need to be told these things? I have spoken to other journalists who were there at the time and they recall similar feelings.

My own notebooks and reports of that period and other reports in the British press give some insight into what the world thought at the time and how they perceived events in Rwanda. Certainly few people thought that the plane crash that killed President Juvénal Habyarimana of Rwanda and President

Cyprien Ntaryamira of Burundi would trigger one of the worst genocides of the twentieth century. Although the disarming and murder of the Belgian paratroopers, part of the UN force, and the open killings in the streets of Kigali, the capital, began the next day, these events were not interpreted as a spur to international action. On the contrary they instigated withdrawal. The reasons for this lie in the failure to understand what was happening in Rwanda at the time and that failure has much to do with the importance – or lack of it – that outsiders gave to Africa, the way in which they thought of Africa and the language they used to describe it.

Rwanda simply wasn't important enough. To British editors, it was a small country far away in a continent that rarely hit the headlines. The words Hutu and Tutsi sounded funny, hardly names that an ambitious news editor or desk officer would want to draw to the attention of a busy boss and claim that they were of immediate and vital importance. Within a few days of the plane crash, *The Times* ran several articles about what it obviously considered an angle to interest its readers: the fate of the Rwandan guerrillas. Being a former Belgian colony and Francophone, it was of little interest to the Foreign Office, which had been forced to cut its staffing levels in Africa in the 1980s and early 1990s. Rwanda was not a country that had historical or commercial links with Britain and Britain had no diplomatic representation there. In London, as the crisis developed, Douglas Hurd's staffers were reduced to telling the foreign secretary what they had seen on CNN that day. This was Britain's main source of information about what was happening on the ground.

On 7 April, all major newspapers reported the plane crash that killed the presidents and followed it with reports of the murder of the Belgian soldiers and then the evacuation of foreigners. There was little attempt to analyze Rwanda's politics beyond the fact there had been a civil war that had been frozen by the Arusha accords. For most newspapers, the foreign story of the moment was Bosnia and its coverage was already stretching budgets and staffing levels.

Furthermore, on 27 April, South Africans were to vote in the country's first democratic elections. That would mark the end of apartheid. The implications for Africa and black people throughout the world were immeasurable. This was clearly going to be a momentous event in itself, but at the time, many Western commentators were also predicting a ghastly bloodbath in South Africa. They said that the African National Congress (ANC) would break its promises and begin a campaign of murder and destabilization. Others, observing the continuing violence in KwaZulu-Natal, predicted a tribal conflict between Xhosa and Zulu. Mangosuthu Buthelezi, the leader of the Zulu Inkatha movement, had not signed up to the national deal, and more and more people were dying in the gang warfare between Inkatha gangs and the ANC.

In the end, Buthelezi signed the agreement days before the election, the voting was vast and peaceful and the miracle was completed by the saintly wisdom and demeanour of Nelson Mandela. The expectations of journalists who headed en masse for Durban in search of a bloodbath, were not fulfilled. As a result they missed the worst bloodbath of all.

This group of journalists included most of the stringers for the world's press based in Nairobi who usually covered East Africa. Normally, they would have been in Rwanda on the next flight, but the world's press could not apparently cover more than one Africa story at a time. Some did not even try. The *Financial Times* of London, always squeamish about stories that involve blood but not business, did not send its Nairobi correspondent to South Africa, but nor was she sent to Rwanda for more than a week after the country collapsed.

Burundi, Rwanda's neighbour and twin, offered more evidence that the world would not be moved by Rwanda's plight. The previous autumn, the first democratically elected president of Burundi, Melchior Ndadaye, had been murdered. He was the country's first Hutu president and his death was followed by the massacre of at least 50,000 people (FIDH 1995). Some said it was five times that number. According to the Commission Internationale, Hutus and Tutsis were killed in about equal numbers. Reviewing the report, Professor René Lemarchand wrote:

> A blind rage suddenly seized Frodebu militants and peasants alike in almost every province, and they killed every Tutsi in sight … the picture that emerges is one of unadulterated savagery. In one commune after another, scores of men, women and children were hacked to pieces with machetes, speared or clubbed to death, or doused with kerosene and burned alive. Of the active involvement of some communal and provincial authorities in the massacres, there can be no doubt … From all appearances, however, little prodding was needed for the crowds to heed their incitements. (Lemarchand 1995)

Not a single staff journalist from the British press had covered this story. It barely made the headlines and was hardly reported in British national newspapers or on national radio in Britain. Any news editor or desk officer who made a check through the records would have found that massacres of Hutus and Tutsis in Rwanda and Burundi had occurred with appalling frequency in the second half of the twentieth century. The word genocide was frequently used to describe these massacres, but no one had ever proposed sending a peacekeeping army to stop them. So why should they now? The United States whose airlift and financial muscle were – and are – essential to any rapid UN peacekeeping operation, had been traumatized by the deaths of 18 of its special forces in Somalia on a single night the previous October. As far as Washington was concerned, Rwanda was Africa and Africa was Somalia. President Clinton was not going to allow the UN – let alone the US – to get sucked into local conflicts that might end in another disaster.

The language used by the press to describe Rwanda reinforced the impression that what was going on was an inevitable and primitive process that had no rational explanation and could not be stopped by negotiation or force. A report in *The Times* warned of an 'eruption of tribal violence' (Bone 1994). The local Reuters correspondent, Thadée Nsengiyaremye (1994), reported 'gangs of youth settling tribal scores hacking and clubbing people to death'. He quoted Western diplomats as saying 'continuing tribal slaughter between the Hutu majority and Tutsi minority in the Central African states was feared'. Lindsey Hilsum (1994a), writing in the *Guardian*, spoke of Kigali descending into chaos and quoted a diplomat as saying it was getting 'messier and messier … various clans are murdering others, there is a general score settling going on in Kigali.'

All this was reported in the context of renewed fighting between the RPF and government troops. After the plane crash, the RPF abandoned the ceasefire and advanced. In Kigali, the presidential guard attacked the 600-strong contingent of RPF fighters that had been allowed to come to Kigali to protect the politicians who had joined the government as part of the Arusha accords. The civil war was resumed.

Most journalists accepted the diplomats' implicit agenda that the killing of civilians was an offshoot of the renewed civil war. Hutus were afraid that the RPF would overrun the country and were attacking their Tutsi neighbours whom they regarded as RPF supporters or even a fifth column. After the killing of President Ndadaye in Burundi by Tutsi soldiers it was easy to persuade them that there was a Tutsi conspiracy to re-establish their supremacy in both countries. They may also have been persuaded that the RPF had shot down the plane and killed President Habyarimana. Those early reports of 'tribal bloodletting' (AFP 1994) also implied that Tutsis were trying to take over Rwanda and were killing Hutus indiscriminately. The assumption was that the anarchy created by renewed fighting had allowed these 'ancient tribal hatreds' to burst forth and that they could only be suppressed by the establishment of a ceasefire.

It was not until 12 April when Catherine Bond (1994a) in *The Times* stated that 'Tutsis were the target plus Hutus who had made the mistake of supporting the [Arusha accords]'. Two days later she wrote:

> The majority of the killings are carried out by militias, trained at the instigation of (President) Juvénal Habyarimana. The militiamen belonged to two political parties, which are opposed to power sharing with rebels from Rwanda's minority Tutsi tribe … Increasingly in the past two days the militiamen have appeared on the streets armed with guns and stick grenades given to them by the remnants of a government led by extremists from the majority Hutu tribe. (Bond 1994b)

There were several references in the media to genocide in Rwanda and Burundi, but these referred to past massacres. This – a week after the killings had begun – was the first hint that what was happening was not mere mayhem or madness but well organized. Three days later, however, the *Guardian* was still reporting 'thousands have died in a orgy of ethnic violence between the majority Hutu and the minority Tutsi tribes' (Hilsum 1994b).

The *Interahamwe* – the organized death squads – was not mentioned in the press until 30 April, when Reuters began to use the name. Meanwhile the use of words and phrases like 'tribe', 'orgy of violence', 'bloodletting' and 'settling old scores' implied that these were something incomprehensible to outsiders and uncontrollable, not amenable to reason or negotiation. There was no sudden breakthrough among outsiders in understanding that this was not just another round of fighting between two ethnic groups but an organized mass murder of an entire population. The language of newspapers gradually changed throughout April from a story about a civil war to a story of genocide.

In a continent not known for the ability of its governments to command obedience, instil discipline or organize huge public works programmes, it is difficult to attribute the genocide purely to mobilization and obedience. Nor do most African people believe or obey everything they are told on state-run radio. Some Rwandans killed out of fear of being killed themselves. The orders to kill Tutsis resonated with long held fears and feelings. They were accepted as a permission – even welcomed – by vast numbers of Hutus. The Hutu refugees that I spoke with in Goma later in 1994 mostly denied that any killings had taken place. The few who admitted that Tutsis had been killed said that it had to happen. 'They were going to do the same to us,' one told me (Henri, personal communication, 1994).

Yet, had the politicians, diplomats and journalists discovered earlier the organizational element that made the genocide – created from the top-down as well as bottom-up – they perhaps would have had a different attitude to the Rwanda government and the RPF. They would have seen that the massacres were not an offshoot of fighting between government and rebels. They would have seen them as the main issue far sooner.

How might that have changed things? As always, might-have-beens are impossible to judge. But had the world's powerful governments realized and accepted sooner that genocide was taking place, they might have ensured that the UN did not see the two parties as equal combatants in a civil war. That might have meant they would not have been so keen to work for a ceasefire. The United States and other Security Council members may not have given the UN orders to abandon Rwanda when they failed to secure that ceasefire but, on the contrary, they might have encouraged the RPF to take over the country more quickly to end the killing and establish order. The UN and aid agencies backed by Western governments may not then have treated the Hutu refugees and the soldiers that accompanied them to eastern Congo as victims in need of aid, but might have taken action earlier to disarm them and start to identify who among them was responsible for the genocide.

REFERENCES

AFP (Agence France-Press). 1994. The *Independent*, 13 April.

Bond, C. 1994a. Cabinet Joins Flight of 100,000 from Kigali. *The Times*, 13 April.

—— 1994b. Kill Injured in Red Cross Van. *The Times*, 15 April.

Bone, J. 1994. Presidents' Deaths Raise UN Fears of Tribal Violence. *The Times*, 7 April.

FIDH (Fédération internationale des ligues des droits de l'Homme). 1995. *Commission internationale d'enquête sur les violations des droits de l'homme au Burundi depuis 21 Octobre 1993*. FIDH, Paris, France.

Hilsum, L. 1994a. Rwandan PM Killed as Troops Wreak Carnage. *Guardian*, 8 April. Available at <www.guardian.co.uk/fromthearchive/story/0,12269,1186802,00.html> (accessed 18 December 2005).

—— 1994b. *Guardian*, 16 April.

Lemarchand, R. 1995. *Burundi: Ethnic Conflict and Genocide*. Woodrow Wilson Centre Press and Cambridge University Press, Cambridge, UK. 232 pp.

Melvern, L. and P. Williams. 2004. Britannia Waived the Rules: the Major Government and the 1994 Rwandan Genocide. *African Affairs*, 103: 1–22.

Nsengiyaremye, T. 1994. Hundreds Die as Tribal Violence Sweeps Rwanda. *Independent*, 8 April.

23
How the Media Missed the Rwanda Genocide

Alan J. Kuperman

From April to July 1994, approximately 500,000 Rwandan Tutsi, some 80 per cent of the country's Tutsi population, were exterminated in the most efficient and complete genocide of modern times. Western media blame the international community for not intervening quickly, but the media must share blame for not immediately recognizing the extent of the carnage and mobilizing world attention to it. They failed to report that a nationwide killing campaign was under way in Rwanda until almost three weeks into the violence. By that time, some 250,000 Tutsi had already been massacred.

During those first weeks, Western reporting was marred by four lapses. First, it mistook genocide for civil war. The country had been wracked by a low-level civil war from 1990 to 1993 between the government, controlled by the Hutu majority, and a rebel force comprising mainly Tutsi. Although a minority, the Tutsi had ruled until the late 1950s when the Hutu took power and forced many Tutsi to flee as refugees. In both the 1960s and 1990s Tutsi refugee rebels had launched intermittent offensives against Rwanda, so on the outbreak of genocide on 6 April 1994, Western correspondents reported the initial burst of violence in Kigali as the resumption of a bloody civil war.

On 11 April, an editorial in London's *The Times* pondered international calls for a ceasefire and asked rhetorically, 'Which parties would be asked to cease fire against whom?' (Times Editors 1994). A 12 April report in Belgium's *De Standaard* on government violence in Kigali added that 'it is absolutely certain that a large number of acts of terror were committed' as well 'in the area controlled by the rebels' (Buyse 1994). Early reports also indicated that the Tutsi rebels were winning the civil war and had rejected government offers of a nationwide ceasefire, which contradicted any notion of Tutsis as victims. By 13 April, Radio France International reported that 'the fall of Kigali seems imminent' (Anon. 1994a). On 14 April, *The Times* and *Le Monde* reported that it was now the Hutu who feared vengeance from Tutsi rebels who had gained the upper hand in Kigali (Bond and Prentice 1994; Hélène 1994a).

A second mistake by international news media was to report that violence was on the wane when in fact it was mounting. On 11 April, just four days after the

This paper first appeared in the *International Press Institute Report*, 6(1), 2000.

fighting started, *The New York Times* reported that violence had 'appeared to slacken' (Schmidt 1994a), and *Le Monde* concurred the next day that fighting had 'diminished in intensity' (Hélène 1994b). Two days later, *Le Monde* said that 'a strange calm reigns in downtown' Kigali (Hélène 1994a). On 15 April, it reported this calm spreading to the capital's suburbs, allowing 'humanitarian organizations to cautiously resume their activities' (Hélène 1994c). Only on 18 April did Brussels' La Une Radio Network question this consensus by explaining that the decline in reports of violence was because 'most foreigners have left, including journalists' (Anon. 1994b). The exodus of reporters was so thorough that it virtually halted Western press coverage. European newspapers that had been providing daily coverage of the violence in Kigali stopped cold on 18 April, for four days in France's *Le Monde* and seven in Britain's *Guardian*. Ironically, this was when the slaughter reached its peak.

The third reporting error was that early published death counts were gross underestimates, sometimes by a factor of ten. On 10 April, three days into the killing, *The New York Times* quoted estimates of 8,000 or 'tens of thousands' dead in Kigali (McFadden 1994). During the second week, media estimates did not rise at all. On 16 April, the *Guardian* still reported only an 'estimated 20,000 deaths' (Hilsum 1994). Two days later, *The New York Times* repeated this same statistic, underestimating the actual carnage at that point by about tenfold. Not until a few days later did the scope of killing rapidly emerge (Schmidt 1994b).

Fourth, for nearly two weeks, Western news organizations focused almost exclusively on Kigali, a city that contained only 4 per cent of Rwanda's population, and did not report the far broader tragedy unfolding around them. The few reports of violence in the countryside seemed to indicate renewal of mutual communal strife or civil war, rather than genocide. On 11 April, Paris Europe No. 1 Radio reported that 'Hutus are hunting down Tutsis throughout the country,' but then added, 'and the other way round' (Giesbert 1994). Brussels' La Une Radio Network reported that killing and looting in Rwanda's southwest was targeted against the 'opposition', rather than an ethnic group (Anon. 1994c). Likewise, on 12 April, the *Washington Post* wrote, 'sketchy reports said fighting has spread to Rwanda's countryside,' but in a context suggesting combat between government troops and armed rebels (Parmelee 1994a). The first report of a large-scale massacre outside the capital came on 16 April (Bond 1994; Parmelee 1994b).

American newspapers failed to convey the nationwide scope of the violence until 22 April when *The New York Times* belatedly reported that fighting bands had reduced 'much of the country to chaos' (Lewis 1994). Still, many foreign observers could not conceive that genocide was under way. On 23 April, the *Washington Post* speculated that the dearth of Tutsi refugees fleeing Rwanda was because 'most of the borders have been sealed' (Parmelee 1994c). Only on 25 April was the riddle solved when the *New York Times* reported that violence had 'widened into what appears to be a methodical killing of Tutsi across the countryside', and that the missing refugees 'either have been killed or are trying to hide' (Lorch 1994).

At least three factors help to account for these reporting lapses. First, the evacuation of foreign nationals left few reporters in the countryside after the first few days or in the capital after the first week. Second, the situation was legitimately confusing. Tutsi rebels were winning the civil war and retaliating against suspected civilian Hutu extremists at the same time that the civilian Tutsi population was being systematically exterminated. Third, even experts were slow to appreciate what was happening. The commander of Belgian peacekeepers stated on 15 April to Radio France International that 'the fighting has ... all but stopped' (Anon. 1994d). No human rights group even suggested the possibility of genocide until 19 April (Human Rights Watch 1994).

In the wake of Rwanda's tragedy, the media harshly criticized the United Nations and its Western members for not immediately recognizing the killing campaign and reacting to prevent it. Such criticism is only partly valid. American and other Western officials did drag their feet after the genocide was reported, avoiding use of the word genocide for weeks afterward for fear of being compelled to intervene.

But the media must share the blame for failing to provide prompt notice of the genocide. In obscure parts of the world, where Western governments do not invest significant intelligence assets, the news business is relied on to serve as a surrogate early-warning system. In Rwanda, it did not fulfil this role.

Partly in reaction to this reporting failure in Rwanda, Western media have suffered from exactly the opposite problem ever since. They now exaggerate the extent of civilian atrocities in ethnic conflict. Around the world, rebels and human rights groups learned the lesson from Rwanda that they must declare 'genocide' to have any hope of Western intervention. Because the press does not want to get caught napping again, it duly reports such claims even though it cannot confirm them. Thus, Western readers were told for months that genocide was raging in Kosovo, but forensic investigators have been able to find just 5,000 corpses to date, some of whom may have been armed rebels (Garvey 2004).

Likewise, Western media reported that genocide was occurring in East Timor after its vote for independence, but now the UN estimates that only 1,000 were killed before and after the referendum (Anon. 2005). This is not to say that a few hundred or thousand deaths are unimportant. But they do not constitute genocide by any reasonable definition. The UN defines genocide as 'acts committed with intent to destroy, in whole or in part, a national, ethnical, racial or religious group as such' (UN 1951: Article II). The definition has been broadened in practice to include destruction of political groups.

Perhaps the main reason that Western correspondents have had difficulty reporting ethnic violence accurately is that at least one of the sides does not want them to, and reporters cannot confirm many allegations without risking their lives by visiting combat zones. There is no moral requirement for journalists to make such a personal sacrifice. But so long as reporters do not confirm the facts on the ground, they must try to do everything else possible to piece together the real story for readers – in full awareness that combatants, governments and private agencies are all trying to manipulate them.

Rwanda's Hutu government wanted reporters to think that violence was civil war rather than genocide. In a similarly manipulative way, the Kosovo Liberation Army wanted reporters to think that Yugoslav government violence prior to NATO's bombing was genocide or ethnic cleansing rather than counter-insurgency. In both cases, Western reporters were fooled. They should take a lesson from this as they continue their vital task of informing Western policymakers and publics about violent conflicts around the world.

REFERENCES

Anonymous. 1994a. Kigali Reportedly About to Fall to RPF [in French]. Radio France International, Paris, 13 April, 2130 GMT. Translated by Foreign Broadcast Information Service (FBIS-AFR-94–072), 14 April 1994: 2.

—— 1994b. Soldier Comments on Military Strategies in Rwanda [in French]. La Une Radio Network, Brussels, 18 April, 1500 GMT. Translated by Foreign Broadcast Information Service (FBIS-WEU-94–075), 19 April 1994: 5.

—— 1994c. Conflict Reportedly Spreading to Zaire Border [in French]. La Une Radio Network, Brussels, 11 April, 1600 GMT. Translated by Foreign Broadcast Information Service (FBIS-AFR-940–070) 12, April 1994.

—— 1994d. Belgian UN Commander Pessimistic [in French]. Radio France International, Paris, 15 April, 1830 GMT. Translated by Foreign Broadcast Information Service (FBIS-AFR-94–074), 18 April 1994: 2.

—— 2005. Truth Commission on East Timor Killings. *The Irish Times*, 2 August: 8.

Bond, C. 1994. Embattled UN Clings to Hope of Rwanda Truce. *The Times*, 16 April: 15.

Bond, C. and E.A. Prentice. 1994. Rwandan Rebels Prepare Last Push. *The Times*, 14 April: 11.

Buyse, A. 1994. Chaos in Rwanda Threatens Stability of Whole Region [in Dutch]. *De Standaard,* 12 April. Translated by Foreign Broadcast Information Service (FBIS-AFR-94–072), 14 April 1994.

Garvey, B. 2004. Weak Case Against Milosevic has Hague in 'a Panic': Massacres in Kosovo Never Happened, Say Canadians Who Investigated Mass Graves. *The Ottawa Citizen*, 29 August: A1.

Giesbert, F.O. 1994. Interview with French Foreign Minister Alain Juppe [in French]. Europe No. 1 Radio, Paris, 11 April, 0540 GMT. Translated by Foreign Broadcast Information Service (FBIS-WEU-94–070), 12 April 1994.

Hélène, J. 1994a. Forces gouvernementales et rebelles se disputent le contrôle de la capitale. *Le Monde*, 14 April: 7.

—— 1994b. Le Rwanda à feu et à sang. *Le Monde*, 12 April: 1.

—— 1994c. Les combats continuent au Rwanda. *Le Monde*, 15 April: 3.

Hilsum, L. 1994. Rwandan Blood Flows as Foreign Forces Depart. *Guardian*, 16 April.

Human Rights Watch. 1994. Letter to UN Security Council. Human Rights Watch, New York, NY, USA, 19 April.

Lewis, P. 1994. Security Council Votes to Cut Rwanda Peacekeeping Force. *The New York Times*, 22 April: A1.

Lorch, D. 1994. Rwandan Refugees Describe Horrors After a Bloody Trek. *The New York Times*, 25 April: A1.

McFadden, R.D. 1994. Western Troops Arrive in Rwanda to Aid Foreigners. *The New York Times*, 10 April: 1.

Parmelee, J. 1994a. Rebels Advance in Rwanda, Vow to Take Over Capital. *Washington Post*, 11 April: A13.

—— 1994b. Rwandans Ever More Isolated: Reporters, Belgian Troops Pulling Out. *Washington Post*, 16 April: A12.

—— 1994c. Fears Mounting for Rwandans: Aid Agencies Say Pullout of U.N. Peacekeepers Endangers Refugees. *Washington Post*, 23 April: A14.

Schmidt, W.E. 1994a. Deaths in Rwanda Fighting Said to be 20,000 or More. *The New York Times*, 11 April: 12.

—— 1994b. Rwanda Puzzle: is Uganda Taking Sides? *The New York Times*, 18 April: A6.

Times Editors. 1994. Carnage in Africa: It Is for the Rwandans Themselves to Cure their Malaise. *The Times*, 11 April.

UN (United Nations). 1951. *Convention on the prevention and punishment of the crime of genocide.* Adopted by Resolution 260 (III) of the UN General Assembly, 9 December 1948. *UN Treaty Series* no. 1021, vol. 78: 277. Available at <www.preventgenocide.org/law/convention/text.htm> (accessed 6 September 2005).

24
An Analysis of News Magazine Coverage of the Rwanda Crisis in the United States

Melissa Wall

From the days of the African nationalist movements, Western news organizations have tended to paint a one-dimensional portrait of intracountry conflict occurring on the African continent. Various organizational constraints have combined with a tendency toward the stereotype to create a shallow type of reporting that has been much criticized in the past. When the ongoing violence in Rwanda suddenly burst into the news in the spring of 1994, some media observers hoped for more meaningful coverage. Many news organizations had acknowledged and pledged to overcome prior shortcomings. In addition, there was no longer a Cold War to provide a means of framing the conflict. Some positive coverage of African politics was coming out of South Africa where the first national elections were going to be held. The Rwanda crisis represented a chance for the media to truly explain to news audiences the real reasons – political, economic and social – for African violence, rather than relying on the old stereotypes of tribe versus tribe, east versus west.

Did the United States media portray the Rwanda crisis in a way that was different from past coverage? To make this assessment, I analyzed news magazine coverage of Rwanda for the entire year of 1994.

PRESS COVERAGE OF AFRICA

Organizational demands

The type of news that gets published about Africa is influenced by the general values and organizational demands of the Western media. News is not merely the random reporting of events, but is rather constructed and shaped by reporters and editors who determine what is worthy of coverage and what is not, and how events will be presented (Chang and Lee 1992; Gitlin 1980; Tuchman 1978; White 1950). Because the media tend to value conflict and crisis, especially when the news is coming from foreign countries, that is the type of story that most often gets reported (Fair 1993; Hachten 1992a; Lent 1977).

Logistic barriers also prevent reporters from covering African nations as well as they could. Reporters are often 'parachuted' into countries and expected to cover rapidly breaking, dramatic events (Rosenblum 1979). They arrive with little

This article first appeared in *International Communication Gazette*, vol. 59, no. 2, pp. 121–34 (1997).

or no knowledge of the country's history, politics and culture and few, if any, local sources. They rarely speak local languages and quickly move on when they or their editors decide the story is growing cold (Hess 1994; Rosenblum 1993). In some countries, governments exercise various forms of censorship, which can make the work of a reporter difficult if not impossible (Hachten 1992a).

Hachten (1992a) believes that there are far too few foreign correspondents bringing news from Africa to American readers. Another problem with international reporting of Africa is the lack of widespread news bureaus. Rather than being evenly distributed throughout the world, bureaus are concentrated primarily in western Europe. In Africa, a correspondent based in South Africa may be expected to cover the entire continent. One of the reasons given is financial (Hachten 1992b). News from Africa is not seen as a money-maker for news organizations (Ebo 1992). This leaves only a handful of reporters covering the continent – correspondents who are sometimes compelled to 'look for news stories that are easy and convenient to gather' (Ebo 1992: 16).

Themes of coverage

Lack of interest in covering Africa and lack of resources devoted to finding reporters who speak the languages and know the culture have contributed to several tendencies in news media treatment of Africa. The first is toward portraying any challenge to the status quo as negative. This can be seen most clearly in the coverage of the African nationalist movements, such as the 1950s independence movement in Kenya (Maloba 1992). A second trend is toward portraying political events in Africa as irrational tribalism; such portrayals rarely probe for the underlying causes of conflicts (Fair 1993; Ibelema 1992). This can be seen in coverage of the Biafran war in Nigeria and other wars since. The third tendency is toward portraying events through an East–West lens, a particularly popular media frame during the Cold War (Fair 1992; Govea 1992). All of these tendencies rely on oversimplification of complex events. Rather than providing context for unfamiliar conflicts and settings, they can create stereotypes that become fixed in the minds of news consumers.

The reporting of Africa's wars of independence set the tone and structure of Western media coverage of African political violence (Hawk 1992). In covering Kenya's struggle for independence in the 1950s, the press relied on inflammatory adjectives and negative descriptions to describe the movement. Often the news coming out of Kenya was shaped by the colonial government, which distributed press handouts almost daily (Edgerton 1989). Colonial propagandists played up two ideas. First, Africans were primitive and irrational; therefore, Western coverage really could not make sense of their politics or positions (Maloba 1992). Second, Africans who challenged colonial powers were brutal and savage. This idea helped dehumanize African leaders in Western press coverage (Hawk 1992).

Another example of the trends in the coverage of African conflict can be seen in the reporting of the Nigerian civil war, also known as the Biafran war. News coverage showed how the Western media continued to see African conflicts in simplified terms, particularly tribe versus tribe. It focused on events, not on issues, background, consequences or other contextual sorts of information

(Himmelstrand 1971). The media fixated on tribal differences because that reinforced ideas about African primitivism (Artis 1970). By attributing events to tribalism, the press did not have to analyze complex political and economic situations (or any genesis of such in colonialism) (Ibelema 1992).

This way of viewing African conflict has yet to change. In looking at Western coverage of *Inkatha*, Brock found news stories about conflict in South Africa reported as senseless tribal violence – 'complex situations are reduced to "tribal"', – and disputes among political groups such as the African National Congress and *Inkatha* are seen not as political and ideological but as primitive clashes (Brock 1992: 151). Fair also found that coverage of the Liberian war focused on African tribalism and primitivism and not the political causes. She interprets the emphasis on tribalism as an attempt to make Africa appear to be located 'back in time' and, therefore, incomprehensible to Western media consumers (Fair 1993: 14).

Studies by Govea (1983, 1992) and Fair (1992) found that conflict in Africa was presented within an East–West frame even when events had little to do with the Cold War. In her examination of *The New York Times* coverage of US food aid to Ethiopia from 1980 to 1989, Fair (1992) found that newspaper stories suggested that the benevolence of the West saved the nation from complete ruin. The news media not only failed to focus on the political and social realities of the Horn of Africa, they failed to relate what was happening to environmental and climactic changes, instead attributing Ethiopia's food shortage to its Marxist form of government. Historical background that might reveal the link between Western policies and tragic events such as the famine are usually left out of reports about Africa (Ebo 1992).

METHODS

In this project, I analyzed all 38 full-length news reports about the Rwandan crisis that appeared in 1994 in *Newsweek*, *Time* and *U.S. News and World Report*. I chose news magazines for analysis because they tend to summarize the dominant view of a news event, and also because the writing used in them is believed to be colourful and full of visual images (Buckman 1993; Schramm 1988).

Shaping my analysis was the idea that news is not a random happening of events, but a carefully selected and constructed version of reality, determined by various gatekeepers and organizational routines, such as relying on official sources (Gans 1979; Tuchman 1978). In addition to following these routines, reporters are also believed to construct news stories as a 'package' of 'condensing devices' that work as shorthand between the journalist and the reader (Gamson and Modigliani 1989: 3). Various researchers have identified these condensing devices as metaphors, keywords, depictions or visual images, agency (the person or thing responsible for the story's action, often identified via headlines) and sources (Entman 1991; Gamson and Modigliani 1989; Pan and Kosicki 1993).

Taking all of these studies into account, I analyzed a set of dimensions that I believe reveals the nature of the coverage of the Rwandan crisis: sources, metaphors, portrayals (depictions of individual people), agencies and keywords. Sources and portrayals were determined by content analysis of the text; keywords were derived by noting what words appeared in both the headlines and the text and what additional words seemed to have a particular salience within the text alone. Agency was measured by examining headlines (who or what was identified as causing the crisis and who or what was identified as solving it). Metaphors were open coded. The data gathered from studying each of these dimensions were then considered as a whole to determine overall themes in coverage.

RESULTS

Content analysis of sources (215 in all) revealed that aid workers (22 per cent) were quoted more frequently than any other source, followed closely by ordinary local people (21 per cent). Other sources included: local opposition members (14 per cent), which included the Rwandan Patriotic Front and people identified as supporting political groups opposed to the extremists; Western officials (13 per cent); United Nations representatives (13 per cent); and local officials (9 per cent), which included the ruling party and the former military leaders. Two other types of sources were infrequently quoted: experts (5 per cent), regional (2 per cent) and other (1 per cent).

That expert sources, such as human rights advocates or academic specialists, made up only 5 per cent of sources is notable as these sorts of sources could easily have been contacted and interviewed in the West. In fact, groups such as Human Rights Watch Africa were releasing regular press bulletins with timely, well-documented information. They were an obvious source of informed background and comment about what was really happening in Rwanda. Also notable was the dearth of sources from other African countries – people who might have been able to provide insights and African points of view on the situation.

Collapsing source categories into non-Rwandan and Rwandan revealed that non-Rwandan sources (including governmental and nongovernmental organizations) made up 48 per cent of all sources. These people, with one exception, were Westerners. Rwandans made up 44 per cent of all sources. Taken alone, this finding might suggest that Africans were given more of a voice in coverage of the conflict (compared with Fair's (1992) earlier finding that they were rarely quoted); however, when other results are considered, the presentation of Rwandans seems far from positive.

For instance, of the 76 portrayals of Rwandans, 74 per cent depicted Rwandans as passive, 10 per cent as causing problems, 9 per cent as neutral and 7 per cent as solving problems. In comparison, of the 19 portrayals of non-Rwandans, usually Westerners, 75 per cent depicted them as solving problems, 19 per cent as passive and 6 per cent as causing problems.

The headline analysis further suggests that Rwandans were not favourably portrayed. Headlines were analyzed to determine whether they listed a cause of the problem, a solution for the problem or neither. Most headlines (71 per cent) listed neither cause nor solution. Of those that did list a cause (16 per cent), tribalism was either directly cited as the cause ('Deeper into the abyss: an orgy of tribal slaughter kills thousands as most foreigners flee for their lives' (Hammer et al. 1994: 32)) or indirectly through reference to the ethnicity of a particular group ('The swagger of defeat: in exile, the Hutu army is stealing food, intimidating refugees and plotting a return to power' (Fedarko 1994a)). Of the headlines that listed solutions (13 per cent), Rwandans were never seen as the solution, only Westerners such as the French: 'The horrific scars of Rwanda's civil war: *France sends in troops* to stop the carnage' (Kiley and Coleman 1994: 51, my emphasis).

The keyword results also contribute to the negative image of Rwandans and to the idea that the entire conflict was based on little more than brutal tribalism: the words 'ethnic' or 'tribal' appeared 55 times in the text and in 4 headlines. Compare this with the word 'political', which appeared 25 times. Also notable was the reliance on ethnic designations: Hutu/Hutus or Tutsi/Tutsis appeared 456 times in the stories about the crisis. Compare the appearance of these tribal designations with the designation 'extremist(s)', which was used 14 times in total. Other keywords that seem to have particular salience include 'slaughter' and 'carnage', which appeared 19 and 9 times respectively, within the text. 'Slaughter' also appeared 5 times in headlines, 'carnage' twice.

Metaphors tended to cluster in particular patterns. The clusters were examined and used to help derive the themes of coverage listed below. Patterns included: comparing the violence to explosions or eruptions; comparing the movement of refugees to natural disasters; and comparing the events to biblical scenes or diseases. Examples of metaphors are included below.

Five themes in coverage

I identified five overall themes in the magazine coverage of the Rwanda crisis:

1. The Rwanda violence was the result of irrational tribalism.
2. Rwandan people are little better than animals, ranging from the barbaric to the helpless and pathetic.
3. The violence is incomprehensible and, thus, is explained through comparison to biblical myths, supernatural causes, natural disasters or diseases.
4. Neighbouring African countries are just as violent and, thus, unable to help solve Rwanda's problems.
5. Only the West is capable of solving Rwanda's problems.

1. The Rwanda violence was the result of irrational tribalism. Instead of explaining political and other causes behind the violence, news magazines chose to present the crisis as another eruption of irrational African violence, fuelled by ethnic hatred. There was a high level of use of words that emphasized the ethnic aspect of the conflict. Consider this headline: 'All the hatred in the world: as *Tutsi rebels* pursue their fast moving offensive, they find they are taking over a once populous country that is now both deserted and embittered' (Purvis 1994: 36, my emphasis). Rather than 'Tutsi rebels,' the headline could have used the more accurate label 'Rwandan Patriotic Front'.

Coverage also suggested that Rwandans were fated to kill each other. 'Once more,' one headline about the Rwandan conflict noted, 'tens of thousands are massacred,' while within the story we read: 'For four centuries, hatred between the minority Tutsi tribe and the majority Hutus has been the curse of Rwanda' – what is happening in Rwanda was only the 'latest' tragedy (Masland et al. 1994: 33). We could only expect more of the same; after all, 'Rwanda is helpless against its demons' (Hammer et al. 1994).

Supporting the idea that events in Rwanda were beyond human control was the consistent use of metaphors comparing the violence to an explosion or conflagration. Stories implied that the plane crash 'sparking the fighting' merely set off the violent tendencies that were already present within all Rwandans (Kiley and Coleman 1994: 51). News accounts made it seem inevitable that the 'violence exploded' (Hammer 1994a). After all, 'Rwanda is a crucible full of explosives' (Gibbs 1994: 57) and the entire nation was 'like a time bomb' (Gibbs, Crumley et al. 1994: 28). What happened was simply another 'tribal meltdown' (Gibbs 1994: 56) or a natural 'spasm of ethnic violence' (Anon. 1994a: 40). These sorts of metaphors implied that the violence was caused by something innate within the Rwandan people who were likely to burst into savage slaughter at any time.

In fact, the idea of this spontaneity was planted in the media by extremists who fled to Nairobi immediately after the killings began and held press conferences to make this claim, which was then reported in the Western press (Omaar and de Waal 1994). Press releases from human rights agencies revealed that extremists carefully planned and carried out the initial killings (Human Rights Watch Africa 1994). Although these releases were made available early on in the crisis, their contents were not reported in the news magazines until months later.

Although the conflict was initiated by particular political groups, we read almost nothing about them. By not bothering to name the specific parties, the magazines promoted the idea that the conflicts were about tribal rivalries and not about named opposition groups challenging the status quo. Only one magazine (*U.S. News and World Report*) named the *Mouvement Républicain National pour la Democratie et le Développement* (MRND), the late president's party, and then only in one story that ran in November, seven months after the genocide. None of the stories mentioned the MRND's ally, the *Coalition pour la Défense de la République* (CDR), which the human rights organizations listed as equally if not more virulent than the MRND, or the political party that opposed both, the Parti Social Démocrate (PSD). Instead, we read only of opposition groups, rebels and, mainly, Hutus and Tutsis.

2. Rwandan people are little better than animals, ranging from the pathetic to the barbaric. The analysis revealed that ordinary people were the second most frequently quoted group of people. If we examine the coverage more closely, however, we find that while Rwandans were given a voice, it was only within a framework that consistently presented them as pathetic and helpless victims, as insensate, animal-like creatures or as barbaric savages. This is despite the fact that some government ministers refused to go along with the massacres and some Hutus put themselves and their families at risk to protect Tutsi neighbours and friends. Some Tutsi and Hutu – armed only with sticks and stones – formed neighbourhood patrols in an attempt to protect their communities (Omaar and de Waal 1994). Such descriptions were practically absent from the magazines.

Instead, ordinary Rwandans were presented as passive victims. In a typical portrayal, we read,

> As a wintry morning wind whips through the camp, a dozen dying people huddle outside a white medical tent, waiting for the French doctors to arrive from the town of Goma. A father pushes his prostrate son in a wheelbarrow; a woman props up her husband as his head lolls. (Hammer 1994b: 17)

Ordinary people were rarely described as helping each other or fighting off the perpetrators of the violence. Instead, we are overwhelmed with descriptions such as this one of Father Oreste Incimatata who recounts what happened when the death squads came to his church: '"The women and children sang religious songs, cried and prayed," said Incimatata who *hid under his bed* in an adjoining rectory during the killing' (Hammer 1994c: 46, my emphasis).

If not passive victims, then Rwandans were compared with animals. Accounts described fleeing Rwandans as 'a mad stampede' of refugees (Watson et al. 1994: 26) or as a 'human swarm' (Hammer 1994d: 34). Comparing their movements with animals suggests that they are not rational, fully evolved human beings, but something less. This sort of metaphor dehumanizes the refugees and can make it difficult for Western media consumers to summon much sympathy. Evidence revealing the humanity of some Rwandans was rarely if ever presented.

Another way in which the animal metaphors were used was in the description of the youth wings that perpetrated much of the violence. In one account, one such group was compared with dogs, noting that the extremist leaders 'let *Interahamwe* off the leash' (Ransdell 1994a: 67). In making those who committed horrendous crimes so abstract, the story made it more difficult for readers to understand that the violence took a great deal of planning and thinking to carry out.

Also contributing to the savage barbarian image were metaphors such as the violence was letting Rwanda 'feed its hatreds' (Gibbs, Marlowe et al. 1994: 38) and Rwanda was 'Central Africa's slaughterhouse' (Ransdell 1994b: 47), as if the people butchered each other with the same regularity that people in other cultures slaughter beef. Stories suggested that Rwandans have little regard for human life, noting that bodies were 'dumped like garbage' (Anon. 1994a: 41).

How can people engage in such brutal behaviour? The stories implied because they are so unfeeling. 'Rayontina Mukansonera, 19, describes being raped repeatedly by Hutu militia before escaping in the confusion following the rebel advance. "They showed no mercy," she says, *matter-of factly*' (Purvis 1994: 36, my emphasis). Another story described this scene outside one of the refugee camps in Zaire: 'A shoemaker mends a pair of battered loafers, only inches ways from a small dead boy. "After a time you don't even notice them," he says, shrugging' (Hammer 1994b: 15). Meanwhile, the United Nations burial squad loads dead bodies onto a truck under the tutelage of a European: 'Louis Biritsen, 37, directs the team's movements. "Softly, softly," he orders, as the workers toss a dead pregnant woman onto the heap of corpses. "You must be compassionate"' (Hammer 1994b: 17).

3. The violence is so incomprehensible, it can only be explained through comparison to biblical myths, supernatural causes, natural disasters or diseases. In refusing to consider political, economic or other causes for the violence, the magazines were left with explanations that seemed to indicate that the violence was simply beyond the comprehension of Western logic. They compared the violence to events from the bible, supernatural causes, natural disasters and diseases – none of which provided the news audience with an understanding of the underlying reasons for violence in Rwanda. Particularly striking was the use of biblical images or myths to explain what was happening in Rwanda. Four headlines referred to Rwanda and the events there as constituting hell: 'Tribal bloodlust and political rivalry turn the country into an unimaginable hell' (Mutiso 1994: 45); 'Hell postponed' (Michaels 1994: 56); 'Escape from hell' (Hammer 1994d: 34); 'Descent into hell' (Ransdell et al. 1994).

The text of the stories contained other biblical references. One story noted, 'There are no devils left in hell ... they're all in Rwanda' (Gibbs 1994: 56). Other metaphors included 'a biblical array of pestilence' (Watson et al. 1994: 26) and an 'exodus of biblical sweep' (Hammer 1994d: 34). These images seem to reflect the idea of a nation, as Fair (1993) puts it, from back in time, so far behind the West that what occurs there can only be related to bible stories. Other comparisons suggested that the violence was the result of supernatural causes, also unfathomable to rational, Western minds: 'Rwanda is helpless against its demons' (Hammer et al. 1994) and 'Rwanda is tormented by its own implacable demons' (Watson et al. 1994: 26). Here, so-called modern reason and rational thought have yet to take root.

Another means of dehumanizing the Rwandans was to describe the movements of great numbers of people so as to suggest that they were a natural occurrence in this region of the world. This naturalness was particularly suggested by metaphors that compared the refugees' exodus to movements of water, which was the most frequent type of metaphor in the news magazines' coverage. Stories included the following water metaphors (emphasis added): '*flood* of refugees' (Fedarko 1994a); 'choking the *flow* of refugees' (Fedarko 1994b: 56); 'terrified men, women and children *poured*' (Hammer 1994d: 34); 'slow moving *river* of humanity' (Fedarko 1994b: 56); '[returning refugees] like trying to turn back a *tidal wave* one teacup at a time' (Gibbs, Marlowe et al. 1994: 38); '*tide* of terrified humanity' (Anon. 1994b: 30); 'latest *tide* [of refugees]' (Fedarko 1994b: 56); '*trickle* of Rwandans' (Nelan 1994: 53); 'few [refugees] *trickled* back' (Watson et al. 1994: 26); '*streams* of misery stretch for miles' (Mutiso 1994: 44); '*stream* of refugees' (Ransdell 1994b: 47).

This type of metaphor implies that these movements of people – like floods or other natural events – cannot be stopped by human intervention. Such terms exclude clear explanations of why the people are fleeing or what other options they have. The use of this metaphor also overlooks some of the man-made problems that created the circumstances for the violence. Rwanda had been trying to carry out Western-dictated economic reforms. Structural adjustment had created incredible strains on the infrastructure with schools, health services and the nation's entire economic system in near collapse (Chossudovsky 1995).

Other imagery suggests that what occurred in Rwanda was like malaria or some other disease that is endemic to Africa and has nothing to do with the rest of the world. Thus, readers find that 'Rwanda is infected by tribal hate' and 'madness spread like an eager germ' (Gibbs, Crumley et al. 1994: 30). This type of metaphor seems to be used merely to 'jazz' up what ought to have been a story compelling enough on its own merits. Thus, readers are told that 'statistics seep out of Rwanda like blood from an open wound' (Roberts 1994: 11). This incurable disease/untreatable wound imagery works only if reporters forget to look into Rwanda's past. Any 'infection' of hatred can be traced back to the colonial occupiers, who stressed tribal designations in ruling the country (Chossudovsky 1995; Kane 1995).

4. Neighbouring African countries are just as violent and, thus, unable to help solve Rwanda's problems. The news magazines suggested that there could be no local solutions because the entire region was just as chaotic and violent. Readers might assume that all African countries are inherently disorderly when they read about the lack of stability in Rwanda's neighbouring countries. One magazine noted that the surrounding nations created a 'logistical nightmare for U.S. forces ... the disorganization, lack of fuel and congestion at all central African airports grounded many planes meant to ferry supplies' (Gibbs, Marlowe et al. 1994: 39). Readers were told that Zaire has 'been tottering on the brink of collapse' (Ransdell et al. 1994), while Zairian troops loot and its ministers drink champagne but refuse to help. Likewise, ethnic violence was 'the trigger that will blow Burundi apart' (Michaels 1994: 56). In only one story do we read that Tanzania was 'one of Africa's most stable countries' (Ransdell et al. 1994: 42). No story discussed Tanzania's willingness to take in and try to care for thousands of refugees, nor did the stories include information about Uganda, which was working to overcome its own history of violence and genocide.

One means of making surrounding nations appear unable to help was by not quoting any sources from them. Thus, a regional perspective was practically non-existent (only 2 per cent of all sources). We do find one quote and a portrayal buried within a detailed story about the horrors of the Rwandan refugee camps. A Kinshasa student had come to help tend ailing refugees. Nevertheless, she was not asked to comment on what the crisis meant to Zaire or Africa, or even why she chose to come and help. If one Zairian was helping, we might assume there were others, although they did not appear in the magazine coverage.

An obvious source to comment on the situation, the Organization for African Unity, was mentioned only twice by the magazines. Government officials or others from Tanzania or Zaire could have perhaps given some perspective on managing the influx of half a million refugees. Only one of the magazines quoted a Tanzanian (a general who advocated military intervention). Zairian officials were only quoted in the context of their country being yet another example of African chaos. The Rwandan Patriotic Front was based in Uganda, where many of its members had previously been part of the Ugandan army. What was the Ugandan perspective on the conflict? Do their officials see any workable solutions? If the magazines were unable to unearth any alternative explanations or solutions from the sources they were relying on, then perhaps they should have considered there might not have been a lack of solutions so much as a lack of broad perspective.

5. *Only the West is capable of solving Rwanda's problems.* Consistently, when the magazines did portray people taking positive steps to deal with the violence in Rwanda, they were almost always Westerners, either French troops or American aid workers. The idea that these were the sorts of people capable of dealing with the troubles was reinforced by relying on them for quotes and portraying them as actively helping solve the problem. The coverage suggested that groups from the North such as the United Nations or international nongovernmental organizations would provide the order the world needs.

One of the ways the stories emphasized the ability of the West to fix Rwanda's problems was by relying on Westerners as the primary sources. Not only were aid workers quoted most often (22 per cent), they were more likely to be portrayed as solving Rwanda's problems. Typical of the coverage is this portrayal: A '27-year-old American noticed an emaciated woman sitting in the dirt with three small children. "She didn't look at me, but I saw her eyeing my water bottle"… [he] sauntered over to the woman and dropped his water bottle next to her. "It's not fun to play God and figure who gets what," he said' (Hammer 1994a: 32).

In the headline analysis, the French were most often mentioned as solving the conflict (named four times in the headlines). The magazines further implied that the preferred saviour among these groups was the United States, noting that diligent American aid workers were in 'a race with death' (Watson et al. 1994: 26), trying to save Rwandans from themselves. Examples of Rwandans (or citizens of Tanzania, Zaire, etc.) helping to cope with the disaster are seldom found. Ultimately, coverage implied that only the US military could truly save Rwanda. As one headline noted, 'Nice idea, wrong army, Rwanda: are the French the ones to make peace?' (Stanger and Hammer 1994: 48). In addition, metaphors referenced the Nazi atrocities of World War II as well as suggesting that just as the United States devised the Marshall Plan (Gibbs, Marlowe et al. 1994: 38) for war-torn Europe after World War II, it now needed to reassemble Rwanda.

CONCLUSION

Western news coverage of Africa has always tended to distort and oversimplify complex events. The Rwanda coverage continued the adherence to old patterns such as interpreting conflicts in Africa as evidence of backwardness. Some new trends seemed evident as well. With the end of East–West rivalry, the Cold War framework has been removed and now the coverage seems to suggest that violence is simply tribal or inexplicable. Western officials played less of a role in the coverage, probably because of the lack of government involvement. Western aid organizations seemed to be filling the gap, although locals were quoted more than has previously been the case. While these were all changes, they did not necessarily herald better, more comprehensive coverage. For instance, if we look at the total portrait of these locals, we find mainly graphic descriptions that confirm that Rwandans are helpless wretches or brutal savages.

While reporting from an area with such violence can be logistically difficult, there were other ways to obtain information. Early on, various human rights organizations publicized the names of those who systematically planned and executed the genocide. These names were made readily available through written press releases as well as via the Rwanda Crisis Web site on the Internet. Yet magazines failed to use this information. Also, reporters could have sought comment from surrounding countries in the region. Instead, these countries were described as more examples of the instability of the entire continent, implying that Rwanda's violence is the rule, not the exception to life on the African continent and that no regional government was competent to comment.

By relying on tribalism as the explanation for the violence, the magazines rarely mentioned who planned and executed the genocide that started the violence. Readers were left to believe that this tribal violence just exploded. By attributing the violence to tribal strife and not to the known individuals who were truly responsible ('an orgy of tribal slaughter kills thousands'), the coverage let the real perpetrators off the hook.

Because Africa is one of the continents about which we often know little, news coverage about it takes on a special importance. In many cases, it represents the only information about that area that many Westerners ever encounter. Instead of supplying readers with full, explanatory portraits of Africa, news organizations have tended to stick with the easy stereotype, the image that can be easily absorbed by readers, however false it may be. The coverage of the Rwanda crisis proves no exception to the negative, shallow coverage of the past. Granted, events such as this conflict were complicated and violent, using metaphors to try to produce 'colourful' reports was a disservice not only to Africans but also to American news consumers. The tendency to write off Rwanda (and perhaps all of Africa) as naturally violent and not worth analyzing on any insightful level made American news coverage one more terrible element in the entire crisis.

REFERENCES

Anonymous. 1994a. Mass Murder. *Newsweek*, 9 May: 40–1.

—— 1994b. It's Too Big. *Newsweek*, 25 July: 30–1.

Artis, W. 1970. The Tribal Fixation. *Columbia Journalism Review*, Fall: 48–9.

Brock, L. 1992. 'Inkatha: Notions of the "Primitive" and "Tribal" in Reporting on South Africa'. In B. Hawk (ed.). *Africa's Media Image*. Praeger, New York, NY, USA: 149–61.

Buckman, R.T. 1993. How Eight Weekly News Magazines Covered Elections in Six Countries. *Journalism Quarterly*, 70(4): 780–93.

Chang, T. and J. Lee. 1992. Factors Affecting Gatekeeper's Selection of Foreign News: a National Survey of Newspaper Editors. *Journalism Quarterly*, 69(3): 554–61.

Chossudovsky, M. 1995. IMF–World Bank policies and the Rwandan holocaust. Rwanda Crisis Web, February.

Ebo, B. 1992. 'American Media and African Culture'. In B. Hawk (ed.). *Africa's Media Image*. Praeger, New York, NY, USA: 15–25.

Edgerton, R.B. 1989. *Mau Mau: an African Crucible*. Free Press, New York, NY, USA.

Entman, R.E. 1991. Framing US Coverage of International News: Contrasts in Narratives of the KAL and Iran Air Incidents. *Journal of Communication*, 41, (4): 6–27.

Fair, J.E. 1992. 'Are We the World?' In B. Hawk (ed.). *Africa's Media Image*. Praeger, New York, NY, USA: 109–20.

—— 1993. War, Famine and Poverty: Race in the Construction of Africa's Media Image. *Journal of Communication Inquiry*, 17(2): 5–23.

Fedarko, K. 1994a. The Swagger of Defeat: in Exile, the Hutu Army is Stealing Food, Intimidating Refugees and Plotting a Return to Power. *Time*, 15 August: 25.

—— 1994b. In Fear of a Nation's Revenge: As the French Pull Out, Hutu Frightened of Reprisals Threaten Another Exodus Across Rwanda's Borders. *Time*, 24 August: 56–7.

Gamson, W.A. and A. Modigliani. 1989. Media Discourse and Public Opinion on Nuclear Power: a Constructionist Approach. *American Journal of Sociology*, 95(1): 1–37.

Gans, H.J. 1979. *Deciding What's News; a Study of CBS Evening News, NBC Nightly News, Newsweek and Time*. Pantheon, New York, NY, USA.

Gibbs, N. 1994. Why? The Killing Fields of Rwanda: Hundreds of Thousands Have Died or Fled as a Result of Tribal Strife. Are These the Wars of the Future? *Time*, 16 May: 56–63.

Gibbs, N., B. Crumley, M. Michaels and A. Purvis. 1994. Cry the Forsaken Country: for More Than 2 Million Refugees, Hunger and Disease Take Up Where a Vicious Civil War Left Off. *Time*, 1 August: 28–37.

Gibbs, N., L. Marlowe and M. Michaels. 1994. Destination Unknown: the U.S., the U.N. and the Country's New Leaders Say the Best Hope for Rwanda's Refugees is To Go Home, but Who Can Convince Them It's Safe? *Time*, 8 August: 38–41.

Gitlin, T. 1980. *The Whole World is Watching: Mass Media in the Making and the Unmaking of the New Left*. University of California Press, Berkeley, CA, USA.

Govea, R. 1983. East–West Themes in the Reporting of African Violence. *Social Science Quarterly*, 64(1): 193–99.

—— 1992. 'Reporting African Violence: Can American Media Forget the Cold War?' In B. Hawk (ed.). *Africa's Media Image*. Praeger, New York, NY, USA: 94–108.

Hachten, W.A. 1992a. 'African Censorship and American Correspondents'. In B. Hawk (ed.). *Africa's Media Image*. Praeger, New York, NY, USA: 38–48.

—— 1992b. *The World News Prism; Changing Media of International Communication*. Iowa State University Press, Ames, IA, USA.

Hammer, J. 1994a. A Generation of Failure. *Newsweek*, 1 August: 32.

—— 1994b. Death Watch Rwanda: a Diary of One Day's Horrors in the Refugee Camps at Kimumba. *Newsweek*, 8 August: 15–17.

—— 1994c. The Killing Fields Rwanda: Even a Church Couldn't Protect Women and Children from Genocide. *Newsweek*, 23 May: 46–7.

—— 1994d. Escape From Hell. *Newsweek*, 16 May: 34–5.

Hammer, J., T. Stanger and R. Sparkman. 1994. Deeper into the Abyss: an Orgy of Tribal Slaughter Kills Thousands as Most of the Foreigners Flee for their Lives. *Newsweek*, 25 April: 32.

Hawk, B. 1992. 'Introduction: Metaphors of African Coverage'. In B. Hawk (ed.). *Africa's Media Image*. Praeger, New York, NY, USA: 3–14.

Hess, S. 1994. Speaking in Tongues: More Foreign Correspondents Know Language of the Country They Cover. *Nieman Reports*, 48(3): 30–2.

Himmelstrand, U. 1971. 'The Problem of Cultural Translation in the Reporting of African Social Realities'. In O. Stokke (ed.). *Reporting Africa*. Africana Publishing, New York, NY, USA: 117–33.

Human Rights Watch Africa. 1994. *Rwanda Crisis Web*, 29 April.

Ibelema, M. 1992. 'Tribes and Prejudice: Coverage of Nigerian Civil War'. In B. Hawk (ed.). *Africa's Media Image*. Praeger, New York, NY, USA: 77–93.

Kane, H. 1995. What's Driving Migration? *World Watch*, January/February: 23–33.

Kiley, S. and F. Coleman. 1994. The Horrific Scars of Rwanda's Civil War. *U.S. News & World Report*, 4 July: 51–2.

Lent, J.A. 1977. Foreign News in American Media. *Journal of Communication*, 27(1): 46–51.

Maloba, W. 1992. 'The Media and Mau Mau: Kenyan Nationalism and Colonial Propaganda'. In B. Hawk (ed.). *Africa's Media Image*. Praeger, New York, NY, USA: 51–61.

Masland, T., J. Hammer, K. Breslau and J. Tanaka. 1994. Corpses Everywhere: Once More, Tens of Thousands Massacred. *Newsweek*, 18 April: 33.

Michaels, M. 1994. Hell Postponed: Burundi's Balance. *Time*, 29 August: 56–7.

Mutiso, C. 1994. Streets of Slaughter: Tribal Bloodlust and Political Rivalry Turn the Country into an Unimaginable Hell of Killing, Looting and Anarchy. *Time*, 25 April: 44–6.

Nelan, B. 1994. Hope Battles Fear: Braving Tales of Tutsi Vengeance, a Few Hutu Have Struggled Safely Back to a Silent, Desolate Capital. *Time*, 22 August: 53.

Omaar, R. and A. de Waal. 1994. Rwanda: death, despair and defiance. *Rwanda Crisis Web*, 29 September.

Pan, Z. and G.M. Kosicki. 1993. Framing Analysis: an Approach to News Discourse. *Political Communication*, 10: 55–7.

Purvis, A. 1994. All the Hatred in the World. *Time*, 13 June: 36–7.

Ransdell, E. 1994a. The Wounds of War: a Reconstruction of Rwanda's Genocide Suggests the Killing Could Return. *U.S. News & World Report*, 28 November: 67–75.

—— 1994b. Why is Rwanda Killing Itself? The Slaughter has Unleashed a Tide of Refugees and Raised Fears That the Fighting Will Spread. *U.S. News & World Report*, 23 May: 46–8.

Ransdell, E., I. Gilmore, L. Lief, B. Auster and L. Fasulo. 1994. A descent into hell. *U.S. News & World Report*, 1 August: 42.

Roberts, S. 1994. Rwanda's Trail of Tears. *U.S. News & World Report*, 16 May: 10–11.

Rosenblum, M. 1979. Coups and Earthquakes: Reporting the Third World for America. Harper and Row, New York, NY, USA.

—— 1993. *Who Stole the News?* John Wiley and Sons, New York, NY, USA.

Schramm, W. 1988. *The Story of Human Communication: Cave Painting to Microchip*. HarperCollins, New York, NY, USA.

Stanger, T. and J. Hammer. 1994. Nice Idea, Wrong Army: Rwanda: Are the French the Ones to Make the Peace? *Newsweek*, 4 July: 48.

Tuchman, G. 1978. *Making News: a Study in the Construction of Reality*. Free Press, New York, NY, USA.

Watson, R., J. Schofield, R. Sparkman, L. Nkaoua, K. Chubuck and J. Babby. 1994. A Race With Death. *Newsweek*, 1 August: 26–30.

White, D.M. 1950. The 'Gatekeeper': a Case Study in the Selection of News. *Journalism Quarterly*, 27: 383–90.

Part Three

Journalism as Genocide: the Media Trial

25
The Verdict: Summary Judgement from the Media Trial

This chapter is a transcript of the summary judgement of the *International Criminal Tribunal for Rwanda* (ICTR). It is also available on the ICTR website, available at <www.ictr.org>.

TRIAL CHAMBER I

Before Judges: Navanethem Pillay, presiding
Erik Møse
Asoka de Zoysa Gunawardana
Registrar: Adama Dieng
Judgement of: 3 December 2003

THE PROSECUTOR
V.
FERDINAND NAHIMANA
JEAN-BOSCO BARAYAGWIZA
HASSAN NGEZE
Case No. ICTR-99-52-T

SUMMARY

Counsel for the Prosecution
Mr Stephen Rapp
Ms Simone Monasebian
Ms Charity Kagwi
Mr William Egbe
Mr Alphonse Van
Counsel for Ferdinand Nahimana
Mr Jean-Marie Biju-Duval
Diana Ellis, Q.C.
Counsel for Jean-Bosco Barayagwiza
Mr Giacomo Barletta-Caldarera
Counsel for Hassan Ngeze
Mr John Floyd, III
Mr René Martel

I. INTRODUCTION

1. Trial Chamber I today delivers its judgement in the trial of three Accused persons: Ferdinand Nahimana, Jean-Bosco Barayagwiza, and Hassan Ngeze. The judgement will be available in written form in English tomorrow and in French upon translation. The Chamber will deliver orally a summary of the judgement. The judgement and not this summary is the authoritative text.
2. Ferdinand Nahimana was born on 15 June 1950, in Gatonde commune, Ruhengeri prefecture, Rwanda. He was a professor of history and Dean of the Faculty of Letters at the National University of Rwanda. In 1990, he was appointed Director of ORINFOR (Rwandan Office of Information) and remained in that post until 1992. He was a founder of RTLM and a member of its *comité d'initiative*, or Steering Committee.
3. Jean-Bosco Barayagwiza was born in 1950 in Mutura commune, Gisenyi prefecture, Rwanda. A lawyer by training, he held the post of Director of Political Affairs in the Ministry of Foreign Affairs. He was a founder of the CDR and of RTLM and a member of the Steering Committee of RTLM.
4. Hassan Ngeze was born on 25 December 1957 in Rubavu commune, Gisenyi prefecture, Rwanda. From 1978, he worked as a journalist, and in 1990, he founded the newspaper *Kangura* and held the post of Editor-in-Chief.
5. The three Accused are charged in separate Indictments; they were tried jointly. The Accused are all charged on counts of genocide, conspiracy to commit genocide, direct and public incitement to commit genocide, complicity in genocide, and crimes against humanity (persecution and extermination). Additionally, Hassan Ngeze is charged with crimes against humanity (murder). The Accused are charged with individual criminal responsibility under Article 6(1) of the Statute for these crimes. Nahimana is additionally charged with superior responsibility under Article 6(3) in respect of direct and public incitement to commit genocide and the crime against humanity of persecution. Barayagwiza and Ngeze are additionally charged with superior responsibility under Article 6(3) in respect of all the counts except conspiracy to commit genocide.
6. In the Indictments, Ferdinand Nahimana and Jean-Bosco Barayagwiza were also charged with the crime against humanity of murder, and Barayagwiza was charged on counts of serious violations of Article 3 common to the Geneva Conventions and of Additional Protocol II. On 25 September 2002, the Chamber granted the Defence motion for acquittal in respect of these counts.
7. The Accused, Jean-Bosco Barayagwiza, elected not to attend his trial, giving as his reasons that he did not have confidence that he would be afforded a fair trial in light of the Appeal Chamber's reversal of its decision ordering his release before the trial.

8. This case raises important principles concerning the role of the media, which have not been addressed at the level of international criminal justice since Nuremberg. The power of the media to create and destroy fundamental human values comes with great responsibility. Those who control such media are accountable for its consequences.

II. FACTUAL FINDINGS

VIOLENCE IN RWANDA IN 1994

9. The Chamber finds that within the context of hostilities between the RPF and the Rwandan Government, which began when the RPF attacked Rwanda on 1 October 1990, the Tutsi population within the country was systematically targeted as suspected RPF accomplices. This targeting included a number of violent attacks that resulted in the killing of Tutsi civilians. The RPF also engaged in attacks on civilians during this period. Following the shooting of the plane and the death of President Habyarimana on 6 April 1994, widespread and systematic killing of Tutsi civilians, a genocide, commenced in Rwanda.

KANGURA

10. Hassan Ngeze was the owner, founder and editor of *Kangura*. He controlled the publication and was responsible for its contents. The first issue of *Kangura* was published in May 1990, the last in 1995. No issues were published between April and July 1994. *Kangura* was very well known in the country as well as internationally. It was probably the most well known newspaper from Rwanda during that period of time. The newspaper had two versions, one primarily in Kinyarwanda and one primarily in French, referred to as the international version.
11. On the cover of each issue of *Kangura*, beginning in February 1991 with the publication of *Kangura* No. 10, appeared the title 'The Voice that Awakens and Defends the Majority People'. The term '*rubanda nyamwinshi*', which means 'majority people', was used by *Kangura* to refer to the Hutu majority. The Chamber has examined a number of articles and excerpts from *Kangura*, focusing primarily on those that addressed issues of ethnicity and on those which called on readers to take action.
12. *The Ten Commandments* were published in *Kangura* No. 6, in December 1990, within an article entitled *Appeal to the Conscience of the Hutu*. The introduction of this article warned readers:

> The enemy is still there, among us, and is biding his time to try again, at a more propitious moment, to decimate us.
>
> Therefore, Hutu, wherever you may be, wake up! Be firm and vigilant. Take all necessary measures to deter the enemy from launching a fresh attack.

13. The second part of the article, entitled 'The Tutsi ambition', described the Tutsi as 'bloodthirsty', and referred to their continuing ideology of Tutsi domination over the Hutu, and to the 'permanent dream of the Tutsi' to restore Tutsi minority rule. The article referred to a plan of 1962, in which the Tutsi were to resort to two weapons they thought effective against the Hutu: 'money and the Tutsi woman'. One part of the article, entitled 'The Tutsi woman', stated that Tutsi women were sold or married to Hutu intellectuals or highly placed Hutu officials, where they could serve as spies in influential Hutu circles and arrange government appointments, issue special import licences, and pass secrets to the enemy. Another part, which included the *The Ten Commandments*, exhorted the Hutu to wake up 'now or never' and become aware of a new Hutu ideology, with roots in and in defence of the 1959 revolution. Reference was made to the historical servitude of the Hutu, and readers were urged to 'be prepared to defend themselves against this scourge.' The Hutu were urged to 'cease feeling pity for the Tutsi!' The article then set forth *The Ten Commandments*.
14. The first commandment warns Hutu men of the dangers of Tutsi women and deems a traitor any Hutu man who marries a Tutsi woman, keeps a Tutsi mistress, or makes a Tutsi woman his secretary or protégée. Another commandment casts as a traitor any Hutu man who enters into business with Tutsi partners, invests his or state money in a Tutsi company, or lends to or borrows from a Tutsi. Other commandments require that strategic political, economic and military positions be entrusted to the Hutu, that students and teachers should be in the majority Hutu, and that the Hutu be united in solidarity and 'seek friends and allies for the Hutu cause.' The ninth commandment concludes, 'The Hutu must be firm and vigilant towards their common Tutsi enemy.'
15. In defence of his publication of *The Ten Commandments*, Ngeze invoked his publication of the Tutsi *19 Commandments* in *Kangura* No. 4, 1990, in an effort to show the even-handedness of *Kangura*. The *19 Commandments* were addressed to Tutsi, implicitly, and called on them to get into positions of authority, to get to know others in authority, befriend them, and then replace them. There was much in the document about the importance of undermining Hutu confidence, with phrases such as 'use the educated Bahutu credulity', 'show them they are incapable', 'ridicule the civil servants under our authority as ignorant Bahutu people', and 'do whatever you can to keep the Bahutu civil servants in an inferiority complex'. Commandment 13 told readers to 'Keep in mind that the Hutu are created to be servant to other', and Commandment 16 issued a special call to the 'youth Tutsi', stating that if 'we fail to achieve our goal, we will use violence'.
16. The Chamber finds that *The Appeal to the Conscience of the Hutu* and *The Ten Commandments* of the Hutu included within it, published in *Kangura* No. 6 in December 1990, conveyed contempt and hatred for the Tutsi ethnic group, and for Tutsi women in particular as enemy agents. *The Appeal to the Conscience of the Hutu* portrayed the Tutsi as a ruthless enemy, determined

to conquer the Hutu, and called on the Hutu to take all necessary measures to stop the enemy. *Kangura* published the *19 Commandments* to alert readers to the evil nature of the Tutsi and their intention to take power and subjugate the Hutu. *The Ten Commandments* of the Hutu and the *19 Commandments* of the Tutsi were complementary efforts to the same end: the promotion of fear and hatred among the Hutu population of the Tutsi minority and the mobilization of the Hutu population against them. This appeal to the Hutu was visibly sustained in every issue of *Kangura* from February 1991 to March 1994 by the title 'The Voice that Awakens and Defends the Majority People'.

17. Other editorials and articles published in *Kangura* echoed the contempt and hatred for Tutsi found in *The Ten Commandments*. These writings portrayed the Tutsi as inherently wicked and ambitious in language clearly intended to fan the flames of resentment and anger, directed against the Tutsi population. The cover of *Kangura* No. 26 answered the question 'What weapons shall we use to conquer the *Inyenzi* once and for all?' with the depiction of a machete. The message conveyed by this cover was a message of violence, that the machete should be used to conquer the *Inyenzi* once and for all. By *Inyenzi*, *Kangura* meant, and was understood to mean, all Rwandans of Tutsi ethnicity, who in this issue of *Kangura* were stereotyped as having the inherent characteristics of liars, thieves and killers.
18. In *Kangura* Nos. 58 and 59, published in March 1994, a competition was launched, consisting of eleven questions, the answers to which were all to be found in past issues of *Kangura*. Various points were allocated to correct answers, and prizes were announced for the winners. Readers were directed to enter the competition by sending their responses to the questions to RTLM.
19. The introduction to the competition stated that the purpose of the competition was to sensitize the public to the ideas of the newspaper. The Chamber finds that this competition was a joint undertaking of *Kangura* and RTLM, intended to acquaint the readers of *Kangura* and the listeners of RTLM with the content and ideas of *Kangura* as set forth in its past issues. The Chamber finds that the competition was designed to direct participants to any and to all of these issues of the publication and that in this manner in March 1994 *Kangura* effectively and purposely brought these back issues into circulation.

CDR

20. The Chamber finds that Jean-Bosco Barayagwiza was one of the principal founders of CDR and played a leading role in its formation and development. Barayagwiza was seen as, and was, a decision-maker for the party, working to some extent behind the scenes in the shadow of CDR President Martin Bucyana, technically as an advisor or councillor. At some time prior to February 1994, Barayagwiza became the head of

the CDR in Gisenyi prefecture and a member of the national Executive Committee. In February 1994, following the assassination of Martin Bucyana, Barayagwiza succeeded Bucyana. The Chamber finds that Hassan Ngeze was a founding member of CDR and active in the party, and held the position of advisor to the party. The Chamber finds that Ferdinand Nahimana was not a member of CDR.

21. The Chamber finds that the CDR was formed to promote unity and solidarity among the Hutu popular majority and to represent its political interests. The CDR equated political interest with ethnic identity and thereby equated the RPF with the Tutsi, effectively defining the enemy as the Tutsi ethnic group. The CDR also identified as the enemy prominent political opposition leaders. The formal policy of the CDR, as reflected in its political manifesto and public statements, initially condemned ethnic violence and called for peaceful co-existence among the various ethnic groups, maintaining that these ethnic groups each had their own fixed political interests and that unity among the groups was not possible. The CDR considered the RPF to be the political representation of Tutsi interest, determined to seize power back for the Tutsi through force. In an early statement of CDR policy, Barayagwiza expressed the view that force could legitimately be used if necessary to counter this aggression. In a communiqué issued in March 1993, the CDR called on the population to rise up and unseat the President and Prime Minister for their betrayal of the country by acceptance of the Arusha Accords, and in a communiqué issued in November 1993, following massacres it attributed to the RPF, the CDR called on the Hutu population to 'neutralize by all means possible its enemies and their accomplices', having defined the enemies as the Tutsi ethnic group.

22. The Chamber finds that the CDR was a Hutu party and party membership was not open to Rwandans of Tutsi ethnicity. This policy was explicitly communicated to members and the public by Barayagwiza and Ngeze. During the year 1994, and in particular, the period 6 April to 17 July 1994, Barayagwiza continued to exercise effective leadership over the CDR Party and its members. The killing of Tutsi was promoted by the CDR.

23. The CDR had a youth wing, called the *Impuzamugambi*, which became the CDR militia. The CDR members and *Impuzamugambi* were supervised by Barayagwiza and acted under his control in carrying out acts of killing and other acts of violence. Roadblocks were erected and manned by *Impuzamugambi*, for the purpose of identifying and killing Tutsi civilians. Barayagwiza gave orders to the *Impuzamugambi* at roadblocks that Tutsi should not be allowed to pass and that they should kill them unless they had CDR or MRND cards. Barayagwiza supplied weapons to the *Impuzamugambi* which were used for purposes of killing Tutsi. The *Impuzamugambi*, together with the *Interahamwe*, killed large numbers of Tutsi civilians in Gisenyi Prefecture.

RTLM

RTLM broadcasts

24. RTLM started broadcasting in July 1993. A number of witnesses testified to the popularity of RTLM when it first came on air, noting that people could be seen everywhere listening to RTLM. Its broadcasts were a common topic of conversation in homes, offices, cafes, and on the street. Almost everyone had a radio and listened to RTLM. After 6 April 1994, militia at the roadblocks listened to RTLM. Radios and weapons were the two key objects to be seen at the roadblocks, according to one witness.
25. Several hundred tapes of RTLM broadcasts have been introduced in evidence, and various particular broadcasts have been discussed at trial. The Chamber has identified several areas of inquiry in its review, looking in particular at broadcasts that raised the issue of ethnicity and broadcasts that called on the population to take action.
26. The Chamber finds that RTLM broadcasts engaged in ethnic stereotyping in a manner that promoted contempt and hatred for the Tutsi population. RTLM broadcasts called on listeners to seek out and take up arms against the enemy. The enemy was identified as the RPF, the *Inkotanyi*, the *Inyenzi*, and their accomplices, all of whom were effectively equated with the Tutsi ethnic group by the broadcasts. After 6 April 1994, the virulence and the intensity of RTLM broadcasts propagating ethnic hatred and calling for violence increased. These broadcasts called explicitly for the extermination of the Tutsi ethnic group.
27. Many RTLM broadcasts are excerpted in the judgement. In one such broadcast, aired on 4 June 1994, RTLM journalist Kantano Habimana told listeners:

> They should all stand up so that we kill the *Inkotanyi* and exterminate them … the reason we will exterminate them is that they belong to one ethnic group. Look at the person's height and his physical appearance. Just look at his small nose and then break it.

28. Both before and after 6 April 1994, RTLM broadcast the names of Tutsi individuals and their families, as well as Hutu political opponents. In some cases, these people were subsequently killed, and the Chamber finds that to varying degrees their deaths were causally linked to the broadcast of their names. RTLM also broadcast messages encouraging Tutsi civilians to come out of hiding and to return home or to go to the roadblocks, where they were subsequently killed in accordance with the direction of subsequent RTLM broadcasts tracking their movement.
29. Radio was the medium of mass communication with the broadest reach in Rwanda. The Chamber finds that RTLM broadcasts exploited the history of Tutsi privilege and Hutu disadvantage, and the fear of armed insurrection, to mobilize the population, whipping them into a frenzy of hatred and violence that was directed largely against the Tutsi ethnic group.

The *Interahamwe* and other militia listened to RTLM and acted on the information that was broadcast by RTLM. RTLM actively encouraged them to kill, relentlessly sending the message that the Tutsi were the enemy and had to be eliminated once and for all.

Ownership and control of RTLM

30. A number of Prosecution witnesses testified as to the creation, ownership and management of RTLM, and the role of two of the Accused, Nahimana and Barayagwiza, in RTLM. The Chamber found the testimony of Georges Ruggiu, who testified for the Prosecution, and Valerie Bemeriki, who testified for the Defence, to be not credible, and it did not rely on the evidence of these two RTLM journalists. The Chamber finds that RTLM was owned largely by members of the MRND party, with Juvénal Habyarimana, President of the Republic, as the largest shareholder. CDR leadership was represented in the top management of RTLM through Barayagwiza as a founding member of the Steering Committee and Stanislas Simbizi, a member of the CDR Executive Committee who was added to the Steering Committee of RTLM in 1993.
31. The Chamber finds that Nahimana and Barayagwiza, through their respective roles on the Steering Committee of RTLM, which functioned as a board of directors, effectively controlled the management of RTLM from the time of its creation through and beyond 6 April 1994. Nahimana was, and was seen as, the founder and director of the company, and Barayagwiza was, and was seen as, his second in command. They represented RTLM externally in an official capacity. Internally, they controlled the financial operations of the company and held supervisory responsibility for all activities of RTLM, taking remedial action when they considered it necessary to do so. Nahimana also played an active role in determining the content of RTLM broadcasts, writing editorials and giving journalists texts to read.
32. The Chamber finds that after 6 April 1994, Nahimana and Barayagwiza continued to have *de jure* authority over RTLM. They expressed no concern regarding RTLM broadcasts, although they were aware that such concern existed and was expressed by others. Nahimana intervened in late June or early July 1994 to stop the broadcasting of attacks on General Dallaire and UNAMIR. The success of his intervention is an indicator of the *de facto* control he had but failed to exercise after 6 April 1994.

Notice of violation

33. The Chamber considered evidence of correspondence and meetings between the Ministry of Information and RTLM. The Chamber finds that concern over RTLM broadcasting was first formally expressed in a letter to RTLM on 25 October 1993, from Minister Faustin Rucogoza. This concern grew, leading to a meeting on 26 November 1993 and another meeting on 10 February, convened by the Minister and attended by Nahimana and Barayagwiza. At these meetings, Nahimana and Barayagwiza were put

on notice of the Ministry's growing concern that RTLM was violating its agreement with the government by promoting ethnic division and opposition to the Arusha Accords, and that it was reporting news in a manner that did not meet the standards of journalism. Nahimana and Barayagwiza both acknowledged that mistakes had been made by RTLM journalists. Various undertakings were made at the meetings, relating to the broadcasts of RTLM. At the meetings Nahimana was referred to as 'the Director' of RTLM, and Barayagwiza was referred to as 'a founding member' of RTLM and represented the management team. Following the second meeting between RTLM and the Ministry of Information on 10 February 1994, RTLM broadcasts publicly derided the efforts of the Minister to raise these concerns and commented on his inability to stop RTLM. Nevertheless, the Minister pressed forward with a case against RTLM which he was preparing to bring to the Council of Ministers, shortly before he and his family were killed on 7 April 1994.

34. It is evident that concerns over RTLM broadcasting of ethnic hatred and false propaganda were clearly and repeatedly communicated to RTLM. RTLM was represented in discussions with the government over these concerns by its senior management, and Nahimana and Barayagwiza both participated in both meetings. Each acknowledged mistakes that had been made by journalists and undertook to correct them, and each also defended RTLM without any suggestion that they were not entirely responsible for its programming.

FERDINAND NAHIMANA

Rwanda: current problems and solutions

35. The Indictment alleges that in an essay he wrote entitled *Rwanda: Current Problems and Solutions*, published in February 1993 and recirculated with a letter in March 1994, Ferdinand Nahimana called on the population to find a final solution to the problem of Rwanda and incited the youth to organize self-defence groups to fight against the RPF. The essay called for the organization of civil defence, consisting of armed youth, to fight 'the enemy', who were defined explicitly as the RPF and implicitly as 'the Tutsi league', a veiled reference to the Tutsi population. In March 1994, Nahimana re-circulated this essay amidst the ongoing initiative at that time to engage armed youth organizations such as the *Interahamwe* in attacks against the Tutsi population as part of an effort to defeat the RPF. However, the essay stated that such initiative should be coordinated by government officials and the army. While the essay called for defeat of 'the enemy', the Chamber does not find that it, or the introductory letter to it, was a direct call for violence other than a civil defence initiative to be coordinated by the Rwandan army.

36. The Prosecution alleges that between January and July 1994, Ferdinand Nahimana organized meetings with the *Interahamwe* in Ruhengeri

Prefecture. Two such meetings are specifically alleged, one on 29 March 1994 at which Nahimana is said to have given orders for the *Interahamwe* to kill Tutsis from Nyarutovu commune, and one on 12 April 1994 at the communal office in Gatonde, after which the killing of Tutsis is said to have started. The Prosecution relied entirely on the evidence of one witness, Witness AEN, to support its allegations concerning the presence and participation of Nahimana at these two meetings. The Chamber did not find the testimony of Witness AEN to be credible. Therefore, the Prosecution has not met its burden of proof with regard to these allegations.

37. A number of Prosecution witnesses testified to discriminatory practices engaged in by Ferdinand Nahimana as a student against fellow Tutsi students, as a professor against his Tutsi students, in university admissions and faculty appointments, and as Director of ORINFOR against Tutsi employees. The Defence led a number of witnesses to counter these allegations, which in some cases date back to the 1970s. The Chamber considers that these allegations are too remote to the criminal charges against Nahimana, and for this reason will not make factual findings with regard to these allegations.

38. The Chamber finds that Ferdinand Nahimana, as Director of ORINFOR, ordered the broadcast on Radio Rwanda of the contents of a communiqué based on a fax from Nairobi, a false document stating that the PL, or Liberal Party, was the internal arm of the RPF and was planning to assassinate Hutu leaders. This broadcast took place within a few days of a PL meeting in Bugesera on 1 March 1992, resulting in the killing of hundreds of Tutsi civilians. It was broadcast four or five times over the course of 3 and 4 March 1992. The editorial team had decided not to broadcast the communiqué because of their inability to confirm its authenticity. This decision was reversed by Nahimana, who by his own admission did not make an effort to ascertain the accuracy of the Radio Rwanda broadcast, which spread fear and provoked violence against the Tutsi population by Hutu who were falsely led to believe that they faced imminent attack.

Evaluation of Nahimana's testimony

39. The Chamber has considered Nahimana's testimony and finds certain patterns in his response to questioning. With great sophistry, Nahimana often pursued many lines of argument sequentially or even simultaneously in his testimony. Nahimana was not forthcoming in his testimony. While he was not entirely untruthful, in the view of the Chamber, he was evasive and manipulative, and there were many credibility gaps in his testimony. For this reason, the Chamber has been cautious in its evaluation of Nahimana's testimony on particular matters of fact, and does not generally accept Nahimana's version of events.

JEAN-BOSCO BARAYAGWIZA

40. A number of Prosecution witnesses testified to Barayagwiza's presence and participation in CDR meetings, demonstrations and roadblock activities. The Chamber finds that Jean-Bosco Barayagwiza convened CDR meetings and spoke at these meetings, ordering the separation of Hutu and Tutsi present at a meeting in Mutura commune in 1991, and asking Bagogwe Tutsi to do the *Ikinyemera*, their traditional dance, at this meeting and at another meeting in Mutura commune in 1993, publicly humiliating and intimidating them and threatening to kill them. Barayagwiza supervised roadblocks manned by the *Impuzamugambi*, established to stop and kill Tutsi. He was present at and participated in demonstrations where CDR demonstrators armed with cudgels chanted '*Tubatsembatsembe*' or 'let's exterminate them', and the reference to 'them' was understood to mean the Tutsi.
41. The Chamber finds, based on the testimony of Witness AHB, that Barayagwiza came to Gisenyi in April 1994, one week after the shooting of the plane on 6 April, with a truckload of weapons, including firearms and machetes, for distribution to the local population to be used to kill Tutsi civilians. Outreach to three cellules was coordinated in advance, to recruit attackers from among the residents of these cellules and bring them together to collect the weapons. That same day at least 30 Tutsi civilians were killed, including children and older people, with the weapons brought by Barayagwiza.
42. Omar Serushago testified that Barayagwiza raised funds for the purchase of weapons. The Chamber decided to consider the evidence of Omar Serushago with caution and require that his testimony be corroborated. This evidence was not corroborated and is not alone enough to sustain a finding by the Chamber that Barayagwiza raised funds for the purchase of weapons.

HASSAN NGEZE

Radio Rwanda/RTLM broadcasts

43. The Chamber has reviewed the Radio Rwanda and RTLM broadcasts that were introduced by the Prosecution to establish that Hassan Ngeze called for the extermination of the Tutsi and Hutu political opponents, and that he defended the extremist Hutu ideology of the CDR. The Chamber considers that through these broadcasts, Ngeze was trying to send a message, or several messages, to those at the roadblocks. One clear message was: do not kill the wrong people, meaning innocent Hutu who might be mistaken for Tutsi because they had Tutsi features, or because they did not have identification, or because they had identification marked 'RPF'. This is not the same as saying that the Tutsi is not the enemy and should not be killed. In the broadcasts, Ngeze did not tell those at the roadblocks not to kill the Tutsi. The message was to be careful and bring

suspects to the authorities, as much to ensure that the enemy does not mistakenly get through the roadblock as to ensure that the wrong people, meaning innocent Hutu, are not killed. In his testimony, Ngeze provided many explanations for what he said, describing various scenarios, including one to suggest he was trying to trick those at the roadblock into letting him pass with Tutsi refugees carrying false Hutu identity cards. Nevertheless, in the Chamber's view, Ngeze also made it clear in his testimony that his message was not to kill Hutu by mistake.

44. The Chamber recognizes that in telling those at the roadblock not to kill Hutu by mistake, Ngeze was also sending a message that there was no problem with the killing of Tutsi at the roadblock. Such message, however, was implicit in the broadcasts, which repeatedly urged that suspects not be killed but rather be brought to the authorities. In these convoluted circumstances, the Chamber is unable to find that these broadcasts constituted a call to kill that would be clearly understood as such.

The killing of Modeste Tabaro

45. The Indictment alleges that on 21 April 1994 in Gisenyi town, Hassan Ngeze ordered the *Interahawme* to kill Modeste Tabaro, a Tutsi and a member of an opposition political party. Of the four Prosecution witnesses who gave evidence on this killing, only two testified to having witnessed the killing of Modeste Tabaro. While the testimony of these two witnesses is not necessarily inconsistent, the two witnesses presented two different accounts of the killing that do not corroborate each other. This evidence is insufficient, in the Chamber's view, to support a finding beyond a reasonable doubt that Ngeze ordered the shooting of Tabaro. Because the Prosecution has not met its burden of proof, the Chamber need not examine inconsistencies among or make a finding on the credibility of the Defence witnesses in respect of the allegation that Hassan Ngeze ordered the killing of Modeste Tabaro.

Distribution of weapons, demonstrations, roadblocks and killings in Gisenyi and at the Commune Rouge

46. A number of witnesses gave evidence on Hassan Ngeze's role in the distribution of weapons, at demonstrations and at roadblocks in Gisenyi, and on his role in killings in Gisenyi and at the *Commune Rouge*, a cemetery in Gisenyi.

47. Witness AHI testified that Ngeze took part in the distribution of weapons on the evening of 8 April 1994. Witness AFX saw at least fifty guns in Ngeze's house, which Ngeze himself showed the witness. Omar Serushago testified that he saw Ngeze on the morning of 7 April transporting weapons, including guns, grenades and machetes. He saw him again between 13 and 20 April in the same vehicle, parked and containing guns, grenades and machetes. The Chamber accepts the evidence of Witness AHI, Witness AFX, and Serushago that Ngeze stored and distributed weapons, and played a role in securing weapons for the *Impuzamugambi*.

48. A number of Prosecution witnesses saw Ngeze dressed in military attire and carrying a gun. A number of Defence witnesses testified that he wore Muslim or civilian attire, not military attire, and that he did not carry a gun. The Chamber accepts the evidence of the Defence witnesses that they saw Ngeze in Muslim or civilian attire, unarmed. This does not preclude the possibility that there were other occasions on which he dressed in military attire and was armed.
49. Witness AHI testified that Ngeze set up and monitored roadblocks and gave instructions to others at the roadblocks: to stop and search vehicles, to check identity cards, and to 'set aside' persons of Tutsi ethnicity. These Tutsi were transported to and killed at the *Commune Rouge*. The Chamber finds that Ngeze played an active and supervisory role in the identification and targeting of Tutsi at roadblocks, who were subsequently killed at the *Commune Rouge*.
50. Many Prosecution witnesses testified that they saw Ngeze in Gisenyi in a vehicle with a megaphone, calling or leading CDR members to meetings, and transporting *Imuzamugambi* to demonstrations, where *Tuzatsembatsembe*, or 'let's exterminate them', was chanted. Witness AEU heard Ngeze say through the megaphone that he was going to kill and exterminate the *Inyenzi*, meaning the Tutsi. A number of Defence witnesses testified that Ngeze did not have, or could not have had, a megaphone in his vehicle, although several did mention other people named Hassan who had megaphones and might have been confused with Ngeze. Again the Chamber notes that this evidence does not preclude the possibility that Prosecution witnesses did see Ngeze with a megaphone. The testimony of the Prosecution witnesses indicates that Ngeze frequently used a megaphone in conjunction with his vehicle to drive around and mobilize CDR members and others against the *Inyenzi*, who were understood to be the Tutsi.
51. The Chamber finds that Ngeze helped secure and distribute, stored, and transported weapons to be used against the Tutsi population. He set up, manned and supervised roadblocks in Gisenyi in 1994 that identified targeted Tutsi civilians who were subsequently taken to and killed at the *Commune Rouge*. Ngeze often drove around with a megaphone in his vehicle, mobilizing the population to come to CDR meetings and spreading the message that the *Inyenzi* would be exterminated, *Inyenzi* meaning, and being understood to mean, the Tutsi ethnic minority. At Martin Bucyana's funeral in February 1994, Ngeze said that if President Habyarimana were to die, the Tutsi would not be spared.
52. Witness EB gave a detailed account of an attack on 7 April against the Tutsi population in Gisenyi by the *Interahamwe*, an attack in which he and his family were targeted as victims. He heard Ngeze tell *Interahamwe* through his megaphone to kill Tutsi and said that some of the *Interahamwe* should go to the *Commune Rouge* to dig holes. Witness EB said they were then attacked. The attackers killed his younger brother and took his body to the side of the road, where the bodies were placed before being taken to

the *Commune Rouge*. He saw the body of his younger sister, and he saw two women, one of whom was Hassan Ngeze's mother, thrusting the metal rods from an umbrella in between his sister's thighs. She was pregnant at the time of her death. There were many bodies, which were loaded on a vehicle and taken to the *Commune Rouge* for burial.

53. Witness EB testified that two hours later, the attackers returned and looted his parents' home. The attackers returned again at 6 p.m., and found Witness EB's mother there. They hit her on the forehead with a nail-studded club. The *Interahamwe* then threw a grenade into the house, and Witness EB was seriously wounded.
54. The Chamber considered Ngeze's defence of alibi for 7 April 1994, based on his evidence and the evidence of Defence witnesses. This evidence is riddled with inconsistencies, in light of which the Chamber finds that the defence of alibi is not credible.
55. The Chamber finds that Hassan Ngeze ordered the *Interahamwe* in Gisenyi on the morning of 7 April 1994 to kill Tutsi civilians and prepare for their burial at the *Commune Rouge*. Many were killed in the subsequent attacks that happened immediately thereafter and later on the same day. The attack that resulted in these and other killings was planned systematically, with weapons distributed in advance, and arrangements made for the transport and burial of those to be killed.
56. Omar Serushago testified to another scene of slaughter a week later, some time between 13 and 20 April at the *Commune Rouge*. Serushago said he saw Ngeze shoot a Tutsi man after asking why the man had been kept waiting and not killed immediately. The shooting was to be an example for others of how to kill. There is no corroboration of Serushago's testimony, and the Chamber cannot rely solely on his testimony to substantiate this charge against Ngeze.
57. Hassan Ngeze challenged many of the Prosecution witnesses on the grounds that they were members of or affiliated with the organization *Ibuka*. The Chamber finds that although several Prosecution witnesses who testified are members of *Ibuka* or otherwise have links with the organization, none of these witnesses was influenced in their testimony by *Ibuka*, which is a non-governmental organization assisting survivors of both Hutu and Tutsi ethnicity in the aftermath of the killings that took place in 1994.

Evaluation of Hassan Ngeze's testimony

58. In addressing the charges against him, Ngeze evidenced little awareness of the lack of consistency in his testimony, often altering or contradicting what he had said within minutes of saying it. Ngeze wavered back and forth in his testimony on fundamental issues, as well as virtually every detail of his evidence. Ngeze repeatedly and insistently denied the obvious in his testimony. Ngeze uses, distorts and fabricates information freely, marshalling it for other ends. In his testimony, as well as his other conduct during the proceedings, Ngeze demonstrated a thorough disregard for the truth, and for the solemnity of his declaration to testify truthfully.

INTERACTIONS AMONG THE ACCUSED

59. Several witnesses testified to having seen various of the Accused together at meetings. Witness AHA, who worked for *Kangura*, accompanied Ngeze to meetings with Barayagwiza in his office and his house, where Barayagwiza and Ngeze discussed the CDR, *Kangura* and RTLM all in the context of the Hutu struggle against the Tutsi. Nahimana and Barayagwiza worked very closely together in the management of RTLM. Barayagwiza and Ngeze worked very closely together in the CDR. The Chamber notes that Nahimana and Ngeze were not seen together as much as they were each seen with Barayagwiza. Nevertheless, as evidenced by the conversation between Ngeze and Barayagwiza, an institutional link among them all was perceived. At a personal level, the point of connection for the three Accused was Jean-Bosco Barayagwiza.
60. The Prosecution introduced evidence of meetings that took place at the Hotel des Milles Collines and Hotel Diplomat, one meeting between Barayagwiza and Nahimana and another at which Barayagwiza was present. Witness WD, a waiter who worked at these hotels, testified to comments made by the two Accused that he overheard as he was serving them. The Chamber finds the testimony of Witness WD to be not credible. As he was the sole witness to the conversations about which he testified, the Chamber finds that the Prosecution did not sustain its burden of proof with regard to these allegations.
61. The Chamber finds that Nahimana, Barayagwiza and Ngeze participated in an MRND meeting in 1993 at Nyamirambo Stadium in Kigali. The meeting was attended by about 15,000 people, including *Interahamwe* and *Impuzamugambi*, who were transported to the meeting by ONATRACOM government-run buses. Nahimana, Barayagwiza and Ngeze were introduced, RTLM and *Kangura* journalists. The President of MRND, Ngirumpatse, spoke first and referred to RTLM as a radio they had acquired. He urged the crowd to listen to RTLM rather than Radio Rwanda, which he referred to as an *Inyenzi* radio. Nahimana addressed the meeting and said RTLM should be used to disseminate their ideas relating to Hutu empowerment, and he requested that people support RTLM with financial contributions. Barayagwiza spoke about collaboration with the CDR and working together to fight the *Inyenzi*. He also spoke of using RTLM to fight against the *Inyenzi*. He said the *Inyenzi* were not far, and were even there among them. RTLM reported on the meeting and broadcast many of the speeches, including Nahimana's.
62. The Chamber considered the interactions among CDR, RTLM and *Kangura*, three institutions controlled by the Accused. The Chamber finds that *Kangura* supported the CDR, claiming the party as its own, publishing a special issue on the occasion of its creation, with a membership application form, and urging its readers to join the party. In *Kangura*, Hassan Ngeze publicly acknowledged his formal role as an advisor to the CDR, and through editorials, photographs, and the publication of

letters and communiqués, *Kangura* endorsed and actively promoted the CDR. *Kangura* and RTLM functioned as partners in a Hutu coalition, of which CDR was also a part. *Kangura* and RTLM presented a common media front, publicly interacting and promoting each other through articles, broadcasts, and the joint initiative represented by the *Kangura* competition in March 1994. *Kangura* portrayed all three of the Accused in a common undertaking relating to RTLM. The purpose of the coalition was to mobilize the Hutu population against the Tutsi ethnic minority.

III. LEGAL FINDINGS

GENOCIDE

The Accused are charged with genocide.

Acts of RTLM

63. The Chamber has found that RTLM broadcasts engaged in ethnic stereotyping in a manner that promoted contempt and hatred for the Tutsi population and called on listeners to seek out and take up arms against the enemy. The enemy was defined to be the Tutsi ethnic group and Hutu opponents. These broadcasts called explicitly for the extermination of the Tutsi ethnic group. In 1994, both before and after 6 April, RTLM broadcast the names of Tutsi individuals and their families, as well as Hutu political opponents who supported the Tutsi ethnic group. In some cases these persons were subsequently killed. A specific causal connection between the RTLM broadcasts and the killing of these individuals – either by publicly naming them or by manipulating their movements and directing that they, as a group, be killed – has been established.

Acts of Kangura

64. The Chamber has found that articles and editorials in *Kangura*, such as *The Appeal to the Conscience of the Hutu*, conveyed contempt and hatred for the Tutsi ethnic group, and for Tutsi women in particular as enemy agents, and called on readers to take all necessary measures to stop the enemy, defined to be the Tutsi population. The cover of *Kangura* No. 26 promoted violence by conveying the message that the machete should be used to eliminate the Tutsi, once and for all. This was a call for the destruction of the Tutsi ethnic group as such. Through fear-mongering and hate propaganda, *Kangura* paved the way for genocide in Rwanda, whipping the Hutu population into a killing frenzy.
65. The nature of media is such that causation of killing and other acts of genocide will necessarily be effected by an immediately proximate cause in addition to the communication itself. In the Chamber's view, this does not diminish the causation to be attributed to the media, or the criminal accountability of those responsible for the communication.

Acts of CDR

66. The Hutu Power movement, spearheaded by CDR, created a political framework for the killing of Tutsi and Hutu political opponents. The CDR and its youth wing, the *Impuzamugambi*, convened meetings and demonstrations, established roadblocks, distributed weapons, and systematically organized and carried out the killing of Tutsi civilians. As well as orchestrating particular acts of killing, the CDR promoted a Hutu mindset in which ethnic hatred was normalized as a political ideology. The division of Hutu and Tutsi entrenched fear and suspicion of the Tutsi and fabricated the perception that the Tutsi population had to be destroyed in order to safeguard the political gains that had been made by the Hutu majority.
67. The Defence contends that the downing of the President's plane and the death of Habyarimana precipitated the killing of innocent Tutsi civilians. The Chamber accepts that this moment in time served as a trigger for the events that followed. That is evident. But if the downing of the plane was the trigger, then RTLM, *Kangura* and CDR were the bullets in the gun. The trigger had such a deadly impact because the gun was loaded. The Chamber therefore considers the killing of Tutsi civilians and Hutu political opponents can be said to have resulted, at least in part, from the message of ethnic targeting for death that was clearly and effectively disseminated through RTLM, *Kangura* and CDR, before and after 6 April 1994.

Acts of Barayagwiza

Barayagwiza distributed a truckload of weapons to the local population, which were used to kill individuals of Tutsi ethnicity. At least 30 Tutsi civilians were killed, including children and older people. Barayagwiza played a leadership role in the distribution of these weapons, which formed part of a predefined and structured plan to kill Tutsi civilians. From Barayagwiza's critical role in this plan, orchestrating the delivery of the weapons to be used for destruction, the Chamber finds that Barayagwiza was involved in planning these acts.

Acts of Ngeze

68. Hassan Ngeze on the morning of 7 April 1994 ordered the *Interahamwe* in Gisenyi to kill Tutsi civilians and prepare for their burial at the *Commune Rouge*. Many were killed in the attacks that happened immediately thereafter and later on the same day. Ngeze helped secure and distribute, stored, and transported weapons to be used against the Tutsi population. He set up, manned and supervised roadblocks in Gisenyi in 1994 that identified targeted Tutsi civilians who were subsequently taken to and killed at the *Commune Rouge*. Ngeze often drove around with a megaphone in his vehicle, mobilizing the population to come to CDR meetings and spreading the message that the *Inyenzi* would be exterminated, *Inyenzi* meaning, and being understood to mean, the Tutsi ethnic minority. In this manner, Ngeze instigated the killing of Tutsi civilians.

Genocidal intent

69. In ascertaining the intent of the Accused, the Chamber has considered their individual statements and acts, as well as the message they conveyed through the media they controlled. On 15 May 1994, the Editor-in-Chief of RTLM, Gaspard Gahigi, told listeners:

> ... they say the Tutsi are being exterminated, they are being decimated by the Hutu, and other things. I would like to tell you, dear listeners of RTLM, that the war we are waging is actually between these two ethnic groups, the Hutu and the Tutsi.

70. Even before 6 April 1994, RTLM was equating the Tutsi with the enemy, as evidenced by its broadcast of 6 January 1994, with Kantano Habimana asking, 'Why should I hate the Tutsi? Why should I hate the *Inkotanyi*?'
71. With regard to *Kangura*, in perhaps its most graphic expression of genocidal intent, the cover of *Kangura* No. 26 answered the question 'What Weapons Shall We Use To Conquer The *Inyenzi* Once And For All?' with the depiction of a machete. That the Tutsi ethnic group was the target of the machete was clear.
72. The newspaper and the radio explicitly and repeatedly, in fact relentlessly, targeted the Tutsi population for destruction. Demonizing the Tutsi as having inherently evil qualities, equating the ethnic group with 'the enemy' and portraying its women as seductive enemy agents, the media called for the extermination of the Tutsi ethnic group as a response to the political threat that they associated with Tutsi ethnicity.
73. The genocidal intent in the activities of the CDR was expressed through the phrase '*tubatsembasembe*' or 'let's exterminate them', a slogan chanted repeatedly at CDR rallies and demonstrations. At a policy level, CDR communiqués called on the Hutu population to 'neutralize by all means possible' the enemy, defined to be the Tutsi ethnic group.
74. The editorial policies evidenced by the writings of *Kangura* and the broadcasts of RTLM, and the organizational policy evidenced by the activity of CDR, constitute, in the Chamber's view, conclusive evidence of genocidal intent. Individually, each of the Accused made statements that further evidence this intent.
75. Ferdinand Nahimana, in a Radio Rwanda broadcast on 25 April 1994, said he was happy that RTLM had been instrumental in awakening the majority people, meaning the Hutu population, and that the population had stood up with a view to halting the enemy. Nahimana associated the enemy with the Tutsi ethnic group. As the mastermind of RTLM, Nahimana set in motion the communications weaponry that fought the 'war of media, words, newspapers and radio stations' he described in his Radio Rwanda broadcast of 25 April as a complement to bullets.
76. Jean-Bosco Barayagwiza himself said in public meetings, 'let's exterminate them' with 'them' being understood by those who heard it as a reference to the Tutsi population. After separating the Tutsi from the Hutu and

humiliating the Tutsi by forcing them to perform the *Ikinyemera*, a traditional dance, at several public meetings, Barayagwiza threatened to kill them and said it would not be difficult. From his words and deeds, Barayagwiza's ruthless commitment to the destruction of the Tutsi population as a means by which to protect the political gains secured by the Hutu majority from 1959 is evident.

77. Hassan Ngeze wrote many articles and editorials, and made many statements that openly evidence his genocidal intent. In one such article he stated that the Tutsi 'no longer conceal the fact that this war pits the Hutus against the Tutsis.' His radio broadcast of 12 June 1994 called on listeners not to mistakenly kill Hutu rather than Tutsi. Crass references to the physical and personal traits of Tutsi ethnicity permeate *Kangura* and his own writings in *Kangura*. Ngeze harped on the broad nose of the Hutu as contrasted with the aquiline nose of the Tutsi, and he incessantly described the Tutsi as evil. His role in saving Tutsi individuals whom he knew does not, in the Chamber's view, negate his intent to destroy the ethnic group as such. Witness LAG heard him say, '[I]f Habyarimana were also to die, we would not be able to spare the Tutsi'. Witness AEU heard Ngeze on a megaphone, saying that he was going to kill and exterminate all the *Inyenzi*, by which he meant the Tutsi, and Ngeze himself ordered an attack on Tutsi civilians in Gisenyi, evidencing his intent to destroy the Tutsi population.

78. Based on this evidence, the Chamber finds that Ferdinand Nahimana, Jean Bosco Barayagwiza and Hassan Ngeze acted with intent to destroy, in whole or in part, the Tutsi ethnic group. The identification of Tutsi individuals as enemies of the state associated with political opposition, simply by virtue of their Tutsi ethnicity, underscores the fact that their membership in the ethnic group, as such, was the sole basis on which they were targeted.

Individual criminal responsibility

79. The Chamber has considered the individual criminal responsibility of Ferdinand Nahimana and Jean-Bosco Barayagwiza for RTLM broadcasts, by virtue of their respective roles in the creation and control of RTLM. Nahimana and Barayagwiza were, respectively, 'number one' and 'number two' in the top management of the radio. They represented the radio at the highest level in meetings with the Ministry of Information; they controlled the finances of the company; and they were both members of the Steering Committee, which functioned in effect as a board of directors for RTLM. Nahimana chaired the Program Committee of this board, and Barayagwiza chaired its Legal Committee.

80. While recognizing that Nahimana and Barayagwiza did not make decisions in the first instance with regard to each particular broadcast of RTLM, these decisions reflected an editorial policy for which they were responsible. The broadcasts collectively conveyed a message of ethnic hatred and a call for violence against the Tutsi population. This message was heard around the world. 'Stop that radio' was the cry Alison Des Forges heard from Rwanda

during the killings, and it was the cry conveyed to the United Nations by Reporters Without Borders in May 1994. As board members responsible for RTLM, including its programming, Nahimana and Barayagwiza were responsible for this message. Both Barayagwiza and Nahimana knew that RTLM programming was generating concern, even before 6 April 1994. Yet RTLM programming followed its trajectory, steadily increasing in vehemence and reaching a pitched frenzy after 6 April. Nahimana and Barayagwiza knew that the hate being spewed by these programmes was of concern and failed to take effective measures to stop their evolution into the deadly weapon of war and genocide that was unleashed in full force after 6 April 1994.

81. After 6 April 1994, although the evidence does not establish the same level of active support, it is nevertheless clear that Nahimana and Barayagwiza knew what was happening at RTLM and failed to exercise the authority vested in them as office-holding members of the governing body of RTLM, to prevent the genocidal harm that was caused by RTLM programming. That they had the *de facto* authority to prevent this harm is evidenced by the one documented and successful intervention of Nahimana to stop RTLM attacks on UNAMIR and General Dallaire. The Chamber notes that Nahimana has not been charged for genocide pursuant to Article 6(3) of its Statute. For his active engagement in the management of RTLM prior to 6 April, and his failure to take necessary and reasonable measures to prevent the acts of genocide caused by RTLM that occurred after 6 April, the Chamber finds Barayagwiza guilty of genocide pursuant to Article 6(3) of its Statute.

82. The Chamber notes Nahimana's particular role as the founder and principal ideologist of RTLM. RTLM was his initiative and his design, which grew out of his experience as Director of ORINFOR and his understanding of the power of the media. Although Nahimana disclaimed responsibility for RTLM broadcasting after 6 April, the Chamber considers this disclaimer too facile. Nahimana's interview on Radio Rwanda, in which he said he was very happy with RTLM's instrumental role in awakening the Hutu population, took place while the genocide was underway; the massacre of the Tutsi population was ongoing. Nahimana may have been less actively involved in the daily affairs of RTLM after 6 April 1994, but RTLM did not deviate from the course he had set for it before 6 April 1994. The programming of RTLM after 6 April built on the foundations created for it before 6 April. RTLM was Nahimana's weapon of choice, which he used to instigate the acts of genocide that occurred. For this reason the Chamber finds Nahimana guilty of genocide pursuant to Article 6(1) of its statute.

83. Jean-Bosco Barayagwiza was one of the principal founders of CDR and played a leading role in its formation and development. He was a decision-maker for the party. The killing of Tutsi civilians was promoted by Barayagwiza himself and by CDR members in his presence at public meetings and demonstrations. Barayagwiza supervised roadblocks manned

by the *Impuzamugambi*, established to stop and kill Tutsi. Barayagwiza was at the organizational helm of CDR. He was also on site at the meetings, demonstrations and roadblocks that created an infrastructure for the killing of Tutsi civilians. For this reason, the Chamber finds him guilty of instigating acts of genocide committed by CDR members and *Impuzamugambi*, pursuant to Article 6(1) of its Statute. For his individual acts in planning the killing of Tutsi civilians, the Chamber finds him guilty of genocide, pursuant to Article 6(1) of its Statute.

84. The Chamber further finds that Barayagwiza had superior responsibility over members of the CDR and its militia, the *Impuzamugambi*, as President of CDR at Gisenyi Prefecture and from February 1994 as President of CDR at the national level. He promoted the policy of CDR for the extermination of the Tutsi population and supervised his subordinates, the CDR members and *Impuzamugambi* militia, in carrying out killings and other violent acts. For his active engagement in CDR, and his failure to take necessary and reasonable measures to prevent the acts of genocide caused by CDR members, the Chamber finds Barayagwiza guilty of genocide pursuant to Article 6(3) of its Statute.
85. The Chamber finds Hassan Ngeze, as founder, owner and editor of *Kangura*, a publication that instigated the killing of Tutsi civilians, as well as for his acts of ordering, inciting and aiding and abetting the killing of Tutsi civilians, guilty of genocide, pursuant to Article 6(1) of its Statute.

DIRECT AND PUBLIC INCITEMENT TO GENOCIDE

86. The Chamber examined the central principles that emerge from the international jurisprudence on incitement to discrimination and violence that serve as a useful guide to the factors to be considered in defining elements of 'direct and public incitement to genocide' as applied to mass media.
87. Editors and publishers have generally been held responsible for the media they control. In determining the scope of this responsibility, the importance of intent, that is the purpose of the communications they channel, emerges from the jurisprudence. The actual language used in the media has often been cited as an indicator of intent. Critical distance is a key factor in evaluating the purpose of the publication.
88. The jurisprudence on incitement also highlights the importance of taking context into account when considering the potential impact of expression. Other factors relating to context that emerge from the jurisprudence, particularly that of the European Court of Human Rights, include the importance of protecting political expression, particularly the expression of opposition views and criticism of the government.
89. In considering whether particular expression constitutes a form of incitement on which restrictions would be justified, the international jurisprudence does not include any specific causation requirement linking the expression at issue with the demonstration of a direct effect. In the well-known Nuremburg case of *Julius Streicher*, there was no allegation

that Streicher's publication *Der Stürmer* was tied to any particular violence. Much more generally, it was found to have 'injected into the minds of thousands of Germans' a 'poison' that caused them to support the National Socialist policy of Jewish persecution and extermination.

90. Counsel for Ngeze has argued that United States law, as the most speech-protective, should be used as a standard, to ensure the universal acceptance and legitimacy of the Tribunal's jurisprudence. The Chamber considers international law, which has been well developed in the areas of freedom from discrimination and freedom of expression, to be the point of reference for its consideration of these issues, noting that domestic law varies widely while international law codifies evolving universal standards. The Chamber notes that the jurisprudence of the United States also accepts the fundamental principles set forth in international law and has recognized in its domestic law that incitement to violence, threats, libel, false advertising, obscenity, and child pornography are among those forms of expression that fall outside the scope of freedom of speech protection.

Charges against the accused

91. The Accused are charged with direct and public incitement to genocide.
92. The crime of incitement is an inchoate offence that continues in time until the completion of the acts contemplated. The Chamber accordingly considers that the publication of *Kangura*, from its first issue in May 1990 through its March 1994 issue, the alleged impact of which culminated in events that took place in 1994, falls within the temporal jurisdiction of the Tribunal. Similarly, the Chamber considers that the entirety of RTLM broadcasting, from July 1993 through July 1994, the alleged impact of which culminated in events that took place in 1994, falls within the temporal jurisdiction of the Tribunal.
93. In its review of *Kangura* and RTLM, the Chamber notes that some of the articles and broadcasts highlighted by the Prosecution convey historical information, political analysis, or advocacy of an ethnic consciousness regarding the inequitable distribution of privilege in Rwanda. Barayagwiza's RTLM broadcast of 12 December 1993, for example, is a moving personal account of his experience of discrimination as a Hutu. The Chamber considers that it is critical to distinguish between the discussion of ethnic consciousness and the promotion of ethnic hatred. This broadcast by Barayagwiza is the former but not the latter. A communication such as this broadcast does not constitute incitement. In fact, it falls squarely within the scope of speech that is protected by the right to freedom of expression. Similarly, public discussion of the merits of the Arusha Accords, however critical, constitutes a legitimate exercise of free speech.
94. The Chamber considers that speech constituting ethnic hatred results from the stereotyping of ethnicity combined with its denigration. In the Chamber's view, the accuracy of a generalization is only one factor to be considered in the determination of whether it is intended to provoke rather than to educate those who receive it. The tone of the statement is as relevant to this

determination as is its content. The Chamber also considers the context in which the statement is made to be important. A statement of ethnic generalization provoking resentment against members of that ethnicity would have a heightened impact in the context of a genocidal environment. It would be more likely to lead to violence. At the same time the environment would be an indicator that incitement to violence was the intent of the statement.

95. The Accused have cited in their defence the need for vigilance against the enemy, the enemy being armed and dangerous RPF forces who attacked the Hutu population and were fighting to destroy democracy and reconquer power in Rwanda. The Chamber accepts that the media has a role to play in the protection of democracy and if necessary the mobilization of civil defence for the protection of the nation and its people. What distinguishes both *Kangura* and RTLM from an initiative to this end is the consistent identification made by the publication and the radio broadcasts of the enemy as the Tutsi population. Readers and listeners were not directed against individuals who were clearly defined to be armed and dangerous. Instead, Tutsi civilians and in fact the Tutsi population as a whole were targeted as the threat.

96. Both *Kangura* and RTLM, as well as CDR in its communiqués, named and listed individuals suspected of being RPF or RPF accomplices. In their defence, the Accused stated that these individuals were, at least in some cases, RPF members. The Chamber accepts that the publication of official information is a legitimate function of the media. Not all lists and names published or broadcast were associated with such sources, however. To the contrary, the evidence reviewed by the Chamber indicates a pattern of naming people on vague suspicion, without articulated grounds, or in those cases where the grounds were articulated they were highly speculative or in some cases entirely unfounded. In these cases, the only common element is the Tutsi ethnicity of the persons named, and the evidence in some cases clearly indicates that their ethnicity was in fact the reason they were named.

97. Also, the names published and broadcast were generally done so in the context of a message, that was at times more or less explicit. An official list of 123 names of suspects was published in *Kangura* No. 40 with an express warning to readers that the government was not effectively protecting them from these people and that they needed to organize their own self-defence to prevent their own extermination. This message classically illustrates the incitement of *Kangura* readers to violence: by instilling fear in them, giving them names to associate with this fear, and mobilizing them to take independent measures to protect themselves. In some instances, names were mentioned by *Kangura* without such an explicit call to action. The message was nevertheless direct. That it was clearly understood is overwhelmingly evidenced by the testimony of witnesses that being named in *Kangura* would bring dire consequences. Similarly, RTLM broadcast a message of fear, provided listeners with names, and encouraged them to defend and protect themselves, incessantly telling them to 'be vigilant'.

98. With regard to causation, the Chamber recalls that incitement is a crime regardless of whether it has the effect it intends to have. In determining whether communications represent a risk of causing genocide and thereby constitute incitement, the Chamber considers it significant that in fact genocide occurred. One witness described what RTLM did as 'to spread petrol throughout the country little by little, so that one day it would be able to set fire to the whole country'.

RTLM

99. RTLM broadcasting was a drumbeat, calling on listeners to take action against the enemy and enemy accomplices, equated with the Tutsi population. The phrase 'heating up heads' captures the process of incitement systematically engaged in by RTLM, which after 6 April 1994 was also known as 'Radio Machete'. The nature of radio transmission made RTLM particularly dangerous and harmful, as did the breadth of its reach. Unlike print media, radio is immediately present and active. The power of the human voice, heard by the Chamber when the broadcast tapes were played in Kinyarwanda, adds a quality and dimension beyond language to the message conveyed. Radio heightened the sense of fear, the sense of danger and the sense of urgency giving rise to the need for action by listeners. The denigration of Tutsi ethnicity was augmented by the visceral scorn coming out of the airwaves – the ridiculing laugh and the nasty sneer. These elements greatly amplified the impact of RTLM broadcasts.

100. The Chamber has found that Ferdinand Nahimana acted with genocidal intent. It has found him responsible for RTLM programming pursuant to Article 6(1) and established a basis for his responsibility under Article 6(3) of the Statute. Accordingly, the Chamber finds Ferdinand Nahimana guilty of direct and public incitement to genocide, pursuant to Article 6(1) and Article 6(3) of the Statute.

101. The Chamber has found that Jean-Bosco Barayagwiza acted with genocidal intent. It has found Barayagwiza responsible for RTLM programming pursuant to Article 6(3) of the Statute of the Tribunal. Accordingly, the Chamber finds Jean-Bosco Barayagwiza guilty of direct and public incitement to genocide, pursuant to Article 6(3) of its Statute.

CDR

102. The killing of Tutsi civilians was promoted by the CDR through the publication of communiqués and other writings that called for the extermination of the enemy and defined the enemy as the Tutsi population. For his failure to take necessary and reasonable measures to prevent the acts of direct and public incitement to commit genocide caused by CDR members, the Chamber finds Barayagwiza guilty of direct and public incitement to commit genocide pursuant to Article 6(3) of its Statute.

KANGURA

103. The Chamber notes that the name *Kangura* itself means 'to wake up others'. This was the clear intent of *Kangura* and the publication is a litany of ethnic denigration presenting the Tutsi population as inherently evil and calling for the extermination of the Tutsi as a preventive measure. The Chamber notes the increased attention in 1994 issues of *Kangura* on the fear of an RPF attack and the killing of innocent Tutsi civilians that would follow as a consequence of such attack.
104. The Chamber notes that not all of the writings published in *Kangura* and highlighted by the Prosecution constitute direct incitement. *A Cockroach Cannot Give Birth to a Butterfly*, for example, is an article brimming with ethnic hatred, but it did not call on readers to take action against the Tutsi population.
105. As founder, owner and editor of *Kangura*, Hassan Ngeze used the publication to instill hatred, promote fear, and incite genocide. It is evident that *Kangura* played a significant role, and was seen to have played a significant role, in creating the conditions that led to acts of genocide. Accordingly, the Chamber finds Hassan Ngeze guilty of direct and public incitement to genocide, under Article 2(3)(c) and in accordance with Article 6(1) of the Statute.
106. For his individual acts, such as driving with a megaphone in his vehicle, mobilizing the population to come to CDR meetings and spreading the message that the Tutsi population would be exterminated, the Chamber finds Hassan Ngeze guilty of direct and public incitement to genocide, pursuant to Article 6(1) of the Statute.

CONSPIRACY

107. The Accused are charged with conspiracy to commit genocide.
108. The *Musema* judgement defined conspiracy to commit genocide as an agreement between two or more persons to commit the crime of genocide. The requisite intent for the crime of conspiracy to commit genocide is the same intent required for the crime of genocide.
109. The Chamber considers that conspiracy can be comprised of individuals acting in an institutional capacity as well as or even independently of their personal links with each other. Institutional coordination can form the basis of a conspiracy among those individuals who control the institutions that are engaged in coordinated action. The Chamber considers the act of coordination to be the central element that distinguishes conspiracy from 'conscious parallelism', the concept put forward by the Defence to explain the evidence in this case.
110. Nahimana and Barayagwiza collaborated closely as the two most active members of the Steering Committee, or provisional board, of RTLM. Barayagwiza also collaborated closely with Ngeze in the CDR. The Chamber finds that Baryagawiza was the lynchpin among the three

Accused, collaborating closely with both Nahimana and Ngeze. Institutionally also, there were many links that connected the Accused to each other through RTLM, *Kangura* and CDR. The evidence establishes, beyond a reasonable doubt, that Nahimana, Barayagwiza and Ngeze consciously interacted with each other, using the institutions they controlled to promote a joint agenda, which was the targeting of the Tutsi population for destruction. There was public presentation of this shared purpose and coordination of efforts to realize their common goal. The Chamber finds that the Accused are guilty of conspiracy to commit genocide, pursuant to Article 6(1) of its Statute.

CRIMES AGAINST HUMANITY (EXTERMINATION)

111. The Accused are charged with crimes against humanity (extermination).

112. Based on its factual findings, and the legal findings set forth under Genocide, the Chamber finds Ferdinand Nahimana guilty of extermination, pursuant to Article 6(1) of the Statute. The Chamber finds Jean-Bosco Barayagwiza guilty of extermination, pursuant to Article 6(3) of the Statute of the Tribunal for the broadcasts of RTLM, pursuant to Article 6(1) and 6(3) for the activities of CDR, and pursuant to Article 6(1) for his own acts. The Chamber finds Hassan Ngeze guilty of extermination, for the publication of *Kangura* and for his own acts, pursuant to Article 6(1).

CRIMES AGAINST HUMANITY (PERSECUTION)

The Accused are charged with persecution.

113. Unlike the other crimes against humanity enumerated in the Statute of the Tribunal, the crime of persecution specifically requires a finding of discriminatory intent on racial, religious or political grounds. In Rwanda the targets of attack were the Tutsi ethnic group and the so-called 'moderate' Hutu political opponents who supported the Tutsi ethnic group. The Chamber considers that the group against which discriminatory attacks were perpetrated can be defined by its political component as well as its ethnic component. RTLM, *Kangura* and CDR essentially merged political and ethnic identity, defining their political target on the basis of ethnicity and political positions relating to ethnicity. The Chamber considers that the discriminatory intent of the Accused falls within the scope of persecution on political grounds of an ethnic character.

114. The crime of persecution has been held by ICTR jurisprudence to require 'a gross or blatant denial of a fundamental right reaching the same level of gravity' as other enumerated crimes against humanity. The Chamber considers it evident that hate speech targeting a population on the basis of ethnicity, or other discriminatory grounds, reaches this level of gravity and constitutes persecution. Hate speech is a discriminatory form of aggression that destroys the dignity of those in the group under attack. It creates a lesser status not only in the eyes of the group members

themselves but also in the eyes of others who perceive and treat them as less than human. The denigration of a person on the basis of his or her ethnic identity or other group membership in and of itself, as well as in its other consequences, can be an irreversible harm.

115. Unlike the crime of incitement, which is defined in terms of intent, the crime of persecution is defined also in terms of impact. Persecution is not a provocation to cause harm. It is itself the harm. Accordingly there need not be a call to action in communications that constitute persecution. For the same reason, there need be no link between persecution and acts of violence. The Chamber notes that Julius Streicher was convicted at Nuremberg of persecution for anti-semitic writings that significantly predated the extermination of Jews in the 1940s. In Rwanda, the virulent writings of *Kangura* and the incendiary broadcasts of RTLM functioned in the same way, conditioning the Hutu population and creating a climate of harm, as evidenced in part by the extermination and genocide that followed. Similarly, the activities of the CDR, a Hutu political party that demonized the Tutsi population as the enemy, generated fear and hatred that created the conditions for extermination and genocide in Rwanda.

116. Freedom of expression and freedom from discrimination are not incompatible principles of law. Hate speech is not protected speech under international law. In fact, governments have an obligation under international law to prohibit any advocacy of national, racial or religious hatred that constitutes incitement to discrimination, hostility or violence. A great number of countries around the world, including Rwanda, have domestic laws that ban advocacy of discriminatory hate, in recognition of the danger it represents and the harm it causes. The Chamber considers, in light of these well-established principles of international and domestic law, and the jurisprudence, that hate speech that expresses ethnic and other forms of discrimination violates the norm of customary international law prohibiting discrimination. Within this norm of customary law, the prohibition of advocacy of discrimination and incitement to violence is increasingly important as the power of the media to harm is increasingly acknowledged.

117. Having established that all communications constituting incitement were made with genocidal intent, the Chamber notes that the lesser intent requirement of persecution, the intent to discriminate, has been met with regard to these communications. Having also found that these communications were part of a widespread or systematic attack, the Chamber finds that these expressions of ethnic hatred constitute persecution. Persecution is broader than direct and public incitement, including advocacy of ethnic hatred in other forms. For example, the *Kangura* article, A Cockroach Cannot Give Birth to a Butterfly, constitutes persecution. In this article, the Tutsi were described as biologically distinct from the Hutu, and inherently marked by malice and wickedness. The Tutsi were portrayed as mean and vengeful, and their weapons were defined to be women and money. The RTLM interview broadcast on June 1994, in which Simbona,

interviewed by Gaspard Gahigi, talked of the cunning and trickery of the Tutsi, also constitutes persecution.

118. The Chamber notes that Tutsi women, in particular, were targeted for persecution. The portrayal of the Tutsi woman as a femme fatale, and the message that Tutsi women were seductive agents of the enemy was conveyed repeatedly by RTLM and *Kangura*. *The Ten Commandments*, broadcast on RTLM and published in *Kangura*, vilified and endangered Tutsi women. By defining the Tutsi woman as an enemy in this way, RTLM and *Kangura* articulated a framework that made the sexual attack of Tutsi women a foreseeable consequence of the role attributed to them.

119. Activities and communications of the CDR, as well as acts personally committed by Barayagwiza, that advocated ethnic hatred constitute persecution.

120. For these reasons, the Chamber finds Ferdinand Nahimana guilty of persecution pursuant to Article 6(1) and Article 6(3) of the Statute for the broadcasts of RTLM. The Chamber finds Jean-Bosco Barayagwiza guilty of persecution, pursuant to Article 6(3) for the broadcasts of RTLM and the activities of CDR, and pursuant to Article 6(1) for the activities of CDR and for his own acts. The Chamber finds Hassan Ngeze guilty of persecution, pursuant to Article 6(1), for articles in the publication *Kangura*.

CRIMES AGAINST HUMANITY (MURDER)

121. Hassan Ngeze is charged with crimes against humanity (murder). The Prosecution conceded during its Closing Arguments that it was not pursuing the allegation in the Indictment of the shooting of a Tutsi girl. The Prosecution failed to prove that Ngeze ordered the killing of or killed Modeste Tabaro, as alleged in the Indictment. The Prosecution also failed to prove that Ngeze killed a man in the *Commune Rouge*, as alleged in the Indictment. The Chamber therefore finds that Hassan Ngeze is not guilty of murder.

IV. VERDICT

FOR THE FOREGOING REASONS, having considered all of the evidence and the arguments:

THE CHAMBER unanimously finds Ferdinand Nahimana:

Count 1: Guilty of Conspiracy to Commit Genocide

Count 2: Guilty of Genocide

Count 3: Guilty of Direct and Public Incitement to Commit Genocide

Count 4: Not Guilty of Complicity in Genocide

Count 5: Guilty of Crimes Against Humanity (Persecution)

Count 6: Guilty of Crimes Against Humanity (Extermination)

Count 7: Not Guilty of Crimes Against Humanity (Murder)

THE CHAMBER unanimously finds Jean-Bosco Barayagwiza:

Count 1: Guilty of Conspiracy to Commit Genocide
Count 2: Guilty of Genocide
Count 3: Not Guilty of Complicity in Genocide
Count 4: Guilty of Direct and Public Incitement to Commit Genocide
Count 5: Guilty of Crimes Against Humanity (Extermination)
Count 6: Not Guilty of Crimes Against Humanity (Murder)
Count 7: Guilty of Crimes Against Humanity (Persecution)
Count 8: Not Guilty of Serious Violations of Article 3 Common to the Geneva Conventions and of Additional Protocol II
Count 9: Not Guilty of Serious Violations of Article 3 Common to the Geneva Conventions and of Additional Protocol II

THE CHAMBER unanimously finds Hassan Ngeze:
Count 1: Guilty of Conspiracy to Commit Genocide
Count 2: Guilty of Genocide
Count 3: Not Guilty of Complicity in Genocide
Count 4: Guilty of Direct and Public Incitement to Commit Genocide
Count 5: Not Guilty of Crimes Against Humanity (Murder)
Count 6: Guilty of Crimes Against Humanity (Persecution)
Count 7: Guilty of Crimes Against Humanity (Extermination)

V. SENTENCING

Having found the three Accused guilty, the Chamber now proceeds to the sentencing of the Accused.

FERDINAND NAHIMANA

I call on Ferdinand Nahimana to rise for sentencing and face the Court.
Ferdinand Nahimana, you were a renowned academic, Professor of History at the National University of Rwanda. You were Director of ORINFOR and founded RTLM radio station as an independent private radio. You were Political Adviser to the Interim Government sworn in after 6 April 1994 under President Sindikubwabo.

You were fully aware of the power of words, and you used the radio – the medium of communication with the widest public reach – to disseminate hatred and violence. You may have been motivated by your sense of patriotism and the need you perceived for equity for the Hutu population in Rwanda. But instead of following legitimate avenues of recourse, you chose a path of genocide. In doing so, you betrayed the trust placed in you as an intellectual and a leader. Without a firearm, machete or any physical weapon, you caused the deaths of thousands of innocent civilians. Representations were made by your witnesses as to your good character and high standing in society but in the Chamber's view, these circumstances are not mitigating. They underscore your betrayal of public trust.

Having considered all the relevant factors, the Chamber sentences you in respect of all the counts on which you have been convicted to imprisonment for the remainder of your life.

HASSAN NGEZE

I call on Hassan Ngeze to rise for sentencing and face the Court.

Hassan Ngeze, as the owner and editor of a well-known newspaper in Rwanda, you were in a position to inform the public and shape public opinion towards achieving democracy and peace for all Rwandans. Instead of using the media to promote human rights, you used it to attack and destroy human rights. You had significant media networking skills and attracted support earlier in your career from international human rights organizations who perceived your commitment to freedom of expression. However, you did not respect the responsibility that comes with that freedom. You abused the trust of the public by using your newspaper to instigate genocide. The Chamber notes that you saved Tutsi civilians from death by transporting them across the border out of Rwanda. Your power to save was more than matched by your power to kill. You poisoned the minds of your readers, and by words and deeds caused the death of thousands of innocent civilians.

Having considered all the relevant factors, the Chamber sentences you in respect of all the counts on which you have been convicted to imprisonment for the remainder of your life.

JEAN-BOSCO BARAYAGWIZA

Jean-Bosco Barayagwiza was Director of Political Affairs in the Ministry of Foreign Affairs and a founder of RTLM. He was also the founder of CDR and its President in Gisenyi Prefecture, later National President of CDR. He is a lawyer by training and in his book professes a commitment to international human rights standards. Yet he deviated from these standards and violated the most fundamental human right, the right to life. He did so both through the institutions he created, and through his own personal acts of participation in the genocide. He was the lynchpin of the conspiracy, collaborating closely with both Nahimana and Ngeze.

Having considered all the relevant factors, the Chamber considers that the appropriate sentence for Jean-Bosco Barayagwiza in respect of all the counts on which he has been convicted is imprisonment for the remainder of his life. However, in its decision dated 31 March 2000, the Appeals Chamber decided:

> [T]hat for the violation of his rights the Appellant is entitled to a remedy, to be fixed at the time of judgement at first instance, as follows:
> If the Appellant is found not guilty, he shall receive financial compensation;
> If the Appellant is found guilty, his sentence shall be reduced to take account of the violation of his rights.

The Chamber considers that a term of years, being by its nature a reduced sentence from that of life imprisonment, is the only way in which it can implement the Appeals Chamber decision. Taking into account the violation of his rights, the Chamber sentences Barayagwiza in respect of all the counts on which he has been convicted to 35 years' imprisonment. Pursuant to Rule 101(D) of the Rules, Barayagwiza is further entitled to credit for time served, to be calculated from the date of his initial arrest in Cameroon, on 26 March 1996. Credit for time served has been calculated as seven years, eight months and nine days. Therefore, Barayagwiza will serve twenty-seven years, three months and twenty-one days, being the remainder of his sentence, as of 3 December 2003.

Pursuant to Rules 102 (A) and 103, the three Accused shall remain in the custody of the Tribunal pending transfer to the State where they will serve their sentences.

26
The Pre-Genocide Case Against Radio-Télévision Libre des Milles Collines

Simone Monasebian

Wars are not fought for territory, but for words. Man's deadliest weapon is language. He is susceptible to being hypnotized by slogans as he is to infectious diseases. And where there is an epidemic, the group mind takes over.

Arthur Koestler (1978)

On 3 December 2003, the judges of the International Criminal Tribunal for Rwanda (ICTR) convicted Ferdinand Nahimana and Jean-Bosco Barayagwiza of genocide, direct and public incitement to commit genocide, conspiracy to commit genocide, crimes against humanity (persecution) and crimes against humanity (extermination). Nahimana and Barayagwiza were the directors of Radio-Télévision Libre des Milles Collines (RTLM), Rwanda's first private radio station. RTLM, which broadcast from July 1993 to July 1994, was found to have fanned the flames of hate and genocide in Rwanda. The case against Nahimana and Barayagwiza, in what was referred to as 'the Media Trial', raised important principles concerning the role of the media, which had not been addressed at the level of international criminal justice since Nuremberg. Nahimana was sentenced to life in prison and Barayagwiza received a sentence of 35 years (ICTR 2003: para. 1106–7).

The jurisdiction of the ICTR was limited to serious violations of international humanitarian law committed between 1 January and 31 December 1994 (ICTR n.d.). However, in their deliberations, the judges also considered RTLM's 1993 broadcasts (ICTR 2003: para. 103–4, 953, 1017). The judgement received worldwide attention. A *New York Times* editorial heralded the verdicts as 'rightly decided', 'welcome', 'pos[ing] no threat to journalistic free speech' and 'demonstrat[ing] that the international community will demand justice for those who committed crimes against all humanity' (NYT Editors 2003). Even renowned American free speech advocates heralded the convictions (Abrams 2003).

If ever there was a textbook case of broadcasting genocide, RTLM's emissions after 6 April 1994, fit the bill – chapter and verse. Most political, legal and humanitarian activists would agree that RTLM's post-6 April broadcasts should have been stopped.[1] Can the same be said of the pre-6 April broadcasts which the judges also criminalized?[2] This paper looks at those earlier broadcasts, so that we may better answer what should have been done about them at the national and international levels. It is only by answering that question that we can know when is it too early or too late to shut down hate media before it begins broadcasting genocide.

Although the ICTR judges found the pre-plane crash broadcasts to be violative of international humanitarian law regulations, such as those in Articles 19 and 20 of the *International Covenant of Civil and Political Rights* (UN 1966), some human rights organizations have found otherwise. In *Broadcasting Genocide: Censorship, Propaganda and State-Sponsored Violence in Rwanda 1990–1994,* Article 19, the international centre against censorship, writes that there is no freedom of expression issue with regard to RTLM broadcasts after the plane crash as 'giving orders to carry out human rights abuses is not protected whether this is done in writing, orally by two-way radio or by public broadcast ... International law clearly permitted external intervention to jam broadcasts at [the post-plane crash] stage, which is the course of action which should have been undertaken' (Article 19 1996: 166–7).

In the view of Article 19, however, RTLM's hate speech before the plane crash should not, and could not, have been banned or jammed. They argue that '[t]he emphasis should rather be on promoting pluralism in privately owned media and supporting attempted reform of the state broadcasting system as a means of marginalizing extremist propaganda and developing the middle ground' (Article 19 1996: 171). They go on to conclude that the owners of RTLM should only be indicted for charges brought in relation to post-plane crash broadcasts.

RTLM'S BROADCASTING AND OPERATIONS BEFORE THE PLANE CRASH

Even so the tongue is a little member, and boasteth great things. Behold how great a matter a little fire kindleth!
And the tongue is a fire, a world of iniquity: so is the tongue among our members, and it defilith the whole body, and setteth on fire the course of nature; and it is set on fire of hell.

Epistle of James, 3: 5–6

Witness GO summed up RTLM's pre-plane crash broadcasts as follows: 'In fact, what RTLM did was almost to pour petrol – to spread petrol throughout the country little by little, so that one day it would be able to set fire to the whole country' (ICTR transcript, 4 June 2001: 33).

By 11 July 1993 (only three days into its broadcasting), the writing was already on the wall. Employing a cynical play on a well known Rwandan proverb, one of the speakers at RTLM's 11 July general assembly of shareholders was quoted as having uttered the words: '*Aho umututsi yanitse ntiriva*,' meaning 'No chance for the Tutsi.'[3] Those same words were also featured on the cover of a July 1993 issue of the notorious hate journal *Kangura*, in relation to RTLM, as well as in an article about RTLM in that issue (Anon. 1993). Those covering that general assembly came away with the clear impression that RTLM would help *Kangura* further extremist objectives and show the Tutsis, and those who did not follow the extremists' line, their true place (Anon. 1993: 13, ICTR transcript, 2 November 2000: para. 166–7, and 7 February 2001: para. 12–14, 26–8, 29, 33–5).

RTLM and its listeners knew early on that its programming was having a potentially violent impact on Rwandan society. On 20 November 1993, for example, an RTLM broadcaster recounted a telephone call from a listener expressing grave concern about being stoned because the radio station had been talking about him (ICTR exhibit 1D50D: 13).

Although the broadcasts showed marks of hatred and persecution in advance of Burundian Hutu President Melanchoir Ndadaye's assassination, after that 21 October 1993 assassination, RTLM broadcasts became exceedingly virulent; RTLM regularly began to employ the mantra '*amakuru ashyushye*' ('we have hot news'). This phrase became Pavlovian, putting listeners in an expectant mood (Chrétien expert report: ICTR exhibits P117B and P163B). This 'hot news' stood out from the cold traditional rhetoric before RTLM (Dr M. Ruzindana expert report, ICTR exhibit P110A: 36).

Ferdinand Nahimana himself testified that, immediately after the events in Burundi, the station became known as a Hutu Power radio station advocating extremism (ICTR transcript, 23 September 2002: 105–8).

Although very few cassettes from RTLM's early broadcasts could be retrieved, notes of those monitoring RTLM at the Rwandan Ministry of Information provide information. Witness GO's notes for 22 October 1993, report broadcasts containing the statements: 'We Hutus must prove to the Tutsis that we are strong' and 'You Hutus, you must be on the look-out. You might meet the fate of the ones in Burundi' (ICTR exhibit P34: 10, quoting RTLM broadcasters Kantano Habimana and Noël Hitimana, respectively).

A few brave members of the government tried to call RTLM to order. Among them were Jean Marie Vianney Higiro, the director of the Rwandan Office of Information (ORINFOR); Faustin Rucogoza, the minister of information; and Alphonse Marie Nkubito and Francois Xavier Nsanzuwera at the Kigali prosecutor's office – all of them Hutu. RTLM responded by targeting, or intensifying its targeting, of them. RTLM was always above the law.

On 25 October 1993, the Ministry of Information sent RTLM a letter of caution asking the station to assess the possible consequences of its programmes (ICTR transcript, 5 April 2001: 112). Before writing the letter, the minister himself had paid a visit to the station's officials to discuss the violative broadcasts (ICTR exhibits P28E and F). The letter was occasioned by the increasingly ethnically divisive broadcasts after the assassination of Burundian President Ndadaye. The very day RTLM received the letter, a high-level Hutu Power official sent RTLM a letter that was read aloud twice by one of the broadcasters. That letter criticized Minister Rucogoza's letter to RTLM and stated that the minister had evil intentions and that his Hutu Power members were 100 per cent behind RTLM (ICTR exhibit 1D49D). Immediately after reading that letter, the broadcaster, eager to whip up revulsion against Tutsis, stated that bloodthirsty Tutsi dog-eaters assassinated Ndadaye, mutilated his body, and then secretly buried him (ICTR exhibit 1D49D: 3).

The broadcaster's words were untrue. According to Human Rights Watch, '[a]ll the reports of torture and mutilation were false' (Commission Internationale 1994).

> Human Rights Watch, the International Federation of Human Rights Leagues, SOS-Torture, and the Human Rights League of the Great Lakes organized an international commission of inquiry similar to that which had [earlier] documented abuses in Rwanda. The commission arranged for an autopsy by a forensic physician who found that Ndadaye had been killed by several blows of a sharp instrument, probably a bayonet. The body had not been mutilated and showed no signs of torture. (Des Forges 1999: 136)

> In the days after the murder of Ndadaye, Hutu attacked Tutsi in many parts of Rwanda. They killed some forty in Cyangugu, twenty each in Butare and Ruhengeri, seventeen in Gisenyi, thirteen in Kigali and drove many others from their homes. Assailants tried to assassinate Alphonse-Marie Nkubito, a high-ranking judicial official and human rights activist who had frequently defended Tutsi, although himself a Hutu. (Des Forges 1999: 137)

For the anti-Tutsi propagandists, the assassination of the Burundian president offered just the kind of tragedy most helpful to their cause. It gave RTLM the chance to establish itself as the most virulent voice in the campaign against Tutsi (ICTR exhibit P181: 135).

In response to the letter from the minister of information, RTML journalists resorted to insults rather than compliance (ICTR exhibit P28E: para. 2).

In a note that witness GO drafted for his boss, the minister of information, in the days after Ndadaye's assassination, he noted RTLM's endless calls for Hutus to be on their guard. GO emphasized that RTLM 'programs do not take into account ... audience sensitivities. Nobody is unaware that Rwandese are very sensitive to ethnic and separatist speeches' (ICTR exhibit P33: K0032662). In another handwritten note drafted shortly after the Ndadaye assassination, witness GO indicated that the station was 'indulg[ing] in an intentional race to misinformation, which stirred up fire, ethnic hatred and led to some innocent people's death' (ICTR exhibit P35: K00032671).

On 26 November 1993, RTLM officials Ferdinand Nahimana, Jean-Bosco Barayagwiza and Felicien Kabuga were called to a meeting at the Ministry of Information. There, RTLM was warned about its broadcasts, which were unsubstantiated, irresponsible and caused ethnic division within the population (ICTR transcript, 5 April 2001: 129–31, and 135–6 and exhibit P28E). Witness GO, who was assigned the task of monitoring RTLM on a daily basis, testified that RTLM's programmes became even worse after that meeting, going further in inciting ethnic hatred (ICTR transcript, 5 April 2001: 112, 159–60). Tensions in the country regarding RTLM also increased thereafter. Witness GO, for example, saw an *Interahamwe* member beat up an acquaintance of GO's, who was saying that RTLM was leading Rwandans 'into an abyss' (ICTR transcript, 9 April 2001: 19–20).

On the day of the 26 November meeting, the Belgian ambassador to Kigali warned his government that RTLM had called for the assassination of Prime Minister Agathe Uwilingiyimana and the Prime Minister-designate Faustin Twagiramungu (Chrétien expert report: ICTR exhibits P117B and P163B: 26930).

In early December 1993, UNAMIR, which received news of suspicious movements of armed militiamen, reported that RTLM continuously broadcast bitter and increasingly passionate propaganda calling on the Hutu to confront the Tutsi (FIDH and HRW 1999: 173, Chrétien expert report: ICTR exhibits P117B and P163B: 26930).

On 3 December 1993, a group of high-ranking Rwandan military officers wrote to UNAMIR's commander, General Dallaire, warning specifically about the dangers of political assassination and widespread killings (ICTR transcript, Des Forges testimony, 22 May 2002: 121). International journalist Collette Braeckman testified that she had met with Prime Minister Agathe Uwilingiyimana in December 1993, 'who of her own initiative, told me that the radio RTLM was mounting a campaign, an ethnic hate campaign' (ICTR transcript, 29 November 2001: 25–60). According to the prime minister, RTLM had also stated that 'the chairman of my party and myself were condemned to die'. In addition, 'in particular the RTLM were launching a denigration campaign with regard to the Belgian contingent in Rwanda'.

On 17, 20 and 21 December 1993, one RTLM broadcaster was heard stating that although the Tutsi minority claim they are being persecuted, they and their women are the ones holding Rwanda's wealth. A Tutsi businessman by the name of Charles Shamukiga was particularly singled out (ICTR exhibit P36/14 E).

Both Human Rights Watch expert witness, Dr Alison Des Forges, and former Kigali prosecutor, Francois Xavier Nsanzuwera, testified that this dangerous propaganda was untrue, that the wealth was not in the hands of Tutsis (ICTR transcript, 22 May 2002: 198–200, and 24 April 2001: 30–8, respectively). Even an expert witness for the Nahimana defence, Helmut Strizek, testified that this broadcast constituted dangerous propaganda under the circumstances (ICTR transcript, 7 May 2003: 45–9).

Dr Des Forges also went on to explain

> There were, of course, a small number of Tutsi who were wealthy, most of them because they were in business. But the great majority of Tutsi who had been excluded from access to secondary education, for example, were ordinary farmers on the hills, living at the same level of poverty as their Hutu neighbours. The assertion that Tutsi were wealthy was one frequently made on RTLM, and in Kangura, and if I'm not mistaken, repeated by Mr Barayagwiza in his book, sometimes associated with the figure that 70 per cent of the wealthy people of Rwanda were Tutsi. This attempt to depict the Tutsi as the wealthy, the unjustifiably wealthy in a country of

enormous poverty, where poverty was getting clearly worse, contributed to the hostility against Tutsi. I mentioned yesterday the importance of land in this agricultural country and how the fields of Tutsi were allocated almost immediately when the genocide began, often to the very people who had killed them. Other kinds of property was allocated as well. I'm thinking particularly of the contents of the small traders' booths at the open-air market in Butare, which were distributed to people who had participated in attacking Tutsi. So the idea that the Tutsi wealth set them apart was unjustifiably earned. And, what's more, the prospect that that wealth could become a reward for people who participated in attacks against Tutsi, all of this is an important theme throughout these months that comes to extraordinary importance in the period of the genocide itself.

I would remark in this context, based on the discussions I have had with colleagues in genocide studies who work particularly on the field of the Holocaust, that the accusation that Jews were extraordinarily wealthy and had an unjustifiably large share of the wealth of Germany was a frequent accusation at the time of the Holocaust. (ICTR transcript, 22 May 2002: 198–200)

Charles Shamukiga, who was spoken about in the context of an RTLM broadcast falsely attributing the wealth to be in Tutsi hands, was often a target of RTLM before 7 April 1994 and this was a matter of great concern. Shamukiga spoke to then-Prosecutor Nsanzuwera about this programme and Nsanzuwera went to see him with a brigade commander. On the morning of 7 April, Shamukiga called Nsanzuwera to ask whether it was true that the president had been killed, because, on 2 April, RTLM had broadcast that Agathe Uwilingiyimana was planning the president's assassination, and then all the Tutsis would be exterminated. Shamukiga stated that if the president was in fact killed then they would be exterminated, and at that point Nsanzuwera could hear the Presidential Guard soldiers break into Shamukiga's house. His last words were 'this is it, I am going to die' and he was killed. Shamukiga and Sebera were two Tutsi businessmen who were often targeted by RTLM before 7 April. Sebera was also killed in the genocide (ICTR transcript, Nsanzuwera, 23 April 2001: 116–21, and 24 April 2001: 30–8).

On 28 December 1993, an RTLM broadcaster acknowledged being told his false programmes were 'heating up heads' and could cause ethnic violence (ICTR transcript, Nahimana testimony, 14 October 2002: 98–9):

Dear listeners who are tuned to Radio RTLM, I am here at Kigali International Trade Fair ... Er, I came from Radio Rwanda. As I said a few moments ago, I invited you, but I have also just met young men some of whom are *Inkotanyi*. The *Inkotanyi* have been here for a long time and we live with them. We live together and have become quite familiar. They said: 'we have listened to Radio RTLM, the things that you have just stated, namely that there are milk containers [*ibyansi*] and there are people who take drums to Nyacyonga in order to welcome the Fearless *Inkotanyi*, those things that you are saying on

Radio RTLM to heat up heads, are they really true, or your intention is to push people to kill one another?'

The minister of information later complained to RTLM officials about that particular broadcast as well as another on that date, which he explained were intended to incite ethnic unrest (ICTR exhibit P32B: 1–2):

> On the 28 December 1993, on the eve of the FPR battalion's arrival in Kigali, the RTLM broadcast throughout their programmes that this battalion was going to travel by a bus which was given to them only up until Nyacyonga but after Nyacyonga, they would get out of the bus and I quote 'march through Kigali.' These false rumours resulted in the soldiers being warned ... [O]n the same day, the RTLM made a statement about a welcome plan according to which the parents and relatives of the *Inkontanyi* must go and meet them in Nyacyonga, with churns full of milk[4] and beating drums. And as though this reference wasn't obvious enough, they had to add that this is what is needed to be done if one had to welcome the King Kigeli as he returned to restore his royalty.
>
> Remarks and references of these kind need no comment. I simply wanted to point out this fact. The same journalist was able to gather statements in Nyamirambo where the International Fair was taking place and one of the people interviewed, it was the journalist himself who recounted this, this person had expressed strong concerns about the false rumours that I have just mentioned. This person was saying expressly that if such remarks continue to be made, they will only incite people to start fighting. This is with regards to an anxiety expressed which was reported by one of the RTLM journalists. I am only making reference to this case because you yourselves broadcasted it. We record these types of complaints everyday.

Jean-Marie Vianney Higiro, the director of ORINFOR, was a frequent target of RTLM's wrath before 7 April 1994. Higiro, who had tried on several occasions to call RTLM to order for its reckless broadcasts, was often denounced by RTLM as a '*inyernzi*' collaborating with the enemy. On 7 January 1994, an RTLM broadcaster warned Higiro that if he continued to insist RTLM should be shut down then the Hutu people would rise up against him and things would turn bad against him (ICTR transcript, 6 November 2002: 33–7). Higiro did not go back to work after 6 April 1994, because he had fled in fear for his life (Higiro, see Chapter 7).

Self-fulfilling prophesies of violence were one of RTLM's specialties before and after 6 April 1994. On 21 January 1994 (ICTR exhibit P36/38D), RTLM broadcasters suggested that moderate opposition politicians Faustin Twagiramungu and Landould Ndasingwa[5] were behind an assassination plot and incited the population against them. They also suggested that Twagiramungu should be tear-gassed (ICTR transcript, 21 January 1994: 5–8). This was neither the first nor the last time that false and incendiary broadcasts against Twagiramungu were made. In October 1993, RTLM suggested Twagiramungu was involved in the assassination of President Ndadaye (ICTR exhibit P54: K0160116–K0160118).

On 21 January 1994, particularly clear warnings are acknowledged by RTLM that its 'heating up heads' was a cause of violence. In this same broadcast Tutsis are repeatedly referred to as 'tricky':

> So, [laughter] ... small children in Nyamirambo near the Café du Peuple —near the Café du Peuple in Nyamirambo – very small children – small Tutsi children came up to me and said, 'Hello Kantano. We like you, but please, do not heat up our heads.' [laughter]. I laughed my head off: 'Hey, kids, how do I heat up your heads?' They answered, 'you see when we walk around, we are few in number and when you talk about Tutsis we are afraid, and we see CDR members are going to pounce on us. Leave that alone and do not heat up our heads!'
>
> No! Of course, you're only kids. That's not what I'm talking about. But of this war, the current war, the period we are in, this difficult period when the Hutus and the Tutsis are deceiving one another and are at conflict ... lying in order to entrap and kill one another. I cannot but explain the situation and mention the liars by name. As long as the Tutsis wish to regain power through trickery, everyone has the duty to alert the majority people and tell them to be on their guard because the achievements they fought for in 1959 are under threat. You are young, you know nothing about the events of 1959 or the current situation. You still have a lot to learn. Nonetheless, listen to your elder brothers and sisters and ask your fathers and mothers, 'What's going to happen to us now that you want to take us back to the past?' Ask them questions.
>
> As for me, all I am doing is explaining events as they unfold. Each and every event calls for commentary. Children, do not be overly upset with me, I have nothing against the Tutsis, the Twas or the Hutus. I am a Hutu, but I have nothing against the Tutsis. However, given the current political situation, I have the duty to explain and say, 'Beware! The Tutsis are trying to appropriate the Hutus' property by force or trickery.' However, my remarks do not in any way imply hatred for the Tutsis. They are simply clarifications. Indeed, every event calls for commentary. (RTLM transcript of broadcaster Kantano Habimana, ICTR exhibit P36/38E)

Although many of the pre-7 April RTLM broadcasts that have been found mention the Rwandan Patriotic Front (RPF), RTLM journalists in that period acknowledged that to them there was no difference between Tutsis and the RPF. In a 1–2 February 1994 emission, an RTLM broadcaster is heard saying that 'Tutsis and RPF are the same' (ICTR exhibit P36/44C). RTLM's incendiary anti-RPF propaganda was not merely anti-RPF, it was also anti-Tutsi. RTLM equated the RPF to the Tutsi.

In February 1994, RTLM was called in by the Ministry of Information for a second time. Ferdinand Nahimana, Jean-Bosco Barayagwiza and Felcien Kabuga, along with Phocas Habimana, represented RTLM (ICTR transcript,

9 April 2001: 35, 40–1). Radio Rwanda covered part of the meeting. The video excerpts were televised by Radio Rwanda (ICTR exhibits P177A and C); the journalist notes in his coverage of that meeting that

> The situation is very hot, but for some, it even heats up the heads. Radio RTLM is loved, but it is also in trouble during these days. While some still want its programs to reach them, others are complaining about it, accusing it of fostering division, especially between Hutus and Tutsis. In a recent meeting that the Minister of Information held with the RTLM bosses, he expressed his views about this radio. He said: 'Your radio misleads the population and its programs can cause ethnic division.' He added: 'It should cease persuading Rwandans that the Tutsis are at the root of the problems that Rwanda is experiencing since this is not true. It should stop slandering and harassing people. If it is not careful, severe measures may be taken against it.'

In the video, the minister himself is seen telling the RTLM officials that:

> The kind of press that I strongly wish to see in Rwanda, our country, is the one that supports democracy and peace, the one that promotes reconciliation among Rwandans. As for the type of press that sets one ethnic group against the other, which *sets the heads on fire*, sets one region against the other, or causes strife between Rwandans and their friends, this has no place and should never have any in this country.
>
> Normally, a good journalist should abide by the following principles:
>
> Principle one: He should avoid slander (calumny)
> Principle two: He should avoid pointing an accusing finger without evidence
> Principle three: He should report unaltered facts
> Principle four: He should avoid reporting lies
>
> Visibly, RTLM journalists have not adhered to these principles, and this is the topic that we are going to discuss during this meeting. During our last meeting, we had agreed that the RTLM programs would be neutral vis-à-vis political parties and ethnic groups. Unfortunately, RTLM continues to show that it is a political party, that it serves the MRND and the CDR, and that it is a Hutus' mouthpiece ... If this attitude is not redressed, the government may take measures against RTLM.

Witness GO testified that the RTLM contingent stated that they would continue to give time to anyone who would come to testify about Tutsi tricks and their Hutu accomplices; they called the Arusha accords, not a peace accord, but rather a trap to neutralize the revolution of 1959. The RTLM contingent threatened the ministry and accused it of becoming perfect *Inyenzis*. The minister appealed to RTLM to stop broadcasting hate (ICTR transcript, 9 April 2001: 49, 54, 58).

A 'working document' prepared by the ministry for that February meeting noted that RTLM would regularly:

- assimilate all the members of the RPF to the iniquitous Tutsi;
- assimilate the political problems of the country to the RPF;
- reduce the political problems of Rwanda to the ethnic hatred between Hutu and Tutsi;
- assimilate the Tutsi from the inside with the *Inkontanyi*;
- explain to the country that all the evil the country suffers is caused by the Tutsi. (ICTR exhibit P29B: 1–3)

The minister's written address for that meeting noted that complaints about RTLM were being received by human rights associations on a daily basis and that RTLM was leading the country into a race war based on incitement and misinformation during particularly dangerous times (ICTR exhibit P32B: 1–3).

Witness GO drafted a report of the meeting. When he took it to Barayagwiza at the Ministry of Foreign Affairs, Barayagwiza grabbed it, read it closely, then threw it in GO's face. Barayagwiza said that he no longer wanted to see an *Inkontanyi* in his office and that if the Ministry of Information people continued to proceed in the manner they were, then its members would see what was going to happen (ICTR transcript, 10 April 2001: 4–6).

On 25 February 1994, the human rights defence association, AVP, condemned the calls for the extermination of the Tutsi that were being broadcast by RTLM. On the same day, *Interahamwe* President Robert Kajuga presided over a meeting of *Interahamwe* leaders calling for great vigilance vis-à-vis Kigali Tutsi, who should be listed (Chrétien expert report: ICTR exhibits P117B and P163B: 26927; FIDH and HRW 1999: 195).

For some time before February 1994, Minister of Information Rucogoza had been telling Kigali Prosecutor Francois Xavier Nsanzuwera that RTLM was inciting ethnic hatred and violence and that he was worried about it (ICTR transcript, 23 April 2001: 39–41). In February 1994, Rucogoza called a third meeting regarding the media and RTLM, which he asked Nsanzuwera to attend. Ferdinand Nahimana attended on behalf of RTLM. Also at the meeting was Andre Kameya, editor-in-chief of the moderate opposition magazine *Rwanda Rushya*. The minister said that although he respected freedom of speech, the inciting broadcasts and newspaper reports must be stopped. Mr Kameya told Nahimana that, although his paper criticized the regime, it did not promote ethnic division like RTLM, which was broadcasting hate messages. He called RTLM journalists criminals, which angered Nahimana, who accused Kameya[6] of behaving like an agent of the RPF. Nahimana would not accept the fact that RTLM was doing anything wrong. After the meeting, RTLM's programmes became even worse (ICTR transcript, 23 April 2001: 33–41).

Rucogoza told Nsanzuwera that he was still worried about RTLM's broadcasts. Although Nsanzuwera had initially favoured fining RTLM as a sanction, he now suggested that it was time to shut the station down. Rucogoza replied that 'if we do so, they are going to kill us; they are going to massacre us' (ICTR transcript, 23 April 2001: 39–41).

Witness GO testified that from the time the minister of information wrote the 25 October 1993 letter to RTLM, RTLM targeted and threatened him on the radio often. On 7 April 1994, Rucogoza and his entire family were exterminated, as were four other Ministry of Information staff working on the RTLM dossier (ICTR transcript, 10 April 2001: 7–11, 39–40).

An RTLM transcript from 18 March 1994 contains one of the threats made against Rucogoza by RTLM's Kantano Habimana:

> We met and then he asked: 'Kantano, why do you really talk about me?' Ha! In fact, I think people told me that he has become wise. Our bone of contention was that he wanted to close down the RTLM, the people's radio ... Ha! He probably realized this was no easy task; he realized that this was like carrying a cross. He has given up and this is no longer one of his topics. Obviously, he reports what his bosses want him to say, but he realized that the idea of closing down the people's radio could cause him a lot of trouble, which is why he gave up. I said to him: 'If you have now given us peace, we will do the same for you. We will then leave you alone.' This was the only bone of contention between us. We here (at the RTLM) harbor no hatred, but we cannot put up with people who look down upon us or who irritate us. That is all. We have nothing against people whosoever, and *Rucogoza* can thus rest easy, if he has given us peace, all we can do is reciprocate. (ICTR exhibit P36/65D)

People were afraid to file complaints against RTLM, but Francois Xavier Nsanzuwera's boss, Alphonse Marie Nkubito, filed one because Kantano Habimana of RTLM made a broadcast stating that Nkubito was part of a plot to murder the president and was receiving large amounts of money for his participation in this plot. This was broadcast shortly after Nkubito escaped a grenade attack. Nkubito asked Nsanzuwera to speak to broadcaster Kantano Habimana; Nsanzuwera mentioned that he also wanted to ask Noël Hitimana about other broadcasts that were inciting hatred. Nsanzuwera summoned both broadcasters in March 1994. Kantano claimed that all he had done (regarding the Nkubito broadcast) was to read a telegram given to him by his supervisor, Ferdinand Nahimana. Kantano said that if Nsanzuwera wanted the original, he should ask Nahimana for the text, because at RTLM the journalists were only small fish and that Nahimana wrote some of the editorials (ICTR transcript, 23 April 2001: 43–50).

Dealing with RTLM was difficult. The station's journalists announced on the radio when they had been summoned to the prosecutor's office. Staff within the prosecutor's office would spend their days listening to RTLM, because the mention of someone's name on the radio was almost a sentence to death. It was especially difficult for Nsanzuwera to summon the RTLM journalists between 1992 and 1994, as it was not easy to ask for gendarmarie reinforcement. Initially the journalists refused to appear. Then, later, when Kantano informed his listeners about being summoned, it was tantamount to calling on the *Interahamwe* and *Impuzamgambi* to besiege the prosecutor's office. When the RTLM journalists were summoned in March, neighbourhoods in Kigali that were controlled by the *Interahamwe* and *Impuzamgambi* were in such a state of continuous violence that people were afraid to set foot outside after dark (ICTR transcript, 23 April 2001: 43–50). A 30 March 1994 RTLM transcript describes youth surrounding the prosecutor's office on behalf of RTLM (ICTR exhibit P41B: 9–10).

After Nsanzuwera informed Nkubito about his conversation with Kantano Habimana, Nkubito replied that, even if Ferdinand Nahimana was behind the broadcast, he could not be summoned because that meant the whole *Akazu* (those close to the president) was behind RTLM. He advised Nsanzuwera not to try to interrogate Nahimana, as he would be killed (ICTR transcript, 23 April 2001: 43–50).

Nkubito was often targeted on RTLM; he was called an accomplice of the RPF. The first time Nsanzuwera heard his own name on RTLM was in late February or early March 1994, when he arrested a suspect in the killing of Minister Gatabazi: he was threatened on the radio (ICTR transcript, 23 April 2001: 85–95). An RTLM transcript of 30 March 1994 contains an exchange regarding two visits of RTLM broadcasters to Prosecutor Nkubito's office (ICTR exhibit P41B: 9–10). The journalists revelled in recounting that youth surrounded the prosecutors office threatening consequences should action be taken against them.[7]

On 30 March 1994, an RTLM broadcaster incited Hutus against Tutsis by making false claims about a supposed plot to exterminate Hutus in the Bugesera region. This was particularly incendiary in light of the massacres of Tutsis that took place in that region in March 1992, after a similar communiqué was read on the air (ICTR exhibit P41B: 1).[8] In the same emission, RTLM broadcaster Valérie Bemeriki called for violence and shooting on the spot.

In RTLM broadcases on 10, 11 and 14 March 1994, Bemeriki acknowledged that RTLM was being called 'Radio *Nkotsa*' (*Nkotsa* is a bird that signifies doom and bad omens (ICTR transcript, 14 October 2002: 2)). She also warned the *conseillier* who used this term, and went on to say that RTLM teaches Rwandans how to behave, and that it awakens all Rwandans including those in the army. She went on to target specific Tutsis in a certain area, referring to them as people 'all from the same ethnic group' congregating for 'dubious purposes' (ICTR exhibit P36/53B).

International journalist Collette Braeckman testified that during a March 1994 conference on the role of the press in Kigali, she was present at a session when Rwandan journalist François Byabyibwanzi spoke, saying that some of the press were emphasizing ethnic groups and telling people to be 'suspicious of our neighbours'; he said that this type of discussion 'could push Rwandans to kill each other'. According to Braeckman, Byabyibwanzi 'particularly questioned RTLM'. Nahimana and Gaspard Gahigi, the editor-in-chief of RTLM attended that conference (ICTR transcript, 29 November 2001: 98–107, 111).

Witness BI testified that in the pre-April period she was mentioned several times on RTLM as an accomplice of the enemy, and each mention was followed by an attack (ICTR transcript, 8 May 2001: 80–98). She and other human rights activists would listen to RTLM because the broadcasters had started to mention specific neighbourhoods and name individual people; some hours later these neighbourhoods and individuals would be attacked and ransacked by members of the *Interahamwe* and *Impuzamugambi*. In March 1994, these youth militias were omnipresent, uniformed, carrying radios and singing songs about the extermination of the enemy (ICTR transcript, 8 May 2001: 61–71).

On 30 March 1994, notorious extremist Coalition pour la Défense de la République (CDR) party member Katumba[9] was killed in Kigali. RTLM transcripts show that immediately on his death, his brother came to RTLM for 'assistance' (ICTR exhibit P103/187B: K0113770). In a 1 April 1994 emission, RTLM broadcasters target people, including a Tutsi doctor, who they claim to be the killers based on what they refer to as rumours (ICTR exhibit P103/189B: K0165912–3).

RTLM was in the business of stirring up trouble by interpreting mundane disputes as part of the enemy's supposed master plan to destroy the majority people (that is, Hutus). According to RTLM, any controversy, no matter how big or small, was due to the RPF and Tutsi. On 30 March 1994, law students at the faculty of law in Mburabutaro were protesting their conditions. On RTLM, Valérie Bemeriki and another journalist both suggested the strike was an *Inkontanyi* trick (ICTR exhibits P41B: 12–13 and P103/187B: K0113761). The second journalist, however, was unprepared for the live response given to him on the scene by a courageous student who protested the station's blaming the strike, and everything else, on Tutsis and demanded that the station verify its reports (ICTR exhibit P103/187B: K0113753–6).

On 2 April 1994, RTLM claimed that moderate Hutu Prime Minister Agathe Uwilingiyimana was planning to assassinate the president and would stage a coup with those who came from her own prefecture. It went on to announce that if the president was killed, the Tutsis be exterminated. Five days later, Agathe Uwilingiyimana was indeed killed by the Presidential Guard (ICTR transcript, Nsanzuwera testimony, 23 April 2001: 95–8).

Also on 2 April, one broadcaster repeatedly attacks two of RTLM's favourite pre-7 April 1994 targets, Agathe Uwilingiyimana, and moderate Joseph Kavaruganda, president of the Supreme Court of Appeal, both of whom were killed violently on 7 April:

> Mrs Uwilingiyimana Agathe is alerting people that she saw a person with a dagger [near her house]. Imagine that this is the first time she sees a person carrying a weapon!! Now if you go to visit Mrs Uwilinigiyimana you have to be thoroughly searched. It is a pity that there is little confidence. (ICTR exhibit P103/190B: K0147056)

> How is Mrs Uwilinigiyimana Agathe, minister of the never ending transitional government? She is also threatened! She says that she spends sleepless nights

> though she is protected by UNAMIR troops. She is terrified by a knife!! People were really astonished when they heard the statement on the radio! They ask themselves why such a statement about the knife is broadcasted before any investigation is made! What would have happened if they had seen a gun! (ICTR exhibit P103/190B: K0147059)

> I think people should know that diamond can cut diamond. What is a shame after all is to hear a statement from the Prime Minister's office that they have seen a simple knife! A knife, which has not even a safety catch! The visitor could even hold a gun or show it to the security service of the Prime Minister. They could then keep it for him! So, there must be 'something in the wind' for those people who think they could be killed. They should not think they are wanted because of power sharing, but it is rather because of their treachery! A person named Kavaruganda, Joseph, President of the Supreme Court of Appeal, is also afraid because of his treachery. That is fine! Should they be afraid since those traitors have betrayed the people! (ICTR exhibit P103/190B: K0147060)

> Kavaruganda is screamingly funny! Because of his wickedness, he has no driver! (ICTR exhibit P103/190B: K0147060)

> Mugenzi Justin, president of PL party, said at Nyamirambo regional stadium that those who plot against our republic will undergo a terrible disaster and that that disaster is death which always threatens people like Kavaruganda and Agathe. (ICTR exhibit P103/190B: K0147061)

In a 3 April 1994 emission, an RTLM broadcaster repeatedly goes after Tutsis as well as Kavaruganda once again:

> There are lots of information. Mr Twiringiyimana Augustin who lives in Sector Rusiga in Shyorongi has just phoned me to ask RTLM to condemn Tutsis who send names of Hutus to the RPF so that they can be exterminated. So we ask you Noel to inform the people about our imminent death. (ICTR exhibit P103/192F: K0147079)

> [People] have sent RTLM a list of persons who are accomplices of *Inkontanyis*. Those persons are the following: Mr Sebucinganda of Butete in Kidaho commune, Ms. Laurencia Kura, wife of Gakenyeri, living in Butete sector, The Counsellor of Butete Sector is also an accomplice of *Inkontanyis*. (ICTR exhibit P103/192F: K0147080)

> And Kavarurganda!? Will he go to Shyorongi to rest there? He will not find a way to go there. People will not allow him to arrive at the place. He cannot dare go there now if he is a man. I saw the people of Kimihurura asking his bodyguards to shoot him but the latter laughed. I was watching. (ICTR exhibit P103/192F: K0147087)

> Mugabo Xavier who lives in Kagarama was seriously beaten by Makuza's relations. They have robbed him of everything. Keep courageous and take care dear brother! Your neighbors are known and they are Tutsi relations of Gastete. The latter has fled and his whereabouts are not known. Among your neighbors we can name the three brothers who work at Rwanda foam and whose names are Marco and Victory. People who beat you are known but we think there is no problem since you are also strong. (ICTR exhibit P103/192F: K0147086)

Two Hutus particularly targeted by RTLM in the pre-7 April period were André Gasesero (a primary school teacher) and Zacharia Serubyobo (a tradesman). Both were horrifically killed in April 1994. For RTLM, the only thing almost as bad as a Tutsi was a 'Hutu who does not remember ... the Revolution of 1959'.[10] Witness GO knew these two men well and testified in detail about several pre-April 1994 RTLM broadcasts inciting violence against them, particularly because they had good relations with their Tutsi neighbours and were falsely said to be involved in plots against Hutus. They became so hated as a result of RTLM's broadcasts that even their valuables were destroyed after they were killed. GO testified to RTLM's pre-April targeting of other moderate Hutus and Tutsis in that same neighbourhood, who were later slain during the genocide (ICTR transcripts, 22 and 23 March 1994, and 10 April 2001: 62–7, 92–3, 100–101; exhibits P36/43D and P33: K0032661–K0032662).

Another witness, FW, testified that even before 7 April 1994, he heard incendiary ethnically oriented songs by the notorious anti-Tutsi musician Simon Bikindi, ethnic propaganda and the notoriously anti-Tutsi 'Ten commandments of Hutus' on RTLM (ICTR transcript, 1 March 2001: 122–3).

Radio Rwanda journalist Thomas Kamilindi testified that from January to April 1994, RTLM broadcast messages that brought fear to the Tutsi people and to the political opponents of the regime. He went on to state that during this period RTLM

> [O]ften talked about the history of Rwanda, how the history of Rwanda evolved, with emphasis on domination and colonization of Tutsis over Hutus. And they referred to 1959, saying that it was the victory of the Hutus over that colonization. But also about the war – they said that the RPF was infiltrating through bars, drinking bars that were being opened in the town, and that young Tutsi girls were infiltrating all the way to the top commandant of UNAMIR. Commander General Dallaire, according to RTLM, the Tutsis of RPF, the *Inyenzi* – the enemy *Inyenzi* had given him a woman to live with him, a companion. (ICTR transcript, 21 May 2001: 68)

Dr Alison Des Forges noted that, well before 6 April 1994: 'Often RTLM's attacks on UNAMIR were personalized at General Dallaire and in many cases involved insinuations of sexual activity between UNAMIR officers and Tutsi women' (ICTR transcript, 22 May 2002: 119).

Even Jean-Marie Biju-Duval, lead counsel for Ferdinand Nahimana, has stated in regard to RTLM's broadcasts of January through March (particularly

March) 1994, 'the propaganda that was being broadcast albeit, this is very unfortunate – was a political propaganda based on ethnic views' (ICTR transcript, 25 April 2001: 21–2).

People were afraid of RTLM, and they nicknamed it 'Radio *Rutswitsi*' even before 7 April 1994 (*rutswitsi* means to burn, which in Rwanda refers to sowing and spreading ethnic violence (ICTR transcript, Nsanzuwera testimony, 24 April 2001: 42–3)). The messages of hate and ethnic violence were so frequent that people were very afraid of RTLM. They believed they had to listen to it constantly. Well before April 1994, one would find little radios in offices, cafés, bars, taxis – everywhere people gathered, they would be listening to RTLM (ICTR transcript, 23 April 2001: 50–5, 75–85, 87–8, and 24 April: 42–3). People told Prosecutor Nsanzuwera that they would even pay journalists not to have their names mentioned on RTLM, because it was considered a death sentence (ICTR transcript, 23 April 2001: 95). The messages of RTLM were messages of hatred and of incitement to violence even before 7 April. Overwhelming evidence suggests that RTLM was created for the reality that came later. As one witness testified: the genocide didn't happen in one day after beginning on 7 April, because before 7 April RTLM prepared the genocide, and after 7 April it implemented it (ICTR transcript, GO testimony, 10 April 2001: 44–5).

Finally, it is important to observe that warning calls to be on guard against the FPR and to prepare for war were accompanied by statements claiming and highlighting the unchangeable nature of ethnic differences: Hutus should recognize each other, assemble together, learn their secret, in the face of the 'international Tutsi community', which is raising funds (RTLM broadcasts of 25 and 26 October 1993). In a programme recorded on 31 October 1993, Ferdinand Nahimana recalled that 90 per cent of RPF members were Tutsis. In November 1993, RTLM affirmed that the *Inkotanyi* were the direct successors of the *Inyenzi*, who had already launched attacks in 1962 and 1967, that President Obote had helped Rwanda, but the *Inyenzi* were allies of Museveni. Concerning the events in Burundi, RTLM broadcaster Noël Hitimana was happy that Mrs Agathe Uwilingiyimana had at last recognized that a Hutu is a Hutu and a Tutsi a Tutsi. He then embarked on commentaries on the cultural, physical and psychological distinctions between a Hutu and a Tutsi. In conclusion, he hurled: 'You can be recognized, irrespective of your physical appearance' or the shape of your nose – the difference is like that between a white and a black (Chrétien et al. expert report: ICTR exhibits P117B and P163B: 26793; ICTR exhibits P117B, P163B, P36/4C: K0146846).

Additional references to pre-7 April 1994, criminal RTLM broadcasts can be found throughout the Chrétien et al. expert report tendered into evidence in the Media Trial (exhibits P117B and P163B).

RTLM'S INFECTIOUS STYLE BEFORE 6 APRIL 1994

speak to me as to thy thinkings,
As thou dost ruminate, and give thy worst of thoughts
The worst of words.

William Shakespeare, *Othello Act 3 Scene 3*

In a conference paper presented in March 1994, RTLM editor-in-chief Gaspard Gahigi claimed that Radio Rwanda's formal and outmoded language was a major reason for its lack of impact on the Rwandan population. According to Gahigi, Rwandans were 'poorly informed' because the 'official media has ... retained its traditional rhetoric' (ICTR exhibit P76: 16). RTLM, on the other hand, presented informal and unstructured commentaries on various subjects, usually in the form of dialogues, and relied on lengthy interviews with guests to fill time. They also introduced the modern concept of audience participation, broadcasting RTLM's studio telephone number and inviting listeners to call in with their comments. Broadcasters often relayed messages from listeners or referred to conversations they had had with those who called the station (Article 19 1996: 84–7).

On many occasions before April 1994, RTLM's broadcasts were crude. The incredibly heavy drinking and unprofessionalism for which Noël Hitimana lost his position as a Radio Rwanda broadcaster became an asset at RTLM. His alcoholism also provided material for jokes that were no doubt intended to shock listeners. On 3 April 1994, Hitimana used shock humour by making light of his drinking with a listener who, supposedly, telephoned to ask why he was always in such a good mood. Hitimana responded by using a traditional expression to broach the taboo subject of alcoholism and joked about the extent of his drinking (ICTR transcript, 5 November 2002: 119–21).

In that same broadcast, Hitimana, who was notorious for his vulgarity, used the act of passing wind as a metaphor – 'If a person breaks wind it's better if it stinks' (ICTR exhibit P103/192F: K0147081). This type of language, although shocking and offensive to some listeners, attracted a certain section of the population who were to form its most avid fans: young people and delinquents. This was an important target audience as young, destitute people formed the vast majority of militia members, with the exception of high-ranking leaders who tended to be older and part of the elite. This was a group that had not been impressed by the standard government propaganda about the RPF and Tutsis, based on uninteresting and obscure references to the past. In his writings, Ferdinand Nahimana (1993: 21) once quoted an elderly informant who said that oral history might be lost because 'our children are more fascinated by the radio'. RTLM set out to be the radio station that fascinated and captured the minds of the youth. In August 1993, Nahimana explained to Reporters Sans Frontières reporter Phillippe Dahinden that RTLM was 'an entertainment radio geared to the youth' (ICTR transcript, 24 October 2000: 68–74).

Witness Z1 for Nahimana's defence noted the immaturity of RTLM's listeners and the danger some messages posed to young minds even before the plane crash (ICTR transcript, 5 November 2002: 100–1). Z1 testified that even before 6 April 1994, RTLM broadcasted 'incendiary messages' and such messages could have been received negatively by listeners who were not 'mature enough to analyze such information' (ICTR transcript, 5 November 2002: 93–4).

THE JOURNALISTS HIRED BY RTLM BEFORE 6 APRIL 1994

According to the accused, Ferdinand Nahimana, RTLM journalists were the cream of the crop and only became unprofessional and unhinged alcoholic, marijuana smokers after 6 April:

> I said that after the 6th of April until July, these were not journalists like the ones I had known before; Kantano, Gahigi, all of them, before the 6th of April, they were normal journalists. Now what happened after the 6th of April, in fact I am able to deduce that their behavior, the way they acted was because of the state of war, amongst other things, the drugs and alcohol, which was exaggerated. And then another element ... which I found that maybe exacerbated the behavior of these journalists, on the 17th of April 1994, when a bomb fell on the RTLM building and journalist Hitimana was hit and his leg had to be amputated ... and these journalists were unnerved ... Otherwise, I do not want to give the impression that before the 6th of April these journalists were not good journalists. They were among the cream of journalists before the 6th of April 1994. (ICTR transcript, 25 September 2002: 27–8)

Nahimana's testimony was rebutted by his own witness, Z1, who was in as good a position as the accused to know the truth (ICTR transcript, 5 November 2002: 99–100):

> Q: I am asking you, did RTLM journalists discredit RTLM before the 6th of April 1994? Yes or no.
> A: Yes.
> Q: ... Why do you say that RTLM journalists were not la crème de la crème before the 6th of April 1994?
> A: According to the information that you gave to me, that is, RTLM journalists being cream of the cream, I would say that I do not agree with that assertion, because I have an experience, and my experience is that among those journalists there were some journalists who had worked at ORINFOR and had been dismissed from ORINFOR due to lack of professionalism and lack of seriousness, and since I was among the leaders, senior officials of ORINFOR, I knew that those journalists were not competent, and they were working in RTLM. I knew that they were not the cream of the crop, because I knew why they had been dismissed.

When asked questions about three of the RTLM journalists (Hitimana, Rucogoza and Gahigi) who had previously worked at ORINFOR, witness Z1 was able to provide specific information about their misconduct (ICTR transcript, 5 November 2002: 102–4). He recounted that he had seen Noël Hitimana (one of the first journalists hired by RTLM in 1993) drunk while he was working at ORINFOR. Although Hitimana was fired after a specific episode of misconduct, his alcoholism was chronic and persistent and he was not fired for that episode alone, but because the administration's patience had finally run out.

Z1 testified that ORINFOR employee Emmanuel Rucogoza, who came to work for RTLM in January 1994, was sacked and dismissed from ORINFOR for misconduct and 'there was also the fact that he was incompetent' (ICTR transcript, 6 November 2002: 17–18). Regarding Gaspard Gahigi, hired by RTLM in 1993, Z1 stated: 'What I can remember about [Mr Gahigi] is that at times he drank a bit, a bit too much, and I believe it was not acceptable' (ICTR transcript, 7 November 2002: 63).

Another RTLM journalist who began working for RTLM in January 1994, Valérie Bemeriki, was an *Interahamwe* (ICTR transcript, 10 April 2003: 33–4). Georges Ruggiu, who also began working for RTLM in January 1994, had no previous journalism experience.

Cream of the crop? – certainly not. RTLM officials employed the bottom of the barrel to assist them in their criminal enterprise. An enterprise often aimed at mobilizing the lowest common denominator. As Hitler wrote in *Mein Kampf*: 'All propaganda has to be popular and has to adapt its spiritual level to the perception of the least intelligent of those towards whom it intends to direct itself.'

CONCLUSION

Long before the common era, Pindar stressed that 'words have a longer life than deeds' (Pindar 518–438 BC). In more modern times, '[Edmund] Burke said there were three estates in parliament; but in the reporters' gallery yonder, there sat a fourth estate more important than them all.' RTLM's broadcasts after 6 April could not have had the impact they did without the several months of conditioning of the population by its earlier emissions. Although this review of RTLM's impact before 6 April can leave no doubt that its broadcasts were violative of international criminal and humanitarian law, the more difficult question remains at what point should the international community have stepped in to ban or jam its airwaves.

In the Media Trial, the ICTR judges held that: 'In considering whether particular expression constitutes a form of incitement on which restrictions would be justified, the international jurisprudence does not include any specific causation requirement linking the expression at issue with the demonstration of a direct effect' (ICTR 2003: para. 1007). The judges cited the Nuremberg verdict against *Der Stürmer* publisher Julius Streicher for the proposition that there need not be such a direct causal link:

> In the ... case of Julius Streicher, there was no allegation that Streicher's publication *Der Stürmer* was tied to any particular violence. Much more generally, it was found to have 'injected into the minds of thousands of Germans' a 'poison' that caused them to support the National Socialist policy of Jewish persecution and extermination. In international humanitarian law

the question considered is what the likely impact might be, recognizing that causation in this context might be relatively indirect.

The Media Trial judges found no problem in criminalizing the pre-plane crash broadcasts along with those thereafter. There is no doubt that the likely impact of those earlier broadcasts was known to all, even if the causation element of these early broadcasts was relatively indirect.

The judges took pains to note that they were not troubled by a possible chilling effect of criminalizing such speech, where the objectionable speech was that of a powerful majority against a vulnerable minority:

> 1008. The Chamber notes that international standards restricting hate speech and the protection of freedom of expression have evolved largely in the context of national initiatives to control the danger and harm represented by various forms of prejudiced communication. The protection of free expression of political views has historically been balanced in the jurisprudence against the interest in national security. The dangers of censorship have often been associated in particular with the suppression of political or other minorities, or opposition to the government. *The special protections developed by the jurisprudence for speech of this kind, in international law and more particularly in the American legal tradition of free speech, recognize the power dynamic inherent in the circumstances that make minority groups and political opposition vulnerable to the exercise of power by the majority or by the government.* ***These circumstances do not arise in the present case, where at issue is the speech of the so-called 'majority population', in support of the government.*** *The special protections for this kind of speech should accordingly be adapted, in the Chamber's view, so that ethnically specific expression would be more rather than less carefully scrutinized to ensure that minorities without equal means of defence are not endangered.*
> 1009. Moreover, the expression charged as incitement to violence was situated, in fact and at the time by its speakers, not as a threat to national security but rather in defence of national security, aligning it with state power rather than in opposition to it. Thus there is justification for adaptation of the application of international standards, which have evolved to protect the right of the government to defend itself from incitement to violence by others against it, rather than incitement to violence on its behalf against others, particularly as in this case when the others are members of a minority group. (ICTR 2003, emphasis added)

Although criminalizing the pre-April speech is justifiable under international law, the practicality and legality of jamming the airwaves of RTLM before 6 April is not as clear. Before the international community resorts to jamming, the government (or moderate elements therein) ought to be given a chance to discipline broadcasters. In Rwanda, the moderate elements were thwarted at every juncture in their courageous attempts to call RTLM to order. The international community failed to support the efforts of those elements through sanctions, financial support and perhaps the creation of another radio station (the cure to objectionable speech often being more speech rather than less). If in future scenarios the international community seriously supports democratic reforms to counter hate speech, the last resort of jamming of a radio station by the international community (after most of the damage has already been done) may not be necessary.

NOTES

1. See, for example, the testimony of Dr Alison Des Forges of Human Rights Watch: 'At the time, when I talked to people on the telephone, and I would say that I talked to General Dallaire; I talked to representatives of the church; I talked to representatives of nongovernmental organizations, as well as to many ordinary people – and I would say that, of those contacts I had, the vast majority talked of the need to silence RTLM. To me, this became an essential point of action. We who were trying to stop the genocide saw RTLM as a crucial aspect of that killing campaign ... in other words, it's what people said to me at the time when I talked to them on the telephone. It was "stop this radio." And the accounts of daily broadcasts – whether they were naming specific targets, whether they were encouraging attacks in general – these struck terror into the hearts of the victims who listened to the radio, who listened to RTLM as much as they could. The victims listened to this radio. They took it seriously, as well as the assailants at the barriers and on the streets' (ICTR transcript: 23 May 2002, para: 265–9; see also, Des Forges 2002).
2. The judges found that RTLM broadcasts, to varying degrees, were criminal both before and after 6 April 1994 (ICTR 2003: para. 485–7, 953, 974, 1017).
3. *Kangura* editor, Hassan Ngeze, testified that this Kinyarwandan phrase appears in *Kangura* 46 because it is a quote from the RTLM general assembly, which both he and witness AHA covered (ICTR transcript, 1 April 2003: 81–6, and 3 April 2003: 5–9). Ngeze also testified that this phrase essentially stems from a Rwandan proverb, '*Aho umutindi yanitse ntilva*' ('where an unfortunate person puts anything to dry, the sun will not shine'). One of the speakers at the general assembly changed the word '*umutindi*' to '*umututsi*', so that it would mean Tutsis have no chance (because of RTLM).
4. See Hassan Ngeze's trial testimony about the word 'milk' being used as reference to the Tutsi group, (ICTR transcript, 2 April 2003).
5. Ndasingwa, a Tutsi, was regularly a target of RTLM prior to 7 April 1994. Ndasingwa was brutally killed on 7 April 1994, at home, alongside his Canadian wife.
6. Kameya was killed during the genocide (ICTR transcript, 23 April 2001: 33–41).
7. Nsanzuwera and Nkubito miraculously survived. The latter was able to exit the country with foreign assistance and the former narrowly escaped death numerous times while hiding in the Milles Collines hotel, and later in Kabuga, all the while still targeted by RTLM (ICTR transcript, Nsanzuwera testimony, 23–24 April 2001)
8. In March 1992, a large massacre of Tutsi civilians by machete occurred after the repeated broadcasting of a controversial incendiary tract on Radio Rwanda. Nahimana was the director of ORINFOR at the time and authorized the broadcast of this unverified tract.
9. For information about Katumba's CDR activities, see ICTR exhibit P128 (as read out in court on 16 May 2002) and testimony of Agnes Murebwayire on 4 December 2001.
10. The Revolution of 1959 signifies the Hutu overthrow of the Tutsi regime, and often involved machetes.

REFERENCES

Note: Most of the documents of the ICTR can be found on its website, available at <www.ictr.org> and in the database of the Netherlands Institute of Human Rights <www.sim.law.uu.nl/>. The transcript and exhibits referred to in this article are from *The Prosecutor v. Ferdinand Nahimana, Jean-Bosco Barayagwiza and Hassan Ngeze*. Case no. ICTR-99–52-T. ICTR, Arusha, Tanzania.

Abrams, F. 2003. [Title unknown]. *The New York Times*, 5 December: 1.

Anonymous. 1993. RTLM: aho umututse yanitse ntiriva [RTLM: no chance for the Tutsi]. *Kangura*, 46 (July): 13.

Article 19. 1996. *Broadcasting Genocide, Censorship, Propaganda and State-Sponsored Violence in Rwanda, 1990–1994.* Article 19, London, UK. Available at <www.article19.org/pdfs/publications/rwanda-broadcasting-genocide.pdf> (accessed 23 August 2005).

Commission internationale d'enquête sur les violation des droits de l'homme au Burundi depuis le 21 octobre 1993. 1994. *Rapport final.* Human Rights Watch, International Federation of Human Rights Leagues, SOS-Torture, and Human Rights League of the Great Lakes, 5 July.

Des Forges, A. 2002. 'Silencing the Voices of Hate in Rwanda'. In M.E. Price and M. Thompson (eds) *Forging Peace, Intervention, Human Rights and the Management of Media Space*. Edinburgh University Press, Edinburgh, UK: 236–58.

FIDH (Fédération Internationale des Ligues des Droits de l'Homme) and HRW (Human Rights Watch). 1999. *Aucun témoin ne doit survivre*. Karthala, Paris, France.

Koestler, A. 1978. *Janus: a Summing Up*. Random House, New York, NY, USA.

Gourevitch, P. 1998. *We Wish to Inform You That Tomorrow We Will be Killed With Our Families: Stories from Rwanda*. Farrar, Straus and Giroux, New York, NY, USA.

ICTR (International Criminal Tribunal for Rwanda). n.d. General information. ICTR, Arusha, Tanzania. Available at <www.ictr.org/ENGLISH/geninfo/index.htm> (accessed 25 September 2005).

—— 2003. *The Prosecutor v. Ferdinand Nahimana, Jean-Bosco Barayagwiza and Hassan Ngeze*. Case no. ICTR-99–52-T: Judgement and sentence. Arusha, Tanzania, 3 December.

Nahimana, F. 1993. *Le Rwanda: emergence d'un État*. L'Harmattan, Paris, France.

NYT Editors. 2003. Editorial. *The New York Times*, 5 December.

Pindar, 518–438 BC. *Nemean odes*, IV, i.10.

UN (United Nations). 1966. *International covenant on civil and political rights*. General Assembly Resolution 2200A (XXI), 16 December. Available at <www.unhchr.ch/html/menu3/b/a_ccpr.htm> (accessed 6 September 2005).

27
The Challenges in Prosecuting Print Media for Incitement to Genocide

Charity Kagwi-Ndungu

> *It is up to the* Inyenzis *now to demonstrate that they are courageous and to know what will happen in the future. They should understand that if they commit the slightest mistake, then all of them will perish, and that if they make a mistake of once again attacking, launching an attack, no accomplice will survive in Rwanda. They should know that today all Hutus have become united; we're united as one man.*
>
> Hassan Ngeze (1994)

The standard arguments for free speech are well known. We cannot know the truth or the value of an hypothesis if its opponents are forbidden to challenge it or if its proponents are not allowed to defend it. Most of an individual's beliefs, including his or her scientific beliefs, are justified by his or her perception that they have emerged unscathed from the free confrontation of ideas and the unrestrained search for facts. We would be hard pressed to find a single idea now generally accepted that was not offensive to the majority at some time in history.

Throughout history, institutions and individuals have engaged in large-scale efforts to persuade and convince others of the rightness of their ideological views, cultural values and beliefs. The truth is that there have always been excuses and rationales for slavery, for the genocide of Jews, Gypsies and American Indians, with racial and cultural terms of 'us and them' and with the theft of land and resources.

The crime of 'incitement to genocide' knocks against the right to freedom of expression. The challenge is how to counter future war propaganda and speeches that jeopardize the lives of minority groups. Some parameters are laid down in the international law, especially in the landmark judgment in *The Prosecutor v. Ferdinand Nahimana, Jean-Bosco Barayagwiza and Hassan Ngeze*, case no. ICTR-99–52-T (the 'Media Trial') on the responsibility of the media and journalists and their role in the crimes committed in conflict situations without jeopardizing press freedom.

The definition of genocide set forth in the genocide convention (UN 1951) is authoritative and has been incorporated verbatim into the statutes of the Yugoslavian and Rwandan tribunals as well as those of the permanent

International Criminal Court. In addition to the crime of genocide itself, the genocide convention provides that the following acts shall be punishable: conspiracy to commit genocide, direct and public incitement to commit genocide, attempt to commit genocide, and complicity in genocide.

Article III(c) of the convention prohibits 'direct and public incitement to commit genocide'. In specifying this distinct act, the crime is crafted in such a way as to preclude any defence of freedom of expression. The crime of direct and public incitement to commit genocide, like conspiracy, is an inchoate crime, in that the prosecution need not make proof of any result. It is sufficient to establish that:

- The act of direct and public incitement took place.
- The direct and public incitement was intentional.
- It was carried out with the intent to destroy a protected group in whole or in part.

The genocide convention is not the only international document that speaks to the concept of freedom of expression. During the relevant period in 1994, Rwanda was a party to the following international conventions and treaties that directly address the limits of freedom of expression:

- *Convention on the Prevention and Punishment of the Crime of Genocide* (UN 1951) – ratified by Rwanda 16 April 1975.
- *International Covenant on Civil and Political Rights* (UN 1966a) – ratified by Rwanda 16 April 1975; Articles 19 and 20 specifically identify the right of freedom of expression, its limits and the responsibilities that are associated with this right.
- *Optional Protocol to the International Covenant on Civil and Political Rights* (UN 1966b) – ratified by Rwanda 16 April 1975.
- *International Covenant on Economic, Social and Cultural Rights* (UN 1966c) – ratified by Rwanda 16 April 1975.
- *International Convention on the Elimination of All Forms of Racial Discrimination* (UN 1965) – ratified by Rwanda 16 April 1975; in Article 5, 'state parties undertake to prohibit and eliminate racial discrimination in all its forms and to guarantee the right of everyone, without distinction as to race, colour, or national or ethnic origin, to equality before the law'.
- *African Charter on Human and Peoples' Rights* (OAU 1981) – ratified by Rwanda 15 July 1983; Article 9 provides that 'every individual shall have the right to receive information' and 'every individual shall have the right to express and disseminate his opinions within the law'.

These conventions show that freedom of expression is not absolute and can be limited in instances where it conflicts with the rights of others. Attaining the right balance between freedom of expression and its limits had indeed proved difficult in international law. 'International law … requires a contextual analysis … The use of the right to freedom of expression, if aimed to destroy the rights of others, constitutes an abuse of that right and as such may be restricted by law' (Farrior 1996). Although under international conventions and treaties all speech is protected, every one of these instruments also recognizes that certain restrictions on speech are permissible and are, in fact, often required to uphold certain other fundamental rights.

A BRIEF COMPARISON OF *KANGURA* AND *DER STÜRMER*

On 20 April 1923, the first copy of *Der Stürmer* ('The Attacker') was published; 71 years later in Rwanda the newspaper *Kangura*[1] ('Awake') first appeared. Fifty-nine issues of *Kangura* were published, more or less monthly, as well as a number of international issues. Publication ceased during the genocide and resumed in September 1994.

Circulation

Der Stürmer circulation amounted to a few thousand, fluctuating throughout the years of its publication. However, the sales figures do not reflect the number of people who actually read *Der Stürmer* or *Kangura. Der Stürmer* was displayed in specially constructed cases all over Germany. Constructed by local supporters in places where people naturally congregated – bus stops, parks, street corners, etc. – these display cases were often large and adorned with phrases from the paper such as '*Die Juden Sind Unser Unglück*' ('The Jews are our misfortune') (Bytwerk 2001).

Before the genocide, approximately 66 per cent of Rwandans were literate. *Kangura* was printed in relatively small numbers, but each issue was circulated to numerous readers. It was common practice for a person to buy a newspaper, photocopy it and distribute it, read it to his neighbour who could not read and read it in public places for people to listen (ICTR transcript, Marcel Kabanda, 13 May 2001: 58–9).

In January 1992, an article written by François Akimana, president of the Executive Committee of the National Parti pour la libération du peuple Hutu (PALIPEHUTU), describes the circulation of *Kangura*'s international edition:

> I do not have words to describe the prevailing situation. When this issue of the *Kangura* newspaper appeared, in some areas of Bujumbura, all the Hutus, particularly PALIPEHUTU members, heaved a deep sigh of relief. They distributed the newspaper everywhere, including prisons, to the extent that a copy could cost up to a 1,000 Burundi francs, that is, if you are lucky enough to get one because some people preferred to frame them so they could enlighten all family members. (Akimana 1992)

During the Media Trial, several witnesses gave evidence of this system of oral reporting. Witness FS (ICTR transcript, 7 February 2000: 40–1) stated that in Rwanda, people commonly read to each other. For example, he said an illiterate person might ask his child who goes to school to help him read articles from newspapers. Thus, people who could not read bought *Kangura* and asked others to read it for them.

Witness ABE (ICTR transcript, 27 February 2000: 49–50) stated that the literacy levels in Rwanda were very low; however, those who could read *Kangura* were able to explain it to those who could not read and thus the messages were widely disseminated. Witness AGX (ICTR transcript, 21 June 2001: 74) testified that although he did not buy *Kangura*, he borrowed copies from his neighbours and friends to read. Witness AFB (ICTR transcript, 6 March 2001: 23) stated that he did not buy *Kangura* but people who bought it would tell him the main points in each issue. Defence witness RM 10 (ICTR transcript, 20 January 2003: 34), who was illiterate, said that she would buy *Kangura* and ask someone to read it to her; she stated that this was a common practice in Rwanda.

Style

Like *Der Stürmer, Kangura* was filled with stories of scandal and crime. The articles were written by the editor Hassan Ngeze, a couple of staff writers and readers who submitted articles. Like *Der Stürmer*, the quality of the publication from a purely journalistic standpoint was lamentable. Nevertheless, both *Kangura* and *Der Stürmer* enjoyed enormous influence and support from leading authorities. Both were written in a style that the average person could easily understand. The writing was simple and straightforward, using short sentences and basic vocabulary. Ideas were repeated. Headlines, such as 'Inhabitants of Kigali remain vigilant: the enemy is still among us' (*Kangura* no. 20, August 1991) grabbed the reader's attention. And the cartoons were easily understood. Both journals adopted their local community's style of speaking, and had a similar effect.

In *Der Stürmer*, caricatures were used to present various themes of anti-Semitism. Jews were depicted as unshaven, short and fat with large, hooked noses and bulging eyes. They were also shown as vermin, snakes and spiders. The female form was often displayed nude or partly nude. In *Der Stürmer*, 'Aryan' women were often illustrated as the victims of Jews. These nude women made the paper especially attractive to young males (Bytwerk 2001).

Kangura also printed caricatures that were easy to comprehend by a largely illiterate community. The images were graphic and reinforce its message of morbid psychological antagonism of the Hutu masses against the Tutsi ethnic group. In *Kangura*, Tutsi women were depicted as seductress spies, and the Tutsi feudal regime was a consistent theme.

While *Der Stürmer* focused on a worldwide conspiracy of the Jews to take over the world based on the protocols of the elders of Zion,[2] *Kangura* propagated the ancient plan of the Tutsi to conquer the Central Africa region.[3] This was a theory based on the 19 Tutsi commandments.[4] It linked Tutsis living inside Rwanda with those who had exploited Hutus in the past, with the Rwandan Patriotic Front (RPF) and with all the Tutsi in the diaspora. For example, in a *Kangura* editorial in July 1991, Hassan Ngeze (1991) asserts: 'Tutsis always seek to reconquer power which Gahutu seized.'[5] He states that it can be proven that 85 per cent of Tutsis within the country have close or loose ties with the refugees and have become *Inyenzi-inkotany*i. He warns that Tutsis within the country always help their brothers, work day and night and never surrender. His message was clear that the *Inyenzi* were supported by Tutsis the world over.

Impact

Albert Forster, Gauleiter of Danzig, wrote:

> With pleasure I say that the *Stürmer*, more than any other daily or weekly newspaper, has made clear to the people in simple ways the danger of Jewry. Without Julius Streicher and his *Stürmer*, the importance of a solution to the Jewish question would not be seen to be as critical as it actually is by many citizens. It is therefore to be hoped that those who want to learn the unvarnished truth about the Jewish question will read the *Stürmer*. (Bytwerk 2001)

Similar letters came from Heinrich Himmler (1937) and other prominent Nazis. In a leading article in *Der Stürmer,* Streicher wrote about the paper's impact and goal:

> The continued work of the *Stürmer* will help to ensure that every German down to the last man will, with heart and hand, join the ranks of those whose aim is to crush the head of the serpent Pan-Juda beneath their heels. He who helps to bring this about helps to eliminate the devil. And this devil is the Jew. (Streicher 1937)

Similarly the impact of *Kangura* in shaping public opinion about the Tutsis in Rwanda and neighbouring countries was phenomenal. In *Kangura* no. 54 published in January of 1994, Hassan Ngeze informs the readers of *Kangura* that he has fulfilled his self-appointed task of uniting the Hutu and revealing to the people who the Tutsi is. He states this in a section titled 'The role of *Kangura* in the salvation of Rwanda':

> Before Rwanda was attacked, *Kangura* revealed the plan. We started urging the Hutus to unite, not to listen to what the enemy was asking them to do, especially as the enemy was the cause of the war amongst them. From that time, the truth preached by KANGURA has played a remarkable role in the reconciliation of Hutus and the return of those who had been misled. Today, Hutus from different parties meet, discuss and share a drink. The irrefutable proof of this is the speech Justin MUGENZI delivered during the MRND meeting the day before yesterday in Nyamirambo. Who could have thought that MUGENZI will one day become an Interahamwe? Kangura's role will be studied in the history of Rwanda and that of the region we live in where a lot of Tutsis reside; Besides, *Kangura has revealed to the coming generation who the Tutsi is.* (ICTR transcript, Marcel Kabanda, 16 May 2002: 176, emphasis added; Ngeze 1994)

It was clear that the message in *Kangura* was read and taken seriously by the Rwandan community. In the Akayesu case, the Trial Chamber held that, 'In light of the culture of Rwanda, acts of incitement can be viewed as direct or not, by focusing mainly on the issue of whether the persons for whom the message was intended immediately grasped the implication thereof' (ICTR 1998a: para. 558).

The message in an article signed by François Akimana, the president of PALIPEHUTU, reflects the effect of *Kangura*. In reference to international issue 3, he states that for the Hutus, 'Kangura has become a culture, an extraordinary culture which reassured them in the same manner as Baby Jesus, and when Christmas Day came' (Akimana 1992: 5; ICTR transcript, Kabanda, 14 May 2002: 131–4). He goes on to describe the reaction of the Tutsis in Burundi when they saw the issue: 'They fell sick, they had liver crisis. They died because of the truth that they had come to see in *Kangura* newspapers.'

CALL FOR EXTERMINATION

In December 1941, Julius Streicher wrote that 'if the danger of ... reproduction of that curse of God in the Jewish blood is finally to come to an end, then there is only one way – the extermination of that people whose father is the devil' (Taylor 1992: 378).

Issue 26 (November 1991) of *Kangura* was titled 'Tutsi: race Of God!? What arms shall we use to conquer the *Inyenzi* once and for all?' (ICTR exhibit P7 translated in P115/26/A: K015110). In this issue, the Tutsi ethnic group was ironically referred to as 'the race of God'.[6] The question about conquering the *Inyenzi* once and for all carried an ominous message calling for a final solution to the evil that, according to *Kangura*, the Tutsi ethnic group posed in Rwanda. An article on page 7, informed readers that:

> Historians and sociologists tell us that Rwanda is inhabited by three ethnic groups, which are the Twas, the Hutu, and the Tutsi. They say that these ethnic groups can co-exist in harmony and work together if Tutsis do not behave themselves in a bragging manner, people who like to boast, talk a lot, tell lies and are hypocrites, people who are never satisfied and people who want to have everything, they're thieves, they are involved in intrigues, they are wicked, they are killers. And they are people who have grudges just like serpents. (ICTR transcript, Hassan Ngeze, 2 April 2003: 87–8; Moustapha 1991)

CHALLENGES FACED DURING THE MEDIA TRIAL

Translation of Kangura

One of the greatest challenges was that not all 73 *Kangura* issues were translated into English and French. This was and still is a subject in contention with the defence. When litigated before the Trial Chamber, it was held that such an exercise would stretch the resources of the Tribunal beyond its capacity. The Trial Chamber noted that the resources of the tribunal were not unlimited and that only the relevant portions need be translated. The defence attourneys were asked to explore less expensive measures, such as securing the cooperation of their clients who were fluent in Kinyarwanda and French or using Kinyarwanda investigators.

Addressing this matter in the judgement, the Chamber noted that: defence counsel availed themselves of the opportunity to select issues for translation and that copies of all issues within the custody of the prosecution were furnished years ago to the defence in hard copy and electronically on a CD-ROM. The Chamber also noted that the extracts of *Kangura* relied on by both the prosecution and the defence were read into the trial record during presentation of both their cases. This included simultaneous translations into English and French. Thus, the relevant translations were provided to the Chamber for its consideration (ICTR 2003a: para. 44).

Temporal jurisdiction of the Tribunal

Article 7 of the statute of the ICTR states:

> The territorial jurisdiction of the International Tribunal for Rwanda shall extend to the territory of Rwanda including its land surface and airspace as well as to the territory of neighboring States in respect of serious violations of international humanitarian law committed by Rwandan citizens. The temporal jurisdiction of the International Tribunal for Rwanda shall extend to a period beginning on 1 January 1994 and ending on 31 December 1994. (ICTR 1994: article 7)

Only five issues of *Kangura* were published in 1994 before the genocide. The famous ten commandments of the Hutu were only republished in December 1990. The 19 Tutsi commandments were also republished in *Kangura* in November 1990.

The defence contention, which is still a matter of appeal, was that the Chamber had no jurisdiction over *Kangura* issues published before 1994. In pre-trial rulings, the Court held that although many of the events referred to in the indictment preceded 1 January 1994, such events 'provide a relevant background and a basis for understanding the Accused's alleged conduct in relation to the Rwanda Genocide of 1994' (ICTR 1999: para. 3). The Appeals Chamber confirmed the Trial Chamber's decision that an accused could not be held accountable for crimes committed before 1994 and that such events would not be referred to 'except for historical purposes or information' (ICTR 2000a: 6).

Evidence was adduced that, in March 1994 (issues 58 and 59: 7–11), *Kangura* called on and directed its readers to read almost all editions of the newspaper by publishing ten questions, whose answers could be found in previous issues, and offered several prizes. In its judgement, the Trial Chamber held that 'the competition was designed to direct participants to any and to all of these issues of the publication and that in this manner in March 1994 *Kangura* effectively and purposely brought these issues back into circulation' (ICTR 2003a: para. 257).

PROSECUTION OF JOURNALISM AT NUREMBURG

The Media Trial marked the first time since Nuremberg that hate speech had been prosecuted internationally as a war crime. The trial of Julius Streicher was characterized in the Akayesu judgement of the tribunal as the 'most famous conviction for incitement' (ICTR 1998a: para. 550). The different treatment of two Nazi defendants at Nuremberg – the publicist Julius Streicher and head of the radio division of the propaganda ministry, Hans Fritzsche – was an early indication of ambiguity in international law regarding the incitement that would well outlast the Nuremberg trials. Streicher, a committed Nazi and the publisher of *Der Stürmer*, was convicted of crimes against humanity and hanged for having provoked hatred against the Jews and having called for the annihilation of the Jewish race. He received this punishment even though he had held no official government or party position and his journal was not an official party or state organ.

The International Military Tribunal at Nuremberg linked Streicher's propaganda with the war crimes that had been carried out to establish a parallel to the specific intent requirement in criminal law. The tribunal held that

> Streicher's incitement to murder and extermination at the time when Jews in the East were being killed under the most horrible conditions clearly constitutes persecution on political and racial grounds in connection with War Crimes, as defined by the Charter, and constitutes a Crime against Humanity. (Avalon Project 2005)

The tribunal's reference to 'crimes committed in the East', and not those committed within Germany, implicitly linked the alleged crimes against humanity with war crimes. The link to the actual killing in the East also established an element of causation in the definition of actionable incitement, which seemed to require both inciting words and the physical realization of their message.

Although not charged with 'direct incitement', Hans Fritzsche was accused of inciting and encouraging the commission of war crimes 'by deliberately falsifying news to arouse in the German people those passions which led them to the commission of atrocities'. The Nuremberg Tribunal held that there was definite evidence of anti-Semitism in his broadcasts, and that he had blamed the war on the Jews. But, said the tribunal, 'these speeches did not urge persecution or extermination of Jews.' Consequently, it was 'not prepared to hold that they were intended to incite the German people to commit atrocities on conquered peoples'. In effect, Fritzsche's anti-Semitic propaganda was not 'direct' enough to consist of incitement to commit genocide.[7]

The Fritzsche holding set a tough standard of causality between targeted words and specific events. Although the tribunal characterized Fritzsche's virulently anti-Semitic statements in his broadcasts as 'strong statements of a propagandist nature', it found no evidence of explicit calls for the extermination of the Jews (Avalon Project 2005). Accordingly, it concluded that it was 'not prepared to hold that [these statements] were intended to incite the German people to commit atrocities on conquered people', and that Fritzsche 'cannot be held to have been a participant in the crimes charged'. His aim was rather to arouse popular sentiment in support of Hitler and the German war effort. The term 'on conquered people' again suggests a focus on crimes against the peace. The tribunal held that Fritzsche was not aware that the information was false. It also noted that he was not aware of the extermination of the Jews in the East. His position and official duties were also held not to be sufficiently important to infer that he took part in the originating or formulating propaganda campaigns. Fritzsche was considered a 'conduit' of propaganda, not a liable participant.

DIRECT AND PUBLIC INCITEMENT AND THE INTERNATIONAL CRIMINAL TRIBUNALS FOR YUGOSLAVIA AND RWANDA

The crime of direct and public incitement to commit genocide is punishable under Article 2(3)(C) of the Statute of the ICTR and Article 4 (3)(e) of the Statute of the International Criminal Tribunal for the (former) Yugoslavia (ICTY). The ICTY has issued no indictments against journalists. In the first conviction of the ICTR, for direct and public incitement to commit genocide, the Trial Chamber described the essential elements of the crime of direct and public incitement to commit genocide:

> directly provoking the perpetrator(s) to commit genocide, whether through speeches, shouting or threats uttered in public places or at public gatherings, or through the sale or dissemination, offer for sale or display of written material or printed matter in public places or at public gatherings, or through the public display of placards or posters, or through any other means of audiovisual communication. (ICTR 1998a: para. 559)

The Akayesu case determined that the *mens rea* required for the crime of direct and public incitement to commit genocide lies in the intent to prompt directly or to provoke another to commit genocide. It implies a desire on the part of the perpetrator to create by his or her actions a particular state of mind necessary to commit such a crime in the minds of the person(s) he or she is engaging. That is to say that the person who is inciting to commit genocide must have the specific intent to commit genocide, that is, to destroy, in whole or in part, a national, ethnical, racial or religious group, as such (ICTR 1998a: para. 560).

The Trial Chamber held that genocide fell within the category of crimes so serious that direct and public incitement to commit such a crime must be punished as such, even when such incitement fails to produce the result expected by the perpetrator (ICTR 1998a: para. 552). Whether a communication constituted incitement depended on the context in Rwanda at the time of these events. The Chamber noted that the facts should be considered

> on a case-by-case basis whether, in light of the culture of Rwanda and the specific circumstances of the instant case, acts of incitement can be viewed

as direct or not, by focusing mainly on the issue of whether the persons for whom the message was intended immediately grasped the implication thereof. (ICTR 1998a: para. 558)

The Akayesu Trial Chamber opined that the direct element of incitement should be viewed in light of its cultural and linguistic content. It noted that a particular speech may be perceived as 'direct' in one country, but not in another depending on the audience (ICTR 1998a: para. 557).

The next conviction for the crime of direct and public incitement was in the case of the *Prosecutor v. Georges Ruggiu* (ICTR 2000b). Others include: *The Prosecutor v. Jean Kambanda* (ICTR 1998b); *The Prosecutor v. Eliézer Niyitegeka* (ICTR 2003b); *The Prosecutor v. Juvénal Kajelijeli* (ICTR 2003c).

PARAMETERS OF PRESS FREEDOM

During the Media Trial, the Chamber examined a number of articles and excerpts from *Kangura*, focusing primarily on those that addressed issues of ethnicity and on those that called on readers to take action. During its deliberations, the Chamber accepted that the media has a role to play in the protection of democracy and, where necessary, the mobilization of civil defence for the protection of a nation and its people. The Chamber noted that what distinguished both *Kangura* and RTLM from an initiative to this end was their consistent identification of the enemy as the Tutsi population. Readers and listeners were not directed against individuals who were clearly defined as armed and dangerous. Instead, Tutsi civilians and in fact the Tutsi population as a whole were targeted (ICTR 2003a: para. 1025).

The Chamber considered that it was critical to distinguish between the discussion of ethnic consciousness and the promotion of ethnic hatred (ICTR 2003a: para. 1020). It also held that speech constituting ethnic hatred results from the stereotyping of ethnicity combined with its denigration (ICTR 2003a: para. 1021).

With regard to the RTLM broadcast stating that the Tutsi 'are the ones who have all the money', the Chamber held that, although this broadcast, which did not call on listeners to take any action, did not constitute direct incitement, it demonstrated the progression from ethnic consciousness to harmful ethnic stereotyping (ICTR 2003a: para. 1021).

The Chamber opined that the context in which the statement is made to be important. A statement provoking resentment against members of an ethnic group would have a heightened impact in the context of a genocidal environment. It would be more likely to lead to violence. At the same time the environment would be an indicator that incitement to violence was the intent of the statement (ICTR 2003a: para. 1022).

Although the Chamber accepted that Hassan Ngeze had only reprinted the ten Bahutu commandments and the 19 commandments of the Tutsi, it found that the clear intent of the publication of the latter was to spread fear that the

Tutsi endanger the Hutu, and of the former to tell the Hutu how to protect themselves from that danger (ICTR 2003a: para. 1022).[8]

The Chamber noted that the positioning of the media with regard to the message indicates the real intent of the message, and to some degree the real message itself. The editor of *Kangura* and RTLM's broadcast journalists did not distance themselves from the message of ethnic hatred; rather they purveyed it (ICTR 2003a: para. 1024).

The Chamber also noted that the editorials and articles reviewed during the trial consistently portrayed the Tutsi as wicked and ambitious, using women and money against the vulnerable Hutu (ICTR 2003a: para. 187). The presentation of Tutsi women as femmes fatales focused particular attention on them and the danger they represented to the Hutu. This danger was explicitly associated with sexuality. By defining Tutsi women as an enemy in this way, *Kangura* articulated a framework that made the sexual attack of Tutsi women a foreseeable consequence of the role attributed to them (ICTR 2003a: para. 188).

CAUSATION

The Chamber reaffirmed the Akayesu decision that incitement was a crime regardless of whether it has the effect it intends to have. In determining whether communications represent intent to cause genocide and thereby constitute incitement, the Chamber considered it significant that in fact genocide occurred. That the media intended to have this effect is evidenced in part by the fact that it did have this effect (ICTR 2003a: para. 1039).

In considering whether particular expression constituted a form of incitement on which restrictions would be justified, the Chamber noted that the international jurisprudence does not include any specific causation requirement linking the expression at issue with the demonstration of a direct effect. In the *Streicher* case, for example there was no allegation that the publication *Der Stürmer* was tied to any particular violence. Much more generally, it was found to have 'injected into the minds of thousands of Germans' a 'poison' that caused them to support the National Socialist policy of Jewish persecution and extermination (ICTR 2003a: para. 1007).

NOTES

1. Beginning with issue no. 10 (February 1991), the slogan 'The voice that awakens and defends the majority people' appeared on the cover.
2. For example, in a lead article that appeared in March 1933 just after the Reichstag fire, the claim was that the fire was part of a worldwide Jewish conspiracy based on the *Protocols of the Elders of Zion*. Julius Streicher (1933a) claimed that the 'Zionist protocols' were agreed on by the Jews at the World Jewish Congress in 1897 in Basel. In July 1933, he wrote the secret goals of the Jewish people are laid out in the 'Protocols of the Elders of Zion', which *Stürmer* had written about more than a hundred times and that 'contain the Jewish plan for world conquest' (Streicher 1933b).
3. Published in *Kangura* issue no. 4 (November 1990) right after the 1 October attack of the Rwandan Patriotic Front.

4. The expert report of Professor Kabanda (exhibit P116(b) page 7 in the Media Trial) states that these commandments were purportedly exhumed in 1962 in the Congo. Their authenticity is yet to be established and their author is unknown.
5. Referring to the 1959 revolution, which was politically orchestrated communal violence that resulted in thousands of mostly Tutsi casualties and forced roughly 300,000 Tutsis to flee to neighbouring Burundi and Uganda.
6. Evidence entered during the testimony of Dr Ruzindana, a sociolinguistic expert (21 March 2002: 124–5). According to the judgement in the Media Trial (ICTR 2003a: para. 246) by *Inyenzi*, *Kangura* meant, and was understood to mean, all Rwandans of Tutsi ethnicity, who in this issue of *Kangura* were stereotyped as having the inherent characteristics of liars, thieves and killers. The Trial Chamber found that the message clearly conveyed to the readers of this issue was that the Hutu population should 'wake up' and take the measures to keep the Tutsi enemy from decimating the Hutu (para. 1035).
7. Fritzsche, acquitted by the tribunal at Nuremberg, was later to be tried in Germany and convicted of similar crimes (Tusa and Tusa 1984: 477–8).
8. In paragraph 156 of the judgement, in the discussion of the evidence on the two sets of commandments the Chamber held that an article in issue 40 (October 1993) of *Kangura* titled 'A cockroach (*Inyenzi*) cannot bring forth a butterfly' explicitly called on the Hutu to follow the ten commandments. Similarly, it could reasonably be held that *Kangura* supported the ten commandments, in substance if not in form, based on the letter published in issue 36 (May 1992) of *Kangura* calling on men to divorce their Tutsi wives. Although the article was signed by someone else, it was published by Ngeze.

REFERENCES

Note: Most of the documents of the ICTR can be found on its website, available at <www.ictr.org> and in the database of the Netherlands Institute of Human Rights <www.sim.law.uu.nl/>. The transcript and exhibits referred to in this article are from *The Prosecutor v. Ferdinand Nahimana, Jean-Bosco Barayagwiza and Hassan Ngeze*. Case no. ICTR-99–52-T. ICTR, Arusha, Tanzania.

Akimana, F. 1992. Dushima inyandiko ya *Kangura*. *Kangura,* 30 (January): 5.

Avalon Project at Yale Law School. 2005. Judgement of the International Military Tribunal for the trial of German major war criminals: Fritzsche. Available at <www.yale.edu/lawweb/avalon/imt/proc/judfritz.htm> (accessed 6 September 2005).

Bytwerk, R.L. 2001. *Julius Streicher: Nazi Editor of the Notorious anti-Semitic Newspaper Der Stürmer.* Chapter 3: Der Stürmer: a Fierce and Filthy Rag. Cooper Square Press, New York, NY, USA.

Farrior, S. 1996. Molding the Matrix: the Historical and Theoretical Foundations of International Law Concerning Hate Speech. *Berkeley Journal of International Law*, 14(1).

Himmler, H. 1937. Letter. *Der Stürmer*, 14 (April). [Translation of document M-22. In *Nazi conspiracy and aggression* (vol. VIII). United States Government Printing Office, Washington, DC, USA, 1946: 13]

ICTR (International Criminal Tribunal for Rwanda). 1994. Statute of the international tribunal. (Security Council Resolution 955). Office of the United Nations High Commissioner for Human Rights, New York, NY, USA. Available at <www.ohchr.org/english/law/itr.htm> (accessed 23 October 2005).

—— 1998a. Judgement. In *The Prosecutor v. Jean Paul Akayesu.* Case no. ICTR-96–4. ICTR, Arusha, Tanzania.

—— 1998b. Judgement and sentence. In *The Prosecutor v. Jean Kambanda*. Case no. ICTR-97–23-S. ICTR, Arusha, Tanzania, 4 September.

—— 1999. Decision on the prosecutor's request for leave to amend the indictment. In *The Prosecutor v. Hassan Ngeze*, Case no. ICTR-97–27-I. ICTR, Arusha, Tanzania, 5 November.

—— 2000a. Decision on the interlocutory appeals. In *Hassan Ngeze and Ferdinand Nahimana v. The Prosecutor.* ICTR, Arusha, Tanzania, 5 September.

—— 2000b. Judgement. In *The Prosecutor v. Georges Ruggiu*. Case no. ICTR-97–32-I. ICTR, Arusha, Tanzania.

—— 2003a. Judgement and sentence. In *The Prosecutor v. Ferdinand Nahimana, Jean-Bosco Barayagwiza and Hassan Ngeze*. Case no. ICTR-99–52-T. ICTR, Arusha, Tanzania, 3 December.

—— 2003b. Judgement and sentence. In *The Prosecutor v. Eliézer Niyitegeka*. Case no. ICTR-96–14-T. ICTR, Arusha, Tanzania, 16 May.

—— 2003c. Judgement and sentence. In *The Prosecutor v. Juvénal Kajelijeli*. Case no. ICTR-98–44a-T. ICTR, Arusha, Tanzania, 1 December.

Moustapha, B. 1991. Ibinyamakuru by'ibyitso birabeshya ntibizagera ku ntego zabyo [The newspapers of the accomplices are wrong, rather they are telling lies. They are never going to achieve their objectives]. *Kangura*, 26 (November): 7.

—— 1994. Politiki yo kubeshya itumye Inkotanyi zicuza icyo zarwaniye. *Kangura,* 54 (January): 3.

OAU (Organization of African Unity). 1981. African [Banjul] charter on human and peoples' rights. OAU, Addis Ababa, Ethiopia. CAB/LEG/67/3 rev. 5, 21 I.L.M. 58 (1982).

Streicher, J. 1937. To Everybody! The 'Stuermer' was Right. The Battle Against the Devil. *Der Stürmer*, 39 (September).

—— 1933a. Der Schuldige. *Der Stürmer,* 10 (March).

—— 1933b. Die Geheimpläne gegen Deutschland enthüllt. *Der Stürmer,* 34 (July).

Taylor, T. 1992. *The Anatomy of the Nuremberg Trials*. Alfred E. Knopf, New York, NY, USA.

Tusa, A. and J. Tusa. 1984. *The Nuremberg Trial*. Scribner, New York, NY, USA.

UN (United Nations). 1951. *Convention on the prevention and punishment of the crime of genocide*. Adopted by Resolution 260 (III) of the UN General Assembly, 9 December 1948. *UN Treaty Series* no. 1021, vol. 78: 277. Available at <www.preventgenocide.org/law/convention/text.htm> (accessed 6 September 2005).

—— 1965. *International convention on the elimination of all forms of racial discrimination*. General Assembly Resolution 2106 (XX), 21 December. Available at <www.unhchr.ch/html/menu3/b/d_icerd.htm> (accessed 6 September 2005).

—— 1966a. *International covenant on civil and political rights*. General Assembly resolution 2200A (XXI), 16 December. Available at <www.unhchr.ch/html/menu3/b/a_ccpr.htm> (accessed 6 September 2005).

—— 1966b. *Optional protocol to the international covenant on civil and political rights*. General Assembly Resolution 2200A (XXI), 16 December. Available at <www.unhchr.ch/html/menu3/b/a_opt.htm> (accessed 6 September 2005).

—— 1966c. *International covenant on economic, social and cultural rights*. General Assembly Resolution 2200A (XXI), 16 December. Available at <www.unhchr.ch/html/menu3/b/a_cescr.htm> (accessed 6 September 2005).

28
'Hate Media' – Crimes Against Humanity and Genocide: Opportunities Missed by the International Criminal Tribunal for Rwanda

Jean-Marie Biju-Duval

On 3 December 2003, nine years after the genocide and three years after the 'Media Trial' began, the International Criminal Tribunal for Rwanda (ICTR) sentenced Hassan Ngeze, Ferdinand Nahimana and Jean-Bosco Barayagwiza to life in prison. (For procedural reasons, Barayagwiza's sentence was later reduced to 35 years.)

These three defendants had initially been charged separately, but the ICTR decided to try them together because of the roles all three had played in the Rwandan media in 1994. Ngeze was editor-in-chief of the newspaper *Kangura*, while Nahimana and Barayagwiza were among the founding members of Radio-Télévision Libre des Milles Collines (RTLM) and sat on its board of directors.

Fifty-six years after the Nuremberg and Tokyo trials, the Media Trial gave the international criminal justice system the opportunity to rule on an issue that has been central to its jurisdiction since its very inception: propaganda in the organs of the press as a crime against humanity and a crime of genocide. In an international context, free of bilateral antagonism and above any suspicion of imposing 'victor's justice', the ICTR's judges could have freely and serenely invoked the enduring principles of international law and applied them with all the rigour that the rules of criminal procedure require. But as the following discussion will show, most of the hope that they would do so has now been dashed.

THE RESPONSE OF INTERNATIONAL CRIMINAL LAW TO PROPAGANDA: FROM THE REQUIREMENTS OF NUREMBERG TO THE BANALIZATION OF GENOCIDE

The principles for determining what types of propaganda constitute international crimes originated in the verdict handed down by the International Military Tribunal (IMT) at Nuremberg on 1 October 1946, when it pronounced the death sentence of Julius Streicher, editor-in-chief of the newspaper *Der Stürmer*, but acquitted Hans Fritzsche, *Ministerialdirektor* (permanent secretary) at the Reich Ministry of Propaganda and chief of radio propaganda for the Nazi party.

In its rulings on Nazi anti-Semitic propaganda, the Nuremberg Tribunal drew a perfectly clear dividing line between propaganda such as Fritzsche's, which was violently anti-Semitic but did not call directly for extermination, and the direct calls for extermination that Streicher was publishing at the very time that the extermination was in progress. Only the latter were deemed to meet the definition of crimes against humanity.

Taking this seminal judgement as its precedent, the United Nations gave this distinction the force of international law on 9 December 1948, when it adopted the *Convention on the Prevention and Punishment of the Crime of Genocide*, which established the international crime of 'direct and public incitement to commit genocide' (UN 1951).

When the constituent elements of this new international crime were being debated, the question of the criminalization of 'hate media' was raised in the clearest possible terms. The USSR demanded that propaganda that tended to incite racial hatred be classified as a crime, inasmuch as such hatred was the source of acts of genocide. To this end, the Soviets proposed two amendments to the convention. The first would have criminalized 'all forms of public propaganda (press, radio, cinema, etc.) aimed at inciting racial, national or religious enmities or hatred'. The second would have criminalized 'all forms of public propaganda (press, radio, cinema, etc.) aimed at provoking the commission of acts of genocide'. Both amendments were rejected by a large majority (28 to 11 against the first, with 4 abstentions, and 30 to 8 against the second, with 6 abstentions) (UN 1948). Only *direct* and public incitement to commit genocide was included in the final definition.

More than 40 years later, the crimes committed in the former Yugoslavia and the genocide of the Rwandan Tutsis obliged international tribunals to again consider when hate speech should be classified as a crime against humanity. The ICTR ruled on the crime of direct and public incitement to commit genocide in its first judgement regarding the Rwanda genocide of 1994:

> Direct and public incitement must be defined … as directly provoking the perpetrator(s) to commit genocide, whether through speeches, shouting or threats uttered in public places or at public gatherings, or through the sale or dissemination … of written material or printed matter … or through the public display of placards or posters, or through any other means of audiovisual communication. (ICTR 1998: para. 559)

Following the Streicher precedent, the ICTR applied this definition to the *bourgmestre* of a commune who, at the very time when the genocide was being committed, made public calls for the people of his commune to participate in the extermination – calls that were immediately followed by action. This case, however, involved speech by a government official to the citizens of his jurisdiction, not a propaganda message disseminated through the press.

In another case heard by the ICTR, charges were laid against Georges Ruggiu, who had been a journalist at RTLM from April to July 1994 and the direct author of incendiary broadcasts at the very time that Rwanda was bursting into flames. This case gave the tribunal the opportunity to rule on the specific question of whether journalists could participate in the commission of the crime of genocide actively, directly and personally, via the airwaves (ICTR 2000).

The Media Trial brought the issue of the 'media of genocide' before the Rwanda tribunal once more and raised a new question – the criminality of the propaganda that was broadcast and published before 6 April 1994, when the attack on the president's plane precipitated the massacres and genocide. On this question, the parties took three clearly different positions:

- The prosecution argued for a very extensive definition of the forms of hate speech that constitute a crime.
- The defence for Hassan Ngeze took a more restrictive position, based on the principle of freedom of expression.
- The defence for Ferdinand Nahimana focused on the necessarily strict interpretation of the concept of crimes against humanity that is imposed by international law.

The judgement in this case rendered on 3 December 2003 appears to mark a break with the principles established at Nuremberg. To make a finding of criminality with regard to RTLM's radio broadcasts before 6 April 1994, which did not contain any direct calls for extermination, the judges of the ICTR chose to extend the definition of crimes against humanity through the press to include all bellicose speeches targeting civilian populations on the basis of 'ethnic stereotyping' (ICTR 2003a).

To the legal scholar, this extension of the definition raises concerns not only about the fundamental rights guaranteed by the principles of the legality and non-retroactivity of the criminal law, but also about the future of a body of international criminal law whose effectiveness depends on consensus among nations. Even more important, this approach tends to blur the criteria set out in the 1948 convention and dangerously to 'banalize' the notion of crimes against humanity and genocide, without contributing in any useful way to their prevention and punishment.

By expanding the sphere of crimes against humanity to include the hateful aberrations of the media in a time of crisis, the judges in the Media Trial have opened a Pandora's box that is all the more dangerous because they have shown such extreme flexibility in the way they interpret the spoken and written word.

Definition of the crime of incitement: an illegitimate and dangerous extension of the criminal sphere

When delegates to the United Nations were debating what kinds of speech could be prosecuted as crimes before international tribunals, they were guided by one major concern. The delegates did not want to create an opportunity for totalitarian states to justify repression of their domestic opposition or to interfere in the domestic affairs of other states.

Everyone agreed that hate speech was dangerous. But everyone also agreed that it was difficult to define and interpret. If the crime's boundaries were to become too blurry, the charge might be misused. In addressing the question of propaganda that leads to genocide, the United Nations decided in 1948 that propaganda would be treated as an international crime only from the moment that this hate speech contained calls for genocidal extermination. This 'moment' must not provide any cause for debate, and the evidence must dispel any dangers of exegesis and interpretation. That is why the incitement must be 'direct and public'.

In the Media Trial, however, the judges refused to accept this limitation to unequivocal calls for genocide. Instead, the judges opted for an extensive approach to criminalization, which inevitably involved them in the business of interpreting speech, to the detriment of the certainties that are essential to the judicial process.

An extensive conception of persecution as a crime against humanity: abandoning the Nuremberg criteria

Article 3 of the Statute of the ICTR (1994) is devoted to crimes against humanity, which consist of 'inhumane acts' including 'persecutions on political, racial and religious grounds', committed 'as part of a widespread or systematic attack against any civilian population on national, political, ethnic, racial or religious grounds'. The concept of persecution as a crime against humanity thus supposes a level of gravity that has no equivalent in the forms of persecution contemplated in human rights law[1] and that must rise to the same degree of inhumanity as the other acts listed in Article 3: murder, extermination, enslavement, imprisonment, torture and rape. And whatever the act, it must be committed as part of a widespread, systematic attack against a civilian population and in full knowledge of this context.

In the Media Trial, the reason that the Office of the Prosecutor attempted to apply the concept of persecution to propaganda was to criminalize RTLM broadcasts before 6 April 1994, whose content would not bear characterization as the crime of 'direct and public incitement to commit genocide'. Taking over where the prosecution left off, the ICTR judges went so far as to extend the concept of crimes against humanity to any hate speech targeting a population on discriminatory ethnic or political grounds, regardless of its actual consequences (ICTR 2003a: para. 1069–82).

This extension is unprecedented and bears no comparison with the other inhumane acts that, as part of a widespread and systematic attack, constitute crimes against humanity: extermination, enslavement, murder, rape, and so on. Belonging to a group targeted by racist, bellicose or discriminatory speech cannot be considered a matter of equal gravity with being physically murdered, raped or enslaved because of one's ethnicity. The extension of the concept of crimes against humanity to any political or ethnic hate speech[2] results in a dilution and hence a dangerous banalization of such crimes.

Paradoxically, the judges in the Media Trial cited the Nuremberg precedent, even though the Nuremberg tribunal refused to apply this very label to the most virulent anti-Semitic speeches broadcast as part of a systematic policy – Fritzsche's policy – simply because these speeches did not unequivocally call for extermination. In reality, the Media Trial judges were making their own law and imposing it retroactively, even though it had been expressly rejected when the convention of 1948 was drafted: they were defining propaganda as a crime against humanity if it was of a kind that could create the conditions for genocide (see ICTR 2003a: para. 1073).

In contrast, when the International Criminal Tribunal for (the former) Yugoslavia (ICTY) dealt with the issue of hate speech, it clearly affirmed that speech inciting hatred cannot, in itself, constitute a crime against humanity (ICTY 2001a: para. 209). This tribunal's analysis, which is faithful to the Nuremberg criteria, is also embraced in the Statute of the International Criminal Court, which criminalizes 'incitement' only to the extent that someone directly and publicly incites others to commit the crime of genocide (ICC 2002: art. 25.3(e)).

Thus, in light of the body of international law that, since 1946, has been completely consistent in refusing to treat propaganda speech, however hateful, as an international crime unless it directly calls for genocide, the judgement in the Media Trial must be seen as an isolated aberration for which there is scarcely any explanation other than considerations of judicial convenience.

An extensive conception of the crime of direct and public incitement to commit genocide: the banalization of genocide

From the outset, the judges in the Media Trial based their approach to the concept of incitement to commit genocide on an excerpt from statements made by the Soviet delegate during the debates in which the 6th Committee of the United Nations General Assembly delimited this concept in October 1948 (UN 1948). The USSR wished to include in this crime all forms of propaganda 'preparatory' to genocide, in other words 'forms of public propaganda that tend to incite racial, national or religious hatreds or that are aimed at provoking the commission of acts of genocide'.

The suggestion was rejected in favour of a more restrictive definition confined to communications calling directly and intentionally for the execution of the crime of genocide. The most intense hostility toward the Soviet amendment was expressed by the delegate from the United States, and a large majority agreed that, as the Greek delegate put it, 'However regrettable these acts may be, they do not come under the convention on genocide' (UN 1948, translated). It is surprising, to say the least, that the ICTR's judges should make this rejected proposal the first argument in their demonstration.

The judges went on to offer an interpretation of the judgement of the IMT at Nuremberg that was also surprising. In particular, they offered an astonishing posthumous defence of Fritzsche, who was Goebbels' right arm, while they failed to stress the violently anti-Semitic nature of his broadcasts.

But what was actually remarkable about the Fritzsche trial was that even though it was held at a time when the public tolerated and even encouraged the summary settling of accounts with anyone suspected of having collaborated with the Nazi occupiers, the judges took the risk of going against public opinion. Although they were fully aware of the violence of the defendant's anti-Semitic hate speech, they nevertheless found that it did not constitute a crime against humanity. In contrast, Streicher's direct calls for extermination earned him a death sentence. Paradoxically, by including hate speech in the sphere of crimes against humanity, the ICTR judges were drawing conclusions from these two precedents that are the opposite of those that actually arise from them.

It goes without saying that hate speech and calls to violence present a special kind of danger. The *International Covenant on Civil and Political Rights* (UN 1966) provides that such acts be prohibited by law, and we should all be pleased that states provide punishments in their domestic legislation to give effect to this prohibition. But it is equally apparent that these acts are not comparable to the absolute crime that genocide represents, and they have never been regarded by international law as having to be incorporated into the international punishment of this crime.

The same applies to RTLM's denunciations of individuals by name over the radio, generally aimed at publicly stigmatizing them as belonging to the rebellion. In this regard, it is significant that to demonstrate the criminality of these denunciations, the ICTR judges repeatedly observed that they were not based on any serious investigation and that the journalist did not provide the evidence of his good faith, much less of the accuracy of his assertions. On the contrary, what the judges' observations actually show is that these oral attacks did not enter the sphere of genocide: by its very nature, a direct and public call to genocide cannot be based on any kind of justification. The question does not arise. When Streicher says 'The Jews of Russia must be killed. They must be extirpated and exterminated,' no judge inquires into whether he has just cause for saying this. Here we come to the very core of what constitutes a crime against humanity: it is unjustifiable by its very nature.

By taking the criminal status of direct and public incitement to commit genocide and extending it to words and actions that cannot bear comparison with the unsurpassable gravity of the crime of genocide, the judges in the Media Trial have encouraged an unacceptable banalization of this crime.

Identification of the crime of incitement in the Rwandan press: the dangers of interpretation versus the requirements of criminal procedure

From the very outset, the circumstances of the Media Trial were exceptionally favourable to the analysis of facts and the establishment of 'proof'. Every issue of *Kangura* ever published was available, and there were nearly 300 recordings of hundreds of hours of RTLM radio broadcasts. Thus it was possible to obtain an extremely representative if not complete sense of the reality of the propaganda that these two press organs were disseminating in Rwanda in 1993 and 1994.

Thus, there was good reason to believe that the judges could fully evaluate the *actus reus* (conduct component) of the crimes being prosecuted, and in any case of the crime of incitement, without recourse to any other, less certain forms of evidence, such as direct or indirect testimony. Instead of vainly attempting to probe the defendants' hearts and minds or presumptuously attempting to lay bare the journalists' implicit suggestions, double meanings and unavowed motives, the judges at Arusha should have stuck to the evidence of the crimes.

This evidence was duly documented in the recordings assembled by the Office of the Prosecutor. From April to July 1994, the very time when the genocidal operations were in progress, RTLM journalists were making broadcasts in which they directly called for the massacre of the Tutsis. These broadcasts on their own sufficed to identify the crime and its perpetrators beyond any reasonable doubt.

This evidence also highlighted the lack of any such calls to extermination in the broadcasts made before 6 April 1994.

Instead of confusedly lumping propaganda speech together with calls for extermination out of some short-sighted judicial opportunism, the ICTR should have seized this historic moment to subject these realities to a judge's impartial eye. By strictly enforcing the applicable law, the judges could have demonstrated that the international criminal justice system can rise above the pressures placed on it by the vagaries of diplomacy and the media.

This opportunity was missed. Instead of applying the simple, steadfast criteria of international law to realities that are so distinct from one another that they can never be confused, the ICTR judges chose to apply new, complex, uncertain methods to a reality that they absurdly oversimplified for this purpose.

The uncertainties of interpretation: condemnation to the benefit of the doubt

The crime of *direct* and public incitement to commit genocide presupposes that the communication in question is unambiguous and unequivocal. As soon as a communication can be interpreted in a variety of ways, it fails to meet the definition of this crime. Streicher's articles were unequivocal. He called for extermination; this is a direct and public incitement to commit genocide. Fritzsche's broadcasts were quite violently anti-Semitic and called for combat against the 'Judeo-Bolshevik enemy', but they were equivocal about the plans for extermination; hence, they did not rise to the level of crimes against humanity. Ever since 1946, this has been the test in law. Regardless of whether a communication is explicit or implicit, it must be unequivocal.

Yet the judgement handed down in the Media Trial makes the equivocal nature of the communications the very cornerstone of its reasoning. According to the judges, if RTLM's broadcasts before 6 April 1994 were criminal, it is because the journalists, under the cover of verbal attacks against the Rwandan Patriotic Front (RPF) rebels, historically referred to by the terms *Inyenzi* or *Inkotanyi*, were actually in certain cases targeting the entire Tutsi population in an equivocal, undifferentiated fashion.

And yet an analysis of the broadcasts themselves does not confirm this interpretation, a fact that the judges themselves acknowledged, citing numerous broadcasts in which the above terms referred unequivocally to the RPF fighters alone, and not to the Tutsi civilian population.

One thing is certain: the meaning that the judges attributed to these broadcasts was based on their interpretation of a language of which none of them had any mastery (Kinyarwanda) and on an assumption that was only hypothetical. They were operating in the shifting sands of interpretation, with their judgement at the mercy of contrary winds.

The case of Léon Mugesera demonstrates this. In November 1992, just a few months after the massacres of the Tutsi population of the Bugesera region, Mr Mugesera, a well-known Rwandan university professor and an influential politician, made a speech in his commune that the ICTR's official historiographers, on the authority of the prosecutor's expert witnesses Alison Des Forges and Jean-Pierre Chrétien, have since cited as the archetype of speech that incites genocide. In this speech, the expressions '*Inyenzi*', 'accomplices of the *Inyenzis*' and '*Inkotanyi*' recur repeatedly, and the speaker repeatedly exhorts his listeners to fight them because, 'the person whose neck you do not cut is the one who will cut yours'. Subsequently, Mr Mugesera was exiled to Canada, where the minister of immigration initiated deportation proceedings against him on the basis of this same speech. Relying on the testimony of Des Forges and Chrétien, the minister represented this speech as constituting an incitement to murder, genocide and hatred and a crime against humanity. Thus, in considering Mr Mugesera's case, the highest Canadian courts also found themselves attempting to interpret this speech.

The judgement that the Canadian court delivered on 8 September 2003, the day after the arguments in the Media Trial had ended, undermined in advance the basic foundations of the judgement that the ICTR was to render three months later. The method of interpretation that the Canadian judges applied led them to conclusions diametrically opposed to those of expert witness Alison Des Forges, who was the key prosecution witness in the Media Trial and whose theories were the basis for the judgement rendered by the ICTR on 3 December 2003. Rejecting with the greatest firmness the interpretation that this expert witness was trying to impose, the Canadian judges expressed a definitive certainty: nothing in this speech could be seriously suspected of constituting an incitement to a crime against humanity or an incitement to murder or even an incitement to hatred.[3]

Such are the vagaries of interpretation. And that is why, when they ventured into interpretation, the judges in the Media Trial were building their judgement on sand.

The uncertainties of causality: abandoning the rules of criminal procedure

The judges' embarrassment becomes most obvious at those points in the proceedings where, uncertain of the exact meaning of a communication, they invoked its supposed effects to prove that it constituted criminal incitement (ICTR 2003: para. 1029).

This subsidiary approach by way of causality is not in itself, devoid of legitimacy. When it is possible to observe concordance and concomitance between a communication and the commission of acts of genocide, it is not unreasonable to suspect that this communication may have constituted a direct call to genocide.

Such was indisputably the case for a significant number of RTLM broadcasts over the months April to July 1994. In the heart of Kigali, at the very time when acts of genocide were being perpetrated there, Kantano Habimana, RTLM's star broadcaster, called on the militiamen at the barriers to identify the 'small noses' and kill them. This is direct and public incitement to commit genocide.

But this was not the case before 6 April. Although RTLM had been broadcasting since July 1993, only when other 'causes' arose that were effective in other ways did massacres break out across the country. They did not occur until the disastrous attack of 6 April killed two Hutu heads of state, the RPF resumed its armed struggle and military, paramilitary and civilian authorities issued the orders for genocide. Not until RTLM's journalists came under the sway of an army engaged in total war did they themselves make the transition from propagandists to combatants and then to criminals. Nothing in the events preceding 6 April 1994 allows the propaganda that was broadcast by RTLM to be interpreted as a call to commit crime. The causal approach that the judges adopted for this period actually leads to the opposite interpretation from the one they reached: from July 1993 to April 1994, no causal link can be established between RTLM's broadcasts and acts of anti-Tutsi violence. During this period, the political assassinations were directed exclusively against Hutu leaders,[4] and in the only collective massacre recorded, the victims were Hutu civilians, mostly members of the *Mouvement Républicain National pour la Democratie et le Développement* (MRND)[5] and the perpetrators were the RPF.[6]

This situation was understood clearly enough by Rwandan civil society. On the eve of the genocide, in mid-March 1994, Father André Sibomana,[7] a priest, journalist and human rights activist, invited RTLM's editor-in-chief to participate in a seminar that the Belgian embassy was hosting in Kigali, on the subject of 'objectivity and honesty in political information'. Thus RTLM was perceived as a radio station engaged in political combat in a context where the ethnic factor played a major role, but not as an instrument of civil war, much less one of planned genocide.

Despite these obvious circumstances, the ICTR judges, assuming the prosecution's role, attempted to establish a connection, a supposed direct causal link, however tenuous, between a very small number of broadcasts and murders of Tutsi civilians committed after 6 April, thus mistakenly thinking that they could provide *a posteriori* proof of criminal incitement. And to this end, they discarded the rules of criminal procedure and gave probatory weight to allegations and documents that were devoid of any value as legal evidence. Instead of sticking to the indisputable evidence of fact and law, the judges, under the cover of excellent intentions to protect human rights and under pressure from public opinion, took the risk of letting their decision rest on infinitely shifting, crumbling foundations.

IDENTIFYING THE GUILTY: THE TEMPTATION TO SCAPEGOAT

Genocide and crimes against humanity imply by their nature a large number of participants or even, in the case of Rwanda, countless perpetrators. The commission of these crimes assumes a form of organization put in place by authorities or at the very least 'leaders' whose responsibility is of the essence even if they are physically remote from the site of the crime and its immediate authors. These are the planners, the organizers, the order givers, the people in charge.

Ever since Nuremberg, international criminal law has developed around the responsibility of those who order and organize the crimes much more than of those who simply carry them out – not only because these are essential responsibilities, but also because no international jurisdiction would have the capacity to judge all of the participants in such crimes. If we cannot judge all of these participants, then we must judge those with the highest degree of responsibility and so, in a sense, judge through them the crimes committed by others.

By virtue of the subject that they deal with and the symbolic role that they necessarily play, international criminal tribunals run a risk that national courts face only rarely: that of using the defendant who is at hand as a means of condemning the guilty parties who are not. This risk becomes even greater when a trial is intended not only to prosecute individuals but also to try a criminal phenomenon, such as propaganda. And when the person accused under these circumstances has been singled out in the media for condemnation by international public opinion before his trial even begins, the risk becomes tremendous. His value as a symbol of guilt makes him a scapegoat too convenient to be spared.

That is what happened to Ferdinand Nahimana, who was left alone in the defendants' box to answer for the actions of RTLM's journalists in the absence of the station's president, its general manager and its editor-in-chief for radio. As early as May 1994, addressing the United Nations Commission on Human Rights, the nongovernmental organization Reporters Sans Frontières groundlessly denounced Nahimana as the archetype of the intellectual extremists who founded RTLM. As the star defendant in the Media Trial, in his accusers' imaginations he became the ideal choice for the role of the Goebbels of the Rwanda genocide.

The crimes of thought and speech that RTLM radio had committed against the Tutsi population were rooted in the history of Rwanda, and so there was a felt need to associate them with a Hutu 'ideologue' and, even better, a renowned historian who was widely known as one of the founders of this station. The opportunity was too good to miss, and the risk of the trial becoming a sacrificial rite rather than a vehicle of justice was immense.

The only way to avoid this risk and resist this temptation would have been to rely on the absolutely rigorous principles of individual criminal responsibility in international law that were established at Nuremberg and that have been further refined in the statutes of the ICTY and the ICTR and the decisions made by those tribunals. These principles distinguish two forms of responsibility, or more precisely, one general principle of responsibility and one exception that is strictly defined to address the specific role of superior authorities:

- A defendant cannot be found guilty unless it is proved that he or she personally committed a positive act aimed at deliberately executing a crime. This is the direct individual responsibility provided for in Article 6.1 of the statute of the ICTR (ICTR 1994).

- The statute of the ICTR also establishes a specific responsibility that represents an exception to this first principle: the responsibility of superiors who did not personally order or commit a crime but did allow their subordinates to do so and failed to take any action to prevent or punish them. This noteworthy exception was designed to hold military commanders accountable for crimes committed by their soldiers. It 'extends to civilian superiors only to the extent that they exercise a degree of control over their subordinates which is similar to that of military commanders' (ICTR 2002: para. 42; ICTY 1998: para. 378). This is the criterion of 'effective control'.

Whichever of these forms of responsibility is involved, the proof on which it is based must be established 'beyond any reasonable doubt' and, once again, with a rigour commensurate with the legal, human, historical and symbolic issues associated with any trial for crimes against humanity. The ICTR judges should, therefore, have gone beyond the rumours and denunciations in the media and insisted on verifying the facts for themselves, hearing the direct witnesses and accessing the original documents. Only by thus strictly adhering both to the principles and to the evidence could the judges at the Media Trial have resisted the siren's song of public opinion or, more prosaically, the pressures from friend and foe in Kigali.

Fifty years after Nuremberg, this extremely political trial provided an opportunity to demonstrate that in the twenty-first century, international criminal justice was not just 'victor's justice' and did not depend on which side won. Instead, it could have been shown to be a solemn vehicle for the triumph of justice, in which the principles of law prevailed over any form of opportunism, whatever the good intentions behind it.

But what actually happened in the Nahimana case (to cite only this example) is that the judges acted just as they had when they redefined the elements of the crime of incitement. They abandoned a strict interpretation of the principles of individual criminal responsibility, they deemed certain facts to be decisive that it is fair to say had not been proven and they remained silent about other well-known facts that had been amply demonstrated in the course of the trial.

The disappearance of the criteria of law

The Nahimana case demanded a new, rigorous form of analysis in light of the principles of international criminal law. Unlike Streicher, Fritzsche and Ruggiu, Ferdinand Nahimana was never prosecuted for statements that he had made personally. (For that matter, he never spoke over the airwaves of RTLM at any time in 1994.) Nor was he being prosecuted for orders that he had given to others. He was being prosecuted mainly for statements made by broadcasters on this radio station when he himself was either outside Rwanda or in the remote western part of the country and was not maintaining any contact of any sort with these journalists or with their manager who remained in Kigali. The presumption that he had the material ability to exercise 'effective control' over these journalists, similar to the control that military commanders exercise over their subordinates, while these journalists were located in Kigali and encircled by the RPF, was extremely audacious not to say completely implausible.

This assumption was all the more tenuous because Nahimana was a civilian and after 7 April 1994, RTLM, like the government radio station and various other private and quasi-public institutions, had been requisitioned by the army, which both controlled it and provided its logistical support and which, moreover, was doing so in a context of war, civil war and genocide. But the ICTR judges carefully refrained from citing these specific circumstances and examining them in light of the demands of international law, that is, the fundamental criterion of the effective ability to control and punish. Their silence on this matter was tantamount to abandoning this criterion entirely.

It is significant that the judges do not cite this fundamental criterion at any point in their lengthy discussion about control over RTLM radio *before* 6 April 1994. Instead, they merely contend that the defendant played 'a very active role in the management' of RTLM as a member of its board of directors. Not a word about his personal ability to give orders or impose punishment, that is, to be a superior in the full sense of the word, with possession of the effective control that the international criminal tribunals, in their judgements, have been careful to distinguish from mere influence that is insufficient to impose criminal liability.[8]

Regarding the key period, from April to July 1994, the judges' 'demonstration' becomes even sketchier. According to them, despite his break with RTLM, Ferdinand Nahimana continued to have authority over it, because they say that in early July 1994, he intervened (under circumstances unknown) to stop the broadcasting of attacks on UNAMIR – an indicator, according to the judges, of his de facto control over this radio station (ICTR 2003a: para. 568). Ferdinand Nahimana absolutely denies having made such an intervention. In any case, this in no way demonstrates that Mr Nahimana possessed this quasi-military power to control and punish from which the responsibility of superior authority arises. The cardinal criterion – the rule of law – has completely disappeared and been replaced with an opportunistic assessment of both the facts and the law – one that totally contradicts earlier decisions made by these same judges (ICTR 2002: para. 43 and 163; ICTR 2003b: para. 474–7).[9]

Identifying the guilty: rejecting the evidence and accepting the hypothesis

'Who is hiding behind RTLM?' Reporters Sans Frontières demanded to know when its spokesperson, Philippe Dahinden, addressed the United Nations Commission on Human Rights on 25 May 1994, at the height of the genocide, while RTLM continued to broadcast its calls for extermination. Who was at the controls? Who commanded this battalion of 'journalists' engaged in this 'war of words', an integral part of the total war and genocide that unfurled before the eyes of a deliberately passive 'international community'?

What was going on between April and July 1994?

Rejecting the evidence

The judges do not dispute that Ferdinand Nahimana was absent throughout this period. The army had seized control over the radio station and the effective day-to-day management was provided by its director, Phocas Habimana, and its editor-in-chief, Gaspard Gahigi. These facts were established incontrovertibly by the only two direct witnesses called to appear, both of them journalists who were present at RTLM from April to July: Georges Ruggiu, a witness for the prosecution, and Valérie Bemeriki, a witness for the defence.

This direct testimony from both sides was completely consistent with the situation then prevailing in Rwanda and especially in Kigali, which was encircled by RPF troops. The only people who had effective control of RTLM were the ones who were in the studios in Kigali, directing, monitoring and sanctioning the actions of the soldier-broadcasters, who wore military uniforms and carried out the orders of the only authority that had the means of commanding obedience in the midst of the massacres: the army.

UNAMIR commander Lieutenant General Roméo Dallaire confirms that when he tried to do something about RTLM's broadcasts, the person he contacted was General Augustin Bizimungu, the chief of staff of the army (Dallaire 2004: 442).

With a wave of their hand and a few scant remarks, the judges dismissed the entire testimony of both these witnesses as lacking credibility, swept this evidence aside and blithely ignored an entire aspect of the reality without which no valid judgements could be made.

Accepting the hypothesis

Conversely, the judges accorded the most uncertain allegations the status of legal proof when they pointed to a hypothetical connection between Ferdinand Nahimana and RTLM. Mr Nahimana's conviction as a superior authority because of criminal broadcasts made from April to July 1994 was based on a single element of proof: the indirect testimony of an expert witness, Alison Des Forges, whose bias and whose willingness to distort the meaning of a text had been so scathingly criticized by the Canadian judges in the Mugesera case.

Ms Des Forges asserted that on 28 February 2000, more than five years after the fact, she had a telephone interview with a French official who told her that he had been present at a conversation in Goma, in late June or early July 1994, between a diplomat from Operation Turquoise and Ferdinand Nahimana, during which Mr Nahimana had promised to intervene to stop the broadcasts against UNAMIR. Ms Des Forges said that the content of this telephone interview was based on a French diplomatic telegram. From this, the judges concluded that Mr Nahimana had effective superior authority over the radio station (ICTR 2003a: para. 568 and 972).

But contrary to what the judges concluded, this supposed conversation, which Ferdinand Nahimana denied, clearly proved nothing, because there was nothing to establish that he did subsequently intervene.[10] Moreover, RTLM stopped broadcasting the day before Kigali was taken by the RPF on 3 July 1994. The station did not resume broadcasting until 9 July, when it set up shop briefly in

Gisenyi, in the extreme northwest of Rwanda, before going silent for good on 14 July. RTLM's broadcasts ceased because of the military victory of the RPF, not because of this hypothetical conversation!

Abandoning the search for the truth

What must be emphasized here is the break down of any thoroughness in the search for the truth in a matter that the judges themselves regarded as one of the essential foundations of their judgement. This was a piece of hearsay evidence; the witnesses cited were known and available, yet none of them was called to appear. The alleged telegram was neither entered into evidence by the prosecutor nor demanded by the judges.

On 9 May 2003, the judges deliberately opposed the appearance of one of the witnesses, stating: 'The Chamber sees no reason to call this witness under Rule 98 and does not find it "essential to truth-seeking" to do so.' Six months later, the same judges made the telephone conversation with expert witness Des Forges the cornerstone of their decision to sentence Ferdinand Nahimana to life imprisonment.

The demonstration beyond any reasonable doubt that a defendant has participated in a crime against humanity cannot be based on confidences that the court refuses to verify and that merely suggest a hypothesis that is refuted by the official statements of direct witnesses.[11] Beyond the fate of the individual who is convicted and sentenced under such circumstances, such laxness on the part of the judiciary can cast discredit on international justice. As always, defending human rights means defending the rights of the individual and, by defending the right of Ferdinand Nahimana to a fair trial, we act to ensure that international justice does not quickly become a laughing stock to its detractors.

The same is true for another essential aspect of participation in a crime under international law: the demonstration of criminal intent.

From the search for criminal intent to the trial for intentions

The law emphasizes that where incitement to genocide is concerned, criminal intent must be demonstrated in its strictest and fullest sense:

> That is to say that the person who is inciting to commit genocide must have himself the specific intent to commit genocide, namely, to destroy, in whole or in part, a national, ethnical, racial or religious group, as such. (ICTR 1998: para. 560)

Unless the accused confesses to such intent, it must be clearly determined from the accused's own words and deeds:

> The Chamber notes, however, that the use of context to determine the intent of an accused must be counterbalanced with the actual conduct of the Accused. The Chamber is of the opinion that the Accused's intent should be determined, above all, from his words and deeds, and should be evident from patterns of purposeful action. (ICTR 2002: para. 63)

To overcome the evidence to the contrary, the judges claimed to discern this genocidal intent in Ferdinand Nahimana on the basis of statements by third parties, of a speech in which he called for the unity of all Rwandans without ethnic distinction and, last, of a deliberately abridged interview whose meaning could be ambiguous only if someone added a word that did not appear in it and removed those words that made its meaning clear.

'Well if not you, it was your brother, or another just like you': the logic of scapegoating

While not disputing the lack of any contact between Ferdinand Nahimana and RTLM's journalists from April through July 1994, the judges made these journalists' broadcasts during this period the proof of his genocidal intent (ICTR 2003a: para. 957–60). The judges thus took criminal intent, that most intimately personal element of the crime, and collectivized it by a logic exemplified in the above line from the French moralist La Fontaine's fable of the wolf and the lamb: the logic of scapegoating.

What makes this detour through the words of third parties all the more unacceptable is that the judges never even suggested that during this period the accused gave any kind of instruction for criminal broadcasts of this kind to be made.

Proof through absurdity

On 21 February 1993, more than a year before the genocide, at the peak of an RPF offensive that brought over a million refugees to the gates of Kigali, Ferdinand Nahimana published an essay entitled 'Rwanda: current problems and solutions'. In it, he wrote:

> Regionalism, 'collinisme',[12] and ethnism, these are the true causes of the disaster that is now befalling Rwanda and its peoples.
>
> In Africa today, ethnic, tribal, regional, and even religious differences continue to impose tremendous burdens that impede the development of peoples and nations. Ethnic identity has been used as a tool to divide and foment hatred among members of the national community. Ethnism has been erected into a system for the mutual exclusion of members of different ethnic groups.
>
> In fact, the Republic was nearly brought down (and this is no secret) by the revenge-seeking mobs of the former monarchists, their descendants, and their supporters who have now organized themselves into what they call the Rwandan Patriotic Front (RPF) *Inkotanyi*.
>
> That is why the leaders of the parties must realize without delay that the number 1 enemy of Rwanda and democracy is the RPF. (Prosecution exhibit P25B in the Media Trial, translation)

There is no ambiguity here: the only enemy of Rwanda is the RPF–*Inkotanyi*, and all of the vital forces in Rwandan society, without ethnic or regional distinction, must unite against it. Nahimana therefore suggested the establishment of a civil defence organization to be overseen by the government authorities:

> For this operation to succeed, all of society must recognize the need for it and stand as one against any form of collective threat or aggression. This recognition will then automatically repudiate hatred and division based on ethnic and regional origin.

Yet according to the judges, this essay must be regarded as proof of the intention to exterminate all or part of the Tutsi population – men, women, and children, the old and the young – a year and a half later. Why? Because its author was imprudent enough to commit the inexpiable crime of alluding to the existence of a 'Tutsi league' from which the RPF may have emerged (ICTR 2003a: 966).

Here we come to the culmination of this logic of ultimate causes that demanded a guilty verdict for Ferdinand Nahimana, as well as of its intrepretive corollary, criticized earlier with regard to the analysis of the propaganda broadcast by RTLM. Taken to its final conclusion, the judges' approach amounts to making a text say the opposite of what it really says, despite all the evidence, even though all of the accused's other writings belie this misleading interpretation.

Manipulating the evidence

On 24 April 1994, when Ferdinand Nahimana again set foot on Rwandan soil in the border town of Cyangugu after twelve days in exile with his family in Burundi and Zaire, a journalist from Radio Rwanda asked him about his journey and the current situation. In response he cited the need to 'stop the enemy', declared his refusal to accept the 'dictatorship' of the *Inkotanyi*, and stated his satisfaction with the way that the country's two radio stations had called on the people to cooperate with the military authorities to confront the invader.

At that time, the international press was still hesitant in its analysis of the events in Rwanda (whether they constituted war or civil war, interethnic massacres or genocide), while the United States and the United Kingdom were working successfully to prevent recognition of the genocide by the Security Council.

Here too, the judges take this single public statement, which lasted only a few seconds, and turn it into an endorsement of ethnic extermination. But they do so only through an incomplete interpretation of a deliberately abridged text. The recording of Nahimana's words came from the archives of the RPF regime and the last part of it was suppressed, but the judges ignored the protests of the defence and refused to discuss its admissibility.

There was nothing in this statement that could be seen as a form of criminal incitement, but the judges claimed to have found that it contained an idiomatic expression with a double meaning – an expression that actually was not even there (the verb *gukora,* which normally means 'to work' but in a certain context can mean 'to kill'). They thus misconstrued a statement from which an essential portion had to be excised and a word that the accused never uttered had to be added simply to make it not explicitly criminal, but just possibly ambiguous. And it was on the basis of these elements alone that the judges decided that Ferdinand Nahimana's intention to exterminate the Tutsi population of Rwanda had been established beyond any reasonable doubt.

In the search for a symbolic scapegoat, the rules of criminal procedure were abandoned in favour of a 'trial for intentions' in which evidence was amalgamated and manipulated – in other words, the first step down the road to political trials, which pose a mortal danger for international criminal justice.

* * *

International criminal justice embodies the defence of the individual's humanity against mass crimes and crimes by the state. When the state is criminal or criminally complicit or impotent, international criminal justice is the last recourse for the individual and, through the individual, for outraged humanity. When faced with violations of human rights so extreme as to constitute dehumanization, this justice must be the highest and most unyielding form of civilization in the defence of the individual, without compromise, connivance or calculation, with complete independence, and with no other concern than to enforce the law rigorously and impartially. That is its sole source of legitimacy; that is what its effectiveness depends upon.

As defenders of the individual, lawyers are by their very nature at the heart of this new struggle between civilization and barbarism. As counsel for a defendant on trial before an international court, the ICTR, I have a duty to point out the dangers that, within this court charged with protecting the rights of humanity, threaten their very foundations: human rights, and among these the right to a fair trial.

As defence counsel for Mr Ferdinand Nahimana, and through him for the rights of any individual accused of a crime, I cannot stand silent and let judicial methods and behaviours that I find contrary to the rules of justice take root to the naïve or cynical applause of public opinion.

Resist the temptation to be arbitrary or opportunistic, and stick to the strict enforcement of the existing rules. Resist the temptation to scapegoat, and convict only on the basis of indisputable evidence. These are the principles that must guide international justice in the twenty-first century.

NOTES

1. The ICTY Trial Chamber defined persecution as 'the gross or blatant denial, on discriminatory grounds, of a fundamental right, laid down in international customary or treaty law, reaching the same level of gravity as the other acts prohibited in Article 5 [of the Statute]' (ICTY 1998: para. 621). 'It would be contrary to the principle of legality to convict someone of persecution based on a definition found in international refugee law or human rights law' (ICTY 1998: para. 589).
2. 'The Chamber considers it evident that hate speech targeting a population on the basis of ethnicity, or other discriminatory grounds, reaches this level of gravity and constitutes persecution under article 3(h) of its Statute' (ICTR 2003a: 1072).
3. The Canadian judges' conclusions were unequivocal: 'The Kabaya speech was made on November 22, 1992 by a political figure before a partisan meeting in a context of armed aggression. The speech was improvised and not based on any notes, and the various speakers were not consulted before beginning to speak. The speaker spoke fluently, used clear and colourful language, sometimes even brutal language. This speaker was a fervent supporter of

democracy, patriotic pride and resistance to invading foreign forces. The themes of his speeches were elections, courage and love. His family life, his personal and professional relationships, his past, did not indicate any tendency toward racism. Even though it is true some of his statements were misplaced or unfortunate, there is nothing in the evidence to indicate that Mr Mugesera, under the cover of anecdotes or other imagery, deliberately incited to murder, hatred or genocide. The principal witnesses for the Minister – Ms Des Forges, Messrs Gillet, Reyntjens, Overdulve and Hnadye – only provided a biased or misinformed view of the events concerning Mr Mugesera.' (*Mugesera v. Canada* 2003: para. 240–1).

4. The murders of Gatabazi, an opponent of President Habyarimana, and Gapyisi, Bucyana, Rwambuka and Katumba, all hostile to the RPF.
5. President Habyarimana's party, to which Ferdinand Nahimana belonged.
6. Massacres at Kirambo on 18 and 19 November 1993.
7. Father Sibomana was a correspondent for Reporters Sans Frontières.
8. The Appeals Chamber of the ICTY clearly condemned the theory that influence, independent of any official command authority, can suffice to impose the responsibility of superior authority: 'It is clear, however, that substantial influence as a means of control in any sense which falls short of the possession of effective control over subordinates, which requires the possession of material abilities to prevent subordinate offences or to punish subordinate offenders, lacks sufficient support in State practice and judicial decisions. Nothing relied on by the Prosecution indicates that there is sufficient evidence of State practice or judicial authority to support a theory that substantial influence as a means of exercising command responsibility has the standing of a rule of customary law, particularly a rule by which criminal liability would be imposed.' (ICTY 2001b: para. 266)
9. Two of the three judges who rendered this decision were also members of the Chamber that rendered the judgement in the Media Trial. In the Media Trial, they went so far as to stress that for a political authority, the minister of information, issuing orders during an attack was not sufficient proof of a superior–subordinate relationship, that is, the ability to prevent and to punish.
10. The judges recognized this expressly in paragraph 62 of their interlocutory decision of 13 May 2003.
11. RTLM journalist, Valérie Bemeriki, officially denied having received any instructions to go easier on UNAMIR.
12. Defined in the judgement as 'a cantonal regionalism consisting of favoritism or preference based on a person's hill of origin.'

REFERENCES

Note: Most of the documents of the ICTR can be found on its website, available at <www.ictr.org> and in the database of the Netherlands Institute of Human Rights <www.sim.law.uu.nl/>.

Dallaire, R.A. 2004. *Shake Hands with the Devil: the Failure of Humanity in Rwanda.* Random House, Toronto, Canada.

ICC (International Criminal Court). 2002. Rome statute of the International Criminal Court. Public Information and Documentation Section of the ICC, The Hague, Netherlands. Available at <http://www.icc-cpi.int/library/about/officialjournal/Rome_Statute_120704-EN.pdf> (accessed 7 September 2005).

ICTR (International Criminal Tribunal for Rwanda). 1994. Statute of the international tribunal. (Security Council Resolution 955). Office of the United Nations High Commissioner for Human Rights, New York, NY, USA. Available at <www.ohchr.org/english/law/itr.htm> (accessed 23 October 2005).

—— 1998. Judgement. In *The Prosecutor v. Jean-Paul Akayesu.* Case no. ICTR-96–4-T. ICTR, Arusha, Tanzania, 2 September.

—— 2000. Judgement. In *The Prosecutor v. Georges Ruggiu.* Case no. ICTR-97–32-I. ICTR, Arusha, Tanzania, 1 June.

—— 2002. Judgement. In *The Prosecutor (Appellant) v. Ignace Bagilishema (Respondent).* Case no. ICTR-95–1A-A. ICTR, Arusha, Tanzania, 3 July.

—— 2003a. Judgement and sentence. In *The Prosecutor v. Ferdinand Nahimana, Jean-Bosco Barayagwiza and Hassan Ngeze*. Case no. ICTR-99–52-T. Arusha, Tanzania, 3 December.

—— 2003b. Judgement and sentence. In *The Prosecutor v. Eliézer Niyitegeka*. Case no. ICTR-96–14-T. ICTR, Arusha, Tanzania, 16 May.

ICTY (Internation Criminal Tribunal for Yugoslavia). 1998. Judgement. In *The Prosecutor v. Zejnil Delalic et al.* (the Celebici case). Case no. IT-96–21-T. ICTY, The Hague, Netherlands, 16 November.

—— 2000. Judgement. In *Prosecutor v. Zoran Kupreskic, Mirjan Kupreskic, Vlatko Kupreskic, Drago Josipovic, Dragan Papic, Vladimir Santic, also known as 'Vlado'*. ICTY, The Hague, Netherlands, 14 January. Available at <www.un.org/icty/kupreskic/trialc2/judgement/index.htm> (accessed 25 October 2005).

—— 2001a. Judgement. In *Prosecutor v. Kordic*. ICTY, The Hague, Netherlands, 26 February.

—— 2001b. Judgement. In *Prosecutor v. Zejnil Delalic et al.* (the Celebici case). Case no. IT-96–21-A. ICTY, The Hague, Netherlands, 20 February.

Mugesera v. Canada (Minister of Citizenship and Immigration) (F.C.A.). 2003. Federal Court of Appeal, Décary, Létourneau and Pelletier JJ.A. Québec, April 28 and 29; Ottawa, 8 September 2003. Available at <recueil.cmf.gc.ca/fc/2004/pub/v1/2004fc33123.html>.

UN (United Nations). 1948. Debates of the 6th Committee of the UN General Assembly. UN, New York, USA, 29 October.

—— 1951. *Convention on the prevention and punishment of the crime of genocide*. Adopted by Resolution 260 (III) of the UN General Assembly, 9 December. 1948. *United Nations Treaty Series* no. 1021, vol. 78: 277. Available at <http://www.preventgenocide.org/law/convention/text.htm> (accessed 6 September 2005).

—— 1966. *International covenant on civil and political rights*. General Assembly Resolution 2200A (XXI), 16 December. Available at <www.unhchr.ch/html/menu3/b/a_ccpr.htm> (accessed 6 September 2005).

29
A Lost Opportunity for Justice: Why Did the ICTR Not Prosecute Gender Propaganda?

Binaifer Nowrojee

> 72. The newspaper and the radio explicitly and repeatedly, in fact relentlessly, targeted the Tutsi population for destruction. Demonizing the Tutsi as having inherently evil qualities, equating the ethnic group with 'the enemy' and portraying its women as seductive enemy agents, the media called for the extermination of the Tutsi ethnic group as a response to the political threat that they associated with Tutsi ethnicity.
>
> 118. ... Tutsi women, in particular, were targeted for persecution. The portrayal of the Tutsi woman as femme fatale, and the message that Tutsi women were seductive agents of the enemy was conveyed repeatedly... [and] vilified and endangered Tutsi women ... defining the Tutsi woman as an enemy in this way... articulated a framework that made the sexual attack of Tutsi women a foreseeable consequence of the role attributed to them. (ICTR 2003, judgement see Chapter 25)

In December 2003, the International Criminal Tribunal for Rwanda (ICTR) delivered a judgement that convicted three media executives for their rôle in instigating hatred and inciting genocide. It was a significant judgement in that it acknowledged the powerful role that the media and hate speech can play in inciting people to mass violence. In Rwanda, the consequences were devastating. In a three-month period, some 800,000 were killed and thousands were raped and mutilated.

Why were none of these men held responsible for their role in provoking the sexual attacks against Tutsi women? Clearly the evidence was there. In strong language, the court found that these media executives had 'targeted', 'vilified' and 'endangered' Tutsi women in such a way that made the sexual attacks 'a foreseeable consequence of the role attributed to them' (ICTR 2003, judgement summary: para. 118).

But the ICTR prosecutor never led charges to hold these three defendants responsible for their part in encouraging the brutal rapes and sexual mutilations. In fact, in arguing the case, the prosecutor paid little or no attention to the vicious gender propaganda, despite the strong evidence that continued to make its way into the courtroom and, ultimately, into the judgement.

This negligence is part of a larger failure of the Prosecutor's Office at the ICTR to fully deliver justice to Rwanda's victims. Given the overwhelming evidence of widespread sexual violence during the genocide, the lack of accountability for these crimes can only be attributed to the lack of a comprehensive strategy on the part of the Prosecutor's Office to effectively investigate and prosecute these crimes.

The legacy is that the crimes against Rwandan women are largely going unpunished by the ICTR. At the tenth anniversary of the genocide (in April 2004), the figures were dismal: of the completed cases, 90 per cent had no sexual violence convictions. In 70 per cent of those cases, the prosecutor had not even brought sexual violence charges.

The 'Media Trial' judgement (ICTR 2003), in particular, stands as a symbol of the neglect of the prosecutor to pursue the sexual violence crimes against women even though she possessed strong evidence, thus making the prosecutor responsible for an injustice to women in the course of administering international justice.

WIDESPREAD SEXUAL VIOLENCE DURING THE GENOCIDE

When Roméo Dallaire, commander of the United Nations peacekeeping force during the Rwanda genocide, testified before the ICTR, he graphically described the female corpses he had witnessed:

> we could notice on many sites, sometimes very fresh – that is, I am speaking of my observers and myself – that young girls, young women, would be laid out with their dresses over their heads, the legs spread and bent. You could see what seemed to be semen drying or dried. And it all indicated to me that these women were raped. And then a variety of material were crushed or implanted into their vaginas; their breasts were cut off, and the faces were, in many cases, still the eyes were open and there was like a face that seemed horrified or something. They all laid on their backs. So there were some men that were mutilated also, their genitals and the like. A number of them were – women had their breasts cut off or their stomach open. But there was, I would say generally at the sites you could find younger girls and young women who had been raped. (ICTR-98–41-T transcript, 20 January 2004)

The following month, when Dallaire's assistant, Major Brent Beardsley, followed as a witness in the same 'Military I' case, the prosecuting lawyer asked: 'With respect to the female corpses, in particular, did you make any observations about any particular characteristics that those corpses may have had?' Beardsley replied:

> Yes, two things, really. One, when they killed women it appeared that the blows that had killed them were aimed at sexual organs, either breasts or

vagina; they had been deliberately swiped or slashed in those areas. And, secondly, there was a great deal of what we came to believe was rape, where the women's bodies or clothes would be ripped off their bodies, they would be lying back in a back position, their legs spread, especially in the case of very young girls. I'm talking girls as young as six, seven years of age, their vaginas would be split and swollen from obviously multiple gang rape, and then they would have been killed in that position. So they were laying in a position they had been raped; that's the position they were in.

Rape was one of the hardest things to deal with in Rwanda on our part. It deeply affected every one of us. We had a habit at night of coming back to the headquarters and, after the activities had slowed down for the night, before we went to bed, sitting around talking about what happened that day, drink coffee, have a chat, and amongst all of us the hardest thing that we had to deal with was not so much the bodies of people, the murder of people – I know that can sound bad, but that wasn't as bad to us as the rape and especially the systematic rape and gang rape of children. Massacres kill the body. Rape kills the soul. And there was a lot of rape.

It seemed that everywhere we went, from the period of 19th of April until the time we left, there was rape everywhere near these killing sites. (ICTR-98–41-T transcript, 3 February 2004)

Sexual violence, directed predominantly against Tutsi women, occurred on a massive scale during the Rwanda genocide. Although the exact number of women raped will never be known, testimonies from survivors confirm that rape was extremely widespread. Thousands of women were individually raped, gang-raped, raped with objects such as sharpened sticks or gun barrels, held in sexual slavery (either collectively by a militia group or singled out by one militia man) or sexually mutilated. These crimes were frequently part of a pattern in which Tutsi women were raped after they had witnessed the torture and killings of their relatives and the destruction of their homes. Many women were killed immediately after being raped or raped to death using sharp sticks or other objects (Nowrojee 1996).

The sexual violence was perpetrated largely by members of the Hutu militia groups known as the *Interahamwe*, by other civilians and by soldiers of the Rwandan armed forces (Forces Armées Rwandaises (FAR)), including the Presidential Guard. Administrative, military and political leaders at the national and local levels, as well as heads of militia, directed, encouraged and allowed both the killings and sexual violence to further their political goal: the destruction of the Tutsi as a group. Sexually subjugating and mutilating Tutsi women was both a way to punish the women and to attack the ethnic group.

GENOCIDE PROPAGANDA AGAINST TUTSI WOMEN[1]

The outpouring of violence directed against Rwandan women on the basis of their gender and ethnicity was fuelled by the hate propaganda before and during the genocide. To this end, the media played a role in propagating and disseminating stereotypes of Tutsi women as devious seductresses who would use their beauty to undermine the Hutu community. The hate propaganda before and during the genocide demonized Tutsi women's sexuality and, as the Media Trial judgement noted, 'made the sexual attack of Tutsi women a foreseeable consequence'.

In the years preceding the genocide, the organizers used propaganda to heighten fear and hatred between Hutu and Tutsi. Through the written press and then through Radio-Télévision des Milles Collines (RTLM), extremists taught that the two were different peoples: the Hutu part of the larger category of 'Bantu' and the Tutsi part of the 'Ethiopid' or 'Nilotic' group. Such categories, once thought to be real, are now recognized to be inaccurate groupings and a legacy of nineteenth century European racism. Simplifying and distorting history, the propagandists insisted that Tutsi were foreign conquerors, who had mastered the majority Hutu through a combination of ruse and ruthlessness. According to these beliefs, the Tutsi had refused to accept the destruction of their power in the 1959 revolution and were determined to re-assert control over the Hutu.

In their drive to dominate, propagandists said, Tutsi used their women – thought to be more beautiful than Hutu women – to infiltrate Hutu ranks. Through the written press and then through RTLM radio, extremists portrayed Tutsi women as devious seductresses who would undermine the Hutu. The propaganda warned Hutu men to beware of Tutsi women. Military men were barred from marrying Tutsi women. The stereotypes also portrayed Tutsi women as arrogant and looking down on Hutu men whom they considered ugly and inferior (Chrétien et al. 1995).

Beginning in 1990, over a dozen newspapers in Kinyarwanda or French were launched, and they systematically exploited ethnic hatred (Chrétien et al. 1995: 45–7). Although these papers had a relatively small circulation, mostly in the capital, Kigali, they were often taken to the countryside by urban workers on the weekends and their message was shared widely in rural communities. In some cases, the local authorities in the rural areas were provided with copies. In addition to articles excoriating the Tutsi community, the magazines printed graphic cartoons portraying Tutsi women using their supposed sexual prowess on UN peacekeepers (Rwandan Patriotic Front (RPF) supporters according to the propaganda) and the moderate Prime Minister Agathe Uwilingiyimana in various sexual poses with other politicians (Chrétien et al. 1995: 336, 368).

Kangura ('wake up' in Kinyarwanda) magazine was the first and most virulent voice of hate. *Kangura* often warned the Hutu to be on guard against Tutsi women. According to *Kangura*, '[t]he *Inkotanyi* [a word used to refer to the RPF meaning 'fierce fighter' in Kinyarwanda] will not hesitate to transform their sisters, wives and mothers into pistols' to conquer Rwanda (Anon. 1991). In the December 1990 issue of *Kangura*, editor Hassan Ngeze published the 'Ten Commandments' of the Hutu, four of which dealt specifically with women (Anon. 1990):

1. Every Hutu should know that a Tutsi woman, wherever she is, works for the interest of her Tutsi ethnic group. As a result, we shall consider a traitor any Hutu who: marries a Tutsi woman; befriends a Tutsi woman; employs a Tutsi woman as a secretary or a concubine.
2. Every Hutu should know that our Hutu daughters are more suitable and conscientious in their role as woman, wife and mother of the family. Are they not beautiful, good secretaries and more honest?
3. Hutu women, be vigilant and try to bring your husbands, brothers and sons back to reason.
7. The Rwandese Armed Forces should be exclusively Hutu. The experience of the October [1990] war has taught us a lesson. No member of the military shall marry a Tutsi.

Another issue of *Kangura* (1992, 29 (January): 16–17) accused Tutsi women of monopolizing positions of employment in both the public and private sectors, hiring their Tutsi sisters on the basis of their thin noses (a stereotypically 'Tutsi feature'), thereby contributing to the unemployment rate of the Hutu, particularly Hutu women. *Kangura* called on Hutu to use the necessary vigilance against the Tutsi, whom it dubbed the *inyenzi* (cockroaches), and accomplice Hutu (*ibyitso*: traitors). One Hutu woman commented, 'According to the propaganda, the Tutsi were hiding the enemy. And their beautiful women were being used to do it. So, everybody knew what that meant' (Human Rights Watch/FIDH interview, 18 March 1996, Kigali).

THE IMPACT OF THE MEDIA PROPAGANDA DURING THE VIOLENCE

When the violence began in 1994, not surprisingly, aggression against Tutsi women targeted their sexuality and was fuelled by both ethnic and gender stereotypes. Rape served to shatter the image of Tutsi women – as spies for the Tutsi community through their sexual prowess – by humiliating, degrading, and ultimately destroying them. Even Tutsi women married to Hutu men were not spared, despite the custom that a wife was protected by her husband's lineage after marriage.

Throughout the genocide, women were consistently raped, with explicit verbal reference to their status as Tutsi women. It is clear that the rapists took up the media message that raping Tutsi women was justified because of their ethnicity and gender. Of the statements that concentrated on the Tutsi stereotype, the overwhelming majority were sexual references. Tutsi women were perceived as overly sexualized, 'destroying the country with their seduction'; therefore, many rapists referred to their right to satisfy their sexual desire by force. Rape witnesses and victims report the following statements, among others: 'Now we can have Tutsi women for free,' 'The tables have turned so now I can satisfy my sexual desires' or 'It is unfortunate to be killing Tutsi women since they taste better than Hutu women.' Rapists repeatedly referred to Tutsi genitalia and the desire to see what Tutsi look or taste like. Rape survivors recount comments such as: 'We want to see how sweet Tutsi women are,' or 'You Tutsi women think that you are too good for us,' or 'We want to see if a Tutsi woman is like a Hutu woman,' or 'If there were peace, you would never accept me,' or 'You Tutsi girls are too proud,' apparently setting the stage for their degradation.

Many statements from broadcasters or in *Kangura* were cast in the form of a proverb. The use of proverbs suggests a concerted effort to promote slogans to motivate rapists and provide a broadly accessible terminology of justification in perpetrating sexual violence. Rape survivors and witnesses recount rapists saying: 'Tutsi caused problems and must be exterminated with their eggs,' 'If you cannot catch the lice, you kill its egg' and 'If you set out to kill a rat, you must kill the pregnant rat.'

Statements during rape also referred to non-sexual Tutsi stereotyped characteristics. Most either labelled Tutsi women as generally arrogant or sexually arrogant in their sexual refusal of Hutu men. Rapists also repeatedly used general ethic insults, such as 'Tutsi snake'.

Different rapists throughout the country repeatedly employed the same terminology – echoing the invectives in the media propaganda – while raping Tutsi women. The statements at the time of rape demonstrate links with the media propaganda that had advocated the same gender and ethnic stereotypes. Specific insults deployed by the radio and print media were repeated by rapists during rape. This direct correlation between media propoganda and statements by rapists demonstrates a causal link between the propaganda and the ensuing sexual violence across the country.

THE MEDIA TRIAL: A SQUANDERED OPPORTUNITY TO PROSECUTE GENDER PROPAGANDA

In December 2003, the ICTR Trial Chamber handed down a judgement in the Media Trial against two founders of RTML and the editor of *Kangura* newspaper. The three were found guilty of genocide, conspiracy to commit genocide, direct and public incitement to commit genocide and crimes against humanity (extermination and persecution). RTLM founder, Ferdinand Nahimana, and former *Kangura* editor, Hassan Ngeze, received life sentences; Jean-Bosco Barayagwiza, another RTLM founder, was sentenced to 35 years.

Despite the strong evidence in the possession of the prosecuting attorneys, the Prosecutor's Office had not brought charges against the accused for their role in inciting sexual violence against women. Throughout the trial, strong evidence of the gender propaganda and its devastating impact on Tutsi women made its way into the courtroom, and in the judgement the court referred to it several times and noted its devastating impact on Tutsi women. Because the prosecutor had not brought sexual violence charges, the Trial Chamber was not able to convict on that basis; it could only note the many references to women that had arisen during the course of the trial.

The Trial Chamber noted that Tutsi women were particularly targeted for persecution: the presentation of Tutsi women as femmes fatales and a danger to the Hutu that was explicitly associated with sexuality. By defining the Tutsi women as enemies in this way, *Kangura* articulated a framework that made the sexual attack of Tutsi women a 'foreseeable consequence'. The court found that *Kangura* played a substantial role in inciting Hutu hatred and violence against Tutsis, especially Tutsi women:

> The newspaper and radio explicitly and repeatedly, in fact relentlessly, targeted the Tutsi population for destruction. Demonizing the Tutsi as having inherently evil qualities, equating the ethnic group with 'the enemy' and portraying its women as seductive enemy agents, the media called for the extermination of the Tutsi ethnic group as a response to the political threat that they associated with Tutsi ethnicity. (ICTR 2003, summary judgement: para. 72)

The Trial Chamber highlighted the Ten Commandments of the Hutu and the *Kangura* article entitled 'Appeal to the conscience of the Hutu,' which contained various myths about the Tutsi people, including that they were all bloodthirsty and that they used the two weapons of 'money and Tutsi women' against the Hutu. The article warned of an impending Tutsi attack and rallied its readers to commit acts of violence against Tutsis to 'deter the enemy'.

An article published in issue 19 of *Kangura* described Tutsi women enemy agents who infiltrated Hutu households through marriage. The Chamber held that this passage promoted the stereotype that Tutsi women intentionally used their sexuality to lure Hutu men into liaisons to promote the ethnic dominance of the Tutsi over the Hutu.

The judgement recounts testimonies from witnesses who described the effect of the *Kangura* publications and the RTLM broadcasts in inciting Hutu men to attack and kill Tutsi women, including their own Tutsi wives.[2] RTLM broadcasts denounced specific Tutsi women, who were later targeted for violence. Witness BI, who was specifically singled out on RTLM broadcasts that alleged her mother was a Tutsi who had married a Hutu man to make him lose his head, was then violently attacked in her home. Another broadcast about her used explicit sexual imagery and resulted in a sexually motivated attack against her (ICTR 2003: para. 442).

THE ICTR'S SHAMEFUL RECORD IN PROSECUTING SEXUAL VIOLENCE CRIMES

The Media Trial is unfortunately symptomatic of a larger neglect by the ICTR prosecutor to fully prosecute crimes of sexual violence directed at Rwandan women during the genocide. The ICTR was tasked with prosecuting serious violations of international humanitarian law committed during 1994 in Rwanda or by Rwandan citizens in neighbouring states. Rape is a prosecutable crime under international law.

Given the evidence and the elements of the crimes that the ICTR was tasked with prosecuting, virtually every defendant coming before this international court should be charged and convicted, where appropriate, for their role in perpetrating such acts against women or for command responsibility in not preventing the acts of their subordinates.

Ten years after the genocide, the ICTR had handed down 21 sentences: 18 convictions and 3 acquittals.[3] This is approximately a third of those in custody. An overwhelming *90 per cent* of those judgements contain no rape convictions. More disturbing, there are double the number of acquittals for rape than rape convictions.

No rape charges were even brought by the Prosecutor's Office in 70 per cent of the adjudicated cases. In the 30 per cent that included rape charges: only 10 per cent were found guilty for their role in the widespread sexual violence. *Double that number*, 20 per cent, were acquitted because the court found that the prosecutor did not properly present the evidence beyond a reasonable doubt.[4] In real numbers, that means *only two* defendants have specifically been held responsible for their role in the sexual violence crimes (a third was convicted by a judgement which was reversed on appeal), despite the tens of thousands of rapes committed during the genocide.[5] How can this be?

It is hard to imagine that anyone present in Rwanda during the genocide would not have been aware that tens of thousands of women were being attacked with such ferocity. Political, administrative and military leaders at the national and local levels as well as heads of militia directed, encouraged or permitted the killings and sexual violence to further their political goals: the destruction of the Tutsi as a group. They bear responsibility for these abuses.

Much has been written by legal scholars celebrating the international tribunals as an important step in ending impunity for sexual violence against women. The widespread evidence of sexual violence as a weapon of conflict in the former Yugoslavia and during the genocide in Rwanda has led to groundbreaking judgements through the UN tribunals set up to try those responsible for crimes against humanity, genocide and war crimes.[6] The ICTR was feted by lawyers for its first landmark judgement in the case of Akayesu that expanded international law on rape – a point of pride that ICTR officials always cite as a manifestation of their commitment to prosecute sexual violence. Yet, as groundbreaking as the Akayesu judgement is, it is increasingly standing alone as an exception – an anomaly.

If the current trend continues, when the doors of the ICTR close, its judgements will not tell the full story of what happened during the Rwanda genocide. They will not correctly reflect responsibility for the shocking rapes, sexual slavery and sexual mutilations that tens of thousands of Rwandan women suffered.

The jurisprudence as it stands now – a growing string of acquittals for rape – in fact will do the opposite. The record of this tribunal in history will not only minimize responsibility for the crimes against women, but will actually deny that these crimes occurred. A reader of the ICTR jurisprudence will be left believing mistakenly that the mass rapes had little or nothing to do with the genocidal policies of the leaders. That indeed is a serious miscarriage of justice.

PROSECUTING SEXUAL VIOLENCE AS AN AFTERTHOUGHT

There is a reason why 90 per cent of the ICTR judgements do not contain rape convictions and why the number of rape acquittals is double the number of convictions. At the ICTR, crimes of sexual violence have never been *fully and consistently* incorporated into the investigations and strategy of the Prosecutor's Office. No comprehensive prosecution strategy or a precise work plan to document and bring the evidence of sex crimes into the courtroom has been pursued consistently for the past decade.

This is not to say that the Prosecutor's Office has neglected this issue entirely – not at all. Approximately half the cases that the court will ultimately hear contain allegations of sexual violence.[7] Commendable efforts have been made, but the problem is that they have not been consistently pursued. The squandered opportunities, periods of neglect and repeated mistakes have caused major setbacks to effective investigations and prosecutions of sexual violence crimes.

Ten years after the genocide, international justice for Rwandan women remains unattainable largely because of a lack of political will in the Prosecutor's Office to comprehensively investigate or reflect the widespread sexual violence in the indictments – particularly during the tenure of Prosecutor Carla Del Ponte. The sporadic attention to gender crimes over the years has implicitly sent a message to the investigations and prosecution staff that this issue is not important. The lack of sustained attention by the leadership has in turn resulted in a weak institutional capacity within the Prosecutor's Office to effectively investigate and develop the evidence to prosecute these crimes.

Some cases have moved forward without rape charges, sometimes even when the prosecutor is in possession of strong evidence. Other cases with rape charges have come to trial without adequate attention to ensuring that the necessary evidence has been collected. In a significant proportion of the cases, rape charges have been added belatedly as amendments, as an afterthought, rather than an integral part of a prosecution strategy to acknowledge that rape was used as a form of genocidal violence. To this day, trial team leaders continue to have differing, and even contradictory, interpretations of legal responsibility for the violence against women and what legal approaches to adopt in the courtroom.

Despite the rhetoric and the repeated pronouncements expressing a commitment to prosecuting rape, the Prosecutor's Office has never articulated and pursued a consistently defined prosecution strategy of how this crime fits into the genocidal policies of the leaders nor has it consistently employed effective investigative techniques to fully document the crimes against women. The four prosecutors that have held this office since 1994 have adopted a variety of approaches to this issue. As a result, there has never been one identified work plan pursued consistently by all investigators and trial lawyers in putting together their cases on this issue over the decade. To date, the lack of a coherent and consistent policy on sexual violence prosecutions remains a major impediment. Prosecuting trial attorneys are quick to blame their shortfalls on inadequate investigations or unwilling rape victims, rather than to reinvigorate their investigations and to find ways to make the process more enabling for rape victims to testify.

MORE MUST BE DONE BY THE ICTR PROSECUTOR

Sexual violence against women and girls in situations of armed conflict or systematic persecution constitutes a clear breach of international law.[8] Perpetrators of sexual violence can be convicted for rape as a war crime, a crime against humanity or as an act of genocide or torture, if their actions meet the elements of each. Leaders in positions of responsibility who knew or should have known of such abuses and who took no steps to stop subordinates who committed sex crimes can also be held accountable.

It is therefore part of the mandate of the ICTR. It is the job of the prosecutor to effectively investigate and prosecute this crime with the same seriousness as other international crimes under his or her brief. Given what happened in Rwanda, accountability for the sexual violence should be integrated in virtually all the cases given its widespread and systematic use during the Rwanda genocide.

Although the Media Trial judgement is a lost opportunity for the ICTR prosecutor to deliver justice to women, it provides an avenue to redress the historic neglect of gender crimes. The Trial Chamber language that identifies the mass rapes as 'a foreseeable consequence' of the gender propaganda provides a strong basis on which the prosecutor can build to argue that the top military and government command should have had reason to know that widespread sexual violence would be directed at Tutsi women and, therefore, bear responsibility for not preventing or punishing their subordinates.

NOTES

1. The report, *Shattered Lives: Sexual Violence During the Rwandan Genocide and its Aftermath* (Nowrojee 1996) published by Human Rights Watch was written by Binaifer Nowrojee, a consultant to the Women's Rights Project. It was based on interviews and research conducted in Rwanda in March and April 1996 by Binaifer Nowrojee and Janet Fleischman. It remains one of the only dedicated studies of the impact of sexual violence against women during the Rwanda genocide. Readers are referred to it for further information and details on the issue of sexual violence during the genocide.
2. For example, witness GO described the effect of RTLM broadcasts of the Ten Commandments in inciting Hutu men to kill their Tutsi wives: 'The goal of mentioning the ten Hutu commandments was to ensure that the population understood that all the Hutus must become united. And they must have a single fighting goal that they should aim for. And that they should have no link or no relationship between Hutus and Tutsis. And it's for that reason that some men started killing their wives who were Tutsis. In other cases, children who, with the result of a mixed marriage, whether they had a Tutsi mother or a Hutu father, but thought that they were more Hutu than Tutsi, killed their own mothers. Just that it was explained to Hutu widows, i.e., Hutu women who had been married to Tutsi men, and whose husbands had been killed and whose children had been killed, that in fact, it was not a problem. That they had just gotten rid of enemies. And that the only persons who had any link with these people were those women. And that is indeed how things happened.' (ICTR 2003: para. 438)

3. As of April 2004, the ICTR had indicted 82 people and made 66 arrests. Sixteen indicted suspects remained at large and six others were no longer in custody: one died before trial, two have had indictments against them withdrawn and three have been acquitted. Among the 60 in custody, 18 were convicted (12 had appeals pending), 21 accused were on trial and another 21 were in detention awaiting trial. The Appeals Chamber has so far confirmed seven convictions and one acquittal. Still in question was whether the ICTR would bring any new indictments for crimes committed by members of RPF credited with ending the genocide before taking power; and whether the ICTR will opt to transfer some of its caseload either to Rwanda or some other national jurisdiction in order to meet the 2008 completion deadline (ICTR detainees – status chart as of 15 March 2004; see <http://196.45.185.38/ENGLISH/factsheets/detainee.htm for updates.).
4. Alfred Musema (ICTR-96–13), life sentence for rape (2000), overturned on appeal and acquitted of rape (2001); Eliezer Niyitegeka (ICTR-96–14), acquitted of rape (2003); Juvénal Kajelijeli (ICTR-98–44A), acquitted of rape (2003); and Jean de Dieu Kamuhanda (ICTR-99–54), acquitted of rape (2004).
5. Jean Paul Akayesu (ICTR-96–4), 15 years for rape (1998), upheld on appeal (2001); Alfred Musema (ICTR-96–13), life sentence for rape (2000), overturned on appeal and acquitted of rape (2001); Laurent Semanza (ICTR-97–20), 7 and 10 years for two counts of rape, appeal pending.
6. In 1998, the ICTR handed down a landmark judgement in the case of Akayesu. It was the first conviction for genocide by an international court; the first time an international court punished sexual violence in an internal conflict; and the first time that rape was found to be an act of genocide to destroy a group. In 2002, the ICTY issued a significant ruling in the Foca case, convicting three men for rape, torture and enslavement as crimes against humanity. It was the first indictment by an international tribunal solely for crimes of sexual violence against women and the first conviction by the ICTY for rape and enslavement as crimes against humanity.
7. Unless of course the rape charges are withdrawn, as was done in the case of Emmanuel Ndindabahizi in 2003.
8. Rape, when committed on a mass scale, is explicitly identified as a crime against humanity. Rape and other forms of sexual violence against civilians are a violation of the *Geneva Conventions and their Additional Protocols* (for both international and internal conflicts). Sexual violence can be a crime under the Genocide Convention (UN 1951) if committed with the intent to destroy, in whole or in part, a national, ethnic, racial or religious group through killing or serious bodily harm. Rape can also be a form of torture.

REFERENCES

Anonymous. 1991. *Kangura*, 19 (July). (Quoted in Chrétien et al. 1995: 161).

Chrétien, J.P., J.F. Dupaquier and M. Kabanda. 1995. *Rwanda: les médias du génocide.* Karthala, Paris, France. 397 pp.

ICTR (International Criminal Tribunal for Rwanda). 2003. Judgement and sentence. *The Prosecutor v. Ferdinand Nahimana, Jean-Bosco Barayagwiza and Hassan Ngeze*. Case no. ICTR-99–52-T: Arusha, Tanzania, 3 December.

——. 2004. Examination-in-Chief of General Roméo Dallaire, former force commander, U.N. peacekeeping mission in Rwanda (UNAMIR). Transcript. In *The Prosecutor v. Bagasora, Kabiligi, Ntabakuze, Nsengiyumva*. Case no. ICTR-98–41-T.

Nowrojee, B. 1996. *Shattered Lives: Sexual Violence During the Rwandan Genocide and its Aftermath.* Human Rights Watch, New York, NY, USA.

UN (United Nations). 1951. *Convention on the prevention and punishment of the crime of genocide.* Adopted by Resolution 260 (III) of the UN General Assembly, 9 December. 1948. UN Treaty Series no. 1021, vol. 78: 277. Available at <www.preventgenocide.org/law/convention/text.htm> (accessed 6 September 2005).

Part Four

After the Genocide and the Way Forward

30
Intervening to Prevent Genocidal Violence: the Role of the Media

Frank Chalk

The media of mass communications today include traditional printed newspapers, magazines and journals, as well as the twentieth century's core electronic resources: radio, television and the Internet. In wealthy nations, the print media, television and the Internet predominate, while in poorer states, often marked by low rates of literacy, the medium of choice for shaping and reinforcing public opinion is radio.

In utilitarian genocides, largely motivated by the desire to create, expand and preserve formal states and empires, the perpetrator calls directly on the professional armed forces of the state to facilitate the acquisition of wealth, eliminate a perceived threat or spread terror. But in genocides motivated by the search for a perfect future inspired by a utopian ideology, the state demonizes the victim group and its members, excluding them from the universe of mutual human obligations. This process usually requires intensive, sustained propaganda to mobilize violence on a grand scale. Crimes against humanity, and especially genocide, require the spread of hate propaganda and disinformation throughout the general population to reinforce key motivating beliefs. Other motives – acquisition of wealth, elimination of a perceived threat and spread of terror – often play a role in ideologically motivated genocides, but largely among the ordinary killers who operate at a social and political level below that of the key architects of the genocide.

ACUTE CURRENT QUESTIONS REGARDING THE ROLE OF THE MEDIA

The media do not make ideologically motivated genocide happen, but they facilitate and legitimate it. Low-level Hutu perpetrators of the Rwanda genocide affirm that broadcasts by radio station RTLM affected their thinking in key ways. Even before the death of President Habyarimana, RTLM reinforced their fear of a Tutsi conspiracy to commit genocide against them, a fear amplified by reports of killings of Hutu civilians by the Rwandan Patriotic Front (RPF) as it advanced into northern Rwanda. Following the death of the president, RTLM created an atmosphere legitimating the elimination of Tutsi through interviews with government officials and eminent Rwandans who identified *all* Tutsi as subversive supporters of the RPF and its alleged plan to commit genocide against the Hutu. And RTLM created a background of pervasive, overwhelming hatred toward the Tutsi, which discouraged ordinary Hutu from refusing orders to serve in well-organized patrols to hunt down and kill Tutsi.

For many of the ordinary Hutu perpetrators interviewed by Aaron Karnell (2003), RTLM's broadcasts made it appear as if all the authorities in the country urging the killing of Tutsi spoke with one voice. And while Karnell found that direct contact with local authorities rather than listening to RTLM was what immediately precipitated anti-Tutsi killing, he concludes that 'RTLM played a critical reinforcing role in the effort of authorities to mobilize Hutu for violence'.

After interviewing a very large sample of ordinary Hutu killers, Scott Strauss (2004) reached similar conclusions.

> The interviews I conducted suggest that the main effect of the radio broadcasts was to help establish killing Tutsis as the new order of the day – as the new 'law,' as the new basis for authority – after Habyarimana's assassination and after the civil war resumed. [Thus, he concludes,] The radio broadcasts did not create that experience of insecurity, but likely contributed to it. (Strauss 2004: 281)

Most of the ordinary killers interviewed by Strauss cited face-to-face mobilization as 'a greater factor in their decision to take part in the killing than were radio broadcasts', but, he found, 'the radio broadcasts shaped the overall atmosphere in which the mobilization occurred and empowered the most violent killers' (Strauss, 2004: chapter 7 and 387).

Current field research in Rwanda makes it evident that broadcasts by RTLM facilitated and legitimated the Rwanda genocide of 1994. Preventing or stopping RTLM's messages of hate would have seriously undermined the ability of its high-level planners to carry out the mass mobilization required for the systematic annihilation of Rwanda's Tutsi.

Real conflicts over territorial boundaries and scarce resources are frequent occurrences in history, but they rarely require the intensive, sustained, eliminationist propaganda that one finds in cases of ideologically motivated genocide. When ethno-nationalist, utopian and racist goals become paramount, perpetrators work most intensively to persuade their subjects of the danger to their security and the need to eliminate whole groups of people portrayed as threatening their very survival. Propaganda and ideology interact synergistically to create panic – fear that allows ordinary people to believe that they are killing to preserve traditional rights imperiled by threatening groups. In such situations, the media's role is to engender fear, hatred and violence, inciting and legitimating the destruction of cultures and groups of innocent human beings as the only possible solution to the threatened loss of life, rights and property. As William Schabas (2000) reminds us, 'Genocide is prepared with propaganda, a bombardment of lies and hatred directed against the targeted group, and aimed at preparing the "willing executioners" for the atrocious tasks they will be asked to perform.' And it is precisely this open mass mobilization of the population by the media through public encouragement of the people to endorse and join in state-supported crimes against humanity and genocide that aids us in predicting and recognizing early warnings of ideologically motivated genocide.

The newspaper *Kangura*, edited by Hassan Ngeze, was a private publication. Radio station RTLM was a private media outlet. Yet both played major roles in inciting Rwandans to commit genocide. *Kangura* and RTLM were closely connected to the Hutu Power wing of the Rwandan government and the Coalition for the Defence of the Republic (CDR) political party through stock ownership, seats on the board of directors, cross consultation, and even the broadcasting of editorials from *Kangura* on radio programmes offered to the largely illiterate public by RTLM. While *Kangura* ceased publication before the genocide, throughout the genocide RTLM urged the killers on to greater zeal and efficiency, even furnishing listeners with the names, addresses and automobile licence plate numbers of those who still needed to be killed.

Before rendering judgement in the Nahimana media case, the judges of the International Criminal Tribunal for Rwanda (ICTR) had to examine once more the meaning of incitement as an element of the crime of genocide as defined in the United Nations genocide convention (UN 1951). And they had to do so in the context of an earlier case, the Akayesu case, in which the court had concluded, 'The prosecution must prove a definite causation between the act characterized as incitement or provocation in this case, and a specific offence' (ICTR 1998: para. 557).

A number of important principles have emerged from the ICTR's decision in the Nahimana media case. The judges set key boundaries defining legitimate expression and elaborated principles for interpreting their guidelines. In summary, the major points of the decision are:

- Incitement to commit genocide is a crime in its own right and the incitement need not have succeeded to be considered a crime.
- Because incitement is a crime in its own right, no causal relationship between the incitement and the acts of the perpetrators of genocide need be demonstrated to prove the accused is guilty of incitement.
- Incitement of ethnic hatred can be distinguished from the legitimate use of the media by focusing on three factors: the tone and not just the content of a communication; the context in which a media statement is made; whether the media distanced itself appropriately when reporting stories incorporating the messages of those who advocated ethnic hatred.
- The media play a legitimate role in a nation's self-defence, but that role requires that the media characterize as threats those individuals who are armed and dangerous rather than entire ethnic groups.
- Ethnic expressions by the media should receive more rather than less scrutiny 'to ensure that minorities without equal means of defence are not endangered' (ICTR 2003: para. 1008).
- International law rather than domestic law should be the point of reference when making determinations of freedom from discrimination and freedom of expression.

Recent history makes us aware that the effective use of the media in preventing genocide requires assessing the stage that the genocidal situation has reached and devising a response strategy appropriate to that stage. Poor, economically developing societies struggling to move from authoritarian, arbitrary rule to establish the democratic foundations of civil society are particularly vulnerable to genocide. Such societies have few competing media outlets, possess no tradition of independent media, lack deeply rooted professional standards for journalism and endure a violent media culture that exhibits no sense of responsibility to society as a whole. Journalists in such societies are frequently manipulated and bribed by the dominant political faction ('envelope journalism'), are dependent on stereotyping and sensationalism for the themes of their news stories and are oblivious to potential news stories that would diminish ethnic and political hatred. Good, highly trained journalists with professional standards are frequently subjected to threats and, in the wake of assassinations and beatings, may surrender to manipulation and intimidation by the purveyors of fear (Frohardt and Temin 2003).

RECOMMENDATIONS FOR INTERVENTION

- ***Early-stage interventions*** – in conflict situations where mass killing has not begun – include domestic and foreign monitoring of the media, training programmes and codes of conduct to raise the skills and standards of local editors and journalists and strengthening of the local independent media. In such situations, local and foreign broadcasts of serial drama programmes addressed to children and soap operas for adults emphasizing the benefits of interethnic cooperation, the real benefits of compromise and peaceful solutions to problems are useful methods for lessening conflict. Local, multi-ethnic production teams have proved to be especially effective and credible originators of such productions (Frohardt and Temin 2003).
- ***Middle-stage intervention*** – in societies just beginning to suffer genocidal massacres – must be swift and aggressive. When government-sanctioned threats and intimidation make it impossible for local journalists, domestic nongovernmental organizations (NGOs) and government ministers to intervene effectively against media promoters of ethnic, religious and racial hatred, foreign governments and NGOs, regional associations of states and international organizations like the United Nations and the European Union must place the disseminators of hate propaganda on notice that their threatening messages are being monitored, recorded and transcribed to enable the prosecution and punishment of culpable media owners, editors and journalists. Foreign broadcasters should broadcast accurate, targeted news in local languages to counter the disinformation and distortions of domestic information providers and to supplement whatever material domestic anti-hate broadcasters are able to beam to their listeners. Electronic jamming of hate transmitters should be initiated.

- ***Late-stage intervention*** – launched when genocide is underway – may require actually destroying the transmitters and printing presses of the hate mongers. Foreign broadcasters should supplement their news broadcasts with frequently repeated warnings that a genocide is underway, report credible threats designed to deter the perpetrators from further killing, provide accurate information to discourage potential victims from congregating in perpetrator-targeted locations, like the churches which became killing-grounds in Rwanda, and appeal to ordinary citizens to conceal and protect members of the victim group. Future rewards should be promised for citizens who can document after the defeat of the genocidal regime that they hid potential victims and refused to participate in the killing. Whenever feasible, routes to safety and practical suggestions for survival should be announced.

Many of these recommendations have already been field-tested in countries such as Afghanistan, Bosnia-Herzegovina, Burundi, Cambodia, Kosovo, Liberia, Macedonia and Sierra Leone by international organizations, governments and NGOs including the United Nations, the European Union, the Organization for Security and Co-operation in Europe (OSCE), the BBC World Service, the BBC Trust, the British Department for International Development (Britain 2000), the United States Agency for International Development's Center for Democracy and Governance, the Internews Network, the Canadian Institute for Media, Policy and Civil Society, Search for Common Ground, the Hirondelle Foundation, the Open Media Research Institute, the Radio Partnership, the Center for War, Peace and the News Media and Lifeline Media.

Still needed is an international code of conduct that recognizes the dual-use possibilities of television and AM, FM, and satellite radio transmitters and subjects those countries already under international arms embargoes initiated by the United Nations Security Council, the OSCE and the European Union (EU 1998) to the same or even tighter export control policies as those for military equipment. Following European Union and other international guidelines, the new code of conduct would prohibit exports of transmitters to countries:

- Not respecting sanctions decreed by the UN Security Council.
- Violating their human rights obligations, including the United Nations *Convention on the Prevention and Punishment of the Crime of Genocide* (UN 1951), the *International Covenant on Civil and Political Rights* (UN 1966) and the *Universal Declaration on Human Rights* (UN 1948).
- Likely to use the equipment to provoke or prolong armed conflicts or aggravate existing tensions in the country of final destination.
- Endangering regional peace, security and stability.
- Threatening the national security of the states subscribing to the code of conduct and of territories whose security is a responsibility of member states, as well as that of friendly and allied countries.
- Demonstrating disrespect for international law, alliances and the need to contain terrorism.

- Likely to divert the equipment within the buyer country or re-export it under undesirable conditions.

To refine and further develop measures to prevent the use of hate radio in inciting genocidal violence, the Montreal Institute for Genocide and Human Rights Studies is organizing an international conference to be held in spring 2007. Specialist scholars, representatives of NGOs, government agencies and manufacturers of radio transmission equipment will convene to discuss the next stage – bringing relevant mobile and stationary radio transmitters under the jurisdiction of the existing dual-use controls for arms exports. Once established, the new regime in radio export controls will ensure that hate-radio transmitters can be legitimately targeted for destruction if and when their operators violate the terms of the revised code of conduct. In this respect, the new code will constructively embody the fateful encounter with hate radio in Rwanda and stand as one of the many memorials to the victims of the Rwanda genocide.

REFERENCES

Britain, Department for International Development. 2000. *Working with the media in conflicts and other emergencies*. Conflict and Humanitarian Affairs Department and Social Development Department, London, UK.

EU (European Union). 1998. *EU Code of Conduct on Arms Exports*. EU, 8 June. Available at <projects.sipri.se/expcon/eucode.htm> (accessed 3 January 2006).

Frohardt, M. and J. Temin. 2003. *Use and abuse of media in vulnerable societies*. Special Report 110. United States Institute of Peace, Washington, DC, USA. Available at <www.usip.org/pubs/specialreports/sr110.pdf> (accessed 3 January 2005).

ICTR (International Criminal Tribunal for Rwanda). 1998. Judgement. In *The Prosecutor versus Jean-Paul Akayesu* (case ICTR-96–4-T). ICTR, Arusha, Tanzania, 2 September.

—— 2003. Judgement and sentence. In *The Prosecutor v. Ferdinand Nahimana, Jean-Bosco Barayagwiza and Hassan Ngeze* (case no. ICTE-99–52-T). ICTR, Arusha, Tanzania, 3 December.

Karnell, A.P. 2003. Role of Radio in the Genocide of Rwanda. College of Communications and Information Studies, University of Kentucky, Lexington, KT, USA. PhD dissertation.

Schabas, W.A. 2000. Hate Speech in Rwanda: the Road to Genocide. *McGill Law Journal*, 46: 141–71.

Straus, S.A. 2004. The Order of Genocide: Race, Power, and War in Rwanda. University of California, Berkeley, CA, USA. PhD dissertation.

UN (United Nations). 1948. *Universal Declaration on Human Rights.* Adopted and proclaimed by the General Assembly Resolution 217 A (III), 10 December. Available at <www.un.org/Overview/rights.html> (accessed 9 September 2005).

—— 1951. *Convention on the prevention and punishment of the crime of genocide*. Adopted by Resolution 260 (III) of the UN General Assembly, 9 December 1948. *UN Treaty Series* no. 1021, vol. 78: 277. Available at <www.preventgenocide.org/law/convention/text.htm> (accessed 6 September 2005).

—— 1966. *International covenant on economic, social and cultural rights*. General Assembly Resolution 2200A (XXI), 16 December. Available at <www.unhchr.ch/html/menu3/b/a_cescr.htm> (accessed 6 September 2005).

31
Information in Crisis Areas as a Tool for Peace: the Hirondelle Experience

Philippe Dahinden

In an interview one day, an African musician said to me, 'Words can save people just as they can kill people.' The artist was Baaba Maal, the singer from Senegal. Why is it that words can save, and kill?

In May 1994, I spent two weeks in Rwanda as a reporter for Swiss Television, at the time the genocide was taking place. I already knew the country. I was also familiar with the media of hate. After the evacuation of most foreigners, my cameraman and I were among the first members of the international media to go as far south as Butare. We saw many, many corpses. We also came to realize how information – or rather disinformation and propaganda – could actually kill. At every roadblock set up by the militia, the *Interahamwe*, I could hear the radio, RTLM, designating the targets to be hit. I could also see that hundreds of thousands of civilians were fleeing or waiting for the violence to stop. But these civilians had no real information. All they heard were rumours or the slogans of the extremists.

When I returned to Europe, I thought that, as journalists, we couldn't just remain impotent in this situation. We did our job as well as we could informing the rest of the world, but the victims of the events, who didn't see our reports, also deserved information. Information is a right that is as vital as the right to food or medical care. People have a right to know. It's a question of human dignity.

This fundamental right of people to be informed is what justified our profession as journalists and the freedom of the press that we advocate. In 1994, the few Rwandan journalists who survived, such as Thomas Kamilindi, were themselves in the massacres; they couldn't do their work. Therefore, we decided that journalists from Europe should go and help our colleagues in Rwanda to meet this urgent need for information by creating an independent media outlet. We decided to set up a radio station, the only medium that could become operational swiftly and reach a large number of people: that was Radio Agatashya.

This independent radio station was initially designed to counterbalance the influence of the media in Rwanda that were spreading hatred and also to address populations in distress, whether they had escaped the genocide, were deprived of all resources, were displaced inside the country or were fleeing outside. In July 1994, as the ground situation rapidly changed, the station refocused its priority on assisting survivors and the humanitarian organizations that were attempting to help them.

It certainly helped save human lives. From its very first broadcasts, however, Radio Agatashya's mission was to provide 'water and bread, but also trustworthy, independent and pluralist news', to quote François Gross, then president of Reporters Sans Frontières, the organization that had launched the radio station. The goal remained to appease hatred by providing non-partisan information, to help reduce tension and to end the spiral of violence by broadcasting programmes carried out on the ground. The genocide had already taken place, but the entire region was afire and antagonism remained as sharp as ever. Reconciliation was still a distant goal, but we had to take initial steps in that direction.

HIRONDELLE FOUNDATION

The Hirondelle Foundation, which grew out of the Rwanda experience, is an organization of journalists that sets up and operates media services in crisis areas. Since its foundation in 1995, Hirondelle has established and managed Radio Agatashya in the Great Lakes Region of Africa; Star Radio in Liberia; the Hirondelle News Agency at the International Criminal Tribunal for Rwanda at Arusha, Tanzania; Radio Blue Sky in Kosovo; Radio Ndeke Luka in Bangui in the Central African Republic; Moris Hamutuk, a radio programme for refugees in Timor; Radio Okapi, a national network in the Democratic Republic of Congo and Radio Miraya, a national network in Sudan, as well as a support project with the Radio-Television of Timor-Leste (RTTL).

The Hirondelle Foundation, 'Media for peace and human dignity', took its name from the first of its radio operations, 'Agatashya', which means little swallow in Kinyarwanda. The appeal of the name is in its simplicity and universality.

An independent media outlet has a fundamental role to play in societies where authoritarian and non-democratic regimes are in power. In such situations, the traditional media fall silent because of insecurity, physical risks and because money invested in development projects could ultimately end up serving no useful purpose. But an independent radio station can play a crucial role in furthering peace by dissipating rumours, avoiding propaganda and focusing attention on hard facts. We feel that by providing a population that is deprived of impartial, professional, hard news with just that kind of information we are doing nothing more than recognizing a fundamental human right, the right to be informed.

Whenever a political, military or economic power uses information as a propaganda instrument to condition the minds of people, to incite hatred, to suppress, to create intolerance, to keep people in ignorance or generally to manipulate them, this violates the dignity of men and women and degrades them. Whenever men and women of a particular national, ethnic or other group are deprived, for political or economic reasons, of information that concerns them directly, this too is a violation of their dignity.

RADIO AGATASHYA

Radio Agatashya acted as a pioneer in this realm. In late May 1994, I addressed the United Nations Commission on Human Rights in the name of Reporters sans Frontières (RSF (Reporters Without Borders)) and proposed the creation of a 'free radio station … that will allow Rwandans to receive honest and independent information'. RSF International gave its Swiss section the mandate to create a radio station that would serve humanitarian ends in fighting against the damaging effects of hate media.

After an assessment mission in June and July 1994, we chose the Bukavu region in the south Kivu area of what was then known as Zaire (now the Democratic Republic of Congo) as the first broadcast site. This location was chosen primarily for security reasons and because we couldn't get permission to operate in Rwanda. On 4 August 1994, Radio Agatashya broadcast for the first time in Kinyarwanda and French. The station employed Rwandan, Zairean and Swiss journalists. A few months later, in March 1995, we created the Hirondelle Foundation in Geneva, to carry on the project and assume its management.

The station was launched with a small team, but millions of listeners were gradually able to pick up its broadcasts in a broad area of the Great Lakes Region. The listening area covered part of eastern Zaire, Rwanda and Burundi. When it became a regional station in 1995, with some 40 journalists, it had studios and news correspondents in Kigali, Goma and Bujumbura. It opened a news correspondents' desk at the International Criminal Tribunal for Rwanda (ICTR), which had recently been set up at Arusha. This office has survived to this day and has become the independent Hirondelle Press Agency (Agence de Presse Hirondelle), which covers ICTR sessions.

Once fully operational, Radio Agatashya had as many as 60 local collaborators plus three expatriates. Every day, the station broadcast eight hours of programming in five languages: French; Kinyarwanda, the language of Rwanda; Kirundi, the language of Burundi; Swahili, the language of the region; and English (twice a week). This included two principal news broadcasts a day, two news summaries, plus hundreds of magazine and feature programmes on such topics as respect for human rights, justice, health conditions and HIV/AIDS prevention.

In all, the station reached an estimated four million listeners. It contributed enormously to making the general public more aware of the activities of the major international agencies and nongovernmental organizations (NGOs) operating in the region. Radio Agatashya rapidly earned the nickname: 'the radio that does not bend' – the impartial radio.

As a matter of policy, only stringently checked facts could be broadcast. Commentary was not allowed. The station was able to pursue its mandate by attentively recruiting quality personnel and by abiding by a charter that sought to ensure complete editorial independence in the content of its broadcasts.

It is worth repeating the charter here in its entirety:

Agatashya Radio Charter

Independent regional radio with a humanitarian vocation

1. Intention of the programme

Agatashya Radio intends to come to the help of civilian populations, victims of events in the Sub-Region of the African Great Lakes, without distinction or discrimination. It uses for this purpose, and for this purpose exclusively, the information it broadcasts.

Agatashya Radio offers the people, victims of the events in the sub-region of the Great Lakes, Rwanda, Burundi, Eastern Zaire and north-west Tanzania, the maximum of useful information, more especially about the situation in the sub-region. It places its reliance on the factual exactitude and neutrality of the information. Every time it is possible, Agatashya Radio will give priority to service information for the civilian population, victims of the events, in particular food and medical services, as well as the search for those who have disappeared and the uniting of separated families.

Agatashya Radio observes strict political neutrality and seeks to remain independent in the eyes of all in the execution of its programmes and the choice of its collaborators. It avoids all useless controversies and gives particular care and attention to any rumour or information likely to arouse a movement of panic in the population. The responsibility for the use thereof can only be entrusted to Swiss reporters chosen by the HIRONDELLE Foundation.

No one, public or private, may demand the broadcasting of information, opinions or works on Agatashya Radio. The management of the Radio, alone, shall decide the contents of its programmes, in particular the form and substance of the information it broadcasts, no matter who the authors or the sources of its information may be.

2. Setting up and contents of programmes

Agatashya Radio is bound to no specific place for broadcasting. Its vocation is to be near those people who are the victims of the events and to request the authorization to broadcast for a limited period from the authorities of the appropriate territories, without any political distinction. Agatashya Radio will make sure, in particular, that the auditors can clearly identify the HIRONDELLE Foundation, its aims, and the donors of the operation.

Agatashya Radio's basic programme is to give factual information on the situation in the sub-region for those people in particular who have escaped, have nothing left, have been dispersed, displaced or are refugees outside their own countries; on the activities of NGOs (non-governmental organizations) having relations with countries affected by the events; information on the defence and the promotion of human rights, the search for peace and action in favour of reconciliation.

The programme may at anytime be developed and include useful pin-point information for those persons victims of acts of war and violence or didactic programmes on human rights, the restoration of peace and reconciliation.

Agatashya Radio also works to make the situation of civilian populations, and victims of events, known outside the sub-region.

3. Sources

Agatashya Radio sources are the international humanitarian assistance organizations and NGOs active in the field, as well as the other usual journalistic sources available. They are verified and processed with the greatest regard to objectivity.

Agatashya Radio collaborates for this purpose with these humanitarian organizations, amongst others. It has, therefore, been agreed with the international organizations and NGO partners to this project that they will transmit to Agatashya Radio, at regular intervals, the information they think useful. This information may concern any geographical area in the sub-region, Rwanda, Burundi, eastern Zaire or north-west Tanzania.

The source shall specify on each occasion if it wishes to be mentioned or not. Agatashya Radio may decide not to mention a source.

4. Developments

Agatashya Radio is developing with the international organizations and NGO partners, specific didactic programmes useful for the victims of the events, the elaboration of which requires several weeks or months.

Agatashya Radio is studying with the international organizations and NGO partners which will be, at the time of broadcasting, the most appropriate vehicle with due regard to the general environment at that time (document in possession of author).

• At the end of October 1996, Radio Agatashya was abruptly forced off the air. This followed the new conflict launched by the Rwanda-backed rebel Banyamulenge and Laurent-Desire Kabila in eastern Zaire. A substantial part of Radio Agatashya's equipment was looted or confiscated. All employees managed to flee, but three were killed. In Rwanda, the editing studio had already been closed since the beginning of 1996 due to official pressure from the government.

Radio Agatashya was launched to respond to an emergency situation. In October 1996, it also broadcast its last programmes in the midst of a serious crisis. In the interval, it had experienced events that persistently imposed emergency requirements, such as the Masisi conflict in Kivu and the civil war in Burundi. But beyond these challenges, the project provided an unique experience concerning the potential role of a mass medium in a conflict-stricken area.

During the two years on the air, we were able to discover in a zone of conflict how important it was to disseminate information on the spot, to have media close by in local languages, offered by local journalists. Information is a weapon that can kill people when it's manipulated. It's a major issue in conflict, and totalitarian regimes, when the belligerents try to control information. We know that information can also be an instrument of peace to counter propaganda, to counter the incitement of violence and, therefore, to help resolve or prevent conflict.

During the 1996 war, when Kabila and his allies reached Bukavu, where our radio station was located, we described as clearly as possible how the fighting was going. This information was a bulwark against rumour and panic, particularly when rebel propaganda falsely or inaccurately announced the presence of soldiers at the gates of the city. Appeals for calm were sent out by people who were respected, such as the Archbishop of Bukavu, and they contributed to reducing tension within the population and reducing hostility toward certain groups, who were considered scapegoats. This didn't stop the conflict, but the radio nevertheless did spare lives and prevented greater suffering.

Lack of official authorization prevented the station from broadcasting from Kigali as was planned initially. We had to face criticism for maintaining our station in an area where extremists and genocide perpetrators were still present. Nonetheless, we think that our choice was correct. First, without our radio station, there would have been no independent information at all. Second, our programmes in Kinyarwanda reached listeners directly, without any risk of being manipulated by extremists and, thereby, helped fight the propaganda. Last, in spite of the closure of Radio Agatashya, the information on judiciary proceedings continued through the Hirondelle Agency at Arusha, in particular via international radio networks.

In terms of the genocide and its consequences, we took a clear editorial line on information. We focused on the need for justice, explaining, in local languages, the role of the international tribunal. We explained legal concepts. As a result, we were able to counter the propaganda of extremists in the camps, who wanted to deny that the genocide had taken place. We explained that if somebody had been convicted of genocide, this did not mean that all of his descendents would also be banished for life from society. We explained in simple terms and in the local language that responsibility here was individual, not passed on to the descendants. We also allowed people who escaped the genocide to speak on the radio to describe their reality.

'PEACE MEDIA'

Propaganda often feeds on real facts – skirmishes, imprisonment, incidents – but tends to exacerbate and amplify them, emphasizing their emotional load and rendering them intolerable for one of the involved parties. Rigorous information, on the other hand, respects facts and conveys them to listeners in a reliable way.

Such strict information also allows people, on both sides, to listen to each other, to talk through live accounts and reports. It re-establishes, without any pathos or judgement, a form of communication and humanity in ravaged countries.

In areas of conflict, the editorial boards of 'peace media' are most frequently mixed. They gather journalists from different and conflicting linguistic, national, ethnic and religious groups – to work together. This is a difficult challenge and the risks taken by our collaborators (as well as the threats they often receive) are real. Such mixed editorial boards can engender respect with listeners – thanks to the quality of their work.

Is a peace medium just another independent medium? Well, almost; however, its editorial line reflects the mission entrusted to it. Radio Agatashya, for example, gave priority to information and programmes that were in the interests of its listeners. The return to peace, compliance with fundamental human rights, justice, tolerance, searching for grounds for agreement between antagonistic groups and reconciliation between opponents – all such issues were part of the priority news reports and programmes. Radio Agatashya could not be anyone's spokesperson; it did not represent a government or an international organization or a political group.

Our various projects generally opened the way to local media. An independent media outlet enjoying international support can often provide information that local media cannot broadcast. However, once the news is on the air, local media may find it less risky to speak up. In addition, in compliance with its written statutes, the Hirondelle Foundation is committed to leaving local media in place after its departure and ensuring that responsible broadcasting by local journalists continues.

This is how the Hirondelle Foundation came to see its role in crisis areas and the role that can be played by peace media. Media cannot stop a conflict, but they can contribute to a better climate. There are two possible approaches. The first consists of producing and broadcasting programmes with explicit pro-peace content. These can be, for example, radio dramas featuring families from hostile parties and revealing, through concrete neighbourhood communication, that differences are actually less significant than similarities.

The other approach consists of offering listeners a non-specialized medium that reflects reality as accurately and as faithfully as possible to counteract the impact of propaganda whatever its nature. This is the preferred approach of the Hirondelle Foundation, in spite of the difficulties it involves. The objective is to manage in a crisis area according to the same rules and techniques as a media outlet in a stable area. Indeed these rules remain fully valid in crisis-stricken areas, all the more so as information fulfils a crucial function in such regions.

HUMAN DIGNITY

Populations who are victims of conflicts are deprived of their dignity and of their fundamental human rights. The attentiveness of a radio station to its listeners – programming designed and implemented for them and broadcast in their language – will be perceived as a mark of respect. This restored dignity is one of the fundamental objectives of the Hirondelle Foundation ('Media for peace and human dignity'). It is also one of the reasons for the popular success of our projects.

To conclude, I would like to quote my colleague Jean-Marie Etter, president of the Hirondelle Foundation, who said,

Information really is a way of restoring responsibility and the dignity of our listeners. A radio of peace is also a radio which tries to give to people, who have been victims of war, or abuse of power, to give them some control over their own destiny.[1]

NOTE

1. Etter, J.-M. 'L'information en zones de crises: construire la credibilite', intervention during a colloquium organized by UNESCO and SIDA on information in zones of violent conflict. Stockholm, May 2003.

32
The Use and Abuse of Media in Vulnerable Societies

Mark Frohardt and Jonathan Temin

In the wake of the deadly and destructive civil conflicts so prominent in the 1990s, academics and practitioners have increasingly focused on predicting and preventing civil conflict, rather than on responding to and recovering from it. Accordingly, various methods have been developed to identify societies in which violent conflict is likely to occur, and significant research has been conducted into the root causes of civil conflict. That work has focused on identifying and understanding such causal factors as economic decline, long-standing grievances between groups and the ethnic and religious make-up of society. But insufficient attention has been devoted to the use of the media to promote violent conflict.

In this paper, we focus on the role of media in vulnerable societies, which are defined as societies highly susceptible to movement toward civil conflict or repressive rule. This often describes societies in developing countries and countries in transition, almost always those struggling to make the transition from authoritarian to democratic government. It frequently describes multi-ethnic societies as well, which, over the past decade, have proved more likely to fall victim to conflict than societies with greater ethnic homogeneity.

Although media outlets can be actively used to promote conflict, media can also contribute to conflict *involuntarily.* Such passive incitement to violence most frequently occurs when journalists have poor professional skills, when the media culture is underdeveloped or when there is little or no history of independent media. Under such circumstances, journalists can inflame grievances and promote stereotypes by virtue of the manner in which they report, even though their intentions are not necessarily malicious and they are not being manipulated by an outside entity.

Perhaps media have generally been overlooked in analyses of conflict because, on their own, they are rarely a direct cause. Nonetheless, as part of a larger matrix of factors, media can be extremely powerful tools for promoting violence, as witnessed in Rwanda, the former Republic of Yugoslavia, the former Soviet republic of Georgia and elsewhere. As Jamie Metzl (1997) observes, 'mass media reach not only people's homes, but also their minds, shaping their thoughts and sometimes their behavior.'

An earlier version of this article was published as special report 110 to the United States Institute of Peace (Frohardt and Temin 2003).

Media behaviour can also provide indicators of impending conflict, as certain characteristics of media structure and media behaviour tend to precede conflict; some are evident early enough that an intervention may be feasible. If preventing conflict is the goal, then influential tools such as media must be closely examined, their pernicious effects mitigated and positive output magnified. The various approaches to precluding or stopping the use of media as a tool to promote division and conflict range from training journalists to advising legislators on drafting media legislation. But for such training or advising to be effective, the role of media in moving societies toward or away from conflict needs to be clearly understood.

CLUES TO CONFLICT

Using a series of indicators, it is possible to identify societies in which media outlets are especially susceptible to abuse or that may be in the early stages of manipulation. These indicators are divided between those dealing with *media structure* (the way the media sector is set up) and those dealing with *media content* (the articles and programming that media outlets produce). None of these indicators constitutes either sufficient or necessary conditions for media manipulation to occur, but when a significant portion of them are evident media outlets are especially vulnerable to abuse.

Structural indicators

Structural indicators can be divided into three categories: indicators concerning the media outlets themselves; indicators concerning the professionals – journalists, editors, managers and owners – associated with the outlets; and indicators concerning the structure of government institutions dealing with the media.

Media outlets

These indicators concern the configuration of the media landscape in a particular country and the influence that media outlets exert over society. They include reach, accessibility and plurality.

The *reach* enjoyed by media outlets is critical for obvious reasons: if the reach of an outlet is minimal, then its capacity to influence a society will also be limited. Factors affecting reach include the strength of radio and television signals and the breadth of newspaper distribution.

Media *accessibility* is equally important. Even if media are widely available, people still need to have access if they are to be influential (recognizing this fact, the Rwandan government handed out free radios before the 1994 genocide). For newspapers this means that people must be literate in the language of the newspaper and have the means to acquire a newspaper, whether that means purchasing one, borrowing one from a friend or other means. For radio and television, it means owning or having access to a radio or television and understanding the language of the programming. In developed countries, media access is taken for granted, but in many developing countries it is not easily achieved.

The degree of media *plurality* is critical because with greater competition, one or a small number of media outlets are less likely to have the capacity to dominate. Plurality applies not only to the number of outlets but also to the number of divergent voices emanating from those outlets. In other words, a multitude of private stations all playing music, or all espousing similar messages, does not constitute plurality. The society in which media can exert the most influence, both positive and negative, is one in which media outlets enjoy wide exposure but have relatively few competitors.

An important variable here concerns whether the media scene is dominated by either state-owned or private outlets or if there is a balanced mixture of the two. Particularly where the media scene is dominated by the state, there is often little or no check on media behaviour.

Another important variable is the receptivity of the population to diversified independent media. This is often taken for granted in developed countries, but in many societies there is little or no history of media diversity and independence. Under these circumstances, when media diversification does occurs, one of the consequences can be the type of situation that developed in the former Soviet republic of Georgia, where suddenly vacant media space was filled by outlets operating from distinctly nationalist and ethnic perspectives.

Media professionals

The second set of indicators concerns media professionals. This includes not only journalists, but also the people behind the scenes, such as editors, station managers and owners. The indicators are journalist capacity; journalist isolation; the political, ethnic, religious and regional composition of the media corps; and the degree of diversity in the ownership of media outlets.

Journalist capacity refers to journalists' ability to carry out their charge with a reasonable degree of professional integrity and skill. More capable journalists tend to make media outlets less susceptible to abuse. Journalism training is an important variable. Questions that should be asked in any society that may be vulnerable to conflict include: Is there a school of journalism or communications in which journalists are trained? Do journalists enter the profession with the skills needed to report responsibly? The degree of fact checking in place is also important: Do journalists write unsubstantiated stories filled with rumours? Or are the origins of most stories clear and are they attributed to credible sources? The answers to these questions go a long way toward determining the susceptibility of journalists to abuse.

The second indicator is the *degree to which journalists are isolated,* physically and metaphorically, from their domestic and international colleagues. An awareness of international standards of professional journalism provides a basis from which journalists may feel justified, beyond their own personal conviction, to resist manipulation, because they enjoy a network of support and feel part of a larger community of journalists who adhere to a common standard. Not only are they emboldened by that support, but they may also be able to use the network to communicate with the outside world if media freedom comes under attack. Consequently, those who intend to manipulate the media may be more hesitant if every time they apply pressure behind the scenes their actions are made public by the local or international media.

Particularly in traditional societies where ethnic bonds are strong, simple peer pressure and an emphasis on the importance of responsibility to clan or group can facilitate media manipulation. In such societies, it may be relatively easy for individuals holding revered positions in their groups to manipulate members of the same group who work as journalists. They can sometimes do so using threats or bribes, without having to revert to overt coercion.

Along the same lines, *diversity in the ownership of media outlets* is critical because, ultimately, it is the owners who exert the most control over content. A society is especially vulnerable to media abuse when all or a significant portion of media outlets are owned by one or a small number of people, particularly if those people are of the same ethnicity or religion, support the same political party or are from the same region. Even a balanced mix of state-owned and independent media outlets may not be sufficient to guard against abuse, because the 'independent' outlets may have strong ties to the government. It is also important to determine whether more subtle links exist between influential members of particular groups and media outlets, such as discrete financial relationships.

Government institutions concerned with media

Perhaps as important as the structure of media outlets and the people involved in them are the independence and effectiveness of government institutions concerned with the media, particularly the legislature and judiciary. The degree of media independence and freedom established in a country's laws and the degree to which those laws are enforced define the space in which media are allowed to operate. The relevant indicators here are media's legal environment and changes in media controls.

Two very different types of legislation are critical to maintaining a healthy legal environment for media: legislation protecting journalists and media outlets from abuse and guaranteeing their freedom to operate without government interference; and legislation, such as libel and slander laws, protecting private individuals from being the subject of unjustified insult or falsehoods appearing in the media. The former allows journalists to operate without fear of government coercion, unwarranted prosecution or personal harm.

If such legislation is in place and consistently enforced, then journalists and media outlets are not likely to be very susceptible to abuse. But if such legislation is absent, journalists and media outlets are essentially 'fair game' for the government, meaning that the state is free to attempt to manipulate them however it chooses. Journalists, in turn, have few options for recourse.

If private individuals have no effective avenue for registering complaints against the media, then few options are available to people or groups who may be unfairly criticized or demonized in the media. The absence of the possibility of punishment emboldens those associated with hate media outlets and may encourage the formation of such outlets, because the risks involved are reduced. To counteract this effect, mechanisms for punishment, such as libel or hate speech legislation that protects both individuals and groups, can be beneficial.

Recent research into the causes of civil conflict suggests that societies in transition (those that are in the process of liberalizing and moving toward a more open, democratic dispensation) are more vulnerable to conflict than societies that have already gone through a transition or those awaiting one. In other words, it is societies 'on the way up' that tend to experience civil conflict. A common characteristic of liberalization is relaxation of controls on the media and, although this is generally a positive development, dangers accompany it. Newly opened media space can quickly be filled by media outlets that mirror political or ethnic centrifugal forces promoting conflict. Thus, a relaxation of media controls can sometimes actually lay the groundwork for future conflict.

On the other hand, a tightening of media controls can also be a precursor to conflict, as it can be indicative of a government's intentions: for example, the Zimbabwean government-imposed tight restrictions on media toward the beginning of its violent land-seizure initiative and its effort to ensure Robert Mugabe's victory in the 2002 presidential elections. By forcing these measures through parliament, Zimbabwean authorities telegraphed their intentions.

CONTENT INDICATORS

Content is critical to the overall analysis because media content helps shape an individual's view of the world and helps form the lens through which all issues are viewed. The content indicators presented here can be evident early in the manipulation process, at a point where intervention may still be feasible. However, once media manipulation is widely apparent it may be too late, and interventions may yield little or no benefit.

Content creating fear

The construction of fear is likely to be a component of any effort to use media to promote conflict. In Rwanda before the genocide, a private radio station tried to instil fear of an imminent attack on Hutus by a Tutsi militia. These efforts were at least partly successful, as many people subscribed to the 'imminent' threat, although only flimsy evidence was provided to support it. When such reporting creates widespread fear, people are more amenable to taking pre-emptive action, which is how the actions taken in Rwanda were characterized. Media were used to make people believe that 'we must strike first in order to save ourselves.' Creating fear laid the foundation for taking violent action through 'self-defence'.

In assessing the construction of fear, one must be circumspect, however, because there is an important distinction between content that criticizes a person or group in a manner that is simply degrading (as seen in many Western tabloids) and printing or broadcasting information that is clearly intended to create a fearful reaction. Although the former can lay the groundwork for the latter, it is most often the latter that increases the likelihood of conflict. Four strategies commonly used to create fear are:

1. *Focus on past conflicts and on a history of ethnic animosity.* By highlighting the fact that violent conflict has occurred in the past and that the same groups behind violent acts then are suspected of planning them now, the potential for future conflict can appear much greater to media consumers than it actually is, and the means and capacity for carrying out such atrocities more attainable. Media can be used to make the point that 'they did it before, they can do it again'.
2. *Manipulation of myths, stereotypes and identities.* This often occurs through the dehumanization of members of the 'other' group. Frequent references to Tutsis as 'cockroaches' in the Rwandan media are an example of this phenomenon. As soon as people in the other group are perceived as 'less than human', engaging in conflict with them and killing them becomes easier to justify. A related strategy is to portray members of a particular group as 'irrational' or 'unpredictable', providing additional justification for pre-emptive action.
3. *Overemphasis on certain grievances, inequities, or atrocities.* This tactic can create the impression that circumstances are worse than they really are and that a particular group is more victimized than it actually is. If the overemphasized grievance or inequity is particularly sensitive, such as a religious issue or an issue concerning the use of natural resources, excessively negative reporting can be particularly inflammatory. Overemphasis adds fuel to the fire by creating the impression that a group is being intentionally discriminated against and that the situation is particularly dire, even though neither of these impressions may be accurate. Discrimination may be present, but the size and scope of the discrimination may be exaggerated in the media; thus, the 'victimized' group is given added incentive and justification for reprisal, regardless of whether their grievances are actually legitimate.
4. *Shift toward consistently negative reporting.* The critical element here is change; if the situation has been bad from the start and consistently negative reporting is the norm, then it is not likely to be inflammatory. But a significant shift in reporting toward a decidedly negative and pessimistic tone creates the impression that the country's situation is worsening considerably and provides justification for people or groups to stop and reverse that slide by taking decisive action, including violence.

Content creating inevitability and resignation

Just as media outlets have been used to create a pervasive sense of fear, they have also been used to convince people that conflict is inevitable. This leaves media consumers resigned to the notion that conflict will happen, and when such resignation is prevalent, efforts to prevent conflict tend to be seen as futile, which makes them increasingly unlikely to succeed.

Portraying conflict as part of an 'eternal' process is a strategy frequently used to create the impression that conflict is inevitable. This often occurs when media promote 'primordial identities' that suggest that people of different ethnicities have, since the beginning of time, been in conflict with one another, have never coexisted peacefully and are somehow preordained to be in perpetual conflict. Rarely, if ever, is this actually the case, as virtually every ethnic conflict involves groups that have lived together peacefully at one stage or another.

A similar strategy for promoting the inevitability of conflict is to *use media to discredit alternatives to conflict.* For example, Alison Des Forges (2002: 241) observes that Rwandan radio 'seized the opportunity to impress upon Hutu that Tutsi could never be trusted and that any form of power-sharing, such as that specified in the Arusha Accords, could never work'.

OPPORTUNITIES FOR INTERVENTION

The term 'intervention', as it is used here, does not denote any sort of military or armed initiative (with one exception in the segment on 'aggressive interventions'). Rather, the term refers to support for the development of diverse, pluralistic independent media outlets giving voice to a variety of views and opinions. Such interventions are not carried out by soldiers or peacekeepers, but by journalists, professional media trainers and nongovernmental organization (NGO) workers.

Structural interventions

The most effective strategy for strengthening a professional media sector and protecting its content from biased influence is through reforms in media structure. Structural reforms have many advantages over interventions that target only content. If carried out early enough they can prevent media abuse from taking place. Structural reforms can also go a long way toward obviating future attempts to manipulate the media during periods of social stress. Once in place, these reforms are no longer dependent on foreign assistance, so they tend to maintain legitimacy and build popular support. Eight types of structural interventions are detailed below.

1. *Strengthening independent media.* Enhancing the ability of independent media outlets to resist unwanted influence from the government or elsewhere is critical to developing their ability to avoid abuse and manipulation. This strengthening is often a product of media plurality and longevity, both of which make using media to incite violence increasingly difficult. Plurality creates strength in numbers; with a variety of diverse independent media outlets in place, if one or even several are co-opted the effect is mitigated. Through media expansion and diversification, hate media can be marginalized; for example, in the United States, hate media exist but are virtually irrelevant. Longevity contributes to the strength of independent media because the longer independent outlets are in place, the more ingrained in society they

become. Consequently, if such ingrained outlets are abused, or shut down, the public outcry is likely to be substantial.

One of the most prominent examples of independent media thwarting government attempts to manipulate information comes from Serbia under Slobodan Milosevic, where the independent radio station B92 is credited with playing an instrumental role in informing and mobilizing the population.

2. *Developing journalist competence.* This intervention involves two basic objectives: enhancing the physical resources available to journalists (such as computers and vehicles) and enhancing human resources (such as writing ability, editing skills and contextual knowledge). If journalists lack physical resources, they are likely to be more susceptible to co-optation and corruption. Human resource needs are more difficult to define and to provide because they are not tangible goods. The principal method of enhancing human resources is through training, often through peer-to-peer training conducted by journalists. Although the results of such training are often difficult to quantify, the benefits accrued by journalists can be substantial.

   Even with the latest technology, ultimately it is the quality of the journalist that determines the quality of the journalism. Improving the technical or material components of the medium does not, in itself, improve the message. Consequently, addressing human resource needs must be a top priority. An added benefit of developing journalist competence is that more competent journalists are more likely to investigate and report on actors attempting to abuse the media and to expose their intentions, which can deter or thwart their efforts. Investigative journalism can be critical to blocking efforts to incite conflict and can debunk some of the inflammatory myths and stereotypes propagated in the media.

3. Another type of structural intervention involves *working with the legislature and judiciary*, the government institutions responsible for protecting citizen's rights, including the rights to free speech and independent media. Particular attention should be paid to the legislature because of its capacity to make and modify legislation. In many societies susceptible to media abuse, the legislation necessary to prosecute media abuse – including laws that protect the independence of private media outlets and that address hateful and antagonistic media content, such as slander and libel laws – is absent, ineffective or poorly designed. Thus it is important for experts in comparative media to work with legislatures to aid them in crafting such legislation.

   Once the necessary legislation is in place, it is equally important that the judiciary has the capacity to enforce the laws. If it is effective and impervious to corruption, the judiciary can provide an important check on media abuse because it can punish actors attempting to use the media maliciously. But in so many of the societies recently succumbing to conflict and in those vulnerable to doing so, rule of law is weak and the legal system is riddled with bribery and corruption. Among the recommendations by the NGO Article 19 following the Rwanda genocide was that government 'should seek to strengthen the judiciary to ensure that the necessary steps can be taken within the domestic legal system to prevent the broadcasting of incitement to violence' (Article 19 1996: 171). But often the government is poorly equipped to do this, and assistance from the NGO community can make a significant difference. NGOs should focus on strengthening the mechanics of the judiciary and on reducing the susceptibility of judges to corruption.

4. *Promoting diversity in the journalist corps and media ownership*. If there is little diversity among journalists and owners of media outlets, they are more vulnerable to abuse by members of the dominant group or groups in society. The way to combat this effect is clear – promote diversity – but strategies for doing so are not as obvious. One way to promote diversity among journalists is to impress on managers and owners of media outlets the importance of diversity and how they can benefit from it, both commercially and through content improvements that result from employing more diverse personnel.

   Another strategy is to work with members of certain political, ethnic, religious or regional groups to help them become involved with media (though this involves the risk of appearing to favour one group over another). A third strategy is to create incentives for outlets to promote diversity in their hiring, for example by having donor organizations provide more support, financial or otherwise, to outlets that are more diverse. Promoting diversity in media ownership is even more complex, because in a market economy it would be difficult and ill-advised to set quotas concerning the demographics of media ownership. Worse yet, in a non-market society, the government controls the media outlets and is unlikely to be convinced of the merits of diversity in ownership. Nonetheless, there are ways both to aid individuals to create new private media outlets and to encourage governments to allow for such outlets. One route is through bilateral aid, particularly aid channelled from development banks through national financial institutions via leasing and other financial support, intended for developing small- and medium-sized businesses.

5. *Licensing and regulation of media outlets*. A balance must be struck in the media regulatory environment so that starting a media outlet is not an overly complex, time-consuming, bureaucratic task, but regulation is not so lax that almost anybody can have a radio station or newspaper. Complete state control over media is not the solution, but neither is the total absence of regulation. Some type of government oversight of the licensing process is often in order, but one that is shielded, to the extent possible, from heavily political or corrupt influences. Again, it may be difficult for governments, particularly in developing countries still building and consolidating their democracies, to design and implement such regulations effectively. Assistance and encouragement from the domestic and international NGO communities can provide a strong impetus for establishing regulations, and international assistance can provide a blueprint for how to implement such regulation. Bilateral relations between donor and developing countries are also important, as they often involve assistance to government institutions

and advice on the overhaul of bureaucratic processes, which can strongly affect the domestic regulatory environment.

6. *Strengthening domestic and international networks*. Because journalists in vulnerable societies are often isolated from both domestic and international colleagues, establishing and strengthening journalist networks can be an effective way to combat media abuse. Domestically, this can be accomplished through journalist organizations or unions. When effective, they serve various purposes – providing journalists with information and ideas on how to report in a particular context (especially when there are personal safety issues involved), defending journalists' rights and freedoms and providing journalists with legal counsel. All of these services are critical, particularly in a society where the state is wary of independent media and eager to crack down on independent journalists.

   International journalist networks can be just as important. Such networks can help journalists operating in difficult circumstances feel part of a larger community of colleagues around the world, which can strengthen their resolve. These networks can also inform journalists on what may be considered international standards of journalism.

   A more programmatic form of international networking involves making international media, such as CNN or the BBC, accessible to journalists in vulnerable societies. The benefits of this are twofold: sometimes journalists use the content verbatim, but even if they do not, they are better informed and are exposed to a different perspective, which helps them in their own reporting.

7. *'Demand-side' intervention*. Too often the 'supply side' of the media equation (meaning the news and information that is supplied by media outlets) is closely scrutinized at the expense of attention to the 'demand side' (the demand by individuals for that news and information). A problem often found in societies in which media abuse occurs and in societies with under-developed media in general is that media consumers – everyday citizens – rarely consider and question the source and credibility of their news. Instead, they take for granted that what they hear on the radio and read in the newspapers is accurate and unbiased. For example, Des Forges (2002: 246) observes that in Rwanda before and during the genocide, 'most ordinary people saw no reason to call into question their practice of taking the radio as the voice of authority'.

   Part of the reason for the absence of critical analysis of the media was that, prior to the genocide, most Rwandans had never been exposed to alternatives to state-owned media, so they were conditioned to believe everything they heard from the few state-controlled outlets to which they had access. It was also due to the fact that most Rwandans had little understanding of the bias inherent in all media outlets.

   The prescription is increased public education and enhanced awareness of how media outlets operate. People need to understand that media outlets report from a particular perspective, one that may represent interests contrary to their own. B92 in Serbia tried to create such an understanding. 'The idea was to provoke the public to start thinking about the information that they were receiving,' according to one of the station's managers. 'So don't be just a passive recipient of this information, think about it and decide, do you believe it or not?' (Glyn-Pickett 1999).

8. *Media monitoring*. The final structural intervention is quite broad: monitoring media behaviour in an effort to identify the indicators described above so that the interventions detailed here can occur. It is imperative that someone keep watch over the media and, just as critical, over forces influencing the media. Such oversight is accomplished most effectively through media monitoring initiatives, organized efforts to monitor for specific characteristics. Some monitoring of broadcasts in various countries already occurs – the United States government runs the Foreign Broadcast Information Service and the BBC has a monitoring service – but it is not broad enough and does not cover media outlets in some of the most vulnerable societies.

Monitoring for the indicators presented above can inform policymakers about societies at risk of media manipulation. In doing such monitoring, it is important to work with local NGOs to develop a local monitoring capacity.

Content-specific interventions

Content-specific interventions are often based on observations of the content indicators detailed above, which tend to appear at a relatively late stage. But content-specific interventions can also be pre-emptive. The interventions described here can occur before the appearance of the indicators, to ensure that they do not appear. Content-specific interventions are most effective when media abuse is involuntary due to a lack of training and competence, rather than calculated.

If the media abuse is intentional, content-specific interventions are unlikely to succeed because journalists are fully aware of the consequences of their actions. But when media abuse is involuntary, such interventions offer alternatives to structural interventions; in circumstances where structural interventions are ineffective, content-specific interventions may be more successful. They may also serve as short-term remedies for some forms of media abuse, allowing more time for structural interventions, which tend to take longer to implement and yield results.

1. *'Repersonalization'*. As described above, one of the strategies for using media to instigate conflict involves the 'dehumanization' and 'depersonalization' of individuals. Through this process, people are portrayed in the media as members of a stigmatized group rather than as individuals.

   Training on how journalists can move beyond the political, ethnic, religious or regional factors to identify the true source of a grievance (be it an economic grievance or another concern) and how they can portray people first and foremost as individuals can ease tensions and move a society away from conflict. These strategies concern not only mitigating the negative effects of media abuse but also using media as a positive tool for reconciliation and conflict prevention.

2. *Issue-oriented training.* Journalists can be trained in reporting issues that tend to be particularly sensitive and possibly explosive. Reports on economic issues and environmental resources, in particular, can be distorted and twisted into tales of ethnic hatred and animosity because they are issues that affect people's livelihood, as they can have a dramatic effect on both personal economic viability and general stability. Thus it is particularly important that they are reported on in a professional manner, and issue-oriented training focusing on how journalists can frame these issues helps ensure that they are.
3. *Entertainment-oriented programming.* Entertainment-oriented programming offers another way to use media as positive tools for preventing and resolving conflict. The work of the NGO Search for Common Ground provides several impressive examples of such programming. Among other projects, they have co-produced a dramatic television series for Macedonian children intended to facilitate cross-ethnic understanding; and they have established radio studios in Burundi, Liberia and Sierra Leone that produce, in addition to other programming, soap operas designed to encourage dialogue and discourage violence. Entertainment-oriented programming can have a direct effect and may be significantly more influential than news programming.

Aggressive interventions

Finally, the third group of strategies for combating media abuse and manipulation involves what may be considered 'aggressive interventions'. Such interventions tend to be a last resort and usually occur after media abuse and manipulation is widely apparent, often after violent conflict has begun. They are more reactive than proactive. They are also externally imposed and some forms are unlikely to be effective if not accompanied by other forms of intervention, such as military intervention. Such aggressive interventions do not usually change media structure or content, although some forms do disable physical infrastructure. Clearly, earlier intervention that stands a chance of preventing media abuse and manipulation before it proliferates is preferable.

1. *Alternative information.* A prominent strategy for aggressive intervention is for foreign entities, including governments, NGOs and political parties to offer sources of information other than those available domestically. In several instances, alternative information has played an important role in mobilizing a population and injecting new ideas into society. Among them are Democratic Voices of Burma, a station broadcasting into Burma out of Norway, and Radio Freedom and Capital Radio in South Africa. Radio Freedom was broadcast by the African National Congress into South Africa from several southern African states in the 1970s, and Capital Radio broadcast from the 'homeland' of Transkei to the rest of South Africa in the 1980s. Both served as valuable sources of news about the realities of apartheid, winning many converts among the white population along the way.

More generally, in many countries major international radio networks, such as the BBC and Voice of America (VOA), are regularly heard on the airwaves and offer citizens reliable information that sometimes contradicts information broadcast by local media outlets.

Alternative information can be specifically designed to counter information broadcast by a single or small number of sources, such as government media or hate media outlets.

A good example of the use of alternative information is the Ring Around Serbia, a multilateral project spearheaded by the United States in 1999. It involved assembling a ring of radio transmitters in countries neighbouring Serbia and broadcasting programming from the BBC, VOA, Deutsche Welle, Radio France International and Radio Free Europe into Serbia. Such an intervention is reactive and occurs late in the manipulation process. It is also expensive, difficult to organize and of questionable legality. Broadcasts prepared specially for transmission into 'hostile territory' are often perceived as propaganda and thus discounted by the intended audience. But if all other opportunities for media intervention have been missed, broadcasting alternative information may merit consideration.

2. *Radio and television jamming.* Perhaps the most frequently discussed strategy for countering hate media is jamming radio and television signals. In looking back at Rwanda, several scholars and practitioners, foremost among them Roméo Dallaire, the UN commander in Rwanda during the genocide, have suggested that jamming Rwandan radio would have made carrying out the genocide significantly more difficult and would have been worth the effort and cost (to his credit, Dallaire proposed radio jamming *before* the genocide as well). But jamming is a blunt instrument that comes with substantial legal concerns and would only be seriously considered once violence is already widespread. The more effective and less costly alternative to radio jamming is removing media from the 'toolkit' belonging to actors intent on inciting conflict, which is what the structural and content-specific interventions detailed above are designed to do.

RECOMMENDATIONS

As this analysis demonstrates, media can be extremely powerful tools used by those intent on instigating conflict. Media are multipliers: they amplify and disseminate messages and opinions. Media spread information and misinformation, shape individuals' views of others and can heighten tensions or promote understanding. This makes controlling media and their messages an important goal for anyone intent on promoting conflict. This analysis concludes with four recommendations to the international community for addressing the use and abuse of media in vulnerable societies:

1. ***Media in vulnerable societies should be monitored.***
Media in vulnerable societies should be monitored for the 'clues to conflict' detailed above. Special attention should be devoted to the structural indicators

– including, in particular, journalist competence, media variety and plurality and media's legal environment – as they can reveal how vulnerable or resistant media are to manipulation and point to specific interventions that might prevent media co-optation and abuse before it occurs. Attention should also be given to content indicators, such as a focus on past atrocities and a history of ethnic hatred; manipulation of myths, stereotypes and identities to 'dehumanize'; and efforts to discredit alternatives to conflict. The monitoring should be comprehensive; put in context with political, economic and social indicators; and conducted by experienced or trained monitors.

2. ***There should be greater collaboration between media organizations and conflict resolution organizations.***
   The role of media in fomenting conflict is seldom addressed comprehensively by either media or conflict resolution NGOs. Media organizations tend to devote limited attention to the dynamics and causes of violent conflict, while conflict resolution organizations often overlook the role of media in fomenting or tempering the conflicts they scrutinize. However, working together, these organizations can pool their knowledge and address the role of media in conflict from both sides of the issue. Particularly in efforts to develop early-warning instruments, media organizations should be consulted and media 'indicators' incorporated into the analysis, so that media are considered, along with other factors, when trying to identify societies highly susceptible to conflict. Such collaboration can enhance understanding of the relevant issues and the design and implementation of early-warning instruments and preventive interventions.
3. ***Media organizations need to build a better case for monitoring and early intervention and encourage appropriate donor support.***
   Early, preventive media intervention, such as the structural interventions described above, can be significantly more effective and beneficial than later, reactive interventions, such as radio jamming. Early interventions are more cost-effective and can lay the foundation for the long-term institutional development necessary to combat political or ethnic instability. Media organizations need to provide donors with reliable research and reports on significant field experience to justify supporting early interventions, even before traditional conflict indicators are visible. Further collaboration and information-sharing between conflict resolution and media organizations, particularly through common methods for identifying critical points for intervention, will contribute greatly to assuring donors that funding early intervention is worthwhile and cost-effective.
4. ***A systematic review of media behaviour in vulnerable societies should be conducted.***
   An effective approach to gaining a better understanding of use and abuse of media in vulnerable societies would be to conduct a comprehensive study by monitoring the characteristics of media behaviour in several countries deemed close to conflict. Such a review could provide the quantitative and qualitative data needed to focus the attention of donors and media

organizations on the role of media in such societies and on the importance of early, preventive intervention.

REFERENCES

Article 19. 1996. *Broadcasting Genocide, Censorship, Propaganda and State-Sponsored Violence in Rwanda, 1990–1994.* Article 19, London, UK. Available at <www.article19.org/pdfs/publications/rwanda-broadcasting-genocide.pdf> (accessed 23 August 2005).

Des Forges, A. 2002. 'Silencing the Voices of Hate Radio in Rwanda'. In M.E. Price and M. Thompson. *Forging Peace: Intervention, Human Rights, and the Management of Media Space.* Edinburgh University Press, Edinburgh, UK.

Frohardt, M. and J. Temin. 2003. *Use and abuse of media in vulnerable societies* (special report 110). United States Institute of Peace, Washington, DC, USA. Available: <www.usip.org/pubs/specialreports/sr110.html> (accessed 13 September 2005).

Glyn-Pickett, J. 1999. Interview on 'Fresh Air'. National Public Radio, Washington, DC, USA, 29 March.

Metzl, J. 1997. Information Intervention: When Switching Channels Isn't Enough. *Foreign Affairs*, November–December: 15.

33
Censorship and Propaganda in Post-Genocide Rwanda

Lars Waldorf

We used communication and information warfare better than anyone.
President Paul Kagame (Pottier 2002: 53)

Rwandans realize perfectly well that there is a significant discrepancy between what they see with their own eyes every day and what they hear through the official media or private newspapers, which support the government line. They can see they are not being told the truth. Once again, we have fallen into an era of suspicion and speculation, which is so favourable to dissemination of the worst kind of propaganda.
André Sibomana (1999: 144)

In the aftermath of the 1994 genocide, in which Radio-Télévision Libre des Milles Collines (RTLM) and *Kangura* played a notoriously galvanizing role, Rwanda's new government faced the task of ensuring that a resurrected press would not voice hate speech again.[1] More than 12 years on, however, an increasingly authoritarian regime dominated by the Rwandan Patriotic Front (RPF) continues to justify censorship and propaganda as a necessary safeguard against the recrudescence of genocide. As the minister of information explained, 'The specter of 1994 makes us a lot more vigilant ... The means of information must not become vectors for germs of discord in the Rwandan population' (Fontemaggi 2003). The RPF portrays RTLM and *Kangura* as cautionary tales about the dangers of too much press freedom and private media. In reality, however, RTLM and *Kangura* testify to the dangers of government control and manipulation of the media.[2]

After taking power in 1994, the RPF retooled the previous regime's information agency and the official media to disseminate its own propaganda. As under the previous regime, the government has promoted private media outlets to create a facade of media pluralism.[3] At the same time, the RPF has successfully suppressed or co-opted independent journals and accused independent journalists of inciting ethnic 'divisionism' and even genocidal ideology. As a result, there is less press freedom and media pluralism in Rwanda today than there was before the genocide.

Johan Pottier (2002: 202) has illuminated how the RPF attained a 'monopoly on knowledge construction' vis-à-vis the international media. The RPF's prowess at propaganda should come as no surprise; after all, President Paul Kagame was head of military intelligence for Yoweri Museveni's National Resistance Movement army, which won the Ugandan civil war. While acknowledging the RPF's propaganda skills, Pottier faults the ignorance of many Western (especially Anglophone) journalists who were covering Rwanda for the first time and who could not see past the RPF as saviour and the international community as guilty bystander. Yet, the RPF's propaganda success with Western donors and media could not have been accomplished without its suppression of competing narratives, alternative voices and independent media within Rwanda.

POST-GENOCIDE POLITICAL DEVELOPMENTS

After the RPF defeated the genocidal forces militarily and installed a transitional government, there was some prospect that Rwanda might finally achieve a non-ethnic and more democratic government. Such hope quickly evaporated as Anglophone Tutsi military elites took control, both within the RPF and the government, marginalizing Francophone Hutu as well as Francophone Tutsi survivors (Reyntjens 2004). The RPF's authoritarianism stems from two main sources: a longstanding commitment to democratic centralism (shared by other well-disciplined guerrilla or vanguard movements) and its understandable fear of democracy in a country where Hutu comprise an overwhelming majority (HRW 2003: 4; ICG 2002: 2).[4]

Since 1995, more than 40 prominent figures – both Hutu and Tutsi – have fled into exile, while several others have been assassinated, imprisoned or disappeared (Human Rights Watch 2003: 8–9; ICG 2002: 28–9). In 1995, three Hutu political leaders resigned: Prime Minister Faustin Twagiramungu (from the Mouvement Démocratique Républicain (MDR)), Interior Minister Seth Sendashonga (from the RPF), and Justice Minister Alphonse Nkubito. Twagiramungu and Sendashonga went into exile, and Sendashonga was assassinated in Nairobi in 1998 after trying to create an opposition movement in exile. In early 2000, President Kagame linked Joseph Sebarenzi, the charismatic, Tutsi parliamentary leader, to monarchists and he fled into exile in the United States. After Assiel Kabera, an influential Tutsi genocide survivor and aide to Hutu President Pasteur Bizimungu, was assassinated, his two brothers fled the country: one was vice-president of Ibuka, the main survivors' association, while the other was head of the survivors' assistance fund. The same year, the government also arrested Jean Mbanda, a Tutsi survivor and parliamentarian, on corruption charges after he publicly criticized the government.[5] Prime Minister Celestin Rwigema, a Hutu MDR politician, fled to the United States in 2000, after which the Rwandan government accused him of genocide. President Bizimungu, a Hutu member of the RPF, resigned in 2000 and attempted to create a new political party, Parti Démocratique pour le Renouveau-Ubuyanja, which was immediately banned. He was arrested in 2002 and, after a show trial in 2004, was sentenced to 15 years for inciting rebellion, plotting to overthrow the government and other crimes (ICG 2002: 30–1; USDS 2005).

The RPF banned three opposition parties and co-opted the remaining parties in advance of the 2003 presidential and parliamentary elections – the first since the 1994 genocide. It levelled unsubstantiated accusations of divisionism against its political opponents – propaganda that the official and pro-government media were only too happy to repeat (EU EOM 2003a: 45). As the European Union Electoral Observer Mission noted, 'Accusations of separatism and divisionism, which are grave in the Rwandan context, had a tendency to be used as arguments for limiting the freedom of speech of political opponents during the election campaigns' (EU EOM 2003a: 10). The RPF accused the Liberal Party of promoting ethnic 'divisionism' by advocating on behalf of Tutsi genocide survivors. A parliamentary commission called for banning the MDR, the leading opposition party, and accused 46 individuals of collaborating with the MDR to promote genocidal ideology (HRW 2003). The former Minister of Defence and the army's parliamentary representative fled the country. Shortly, thereafter, five people disappeared, including the former vice-president of the Supreme Court and an MDR parliamentarian.[6]

President Kagame won 95 per cent of the vote and the RPF 76 per cent in the 2003 elections which marred by fraud, intimidation, a lack of transparency, and an 'absence of pluralism of opinion' (EU EOM 2004a: 4, 28–40; EU EOM 2003b: 3). After the elections, the EU Mission concluded, 'Political pluralism is more reduced than during the period of transition [July 1994 to July 2003]' (EU EOM 2003a: 4).

Following its electoral victories, the RPF further tightened control over the media and civil society. In early 2004, Parliament formed a commission to investigate the supposed persistence of genocidal ideology in Rwanda. The commission construed any criticism of RPF policies as genocidal ideology. In its June 2004 report, it accused a wide range of media and civil society actors – including CARE International, the BBC, and Voice of America (VOA) – of promoting genocidal ideology. The report made similar accusations against *La Ligue Rwandaise pour la Promotion et la Défense des Droits de l'Homme* (LIPRODHOR), a human rights NGO, and the staff of its two monthly journals, *Umukindo* and *Le Verdict*. Several of LIPRODHOR's human rights defenders, including most of the top leadership, subsequently fled the country. The US Department of State observed: 'After the release of the [parliamentary] report, independent human rights organizations were effectively dismantled, and all independent sources on the human rights conditions in the country disappeared in the second half of the year [2004]' (USDS 2005).

LEGAL RESTRICTIONS ON PRESS FREEDOM

The RPF has imposed a legal regime that greatly restricts press freedom. A 2002 criminal law punishes public incitement to discrimination or divisionism:

> Any person who makes public any speech, writing, pictures or images or any symbols over radio airwaves, television, in a meeting or public place, with the

> aim of discriminating [against] people or sowing sectarianism [divisionism] among them is sentenced to between one year and five years of imprisonment and fined between five hundred thousand (500,000) [US$ 1000] and two million (2,000,000) Rwandan francs [US$ 4,000] or only one of these two sanctions. (Rwanda 2002a: Article 8)

The law defines divisionism in sweeping terms as 'the use of any speech, written statement, or action that divides people, that is likely to spark conflicts among people, or that causes an uprising which might degenerate into strife among people based on discrimination' (Rwanda 2002a: Article 1).

The July 2002 press law (Rwanda 2002b) imposes criminal sanctions on the media for a wide range of ill-defined offences.[7] The law mandates maximum criminal sentences for publications that endanger law and order, threaten public decency, publish false news, hold the president in contempt and defame or abuse public authorities. Journalists can be taken into custody if they excuse genocide, incite soldiers to disobedience or publish false information likely to undermine army morale. In addition, the law forbids journalists from making unfounded accusations and writing propaganda. Under the law, anyone involved in production and circulation is potentially liable for criminal sanctions: 'The following persons ... shall be prosecuted as perpetrators for offences committed using the written press: the director of the publication or the publisher, failing that, the editor-in-chief, failing that, the authors, failing that the printers, and failing that, the sellers, distributors or bill posters' (Rwanda 2002b: Article 88). The law also requires journalists to reveal their sources on demand from the judicial organs (including, presumably, the judicial police). Finally, the law created the High Council of the Press, under the Office of the President, which accredits journalists and advises the government on censorship.[8]

TARGETING INDEPENDENT JOURNALISTS

Shortly after coming to power, the RPF began to censor independent journals and persecute independent journalists. Andre Sibomana, the editor of the Catholic newspaper, *Kinyamateka*, observed:

> At first the government allowed the press to resume its activities freely; then it continually restricted its freedom. It was quite understandable and desirable to limit the scope of the extremist press ... Yet, behind the official objective of raising the moral standards of the press, a real censorship has gradually settled in. It started at the grassroots, within the editorial teams of public and private newspapers, and rose to the top: even the Minister of Information ended up fleeing the country....
>
> Persecution of journalists started again in the autumn of 1994. Arrests, disappearances, attacks and various forms of intimidation increased in early 1995. One event marked the turning point: the attack on Edouard Mutsinzi, the director of the independent weekly *Le Messager*. Towards the ends of the day, in a café in the center of Kigali, a group of Tutsi extremists beat him

for a long time without anyone intervening ... the message got through: from then on, anyone criticizing the government knew what to expect. (Sibomana 1999: 143–4)

Speaking in mid-1997, Sibomana (1999: 144) noted that 'apart from *Kinyamateka*, there is virtually no opposition press.' By September that year, the Catholic Church hierarchy had replaced him with a more pliant editor and, by March 1998, he was dead after the government denied him a passport in time to seek medical treatment in Europe (Sibomana 1999: 159–62). In the years since, *Kinyamateka*'s editorial line has been practically indistinguishable from that of the government-controlled press.

Since 1994, three journalists have been assassinated or disappeared in apparent retaliation for their work. Manasse Mugabo, director of the United Nations radio station's Kinyarwanda service, disappeared in August 1995 (RSF 2001; Sibomana 1999: 143–4). Appolos Hakizimana, editor of *Umuravumba*, was assassinated in April 1997, a week after the authorities seized the journal for describing RPF massacres (LDGL 2002: 62–3).[9] In May 1998, Emmanuel Munyemanzi, former head of production at TV Rwanda, was killed, two months after the director of ORINFOR (Rwanda Information Office) accused him of sabotaging a programme (CPJ 1998).

Over the years, the government has arrested several journalists on accusations of having incited genocide in 1994. Despite international attention from Reporters Sans Frontières, most of them have never been brought to trial (LDGL 2002: 62–3; RSF 2001: 1).[10] One of them, Hélène Nyirabikali, former editor of the government-owned *Imvaho*, died in detention even though she had been awarded a government prize for reconciliation in 1998 (Price 2000: 43). A former Radio Rwanda journalist, Albert-Baudouin Twizeyimana, was released after three and a half years in pretrial detention and a former TV Rwanda journalist, Gideon Mushimiyimana, after six years. Mushimiyimana had been accused of genocide shortly after he gave information to a Radio France International (RFI) journalist (LDGL 2002: 62–3; RSF 2001).

In a remarkable development, the Rwandan government arrested Father Guy Theunis, a Belgian priest, at Kigali airport in September 2005. At a preliminary hearing, several prominent RPF figures – including the vice-president of the High Council of the Press – accused Theunis of incitement to genocide for having translated and republished *Kangura* articles in *Dialogue*, a French journal, in the early 1990s. Defending himself, Theunis argued that *Dialogue* had published extracts from a wide variety of Rwandan journals as part of its review of the Kinyarwanda press (personal notes 2005). It is unclear how republication of *Kangura* excerpts in French (a language not understood by the great majority of Rwandans) could have constituted direct and public incitement to genocide. Nonetheless, the *gacaca* (community) court indicted Theunis for incitement to genocide, referred his case to the formal courts for trial and ordered him detained in Kigali's central prison. In November 2005, Rwanda released Father Theunis on Belgium's agreement to investigate the charges against him. In a subsequent interview, President Kagame stated that Theunis 'was indeed involved' in the genocide (Spiegel, 2006).

Several journalists have been forced into exile. The founder of *Tribun du Peuple*, Jean-Pierre Mugabe, left in 1998. After Joseph Sebarenzi, the popular Tutsi speaker of Parliament, was forced to step down, *Imboni* revealed the RPF's behind-the scenes role. The government then seized the journal and banned it. Following President Kagame's attack on the paper, its two Tutsi journalists left the country: Deo Mushayidi (also president of the Rwandan Association of Journalists) and Jason Muhayimana. Another Tutsi journalist, Jean-Claude Nkubito with Agence France Presse, followed them into exile (ICG 2002: 28–9). At the end of 2001, police briefly detained Amiel Nkuliza, editor of *Le Partisan*, after he published an interview with the MDR secretary general who had accused the RPF of fomenting divisions within the MDR.[11] After reportedly receiving death threats from security forces, Nkuliza fled to Uganda in January 2002, and *Le Partisan* collapsed (Front Line 2005: 70–1; ICG 2002: 27).[12]

In mid-2002, the government expelled Asuman Bisiika, the Ugandan-born Tutsi editor of *The Rwanda Herald*, on immigration charges shortly after he published an editorial calling for the release of former President Bizimungu.[13] With Bisiika ousted, the newspaper folded. At the time, the British Department for International Development (DFID), Rwanda's largest bilateral donor, was funding the newspaper as part of its efforts to promote civil society. The government's action and DFID's lack of public response sent a powerful message to journalists: international donors would not defend Rwanda's independent media.

In early 2002, the government arrested Laurien Ntezimana and Didace Muremangingo, editors of *Ubuntu*, and charged them with attacking state security and inciting divisionism for using the word '*ubuyanja*' (spiritual renewal) in their masthead.[14] The same word figures in the name of the banned political party created by former President Bizimungu. Although an appeals court provisionally released them after a month in detention, Butare's provincial government banned the publication and distribution of *Ubuntu* (HRW 2002; ICG 2002: 14).

UMUSESO AND UMUCO: CASE STUDIES IN PRESS HARASSMENT

Umuseso was a lively, provocative, and occasionally partisan weekly that published critical articles about the government and broke stories on government corruption.[15] The government repeatedly accused the newspaper of inciting divisionism and genocide. In January 2002, the minister responsible for the press compared *Umuseso* to *Kangura* on Radio Rwanda (RSF 2002). In March 2003, a parliamentary commission investigating the MDR labelled *Umuseso* journalists 'propagandists of divisionism' and charged them with disseminating genocidal ideology (Rwanda 2003a). The June 2004 parliamentary commission on genocidal ideology accused *Umuseso* of having 'incited the population to civil disobedience against the government in place' (Rwanda 2004). The charges of genocidal ideology seemed grotesque given that almost half *Umuseso*'s journalists have been Tutsi and one, Kalisa McDowell, fought with the RPF in 1994 (Fontemaggi 2003).

Government authorities have used both existing laws and extra-judicial methods to harass *Umuseso*, driving several of the newspaper's editors and journalists into exile. In May 2001, the founding editor, John Mugabi, sought asylum abroad after being threatened over his exposé of the Rwandan military's resource exploitation in eastern Democratic Republic of the Congo (LDGL 2002: 65, 71; RSF 2001: 4).[16] Around the same time, one of his colleagues, Shyaka Kanuma, left the country after trying to garner an interview with former President Bizimungu (ICG 2002: 15).[17]

In January 2003, Ismail Mbonigabo, then editor, was jailed for a month on charges of divisionism for an article correctly predicting that former prime minister Faustin Twagiramungu of the MDR would challenge President Kagame in the August presidential elections (and for an accompanying cartoon showing President Kagame cutting a baby, labelled MDR, in half).[18] In November 2003, shortly after the RPF won the parliamentary elections, the authorities arrested the current editor, Robert Serufifira, and four journalists for two days for inciting divisionism and defamation with an article about the planned demobilization of the former army chief of staff. Some of the journalists stated they were beaten while in detention. The authorities seized 4,000 copies of the journal to prevent its distribution (AFP 2003; CPJ 2003).

In January 2004, police again seized issues of *Umuseso* after it published several articles alleging corruption by Gerald Gahima, vice-president of the Supreme Court (and the former prosecutor general), and his brother, Théogène Rudasingwa, director of the cabinet.[19] The following month, security forces intimidated Serufifira and another *Umuseso* journalist and labelled them *Interahamwe*. Five days later, after being threatened by armed men, Serufifira fled the country, along with the paper's best known journalist, Kalisa McDowell, and a driver (CPJ 2004). More *Umuseso* journalists have since left Rwanda. Tharcisse Semana was threatened and fled in April 2004 after publishing articles critical of Bizimungu's trial and the parliamentary commission on genocidal ideology (CPJ 2004). In January 2005, Didas Gasana and Rwango Kadafi went into exile. Gasana claimed he had been detained by armed men and threatened with death the day before he left. Kadafi and another *Umuseso* journalist had been attacked in mid-December by six men with knives (CPJ 2004).

In August 2004, the new editor, Charles Kabonero, published an article alleging that Dennis Polisi, the vice-president of Parliament's lower house, had formed a clique of Tutsi returnees from Burundi and was challenging President Kagame's leadership of the RPF and the country. The article also accused Polisi of nepotism and corruption. Polisi filed suit against *Umuseso* for criminal defamation and divisionism. After investigating *Umuseso*, the High Council of the Press demanded that Kabonero reveal his sources and ask pardon. Kabonero refused, arguing that any apology would compromise his legal defence. In September 2005, the council recommended that *Umuseso* be suspended for four months. The minister of information declined to suspend *Umuseso*, but expressed hope that the council's action might serve as a lesson to the paper and other journalists (personal communication 2004). A Rwandan court acquitted Kabonero of divisionism in November 2004, but convicted him of criminal defamation and insulting the dignity of a public official and fined him US$ 15 and 1 franc (US$ 0.001) in symbolic damages payable to Polisi (AFP 2004). On appeal, a higher court increased the sentence to a one-year suspended prison term, a US$ 100 fine and a US$ 1,800 damage award to Polisi (CPJ 2005a).

By mid-2005, *Umuco*, a Kinyarwanda journal had replaced *Umuseso* as the main target of government harassment. In August 2005, police twice questioned the editor, Bonaventure Bizumuremyi, after he published an article on police corruption and another calling for the release of former President Bizimungu. Later that month, police seized copies of the newspaper and conducted a lengthy interrogation of the editor after he published several critical articles, one of which condemned the arrest of the Belgian priest, Father Theunis (CPJ 2005 b,c).

In August 2006, the government's High Council of the Press ruled that several articles in *Umuco*, which criticized the government, had violated the Constitution, the 2002 press law, and the code of professional ethics for journalists. That same month, Bizurnuremyi fled the country to avoid a police summons. Another *Umuco* journalist, Jean-Leonard Rugambage, spent 11 months in prison on the orders of community genocide courts (*gacaca*) after writing an August 2005 article reporting corruption and false accusations by several of those courts.

LIMITING COMMERCIAL RADIO

Radio remains the most important means of communication in Rwanda given the 34 per cent illiteracy rate (Ministry of Finance and Economic Planning 2001: 44) and the limited circulation of newspapers in Kigali and Butare.[20] The 2002 press law had one positive feature: it authorized private radio and television stations for the first time since the genocide. Yet, the government displayed little interest in issuing radio broadcast licences until after the 2003 elections (EU EOM 2003b: 41).

By late 2006, Rwanda had 14 radio stations but that has not led to real media pluralism. For a start, only four of the stations are private.[21] Also, the minister of information has made it clear that the state will retain a monopoly on information broadcast over the airwaves: 'The public radio and television are there for relaying the action of the government. The private media, rather, should be interested in other things, like music and entertainment' (Fontemaggi 2003). Indeed, the private commercial stations have mostly shied away from news and commentary. One independent Rwandan journalist criticized the new commercial stations, saying 'They don't take any risks to inform people' (personal communication 2004).

RESTRICTING THE INTERNATIONAL MEDIA

The government has not been content with harassing the independent Rwandan media; it has also retaliated against foreign journalists and foreign media that portrayed the RPF in an unflattering light. It expelled Christian Jennings (Reuters) in 1997, denied a visa to Stephen Smith (*Libération*) and refused visas to Reporters Sans Frontières (RSF 2001: 1). In June 2006, the Rwandan government ordered Sonia Rolley, Radio France International's correspondent since October 2004, to leave the country within 48 hours after refusing to renew her visa – even though she had received her press accreditation from the Ministry of Information a month earlier. The government offered no explanation for that expulsion.

In 2001, security forces pressured local correspondents for the BBC and VOA to turn over recordings of their interviews with former President Bizimungu (RSF 2001: 4). Police also confiscated recordings made by an international station's local correspondent in mid-2004 (personal communication 2004).

Government officials have repeatedly criticized the BBC, VOA and RFI for promoting divisionism.[22] The 2004 parliamentary commission report on genocidal ideology recommended that the government

> see if strong (or international) radio stations which have become a network of genocidal ideology should be made to reveal their sources on what is happening in Rwanda and should help condemn the genocide and those who always want to perpetrate it. (Rwanda 2004)

The commission also expressed concern that residents in southwest Rwanda only receive information from Congolese radio stations that 'propagate a genocidal ideology in the Great Lakes region' (Rwanda 2004). One of the named Congolese stations is Radio Okapi, a joint venture between the United Nations Observer Mission in Congo (MONUC) and the Swiss media NGO Hirondelle.[23]

At a January 2006 conference, the Minister of Information and the head of the state information agency took turns criticizing Lucie Umukundwa, a VOA correspondent, and Jean-Claude Mwambutsa, a BBC correspondent, for biased reporting, as indicated by their on-air references to critical reports by Amnesty International and Human Rights Watch. The police spokesman also stated that police would investigate their 'ideology' a clear reference to a 2004 parliamentary commission's accusations of 'genocidal ideology' against VOA and the BBC. In July 2006, unidentified men assaulted Umukundwa's brother, reportedly saying the attack was in response to her VOA broadcasts.

International media NGOs working in Rwanda have been very careful not to antagonize the government or its international donors. For example, Internews regularly screened its documentary films for government officials so they could suggest changes before the films were shown throughout the country. In 2003, the United States Agency for International Development (USAID) gave Internews US$ 250,000 to produce four films on the national elections. The first presented the four presidential candidates answering the same set of policy questions, while the second featured interviews with legislative candidates about their policy positions. The government refused to allow distribution of the films until after the elections and USAID abandoned the project (EU EOM 2003b: 48).

CONCLUSION

Post-genocide Rwanda reveals just how easy it is to abuse hate speech laws in post-conflict societies. The RPF justifies its censorship and propaganda on the grounds that political pluralism and press freedom have led – and will lead – inexorably to hate media and incitement to genocide. By uncritically accepting that argument, international donors may be salving their guilty consciences in the short term, but they run the risk of 'aiding violence' (Uvin 1998) in the long term and setting a terrible precedent for other authoritarian regimes. The best way to prevent regimes from inciting hatred and violence through the mass media is to foster independent, pluralistic and professional media that can serve as a counterweight to government propaganda and manipulation. As an independent Rwandan journalist observed:

> The government is the one that can put propaganda in the minds of the people. The shareholders of RTLM were also members of the government ... *Kangura* was trying to write the propaganda of the government. If a government goes wrong with its politics, [government-controlled media] will help to write the propaganda of a government that has already gone astray. (personal communication 2004, initially published in Front Line 2005: 67)

ACKNOWLEDGEMENTS

Thanks to Alison Des Forges, Julia Crawford, Mary Kimani, and several courageous Rwandan journalists who are best left unnamed. All translations from the French are by the author.

NOTES

1. Other vulnerable, post-conflict societies have faced similar problems. See Price (2000) discussing Bosnia, Kosovo, Cambodia, and Rwanda; Palmer (2001) comparing the situation in post-war Kosovo to that of post-Nazi Germany. See also Frohardt and Temin (2003) discussing various interventions to assist independent media in vulnerable states.
2. As a prominent Rwanda academic observed: 'the [pre-genocide] government created media that looked independent to outsiders, but which was under its full control behind the scenes. These outlets conveyed messages of hatred and violence that could not have been published in the official media. Thus, under the guise of promoting the freedom of expression, the government achieved its objective of controlling the press while spreading its propaganda.' (Kamatali 2002: 67) Indeed, it was Rwanda's truly independent journalists – those who challenged government propaganda and the hate media – who were targeted during the genocide.
3. Pro-government newspapers, like *The New Times*, subsist on advertising revenues from government agencies, parastatals and private monopolies. By contrast, newspapers critical of the government have had difficulty in attracting and retaining their advertisers (ICG 2002: 15; RSF 2001).
4. To be fair, the early years of RPF control could be partly understood as a response to an armed insurgency in northwest Rwanda led by remnants of the former genocidal army and

militias, as well as war with those elements in the Democratic Republic of Congo (DRC). Some Hutu Power propagandists, like *Kangura*'s Hassan Ngeze, continued to publish from exile. Yet, even after the insurgency had been largely defeated in 2001 and a peace accord signed in the DRC in 2002, the RPF increased its persecution of political opponents, civil society and independent media.

5. Mbanda was finally released from pretrial detention in early 2003 and later left Rwanda.
6. The charges of divisionism against the MDR parliamentarian, Dr Leonard Hitimana, were particularly baseless: he was well known for having saved Tutsi during the 1994 genocide and for testifying as a prosecution witness at the ICTR (African Rights 2002).
7. President Kagame refused to sign an earlier version of the law that would have imposed sentences ranging from 20 years to death for incitement to genocide. He was reportedly swayed by arguments that such explicit criminal provisions belonged in the penal law.
8. With funding from the British Department for International Development (DFID) and the Netherlands, Internews, an international NGO, prepared a strategic plan for the Ministry of Information, which, among other things, recommended liberalizing the 2002 press law and replacing criminal libel with civil libel (Ministry of Information 2004b: 30–4). In late 2006, the government was drafting a new press law, which represents a marginal improvement over the 2002 press law (personal communications 2006). Though, as one journalist cynically noted, 'the press law is largely irrelevant in a country like Rwanda' (personal communication 2006).
9. In July 1996, the government had banned his prior journal, *Intego*, confiscated that month's issue, arrested him for three weeks and labelled him an *Interahamwe* (a genocidal militia member) over an article criticizing a security campaign (CPJ 1996).
10. As of late 2006, the government had still not tried Valérie Bemeriki, one of the most notorious RTLM broadcasters, even though she has been in custody since 1999.
11. The MDR secretary general, Pierre Gakwandi, was arrested for giving that interview in January 2002. After lengthy pretrial detention, he was finally tried, convicted and sentenced to four years.
12. Nkuliza had already spent two years in detention (from 1997 to 1999) on a charge of attacking state security for having published photos of inmates in the overcrowded Kigali central prison (RSF 2001: 3).
13. Like many other Ugandan-born Tutsi, Bisiika returned to Rwanda after the genocide and began working without obtaining a work permit. Even though Bisiika started *The Rwanda Herald* in October 2000, his work status appears to have been investigated only after he published the editorial on former president Bizimungu.
14. Ntezimana, a respected lay theologian and past recipient of the Pax Christi Award, worked for reconciliation between Hutu and Tutsi before and after the genocide. Although a Tutsi survivor, Muremangingo was mixed with the general population at Butare's central prison, most of whom are accused of genocide.
15. The newspaper also displays the lack of professionalism endemic among Rwandan journalists: most of the stories are unsourced and traffic in rumour and innuendo.
16. Mugabi, who was originally close to the RPF, was detained for three months in 1999 on charges of defamation and false information for an article alleging that the secretary general of the defence ministry had received an illegal kickback on the purchase of helicopter parts. The prosecutor ordered Mugabi's arrest after he refused to name his source.
17. Kanuma subsequently returned to Rwanda and, in 2005, he launched an English-language monthly *Focus*. The paper has offered some investigative reporting and modest criticism, while proclaiming '[t]oday in Rwanda we enjoy press freedoms on a par with any Western democracy.' As editor, Kanuma has repeatedly published inflammatory – and unproven – accusations against his main competitor, the editor of *Umuseso*, including accusations that he was plotting to overthrow the government with a series of bomb attacks.
18. Mbonigabo did not help the cause of independent journalism when he later became the press spokesman for Twagiramungu during the 2003 presidential elections. After Twagiramungu lost the elections, Mbonigabo fled to Uganda.
19. Gahima was forced to resign as Supreme Court judge. Rudasingwa was acquitted by a military court. Both are now in exile.

20. The illiteracy rate is for 1999. In a country where approximately 90 per cent of the population are engaged in subsistence farming, and many earn less than a dollar a day, newspapers are an unaffordable luxury for most people.
21. The remaining ten stations consist of state-owned Radio Rwanda and its three affiliated community stations, four private religious stations and two private community stations. Television broadcasting remains a state monopoly.
22. Both the BBC and VOA present some of their programmes in Kinyarwanda and Swahili, thus reaching a broad audience.
23. After the genocide, the government rejected Hirondelle's application to establish a radio station in Rwanda that would address human rights issues (LDGL 2002: 59).

REFERENCES

AFP (Agence France-Presse). 2003. Remise en liberté provisoire des journalistes arrêtés au Rwanda. AFP, Paris, France, 22 November. Available at <www.abarundi.org/actualite/reg2/afp_211103_r3.html> (accessed 13 September 2005).

—— 2004. Un journaliste rwandais accusé de divisionnisme sera rejugé en appel. AFP, Paris, France, 26 November. Available at <www.africatime.com/rwanda/nouvelle.asp?no_nouvelle=158398&no_categorie> (accessed 22 October 2005).

African Rights. 2002. *Tribute to Courage*. Kigali, Rwanda.

CPJ (Committee to Protect Journalists). 1996. Rwanda: Attacks on the Press in 1996. Committee to Protect Journalists, New York, NY, USA. Available at <www.cpj.org/attacks96/countries/africa/cases/rwandaimp.html> (accessed 13 September 2005).

—— 1998. Journalists Who Disappeared. Committee to Protect Journalists, New York, NY, USA. Available at <www.cpj.org/Briefings/missing_list.html> (accessed 13 September 2005).

—— 2003. CPJ Concerned About Detention of Journalists and Seizure of Newspaper. Committee to Protect Journalists, New York, NY, USA, 21 November. Available at <www.cpj.org/news/2003/Rwanda21nov03na.html> (accessed 13 September 2005).

—— 2004. Cases of Attack 2004: Rwanda. Committee to Protect Journalists, New York, NY, USA, 21 November. Available at <www.cpj.org/cases04/africa_cases04/rwanda.html> (accessed 13 September 2005).

—— 2005a. Editor's Conviction Upheld, Sentence Toughened. Committee to Protect Journalists, New York, NY, USA, 22 March. Available at <www.cpj.org/news/2005/Rwanda22mar05na.html> (accessed 22 October 2005).

—— 2005b. Journalist Held After Criticizing Traditional Court Judges. Committee to Protect Journalists, New York, NY, USA, 15 September. Available at <www.cpj.org/news/2005/Rwanda15sept05na.html> (accessed 22 October 2005).

—— 2005c. Newspaper Seized, Editor Questioned by Police. Committee to Protect Journalists, New York, NY, USA, 20 September. Available at <www.cpj.org/news/2005/Rwanda20sept05na.html> (accessed 22 October 2005).

EU EOM (European Union Electoral Observation Mission). 2003a. *Rwanda: élection présidentielle 25 août 2003 et élections législatives 29 et 30 septembre, 2 octobre 2003* (final report). European Union, Brussels, Belgium. Available at <www.europa.eu.int/comm/external_relations/human_rights/eu_election_ass_observ/rwanda/moe_ue_final_2003.pdf> (accessed 22 October 2005).

—— 2003b. *Déclaration préliminaire des elections présidentielles*. European Union, Brussels, Belgium, 27 August. Available at <www.europa.eu.int/comm/external_relations/human_rights/eu_election_ass_observ/rwanda/prelim.htm> (accessed 13 September 2005).

Frohardt, M. and J. Temin. 2003. *Use and Abuse of Media in Vulnerable Societies*. United States Institute of Peace, Washington, DC, USA. Available at <www.usip.org/pubs/specialreports/sr110.html> (accessed 13 September 2005).

Fontemaggi, F. 2003. Au Rwanda, l'information hantée par le genocide. *Liberation*, 4 December. Available at <www.liberation.fr/page.php?Article=162257> (accessed 22 October 2005).

Front Line. 2005. Front line Rwanda: Disappearances, Arrests, Threats, Intimidation and Co-option of Human Rights Defenders 2001–2004. Front Line, Dublin, Ireland. Available at <www.frontlinedefenders.org/pdfs/1965_Front%20Line%20Rwanda%20Report.pdf> (accessed 22 October 2005).

HRW (Human Rights Watch). 2000. *The Search for Security and Human Rights Abuses*. Human Rights Watch, New York, NY, USA. Available at <www.hrw.org/reports/2000/rwanda/> (accessed 13 September 2005).

—— 2002. *Rwanda: Activists in Detention*. Human Rights Watch, New York, NY, USA. Available at <www.hrw.org/english/docs/2002/01/31/rwanda3716.htm> (accessed 13 September 2005).

—— 2003. *Preparing for Elections: Tightening Control in the Name of Unity*. Human Rights Watch, New York, NY, USA. Available at <www.hrw.org/backgrounder/africa/rwanda0503bck.htm> (accessed 13 September 2005).

ICG (International Crisis Group). 2002. *Rwanda at the End of the Transition: a Necessary Political Liberalization*. ICG, Brussels, Belgium. Available at <www.icg.org//library/documents/report_archive/A400817_13112002.pdf> (accessed 13 September 2005).

Kamatali, J.M. 2002. Freedom of Expression and its Limitations: the Case of the Rwandan Genocide. *Stanford Journal of International Law* 38(5): 57.

LDGL (Ligue des droits de la personne dans la région des Grands Lacs). 2002. La problematique de la liberté d'expression au Rwanda: cas de la presse. *Dialogue*, January–February: 35–81. Available at <www.ldgl.org/presse1.htm> (accessed 13 September 2005).

Ministry of Finance and Economic Planning. 2001. *Rwanda Development Indicators, 2001*. Republic of Rwanda, Kigali, Rwanda, July.

Ministry of Information. 2004. *Strategic Plan for the Development of the Rwandan Media Sector*. Kigali, Rwanda, September.

Palmer, L.R. 2001. A Very Clear and Present Danger: Hate Speech, Media Reform, and Post-Conflict Democratization in Kosovo. *Yale Journal of International Law*, 26(1): 179.

Pottier, J. 2002. *Re-imagining Rwanda: Conflict Survival and Disinformation in the Late Twentieth Century*. Cambridge University Press, Cambridge, UK.

Price, M.E. (ed.). 2000. Restructuring the Media in Post-Conflict Societies: Four Perspectives on the Experience of Intergovernmental and Non-Governmental Organizations. *Cardozo Online Journal of Conflict Resolution*, 2(1). Available at <www.cardozo.yu.edu/cojcr/final_site/articles_notes/vol2_an/Price.htm> (accessed 13 September 2005).

Reyntjens, F. 2004. Rwanda, Ten Years On: From Genocide to Dictatorship. *African Affairs*, 103(441): 177.

RSF (Reporters Sans Frontières). 2001. The President Paul Kagame is a Predator of Press Freedom. RSF, Paris, France, 7 November. Available at <www.rsf.org/rsf/uk/html/afrique/rapport_01/rwanda.html> (accessed 13 September 2005).

—— 2002. Rwanda: Annual Report 2002. RSF, Paris, France. Available at <www.rsf.org/article.php3?id_article=6437> (accessed 13 September 2005).

Rwanda, Republic of. 2002a. *Law 47/2001 of 18/12/2001 instituting punishment for offences of discrimination and sectarianism*. Republic of Rwanda, Kigali, Rwanda, 15 February.

—— 2002b. *Law 18/2002 of 11/05/2002 Governing the Press*. Republic of Rwanda, Kigali, Rwanda, 1 July.

—— 2003a. *Rapport de la Commission Parlementaire de controle mise en place le 27 decembre 2002 pour enqueter sur les problemes du MDR*. Parliamentary Commission, Kigali, Rwanda, 14 April.

—— 2004. *Rapport de la Commission Parlementaire ad hoc, crée en date du 20 janvier 2004 par le Parlement, Chambre des Députes pour analyser en profondeur les tueries perpétrées dans la province de Gikongoro, idéologie génocidaire et ceux qui la propagent partout au Rwanda*. Parliamentary Commission, Kigali, Rwanda, 28 June.

Sibomana, A. 1999. *Hope for Rwanda: Conversations with Laure Guilbert and Herve Deguine*. Pluto Press, Sterling, VA, USA.

Spiegel Online. 2006. Spiegel Interview with Rwandan President Paul Kagame: 'You Can't Trust the UN.' Spiegel, Germany, 28 February. Available at <www.service.spiegel.de/cache/international/spiegel/0,1518,403586,00.html> (accessed 15 May, 2006).

USDS (United States Department of State). 2005. *Country Reports on Human rights Practices 2004: Rwanda*. USDS, Washington, DC, USA, 28 February. Available at <www.state.gov/g/drl/rls/hrrpt/2004/41621.htm> (accessed 23 October 2005).

Uvin, P. 1998. *Aiding Violence: the Development Enterprise in Rwanda*. Kumarian Press, West Hartford, CT, USA.

34

PG – Parental Guidance or Portrayal of Genocide: the Comparative Depiction of Mass Murder in Contemporary Cinema

Michael Dorland

In the hour of brief interviews with film stars preceding the 2005 Oscars, Don Cheadle, nominated for best actor for his role as Paul Rusesabagina, the courageous hotel manager in *Hotel Rwanda*, stated that he was honoured to be associated with a film that told the story of 'a little known genocide' (CTV 2005). Cheadle's remarks indicate a problem relating to the filmic, and often fictionalized, depiction of genocides generally. Whether in Rwanda in the 1990s, Cambodia in the 1970s or Nazi-occupied Poland of the 1940s, genocides are always seemingly, and remain often decades after the fact, 'little known'.

Genocides always take place off-screen, so to speak. There are no images from within the Nazi gas chambers to establish once and for all (if such proof were still required) that the Holocaust happened.[1] There are very few images of the mass slaughter with clubs and machetes of the approximately 800,000 Tutsis killed in Rwanda.[2] There are, however, images of numerous bodies *after* the slaughter and of cleaned skulls in rows and rows at memorial sites in Rwanda, as in Cambodia, that show that mass killings did occur.

There are also the mental images imprinted in the minds of those who witnessed or survived such events, in the form of flashbacks or related associations reactivated by location, smell, etc. These internalized images are, of course, impossible to show and so become the source of acute personal suffering labelled 'post-traumatic stress disorder'.[3]

Such dilemmas of representation leave the actual perpetration of genocide open to doubt, most notably in the case of Holocaust deniers (see, for example, Shermer and Grobman 2000). Curiously, regarding the genocide of non-Jewish populations (the Armenian case being something of an exception), doubts about the actual occurrence of the slaughter seldom arise, although generalized ignorance at the time, or worse impotent indifference, serve a somewhat equivalent function. This may have to do with the fact that we live in a post-Holocaust era, in the sense that the Holocaust set new standards for the acceptability of mass murder on a scale never previously known to humankind.[4] Either way, the actual killings remain off-screen. This is both a problem and a challenge for film-makers, as much for documentary film-makers as for those who have opted to deal fictionally with these issues. (It is equally a problem for historians, philosophers, theologians and the like, different again for novelists, although these will not concern us here.)

What will concern us is some of the problems encountered by certain film-makers who have attempted to represent genocide. For reasons of space, this will be a selective analysis, focusing on differences between 'Holocaust films' and 'genocide films', in which the victims are non-Jews.

THE G WORD

A first step must involve some definitional discussion of the problematic term 'genocide'.

One of the 'diplomatic' issues surrounding the lack of intervention in the Rwandan case was the Western powers' inability to agree on when a genocide actually is one, as opposed to, for example, 'an "acceptable" (if tragic) round of ethnic murder' (Power 2002: 346). Coined by the refugee Polish lawyer Rafael Lemkin, 'genocide' – from the Greek *geno* (race or tribe) and the Latin *caedere* (killing) – meant 'a coordinated plan of *different* actions aiming at the destruction of the essential foundations of the life of national groups, with the aim of annihilating the groups themselves' (Lemkin 1944).

He did not intend the term to capture or communicate the Nazi 'Final Solution'; rather 'genocide' was meant as an 'ideal–typical' concept in international law, a standard by which 'civilization' could begin to come to grips with the novel twentieth century problem of unprecedented mass murder (Power 2002: 43). Through Lemkin's own tireless personal efforts, combined with the legal problems posed by the (equally unprecedented) Nuremberg Trials, the term genocide rapidly did become not only widely accepted (if in other ways unclear) but also entrenched in international law in the 1948 United Nations *Convention on the Prevention and Punishment of the Crime of Genocide* (as specified acts 'committed with intent to destroy, in whole or in part, a national, ethnical, racial or religious group' (UN 1951)).

If not intended to be conflated with the Nazi Judeocide, in fact it was. Genocide and the Holocaust soon became equivalent ideas, if not in international law, then in the broader post-Holocaust culture. Paradoxically, this conflation would make it harder to reach agreement on genocides that did not involve the extermination of millions (by implication, of Jews; this being the standard).

One of the difficulties, then, in the case of the 'diplomatic' debate attempting to come to grips with what was going on in Rwanda in 1993, was the following, in Roméo Dallaire's words:

> I was self-conscious about saying the killings were 'genocidal' because to us in the West, genocide was the equivalent of the Holocaust or the killing fields of Cambodia – I mean millions of people. 'Ethnic cleansing' seemed to involve hundreds of thousands of people. 'Genocide' was the highest scale of crimes against humanity imaginable. It was so far up there, so far off the

charts, that it was not easy to recognize that *we* could be in such a situation. (Power 2002: 358)

Note that Dallaire's reference to Cambodia indicates a shifting downward of the scale of 'acceptable' genocidal killing from the canonical figure of six million to a mere 1.7 million in Cambodia.[5] If the conflation of genocide with the Holocaust compounded the difficulty of rating a mass killing for diplomats and generals, how much more difficult would the issue be for the non-specialist, popular culture at large?

THE HOLOCAUST FILM[6]

As Barbie Zelizer (1998) remarked in her important study of Holocaust memory through the camera's eye, *Remembering to Forget*, the initial dissemination of newsreels of British army bulldozers plowing thousands of emaciated cadavers into the lime pits of Bergen-Belsen raised some of the many problems relating to the depiction of the Holocaust. The main one concerns the problematic status of 'the image' in mass media cultures. The paradox here is that for all the proliferation of mediated images that we have lived with since the mass dissemination of first the movies and then television, we still do not fully understand, scientifically, philosophically and otherwise, how human beings respond to images individually and collectively.

The naïve belief that 'a picture is worth a thousand words' is a highly dubious proposition, especially if the picture depicts something never seen before; just consider modern art's scandalous reception since the beginning of the twentieth century. Thus, the unleashing of images of the Nazi concentration camps, after their liberation by the allied armies in the spring of 1945, of mountains of dead or near-dead staggering survivors, a dissemination widely encouraged by the highest authorities of the Supreme Headquarters Allied Expeditionary Force, posed whole new problems. As Zelizer notes, these images had no 'framing' – they were just suddenly there. She notes as well that this was in a context of a rising professional rivalry between print journalists and photographers, as attested to by *Life* magazine, which, during World War II and the Pacific War in particular, had become increasingly 'realistic' in its photographs of dead American soldiers.[7]

Similarly, it was the showing of the same footage of the bulldozing of murdered concentration camp inmates that caused the uproar at the Nuremberg Trials of the major Nazi war criminals, rather than the massive documentary, textual evidence assembled by the prosecution that journalists covering the trials found so 'boring' (Douglas 2001). In his feature film *Judgment At Nuremberg*, director Stanley Kramer (1961) recaptures precisely the shock of the showing of these same images within the film's depiction of one of the smaller trials involving lesser figures of the Nazi leadership. It was all so shocking and incomprehensible that the most widespread collective response was to repress the whole business for several decades.[8]

'HOLOCAUST' TV SERIES

Hot on the heels of ABC's enormously successful mini-series *Roots* in 1977, NBC responded the year after with the 9.5-hour mini-series *Holocaust*. As historian Peter Novick (1999: 209) writes, 'more information about the Holocaust was imparted to more Americans over those four nights than over all the preceding thirty years.' Nearly 100 million Americans watched all or part of the mini-series, written by screenwriter Gerald Green who also wrote the subsequent novelization (Green 1978). Although both teleplay and novelization have been criticized for their stereotypical characterizations, wooden dialogue and patronization of Holocaust victims (Schartz 1999: 162),[9] the critical reception of *Holocaust* was 'rhapsodic' (Novick 1999: 211). Novick describes the millions of copies of special inserts, study guides and other promotional and educational materials about the Holocaust prepared around the mini-series by American Jewish organizations in an attempt to sensitize gentiles as well as a developing (American) Jewish identity. As for the lasting effects of this first depiction of the Holocaust before a mass audience, Novick is less sanguine. His 'guess is that it hasn't mattered that much' (Novick 1999: 212).

The notable exception concerns the showing of the mini-series in West Germany in January 1979. Not only is *Holocaust* credited with helping persuade the Bundestag later that year to abolish the statute of limitations on war crimes, but as one German journalist wrote: 'It is absolutely fantastic ... *Holocaust* has shaken up post-Hitler Germany in a way that German intellectuals have been unable to do. No other film has ever made the Jews' road to suffering leading to the gas chambers so vivid' (Herf 1986: 214). If *Holocaust* incontestably acted as a turning point in the German popular culture's reluctance to confront the Nazi Final Solution (in part perhaps because the mini-series was a major American production and so a perspective from outside), in America itself, the effect was less clear. Despite many subsequent attempts to bring the Holocaust to American television (Shandler 1999), none would turn out to have the fanfare and audience that *Holocaust* first garnered until the release, 15 years later, of Steven Spielberg's 197-minute feature film *Schindler's List*.

Thus, the representation of the Holocaust by the mass media entailed a gamut of responses, from initial celebration of a medium's ability to partly, if fictionally, depict events drawn from the historical record – technically speaking, what Barbara Foley (1982) terms the 'pseudofactual' in the sense that it replaces literary effects with some form of engagement with the historical – to the posing of such problems as the representability of the Holocaust itself. But these would be issues taken up, in the interim, by film-maker intellectuals, most notably Claude Lanzmann.

LANZMANN'S *SHOAH*

The fact that the first documentary images of the Holocaust appeared 'out of the blue' posed a range of problems, particularly concerning the place of the image not only in contemporary culture, but also in respect to the making of collective memory. There is arguably a demand for understanding history and especially our human relation to it, but there are two contradictory responses to this. On the one hand, there is a popular demand for understanding history that is greater than the kind of history produced by professional, academic historians; for example, the contemporary fascination with biography both in book form and television documentaries (indeed, entire television channels!). On the other hand, and precisely because of the surrounding proliferation of images, there is also an equivalent sense of fragmentation and of conflicting representations of the past, a problem that is only enhanced by the increased technical capacity to turn black-and-white images (formerly signifiers of 'pastness') into colour as well as to redigitize images such that they no longer have any basis in any reality outside of their own.

Thus the debate over the representability of the Holocaust – denounced by Elie Wiesel (1978) as a sacrilege at the time of the airing of *Holocaust* – was the starting-point for Claude Lanzmann's (1985a) nine and a half hour 'documentary' *Shoah* in which there is not a single shot of what we conventionally understand as documentary archival footage. Indeed, Lanzmann has claimed repeatedly that no such images of the Holocaust exist – and even if he had found such images, he would have destroyed them. Arguably they do not exist, just as no document, blueprint or written order of any kind stating 'Now the Jews will be killed' exists either (Lanzmann 1985b: 72). *Shoah* does include footage of present-day Sobibor, Chelmno, Treblinka and Auschwitz, or what remains of these major killings centres. As Simon Srebnik says, when taken back to the present-day site of Chelmno of which nothing remains except the forest,

> It's hard to recognize, but it was here. They burned people here ... Yes, this is the place ... I can't believe I'm here ... It was always this peaceful here. Always. When they burned two thousand people – Jews —every day, it was just as peaceful. (Lanzmann 1985b: 6)

The film's only access to the past is through the voices, expressions and memories of those speaking, the survivors of the Holocaust, the 'technicians' of the Final Solution, the contemporary Polish bystanders. As Ilan Avisar (1997: 38–58) writes,

> the principal channel to the past is ultimately memory. The avoidance of any archival footage further enhances the reliance on personal memories as the sources of knowledge, while the camera documents the ongoing dramatic processes of painful recollection ... Indeed, Lanzmann's '*Shoah*' conveys the painful recognition that memory is the only cognitive avenue to the unimaginable.

Seeing and hearing the tormented workings of memory in the testimonies of the survivors, compounded by the sheer length of the film, its long takes and pauses, not to mention Lanzmann's presence urging his witnesses to remember no matter how painful it is to do so, makes *Shoah* a living (not re-living) present, in which the past is abolished because it is still here, 40 years later – thus the force of the film and its justly celebrated status as the masterpiece of Holocaust film. Not only did *Shoah* single-handedly entail the abandonment of the use of the word 'Holocaust' in France for the more accurate Hebrew term, but one of the reasons that motivated the making of the film was a furious response to the kind of depictions that *Holocaust*, the mini-series, had evoked in Lanzmann as how not to make a film about the Judeocide.[10]

Still, for all the controversy and debate that *Shoah* sparked – not least a colloquium at Oxford over Lanzmann's unflattering depiction of the Poles – it remained, like much of the extensive academic scholarship on the Shoah itself, confined within specialist film or intellectual circles. The biggest Holocaust film of them all was still to come.

'SCHINDLER'S LIST'

Steven Spielberg's *Schindler's List* has been compared to both D.W. Griffith's *Birth of a Nation* and Orson Welles' *Citizen Kane*, arguably the two greatest films in the American cinema (Hansen 2001: 127–51). Released to a torrent of publicity preceded by the director's not inconsiderable reputation for such films as *E.T.* and *Jurassic Park*, it would sweep the Oscars, much as the *Holocaust* mini-series had swept the Emmys in 1978. Because the film's release coincided with the opening of the United States Holocaust Memorial Museum in Washington, DC, publicists for the film included no less a figure than the President of the United States (Novick 1999: 214). If *Time* magazine would write that the film showed 'the greatest sequences of chaos and mass terror ever filmed' (Avisar 1997: 21), other critics such as J. Hoberman wondered whether it was 'possible to make feel-good entertainment about the ultimate feel-bad experience of the twentieth century' (Hansen 2001: 130). The issue, however, is less the critical response to what is certainly, on many levels, an extremely powerful attempt to come as close as possible to a filmed depiction of what aspects of the Holocaust may have been like. This is particularly the case with the sequences concerning the 'liquidation' of the Kraków ghetto. As for Spielberg's depiction of concentration camp 'life' as a state of relentless, unpredictable terror, he tends to personalize this, particularly through the evil character of Plazsow labour camp commander Amon Goeth (Ralph Fiennes), who enjoys pre-prandial random target shooting of prisoners. Italian writer Primo Levi (1960: 29) managed to better grasp the state of constant terror in four words spoken to him by a guard ('*Hier ist kein Warum*' [There is no why here]).

It is interesting that Spielberg declared his film to be 'a document', a claim apparently supported by the fact that much of it was shot in Kraków where many of the historical events depicted took place, and in black-and-white photography, which as we noted earlier serves to signify 'the real past'.[11] Such claims seem disingenuous, to the extent that Spielberg owes his reputation to his virtuosity in manipulating the codes of Hollywood cinema.

Still, there is more involved than predictable arguments about trivialization or Americanization, as Miriam B. Hansen recognizes in elaborating the term 'popular modernism'. This concept, which she compares to Fordism, for example, is the fusion of capitalist means of production with an aesthetic, in a modern vernacular of its own. Such an approach gives her the means of situating *Schindler's List* as 'more sophisticated, elliptical and self-conscious ... than its critics acknowledge' in its capacity for 'reflecting upon the shocks and scars inflicted by modernization on people's lives in a *generally accessible, public horizon*' (Hansen 2001: 135, emphasis added).

Thus there is little question regarding the visual and aural sophistication of *Schindler's List* (as Hansen demonstrates in a series of frame analyses). It's certainly self-conscious, not only as Hansen argues by its references to Kane, but also by the homage it pays to Lanzmann's *Shoah*. In the latter, as survivor Richard Glazer talks about the train trip to Treblinka: '[W]e'd been able to open a window – the old man in our compartment saw a boy ... cows were grazing ... and he asked the boy in signs, "Where are we?" And the kid made a funny gesture. This (draws finger across his throat).' The same gesture is also made by a farmhand. 'And he made that gesture. Like this. We didn't really pay much attention to him. We couldn't figure out what he meant' (Lanzmann 1985b: 34).

In *Schindler's List*, during the train trip to Auschwitz in which a group of Schindler women is accidentally embarked, Spielberg recreates the scene – two shots – described by Glazer of a small boy in a snow-covered field shown making 'that gesture' at the passing boxcars. It's a visual quote from *Shoah*, but we, of the after-*Shoah*, now know what it means.

Still, and because the idea of popular modernism doesn't exclude cheap tricks, Spielberg seemingly can't resist *not* showing off, this time in a perverse homage to Hitchcock's *Psycho*. Soon after their arrival at Auschwitz, among sweeping lights and snarling dogs, the Schindler women, their hair cut badly to the length of Janet Leigh's, are sent naked to the *Bad und Disinfektion* rooms of what we fear – as do they – are the gas chambers, spewing out their greasy flakes of ashened flesh that look like snow. After the door is bolted, we see them through the peephole, huddling together in dreaded anticipation. The camera tilts up to the 'showerheads'; we – and they – wait for what seems the inevitable. And then real water begins to spurt down onto the naked bodies that burst into relieved laughter. There's another shot of the showerheads, to remind us of their double function (life-giving water/death by Zyklon B gas). But we've been had, and are disgusted at our own relief. When the women, sprung by Schindler's tractations, are leaving Auschwitz, they pass a long line of people going the other way who, as we all now know, are about to shortly feel the showerheads' other function. Just to make the point crystal clear, this is followed by a shot of the smoking chimneys of the crematoria. Now that's 'Shoah' business, as the grim joke has it.[12]

A third point, made by the Israeli critic Ilan Avisar, concerns the two endings of *Schindler's List*. The first is within the story when Oskar Schindler, after receiving the ring made for him by his Jews from their gold teeth fillings, bursts into tears and reproaches himself for not having saved more Jews. He launches into a bizarre calculation: his car, had he sold it, would have been worth ten more Jews; the ring two more. The second ending, as a coda to the film, which follows a dissolve as the former prisoners seem to march in a long line from Czechoslovakia to Israel singing sabra songs, shows real Schindler Jews and the actors who played them placing stones in the commemorative ritual gesture on Schindler's Jerusalem grave with its visible Christian cross. Avisar argues – not totally convincingly – that in the first ending it is 'the Christian "savior" who ends in the highest moral position.' More important is what he writes about the second ending that links the Holocaust and the founding of the Jewish state. Avisar (1997: 52) writes that 'in Spielberg's film, ideology combines with aesthetic effect as the linkage creates a narrative closure that deemphasizes the horrors of the genocide in the context of Jewish revival and independence in Israel.'[13] Hansen (2001: 129) also notes with some ambivalence the film's 'enormous success in Germany ... and the discovery of local Schindlers everywhere'. If *Holocaust* inadvertently helped Germany begin to cope with its repression of the Final Solution, Spielberg, by the same token, de-emphasizes the long history of Christian anti-Semitism by the good deeds of one Christian opportunist and, to be doubly safe, redeems the Judeocide since it 'caused' the founding of the Jewish State.

THE GENOCIDE FILM

The genocide film plunges us into a different set of problems, although with the occasional parallel to the Holocaust film, but steering clear of the politico-theological issues raised in the previous paragraph. As with the Holocaust film, the genocide film does not 'show' genocide, except metonymically. Instead, it deals more with questions of racism and, more important, it raises once again, although not directly, the very problem that confronted what Dallaire terms 'the failure of humanity' with respect to Rwanda; namely, what makes a genocide a genocide?

The 1948 UN convention that came into force in 1951 is not terribly helpful in defining what constitutes a genocide. Article II defines genocide as:

a. Killing members of the [national, ethnical, racial or religious] group;
b. Causing serious bodily or mental harm to members of the group;
c. Deliberately inflicting on the group conditions of life calculated to bring about its physical destruction in whole or in part;
d. Imposing measures intended to prevent births within the group;
e. Forcibly transferring children of the group to another group. (UN 1951)

Although such a definition might seem fairly encompassing, some critics have written that it is not broad enough in that it does not cover the killings of certain subgroups, for example, the Soviet killing of the Kulaks as a social class. Others have noted that it focuses on 'physical' extermination as opposed to 'cultural' destruction, linguicide and so on (Kuper 1981; Stein 1996). As Stein, for example, observes, international law until recently was of little help in clarifying the parameters of the 1948 convention, among other reasons because one state has to accuse another of genocide. As noted earlier, the conflation of the Holocaust with a normative conception of genocide has made coming to grips with genocide harder, particularly once such acts occur outside of the European context. The case of Cambodia is a useful illustration of these problems.

CAMBODIA

Today, it is widely assumed that '(t)he Cambodian genocide of 1975–1979, in which approximately 1.7 million people lost their lives (21 per cent of the country's population), was one of the worst human tragedies of the last century' (Yale n.d.). However, it was not until March 2003 that the UN signed an agreement with Cambodia to try the surviving members of the Khmer Rouge leadership for crimes under Cambodian law, international law and custom and international conventions recognized by Cambodia. The latter include genocide, war crimes and breaches of the Geneva Convention. Thus, it took about a decade, since the 1993 elections that outlawed the Khmer Rouge, for the legal machinery to get itself together. A key turning point was the United States Congress' passage in 1994 of the *Cambodian Genocide Justice Act*. In other words, it is a complex process to try the leadership of a state for a range of crimes, of which genocide *may* be one.

The Cambodian case is further complicated by the fact that it is far from clear that what went on under the Khmer Rouge's radical attempt at massive social engineering between 1975 and 1979 was actually a genocide. One of the leading Western historians on Cambodia, the Australian David P. Chandler, does not use the word in his numerous books on the period. The closest he comes to it, because the Khmer Rouge's crimes were largely committed against other Khmers, is French author Jean Lacouture's term 'autogenocide' (Chandler 1999: vii).[14] For Chandler, what distinguishes the Cambodian case is the fusion of the (catastrophic) attempts of other Communist regimes to surpass Western economic development – the Soviet collectivization of agriculture in the 1930s, China's Great Leap Forward in industrial production of the 1950s, the Chinese Cultural Revolution of the 1960s and the Vietnamese and North Korean equivalents – but, in the Cambodian instance, pushed to unprecedented heights of Marxist and indigenous utopianism (such as in the Super Great Leap Forward of 1976). It is something of an oversimplification to lump all these processes together under the rubric 'genocide'. In his book on the workings of the main Khmer Rouge torture centre, S-21, where some 14,000 men, women and children were interrogated, tortured and killed (only seven people emerged alive), Chandler (1999) uses the term 'crimes of obedience'[15] to explain what went on there. These distinctions, while in no means meant to minimize the far-reaching effect of what Chandler (1991) terms 'the Typhoon', do, however, blur the picture somewhat when it comes to 'genocide films' dealing with Cambodia.

THE KILLING FIELDS

'*The Killing Fields*' (Joffé 1984) is probably the best-known film in the West about the fall of Phnom Penh to the Khmer Rouge armies in the spring of 1975 and the almost instantaneous evacuation of the cities' populations into forced rice-growing in the countryside. Despite its title, the film is not really about the killing fields at all. Rather it is mainly about the friendship between *The New York Times* correspondent Sidney Schanberg and his Cambodian translator, coffee boy and apprentice journalist, Dith Pran. Second, it is about the hardships faced by the Western press corps attempting to cover civil wars in dangerous faraway places, with very strong parallels to the chaotic evacuation of Saigon by the panic-stricken Americans at the end of the Vietnam War. Third, much like *Hotel Rwanda*, *The Killing Fields* is at its most general level about the complex links between white foreigners and non-white locals and what happens to the locals once they are abandoned to a local fate.

Ultimately, the film is about the slippery notion of identity in a world or region being globalized by war. Dith Pran survives his capture by the Khmer Rouge, escapes to the Cambodia–Thai border, is reunited with Schanberg and ends up working as a photographer for the *Times* in New York. Dr Haing S. Ngor, who plays Dith Pran, became the first Southeast Asian – and Buddhist – to receive an academy award.

S-21: THE KHMER ROUGE KILLING MACHINE

Rithy Panh's (2003) 101-minute documentary is, as critics have noted,[16] more modestly the Cambodian *Shoah*, using similar strategies as the Lanzmann film. Panh, who fled to France in 1979, returns to Cambodia and the infamous S-21 former prison, now the Tuol Sleng Museum of Genocidal Crimes, where some of the former guards serve as guides. Panh's film documents two of the surviving former prisoners, notably the painter Vann Nath who survived by drawing official portraits of his guards and today reproduces on canvas scenes of the atrocities he witnessed. Unlike the Lanzmann film, former guards, torturers and interrogators are confronted with survivors, Nath and Chum Mey. Like the Lanzmann film, *S-21* details the tortured workings of memory; guards and torturers 'act out' in minute detail the actions committed on the job. But the strength of Panh's film is as a study of the power of affect – how expressions and body language change according to the memory – and also of the human mind's capacity for rationalizing awful deeds. Thus the guard 'explains' that they were victims too and just as terrorized as their victims. *S-21* is an almost clinical analysis of the psychology of torture, and its effects 20 years later.

BACK TO RWANDA

Returning, then, to the case of Rwanda, we find that some of the problems raised initially have gained in contextualization. As we saw in the case of Cambodia, the slow legal process of actually trying crimes of genocide would at last see fruit in Rwanda with the establishment of the International Criminal Tribunal for Rwanda (ICTR) and the first trial as of January 1997. The Akayesu case decided by the ICTR in 1998 was the first in which an international tribunal was called upon to interpret the definition of genocide based on the 1948 convention. The subsequent conviction of former Prime Minister Jean Kambanda was the first time that an accused acknowledged guilt for the crime of genocide before an international tribunal and the first time that a head of government was convicted for the crime of genocide. As the legal process grinds on (it is expected to have completed all trials and appeals by 2010), films about the Rwanda genocide are filling in the blanks in public memory. As of this writing, three films have been released so far: *Hotel Rwanda* (George 2004), *100 Days* (Hughes 2001) – two films that in many ways could hardly be more different – and *Shake Hands with the Devil* (Raymont 2004).

Several more features were released by summer 2005: the United Kingdom/Germany co-production *Shooting Dogs*, starring British actor John Hurt as a Catholic priest, is described as focusing on 'the human aspects of the story', as it frankly admits '(i)t can't ... say everything about the genocide' (Caton-Jones 2005). *Sunday by the Pool*, based on the novel *A Sunday at the Pool in Kigali* (Courtemanche 2004), was produced by Montreal company Equinox Productions. *Sometimes in April* (Peck 2005), another Rwanda genocide feature that was a success at the recent Berlin Film Festival, was aired on HBO in March 2005 and on PBS in April. A feature film version of Dallaire's memoir *Shake Hands with the Devil*, co-produced by Barna-Alper Productions and Halifax Film Company, was shot on location in Rwanda and will be in theatres in 2007.

HOTEL RWANDA: AFRICAN SCHINDLER?

As is by now well known, *Hotel Rwanda* tells the story of a good man caught in terrible times. It is the story of Mille Collines hotel's 'local', that is, African, manager, Paul Rusesabagina, and how he saved some 1,200 people from the slaughter raging outside in Kigali. Earlier, I suggest a parallel with Oskar Schindler, although one that needs qualifying. Rwanda's strategic unimportance – landlocked, no significant minerals, or for that matter of any compelling interest to any of the Western powers, except perhaps Belgium whose former colony it was[17] – means that whereas Schindler was an industrialist (in enamel-work at first and then armaments), Rusesabagina is in the hospitality industry. Which doesn't mean that he can't grease local palms with Cuban cigars or Scotch in an attempt to gain the protection of high-ranking RGF officers.

Rusesabagina's adeptness is in keeping his customers happy, and his Belgian bosses in Brussels informed. His seeming servility is what allows him to be able to bend the rules and provide a refuge for threatened Rwandan Tutsis in what is, first of all, a hotel for white tourists and prominent locals. Unlike Schindler, who despite his breakdown of remorse at the end of '*Schindler's List*' maintains a proprietorial relationship to 'his' Jews, Rusesabagina falls into his subversive role after French and Belgian troops, armed to the teeth, come to repatriate their white fellow nationals. And when he also realizes that his 'masters' in Brussels, whom he has loyally served, can't do very much for him at all. As he tells his wife in a powerful scene of his own coming to self-consciousness: 'I am not even a nigger, I'm an African.' Out of this realization of his own 'nothingness', however, comes altruism.

Unlike Dith Pran in *The Killing Fields*, who seems to bear no ill will at all to the whites who abandoned him, for Rusesabagina, the realization that no white can help him or his endangered fellow citizens is a crucial moment of utter loneliness. (The irony is that he will end up in exile in Belgium.) Similar to *The Killing Fields*, *Hotel Rwanda* is about 'identity': on the one hand, the Tutsi–Hutu identities that were a by-product of Belgian colonial anthropology mired in classical nineteenth century race science in the sense that the Tutsi were 'whiter' anthropomorphically; and the subsequent murderous frenzy of the Hutu attempt to reassert their 'threatened' identity. But on the other hand, the film is also about the illusions of 'identity' – except, of course, for the 'big other' provided by skin colour and especially the difference between being white and being black. In this sense, it is racism, both in *Hotel Rwanda* and in *The Killing Fields* that screens out the genocide; whereas in the Holocaust film, it is the 'racism' that leads inexorably to the killings.

100 DAYS

Oddly for a 'genocide' film, Nick Hughes' (2001) *100 Days* is an astonishingly gentle film about a gentle people, some of whom are directed by state authority to suddenly begin to murder their long-time neighbours. The French word '*pudique*' (discreet but in a bodily sense) is perhaps better than gentle to describe what I'm getting at. The film keeps its gaze turned away from the horrors – except for the sequence of the massacre at the Kibuye Church; and the suggestion of the rape by the priest of Josette and the other Tutsi women (that echoes the tactical use of rape in the former Yugoslavia as a means of eliminating one ethnic group by forced insemination by members of the rival group). *100 Days* in its gentleness is the love story of Josette and Baptiste, and how the genocide comes to kill that love. With the exceptions mentioned, the genocide itself is at times referred back to in time, after the fact, by the memorial markers that are set up at the Church's mass grave site. Or conversely, that remains off-screen, in that for the film's Rwandan actors who had lived through the events and the film's investors and co-producers who had lost countless family members, the making of *100 Days* becomes more an extra-diegetical act of 'working through' memory than what the film itself actually shows.

CONCLUSION: THE GENOCIDE COMMODITY[18]

Like the Marxist conception of the commodity, a film is two-sided and full of metaphysical subtleties. It has use-values (aesthetics, narrative, psychology of characters, action, etc.). It also has exchange-value: a film is capital-intensive and that capital must ideally be recouped through the rental of seats by ticket sales, the selling of foreign and other distribution rights, and the like. However, these two sides of a film are hard to separate. On the contrary, they tend to blur into each other.

As various critics have remarked, conceptual entities referring to historical events such as the Holocaust or, more loosely, genocide, are themselves 'word-commodities' whose value also changes over time. Largely going from neglect, indifference, and lack of knowledge, to varying degrees of approximation to what they refer to. Both the film commodity and the word commodity are subject to fluctuations. As historians like Peter Novick have shown, the meanings attributed to the Holocaust in the American case have followed such a pattern of fluctuation, from an initial shocked high, then to low, and subsequently increasingly higher again, tied as well to the United States' changing relationship to Israel after the Six Day War, and other factors related to the American sense of Jewish identity. Norman Finkelstein's (2000) really bad book, *The Holocaust Industry*,[19] attempts to make something of a similar point, if ham-fistedly: namely that 'Holocaust' is not only a word but also a veritable cultural industry. Yet words, like films, rise and fall in currency. If the Holocaust commodity, so to speak, has had a fairly good run, it would seem these days that it has been largely replaced by the genocide commodity, perhaps because the latter better satisfies our contemporary obsession with victimhood as *the* signifier of historical identity – to wit, the website of Yale University's genocide studies programme: 'As in the Ottoman Empire during the Armenian genocide, the Soviet Union under Stalin, Nazi Germany during the Holocaust, and more recently in East Timor, Guatemala, Yugoslavia and Rwanda' (Yale n.d.). Or that of Latrobe University in Australia on a 2003 conference on the topic of colonialism and genocide. The latter is viewed as an integral part of not only Australian history, but of settler societies more generally (Canada and the United States, for instance), with their Indigenocides; or the nineteenth century German colonization of Namibia that foreshadowed the Holocaust; and the very barbarism of 'civilization' itself with its many forms of cultural genocide (of languages and demographics) (Veracini 2003). World history, in a word, is one long series of genocides. As well it may be: the nineteenth century philosopher Hegel referred to world history as the butcher's block of nations. So, if the general idea is not exactly novel, having a word for it, thanks to Lemkin, seems to be. And where there is a word commodity, the film commodity will surely follow.

This is not, to be sure, a state of affairs to be lamented. On the contrary, the more we learn about the world we live in, the better, presumably. But to expect that words, or even less so, films, will significantly change the world any time soon is perhaps setting the bar too high. Because, in the words of another German philosopher (Martin Heidegger), the world 'worlds'. For all else, there's always the movies.

ACKNOWLEDGEMENTS

My journalism colleague, the late Professor Tim May, suggested the title of this paper.

NOTES

1. I use the conventional term 'Holocaust' for the Nazi extermination of the Jews of Europe. The lengthy debate, particularly in France, over the existence of images of the Holocaust is discussed in detail in Didi-Huberman (2004).
2. According to my colleague, Professor Allan Thompson, the images that did appear in the global media and were universally disseminated as 'the Rwanda genocide' consisted of a short sequence in long-shot from the top of a building showing members of the *Interahamwe*, the young Hutu militants deemed responsible for the killings, hacking away at prone bodies. The footage was shot by British journalist Nick Hughes, seemingly the only journalist to have filmed actual killings.
3. In the Rwanda context, the subsequent breakdown of Canadian Brigadier General Roméo Dallaire, who was helplessly in charge of the UN military contingent there, is probably the best-known such case. See Dallaire (2004) as well as the documentary depicting Dallaire's return to Rwanda a decade later (Raymont 2004).
4. Some of the implications are drawn out in Dorland (2005).
5. From the six million or eleven million on, if one tries to come up with a total figure including Holocaust victims from all sources – a figure which Simon Wiesenthal claims to have invented, which is unlikely as it corresponds so closely to the Wannsee Conference estimates; the statistical evaluation of such data has been a problem ever since. For some perspective on establishing numbers that are often also rhetorical devices, see Marrus (1987). The Wiesenthal claim was purportedly made to Israeli historian Yehuda Bauer (Novick 1999: 215).
6. Although Holocaust is the commonly used term for the extermination of the Jews, Roma and other nationalities, as well as political and military prisoners, by the Nazis, Jews nevertheless constituted over 50 per cent of those exterminated. What then to properly call this catastrophe has been a matter of debate since 1945; Jews in Israel and in France term it the *Shoah*, Hebrew for 'the catastrophe', as opposed to Holocaust which derives from the Greek and connotes a religious sacrifice by burning.
7. See for example Zelizer's reproduction George Strock's photo for *Life*, 'American Dead at Buna Beach, September 1943' (Zelizer 1998: 37).
8. For reasons of space, I'm only slightly exaggerating here. Alain Resnais' '*Nuit et brouillard*' (1955) and Gillo Pontecorvo's '*Kapo*' (1959) are distinguished precursors of the Holocaust film. American film generally since the 1940s has struggled with understanding Nazism in particular and the Holocaust subsequently. For a quick history of Hollywood's ambivalence and clips from these films, see Daniel Anker's 2004 documentary film, '*Imaginary Witness: Hollywood and the Holocaust*.'
9. The most vocal critic of the mini-series was Elie Wiesel (1978), who wrote 'This series treats the Holocaust as if it were just another event ... Auschwitz cannot be explained nor can it be visualized.'
10. Lanzmann remarks somewhere that the mini-series' depiction of Jews marching stoically into the gas chambers 'like ancient Romans' sickened him.
11. The colour red is used as a symbol for blood with the little girl's coat during the 'liquidation' of the Kraków ghetto. It reappears as her body, still wearing its red coat, is wheelbarrowed onto the piles of bodies now being burned outside as the arrival of some 400,000 Hungarian Jews as of 1944 overtaxed the burn capacity of the crematoria. And the final sequence of Schindler Jews paying homage at the grave of their saviour is shot in full colour.
12. A film that does make the attempt to depict the gassing process and the subsequent disentanglement of twisted bodies for disposal to the crematoria is Tim Blake Nelson's '*The Grey Zone*' (2001a), directed from his play of the same title (Blake Nelson 2001b). The idea of 'the grey zone' is famously elaborated on by Primo Levi in his book *The Drowned and the Saved* (1989). The film's credits bizarrely attribute the story to Dr Miklos Nyisli's *Auschwitz: a Doctor's Eyewitness Account* (1960). Given that '*The Grey Zone*' is the story of a failed Sonderkommando revolt and that Nyisli, while he does describe the Sonderkommando process, is better known as Mengele's (reluctant) assistant, the attribution here is curious.

13. However, as '*Schindler's List's*' closing over titles point out: there are less than 4,000 Jews still alive in Poland today, whereas the 1,100 Jews saved by Schindler have 6,000 descendants.
14. Note too, as we saw with the difficulty of establishing the number of victims of the Holocaust, that in Chandler's earlier, *The Tragedy of Cambodian History* (1991), the estimates of how many died in those four fatal years is half of what it would be in the later book. It is important to recall as well that those who died did so 'from warfare, starvation, overwork, misdiagnosed diseases, and executions' (Chandler 1991: 1).
15. A concept drawn from the experimental studies of Stanley Milgram (1974) and others.
16. Notably the ever-perceptive J. Hoberman in *The Village Voice*.
17. But, as Dallaire (2004) points out, not permitted by UN rules to intervene militarily as the former colonial power.
18. I'm drawing here on Thion (1993).
19. But tellingly translated into 17 languages.

REFERENCES

Anker, D. (director). 2004. *Imaginary witness: Hollywood and the Holocaust*. USA, 92 min.

Avisar, I. 1997. 'Holocaust Movies and the Politics of Collective Memory'. In A.H. Rosenfeld (ed.). *Thinking About the Holocaust*. Indiana University Press, Bloomington, IN, USA.

Blake Nelson, T. (director). 2001a. *The grey zone*. USA, 108 min.

—— 2001b. *The grey zone*. USA, 108 min.

Caton-Jones, M. 2005. *Shooting dogs: the director's statement*. Renaissance Films, London, United Kingdom. Available at <www.renaissance-films.com/index.asp?page=films/shootingdogs.html&nav=02> (accessed 15 September 2005).

Chandler, D.P. 1991. *The Tragedy of Cambodian History*. Yale University Press, New Haven, CT, USA.

—— 1999. *Voices from S-21: Terror and History in Pol Pot's Secret Prison*. University of California Press, Berkeley, CA, USA.

Courtemanche, G. 2004. *A Sunday at the Pool in Kigali*. Vintage Canada, Toronto, Ontario, Canada.

CTV. 2005. *CTV at the Oscars*. 27 February. CTV, Scarborough, Ontario, Canada.

Dallaire, R.A. 2004. *Shake Hands With the Devil: the Failure of Humanity in Rwanda*. Random House, Toronto, Ontario, Canada.

Didi-Huberman, G. 2004. *Images malgré tout*. Les Éditions de minuit, Paris, France. 272 pp.

Dorland, M. 2005. Psychoanalysis After Auschwitz? The 'Deported Knowledge' of Anne-Lise Stern. *Other Voices*, 2(3). Available at <www.othervoices.org/2.3/mdorland/index.html> (accessed 13 September 2005).

Douglas, L. 2001. *The Memory of Judgment: Making Law and History in the Trials of the Holocaust*. Yale University Press, New Haven, CT, USA.

Finkelstein, N. 2000. *The Holocaust Industry: Reflections on the Exploitation of Jewish Suffering*. Verso, New York, NY, USA.

Foley, B. 1982. Fact, Fiction, Fascism: Testimony and Mimesis in Holocaust Narratives. *Comparative Literature*, 34(4): 330–60.

George, T. (director). 2004. *Hotel Rwanda*. United Kingdom/Italy/South Africa, 121 min.

Green, G. 1978. *Holocaust*. Rosettabooks, New York, NY, USA. 408 pp.

Hansen, M.B. 2001. 'Schindler's List is Not Shoah: Second Commandment, Popular Modernism, and Public Memory'. In B. Zelizer (ed.). *Visual Culture and the Holocaust*. Rutgers University Press, Piscataway, NJ, USA.

Herf, J. 1986. 'The "Holocaust" Reception in West Germany'. In A. Rabinbach and J. Zipes (eds). *Germans and Jews Since the Holocaust: the Changing Situation in West Germany*. Holmes & Meier, New York, NY, USA.

Hughes, N. (director). 2001. *100 days*. United Kingdom/Rwanda, 100 min.

Joffé, R. (director). 1984. *The killing fields*. United Kingdom, 141 min.

Kramer, S. (director). 1961. *Judgment at Nuremberg*. USA, 186 min.

Kuper, L. 1981. *Genocide: Its Political Use in the Twentieth Century*. Penguin Books, Markham, Ontario, Canada.

Lanzmann, C. (director). 1985a. *Shoah*. France, 9.5 hours.

—— 1985b. *Shoah: An Oral History of the Holocaust: the Complete Text of the Film*. Pantheon, New York, NY, USA.

Lemkin, R. 1944. *Axis Rule in Occupied Europe: Laws of Occupation, Analysis of Government, Proposals for Redress*. Carnegie Endowment for International Peace, Washington, DC, USA. 670 pp.

Levi, P. 1960. *Survival in Auschwitz*. Macmillan Collier, New York, NY, USA.

—— 1989. *The Drowned and the Saved*. Vintage International New York, NY, USA.

Marrus, M. 1987. *The Holocaust in History.* Penguin, Markham, Ontario, Canada.

Novick, P. 1999. *The Holocaust in American Life.* Houghton Mifflin, Boston, MA, USA.

Nyisli, M. 1960. *Auschwitz: a Doctor's Eyewitness Account*. Arcade Publishing, New York, NY, USA.

Panh, R. (director). 2003. S-21: *the Khmer Rouge killing machine* (documentary). Cambodia/France, 101 min.

Peck, R. (director). 2005. *Sometimes in April*. France/USA/Rwanda, 140 min.

Pontecorvo, G. (director). 1959. *Kapo*. France/Italy, 116 min.

Power, S. 2002. '*A Problem From Hell': America and the Age of Genocide.* Basic Books, New York, NY, USA.

Raymont, P. (director). 2004. *Shake hands with the devil: the journey of Roméo Dallaire*. Canada, 91 min.

Resnais, A. (director). 1955. *Nuit et brouillard*. France.

Schartz, D.R. 1999. *Imagining the Holocaust*. St. Martin's Press, New York, NY, USA.

Shandler, J. 1999. *While America Watches: Televising the Holocaust.* Oxford University Press, New York, NY, USA.

Shermer, M. and A. Grobman. 2000. *Denying History: Who Says the Holocaust Never Happened and Why Do They Say It?* University of California Press, Berkeley, CA, USA.

Stein, S.D. 1996. 'Genocide'. In E. Cashmore (ed.). *Dictionary of Race and Ethnic Relations* (4th edn.). Routledge, London, UK.

Thion, S. 1993. 'Genocide as a Political Commodity'. In B. Kiernan (ed.). *Genocide and Democracy in Cambodia*. Yale University Press, New Haven, CT, USA. Southeast Asian Monographs no. 41.

UN (United Nations). 1951. *Convention on the prevention and punishment of the crime of genocide*. Adopted by Resolution 260 (III) of the UN General Assembly, 9 December 1948. *UN Treaty Series* no. 1021, vol. 78: 277. Available at <www.preventgenocide.org/law/convention/text.htm> (accessed 6 September 2005).

Veracini, L. 2003. Genocide and Colonialism, II: Discussing a Recent International Conference on 'Genocide and Colonialism' and its Implications for Australian Debates. Australian Humanities Review, 30, October. Available at <www.lib.latrobe.edu.au/AHR/archive/Issue-October-2003/veracini.html> (accessed 13 September 2005).

Wiesel, E. 1978. Trivializing the Holocaust: Semi-Fact and Semi-Fiction. *The New York Times*, 16 April.

Yale. n.d. Cambodian Genocide Program: Introduction. Yale University, New Haven, CT, USA. Available at <www.yale.edu/cgp/cgpintro.html> (accessed 14 September 2005).

Zelizer, B. 1998. *Remembering to Forget.* University of Chicago Press, Chicago, IL, USA.

35
The Responsibility to Report: a New Journalistic Paradigm

Allan Thompson

Hands rose up from the grave to grasp each coffin, as if the dead were welcoming the remains of the genocide victims. The simple wooden boxes contained bones recovered from mass graves and pit latrines so that they could be re-interred during ceremonies marking the tenth anniversary of the Rwanda genocide. It was 7 April 2004 in Kigali, and a gaggle of television crews, reporters and photographers jostled for space around a concrete tomb where victims of the 1994 genocide were finally being given a dignified burial. Earlier, pall bearers had descended into the crypt, climbing down a ladder so they could be in place to receive the coffins. The boxes were gingerly passed one by one into their final resting place at Rwanda's national memorial to the 1994 slaughter.

Ten years after the genocide, Rwanda was still burying its dead and representatives of the international media were there, watching. Heading the dignitaries assembled to take part in the ceremony was Paul Kagame, president of Rwanda and in 1994, leader of the Tutsi-dominated Rwandan Patriotic Front, which ended the genocide and took over the country. Retired Canadian General Roméo Dallaire, who led the ill-fated United Nations mission to Rwanda during the catastrophe, joined Kagame at the ceremony.

Both Kagame and Dallaire could have been forgiven for asking a pointed question as they regarded the international media throng gathered for the ceremonies: where were the world's media a decade earlier when a campaign to exterminate the Tutsi minority and Hutu moderates resulted in the massacre of more than 800,000 innocents?

In hindsight, the media shorthand for the Rwanda genocide goes something like this: the world community failed to intervene and abandoned Rwanda while dead bodies clogged the rivers and piled up on roadsides. These events were reported by the news media, but not very prominently. When the media finally descended on the story, it was to cover the cholera epidemic in refugee camps across the border in Zaire, camps populated by Hutu who fled Rwanda at the tail end of the genocide.

Looking back, it is easy to see what the news media did wrong, both inside Rwanda and without. Many journalists within Rwanda were implicated in the killing. Hate media were instrumental in the extermination campaign. International news media misconstrued or downplayed the Rwanda story.

Political figures, such as US President Bill Clinton (1998), later claimed that they did not have enough information to fully grasp what was going on in Rwanda. More likely, because the public was not very engaged by the Rwanda story, there was little pressure for leaders to do anything.

This collection of papers set out to examine the role of the news media in the 1994 catastrophe, inside and outside Rwanda. More than a decade later, are we any wiser? What has changed and what have we learned from what went wrong? In part, the answer lies in Darfur, the region in western Sudan widely acknowledged in early 2006 to be a humanitarian and human rights tragedy of the first order. By some accounts, as many as 5,000 people continued to die each month in a deteriorating situation of massive atrocities against civilians, blamed primarily on the government and its allied Janjaweed militias.

In the face of reliable accounts of what is at best ethnic cleansing and at worst genocide – a situation that some have described as Rwanda in slow motion – the world community did little. By most accounts, North American media have drastically underplayed the situation in western Sudan, just as they did in Rwanda, despite evidence of massive violations of human rights and a government supporting forces wreaking havoc on innocent civilians. Perhaps, just perhaps, content analysis would demonstrate that Darfur has registered on the media radar screen to a greater degree than did Rwanda. But it has not become a mega-story, or a media sensation. It has not captured our imaginations. And that signals, once again, a media failure.

For what it's worth, the international community has shown a measure of contrition with regard to the events of 1994. Rwanda is now a synonym for the world community's failure to intervene in the face of gross violations of human rights, a genocide. Rwanda is invoked repeatedly, often in sentences that contain the phrase 'never again.' Key figures in the Rwandan drama have apologized, or at least expressed regret, for their failure to act to the best of their abilities.[1] And in large part because of Rwanda, a new paradigm emerged and eventually won formal recognition on the world stage. The Canadian-inspired doctrine called *The Responsibility to Protect* (ICISS 2001) was formally adopted by the United Nations in September 2005. (Whether it is ever put into force is another matter.) The doctrine was set out in the December 2001 report of the International Commission on Intervention and State Sovereignty. It overturns the notion of absolute national sovereignty when it comes to massive violations of human rights and genocide, marking the first time that state sovereignty and non-interference in internal affairs have been qualified. In effect, the UN declaration enshrines in international law the notion that the world community has a right to intervene – a responsibility to protect – to stop a government from massive violation of the human rights of its citizens.

But the document is virtually silent on the role of the news media, and there is little discussion of the part journalists and news organizations could or should play in the face of the kind of atrocities witnessed in Rwanda. All these years later, we don't yet seem to have figured out that part of the puzzle. Perhaps it is time to advance a new paradigm for journalists: the responsibility to report. If we cannot adequately address the kind of structural constraints that handicapped the media in the case of Rwanda, at least we can deal with the behavioural aspects of the media – the way individual journalists conduct themselves.

In the years since 1994, Rwanda has become a case study in hate media, a textbook example of how journalism and particularly the broadcast media can be perverted in the name of hate. And, since Rwanda, considerable attention has been devoted to defining how monitoring the media in zones of actual or potential conflict can help policymakers to grasp more accurately what is going on and to use that information to frame responses with the best chance of preventing or mitigating violence. In Britain, the Foreign and Commonwealth Office (FCO) and BBC Monitoring (BBCM) have established a specialized 'tension and hate speech monitoring' project. BBCM aims to track the world's media for its clients (four main stakeholders: the BBC World Service, the FCO, the Ministry of Defence and the Cabinet Office). BBCM also has a 50-year old partnership with the Foreign Broadcast Information Service in the United States. In August 2002, BBCM began intensively monitoring media in 15 countries of interest, then providing monthly transcripts. A small-scale project, begun in September 2003, involved a focus on media and hate speech and incitement in the former Soviet Union, Israel–Palestine, Kosovo, Albania and Côte d'Ivoire.[2]

Clearly, media monitoring for hate speech has taken on a high profile because of Rwanda. As one observer quipped, we are all now well prepared to stop the Rwanda genocide – ten years too late.[3] And yet, what are the chances of once again coming across such a textbook example of hate media and incitement as Rwanda? We should probably be focused on media interventions that come much earlier in the trajectory that culminates in hate media. In fact, rather than using monitoring reports to try and shut down media outlets, a more useful exercise would be to use the material to design programmes to improve media standards, conduct media training and develop codes of conduct for journalists – behavioural rather than structural solutions.

More than a decade after the genocide, the media sector in Rwanda is still in need of this kind of assistance with training and development. There was no school of journalism in Rwanda until the late 1990s. Before the genocide, Rwanda's journalists were either professionally trained outside the country or trained 'on the job', in some cases with seminars and workshops to improve their skills. The School of Journalism and Communication was founded in 1996 at the National University of Rwanda in Butare. In early 2006, Carleton University's School of Journalism and Communication launched a collaborative effort with its counterpart in Butare to work together on staffing and curriculum development through a project called The Rwanda Initiative.

But efforts to foster a more professional media sector in Rwanda come at a time when respect for human rights and press freedom in the country is a genuine cause for concern. Major human rights organizations, such as Amnesty International and Human Rights Watch, have been highly critical of the Kagame government's treatment of human rights organizations and the news media. The government has been accused of an intimidation campaign that prompted Rwanda's primary human rights organization, LIPRODHOR, to close its doors in early 2005 (AI 2005). Amnesty International accused the Rwandan government of 'inappropriately manipulating the concept of genocide to silence not only organizations and individuals critical of the government but organizations who have a close relationship with the Rwandese people and whose loyalty the government questions' (AI 2004a). And in November 2004, Amnesty International urged the government of Rwanda to do its utmost to foster the independence of the press and to refrain from using the law to repress journalistic activities (AI 2004b). Reporters Without Borders went so far as to label President Kagame an enemy of press freedom. More than a decade after a genocide that deeply implicated the news media, there are still lessons to be learned in Rwanda.

What lessons have the international media drawn from the debacle of Rwanda? Like other international actors, the news media have been slow to acknowledge their failures during the genocide. Journalists tend to look forward, not back. For that reason, it took nearly 60 years for *The New York Times* to come to terms with the impact of its coverage of the Nazi Holocaust. In a 14 November 2001 feature headed 'Turning Away From the Holocaust,' former *Times* executive editor Max Frankel described the influential newspaper's 'staggering, stunning failure' to properly depict Hitler's methodical extermination of the Jews of Europe. Frankel noted that only six times in nearly six years did the front page of the *Times* mention Jews as Hitler's unique target for total annihilation. Sound familiar? The belated media mea culpa about coverage of the Holocaust has not been replicated when it comes to Rwanda, despite all the evidence of an abysmal media failure.

Instead, history continues to repeat itself. Stories like Rwanda continue to be downplayed. Year after year, the international news media devote less and less attention to foreign affairs, with the exception of the 'big' stories, such as the war in Iraq, the war on terror or the disaster *du jour*. Claude Moisy, former chairman and general manager of Agence France-Presse, described an inescapable paradox that 'the amazing increase in the capacity to produce and distribute news from distant lands has been met by an obvious decrease in its consumption' (Moisy 1997). Writing in the late 1990s, Moisy described a clear pattern: with the exception of a surge of international coverage in 1990 and 1991 due to the first Gulf War, the number and length of foreign topics covered in the evening news had declined far below Cold War levels. In early 2006, chances are that a rigorous content analysis would show, pound for pound, a significant up-tick in media coverage of foreign affairs. But factor out the overwhelming focus on Iraq and we are almost certainly looking at a continuation of the trend away from media coverage of international affairs.

Once again, journalists and critics cite a number of factors affecting the limited coverage of Darfur: the difficulty of getting into the region, tight budgets, the news focus on the war in Iraq and the presumed lack of audience interest in Africa (Ricchiardi 2005). For example, one researcher calculated that the nightly newscasts of ABC, CBS and NBC devote a total of roughly 24,900 minutes to news each year – an average of 20 minutes of news in each of these newscasts every night. In 2004, all three networks combined aired a total of only 26 minutes on fighting in Sudan, which has been described by some as genocide. (ABC devoted 18 minutes to Darfur coverage, NBC 5 and CBS only 3.) By contrast, houseware maven Martha Stewart's legal woes garnered 130 minutes of nightly news coverage (Tyndall Report 2004). More recently, a quantitative monitoring of all news segments aired in June 2005 on ABC, CBS, NBC, CNN, FoxNews and MSNBC demonstrated that coverage of Darfur was overshadowed by reporting on the so-called 'runaway bride' (the Georgia woman who drove across the country and concocted a fake kidnapping to escape her wedding in April 2005), the Michael Jackson trial and Tom Cruise's new movie and relationship with actress Katie Holmes.[4]

The shocking thing about these findings is that they no longer shock us. They haven't shocked us for a long time. In fact, we now take this kind of media coverage for granted. There is a vast academic literature on media coverage of international affairs and more specifically, coverage of Africa and the developing world. Some go at this empirically, with an eye to figuring out what the news media are actually doing. Others take a normative approach, prescribing what the media and journalists should do. We need more of both lines of enquiry.

But the problem with media prescriptions is that they are often so general that they are beyond implementation. In essence, the prescriptions end up being variants on the symptoms: news organizations should devote more resources to coverage of Africa and the developing world; the media should train more professionals in coverage of conflict and development issues; news from the developing world should be given more prominence on news pages and in broadcasts; news organizations should deploy more full-time foreign correspondents; rather than just covering wars, the media should pay more attention *before* a conflict erupts and after the fact, examine efforts at conflict resolution and ways the news media could actually support reconciliation and peace (for examples of this prescriptive approach, see Carnegie Commission 1997: 121–3 and Manoff 1997).

All of these prescriptions are really just reworded descriptions of the problem. Clearly, we need more information and more first-hand, eyewitness reporting from places like Darfur. We need to hear more and different voices. But how can we make that happen? Who moves the media? And what is 'the media' anyway? How can we talk coherently about such a disparate, diverse group of commercial and state enterprises that differ vastly across continents? Media organizations are populated by individual journalists, editors, media executives and others. More broadly speaking, 'the media' includes anyone who can apply some code of professional standards and disseminate news and information. So is it even realistic to look for discernible patterns of coverage in the media with an eye to recommending a different course of action?

And yet, some simple truths seem to be borne out by the evidence, and one of those truths is that media coverage does matter. There is a vast literature on how media coverage influences or is interwoven with foreign policy decisions: either directly through the provision of information that ignites public opinion (the so-called 'CNN effect') or indirectly through what Bernard Cohen (1963) described as the media's remarkable agenda-setting power to instruct people as to what they should be thinking about. Others have suggested that media influence is most likely to occur when policy is uncertain and media coverage is critically framed and empathizes with suffering people. But when policymakers have made up their minds and a policy track has been chosen, the news media can have much less influence (Robinson 2000: 614). We probably can't resolve the debate over whether media reports prod decision-makers into action or simply manufacture consent, but there can be no disagreement about the fact that more coverage of an issue or a region is more likely to generate policy action than less coverage (for more on this, consult Robinson 2002 and Wanta et al. 2004).

Media coverage, or lack of it, also matters in the inverse. The media glare of the big story casts a deep shadow on its fringes. Some argue that rather than seeking to measure the impact of media coverage, we should pay more attention to the 'nether world of absence of news' (Sonwalkar 2004: 207) and what happens when the news media methodically downplay or ignore a story.

The crux of the Rwanda piece is that more extensive media coverage might have made a difference, might have pushed international actors to do something in the spring of 1994. Roméo Dallaire argues that media coverage of Rwanda never gained momentum during the genocide, never reached the kind of critical mass needed to move leaders. That momentum only emerged in July 1994, when media descended in droves to cover the plight of those living in the refugee camps in Goma and sparked an international response.

We keep asking ourselves, why did the news media clamber to cover Biafra in 1968, Ethiopia in 1984, Somalia in 1992–93, but not the Rwanda genocide? And why have news media systematically downplayed events in Sudan for the past two decades and virtually ignored other locales (Livingston 1996)?

Could the answer be that 'the media', writ large, the 'cyclops' as some have called it (Bierbauer 1994), can only focus its gaze on one major story at a time? And in choosing such stories, are journalists more likely to seize on a simple, dramatic storyline, featuring good and evil, without the complexities of ethnicity and power politics to clutter the narrative?

According to analysis of 200 English-language newspapers worldwide, the 2004 tsunami in South East Asia generated more column inches in six weeks than the world's top ten 'forgotten' emergencies combined over the previous year (IFRC 2005). The media blitz prompted unprecedented generosity. By February 2005, the international community had donated US$ 500 for every person affected by the tsunami, compared with just 50 cents for each person affected by Uganda's 18-year war (IFRC 2005). Why did the tsunami and the subsequent relief efforts generate so many headlines? There was a simple storyline – a natural disaster. There were no complex political relationships to explain. And even though events were unfolding on the other side of the world, the tsunami met some 'proximity' criteria for Western news editors because many Western tourists were involved.

In *World Disasters Report 2005*, the International Federation of Red Cross and Red Crescent Societies put it bluntly: 'Editors sort stories by death tolls. Disasters that are unusual yet explicable, and that cause considerable death or destruction in accessible places which the audience is believed to care about, get covered. Baffling stories get less attention' (IFRC 2005). Rwanda was a baffling story, as is Darfur. As the Red Cross points out, news can be driven by ratings and circulation. So TV news is part news and part entertainment. No surprise then that 'sudden, dramatic disasters like volcanoes or tsunamis are intensely newsworthy, whereas long-drawn-out crises (difficult to describe, let alone film) are not.' By that score, the estimated 3.8 million deaths in the Democratic Republic of Congo since 1998 from war, disease and malnutrition have generated scant media coverage. But the dramatic eruption of the Nyiragongo volcano near Goma in early 2002 sparked an influx of journalists, even though it killed fewer than 100 people.

But when the cyclops turns its 'monocular gaze', the news media can become a major humanitarian actor, particularly, as Piers Robinson (2000) points out, when decision-makers are uncertain how to proceed. But that media role is very ill-defined and hard to predict with any degree of certainty. That is in part because the media are no less complex as an institution than government or humanitarian organizations. And yet, most studies treat the news media as a monolithic actor (Minear et al. 1994: 31). As Minear and colleagues suggest, rather than seeing the media as an actor with a purpose, it is probably more instructive to see the media as an institution with a process. And that process is inclined toward gatekeeping principles regarding what is news and what is not, what warrants the cost of news coverage and is likely to garner the interest of the audience (Chang and Lee 1992). And often, media attention to one emergency comes at the expense of another. The devastating earthquake in Pakistan in the autumn of 2005 overshadowed coverage of the hurricane and mudslides in Guatemala, just as, in some ways, Michael Jackson overshadowed Darfur.

And ironically, the 24-hour news cycle, rather than leading to more in-depth, comprehensive reporting, has arguably driven coverage in the other direction – toward fleeting, episodic encounters with events outside our daily lives. That makes the news media a bad early warning system. As journalists, we seem to be best at recording and reporting conflict once it has reached a certain pitch, by acting as witnesses to genocide and other atrocities. The economics of the news business is a key factor here. Although it would seem to make sense to go where the news is about to happen, to get ahead of the story, we are more likely to go where the news is happening, where conflict has broken out. It is a sure bet; you're not going to buy a plane ticket and end up with no story. Not much preventive value there. Journalists react to the same impulses as political decision-makers, and conflicts often show up on journalists' radar screen at about the same time as that of the decision-makers and diplomats – or more likely much later.

Not surprisingly, journalists largely reflect the societies in which they live and share the same ambivalence toward what is going on outside their borders, the same focus on domestic issues and selected international issues that are deemed to be relevant. In my view, it is up to individual journalists to crawl outside their skin, to get beyond that domestic focus and to exercise their role fully. Just as nation states have begrudgingly acknowledged the *Responsibility to Protect*

– driven by the simple realization that we have a responsibility to others – I think journalists, as individuals, must accept the responsibility to report.

I suppose my simple point is that we've been lamenting for three decades how 'the media' fail to cover stories like Rwanda and Darfur. I echo the lament, which is backed up by a stream of qualitative and quantitative research. But normative prescriptions for what 'the media' should be doing differently have little application. Could it be that everyone is going about it the wrong way, looking top-down at the media, which is an amorphous, disparate beast anyway, when they should be looking from the ground up, at individual journalists and the role they can play?

British journalist-cum-politician Martin Bell (1998) has spoken about the 'journalism of attachment', a call for empathy with humanity among journalists, something that some regard as an affront to the classical notion of journalistic objectivity and neutrality. But surely journalists can talk about an ethic of responsibility, a responsibility to report on people, places and events that have been excluded from the agenda of news organizations for a myriad of reasons. Surely individual journalists can try to make a difference, even if news organizations and the media are unable or unwilling to fully exercise their role.

Journalists such as Nicholas Kristof of *The New York Times* and Sudarsan Raghavan – now with the *Washington Post* and formerly Africa correspondent for Knight Ridder – have made it their mission to keep the Darfur story on the world's radar screen. They have demonstrated that individual journalists can make a difference. Canadian journalist Stephanie Nolen, Africa correspondent for the *Globe and Mail* newspaper, has single-handedly kept the issue of HIV/AIDS on the Canadian agenda through dogged, persistent reporting on a scourge that is decimating Africa in its own kind of genocide. In my own way, during 17 years as a reporter with the *Toronto Star* – Canada's largest circulation daily newspaper – I made every effort to use my position to interest the newspaper's powerful editors in stories that were not immediately on their radar screen, stories that took me on assignment to such places as Rwanda, Somalia, Sierra Leone and Kazakhstan. My personal interest and sense of responsibility as a journalist were shaped by a seminal experience in the early 1990s, when a development organization saw fit to invest in me and financed a media internship that took me to Africa for an extended period.

Since then, at every opportunity I have urged development assistance agencies, government and nongovernmental organizations, and advocates interested in media coverage of the developing world to invest in individual journalists – those new to the profession and also veterans – by endowing research grants, fellowships and awards that make it possible for journalists to visit the developing world or to explore areas that otherwise fall into that nether world of media absence. In my experience, journalists exposed to the developing world want to go back again and again. And their reporting can make a difference.[5]

In the carnage in Rwanda in 1994, individual journalists tried to fulfil their mandate, even though they were constrained by the chaos and the world's indifference. Thomas Kamilindi, who quit his job at Radio Rwanda on the eve of the genocide, wrote in this collection of his attempts to reach the outside world from his hiding place in the Milles Collines Hotel. Kamilindi kept trying the phone lines until he could get on the air and describe what was happening on the streets of Kigali. One of the attempts on Kamilindi's life came after he managed to get through to radio colleagues in France and describe the atrocities in Rwanda. Imagine the impact if journalists of good conscience, like Kamilindi, had been able to publish blogs in 1994, to circumvent the media inertia of budgets, racism and competing news interests.

Another Rwandan journalist, whose identity remains unknown, managed to capture on videotape some of the atrocities in the streets of Kigali. The journalist, believed to have been a camera operator with Rwandan television at the time, travelled with a group of *Interahamwe* through the streets of Kigali at some point in April 1994. According to one report, the camera operator had apparently befriended members of the death squads, even though he was opposed to the killing. As a journalist, he took considerable risk to gain permission to ride with the death squads through the streets of Kigali, filming some of the scenes and capturing rare footage that has become the mainstay of later documentary accounts of the genocide and a key part of the historical record (Hughes 1998). The world needs more journalists like Kamilindi and the unknown Rwandan TV camera operator.

The concept of media intervention to foster a more highly professional cadre of journalists in the developing world flourished in the decade after the Rwanda genocide. In 2003, Ross Howard, an associate at the Vancouver-based Institute for Media, Policy and Civil Society (IMPACS) estimated that in the previous ten years, US$ 1 billion had been invested in media-related interventions in conflict-stressed societies. Howard (2003) pointed to the emerging belief that news media may well be the most effective means of preventing war and conflict. Such media interventions abound. The Washington-based Search for Common Ground and its European counterpart operate radio studios in Burundi, Liberia and Sierra Leone, producing news, features, drama, music and speciality soap operas for social change as well as television productions. The organization also supports media training workshops in Africa, the Middle East and the Aegean region. The Panos network of organizations works to stimulate debate around key development issues, in part through a media programme. The network includes offices in the Caribbean, Eastern Africa, London, Paris, South Asia, Southern Africa, Washington DC and West Africa, with a combined staff of well over 100 people. Vancouver-based IMPACS supports programmes to foster free, responsible, independent media in emerging democracies by enhancing the contribution of the media to democratic development, good governance and public sector accountability. The Soros Foundation's Open Society Institute, the London-based Institute for War and Peace Reporting and others are also active in vital media training.

We need more voices, more first-hand accounts of events from journalists in the North and the South. Technology makes the arguments about newsroom budgets increasingly less relevant. Simply put, it is much, much cheaper to travel to the developing world and do journalism than it used to be. And why not use more locally based correspondents as well? Isn't it about time that Western news organizations re-examined their assumption that visiting foreign correspondents are of more value than locally based journalists?

One need look no further than the body of work of journalists like Sorious Samura, the documentary film-maker originally from Sierra Leone who has made it his mission to tell African stories. Samura's very personal and engaged form of journalism has resulted in documentaries broadcast widely in North America and Europe on such topics as the atrocities of Sierra Leone's civil war, the real stories of people living with hunger in Ethiopia, the plight of refugees in Darfur, the exodus of migrants through North Africa and the scourge of HIV/AIDS in a country like Zambia. Samura's work is powerful and emotional stuff. But it also far exceeds the professional threshold for broadcast to an international audience. Surely he is not the only journalist in Africa capable of producing top-quality material for a Northern audience.

And Africans don't just need to tell their stories to the outside world. They need to tell them to each other. For decades, London-based Gemini News Service pioneered the notion of South–South journalism, maintaining a network of journalists in the developing world. These local correspondents filed their copy to Gemini's London office, where it was edited, packaged and transmitted through Gemini to be published elsewhere in the developing world. Gemini broke the cycle of dependence that previously forced many Southern news outlets to see themselves through stories written by reporters from the North. And in turn, Gemini News Service provided some news organizations in the developed world – such as *The Toronto Star* and Southam News Service in Canada – with a steady stream of quality news features written by authors based in the developing world. One of Gemini's most innovative projects was a village reporting exercise that saw more than 15 reporters from such countries as India, Sri Lanka, Fiji and Lesotho head off to spend two months living in a village to report on daily life.

Gemini was truly a pioneer in recruiting and cultivating homegrown journalists and using them as correspondents to report on matters of interest to developing countries. Gemini's founder, former *Daily Mail* journalist Derek Ingram, always objected to the notion that he was running an alternative news agency. He wanted Gemini to be regarded as a mainstream source of copy that would also appeal to newspapers in the developed world (for an excellent history of Gemini News Service, see Bourne 1995). Along the way, Gemini served as a springboard for legions of promising young journalists from the developing world as well as a generation of young Canadians who worked at the news agency through fellowships funded by the International Development Research Centre.[6] Sadly, Gemini struggled for years to be financially viable and finally closed its doors in 2003 after nearly 30 years in operation. Perhaps it is time for an agency like Gemini News Service to be reborn.

Other individual journalists are joining forces to try to make innovative use of new technology and web-based information platforms to bring the stories of the developing world to a wider audience. Early in this century, news consumers were introduced to the 'blog', short for weblog. These online journals by individual writers usually consist of frequently updated commentaries, posted to a World Wide Web address. Now, millions of bloggers are sharing their opinions with a global audience in postings that combine content drawn from mainstream media and the web. As Daniel Drezner and Henry Farrell (2004) suggest in a recent paper, 'What began as a hobby is evolving into a new medium that is changing the landscape for journalists and policymakers alike.'

Drezner and Farrell argue that blogs are gaining more influence over the content of international media coverage, primarily through their agenda-setting function and by focusing on new or neglected issues. 'Increasingly, journalists and pundits take their cues about "what matters" in the world from weblogs. For salient topics in global affairs, the blogosphere functions as a rare combination of distributed expertise, real-time collective response to breaking news, and public-opinion barometer,' they write.

And television networks, with their notoriously top-heavy news operations, have begun to deploy 'video journalists', or VJs, individual journalists who carry small hand-held cameras and shoot and edit their own material. The work of some of these VJs is akin to a televised blog, with a mainstream connection. In Canada, the national broadcaster, CBC-Television, has deployed video journalist Saša Petricic in this way. Another such effort is the International Reporting Project at the Johns Hopkins University School of Advanced International Studies (see the International Reporting Project website at <www.journalismfellowships.org/>). The group proposes a new programme concept for international news, an approach designed to bypass current distribution systems and build a new audience. The project aims to produce a new international news series using small teams of video journalists to explore an array of political, economic, health and cultural issues in a given country each month. The plan is to produce content for multiple platforms – including television, the Internet, DVDs, print and radio – and to promote it aggressively. For its part, Carleton University has expanded its Rwanda Initiative to include a media internship programme for Canadian journalism students who want to do work terms with a news organization in Africa. The initiative is also helping student journalists in Rwanda to produce freelance material for an outside audience.

It is difficult to fashion a strategy to deal with the structural flaws in the news media that resulted in the failure to provide adequate coverage of the Rwanda genocide or the crisis in Darfur. But surely that difficulty should not prevent us from trying to change the structure one small piece at a time, through the work of individual journalists. This is a rallying cry to those who call themselves journalists, who practise this profession. Rwandan journalist Thomas Kamilindi recounts an encounter he had in Côte d'Ivoire with a group of young reporters who wondered how to avoid being drawn into the hate media in their country. Kamilindi's admonition was simple: stand up and be reporters, do your job. He is echoed by Roméo Dallaire, who reminds journalists that they can be powerful individually and collectively and must stay dynamic in the search for truth. As Maxwell McCombs notes in a recent review of the literature on media agenda-setting, the space on the media agenda and public attention to that agenda are both rare commodities. 'Setting the agenda is an awesome responsibility,' McCombs (2005: 556) concludes. 'Arguably the most fundamental, overarching ethical question for journalists concerns their stewardship of these resources.'

This collection of papers ends on a simple note, a plea to journalists: do your job, use the power that this profession affords and take up your responsibilities, starting with the responsibility to report.

NOTES

1. United Nations Secretary General Kofi Annan used remarks to a 26 March 2004 memorial conference on the genocide, held at the UN headquarters in New York, to declare that he personally should have done more to 'sound the alarm and rally support', for Rwanda; Bill Clinton used the 25 March 1998 speech in Kigali to acknowledge that the international community must bear its share of responsibility for the genocide, didn't act quickly enough and did not call the crimes by their rightful name: genocide; Roméo Dallaire has stated on numerous occasions since 1994 that he feels he failed personally to fulfil his mission in Rwanda.
2. The author took part in a 25 May 2004 roundtable discussion in London, conducted under Chatham House rules of non-attribution, during which the BBCM tension and hate speech project was described in detail. The roundtable – Hate speech, incitement and conflict: can media monitoring help prevent violence? – was organized by Oxford University's Programme in Comparative Media Law and Policy.
3. The remark was made by one of the participants in the May 2004, London roundtable.
4. Research compiled by the American Progress Action Fund, which operates the BeAWitness.org website. Research for the June 2005 analysis was conducted using the TVEyes media tracking service <www.TVEyes.com>.
5. For example, the author made this argument in testimony before the Senate Standing Committee on Transport and Communications on 1 December 2004, in the context of the committee's examination of the current state of the news media in Canada (Senate 2004).
6. The author took up one of IDRC's Gemini internships in 1990–91 and worked as a copy-editor and writer at Gemini for eight months in addition to making a five-month field trip to North Africa to examine the fledgling Arab Maghreb Union. The time at Gemini was a formative experience.

REFERENCES

AI (Amnesty International). 2004a. Rwanda: deeper into the abyss – waging war on civil society (public statement). Amnesty International, London, UK. AI index: AFR 47/013/2004 (public) News Service no. 169, 6 July.

—— 2004b. Rwanda: government should honour its commitment to respect press freedom (press release). Amnesty International, London, UK. AI index: AFR 47/015/2004 (public) News Service no. 297, 22 November.

—— 2005. Rwanda: human rights organisation forced to close (press release). Amnesty International, London, UK, 7 January.

Bell, M. 1998. 'The Journalism of Attachment'. In M. Kieran (ed.). *Media Ethics*. Routledge, London, UK: 15–22.

Bierbauer, C. 1994. 'Foreword'. In L. Minear, C. Scott and T.G. Weiss (eds). *The News Media, Civil War, and Humanitarian Action*. Lynne Rienner, Boulder, CO, USA.

Bourne, R.1995. *News on a Knife-edge: Gemini Journalism and a Global Agenda*. J. Libbey, London, UK.

Carnegie Commission on Preventing Deadly Conflict. 1997. *Preventing deadly conflict, final report*. Carnegie Commission, New York, NY, USA. Available at <www.wwics.si.edu/subsites/ccpdc/pubs/rept97/finfr.htm> (accessed 1 January 2006).

Chang, T.K. and J.W. Lee. 1992. Factors Affecting Gatekeepers' Selection of Foreign News: a National Survey of Newspaper Editors. *Journalism Quarterly*, 69(3): 554–61.

Clinton, W. Remarks by the president to genocide survivors, assistance workers, and the US and Rwanda government officials. Kigali Airport, Rwanda, 25 March 1998. Clinton Foundation, New York, NY, USA. Available at <www.clintonfoundation.org/legacy/032598-speech-by-president-to-survivors-rwanda.htm> (accessed 10 December 2005).

Cohen, B.C. 1963. *The Press and Foreign Policy*. Princeton University Press, Princeton, NJ, USA.

Drezner, D.W. and H. Farrell. 2004. Web of influence. *Foreign Policy*, November/December. Available at <www.foreignpolicy.com/story/cms.php?story_id=2707&popup_delayed=1> (accessed 10 December 2005).

Howard, R. 2003. The media's role in war and peacebuilding. Presented at the conference on The Role of the Media in Public Scrutiny and Democratic Oversight of the Security Sector, Budapest, 6–9 February 2003. Working Group on Civil Society, Centre for the Democratic Control of Armed Forces, Geneva, Switzerland. Available at <www.impacs.org/files/MediaPrograms/media%20in%20war%20and%20peacebuilding.PDF> (accessed 1 January 2006).

Hughes, N. 1998. Testimony before the International Criminal Tribunal for Rwanda, 25 May. In *The Prosecutor v. George Rutaganda*, case no. ICTR-96–3-T. ICTR, Arusha, Tanzania.

ICISS (International Commission on Intervention and State Sovereignty). 2001. *The responsibility to protect: report of the International Commission on Intervention and State Sovereignty*. International Development Research Centre, Ottawa, Canada. Available at <www.iciss.ca/report-en.asp> (accessed 10 December 2005).

IFRC (International Federation of Red Cross and Red Crescent Societies). 2005. 'Humanitarian media coverage in the digital age' (ch. 5). In *World disasters report 2005*. IFRC, Geneva, Switzerland.

Livingston, S. 1996. 'Suffering in Silence: Media Coverage of War and Famine in Sudan'. In R.I. Rotberg and T.G. Weiss (eds). *From Massacres to Genocide: the Media, Public Policy and Humanitarian Crises*. World Peace Foundation, Cambridge, MA, USA: 68–92.

Manoff, R.K. 1997. The media's role in preventing and moderating conflict. Presented at the conference on Virtual Diplomacy, 1 April 1997. United States Institute of Peace, Washington, DC, USA. Available at <www.usip.org/virtualdiplomacy/publications/papers/manoff.html> (accessed 1 January 2006).

McCombs, M. 2005. A Look at Agenda-Setting: Past, Present and Future. *Journalism Studies*, 6(4): 543–557.

Minear, L., C. Scott and T.G. Weiss. 1994. *The News Media, Civil War, and Humanitarian Action*. Lynne Rienner, Boulder, CO, USA.

Moisy, C. 1997. Myths of the Global Information Village. *Foreign Policy*, 107 (Summer): 78–87.

Ricchiardi, S. 2005. Déjà vu. *American Journalism Review*, February/March. Available at <www.ajr.org/Article.asp?id=3813> (accessed 1 January 2006).

Robinson, G. 2002. 'If you leave us, we will die.' *Dissent*, 49(1): 87–99.

Robinson, P. 2000. The Policy–Media Interaction Model: Measuring Media Power During Humanitarian Crisis. *Journal of Peace Research*, 37(5): 613–33.

Senate of Canada. 2004. *Proceedings of the Standing Senate Committee on Transport and Communications, issue 3 – evidence for December 1, 2004*. Parliament of Canada, Ottawa, Canada. Available at <www.parl.gc.ca/38/1/parlbus/commbus/senate/Com-e/tran-e/03eva-e.htm?Language=E&Parl=38&Ses=1&comm_id=19> (accessed 1 January 2006).

Sonwalkar, P. 2004. 'Out of Sight, Out of Mind: the Non-Reporting of Small Wars and Insurgencies'. In S. Allan and B. Zelizer (eds). *Reporting War: Journalism in Wartime*. Routledge, New York, NY, USA: 206–23.

Tyndall Report. 2004. *Year in review 2004*. Tyndall Report, New York, NY, USA. Available at <www.tyndallreport.com/yearinreview.php3> (accessed 1 January 2006).

Wanta, W., G. Golan and C. Lee. 2004. Agenda Setting and International News: Media Influence on Public Perceptions of Foreign Nations. *Journalism and Mass Communication Quarterly*, 81(2): 364–77.

Bibliography

GENERAL READING

Adelman, H. 2000. Genocidists and saviours in Rwanda. *Other Voices*, 2(1). Available at <www.othervoices.org/2.1/adelman/rwanda.html>.

Adelman, H. and A. Suhrke (eds). 1999. *The Path of a Genocide: the Rwanda Crisis From Uganda to Zaire.* Transaction, New Brunswick, NJ, USA.

Africa Watch. 1992. *Rwanda: Talking Peace and Waging War: Human Rights Since the October 1990 Invasion.* Africa Watch, Washington, DC, USA.

African Rights. 1995. Rwanda: Death, Despair and Defiance. *Review of African Political Economy*, 21(61).

Amnesty International. 1990. *The Republic of Rwanda: a Spate of Detentions and Trials in 1990 to Suppress Fundamental Rights.* Amnesty International, London, UK, October.

—— 1992. *Rwanda: Persecution of Tutsi Minority and Repression of Government Critics.* Amnesty International, London, UK.

—— 1994. *Rwanda: Cases for Appeals.* Amnesty International, London, UK, November.

—— 1994. *Rwanda: Government Supporters and Regular Troops have Committed Massacres All Over the Country.* Amnesty International, London, UK, May.

—— 1994. *Rwanda: Reports of Killings and Abductions by the Rwandese Patriotic Army.* Amnesty International, London, UK, October.

Arno, A. 1984. 'Communication, Conflict and Storylines: the News Media as Actors in a Cultural Context'. In A. Arno and W. Dissanayake (eds). *The News Media in National and International Conflict.* Westview Press, Boulder, CO, USA: 1–15.

Barnett, M.N. 1996. 'The Politics of Indifference at the United Nations and Genocide in Rwanda and Bosnia'. In T. Cushman and S.G. Mestrovic (eds). *This Time we Knew: Western Responses to Genocide in Bosnia.* New York University Press, New York, NY, USA: 128–62.

—— 1997. The UN Security Council, Indifference, and the Genocide in Rwanda. *Cultural Anthropology*, 12(4).

Braeckman, C. 1994. *Rwanda, histoire d'un génocide.* Fayard, Paris, France.

Brauman, R. 1995. 'Genocide in Rwanda: We Can't Say We Didn't Know'. In E. Queinnec and J. Rigal (eds). *Populations in Danger: a Médecins Sans Frontières report.* La Découverte, Paris, France.

Carlsson, I., H. Sung-Joo and R. Kupolati. 1999. *Report of the independent inquiry into the actions of the United Nations during the 1994 genocide in Rwanda.* United Nations, New York, NY, USA.

Carver, R. 2000. 'Broadcasting and Political Transition'. In R. Fardon and G. Furniss (eds). *African Broadcast Cultures: Radio in Transition.* James Currey, Oxford, UK. 192 pp.

Castonguay, J. 1998. *Les casques bleus au Rwanda.* Éditions Harmattan, Paris, France.

Clapham, C. 1998. Rwanda: the Perils of Peacemaking. *Journal of Peace Research*, 35(2).

Dallaire, R. and B. Poulin. 1995. Rwanda: From Peace Agreement to Genocide. *Canadian Defence Quarterly*, 24(3).

Des Forges, A. 1999. *Leave None to Tell the Story: Genocide in Rwanda.* Human Rights Watch and the International Federation of Human Rights Leagues, New York, NY, USA. Available at <www.hrw.org/reports/1999/rwanda/>.

Destexhe, A. 1995. *Rwanda and Genocide in the Twentieth Century.* New York University Press, New York, NY, USA.

Gourevitch, P. 1998. *We Wish to Inform You That Tomorrow We Will be Killed With Our Families: Stories from Rwanda.* Farrar, Straus, and Giroux, New York, NY, USA.

Hatzfeld, J. 2003. *Une saison de machettes.* Seuil, Paris, France.

Hintjens, H.M. 2001. When Identity Becomes a Knife: Reflecting on the Genocide in Rwanda. *Ethnicities*, 1(1): 25–55.

Human Rights Watch. 1993. *Beyond the Rhetoric: Continuing Human Rights Abuses in Rwanda.* Human Rights Watch, New York, NY, USA, June: 1–29.

—— 1994. *Arming Rwanda: the Arms Trade and Human Rights Abuses in the Rwandan War.* Human Rights Watch, New York, NY, USA, January.

—— 1994. *The Aftermath of Genocide in Rwanda: Absence of Prosecution, Continued Killings.* Human Rights Watch, New York, NY, USA, September.

—— 1994. *Rwanda: a New Catastrophe?* Human Rights Watch, New York, NY, USA, December.

—— 1995. *Rearming with Impunity: International Support For the Perpetrators of the Rwandan Genocide.* Human Rights Watch, New York, NY, USA, May. Available at <www.hrw.org/reports/1995/Rwanda1.htm>.

Huyssen, A. 2000. Present Pasts: Media, Politics, Amnesia. *Public Culture,* 12(1): 21–38.

Jennings, C. 1998. *Across the Red River: Rwanda, Burundi and the Heart of Darkness.* Weidenfeld & Nicolson, London, UK.

Kamukama, D. 1993. *Rwanda Conflict: Its Roots and Regional Implications.* Fountain Publishers, Kampala, Uganda.

Klinghoffer, A.J. 1998. *The International Dimension of Genocide in Rwanda.* Macmillan, London, UK.

Kuperman, A. 2000. Rwanda in Retrospect: Could the Genocide Have Been Stopped? *Foreign Affairs*, January/February: 94–5.

Mackintosh, A. 1997. Rwanda: Beyond 'Ethnic Conflict.' *Development in Practice,* 7(4): 464–74.

Melvern, L. 1995. *The Ultimate Crime: Who Betrayed the UN and Why.* Allison and Busby, London, UK.

—— 2000. *A People Betrayed: the Role of the West in Rwanda's Genocide.* Zed Books, London, UK.

—— 2004. *Conspiracy to Murder: the Rwandan Genocide*. Verso, New York, NY, USA.

Prunier, G. 1995. *The Rwanda Crisis 1959–1994: History of a Genocide.* Hurst and Company, London, UK.

Roach, C. (ed.). 1993. *Communication and Culture in War and Peace.* Sage Publications, Newbury Park, CA, USA.

Smith, D.N. 1995. The Genesis of a Genocide in Rwanda: the Fatal Dialectic of Class and Ethnicity. *Humanity and Society,* 19(4): 57–73.

UN Department of Peacekeeping Operations. 1996. *Comprehensive report on lessons learned from UNAMIR, October 1993–April 1996*. United Nations, New York, NY, USA, December.

Uvin, P. 1997. Prejudice, Crisis, and Genocide in Rwanda. *African Studies Review,* 40(2).

—— 1998. *Aiding Violence: the Development Enterprise in Rwanda.* Kumarian Press, West Hartford, CT, USA.

Windrich, E. 1999. Revisiting Genocide in Rwanda. *Third World Quarterly,* 20(4): 855–60.

MEDIA AND RWANDA

Books and journal articles

1998. Hate Speech. *Index on Censorship,* 27(1): 30–59, 61–71.

Artis, W. 1970. The Tribal Fixation. *Columbia Journalism Review*, Fall: 48–9.

Backmann, R. and R. Brauman. 1996. *Les médias et l'humanitaire. Éthique de l'information ou charité-spectacle.* CPFJ Éditions, Paris, France.

Benthall, J. 1993. *Disasters, Relief and the Media.* Tauris & Co, London, UK.

Berger, G. 1998. Media and Democracy in Southern Africa. *Review of African Political Economy,* 78(25): 599–610.

Berkeley, B. 1994. Sounds of Violence: Rwanda's Killer Radio. *New Republic*, 21(8–9): 18–19.

Berry, A.J. and C.P. Berry. 1999. 'The Voice of Extremism'. In A.J. Berry and C.P. Berry (eds). *Genocide in Rwanda: a Collective Memory.* Howard University Press, Washington, DC, USA: 87–122.

Birck, D. 1995. La télévision et le Rwanda ou le génocide de programme. *Temps Modernes*, 583 (July-August): 181–97.

Boisserie, P. and D. Birck. 1995. Retour sur images. *Temps Modernes,* 583 (July-August): 198–216.

Borst, B. 1995. Burundi-Media: Journalists Combat Influence of 'Hate Media.' *Inter Press Service,* 9 August.

Bourgault, L.M. 1995. *Mass Media and sub-Saharan Africa.* Indiana University Press, Bloomington, IN, USA.

Brauman, R. 1994. *Devant le mal Rwanda: un génocide en direct.* Arlea, Paris, France.

Chalk, F. 1999. 'Hate Radio in Rwanda'. In H. Adelman and A. Suhrke (eds). 1999. *The Path of a Genocide: the Rwanda Crisis from Uganda to Zaire.* Transaction, New Brunswick, NJ, USA. 414 pp.

—— 1999. 'Radio Broadcasting in the Incitement and Interdiction of Gross Violations of Human Rights, Including Genocide'. In R.W. Smith (ed.). *Genocide: Essays Toward Understanding, Early Warning, and Prevention.* Association of Genocide Scholars, Department of Government, College of William and Mary, Williamsburg, VA, USA: 85–103.

Chrétien, J.P. 1991. 'Presse libre' et propaganda raciste au Rwanda: *Kangura* et le 10 commandements du Hutu. *Politique Africaine,* 42: 109–20.

—— 1995. La propaganda du génocide. In R. De La Brosse (ed.). *Les médias de la haine.* La Découverte, Paris, France: 22–55.

—— 1998. Rwanda: la médiatisation d'un génocide. In F. d'Almedia (ed.). *La question médiatique.* Seli Arslan, Paris, France: 53–63.

Chrétien, J.P., J.F. Dupaquier, M. Kabanda and J. Ngarambe. 1995. *Rwanda: les médias du génocide.* Karthala, Paris, France.

Coo, S.E. 1997. Documenting Genocide: Cambodia's Lessons for Rwanda. *Africa Today,* 44(2): 223–37.

Dallaire, R. 2003. *Shake Hands With the Devil: the Failure of Humanity in Rwanda.* Random House, Canada.

Deguine, H. and R. Menard. 1994. Are There Any Journalists Left in Rwanda? *Index on Censorship,* 23(6): 55–9.

Des Forges, A. 2002. 'Silencing the Voices of Hate in Rwanda'. In M.E. Price and M. Thompson (eds). *Forging Peace: Intervention, Human Rights and the Management of Media Space.* Edinburgh University Press, Edinburgh, UK. 240 pp.

Domatob, J. 1994. Coverage of Africa in American Popular Press. *Issue,* 22(1): 24–9.

Dowden, R. 1995. 'Media Coverage: How I Reported the Genocide'. In O. Igwara (ed.). *Ethnic Hatred: Genocide in Rwanda.* Association for the Study of Ethnicity and Nationalism, London, UK: 86–92.

Ezell, W.K. 1992. 'Newspaper Responses to Reports of Atrocities: Burundi, Mozambique, Iraq'. In H. Fein (ed.). *Genocide Watch.* Yale University Press, New Haven, CT, USA: 87–112.

Fair, J.E. 1993. War, Famine and Poverty: Race in the Construction of Africa's Media Image. *Journal of Communication Inquiry,* 17(2): 5–23.

Fair, J.E. and L. Parks. 2001. Africa on Camera: Television News Coverage and Aerial Imaging of Rwandan Refugees. *Africa Today,* 48(2): 35–57.

Fardon, R. 1999. 'Ethnic Pervasion'. In T. Allen and J. Seaton (eds). *The Media of Conflict: War Reporting and Representations of Ethnic Violence.* Zed Books, London, UK.

Fardon, R. and G. Furniss (eds). 2000. *African Broadcast Cultures: Radio in Transition.* James Currey Publishers, Oxford, UK.

Fox, F. 1996. Rwanda: the Journalist's Role. *Month,* 29(5): 186–89.

Franklin, A. and R. Love. 1998. Whose News? Control of the Media in Africa. *Review of African Political Economy,* 78(25): 545–50.

Frilet, A. 1995. Reportages en situation de guerre et de génocide. *Temps Modernes,* 583 (July-August): 149–60.

Fujii, L.A. 2004. Transforming the Moral Landscape: the Diffusion of a Genocidal Norm in Rwanda. *Journal of Genocidal Studies,* 6(1): 99–114.

Gatwa, T. 1995. Ethnic Conflict and the Media: the Case of Rwanda. *Media Development,* 42(3): 18–20.

Gibney, M.J. Kosovo and Beyond: Popular and Unpopular Refugees. *Forced Migration Review, 5.* Available at <www.fmreview.org/text/FMR/05/10.htm>.

Gouteux, J.P. 1992. 'Reporting African Violence: Can America's Media Forget the Cold War?' In B.G. Hawk (ed.), *Africa's Media Image.* Praeger, New York, NY, USA: 94–108.

—— 1999. *Le monde, un contre-pouvoir? Desinformation et la manipulation sur le génocide rwandais.* L'Esprit Frappeur, Paris, France.

Gowing, N. 1994. *Real-time television coverage of armed conflicts and diplomatic crises: does it pressure or distort foreign policy decisions?* Joan Shorenstein Barone Center, John F. Kennedy School of Government, Harvard University, Cambridge, MA, USA.

—— 1996. Moving Images – Why Do They Move? *Red Cross, Red Crescent*, 1: 6–7.

Hachten, W.A. and B. Beil. 1985. Bad News or No News? Covering Africa 1965–1982. *Journalism Quarterly,* 62(Autumn): 626–30.

Harrison, P. and R. Palmer. 1986. *News Out of Africa: Biafra to Band Aid.* Hilary Shipman Ltd, London, UK.

Hawk, B. 1992. *Africa's Media Image.* Praeger, New York, NY, USA.

—— 1994. The News Media and Africa. *Issue: A Journal of Opinion,* 12(1).

Hieber, L. 1998. Media as Intervention: a Report from the Field. *Track Two,* 7(4).

Higiro, J.M.V. 1996. Distorsions et omissions dans l'ouvrage Rwanda, les médias du génocide. *Dialogue*, 190: 160–78.

Hilsum, L. 1995. Where is Kigali? *Granta,* Autumn: 147.

Hoge, J.F. Jr. 1997. Foreign News: Who Gives a Damn? *Columbia Journalism Review*, November/December: 49.

Jackobson, P.V. 1996. National Interest, Humanitarianism, or CNN: What Triggers UN Peace Enforcement After the Cold War? *Journal of Peace Research.* 33: 205–15.

Jefremovas, V. 1997. Contested Identities: Power and the Fictions of Ethnicity, Ethnography and History in Rwanda. *Anthropologica,* 23: 1–14.

Kabamba, B. 2000. Francophonie in the African Great Lakes Region in the Local Press: the Case of Rwanda and the Democratic Republic of Congo. *Studia Diplomatica,* 53(3): 135–45.

Karegeye, J.P. 2001. Rwanda: génocide et trouble des discourse. *La langue de bois,* 47: 131–48.

Karnell, A.P. 2002. Counteracting 'Hate Radio' in Africa's Great Lakes Region: Responses and Lessons. *Journal of International Communications*, 8(1): 111–26.

Karnik, N.S. 1998. Rwanda and the Media: Imagery, War and Refuge. *Review of African Political Economy,* 78: 611–23.

—— 1998. The Photographer, His Editor, Her Audience, Their Humanitarians: How Rwanda's Image Travels Through the American Psyche. *ACAS Bulletin*, 50/51: 35–42.

Kellow, C.L. and H. Leslie Steeves. 1998. The Role of Radio in the Rwandan Genocide. *Journal of Communication,* 48(3): 107–28.

Kelman, H.C. 1998. 'Social-Psychological Dimensions of International Conflict'. In W. Zartman and J. Rasmussen (eds). *Peacemaking in International Conflicts: Methods and Techniques.* United States Institute of Peace, Washington, DC, USA.

Lehmann, I.A. 1999. *Peacekeeping and Public Information: Caught in the Crossfire.* Frank Cass, London, UK.

Lemarchand, R. 1994. *Ethnocide as Discourse and Practice.* Cambridge University Press, Cambridge, UK.

—— 1995. Rwanda: the Rationality of Genocide. *Issue: A Journal of Opinion*, 23(2).

Le Pape, M. 1996. Des journalistes au Rwanda: l'histoire immédiate d'un génocide. *Temps Modernes*, 583: 161–80.

Li, D. 2004. Echoes of Violence: Considerations on Radio and Genocide in Rwanda. *Journal of Genocide Research*, 6(1): 9–27.

Livingston, S. and T. Eachus. 1995. Humanitarian Crises and U.S. Foreign Policy: Somalia and the CNN Effect Reconsidered. *Political Communication.* 12: 413–29.

—— 1999. 'Too Little Too Late: American Television Coverage of the Rwandan Crisis of 1994'. In H. Adelman and A. Suhrke (eds). *Path to a Genocide: the Rwandan Crisis from Uganda to Zaire.* Transaction, New Brunswick, NJ, USA.

Mackintosh, A. 1996. 'International Aid and the Media'. In T. Allen, K. Hudson and J. Seaton (eds). *War, Ethnicity and the Media.* South Bank University School of Education, London, UK: 37–56.

Mamdami, M. 2002. *When Victims Become Killers: Colonialism, Nativism and Genocide in Rwanda.* Princeton University Press, Princeton, NJ, USA.

Martin, R. 1994. The Mass Media: Image and Reality. *Journal of Modern African History,* 32(1): 183–89.

Mathien, M. 1998. Les médias et l'actualité de défense. Les journalists face aux militaries ou vice-versa. *Quaderni,* 36: 15–31.

McNulty, M. 1999. 'Media Ethnicization and the International Response to War and Genocide in Rwanda'. In T. Allen and J. Seaton (eds). *The Media of Conflict: War Reporting and Representations of Ethnic Violence.* Zed Books, London, UK: 268–86.

Melvern, L. 2001. Missing the Story: the Media and the Rwandan Genocide. *Contemporary Security Policy,* 22: 91–106.

Menard, R. and Reporters sans Frontières. 1996. *De la radio de la haine à la radio des droits de l'homme*. European Parliament, Brussels, Belgium, 25 April.

Metzl, J.F. 1997. Information Intervention: When Switching Channels Isn't Enough. *Foreign Affairs,* November/December.

—— 1997. Rwandan Genocide and the International Law of Radio Jamming. *American Journal of International Law*, 91.

Mikekemo, K. 1996. The Conspiracy of Silence. *New Times,* October.

Minear, L., C. Scott and T.G. Weiss. 1996. *The News Media, Civil War, and Humanitarian Action.* Lynne Rienner Publisher, Boulder, CO, USA.

Misser, F. and Y. Jaumain. 1994. Death by Radio. *Index on Censorship,* 23(4–5): 72–4.

Moeller, S.D. 1999. *Compassion Fatigue: How the Media Sell Disease, Famine, War and Death.* Routledge, New York and London.

Myers, G., T. Klak and T. Koehl. 1996. The Inscription of Difference: News Coverage of the Conflicts in Rwanda and Bosnia. *Political Geography,* 15(1): 21–46.

Nastios, A. 1996. 'Illusions of Influence: the CNN Effect in Complex Emergencies'. In R.I. Rothber and T.G. Weiss (eds). *From Massacres to Genocide: the Media, Public Policy, and Humanitarian Crises.* Brookings Institution, Washington, DC, and World Peace Foundation, Cambridge, MA, USA.

Olorunnisola, A.A. 1995. When Tribal Wars are Mass Mediated: Re-evaluating the Policy of 'Non-interference.' *Gazette*, 56: 123–38.

Palmer, R.H. 1987. Africa in the Media. *African Affairs,* 86: 241–47.

Pottier, J. 1995. 'Representations of Ethnicity in Post-Genocide Writings on Rwanda'. In O. Igwara (ed.). *Ethnic Hatred: Genocide in Rwanda.* ASEN Publications, London, UK.

—— 2002. *Re-imagining Rwanda: Conflict, Survival and Disinformation in the Late 20th Century.* Cambridge University Press, Cambridge, UK.

—— 2000. 'Reporting the New Rwanda: the Rise and Cost of Political Correctness, With Reference to Kibeho'. In R. Doom and J. Gorus (eds). *Politics of Identity and Economics of Conflict in the Great Lakes Region.* VUB University Press, Brussels, Belgium: 121–47.

Price, M.E. and M. Thompson (eds). 2002. *Forging Peace: Intervention, Human Rights and the Management of Media Space.* Edinburgh University Press, Edinburgh, UK.

Rabechault, M. 2000. *La presse au Rwanda: des massacres à la mission d'information parlementaire.* Institut d'Études Politiques, Université de Strasbourg III, Strasbourg, France, June.

Reporters sans Frontières. 1994. *Rwanda: médias de la haine ou press democratique.* ASF, Paris, France, November.

Reyntjens, F. 1999. A Dubious Discourse on Rwanda. *African Affairs,* 98(1): 119–22.

Roskis, E. 1994. Un génocide sans images. Blancs filment Noirs. *Le Monde Diplomatique,* November: 32.

Rotberg, R. and T. Weiss (eds). 1996. *From Massacres to Genocide: the Media, Public Policy, and Humanitarian Crises.* Brookings Institution Press, Washington, DC, USA.

Semelin, J. 2000. 'Radio'. In D. Shelton, H. Adelman, F. Chalk, A. Kiss and W. Schabas (eds). *The Encyclopedia of Genocide and Crimes Against Humanity.* Thomson Gale, New York, NY, USA.

Silverstein, K. 1994. Guerrillas in the Mist: Media Misrepresentation of Rwanda. *Washington Monthly*, 26(9): 21–3.

Smith, S. 1993. *Somalie: la guerre perdue de l'humanitaire.* Calmann-Levy, Paris, France.

Stephen, M. 1995. Ethnocide – Discourse and Perceptions. *Review of Africa Political Economy*, 65: 367–71.

Thompson, M. and M.E. Price. 2003. Intervention, Media and Human Rights. *Survival*, 45(1): 183–202.

Umurerwa, M.A. 2000. *Comme la langue entre les dents: fratricide et piege identitaire au Rwanda.* Harmattan, Paris, France.

Utley, G. 1997. The Shrinking of Foreign News. *Foreign Affairs.* 76(2): 2–10.

Vidal, C. 1998. Le génocide des Rwandais tutsi et l'usage publique de l'histoire. *Cahiers d'Etudes Africaines,* 38(2–4): 653–63.

Wall, M. 1997. The Rwanda Crisis: an Analysis of News Magazine Coverage. *Gazette,* 59(2): 121–34.

Williams, K. 1992. 'Something More Important Than the Truth: Ethical Issues in War Reporting'. In A. Belsey and R. Chadwick (eds). *Ethical Issues in Journalism and the Media.* Routledge, London, UK: 154–70.

Wolton, D. 1991. *Wargame. L'information et la guerre.* Flammarion, Paris, France.

Web resources

Belgian Senate Session of 1997–8. Parliamentary commission of inquiry regarding the events in Rwanda. Available at <www.senate.be/www/webdriver?MIval=/Dossiers/DossierFiche.html&LEG=1&NR=611&PUID=1006&LANG=fr>.

Hay, Robin. The Media and Peacebuilding. A Discussion Paper. IMPACS (Institute for Media, Policy and Civil Society). Available at <www.impacs.org/pdfs/roundtable.pdf>.

Institute for Media, Peace and Security. Available at <www.mediapeace.org/>.

Montreal Institute for Genocide and Human Rights Studies, *Radio propaganda and genocide: occasional paper*. Available at <migs.concordia.ca/occpapers/radio_pr.html>.

Netherlands Institute of Human Rights. Available at <www.uu.nl/uupublish/homerechtsgeleer/onderzoek/onderzoekscholen/sim/english/18199main.html>.

Radio Netherlands. Folder on Hate Media. Available at <www.rnw.nl/realradio/dossiers/html/burundi-h.html>.

Remembering Rwanda Project. Available at <www.visiontv.ca/RememberRwanda/main_pf.htm>.

Organization of African Unity, *Rwanda: the preventable genocide*. Available at <www.carleton.ca/jmc/mediagenocide/documents/pdf/preventablegenocidereport.pdf>.

United Nations Assistance Mission for Rwanda. Available at <www.un.org/Depts/dpko/dpko/co_mission/unamirS.htm>.

United Nations International Criminal Tribunal for Rwanda. Available at <www.ictr.org/>.

University of the West of England's Web Genocide Documentation Centre. Available at <www.ess.uwe.ac.uk/genocide/gendef.htm>.

War, Propaganda, and the Media. Available at <www.globalissues.org/HumanRights/Media/Propaganda/Rwanda.asp>.

Reports and papers

Africa News Service. 1995. *Special reports: media coverage of Africa*. Available at <www.africanews.org/info/medcont.html>.

Alexis, M. and I. Mpambara. 2003. *IMS assessment mission: the Rwanda media experience from the genocide.* International Media Support, Copenhagen, Denmark, March.

Amnesty International. 1998. *Amnesty International Report 1999: Rwanda*. Available at <www.amnesty.org/ailib/aireport/ar1999/afr47>.

Article 19. 1996. *Broadcasting genocide: censorship, propaganda and state-sponsored violence in Rwanda 1990–1994.* Article 19, London, UK.

BBCM. 1995. Burundi: Reporters Sans Frontières Condemns Media for Encouraging Ethnic Killings. BBC Monitoring Services, Reading, UK, 23 June.

Carlsson, L. 1999. *Report on the independent inquiry into the actions of the UN during the 1994 genocide in Rwanda*. African Policy Information Center, Washington, DC, USA, 16 December.

Cater, N. 1996. Why Does the Media Always Get it Wrong in Disasters: Stereotypes, Standards and Free Helicopter Rides. Presented at the review conference launching *World Disasters Report* by the International Federation of Red Cross and Red Crescent Societies, 23 May. Oxford University Press, Oxford, UK.

Chalk, F. 1999. 'Hate Radio in Rwanda'. In H. Adelman and A. Suhrke (eds). 1999. *The Path of a Genocide: the Rwanda Crisis from Uganda to Zaire.* Transaction, New Brunswick, NJ, USA.

Clinton, W.J. 1998. Remarks by the president to genocide survivors, assistance workers and US and Rwanda government officials, Kigali, Rwanda. Office of the Press Secretary, US Government Printing Office, 25 March. Available at <www.access.gpo.gov/index.html>.

Connaughton, R.M. 1996. *Media of hate*. Strategic and Combat Studies Institute, Camberley, UK.

Glasgow Media Group. 1994. British Television News and the Rwanda Crisis, July 15–21. 1994 (part 4). Glasgow Media Group, University of Glasgow, Glasgow, UK.

Gowing, N. 1998. New Challenges and Problems for Information Management in Complex Emergencies: Ominous Lessons From the Great Lakes and Eastern Zaire. Background paper for the Dispatches from Disaster Zones Conference, Oxford, UK, 28 May. Save the Children Fund and European Commission Humanitarian Aid Office, London, UK.

Gulseth, H.L. 2004. The Use of Propaganda in the Rwandan Genocide: a Study of Radio-Télévision Libre des Milles Collines (RTLM). Department of Political Science, University of Oslo, Oslo, Norway. Cand. Polit. dissertation.

Hilsum, L. 1996. Reporting Rwanda: the media and aid agencies. Report prepared for study III of *The international response to conflict and genocide: lessons from the Rwanda experience.* Joint Evaluation of Emergency Assistance to Rwanda, Danish Foreign Ministry, Copenhagen, Denmark.

International Criminal Tribunal for Rwanda (ICTR). 2000. *Le Procureur contre Georges Ruggiu: convention de plaidoyer aux fins de donner acte d'un accord d'aveu entre Georges Ruggiu et le bureau du procureur*. ICTR, Arusha, Tanzania, April. ICTR-97-32-DP.

Johansson, P. 1996. International press coverage of the Rwanda conflict. Report prepared for study II of *The international response to conflict and genocide: lessons from the Rwanda experience.* Joint Evaluation of Emergency Assistance to Rwanda, Danish Foreign Ministry, Copenhagen, Denmark.

Karnell, A.P. 2003. Role of Radio in the Genocide of Rwanda. University of Kentucky, Lexington, KY, USA. PhD dissertation, July. 373 pp.

Kimani, M. 2002. Rwandan Media on the Dock. University of Warnborough, Canterbury, UK. Master's thesis in communication psychology.

Kirschke, L. 1996. *Broadcasting genocide: censorship, propaganda and state-sponsored violence in Rwanda 1990–1994.* Article 19, London, UK.

Kirschke, L. Multiparty transitions, elite manipulation and the media: reassessing the Rwandan genocide. Unpublished.

Kroslak, D. 1997. The media in wartime: international history and international politics. University of Wales, Aberystwyth, Wales. Unpublished.

Kuperman, A.J. 2000. No More Heroes: War Correspondents Retreat From the Front Line. How the Media Missed Rwandan Genocide. International Press Institute, New York, NY, USA.

Lowe, C. 1997. Talking About 'Tribe': Moving from Stereotypes to Analysis. In *Africa Policy E-Journal*. Africa Policy Information Center, Washington, DC, USA. Available at <www.africaaction.org/docs97/eth9711.1.htm> (accessed 3 January 2006).

Musa, B.A. 1990. New communication technologies in Africa: combative or cooperative systems? Presented at the 7th biennial conference of the African Council for Communication Education, Ouagadougou, Burkina Faso, 22–27 October. ACCE, Nairobi, Kenya.

Nkusi, L., M. Ruzindana and B. Rwigamba. 1998. *The Kinyarwanda language: its use and impact in the various media during the period 1990–1994. A sociolinguistic study*. Internal report commissioned by the United Nations International Criminal Tribunal for Rwanda, Arusha, Tanzania, March.

Prostituting the Facts: aid and the media. 1995. *Crosslines Global Report 14–15*, April/May.

Reporters Sans Frontières. 1995. Rwanda: l'impasse? La liberté d'expression après le génocide. Reporters Sans Frontières, Paris, France.

Sénat commision d'enquête parlementaire concernant les évenements du Rwanda. 1997. *Rapport d'ensemble enseignements tirés de la mission des Nations Unies pour l'assistance au Rwanda (MINUAR), octobre 1993 – avril 1996*. Sénat de Belgique, Brussels, Belgium.

Sorenson, J. 1989. An African Nightmare Discourse on War and Famine in the Horn of Africa. York University, Toronto, Ontario, Canada. PhD dissertation.

Storey, A. 2000. Story-lines and scapegoats: discourse, the Rwandan economy and genocide. Holy Ghost College, Dublin, Ireland. Unpublished manuscript.

United Nations. 1997. Seminar on Public Information Policies and Practices of Field Missions. Harrison Conference Center, Glen Cove, New York, 5–6 March 1997. United Nations Reproduction Section, New York, NY, USA, October.

World Peace Foundation. 1995. *The media, humanitarian crisis and policymaking* (report of an international meeting). World Peace Foundation, Cambridge, MA, USA.

Newspaper articles and radio broadcasts

Anonymous. 1994. L'extermination des Tutsis: les massacres du Ruanda sont le manifestation d'une haine raciale soigneusement entretenue. *Le Monde,* 4 February.

—— 1996. BBC Man Attacks Neutral War Reports. *Guardian*, 23 November.

Bonino, E. 1996. Bringing Humanitarian News into Prime Time. *International Herald Tribune,* 28 June.

Dahlburg, J.T. 1994. Why the World Let Rwanda Bleed: Chastened by Somalia, a Gun-shy U.S. Urged Caution on an Already Weary United Nations, Braking Efforts to Stem the Brutality. *Los Angeles Times,* 10 September: A1.

Glenny, M. 1998. War Radio. BBC Radio 4, London, UK, 10 December.

Gowing, N. 1994. Behind the CNN Factor: Lights! Cameras! Atrocities! But Policymakers Swear They are Not Swayed by the Images. *Washington Post,* 31 July.

Kaban, E. 1995. Rwanda Genocide Probers Want Journalist Testimony. Reuters News Service, 19 September.

Meller, P. 1996. The Dead and the Deadline. *Guardian,* 25 March.

Misser, F. 1994. Rwanda: médias et génocide: la 'radio qui tue.' *Le Monde Diplomatique*, 41, 13 August.

Nolen, S. 1999. The Semantics of Genocide. *Globe and Mail,* 17 November: C1, C2.

Rwanda: Hutu Extremist Radio Reportedly Broadcasting From Gisenyi. Reuters News Service, 13 July 1994.

Index

Compiled by Sue Carlton

100 Days 427, 428
ABC 14, 192, 420, 436–7
Africa, media coverage 8, 165, 211–27
African Charter on Human and Peoples' Rights 331
African National Congress (ANC) 251, 263, 400
Afrika, Janvier 82
Agatashya Radio 381–2, 383–6, 387
  Charter 384–6
Agence France-Presse (AFP) 160–5
aid agencies 167–87
airdrops 180–1, 183
AJR (Association des Journalistes du Rwanda) 83
Akayesu, Jean Paul 335, 337, 338–9, 340, 369, 377, 427
Akazu 23, 24–5, 319
Akimana, François 332, 335
Alagiah, George 170
Albright, Madeleine 248
Alozie, Emmanuel C. 8, 211–30
Amalric, Jacques 59–60
Americares 180–1
Amnesty International 153, 208, 242–3, 245–6, 435–6
Anderson, Benedict 107, 128
Anglican Church 25–6, 28, 29
Annan, Kofi 207, 248
Arnott, Dr Bob 181
Arusha accords (1993) 2, 43–4, 59, 75, 85, 199, 218, 224, 249, 282
  and Hutu Power 45, 57
  and media 86, 98, 122–3, 127, 170, 171, 253, 285, 316, 395
Auerbach, Y. 216
Avisar, Ilan 421, 423–4

Bagosora, Théoneste 43, 47
Bahutu Manifesto 62, 63, 66
Bamwanga, Jean Baptiste 114
Banyamulenge 385
Barayagwiza, Jean-Bosco 9, 277, 278, 287, 293, 308
  and conspiracy 291, 301–2, 306
  genocidal intent 294–5, 300
  role in CDR 281–2, 287, 296–7
  role in RTLM 284–5, 291, 295–6, 298, 300
  sentence 306–7, 343, 367
  trial verdict 297, 302, 304–5
  warnings given to 311, 315–17
Barton, Brenda 180
BBC 36, 87, 154–5, 158, 162, 164, 170–1, 236–7, 401, 406, 412
BBC Monitoring (BBCM) 399, 435
BBC World Service 170, 172, 212, 213
Beardsley, Major Brent 199, 363–4
Belgium 13, 20–1, 27, 29, 46–7, 58–9, 77, 220, 246
  media coverage 168, 170
  withdrawal of troops 48, 151
Bell, Martin 440
Bemeriki, Valérie 95, 116, 139, 284, 319, 320, 326, 355
Benaco 173
Biju-Duval, Jean-Marie 9, 322–3, 343–61
Bikindi, Simon 99, 100, 133, 322
Bisiika, Asuman 409
Bizimungu, Augustin 151, 355, 405, 409, 410, 411, 412
Bizumuremyi, Bonaventure 411
Bloch-Elckon, Y. 216
Bolton, Samantha 169, 171, 175, 183, 185
Bond, Catherine 156, 158, 172, 253
Bosnia 162, 192–3, 196, 208, 251
Boston Globe 162
Bourgault, L.M. 128
Boutros-Ghali, Dr Boutros 206
Boutroue, Joel 176–7, 185
Braeckman, Collette 312, 319
Brauman, Rony 238
Bray, Ian 181
Brock, L. 263
Bucyana, Martin 281–2, 289
Bugesera massacre 42, 46, 70, 319, 350
Bukava 178, 184, 383, 386
Burundi 32, 34–5, 170–1, 184, 219, 236, 243, 245
  assassination of president (1993) 25, 34, 45, 85, 111, 163, 252, 253, 310–11, 315
  president killed in plane crash (1994) 47, 139, 146, 218, 219, 224, 250–1
Bush, George H.W. 195
Butare 48–9, 151

Buthelezi, Mangosuthu 171, 251
Byabyibwanzi, François 319
Byumba 147, 152

Cambodia 17, 417, 418–19, 425–6
camera footage 231–4, 238–41
Campbell, Alison 182–3, 185
Capital Radio, South Africa 400
Caplan, Gerald 6, 20–37
CARE 175, 177, 180, 181, 182–3, 406
Carragee, K.M. 217
Carver, Richard 125–6
Catholic Church 21, 22, 25–6, 28, 29, 77, 96, 136, 408
CDR (Coalition for the Defence of the Republic) 24, 44, 45, 57, 266, 377
  and Media Trial judgement 281–2, 287, 291–2, 293, 294, 296–7, 300, 302–4
  newspapers aligned with 73, 74, 78, 83, 84
  portrayed in cartoons 75–6, 86
Ceppi, Jean-Philippe 201
Chalk, Frank 10, 375–80
Chalker, Baroness Lynda 179, 207, 248
Chandler, David P. 425
Chaon, Anne 5, 7, 160–6
Chicago Tribune 162
Chrétien, Jean-Pierre 6, 55–61, 92, 125, 323, 350
Christian Broadcasting Network 176
Christian Science Monitor 162
Clark, David 207
Clinton, Bill 18, 26, 53, 169, 179, 195, 203, 209, 248, 252, 434
CNN 14, 15, 169, 175, 183, 192, 195, 251
CNN effect 176, 188, 437
Cohen, Bernard 437
Comité d'étude du Conseil supérieure du pays 64
Commune Rouge 289–90, 293
Crocker, Stuart 178
Cyangugu 59, 311

Dahinden, Phillippe 10, 324, 354, 381–8
Daily Nation (Kenya) 211, 215–16, 217, 218–19, 220–1, 222–6
Dallaire, Roméo 2, 5, 6, 12–19, 27, 146, 150, 153, 208, 224, 363, 433
  call for radio jamming 401
  calls for reinforcements 4, 202, 203, 204, 205, 206, 207
  and genocide 418–19, 424
  and international media 147, 157, 438, 443
  interview on French TV 165
  RTLM attacks on 49, 52, 120, 284, 296, 322, 355
  warnings given by 25, 46, 164, 202

Damien, Nkezabera 69
Darfur, Sudan 434, 436–7, 438, 439, 440
De Beer, A. 212
Delahaye, Luc 238–9, 241
Democratic Republic of Congo (DRC) 29, 33–4, 35, 36, 245, 439
Democratic Voices of Burma 400
Department for International Development (DFID) 409
Des Forges, Alison 6, 41–54, 55, 81, 125, 174, 312–13, 322, 350, 355, 356, 395
Deutsche Welle 213, 401
Diallo, Alpha-Abdoulaye 245
Dorland, Michael 10, 417–32
Dottridge Mike 8, 242–7
Dowden, Richard 8, 181, 183, 248–55
Doyle, Mark 5, 7, 14, 16, 145–59, 161, 172, 179, 195, 236
Drezner, Daniel 443

Eachus, T. 195
Eades, David 146
Edeani, D. 214
Enright, Michael 16
Entman, R.M. 217
L'Ère de Liberté 80
Etter, Jean-Marie 387–8

Facelly, Albert 241
Fair, J.E. 263, 268
FAR (Forces Armées Rwandaises) 32, 33, 35, 73, 76, 364
Farrell, Henry 443
Feed the Children 178
Financial Times 252
Finkelstein, Norman 429
Le Flambeau 76, 80, 83
Foa, Sylvana 156, 182
Foley, Barbara 420
Forces Démocratiques pour la Libération du Rwanda (FDLR) 34
Foreign and Commonwealth Office (FCO) (UK) 435
Forster, Albert 334
France 4, 23, 25–6, 28–9, 32, 43, 49–50, 52, 168, 174–5
  see also Operation Turquoise
Frankel, Max 436
freedom of expression 82–3, 330–1, 339–40, 377, 406–9, 436
Friedrich Naumann Foundation 79
Fritzsche, Hans 337–8, 344, 348
Frohardt, Mark 10, 389–403

Gahigi, Gaspard 56, 57, 58, 78, 98, 116, 126, 137, 294, 319, 324, 326, 355

Gahima, Gerald 410
Gaillard, Philippe 157, 201, 208, 209, 249
Gasana, Didas 410
Gasesero, André 322
Gatabazi, Félicien 79, 319
Gemini News Service 442
gender propaganda 362–71
genocide
  definition of 31, 258, 330–1, 418–19, 424, 427
  depicted in films 417–18, 424–9
  interviews with perpetrators 126, 127–34
  use of word 154, 163, 201, 205, 206–7, 418, 424
  as 'work' 49, 50, 93, 96, 101, 110, 133–4
  see also Holocaust
Gersony, Robert 185
Gikondo massacre 199–201, 238
Gikongoro 58, 69
Giles, Tom 8, 235–7
Girard, Eric 239
Gisenyi 158–9, 282, 288, 289, 290, 293, 295
Gitera, Joseph 68, 71
Glazer, Richard 423
Globe and Mail 202
Goma 4, 7, 16, 164, 167–70, 175–85, 194, 239–40, 383, 438, 439
Gourevitch, Philip 104, 208
Govea, R. 263
Gowing, Nik 168
Grain, John 176
Green, Gerald 420
La Griffe 79
Grosser, Alfred 60
Guardian (Nigeria) 211, 215, 216, 217, 219, 220, 221, 222–6
Guardian (UK) 253, 257

Habimana, Festo 77
Habimana, Kantano 56, 57–8, 94, 95, 99, 113, 127, 139, 294, 318–19, 351
  direct and public incitement 283, 351
  interview with Rutaremara 97–8
  popularity of 98, 116–17
  pre-genocide broadcasts 315
Habimana, Phocas 315–16, 355
Habyarimana, Juvénal 14, 22–3, 24, 30, 41–2, 43, 102, 245
  and Arusha Accords 171
  death of 1–2, 5, 25, 27, 36, 47, 96, 103, 119, 122, 132, 138–9, 146, 172, 223, 250–1, 253, 293, 375
  French support for 23, 59, 174
  military coup 66, 67, 244
  and printed press 67, 68, 74–7, 82, 83–4
  and Radio Rwanda 137, 138
  and RTLM 44, 47, 136, 284
Hachten, W.A. 212, 262
Hakizimana, Appolos 408
Hangimana, Augustin 80
Hannay, Sir David 203, 205–6
Hansen, Miriam B. 423
Harelimana, Dr Froduald 78
Harelimana, Gaspard 244
Hatzfeld, Jean 55
Hélène, Jean 59, 161, 201
Higiro, Jean-Marie Vianney 6, 17, 73–89, 92, 310, 314
Hilsum, Lindsey 5, 7, 167–87, 253
Himmler, Heinrich 334
Hirondelle Foundation 382, 383, 384, 387, 412
Hirondelle Press Agency 383, 386
Hitchens, Christopher 209
Hitimana, Noël 57, 101–3, 117, 318, 323, 324, 325–6
Hoberman, J. 422
Hogg, Douglas 207
Holocaust 236, 417–18, 429
  depicted in film 419–24
Holocaust (TV series) 420, 422
Hotel Mille Collines 49, 104, 137, 139, 140, 156–7, 427–8, 441
Hotel Rwanda 417, 427–8
Howard, Ross 441
Huby, Anne-Marie 169, 175, 184
Hughes, Nick 3, 8, 163, 231–4, 428
Huguier, François 238
Human Rights Watch 51, 163, 174, 208, 264, 311, 435
Hurd, Douglas 248, 251
Hutu Power 2, 24, 25, 28, 32, 36, 45, 46, 47–9, 56, 57, 100, 110, 139, 199, 293, 310, 377
Hutus 20–5, 56, 88
  CDR and 282, 287, 293, 294–5
  held in prisons 31
  incitement by press 63–71, 74, 86, 87
  incitement by radio 41–9, 56–8, 87, 90, 93, 94–5, 99, 100–1, 110–13, 119–23, 125–7, 131–4, 283, 287–8, 291–2, 294, 296, 303, 310–23, 352, 365, 375–6
  and international media 145–6, 148, 150, 152–6, 161, 176, 185, 186, 194–5, 201, 206, 218–21, 250–4, 256–9, 265–7
  moderates 27, 138–9, 145, 168, 198, 219, 239, 302, 433
  portrayed in films 428
  in post-genocide era 31, 34, 405
  refugees 4, 23, 28, 38, 53, 164, 194, 235–6, 241
  and Tutsi diaspora publications 77, 78

Ibru, Alex 216
Ibuka 31, 290, 405
Ijambo 75
Ikindi 80
Imbaga 83
Imboni 409
Impuruza 77, 78
Impuzamugambi 282, 287, 288, 289, 291, 293, 297, 319, 320
Incimatata, Father Oreste 267
incitement, direct and public 335, 338–9, 340, 344, 345–6, 347–51, 356–7, 377
ingangurarugo 84–5
Inglish, Sue 170–1, 172
Ingram, Derek 442
Inkhata 251, 263
Inkotanyi 57, 95, 115, 283, 313, 323, 349, 350, 357, 365
Institute for Media, Policy and Civil Society (IMPACS) 441
Institute for War and Peace Reporting 441
Interahamwe 24, 42, 104, 137, 199, 282, 285–6, 289–90, 293, 317, 441
  in DRC 33, 34, 36
  and international media 149, 154, 200–1, 253, 267
  and refugee camps 32, 33
  and roadblocks 149, 234, 381
  and RTLM 45–6, 90, 92, 95, 127, 132–3, 137, 284, 319, 320, 326, 381
  and sexual violence 364
  warnings about 16, 25
Interahamwe (newspaper) 86
International Committee of the Red Cross (ICRC) 150, 153, 173, 178, 201, 208, 209, 245, 438–9
International Conference on the Status of Banyarwanda Refugees 77–8
International Criminal Tribunal for Rwanda (ICTR) 2, 9, 30–1, 113–14, 136, 165, 231, 427
  and gender propaganda 362–3, 367–71
  missed opportunities 18, 343–59, 362–3, 367–71
  and pre-genocide case against RTLM 308–28
  and prosecution of print media 330–40
  summary judgement 111–12, 277–307
International Criminal Tribunal for (the former) Yugoslavia 338, 347, 352
International Monetary Fund 63, 81
Internet 87, 212, 271
  weblogs 443
Internews 412
Intumwa/Le Méssager 75
inyenzi, use of term 48, 68, 84–5, 88, 93, 115, 283, 289, 293, 295, 349–50, 366
Isibo 80, 83
Izuba/Le Soleil 79

Jennings, Christian 412
Jermey, Mike 172, 175
journalism/journalists
  and accountability 136–42
  and blame 160–5, 433–4, 440–1
  local-based correspondents 442
  and opportunities for intervention 395–401
  persecution in post-genocide era 407–9
  and political activism 78–9
  responsibility to report 433–44
  video journalists 443
Judgement at Nuremburg 419
Juppe, Alain 163

Kabanda, Marcel 6, 62–72
Kabera, Assiel 405
Kabila, Joseph 34
Kabila, Laurent-Desire 33, 34, 385, 386
Kabonero, Charles 410–11
Kabuga, Felicien 311, 315–16
Kadafi, Rwango 410
Kagabo, Jose 76
Kagame, Paul 29, 36, 146, 404, 405, 406, 409, 410, 433, 436
Kagwi-Ndungu, Charity 9, 330–42
Kahabaye, Joseph 49
Kajeguhakwa, Valens 74, 80
Kajelijeli, Juvénal 339
Kajuga, Robert 317
Kambanda, Jean 113, 117, 121, 339, 427
Kameya, André 76, 79, 317
Kamilindi, Thomas 7, 136–42, 322, 381, 441, 443
Kanamugire, Charles 76
Kanguka 74, 76, 79, 80
Kangura 6, 58, 62–71, 74, 87, 111–12, 115, 136–7, 309–10, 377, 404, 408
  compared to *Der Stürmer* 332–5
  and gender propaganda 9, 365–6, 367–8
  and Media Trial judgement 2, 279–81, 291–2, 294, 298–9, 301, 302–4, 335–6, 339–40, 348–9
Kanuma, Shyaka 410
Kanyarwanda 75–6
Karamira, Froduald 85, 117, 121
Karnell, Aaron 376
Kassir, Hassan 176
Katale camp 180
Katumba 320
Kavaruganda, Joseph 320, 321

Kayibanda, Grégoire 21–2, 66, 67, 70, 71, 243, 245
Keane, Fergal 172, 195
Keating, Colin 204, 205
Kellner, D. 215
Kellow, C. 92
Kennan, George 188
Kennedy, Ted 51
Kenya 195, 211, 212, 215–16, 217, 225–6, 262
Khmer Rouge 425–6
Kiberinka 76
Kibilira 42
Kibumba 181
Kibuye 59, 164, 428
Kigali 2, 35, 46, 49, 123, 148–53, 156–8, 199, 201, 209, 219, 231, 234, 237, 251, 253, 256–7
Kigali hospital 161
The Killing Fields 426, 428
Kimani, Mary 7, 110–24
Kimenyi, Alexander 76, 77, 78
Kinyamateka 74, 80, 83, 407–8
Kinyarwanda 16–17, 79, 87, 96, 98, 104, 112, 136, 243, 350, 383
Kirschke, L. 103
Kirundi 87, 383
Kivu refugee camps 57
Kovanda, Karel 174, 204
Kramer, Stanley 419
Kristof, Nicholas 440
Kubwabo, Theodore 221
Kuperman, Alan J. 8, 160, 164, 256–60

Laber, Jeri 208
Lacouture, Jean 425
Lake, Anthony 51
Lanzmann, Claude 420–2, 423
Lemarchand, René 252
Lemkin, Rafael 418, 429
Leonard, Terry 195
Levi, Primo 422
Li, Darryl 6, 90–109
Libération 59, 174, 201, 239
LIPRODHOR 406, 435–6
Livingston, Steven 7–8, 188–97
Lizinde, Théoneste 245
Lone, Geoff 173, 177–8
Lorch, Donatella 195
Los Angeles Times 162
Lusaka agreement 33

Maal, Baaba 381
McCombs, Maxwell 443–4
MacDowell Kalisa, Elly 410
Machiavelli, Niccolo 98–9
Magrath, John 204
Maindron, Father 59
Major, John 203, 248
Makusa, Anasthase 70, 71
Mamdani, Mahmood 30, 125
Mandela, Nelson 34, 251
Mass, Monique 161
Matthews, Jenny 180
Mbanda, Jean 405
Mbilizi, Phillipe 117
Mbonigabo, Ismail 410
MDR-Parmehutu (Mouvement Démocratique Républicain) 62, 66, 75, 409
La Médaille/Nyiramacibili 83
Médecins Sans Frontières 60, 163, 169–70, 171, 174–5, 178, 181–2, 183–5, 204
media
  and alternative information 400–1
  failure of 160–5, 235–7, 248–54, 256–9
  indicators of impending conflict 390–5
  intervention in 378–80, 395–403, 435–6, 441
  monitoring 399, 425
  in post-genocide Rwanda 404–13
  regulation 397–8
  as tool for peace 381–8
  see also journalism/journalists; newspapers
Melvern, Linda 8, 198–210, 248
Meridien Hotel 157
Metzl, Jamie 389
Minear, Larry 439
Mironko, Charles 6–7, 125–35
Mitterand, François 59, 174
Mobutu Sese Seko 32, 33, 249
Moeller, Susan 196
Moisy, Claude 436
Monasebian, Simone 9, 308–29
Le Monde 59, 162, 201, 256, 257
Montreal Institute for Genocide and Human Rights Studies 380
Moose, George 51
Morris, Harvey 249
Mpayimana, Elie 80
Mpongebuke, Édouard 80
MRND (*Mouvement Républicain National pour la Democratie et le Développement*) 24, 41, 42, 45, 59, 82, 87, 95–6, 111, 138, 266, 351
  and control of RTLM 44, 284
  membership of 84, 86
  newspapers aligned with 73, 74, 78, 79, 83, 84, 86
  and opposition newspapers 75–6, 82
Muberantwali, Théoneste 80, 82
Mucchielli, Roger 55
Mudatsikira, Joseph 102–3

Mugabe, Jean-Pierre 76, 409
Mugabi, John 410
Mugabo, Manasse 408
Mugemana, Jean-Marie Vianny 246
Mugenzi, Justin 321, 334
Mugesera, Léon 350
Muhayimana, Jason 409
Munyaneza, Aloys 244
Munyango, Bruce 159
Munyemanzi, Emmanuel 408
Muremangingo, Didace 409
Musabe, Pasteur 74
Musamganfura, Sixbert 82
Museveni, Yoweri 244–5, 323
Mushayidi, Deo 409
Mushimiyimana, Gideon 408
Mutsinzi, Édouard 80, 407–8
Mwambutsa, Jean-Claude 412
Myers, Garth 162

Nahimana, Ferdinand 9, 42–3, 277, 278, 282, 285–6, 308
  and conspiracy 291, 301–2
  genocidal intent 294–5, 300
  as head of ORINFOR 42–3, 79, 82, 278, 286, 296, 305, 325
  role in RTLM 44, 121, 284–5, 291, 295–6, 300, 318–19, 324
  scapegoating of 352–9
  sentence 305, 343, 367
  and trial verdict 296, 302, 304, 377
  warnings given to 311, 315–17
Nath, Vann 426
Nation Media Group (NMG) 215–16
Ndadaye, Melchior, assassination of (1993) 34, 45, 85, 111, 163, 218, 252, 253, 310–11, 315
Ndasingwa, Landould 314
New York Times 162, 167, 181, 192, 201–2, 257, 263, 308, 436
newspapers 73–89
  African 211, 213
  American 162, 175
  British 176, 179, 251–3
  distribution in countryside 81–2
  freedom of press 82–3, 330, 339–40, 406–9, 436
  impact on Rwandan politics 83–6
  and profit 79–81
  types of 73–8
Newsweek 263
Ngango, Félicien 79
Ngara 173, 235, 236
Ngeze, Hassan 9, 67–71, 74, 81, 277, 278, 287–90, 293, 295, 330, 333, 334, 339–40
  and conspiracy 291, 301–2, 306
  and gender propaganda 365–6
  genocidal intent 295
  role in CDR 78, 282
  role in *Kangura* 62, 63, 74, 136, 279–81, 297, 301
  sentence 306, 343, 367
  trial verdict 297, 301–2, 304–5
Ngurumbe, Aloys 84–5
Nigeria 211, 212, 213, 214, 216, 217, 225–6, 262–3
Niyitegeka, Eliézer 339
Nkomati 117
Nkubili, Sylvestre 78–9
Nkubito, Alphonse Marie 310, 311, 318, 319, 405
Nkubito, Jean-Claude 409
Nkuliza, Amiel 409
Nkurunziza, Ananie 58, 98, 112–13, 116–17, 127
Nolen, Stephanie 440
Noone, Kevin 175
Le Nouvel Observateur 59
Novick, Peter 420, 429
Nowrojee, Binaifer 362–72
Nsanzimana, Sylvestre 75
Nsanzuwera, François Xavier 139, 310, 312, 313, 317, 318–19
Nsengiyaremye, Dismas 76, 84
Nsengiyaremye, Thaddée 82, 252
Ntaryamira, Cyrien 146, 172, 218, 223, 251
Ntezimana, Laurien 409
Nuremburg International Military Tribunal (IMT) 337–8, 343–4, 345, 347–8, 352
Nwankwo, R. 214
Nwokeafor, C. 214
Nyamata church 158
Nyerere, Julius 34
Nyirabikali, Hélène 408
Nzirorera, Joseph 57, 79, 82

Obinor, F. 226–7
Obote, Milton 323
Open Society Institute 441
Operation Blessing 176
Operation Turquoise 5, 28, 32, 52, 57, 59, 164, 174–5, 239, 240, 355
Operation USA 176, 179, 182
Orbinski, Dr James 208
Organization of African Unity (OAU) 23, 24, 28, 165, 207, 223, 224, 269
ORINFOR 243, 325–6
Oxfam 163, 170–1, 173, 176, 177, 178, 181, 183, 204, 208

Panh, Rithy 426

Le Partisan 409
Pate, Umaru 214
Patterson, T.E. 190
Pazik, Maric 199
Petricic, Sasa 443
Pew Project for Excellence in Journalism 190
Polisi, Dennis 410
Ponte, Carla Del 370
Pottier, Johan 405
Pran, Dith 426
PSD (Parti Social Démocratique) 84, 266

Quotidien de Paris 239

Radio France International (RFI) 58, 140, 161, 162, 212, 256, 258, 401, 412
Radio Free Europe 401
Radio Freedom, South Africa 400
radio jamming 51–3, 309, 378, 401
Radio Muhabura 17, 43, 76, 79, 93, 96–7, 105, 127, 130
Radio Okapi 412
Radio Rutomorangingo 53
Radio Rwanda 17, 42, 44, 47, 48–9, 52, 73, 82, 85, 93, 96–7, 101–2, 136–9, 287–8, 316, 324
radio trottoir 128
Raghavan, Sudarsan 440
RANU (Alliance National Unity) 76
Rassemblement Démocratique Rwandais 69
RDP (Republican Democratic Party) 67
Red Cross hospital 156–7, 173
Redding, Don 177
refugee crisis 4, 16, 29, 32–3, 35, 167–87, 235–6, 239
Register, Larry 169
Reporters Sans Frontières (RSF) 352, 353, 383, 408, 412, 436
Rifkind, Malcolm 207
Ring Around Serbia 401
Riza, Syed Iqbal 248
Robert, Patrick 4, 163, 238–9
Robertson, Pat 176
Robinson, Piers 195, 439
Roefs, W. 217
Rolley, Sonia 412
Roskis, Edward 4, 8, 238–41
Rosper, Manuela 177
Roth, Kenneth 163
Royal Electrical and Mechanical Engineers (REME) 207
RPA (Rwandan Patriotic Army) 111, 113, 115, 118–19, 120, 121, 132
RPF (Rwandan Patriotic Front) 2, 24–5, 36, 127, 130, 282, 349, 357–8
  and African media coverage 218, 219, 220–1, 223, 225
  and Arusha accords 24–5, 43–4, 199–200, 249
  and censorship and propaganda 10, 87, 88, 404–13
  and death of Habyiarama 27, 36, 132
  and France 28, 52, 205
  and Hutu sympathisers 138
  and international media 145–59, 168, 170, 172, 195, 239, 246, 249–50, 254
  invasion of Rwanda 22–3, 41–2, 78, 170, 218, 219, 223, 243–4, 253
  newspapers aligned with 75–6, 79, 80, 83, 86
  and radio propaganda against 46–8, 50, 85, 94, 102, 110–13, 115, 132, 283, 287, 315, 320, 322, 323, 351
  victory of 53, 174, 355–6
RTLM (Radio-Télévision Libre des Mille Collines) 2, 6–7, 12, 16–18, 24, 44–53, 55–60, 87, 90–105, 110–23, 136–9, 375–7
  analysis of broadcasts 113–22, 125–34
  broadcasters 110, 114, 116–17, 122–3, 126–7, 325–6
  discourse of democracy 93, 94–5
  discourse of development 93, 95–6
  discourse of history 93–4
  and gender propaganda 365, 368
  and Media Trial 281, 283–5, 287–8, 291–2, 294–6, 298–300, 302–4, 339–40, 348–9
  pre-genocide case against 9, 308–28, 345, 346, 351
Rubwiliza, Tharcisse 82
Rucogoza, Emmanuel 117, 326
Rucogoza, Faustin 137, 284–5, 310, 317–18qq
Rudahigwa, Mwami Mutara 69
Rudasingwa, Théogène 147, 410
Rugambage, Jean-Leonard 411
Ruggiu, Georges 58, 59, 94, 96, 98, 117, 284, 326, 339, 345, 355
Ruhengeri prison 69, 245, 246
Rusesabagina, Paul 104, 139, 140, 417, 427–8
Russell, Bertrand 69
Rutanga, François 76
Rutaremara, Tito 97–8
Rwabugili, Kigeli 84–5
Rwabugiri, Mwami 20
Rwabukumba, Seraphin 74
Rwabukwisi, Vincent 76, 79
The Rwanda Herald 409
Rwanda Initiative 435, 443
Rwanda Rushya 75–6, 79, 80, 83
Rwigema, Celestin 405
Rwigema, General Fred 76, 78

S-21 425, 426
Samura, Sorious 442
Save the Children Fund, United Kingdom (SCF–UK) 177
Schabas, William 376
Schanberg, Sidney 426
Schindler's List 420, 422–4, 427
Schoepf, B.G. 128
Schoot, Katrin van der 5, 172
Schulz, William F. 208
SCR (Service Central de Renseignements) 82
Search for Common Ground 441
Sebarenzi, Joseph 405, 409
Sebera, Antoine 49, 313
Semana, Tharcisse 410
Semusambi, Félicien 74, 82
Sendashonga, Seth 405
Serubyobo, Zacharia 322
Serufifira, Robert 410
Serushago, Omar 287, 288
sexual violence 363–4, 366–71
Shake Hands with the Devil 427
Shamukiga, Charles 312, 313
Shoah 420–2, 423
Shooting Dogs 427
Sibomana, Father André 83, 111, 351, 404, 407–8
Simbizi, Stanislas 117, 121
Sindambiwe, Father Silvio 82, 83
Sindikubwabo, Theodore 158
Smith, Stephen 174, 175, 412
Somalia 4, 12–13, 174, 188–9, 195, 252, 438
Sometimes in April 427
Southam News Service 442
Spielberg, Steven 420, 422–4
Spitulnik, Debra 128–9, 131, 134
Srebnik, Simon 421
De Standaard 256
Stec, Stefan 199
Steeves, H. 92
Stein, S.D. 425
Stephen, D. 190
Stockton, Nic 177, 180, 181
Strauss, Scott 376
Streicher, Julius 297–8, 303, 326, 334, 335, 337, 340, 343–4, 347, 349
Strizek, Helmut 312
Der Stürmer 298, 326, 332–5, 337, 340, 343
Sunday by the Pool 427
Sygma photo agency 4, 163, 238

Tabaro, Modeste 288
Tanzania 32, 173, 204, 235, 239, 249, 269, 270
Temin, Jonathan 10, 389–403
Témoignage Chrétien 69
Ten Commandments 62, 137, 279–81, 304, 322, 336, 365–6, 368
Theunis, Father Guy 408, 411
Thomas, Annie 160–1, 162
Thompson, Allan 1–11, 433–45
Tikoca, Colonel 200
Time magazine 263, 422
The Times 251, 252, 253, 256
Toronto Star 4, 440, 442
Touré, Sékou 245
tribalism 8, 206, 262–3, 265–6, 268, 269, 271
Le Tribun du Peuple 76, 79, 409
Turpin, Jean-Michel 240
Tutsis 20–5
 CDR and 282, 287, 293, 297, 300
 and international media 145, 150–6, 195, 198, 200–1, 218–21, 243–4, 249–54, 256–8, 266–7
 portrayed in film 427–8
 in post-genocide era 405–6
 and print media 62–71, 74–9, 280–1, 285–6, 292, 294–5, 299, 301, 333–6, 339–40
 radio propaganda against 2, 6–7, 16, 41–53, 56–60, 90–103, 110–13, 119–23, 125–7, 130–4, 283–4, 287–90, 292, 293–4, 296, 299, 300, 303–4, 309–24, 339–40, 349, 351–2, 375–6
 women and gender propaganda 2, 9, 120, 280, 292, 304, 333, 340, 362–71
Twagiramungu, Faustin 17, 312, 314–15, 405, 410
Twizeyimana, Albert-Baudouin 408

Ubuntu 409
Uganda 34, 35, 173, 219, 244–5, 249–50, 270
UJR (Union des Journalistes du Rwanda) 83
Umuco 405
umuganda (communal labour) 96, 104
Umukundwa, Lucie 412
Umuranga 74, 75
Umurangi 75, 83
Umuseso 409–11
UNAMIR (United Nations Assistance Mission for Rwanda) 12, 26–7, 44, 137–8, 175, 199–200, 202, 203, 205, 208
 attacked by RTLM 284, 296, 322, 354, 355, 365
 Belgian contingent 120, 121
 limitations of 16–17, 224
UNAR (Union Nationale Rwandaise) 69
La Une Radio Network 257
UNHCR 173, 180, 181, 182, 183, 185
UNICEF 5, 172, 182
United Kingdom 4, 27, 29, 155, 176, 179, 182, 203, 206–7, 248, 251–2

United Nations 4, 21, 157, 203–7
and concept of incitement 345–6, 347, 377
Convention on the Prevention and Punishment of the Crime of Genocide 204, 205, 207, 209, 330–1, 344, 377, 379, 418
failure of 15, 17–18, 26, 163, 169, 202, 223–4, 248, 254, 258
International Convention on the Elimination of All Forms O Racial Discrimination 331
International Covenant on Civil and Political Rights 331, 348, 379
International Covenant on Economic, Social and Cultural Rights 331
and limits to freedom of expression 331–2, 377
and media pressure 171, 181, 183, 185–6
Observer Mission in Congo (MONUC) 34, 412
and *Responsibility to Protect* 434, 439–40
United States 4, 26, 27, 29, 179, 180–1
failure of 26–7, 29, 165, 188–96, 254
Foreign Broadcast Information Service 399, 435
news magazine coverage of Rwanda 261–72
and Somalia 13, 174, 188, 189, 252
U.S. News and World Report 263, 266
USAID 412
Uwamugira, Zakia 104
Uwilingiyimana, Agathe 73, 75, 219, 312, 313, 320–1, 323
Uwimana, Julien 82

Voice of America (VOA) 36, 87, 141, 212, 213, 401, 406, 412
Vuillemin, Giles-Denis 69–70
vulnerable societies, and media 389–403

Walden, Richard 176, 179, 181, 182
Waldorf, Lars 10, 404–16
Wall, Melissa 8, 261–73
Washington Post 162, 192, 201, 257
Watson, Paul 4
Weaver, Timothy 170
Wiesel, Elie 421
Wilkinson, Ray 180, 182, 183–4
Williams, Paul 248
Willis, Stuart 208
Winter, Roger 77–8, 201–2
World Food Programme (WFP) 171, 180, 182, 249
Worthington, Tony 206–7

Yugoslavia 13–14, 162

Zaffiro, J.J. 212
Zaire 28, 32–3, 56, 159, 162, 164, 195, 239–40, 245, 249, 269–70, 383, 385
Zelizer, Barbie 419